19th Conference on Natural Language Processing/Konferenz zur Verarbeitung naturlicher Sprache (KONVENS 2023)

AA001645

Ingolstadt, Germany
18-23 September

ISBN: 979-8-3313-1645-7

Printed from e-media with permission by:

Curran Associates, Inc.
57 Morehouse Lane
Red Hook, NY 12571

Some format issues inherent in the e-media version may also appear in this print version.

Copyright© (2023) by the Association for Computational Linguistics
All rights reserved.

Printed with permission by Curran Associates, Inc. (2025)

For permission requests, please contact the Association for Computational Linguistics at the address below.

Association for Computational Linguistics
209 N. Eighth Street
Stroudsburg, Pennsylvania 18360

Phone: 1-570-476-8006
Fax: 1-570-476-0860

acl@aclweb.org

Additional copies of this publication are available from:

Curran Associates, Inc.
57 Morehouse Lane
Red Hook, NY 12571 USA
Phone: 845-758-0400
Fax: 845-758-2633
Email: curran@proceedings.com
Web: www.proceedings.com

KONVENS 2023

The 19th Conference on Natural Language Processing (KONVENS 2023)

Proceedings of the Conference

September 18 - 22, 2023

©2023 The Association for Computational Linguistics

Order copies of this and other ACL proceedings from:

Association for Computational Linguistics (ACL)
209 N. Eighth Street
Stroudsburg, PA 18360
USA
Tel: +1-570-476-8006
Fax: +1-570-476-0860
acl@aclweb.org

Message from the Organizers

KONVENS (Konferenz zur Verarbeitung natürlicher Sprache/Conference on Natural Language Processing) is a conference series on computational linguistics established in 1992. It is held annually in Germany, Austria, and Switzerland. KONVENS is organized under the auspices of the German Society for Computational Linguistics and Language Technology, the Special Interest Group on Computational Linguistics of the German Linguistic Society, the Austrian Society for Artificial Intelligence and SwissText.

The papers in these proceedings were presented at the 19th edition of KONVENS, which took place from September 19 to September 21, 2023, at Technische Hochschule Ingolstadt (THI) in Germany. The KONVENS 2023 main conference received over 50 submissions, which were peer-reviewed by three reviewers each. After the review, 22 papers were accepted for presentation at the conference and archived in these proceedings. Several non-archival works have also been presented at the conference. The KONVENS main conference was accompanied by several complementary events: three workshops, a shared task on speaker attribution in newswire and parliamentary debates, a tutorial on learning from task instructions and an event for PhD students. In addition, KONVENS 2023 featured the GSCL Awards for bachelor's and master's theses.

Many thanks to all who submitted their work to KONVENS and our board of reviewers for supporting us greatly with evaluating the submissions. Moreover, we would like to thank Technische Hochschule Ingolstadt, everyone involved in organizing and conducting the conference, and, of course, our sponsors. Without their support, KONVENS 2023 would not have been possible.

Munir Georges (General Chair)
Aaricia Herygers (Local Chair)
Annemarie Friedrich (Program Co-Chair)
Benjamin Roth (Program Co-Chair)

Sponsors

We extend our heartfelt gratitude to our sponsors for their generous support of the KONVENS conference. Their commitment has been instrumental in the success of this event, enabling a vibrant platform for knowledge sharing and innovation.

Gold Sponsors

Bundesdruckerei

Careers in the Bundesdruckerei Group
Tradition and innovation in harmony, that's what Bundesdruckerei is all about. Secure identities, secure data and infrastructures are our core expertise, enabling us to shape digital transformation in a responsible manner. What do we need? We need great people full of ideas and energy who give their best every day. What you can expect is a wide range of activities and countless opportunities for further development.

Secure. Satisfying. Career.
We are all about digital data and identities. With innovative products and advanced technologies. Our customers and the public particularly appreciate the fact that we provide security and trust. We have been providing security "Made in Germany" since 1868. Do innovative products and new concepts excite you too? Are you keen to push new developments? Are you looking to get progress moving and shape the future? Then we should get together.

Start your career at the Bundesdruckerei Group
Join our team and find the job you're looking for in our job vacancies:
`https://www.bundesdruckerei.de/de/karriere/jobs`

Bosch Center for Artificial Intelligence

The Bosch Center for Artificial Intelligence (BCAI) is leading among the industrial AI research centers in Europe. BCAI develops modern AI technologies for Bosch products and services "invented for life." Together with experts from all over the globe, Bosch conducts cutting edge research in applied AI.

`https://www.bosch-ai.com/`

Copper Sponsors

Organizing Committee

Munir Georges (General Chair)

Aaricia Herygers (Local Chair)

Annemarie Friedrich (Program Co-Chair)

Benjamin Roth (Program Co-Chair)

Program Committee

Adrien Barbaresi (Berlin-Brandenburgische Akademie der Wissenschaften)

Agnieszka Faleńska (Universität Stuttgart)

Alexander Fraser (Ludwig-Maximilians-Universität München)

Alexander Mehler (Goethe-Universität Frankfurt)

Andrea Horbach (FernUniversität Hagen)

Anke Holler (Universität Göttingen)

Asad Sayeed (University of Gothenburg)

Barbara Plank (Ludwig-Maximilians-Universität München)

Barbara Schuppler (Technische Universität Graz)

Bernhard Fisseni (Universität Duisburg-Essen)

Bernhard Schröder (University of Duisburg-Essen)

Brigitte Krenn (Österreichisches Forschungsinstitut für Artificial Intelligence)

Casey Kennington (Boise State University)

Cerstin Mahlow (Zürcher Hochschule für Angewandte Wissenschaften)

Chris Biemann (Universität Hamburg)

Christian Chiarcos (Universität zu Köln)

Christian Wartena (Hochschule Hannover)

Clemens Neudecker (Staatsbibliothek zu Berlin - Preußischer Kulturbesitz)

David Schlangen (Universität Potsdam)

Debayan Banerjee (Universität Hamburg)

Ekaterina Lapshinova-Koltunski (Universität Hildesheim)

Eva Maria Vecchi (Universität Stuttgart)

Gabriella Lapesa (Universität Stuttgart)

Georg Rehm (Deutsches Forschungszentrum für Künstliche Intelligenz)

Gertrud Faaß (Universität Hildesheim)

Heike Zinsmeister (Universität Hamburg)

Hendrik Schuff (Bosch Center for Artificial Intelligence, Universität Stuttgart)

Henning Wachsmuth (Leibniz Universität Hannover)

Irina Nikishina (Universität Hamburg)

Josef Ruppenhofer (IDS Mannheim)

Katharina Kann (University of Colorado Boulder)

Kerstin Jung (Universität Stuttgart)

Kilian Evang (Heinrich-Heine-Universität Düsseldorf)

Korbinian Riedhammer (Technische Hochschule Nürnberg)

Manfred Stede (Universität Potsdam)

Marc Schulder (Universität Hamburg)

Marcel Bollmann (Linköping University)

Margot Mieskes (Hochschule für Angewandte Wissenschaften Darmstadt)

Maria Berger (Ruhr-Universität Bochum)

Melanie Andresen (Universität Stuttgart)

Michael Roth (Universität Stuttgart)

Nicolai Erbs (DB Fernverkehr)

Odette Scharenborg (Delft University of Technology)

Peter Bourgonje (Universität Potsdam)

Rainer Osswald (Heinrich-Heine-Universität Düsseldorf)

Roman Klinger (Universität Stuttgart)

Saba Anwar (Universität Hamburg)

Sabine Schulte im Walde (Universität Stuttgart)

Sebastian Pado (Universität Stuttgart)

Seid Muhie Yimam (Universität Hamburg)

Simone Ponzetto (Universität Mannheim)

Sophie Henning (Bosch Center for Artificial Intelligence, Ludwig-Maximilians-Universität München)

Tanja Samardzic (Universität Zürich)

Tatjana Scheffler (Ruhr-Universität Bochum)

Tobias Bocklet (Technische Hochschule Nürnberg)

Torsten Zesch (FernUniversität Hagen)

Udo Kruschwitz (Universität Regensburg)

Valia Kordoni (Humboldt-Universität zu Berlin)

Yves Scherrer (University of Helsinki)

Table of Contents

Conference Program

Tuesday, September 19, 2023

8:45–9:00	***Opening Remarks***
9:00–10:00	*Keynote 1 by Marc Schulder: Being a computational linguist in sign language research*
10:00–10:30	***Coffee Break***
10:30–12:00	**Session 1: Paper Presentations & Sponsor Talk**
10:30–10:45	*Is Prompt-Based Finetuning Always Better than Vanilla Finetuning? Insights from Cross-Lingual Language Understanding* Bolei Ma, Ercong Nie, Helmut Schmid and Hinrich Schuetze
10:45–11:00	*Comparing Pre-Training Schemes for Luxembourgish BERT Models* Cedric Lothritz, Saad Ezzini, Christoph Purschke, Tegawendé Bissyandé, Jacques Klein, Isabella Olariu, Andrey Boytsov, Clément LeFebvre and Anne Goujon
11:00–11:15	*LLpro: A Literary Language Processing Pipeline for German Narrative Texts* Anton Ehrmanntraut, Leonard Konle and Fotis Jannidis
11:15–11:30	*Classifying Noun Compounds for Present-Day Compositionality: Contributions of Diachronic Frequency and Productivity Patterns* Maximilian M. Maurer, Chris Jenkins, Filip Miletić and Sabine Schulte im Walde
11:30–11:45	*From Qualitative to Quantitative Research: Semi-Automatic Annotation Scaling in the Digital Humanities* Fynn Petersen-Frey, Tim Fischer, Florian Schneider, Isabel Eiser, Gertraud Koch and Chris Biemann
11:45–12:00	*Sponsor Presentation by Bosch*
12:00–14:00	***Lunch Break***

14:00–14:40 Session 2: Poster Session 1 Flashlights & Sponsor Talk

14:00–14:20 *Poster Session 1 Flashlights: Advertisement*

14:20–14:40 *Sponsor Presentation by Bundesdruckerei*

14:40–16:00 *Poster Session 1 Projects & PhD Thesis Presentations*

Data and Approaches for German Text simplification – towards an Accessibility-enhanced Communication
Thorben Schomacker, Michael Gille, Marina Tropmann-Frick and Jörg von der Hülls

Steps towards Addressing Text Classification in Low-Resource Languages
Maximilian Weißenbacher and Udo Kruschwitz

15:30–16:00 *Coffee Served*

16:00–17:00 Session 3: Fun Networking Session

17:00–17:15 *Thierry Declerck Memorial*

17:15–17:30 *Break*

17:30–19:00 *GSCL Members Meeting*

19:00– *Welcome Reception*

Wednesday, September 20, 2023

9:00–10:00 *Keynote 2 by Ivana Kruijff-Korbayová*

10:00–10:30 ***Coffee Break***

10:30–12:00 *Thesis Presentations*

12:00–14:00 ***Lunch Break***

14:00–14:45 **Session 4: Paper Presentations**

14:00–14:15 *Toward a Multilingual Connective Database: Aligning German/French Concessive Connectives*
Peter Bourgonje, Sophia Rauh and Karolina Zaczynska

14:15–14:30 *Factuality Detection using Machine Translation – a Use Case for German Clinical Text*
Mohammed Bin Sumait, Aleksandra Gabryszak, Leonhard Hennig and Roland A. Roller

14:30–14:45 *Poster Session 2 Flashlights*

14:40–16:00 **Poster Session 2 Projects & PhD Thesis Presentations**

Linking Danish Parser Output to a Central Word Repository - From Morphosemantic Disambiguation to Unique Identifiers
Eckhard Bick

Automatic Dictionary Generation: Could Brothers Grimm Create a Dictionary with BERT?
Hendryk Weiland, Maike Behrendt and Stefan Harmeling

Towards UkrainianWordNet: Incorporation of an Existing Thesaurus in the Domain of Physics
Melanie Siegel, Maksym Vakulenko and Jonathan Baum

Pointer Networks: A Unified Approach to Extracting German Opinions
Julia Wunderle, Jan Pfister and Andreas Hotho

Exploring Automatic Text Simplification of German Narrative Documents
Thorben Schomacker, Tillmann Dönicke and Marina Tropmann-Frick

Are idioms surprising?
Jonas Nathanael Phlipp, Michael Richter, Erik Daas and Max Kölbl

Answer Candidate Type Selection: Text-To-Text Language Model for Closed Book Question Answering Meets Knowledge Graphs
Mikhail Salnikov, Maria Lysyuk, Pavel Braslavski, Anton Razzhigaev, Valentin A. Malykh and Alexander Panchenko

HS-EMO: Analyzing Emotions in Hate Speech
Johannes Schäfer and Elina Kistner

Evaluating Data Augmentation Techniques for the Training of Luxembourgish Language Models
Isabella Olariu, Cedric Lothritz, Tegawendé Bissyandé and Jacques Klein

Information Type Classification with Contrastive Task-Specialized Sentence Encoders
Philipp Seeberger, Tobias Bocklet and Korbinian Riedhammer

15:30–16:00 ***Coffee Served***

16:00–18:00 ***Social Event***

18:00– ***Conference Dinner***

Thursday, September 21, 2023

9:00–10:00 *Keynote 3 by Hinrich Schuütze: Glot500: Scaling Multilingual Corpora and Language Models to 500 Languages*

10:00–10:30 ***Coffee Break***

10:30–11:30 Session 5: Paper Presentations

11:30–12:00 ***GSCL Thesis Awards & Closing***

Is Prompt-Based Finetuning Always Better than Vanilla Finetuning? Insights from Cross-Lingual Language Understanding

Bolei Ma[⋆ 1] **Ercong Nie**[⋆ 1,2] **Helmut Schmid**[1] **Hinrich Schütze**[1,2]
[1]Center for Information and Language Processing (CIS), LMU Munich, Germany
[2]Munich Center for Machine Learning (MCML), Munich, Germany
bolei.ma@campus.lmu.de nie@cis.lmu.de

Abstract

Multilingual pretrained language models (MPLMs) have demonstrated substantial performance improvements in zero-shot cross-lingual transfer across various natural language understanding tasks by finetuning MPLMs on task-specific labelled data of a source language (e.g. English) and evaluating on a wide range of target languages. Recent studies show that prompt-based finetuning surpasses regular finetuning in few-shot scenarios. However, the exploration of prompt-based learning in multilingual tasks remains limited. In this study, we propose the **PROFIT** pipeline to investigate the cross-lingual capabilities of **Prompt**-based **Fi**ne**t**uning. We conduct comprehensive experiments on diverse cross-lingual language understanding tasks (sentiment classification, paraphrase identification, and natural language inference) and empirically analyze the variation trends of prompt-based finetuning performance in cross-lingual transfer across different few-shot and full-data settings. Our results reveal the effectiveness and versatility of prompt-based finetuning in cross-lingual language understanding. Our findings indicate that prompt-based finetuning outperforms vanilla finetuning in full-data scenarios and exhibits greater advantages in few-shot scenarios, with different performance patterns dependent on task types. Additionally, we analyze underlying factors such as language similarity and pretraining data size that impact the cross-lingual performance of prompt-based finetuning. Overall, our work provides valuable insights into the cross-lingual prowess of prompt-based finetuning.

1 Introduction

Pretrained language models (PLMs) (Devlin et al., 2019; Yang et al., 2019b; Radford et al., 2019), trained on massive amounts of unlabelled data in a self-supervised manner, have shown strong performance after finetuning on task-specific labelled data for a given downstream task, such as sentence classification (Zhuang et al., 2021), text summarization (Zhang et al., 2020), or dialogue generation (Liu et al., 2023c). *Prompt-based learning* (Brown et al., 2020; Schick and Schütze, 2021a,b,c) has recently emerged as a notable advancement, surpassing regular finetuning approaches in few-shot scenarios (Liu et al., 2023a). In prompt-based learning, downstream tasks are reformulated to resemble the types of problems tackled during the PLM's original pretraining by using a textual prompt. For example, in Figure 1(b), an input sentence of the binary sentiment analysis task "`Works as stated!`" can be reformulated with a prompt pattern $P(X) = X \circ$ "`It was [MASK].`" as "`Works as stated! It was [MASK].`" where $\circ$ is the string concatenation operator. We use a *verbalizer* which maps the class label to a *label word*. In this example, the class labels POSITIVE and NEGATIVE can be verbalized as "`great`" and "bad". By comparing the probabilities of the label words "`great`" and "bad" as fillers of the `[MASK]` token, we can predict the correct class label. In the example above, a natural language understanding (NLU) task is transformed into a masked language modeling (MLM) problem, which is the same as the PLM's pretraining objective.

The reformulated input can be used for finetuning, i.e. *prompt-based finetuning*. Figure 1 shows the difference between prompt-based finetuning and vanilla finetuning. Vanilla finetuning solely relies on the hidden embedding of the `[CLS]` token. In contrast, prompt-based finetuning makes use of both the semantic information from the task labels and the prior knowledge encoded in the pretraining phase. Recent empirical studies of few-shot learning showed advantages of prompt-based finetuning over vanilla finetuning (Gao et al., 2021; Li and Liang, 2021).

When applied to multilingual pretrained lan-

[⋆] Equal Contribution.

Proceedings of the 19th Conference on Natural Language Processing (KONVENS 2023), pages 1–16
September 18–22, 2023. ©2023 Association for Computational Linguistics

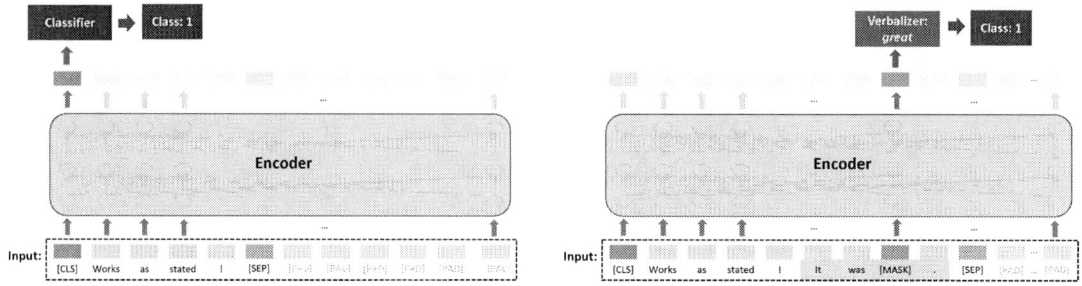

(a) Vanilla finetuning (b) Prompt-based finetuning

Figure 1: The comparion of vanilla finetuning and prompt-based finetuning. [CLS], [SEP], [MASK], [PAD] are special tokens in the encoder vocabulary. The verbalizer is a function mapping from the task label set to a subset of the encoder vocabulary. Input tokens in blue represent the prompt pattern.

guage models (MPLMs), prompt-based finetuning also enables zero-shot[1] cross-lingual transfer. MPLMs such as mBERT (Devlin et al., 2019) and XLM-R (Conneau et al., 2020) are pretrained on huge multilingual corpora and show strong multilinguality (Pires et al., 2019; Dufter and Schütze, 2020; Liang et al., 2021). They have become the dominant paradigm for zero-shot cross-lingual transfer, where annotated training data is available for some source language (e.g. English) but not for the target language (Wu and Dredze, 2019; Hu et al., 2020a). Zhao and Schütze (2021) proposed prompt-based finetuning for cross-lingual transfer. Their work focused on few-shot finetuning. Their experimental results for the natural language inference task showed that prompt-based finetuning performed better in few-shot cross-lingual transfer than vanilla finetuning. However, prior studies failed to examine whether prompt-based learning is also advantageous when training data is not scarce. Therefore, we conduct a comprehensive investigation on diverse cross-lingual language understanding tasks in both full-data and few-shot settings in order to shed more light on the cross-lingual capabilities of prompt-based finetuning.

In contrast to most previous research on prompting, our work is not restricted to monolingual or few-shot scenarios. Instead we explore a wide range of few-shot settings. We adopt a multilingual perspective and aim to uncover the nuances of performance variations associated with prompt-based finetuning. To this end, we implement the PROFIT pipeline and carry out an extensive set of experiments encompassing three representative cross-lingual language understanding tasks: sentiment analysis (Amazon Reviews), paragraph identification (PAWS-X), and natural language inference (XNLI). Our task selection covers single-sentence classification, sentence pair classification and inference task, considering both binary and multi-fold classifications. Our work provides insights into the effectiveness and versatility of prompt-based finetuning in cross-lingual language understanding.

Research Questions and Contributions. In this work, we analyze how the performance of prompt-based finetuning varies with the size of the labelled source language data for zero-shot cross-lingual transfer tasks. We examine a wide range of factors which could have an impact on cross-lingual transfer performance. We attempt to address the following pivotal research questions:

RQ1 *Does prompt-based finetuning outperform vanilla finetuning in the full-data scenario in different NLU tasks?*

We propose the PROFIT pipeline for systematically conducting the cross-lingual transfer experiments. We carry out zero-shot cross-lingual transfer experiments on three different NLU tasks using all the available English training data. By comparing the results of vanilla finetuning and PROFIT for different MPLMs, we find that in the full-data scenario, PROFIT still achieves better cross-lingual performance than vanilla finetuning.

RQ2 *Is prompt-based finetuning always better than vanilla finetuning?*

[1] In this paper, "zero-shot" in "zero-shot cross-lingual transfer" refers to the number of target language training data, i.e., no target language data is provided, while "few-shot" in "few-shot finetuning" refers to the source language used for finetuning, i.e., a few source language data is provided for the finetuning of the MPLM. The finetuned model is then zero-shot transferred to target language.

We investigate how the cross-lingual performance depends on the size of the English training data. Our findings substantiate that the PROFIT exhibits greater advantages in few-shot scenarios compared to full-data scenarios. The specific patterns of performance change are contingent upon the task types.

RQ3 *What underlying factors could affect the cross-lingual performance of* PROFIT*?*

We extensively analyze the factors that could influence the cross-lingual performance of PROFIT, encompassing language similarity, pretraining data size of target languages, etc.

2 Related Work

Prompt-Based Learning GPT-3 (Brown et al., 2020) has sparked research in prompt-based methods. Recent advances include automatic generation of prompt verbalizers and patterns (Schick et al., 2020; Shin et al., 2020), soft prompting (Qin and Eisner, 2021), prefix tuning (Li and Liang, 2021), P-tuning (Liu et al., 2022a), and retrieval-augmented prompting (Liu et al., 2022b). Most of these methods focus on monolingual scenarios, leaving the cross-lingual capabilities of prompt-based methods largely unexplored.

MPLMs and Zero-Shot Cross-Lingual Transfer The advances of MPLMs have positioned them as the standard approach for cross-lingual transfer. MPLMs usually adopt the architecture of some monolingual Transformer-based language model (Vaswani et al., 2017) and are jointly pretrained on large unlabelled multilingual data. For instance, mBERT (Devlin et al., 2019) is based on BERT; XLM-R (Zhuang et al., 2021) and Glot500-m (ImaniGooghari et al., 2023) are based on RoBERTa (Conneau et al., 2020). A multitude of studies have validated the robust multilinguality exhibited by MPLMs, either through probing the MPLMs themselves (Pires et al., 2019) or by identifying the key factors that contribute to their impressive multilinguality (Dufter and Schütze, 2020). Recent empirical studies have further demonstrated the remarkable cross-lingual capabilities of MPLMs by finetuning MPLMs on English training sets and then predicting on test sets of other languages (Karthikeyan et al., 2020; Turc et al., 2021). Several benchmarks have been proposed to evaluate the performance of multilingual encoders, including XTREME (Hu et al., 2020b), XTREME-R (Ruder et al., 2021), Taxi1500 (Ma et al., 2023) and XGLUE (Liang et al., 2020).

Multilingual Prompt Learning While prompting has proven successful in English, the application of prompting techniques in multilingual tasks has yet to be thoroughly explored and extensively studied. Zhao and Schütze (2021) first investigated prompt-based methods for cross-lingual transfer with different prompt forms and verbalizers. Recent follow-up studies introduced mask token augmentation (Zhou et al., 2022) and unified multilingual prompts (Huang et al., 2022) for zero-shot cross-lingual transfer. Despite the growing attention garnered by these methods in the context of few-shot scenarios across various NLP tasks, there remains a dearth of comprehensive investigations into the variations of prompt-based learning methods across different few-shot settings and full-data settings. Tu et al. (2022) focused on an alternative prompting approach for cross-lingual transfer in full-data scenarios. In contrast to prompt-based finetuning, they introduced additional prompt parameters to PLMs and exclusively updated these parameters during the finetuning process. A more recent work (Shi and Lipani, 2023) combined prompt-based finetuning and continued pretraining, but it was limited to monolingual scenarios.

In contrast to the aforementioned previous studies, our work provides a comprehensive investigation of prompt-based finetuning for cross-lingual transfer in both few-shot and full-data scenarios. Furthermore, we empirically analyze the variation of prompt-based finetuning performance across different few-shot settings.

3 Methodology

The purpose of this study is to improve the cross-lingual transfer performance of vanilla finetuning. In vanilla settings of zero-shot cross-lingual transfer, the MPLM is directly finetuned with training data in a source language (English). The finetuned model is then applied to predict the test data in target languages.

In prompt-based learning, we need a pattern-verbalizer pair (PVP) (Schick and Schütze, 2021a) consisting of (i) a *prompt pattern* which converts the input text into a cloze-style question with a mask token, and (ii) a representative word (called *verbalizer*) for each possible class. In our PROFIT approach, a PVP is combined with training data in English during finetuning. As the *training*

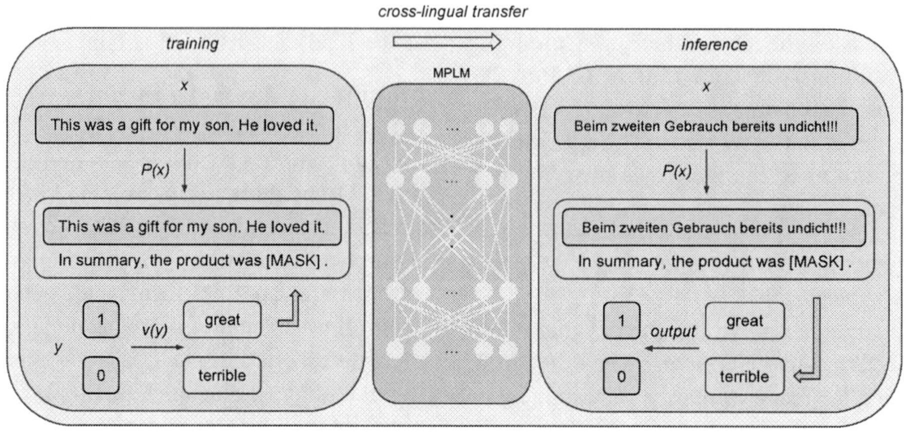

Figure 2: PROFIT pipeline of training and cross-lingual transfer with examples. X is an input sentence and $P(X)$ denotes the prompt pattern which reformulates the input into a prompt. $v(y)$ is the verbalizer which maps each class label y onto a word from the source language vocabulary.

block in Figure 2 shows, a prompt pattern such as $P(X) = X\circ$ "`In summary, the product was [MASK].`" is filled with an input example X "`This was a gift for my son. He loved it.`" A verbalizer such as $\{0 \rightarrow$ "terrible", $1 \rightarrow$ "great"$\}$ is used to map the original labels $\{0,1\}$ onto words. The MPLM takes the filled pattern "`This was a gift for my son. He loved it. In summary, the product was [MASK].`", as input and returns for each of the two verbalizers "terrible" and "great" its probability of being the masked token. Thus, it uses the PVP to reformulate the sentence classification task of vanilla finetuning into a masked token prediction task.

More formally, let D=$\{(X_1, y_1), ..., (X_n, y_n)\}$ denote the set of training examples in the source language, where $X_1, ..., X_n$ are text samples and $y_1, ..., y_n$ are class labels from a label set Y. The prompt pattern $P(.)$ transforms an input sentence X into a cloze-style question with a masked token. The pretrained language model M with trainable parameters θ performs masked token prediction and returns the probabilities $p = M(P(X), \theta)$ of all candidate words for the masked token in $P(X)$. The verbalizer $v(.)$ is a bijective mapping from the set of class labels Y to a set of verbalised words V from the source language vocabulary. We predict the class $\hat{y}$ whose verbalizer $v(\hat{y})$ received the highest probability from model M:

$$\hat{y} = \arg\max_{y \in Y} p(v(y)) \tag{1}$$

We finetune the parameters θ of model M by minimizing the cross-entropy loss function ℓ on D:

$$\hat{\theta} = \arg\max_{\theta} \sum_{(X,y)\in D} \ell(v(y), M(P(X), \theta)) \tag{2}$$

The model with the finetuned parameters $\hat{\theta}$ is used to predict the class labels of the target language examples $D' = \{X'_1, ..., X'_n\}$ using the same prompt pattern and verbalizer as during finetuning (see *inference* block in Figure 2). The best label y'_i for each example X'_i is predicted according to Eq. 1.

In contrast to vanilla finetuning, prompt-based methods such as PROFIT only transform the training data with the prompt pattern P and the verbalizer v, but leave the model architecture unchanged. thus not hindering the efficiency of Vanilla much (Shi and Lipani, 2023). No extra parameters have to be trained from scratch. By reformulating the sentence classification task into a masked token prediction (MTP) task, we can better take advantage of the knowledge that the model has acquired during MTP pretraining.

In the cross-lingual setting, we simply apply the same functions P and v to the target language examples without further modifications.

4 Experimental Setups

4.1 Datasets

In order to investigate the performance on diverse NLU tasks, three representative different classification tasks on NLU are selected for evaluation in this work: sentiment analysis on Amazon product reviews (Keung et al., 2020), paraphrase identification on PAWS-X (Yang et al., 2019a), and natural language inference on XNLI (Conneau et al., 2018).

Amazon Reviews Dataset (Keung et al., 2020) contains product reviews with 5 star ratings from 1 to 5. The multilingual version of this dataset consists of test data in English and 5 other languages. We use the following prompt pattern $P(X)$ and verbalizer $v(y)$ for each review example (X, y):

- $P(X) = X \circ$ "All in all, it was [MASK]."
- $v(1) =$ "terrible", $v(2) =$ "bad", $v(3) =$ "ok", $v(4) =$"good", $v(5) =$ "great"

PAWS-X is a multilingual version of PAWS (Zhang et al., 2019), which consists of challenging paraphrase identification pairs from Wikipedia and Quora. Each data item comprises two sentences. The task is to predict whether the two sentences are paraphrases. The labels are binary: 1 for paraphrase, 0 for non-paraphrase. PAWS-X consists of datasets in English and 6 other languages. For a given sentence pair X_1 and X_2, we design the pattern and verbalizer as:

- $P(X_1, X_2) = X_1 \circ$"? [MASK], " $\circ X_2$
- $v(0) =$ "Wrong", $v(1) =$ "Right"

XNLI is a multilingual version of the MultiNLI dataset (Williams et al., 2018). The text in each data item consists of two sentences. Sentence A is the premise and sentence B is the hypothesis. The task is to predict the type of inference between the given premise and hypothesis among the three types: "entailment" (0), "neutral" (1), and "contradiction" (2). It is a kind of multi-class natural language inference task. XNLI consists of datasets in English and 14 other languages. For a given sentence pair X_1 and X_2, we design the pattern and verbalizer as:

- $P(X_1, X_2) = X_1 \circ$ "? [MASK], " $\circ X_2$
- $v(0) =$ "Yes", $v(1) =$ "Maybe", $v(2) =$ "No"

4.2 Baseline

The following baselines are considered and compared to our PROFIT approach:

MAJ The majority baseline. It always assigns the majority class from the training data.

Direct The pattern filled with the input sample is directly fed to the MPLM for prediction, without finetuning. This is the zero-shot scenario.

Vanilla The standard finetuning method which predicts the class from the hidden embedding of the `[CLS]` token without using a prompt pattern. We use the cross-entropy loss as the objective function for finetuning and AdamW for optimization with a learning rate of 1e-5 and 5 training epochs. The finetuned models are then used to predict the test data.

4.3 Multilingual Models

In order to solve the classification tasks with cross-lingual transfer, we use the pretrained multilingual BERT model (Devlin et al., 2019) "`bert-base-multilingual-cased`" (M) and the XLM-R model (Conneau et al., 2020) "`xlm-roberta-base`" (X) from the Huggingface Transformers library (Wolf et al., 2020). Both models are evaluated with the methods Vanilla and PROFIT. We repeat all our experiments 5 times with different random seeds. The details about model training and hyperparameter settings can be found in Appendix §A.1.

5 Results

5.1 Main Results

	Amazon	PAWS-X	XNLI	Avg.
MAJ	20	55.81	33.33	36.17
Direct-mBERT	20.21	45.05	35.05	33.44
Vanilla-mBERT	42.97	80.24	65.05	62.75
PROFIT-mBERT	**43.98**	**82.16**	**65.79**	**63.98**
Direct-XLM-R	21.98	51.10	35.68	36.25
Vanilla-XLM-R	54.56	82.51	73.61	70.22
PROFIT-XLM-R	**54.66**	**82.73**	**73.82**	**70.40**

Table 1: Overview of results

Table 1 gives an overview of the experimental results. PROFIT outperforms the MAJ baseline with both mBERT and XLM-R for all three classification tasks. PROFIT also outperforms the Direct and Vanilla baselines in both mBERT and XLM-R settings: When trained with mBERT, the performance is improved by **23.77%**, **37.11%** and **30.74%** compared to Direct on Amazon, PAWS-X and XNLI respectively, and by **1.01%**, **1.92%** and **0.74%** compared to Vanilla. When trained with XLM-R, the performance is improved by **32.68%**, **31.63%** and **38.14%** compared to Direct, and by **0.10%**, **0.22%** and **0.21%** compared to Vanilla respectively.

Task	Model	en	ar	bg	de	el	es	fr	hi	ja	ko	ru	sw	th	tr	ur	vi	zh	avg.
Amazon	Vanilla-M	58.92	-	-	45.69	-	48.02	47.45	-	35.07	-	-	-	-	-	-	-	**38.63**	42.97
	PROFIT-M	**59.05**	-	-	**46.66**	-	**49.30**	**48.38**	-	**37.31**	-	-	-	-	-	-	-	38.26	**43.98**
	Vanilla-X	59.61	-	-	**60.14**	-	55.24	55.66	-	51.93	-	-	-	-	-	-	-	49.82	54.56
	PROFIT-X	**60.06**	-	-	59.60	-	**55.72**	**55.89**	-	**52.34**	-	-	-	-	-	-	-	**49.75**	**54.66**
PAWS-X	Vanilla-M	93.85	-	-	84.94	-	87.11	86.55	-	73.39	72.44	-	-	-	-	-	-	77.01	80.24
	PROFIT-M	**94.21**	-	-	**86.06**	-	**88.17**	**87.91**	-	**75.79**	**75.82**	-	-	-	-	-	-	**79.22**	**82.16**
	Vanilla-X	94.33	-	-	86.92	-	88.55	89.04	-	**76.07**	74.71	-	-	-	-	-	-	79.75	82.51
	PROFIT-X	**94.90**	-	-	**87.06**	-	**88.87**	**88.86**	-	75.53	**75.40**	-	-	-	-	-	-	**80.63**	**82.73**
XNLI	Vanilla-M	82.57	65.12	68.97	71.40	66.30	74.22	73.68	60.02	-	-	68.95	50.24	53.15	62.02	57.96	69.80	68.91	65.05
	PROFIT-M	82.57	**65.55**	**69.47**	**71.57**	**67.43**	**75.10**	**74.57**	**60.57**	-	-	**69.55**	**51.13**	**54.58**	**62.64**	**58.04**	**70.74**	**70.08**	**65.79**
	Vanilla-X	84.91	**71.86**	77.78	76.86	75.96	79.25	78.21	69.92	-	-	**75.79**	**65.21**	72.02	73.12	66.07	74.71	73.72	73.61
	PROFIT-X	**84.97**	71.81	**77.92**	**77.35**	**76.11**	**79.31**	**78.75**	**70.10**	-	-	75.43	65.13	**72.39**	**73.23**	**66.95**	**75.05**	**73.92**	**73.82**

Table 2: Detailed cross-lingual performance results on three classification tasks. When calculating the average (avg.), due to the aim of zero-shot cross-lingual transfer, the performance results of the source language English are not taken into account. Model M stands for mBERT, and X for XLM-R.

While PROFIT outperforms all baselines on all three tasks, the degree of improvement differs. The improvements of PROFIT over Vanilla when trained with mBERT (**+1.23%**) are larger than the improvements when trained with XLM-R (**+0.18%**).

We further conducted T-tests for results of Vanilla and PROFIT with different random seeds (see §A.1 for the seeds). Table 3 shows the T-test results with p values for each task with mBERT and XLM-R models. We can see that the p values of all three tasks with mBERT model are under 0.05, indicating that the performance gain of PROFIT is significant with mBERT, while the p values of all three tasks with XLM-R model are bigger than 0.05, showing no significant performance difference.

Model	Amazon	PAWS-X	XNLI
mBERT	0.005	0.003	0.005
XLM-R	0.40*	0.46*	0.44*

Table 3: T-Test results (p) for results of Vanilla and PROFIT with different random seeds. Insignificant results with a p value > 0.05 are marked with *.

One reason for the performance difference of the two models could be that the XLM-R model was pretrained on far more data than mBERT and is also much bigger, so that the Vanilla performance with XLM-R finetuning is much better than with mBERT in cross-lingual context (Conneau et al., 2020; Lauscher et al., 2020), leaving less space for improvement.

A detailed overview of the cross-lingual performance of PROFIT compared to Vanilla for each target language is presented in Table 2. Although the overall performance of PROFIT is better than Vanilla for all three tasks in both mBERT and XLM-R settings, individual differences between languages can be noticed. On Amazon, with mBERT, the improvement in Japanese (ja) (**+2.24%**) is far greater than on average, whereas Chinese (zh) shows no improvement (**-0.37%**); with XLM-R, PROFIT performs slightly worse than Vanilla on both Chinese with **-0.07%** and German (de) with **-0.54%**. On PAWS-X, Korean (ko) shows a larger improvement (**+3.38%**) than average with mBERT, and with XLM-R, whereas French (fr) (**-0.18%**) and Japanese (**-0.54%**) show a slightly worse performance than Vanilla. On XNLI, we find improvements for all languages with mBERT, and with XLM-R, Arabic (ar) (**-0.06%**), Russian (ru) (**-0.36%**), and Swahili (sw) (**-0.08%**) show slightly worse performance than Vanilla.

We conclude that the performance gain of PROFIT over Vanilla depends on the models and languages. In §6, we will further investigate how linguistic factors influence cross-lingual transfer performance.

5.2 Few-shot Ablations

Previous studies show that the prompt framework is more effective than finetuning when training data is scarce (Zhao and Schütze, 2021; Qi et al., 2022). We investigated how the performance changes as the number of training samples K increases in few-shot settings. The training and validation data are randomly sampled with $K \in \{1, 2, 4, 8, 16, 32, 64, 128, 256, 512, 1024\}$

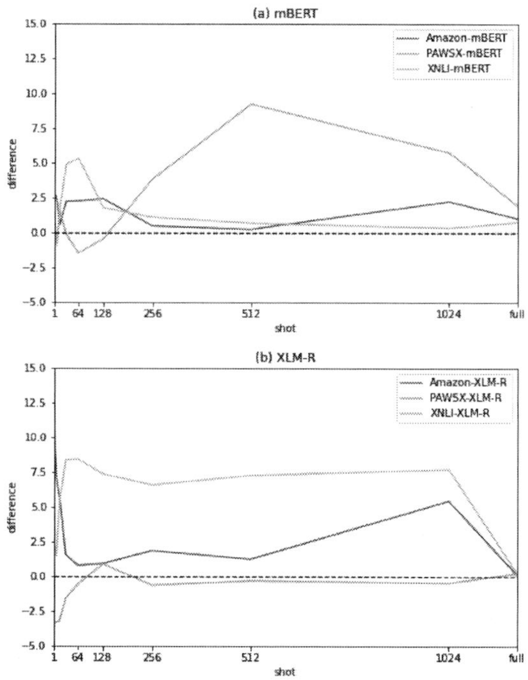

Figure 3: Performance difference between PROFIT and Vanilla in different few-shot settings and full training setting on three NLU tasks with both mBERT and XLM-R models.

shots per class from the English training data.

The detailed results of few-shot ablations can be found in Table 9, Table 10 and Table 11 in Appendix §A.4. Figure 3 shows the performance changes on all three tasks with both mBERT and XLM-R models. On the Amazon task, the performance improvement for smaller numbers of shots is greater than for full training. As the number of shots increases, the improvement decreases accordingly. This implies that on the sentiment analysis task, PROFIT is most valuable with small training data. On XNLI, the improvement of PROFIT over Vanilla is first small with in small shots. It then gets greater, as K increases, and drops again, as bigger K towards full data size shows up. We conclude that on NLI tasks such as XNLI, PROFIT is most effective in few-shot settings with a certain number of K. On PAWS-X, no obvious difference in few-shot settings can be found with mBERT in small shots, but in bigger shots there is greater improvement with $K \in \{256, 512, 1024\}$; however, with XLM-R, PROFIT shows almost no performance improvement over Vanilla.

Overall, sentiment analysis exhibits a clearer performance improvement for smaller numbers of shots, whereas the language inference and paraphrase tasks show greater performance enhancements in few-shot scenarios with larger K. This might be due to difficulties with pairwise inputs in these tasks, where we aim to identify the relationship between a pair of sentences. When it comes to transferring knowledge of sentence relationships, more examples are needed for successful learning than in sentiment analysis tasks where semantic information from comparable cross-lingual sentences can be directly transferred.

6 Cross-Lingual Analysis

In previous empirical studies of cross-lingual transfer learning (Lauscher et al., 2020; Nie et al., 2023), several key factors were identified to exert great effect on the cross-lingual performance, including (1) the size of the pretraining corpus for the target language and (2) the similarity between the source and target languages. We analyze how these two factors influence PROFIT's effectiveness for the languages on three tasks.

The pretraining corpus size of the target languages can be simply measured by the log_2 of the number of articles in Wikipedia[2].

For measuring the similarity between languages, we employ methods from recent studies of language representations. In these studies, languages are encoded as vectors according to their various linguistic and typological features. With these language vectors, a range of distance metrics, such as Euclidean distance and cosine similarity, can be used to measure the similarity between languages. Littell et al. (2017) proposed LANG2VEC which encodes languages using 5 vectors, with each vector representing a specific language feature. Östling and Kurfalı (2023) measured the lexical similarity by calculating language vectors based on the ASJP word list database (Wichmann et al., 2022). Liu et al. (2023b) recently proposed a novel language similarity metric from the perspective of conceptualization across multiple languages. In our work, we compute two similarity metrics: (i) a comprehensive linguistic similarity metric based on LANG2VEC (Littell et al., 2017) and (ii) a lexical similarity metric based on the ASJP word list database (Östling and Kurfalı, 2023).

The LANG2VEC approach provides information-rich vector representations of languages from dif-

[2] https://meta.wikimedia.org/wiki/List_of_Wikipedias

lang	Typological & Phylogenetic Sim.						Lexical Sim.			Size	Task Performance					
	SYN	PHO	INV	FAM	GEO	**Sim$_1$**	*UMAP*	*SVD*	**Sim$_2$**		amazon-M	amazon-X	pawsx-M	pawsx-X	xnli-M	xnli-X
ar	65.47	70.06	75.88	0.00	97.04	**61.69**	-1.90	4.87	**1.49**	**20.20**	-	-	-	-	65.55	71.81
bg	78.78	90.45	70.02	13.61	99.01	**70.38**	8.65	33.21	**20.93**	**18.15**	-	-	-	-	69.47	77.92
de	79.05	83.62	77.62	54.43	99.76	**78.90**	83.42	76.83	**80.13**	**21.42**	46.66	59.60	86.06	87.06	71.57	77.35
el	73.19	95.35	64.75	14.91	98.95	**69.43**	1.24	24.81	**13.03**	**17.76**	-	-	-	-	67.43	76.11
es	84.97	85.81	64.99	9.62	99.59	**69.00**	1.61	28.30	**14.96**	**20.83**	49.30	55.72	88.17	88.87	75.10	79.31
fr	76.83	75.26	73.64	9.62	99.93	**67.06**	1.34	31.76	**16.55**	**21.27**	48.38	55.89	87.91	88.86	74.57	78.75
hi	58.79	85.81	76.53	12.60	91.10	**64.97**	1.20	21.11	**11.16**	**17.26**	-	-	-	-	60.57	70.10
ja	49.63	64.44	65.92	0.00	85.65	**53.13**	-	-	-	**20.39**	37.31	52.34	75.79	75.53	-	-
ko	55.66	74.62	71.04	0.00	86.93	**57.65**	-0.22	12.42	**6.10**	**19.28**	-	-	75.82	75.40	-	-
ru	75.74	90.45	63.17	16.67	95.81	**68.37**	8.63	32.60	**20.62**	**20.87**	-	-	-	-	69.55	75.43
sw	42.26	90.91	76.16	0.00	91.50	**60.17**	-9.05	-7.18	**-8.12**	**16.23**	-	-	-	-	51.13	65.13
th	65.20	81.82	78.88	0.00	85.25	**62.23**	-0.21	3.82	**1.81**	**17.25**	-	-	-	-	54.58	72.39
tr	43.36	85.81	68.49	0.00	98.25	**59.18**	-7.80	-1.56	**-4.68**	**19.00**	-	-	-	-	62.64	73.23
ur	50.01	0.00	71.56	12.60	92.54	**45.34**	1.35	24.92	**13.14**	**17.54**	-	-	-	-	58.04	66.95
vi	64.92	78.33	74.76	0.00	85.25	**60.65**	0.86	-18.50	**-8.82**	**20.29**	-	-	-	-	70.74	75.05
zh	73.49	78.33	74.91	0.00	88.42	**63.03**	-	-	-	**20.37**	38.26	49.75	79.22	80.63	70.08	73.92

Table 4: Overview of language features and task performances with PROFIT for correlation analysis. Language features include typological & phylogenetic similarities (**Sim$_1$**), lexical similarities (**Sim$_2$**), and target language size (**Size**). Task performance contains the PROFIT results on the three datasets with both mBERT and XLM-R models.

ferent linguistic and ethnological perspectives. We adopt five linguistic categories: syntax (SYN), phonology (PHO), phonological inventory (INV), language family (FAM), and geography (GEO). SYN, PHO and INV are typological categories, and FAM and GEO are phylogenetic categories. Given these vectors, we calculate 5 different cosine similarity metrics between English and each target language.

The lexical similarity metric is based on a mean normalized pairwise Levenshtein distance matrix from ASJP. The language vectors used for calculating the lexical similarity are reduced in dimensionality. Two dimensionality reduction methods are employed for calculating the lexical similarity: Uniform Manifold Approximation and Projection (*UMAP*) (McInnes et al., 2018) and Singular Value Decomposition (*SVD*) (Stewart, 1993).

The final typological and phylogenetic similarity score **Sim$_1$** for each language pair is calculated by averaging the 5 similarities of LANG2VEC. Similarly, the lexical similarity score **Sim$_2$** is calculated by averaging the similarities of the *UMAP* and *SVD* vectors. More formally, as Eq. 3 shows, let f denote a feature from the feature set $\mathcal{F}_n$ for metric n, and let v_f denote the corresponding feature vector. The sim$_1$ and sim$_2$ scores for the source language English (e) and some target language j are then calculated by:

$$sim_n(e,j) = \frac{1}{|\mathcal{F}_n|} \sum_{f \in \mathcal{F}_n} \frac{v_f(e) \cdot v_f(j)}{\|v_f(e)\|_2 \, \|v_f(j)\|_2} \quad (3)$$

Table 4 shows a list of language features (typological & phylogenetic similarities, lexical similarities, and target language size) and task performances with PROFIT for the following correlation analysis. The language similarities, namely the typological & phylogenetic similarities (**Sim$_1$**) and lexical similarities (**Sim$_2$**) refer to the similarity between each language and English, based on the above introduced language vectors. Sim$_1$ and Sim$_2$ are calculated by Eq. 3. *ja* and *zh* are not included in Östling and Kurfalı (2023)'s original language sets, thus these two values are missing for the lexical similarities. The target language size (**Size**) is calculated by the log_2 of the number of articles in Wikipedia.

Based on the obtained language features and experimental results of task performance with PROFIT, we did a correlation analysis. Table 5 shows the results of the two correlation tests on each task.

According to the results of Pearson and Spearman tests and the p values, the two factors, namely, both the size of pretraining data for the target language and the similarity of typological and phylogenetic features of languages (sim$_1$) have a significant positive correlation with the improvement

Task	Model	Stat.	sim$_1$		sim$_2$		Size	
			corr.	*p*	*corr.*	*p*	*corr.*	*p*
Amazon	ProFiT-M	P	0.73	0.16*	-0.95	0.21*	0.81	0.09*
		S	0.70	0.19*	-1.00	0.00	0.50	0.39*
	ProFiT-X	P	0.80	0.10*	1.00	0.01	0.92	0.03
		S	0.80	0.10*	1.00	0.00	1.00	1e-24
PAWS-X	ProFiT-M	P	0.82	0.05	0.31	0.69*	0.82	0.04
		S	0.83	0.04	0.20	0.80*	0.60	0.21*
	ProFiT-X	P	0.83	0.04	0.34	0.66*	0.84	0.04
		S	0.77	0.07*	0.20	0.80*	0.71	0.11*
XNLI	ProFiT-M	P	0.57	0.03	0.43	0.14*	0.86	9e-05
		S	0.59	0.03	0.53	0.06*	0.90	1e-05
	ProFiT-X	P	0.72	4e-03	0.43	0.14*	0.70	5e-03
		S	0.77	1e-03	0.63	0.02	0.72	4e-03

Table 5: Correlations between task performance and language similarities (sim$_1$ & sim$_2$) and target language size. P stands for Pearson test and S for Spearman test. Insignificant results with a p value > 0.05 are marked with *.

of cross-lingual performance especially on XNLI, with both ProFiT-M and ProFiT-X models. Only the correlations calculated with the similarity of lexical features (sim$_2$) show some insignificant results. Furthermore, on XNLI, the correlation with language similarity is stronger with ProFiT-X, while the correlation with target data size is stronger with ProFiT-M. We argue that the XLM-R model is bigger than mBERT, so that the linguistic features have more effect on the performance, while for the smaller model mBERT the data size plays a greater role, which further reveals our findings in §5.1 that the applied pretrained model for finetuning has an impact on the ProFiT performance.

On PAWS-X and Amazon, we find weak correlations with the proposed factors, which could result from the limitation of languages in test data: XNLI comprises 15 different languages, whereas PAWS-X and Amazon only contain 7 and 6 languages in the test set, respectively. Thus weaker correlations have been found.

To sum up, language similarity and size are two factors that impact the cross-lingual performance in our study, and we find significant correlations when the test set contains a larger amount of languages.

7 Conclusion

In our work, we introduce ProFiT for zero-shot cross-lingual transfer, a pipeline which reformulates input examples into cloze-style prompts and applies the input examples with the prompts and its verbalizers as masked token to finetuning, changing the sentence classification task of vanilla finetuning into a masked token prediction task. We finetune the multilingual pretrained language model (MPLM) on source language prompts and apply it to target language data. We use ProFiT with the two MPLMs mBERT and XML-R, and evaluate its efficacy on three different types of multilingual classification tasks in natural language understanding – multi-class sentiment classification, binary paraphrase identification, and multi-class natural language inference. Our experiments show that ProFiT outperforms vanilla finetuning with both mBERT and XML-R on all three tasks. We further discovered that the performance improvement of ProFiT is generally more obvious in few-shot scenarios. Additionally, we demonstrate that the similarity of the source and target language and the size of the target language pretraining data significantly correlate with the cross-lingual transfer performance of ProFiT, especially on a big dataset with a variety of test languages.

Limitations

This study presents the ProFiT pipeline, which aims to enhance zero-shot cross-lingual transfer performance. Our approach was evaluated on various multilingual datasets and showed improved performance. However, due to the limitations of the datasets, only a few languages could be evaluated, thus making it difficult to draw a typological conclusion for all languages. Besides, our exploration in using the prompt-based learning method for cross-lingual language understanding is restricted to single-sentence and sentence pair classifications. As future work, our investigation should be extended to more types of language understanding tasks, such as sequence labelling tasks, e.g. slot detection, named entity recognition, etc.

Ethics Statement

This research was conducted in accordance with the ACM Code of Ethics. All the datasets that we use are publicly available. We report only aggregated results in the main paper. We have not intended or do not intend to share any Personally Identifiable Data with this paper.

Acknowledgements

We thank the anonymous reviewers for their efforts and helpful advice. This work was partly supported by Munich Center for Machine Learning (MCML) and China Scholarship Council (CSC).

References

Tom Brown, Benjamin Mann, Nick Ryder, Melanie Subbiah, Jared D Kaplan, Prafulla Dhariwal, Arvind Neelakantan, Pranav Shyam, Girish Sastry, Amanda Askell, et al. 2020. Language models are few-shot learners. *Advances in neural information processing systems*, 33:1877–1901.

Alexis Conneau, Kartikay Khandelwal, Naman Goyal, Vishrav Chaudhary, Guillaume Wenzek, Francisco Guzmán, Edouard Grave, Myle Ott, Luke Zettlemoyer, and Veselin Stoyanov. 2020. Unsupervised cross-lingual representation learning at scale. In *Proceedings of the 58th Annual Meeting of the Association for Computational Linguistics*, pages 8440–8451, Online. Association for Computational Linguistics.

Alexis Conneau, Ruty Rinott, Guillaume Lample, Adina Williams, Samuel Bowman, Holger Schwenk, and Veselin Stoyanov. 2018. XNLI: Evaluating cross-lingual sentence representations. In *Proceedings of the 2018 Conference on Empirical Methods in Natural Language Processing*, pages 2475–2485, Brussels, Belgium. Association for Computational Linguistics.

Jacob Devlin, Ming-Wei Chang, Kenton Lee, and Kristina Toutanova. 2019. BERT: Pre-training of deep bidirectional transformers for language understanding. In *Proceedings of the 2019 Conference of the North American Chapter of the Association for Computational Linguistics: Human Language Technologies, Volume 1 (Long and Short Papers)*, pages 4171–4186, Minneapolis, Minnesota. Association for Computational Linguistics.

Philipp Dufter and Hinrich Schütze. 2020. Identifying elements essential for BERT's multilinguality. In *Proceedings of the 2020 Conference on Empirical Methods in Natural Language Processing (EMNLP)*, pages 4423–4437, Online. Association for Computational Linguistics.

Tianyu Gao, Adam Fisch, and Danqi Chen. 2021. Making pre-trained language models better few-shot learners. In *Proceedings of the 59th Annual Meeting of the Association for Computational Linguistics and the 11th International Joint Conference on Natural Language Processing (Volume 1: Long Papers)*, pages 3816–3830, Online. Association for Computational Linguistics.

Junjie Hu, Sebastian Ruder, Aditya Siddhant, Graham Neubig, Orhan Firat, and Melvin Johnson. 2020a. XTREME: A massively multilingual multi-task benchmark for evaluating cross-lingual generalisation. In *Proceedings of the 37th International Conference on Machine Learning*, volume 119 of *Proceedings of Machine Learning Research*, pages 4411–4421. PMLR.

Junjie Hu, Sebastian Ruder, Aditya Siddhant, Graham Neubig, Orhan Firat, and Melvin Johnson. 2020b. Xtreme: A massively multilingual multi-task benchmark for evaluating cross-lingual generalisation. In *International Conference on Machine Learning*, pages 4411–4421. PMLR.

Lianzhe Huang, Shuming Ma, Dongdong Zhang, Furu Wei, and Houfeng Wang. 2022. Zero-shot cross-lingual transfer of prompt-based tuning with a unified multilingual prompt. *arXiv preprint arXiv:2202.11451*.

Ayyoob ImaniGooghari, Peiqin Lin, Amir Hossein Kargaran, Silvia Severini, Masoud Jalili Sabet, Nora Kassner, Chunlan Ma, Helmut Schmid, André Martins, François Yvon, and Hinrich Schütze. 2023. Glot500: Scaling multilingual corpora and language models to 500 languages. In *Proceedings of the 61st Annual Meeting of the Association for Computational Linguistics (Volume 1: Long Papers)*, pages 1082–1117, Toronto, Canada. Association for Computational Linguistics.

Kaliyaperumal Karthikeyan, Zihan Wang, Stephen Mayhew, and Dan Roth. 2020. Cross-lingual ability of multilingual bert: An empirical study. In *International Conference on Learning Representations*.

Phillip Keung, Yichao Lu, György Szarvas, and Noah A. Smith. 2020. The multilingual Amazon reviews corpus. In *Proceedings of the 2020 Conference on Empirical Methods in Natural Language Processing (EMNLP)*, pages 4563–4568, Online. Association for Computational Linguistics.

Anne Lauscher, Vinit Ravishankar, Ivan Vulić, and Goran Glavaš. 2020. From zero to hero: On the limitations of zero-shot language transfer with multilingual Transformers. In *Proceedings of the 2020 Conference on Empirical Methods in Natural Language Processing (EMNLP)*, pages 4483–4499, Online. Association for Computational Linguistics.

Xiang Lisa Li and Percy Liang. 2021. Prefix-tuning: Optimizing continuous prompts for generation. In *Proceedings of the 59th Annual Meeting of the Association for Computational Linguistics and the 11th International Joint Conference on Natural Language Processing (Volume 1: Long Papers)*, pages 4582–4597, Online. Association for Computational Linguistics.

Sheng Liang, Philipp Dufter, and Hinrich Schütze. 2021. Locating language-specific information in contextualized embeddings. *arXiv preprint arXiv:2109.08040*.

Yaobo Liang, Nan Duan, Yeyun Gong, Ning Wu, Fenfei Guo, Weizhen Qi, Ming Gong, Linjun Shou, Daxin Jiang, Guihong Cao, Xiaodong Fan, Ruofei Zhang, Rahul Agrawal, Edward Cui, Sining Wei, Taroon Bharti, Ying Qiao, Jiun-Hung Chen, Winnie Wu, Shuguang Liu, Fan Yang, Daniel Campos, Rangan Majumder, and Ming Zhou. 2020. XGLUE: A new benchmark datasetfor cross-lingual pre-training, understanding and generation. In *Proceedings of the 2020 Conference on Empirical Methods in Natural Language Processing (EMNLP)*, pages 6008–6018, Online. Association for Computational Linguistics.

Patrick Littell, David R. Mortensen, Ke Lin, Katherine Kairis, Carlisle Turner, and Lori Levin. 2017. URIEL and lang2vec: Representing languages as typological, geographical, and phylogenetic vectors. In *Proceedings of the 15th Conference of the European Chapter of the Association for Computational Linguistics: Volume 2, Short Papers*, pages 8–14, Valencia, Spain. Association for Computational Linguistics.

Pengfei Liu, Weizhe Yuan, Jinlan Fu, Zhengbao Jiang, Hiroaki Hayashi, and Graham Neubig. 2023a. Pretrain, prompt, and predict: A systematic survey of prompting methods in natural language processing. *ACM Computing Surveys*, 55(9):1–35.

Xiao Liu, Kaixuan Ji, Yicheng Fu, Weng Tam, Zhengxiao Du, Zhilin Yang, and Jie Tang. 2022a. P-tuning: Prompt tuning can be comparable to fine-tuning across scales and tasks. In *Proceedings of the 60th Annual Meeting of the Association for Computational Linguistics (Volume 2: Short Papers)*, pages 61–68, Dublin, Ireland. Association for Computational Linguistics.

Yanchen Liu, Timo Schick, and Hinrich Schütze. 2022b. Semantic-oriented unlabeled priming for large-scale language models. *arXiv preprint arXiv:2202.06133*.

Yihong Liu, Haotian Ye, Leonie Weissweiler, Philipp Wicke, Renhao Pei, Robert Zangenfeind, and Hinrich Schütze. 2023b. A crosslingual investigation of conceptualization in 1335 languages. In *Proceedings of the 61st Annual Meeting of the Association for Computational Linguistics (Volume 1: Long Papers)*, pages 12969–13000, Toronto, Canada. Association for Computational Linguistics.

Yongkang Liu, Shi Feng, Daling Wang, Yifei Zhang, and Hinrich Schütze. 2023c. PVGRU: Generating diverse and relevant dialogue responses via pseudo-variational mechanism. In *Proceedings of the 61st Annual Meeting of the Association for Computational Linguistics (Volume 1: Long Papers)*, pages 3295–3310, Toronto, Canada. Association for Computational Linguistics.

Chunlan Ma, Ayyoob ImaniGooghari, Haotian Ye, Ehsaneddin Asgari, and Hinrich Schütze. 2023. Taxi1500: A multilingual dataset for text classification in 1500 languages. *arXiv preprint arXiv:2305.08487*.

Leland McInnes, John Healy, Nathaniel Saul, and Lukas Großberger. 2018. Umap: Uniform manifold approximation and projection. *Journal of Open Source Software*, 3(29).

Ercong Nie, Sheng Liang, Helmut Schmid, and Hinrich Schütze. 2023. Cross-lingual retrieval augmented prompt for low-resource languages. In *Findings of the Association for Computational Linguistics: ACL 2023*, pages 8320–8340, Toronto, Canada. Association for Computational Linguistics.

Telmo Pires, Eva Schlinger, and Dan Garrette. 2019. How multilingual is multilingual BERT? In *Proceedings of the 57th Annual Meeting of the Association for Computational Linguistics*, pages 4996–5001, Florence, Italy. Association for Computational Linguistics.

Kunxun Qi, Hai Wan, Jianfeng Du, and Haolan Chen. 2022. Enhancing cross-lingual natural language inference by prompt-learning from cross-lingual templates. In *Proceedings of the 60th Annual Meeting of the Association for Computational Linguistics (Volume 1: Long Papers)*, pages 1910–1923, Dublin, Ireland. Association for Computational Linguistics.

Guanghui Qin and Jason Eisner. 2021. Learning how to ask: Querying LMs with mixtures of soft prompts. In *Proceedings of the 2021 Conference of the North American Chapter of the Association for Computational Linguistics: Human Language Technologies*, pages 5203–5212, Online. Association for Computational Linguistics.

Alec Radford, Jeffrey Wu, Rewon Child, David Luan, Dario Amodei, Ilya Sutskever, et al. 2019. Language models are unsupervised multitask learners. *OpenAI blog*, 1(8):9.

Sebastian Ruder, Noah Constant, Jan Botha, Aditya Siddhant, Orhan Firat, Jinlan Fu, Pengfei Liu, Junjie Hu, Dan Garrette, Graham Neubig, and Melvin Johnson. 2021. XTREME-R: Towards more challenging and nuanced multilingual evaluation. In *Proceedings of the 2021 Conference on Empirical Methods in Natural Language Processing*, pages 10215–10245, Online and Punta Cana, Dominican Republic. Association for Computational Linguistics.

Timo Schick, Helmut Schmid, and Hinrich Schütze. 2020. Automatically identifying words that can serve as labels for few-shot text classification. In *Proceedings of the 28th International Conference on Computational Linguistics*, pages 5569–5578, Barcelona, Spain (Online). International Committee on Computational Linguistics.

Timo Schick and Hinrich Schütze. 2021a. Exploiting cloze-questions for few-shot text classification and natural language inference. In *Proceedings of the 16th Conference of the European Chapter of the Association for Computational Linguistics: Main Volume*, pages 255–269, Online. Association for Computational Linguistics.

Timo Schick and Hinrich Schütze. 2021b. Few-shot text generation with natural language instructions. In *Proceedings of the 2021 Conference on Empirical Methods in Natural Language Processing*, pages 390–402, Online and Punta Cana, Dominican Republic. Association for Computational Linguistics.

Timo Schick and Hinrich Schütze. 2021c. It's not just size that matters: Small language models are also few-shot learners. In *Proceedings of the 2021 Conference of the North American Chapter of the Association for Computational Linguistics: Human Language Technologies*, pages 2339–2352, Online. Association for Computational Linguistics.

Zhengxiang Shi and Aldo Lipani. 2023. Don't stop pre-training? make prompt-based fine-tuning powerful learner.

Taylor Shin, Yasaman Razeghi, Robert L. Logan IV, Eric Wallace, and Sameer Singh. 2020. AutoPrompt: Eliciting Knowledge from Language Models with Automatically Generated Prompts. In *Proceedings of the 2020 Conference on Empirical Methods in Natural Language Processing (EMNLP)*, pages 4222–4235, Online. Association for Computational Linguistics.

Gilbert W Stewart. 1993. On the early history of the singular value decomposition. *SIAM review*, 35(4):551–566.

Lifu Tu, Caiming Xiong, and Yingbo Zhou. 2022. Prompt-tuning can be much better than fine-tuning on cross-lingual understanding with multilingual language models. In *Findings of the Association for Computational Linguistics: EMNLP 2022*, pages 5478–5485, Abu Dhabi, United Arab Emirates. Association for Computational Linguistics.

Iulia Turc, Kenton Lee, Jacob Eisenstein, Ming-Wei Chang, and Kristina Toutanova. 2021. Revisiting the primacy of english in zero-shot cross-lingual transfer. *arXiv preprint arXiv:2106.16171*.

Ashish Vaswani, Noam Shazeer, Niki Parmar, Jakob Uszkoreit, Llion Jones, Aidan N Gomez, Łukasz Kaiser, and Illia Polosukhin. 2017. Attention is all you need. *Advances in neural information processing systems*, 30.

Søren Wichmann, Eric W. Holman, and Cecil H. 2022. The asjp database. Version 20.

Adina Williams, Nikita Nangia, and Samuel Bowman. 2018. A broad-coverage challenge corpus for sentence understanding through inference. In *Proceedings of the 2018 Conference of the North American Chapter of the Association for Computational Linguistics: Human Language Technologies, Volume 1 (Long Papers)*, pages 1112–1122, New Orleans, Louisiana. Association for Computational Linguistics.

Thomas Wolf, Lysandre Debut, Victor Sanh, Julien Chaumond, Clement Delangue, Anthony Moi, Pierric Cistac, Tim Rault, Remi Louf, Morgan Funtowicz, Joe Davison, Sam Shleifer, Patrick von Platen, Clara Ma, Yacine Jernite, Julien Plu, Canwen Xu, Teven Le Scao, Sylvain Gugger, Mariama Drame, Quentin Lhoest, and Alexander Rush. 2020. Transformers: State-of-the-art natural language processing. In *Proceedings of the 2020 Conference on Empirical Methods in Natural Language Processing: System Demonstrations*, pages 38–45, Online. Association for Computational Linguistics.

Shijie Wu and Mark Dredze. 2019. Beto, bentz, becas: The surprising cross-lingual effectiveness of BERT. In *Proceedings of the 2019 Conference on Empirical Methods in Natural Language Processing and the 9th International Joint Conference on Natural Language Processing (EMNLP-IJCNLP)*, pages 833–844, Hong Kong, China. Association for Computational Linguistics.

Yinfei Yang, Yuan Zhang, Chris Tar, and Jason Baldridge. 2019a. PAWS-X: A cross-lingual adversarial dataset for paraphrase identification. In *Proceedings of the 2019 Conference on Empirical Methods in Natural Language Processing and the 9th International Joint Conference on Natural Language Processing (EMNLP-IJCNLP)*, pages 3687–3692, Hong Kong, China. Association for Computational Linguistics.

Zhilin Yang, Zihang Dai, Yiming Yang, Jaime Carbonell, Russ R Salakhutdinov, and Quoc V Le. 2019b. Xlnet: Generalized autoregressive pretraining for language understanding. *Advances in neural information processing systems*, 32.

Jingqing Zhang, Yao Zhao, Mohammad Saleh, and Peter Liu. 2020. Pegasus: Pre-training with extracted gap-sentences for abstractive summarization. In *International Conference on Machine Learning*, pages 11328–11339. PMLR.

Yuan Zhang, Jason Baldridge, and Luheng He. 2019. Paws: Paraphrase adversaries from word scrambling.

Mengjie Zhao and Hinrich Schütze. 2021. Discrete and soft prompting for multilingual models. In *Proceedings of the 2021 Conference on Empirical Methods in Natural Language Processing*, pages 8547–8555, Online and Punta Cana, Dominican Republic. Association for Computational Linguistics.

Meng Zhou, Xin Li, Yue Jiang, and Lidong Bing. 2022. Enhancing cross-lingual prompting with mask token augmentation. *arXiv preprint arXiv:2202.07255*.

Liu Zhuang, Lin Wayne, Shi Ya, and Zhao Jun. 2021. A robustly optimized BERT pre-training approach with post-training. In *Proceedings of the 20th Chinese National Conference on Computational Linguistics*, pages 1218–1227, Huhhot, China. Chinese Information Processing Society of China.

Robert Östling and Murathan Kurfalı. 2023. Language embeddings sometimes contain typological generalizations.

A Appendix

A.1 Training Details

During training, we used the same hyperparameters for Vanilla and PROFIT to keep the variables consistent for comparison. The chosen hyperparameters for both full-shot training and few-shot training are documented in Table 6. To avoid random effects on training, we trained each experiment with 5 different random seeds $\{10, 42, 421, 510, 1218\}$ and take the average results.

Hyperparameter	Full	Few-shot
EPOCHS	5	50
LEARNING_RATE	1e-5	1e-5
BATCH_SIZE	8	1
GRADIENT_ACCUMULATION_STEPS	4	2
MAX_SEQ_LENGTH	128	128
EARLY_STOPPING_PATIENCE	-	3

Table 6: Hyperparameters

A.2 Dataset Statistics

In Table 7 we show a basic statistic view of the Amazon Review (Keung et al., 2020) , PAWS-X (Zhang et al., 2019) and XNLI (Williams et al., 2018) datasets. We use the original train-dev-test split from the datasets. For training and validation we use the English train and dev dataset, and for test we use the test sets of all languages. The test data size for each target language is the same in all tasks.

Task	Size			#Labels
	| Train |	| Dev |	| Test |	
Amazon	200 000	5 000	5 000	5
PAWS-X	49 401	2 000	2 000	2
XNLI	392 702	2 490	5 010	3

Table 7: Overview of the three datasets. Train and dev data size refers to the number of samples for English. Test data size refers to the number of samples for each target language.

A.3 Reproducibility

The code for data processing and model training is available at the following Github repository: `https://github.com/boleima/ProFiT`.

A.4 Detailed Results

We present the detailed results of few-shot training performance of Vanilla and PROFIT for all three tasks in Table 9 (Amazon Review), Table 10 (PAWS-X) and Table 11 (XNLI), as well as the T-test results for all tasks in few-shot conditions in Table 8.

Shot	Amazon		PAWS-X		XNLI	
	M	X	M	X	M	X
1	0.001	0.001	0.50	0.56*	0.01	0.12*
2	0.10	0.01	0.22*	0.08*	0.89*	0.18*
4	0.09*	0.02	0.80*	0.10*	0.05	0.07*
8	0.23*	0.04	0.83*	0.04	0.86*	0.14*
16	0.78*	0.11*	0.30*	0.05	0.27*	0.03
32	0.06*	0.16*	1.00*	0.58*	0.11*	0.01
64	0.03	0.18*	0.02	0.80*	0.09*	0.002
128	0.07*	0.11*	0.15*	0.82*	0.34*	0.01
256	0.73*	0.21*	0.12*	0.78*	0.07*	0.02
512	0.86*	0.01	0.04	0.90*	0.61*	0.004
1028	0.003	0.31*	0.03	0.55*	0.74*	0.03
full	0.005	0.40*	0.003	0.46*	0.005	0.44*

Table 8: T-Test results (p) for results of Vanilla and PROFIT in different few-shot conditions. M stands for mBERT and X stands for XLM-R. Insignificant results with a p value > 0.05 are marked with *.

Shot	Model	en	de	es	fr	ja	zh	avg.
1	Vanilla-M	22.30	20.66	19.82	20.02	20.14	20.08	20.14
	ProFiT-M	**28.52**	**26.05**	**26.98**	**26.18**	**25.96**	**25.01**	**26.04**
	Vanilla-X	21.98	22.15	21.69	21.79	21.42	21.52	21.71
	ProFiT-X	**37.09**	**29.86**	**35.06**	**36.10**	**33.13**	**34.00**	**33.63**
2	Vanilla-M	24.37	23.14	23.00	22.70	21.27	21.36	22.29
	ProFiT-M	**27.63**	**25.78**	**26.04**	**25.05**	**23.24**	**23.73**	**24.77**
	Vanilla-X	21.31	21.08	21.52	20.67	20.76	21.41	21.09
	ProFiT-X	**35.63**	**31.82**	**33.46**	**34.40**	**33.35**	**32.70**	**33.14**
4	Vanilla-M	27.04	24.94	23.95	23.93	23.86	22.20	23.78
	ProFiT-M	**30.63**	**26.87**	**27.67**	**26.34**	**25.44**	**26.05**	**26.47**
	Vanilla-X	29.74	29.96	29.67	30.87	26.12	28.89	29.10
	ProFiT-X	**40.23**	**37.91**	**38.60**	**38.75**	**38.84**	**37.11**	**38.24**
8	Vanilla-M	29.95	26.82	26.75	26.91	24.18	25.70	26.07
	ProFiT-M	**32.67**	**29.07**	**30.20**	**29.38**	**26.24**	**27.12**	**28.40**
	Vanilla-X	32.02	32.84	33.02	32.60	28.84	31.51	31.76
	ProFiT-X	**42.23**	**35.63**	**40.55**	**39.79**	**39.65**	**38.33**	**38.79**
16	Vanilla-M	33.92	30.87	32.01	30.29	28.94	28.36	30.09
	ProFiT-M	**35.27**	**31.66**	**32.10**	**31.37**	**29.70**	**28.58**	**30.68**
	Vanilla-X	38.97	39.42	38.70	38.84	34.61	35.72	37.45
	ProFiT-X	**44.78**	**44.40**	**43.89**	**43.55**	**42.57**	**41.26**	**43.13**
32	Vanilla-M	36.73	31.26	31.64	31.69	28.94	29.08	30.52
	ProFiT-M	**37.90**	**33.44**	**34.68**	**33.72**	**31.18**	**30.77**	**32.76**
	Vanilla-X	44.92	45.42	44.45	44.78	42.16	41.85	43.73
	ProFiT-X	**47.51**	**47.12**	**46.67**	**45.78**	**44.24**	**42.70**	**45.30**
64	Vanilla-M	39.85	33.76	35.20	34.65	30.98	29.90	32.90
	ProFiT-M	**41.62**	**36.25**	**37.84**	**36.15**	**32.97**	**32.56**	**35.15**
	Vanilla-X	48.06	**48.48**	46.77	**47.34**	44.01	42.05	45.73
	ProFiT-X	**49.42**	48.16	**47.99**	46.93	**45.58**	**44.00**	**46.53**
128	Vanilla-M	43.29	35.52	37.50	36.38	32.36	31.51	34.65
	ProFiT-M	**44.19**	**38.39**	**39.84**	**38.74**	**34.62**	**33.71**	**37.06**
	Vanilla-X	50.40	50.75	48.37	48.12	46.26	44.80	47.66
	ProFiT-X	**50.75**	**51.24**	**49.75**	**49.22**	**47.39**	**45.35**	**48.59**
256	Vanilla-M	**45.64**	37.15	39.23	38.20	**33.54**	**32.86**	36.20
	ProFiT-M	45.39	**37.71**	**39.99**	**40.31**	32.55	32.82	**36.68**
	Vanilla-X	51.21	50.92	47.15	47.85	46.01	44.23	47.23
	ProFiT-X	**51.40**	**52.18**	**50.22**	**49.81**	**47.65**	**45.60**	**49.09**
512	Vanilla-M	**47.66**	**37.57**	39.90	39.16	**33.82**	**33.64**	36.82
	ProFiT-M	47.64	37.48	**40.63**	**40.99**	32.76	33.40	**37.05**
	Vanilla-X	51.90	51.69	49.21	49.67	46.23	43.96	48.15
	ProFiT-X	**52.94**	**52.79**	**50.21**	**50.06**	**48.16**	**45.82**	**49.41**
1024	Vanilla-M	49.26	38.47	41.24	39.88	33.52	33.79	37.38
	ProFiT-M	**49.63**	**41.47**	**43.54**	**41.97**	**36.52**	**34.54**	**39.61**
	Vanilla-X	51.33	48.55	45.06	44.91	42.85	41.79	44.63
	ProFiT-X	**54.55**	**53.15**	**51.98**	**51.18**	**47.98**	**46.08**	**50.07**
full	Vanilla-M	58.92	45.69	48.02	47.45	35.07	**38.63**	42.97
	ProFiT-M	**59.05**	**46.66**	**49.30**	**48.38**	**37.31**	38.26	**43.98**
	Vanilla-X	59.61	**60.14**	55.24	55.66	51.93	**49.82**	54.56
	ProFiT-X	**60.06**	59.60	**55.72**	**55.89**	**52.34**	49.75	**54.66**

Table 9: Few-shot performance on Amazon

Shot	Model	en	de	es	fr	ja	ko	zh	avg.
1	Vanilla-M	**54.38**	53.29	54.22	54.25	53.37	54.01	53.20	53.72
	ProFiT-M	53.21	**54.18**	**54.44**	**54.34**	**55.31**	**54.35**	**53.80**	**54.40**
	Vanilla-X	**51.95**	**51.75**	**51.57**	**51.62**	**51.95**	**51.73**	**51.80**	**51.74**
	ProFiT-X	50.19	48.53	50.68	46.83	50.80	44.55	49.91	48.55
2	Vanilla-M	**53.54**	**53.60**	**53.81**	**54.18**	**54.43**	**54.54**	**53.77**	**54.06**
	ProFiT-M	52.38	53.04	53.34	53.13	54.35	53.90	51.82	53.26
	Vanilla-X	**54.95**	**54.73**	**54.30**	**54.57**	**54.25**	**54.05**	**54.32**	**54.37**
	ProFiT-X	51.59	50.25	51.65	48.86	51.31	46.30	50.70	49.85
4	Vanilla-M	**53.93**	**53.11**	53.38	**53.94**	53.85	**54.28**	**53.71**	**53.71**
	ProFiT-M	52.40	53.07	**53.64**	53.41	**54.79**	53.53	51.20	53.27
	Vanilla-X	53.15	**54.45**	**53.99**	**53.90**	**53.81**	**53.79**	**53.64**	**53.93**
	ProFiT-X	**53.54**	51.25	53.00	49.05	53.46	45.29	51.83	50.65
8	Vanilla-M	**54.30**	53.50	**53.51**	**54.02**	**54.03**	**53.94**	**54.15**	**53.86**
	ProFiT-M	52.81	**54.12**	53.42	53.31	53.98	53.51	51.93	53.38
	Vanilla-X	**54.60**	**55.13**	**54.68**	**54.80**	**55.46**	**55.10**	**55.14**	**55.05**
	ProFiT-X	53.18	52.65	53.03	51.22	52.48	48.83	52.21	51.74
16	Vanilla-M	**54.08**	50.86	52.04	52.66	51.77	52.27	51.23	51.81
	ProFiT-M	52.81	**53.08**	**53.80**	**53.20**	**53.51**	**53.95**	**52.09**	**53.27**
	Vanilla-X	**54.45**	**54.84**	**54.45**	**54.54**	**54.96**	**54.56**	**54.78**	**54.69**
	ProFiT-X	53.73	51.58	53.24	49.95	53.21	48.28	52.31	51.43
32	Vanilla-M	**54.03**	52.94	53.48	**53.65**	53.13	53.58	**53.08**	**53.31**
	ProFiT-M	52.99	**52.97**	**53.75**	53.14	**53.57**	**54.16**	51.42	53.17
	Vanilla-X	52.44	**53.95**	52.96	**53.21**	53.46	**54.05**	**53.94**	**53.60**
	ProFiT-X	**53.63**	51.96	**53.44**	50.51	**53.61**	49.84	52.73	52.01
64	Vanilla-M	**55.44**	**55.42**	**55.46**	**55.97**	**54.80**	**55.92**	**56.41**	**55.66**
	ProFiT-M	53.95	54.59	54.05	54.48	54.51	54.95	52.61	54.20
	Vanilla-X	55.20	**55.35**	54.69	**54.95**	**55.84**	**55.09**	**55.39**	**55.22**
	ProFiT-X	**56.60**	54.95	**55.90**	54.59	55.63	51.51	55.29	54.64
128	Vanilla-M	**56.63**	**56.29**	**56.69**	**56.43**	55.31	55.70	**55.75**	**56.03**
	ProFiT-M	55.54	55.76	55.28	55.26	**55.88**	**55.75**	55.61	55.59
	Vanilla-X	54.61	54.99	54.44	54.80	55.24	**55.14**	54.98	54.93
	ProFiT-X	**58.66**	**56.28**	**57.95**	**54.91**	**56.09**	52.39	**57.35**	**55.83**
256	Vanilla-M	58.66	56.00	56.38	56.93	55.36	55.77	55.65	56.02
	ProFiT-M	**61.84**	**60.51**	**60.65**	**60.90**	**58.56**	**58.70**	**59.70**	**59.84**
	Vanilla-X	59.30	**58.23**	58.79	**58.54**	57.18	**57.54**	**57.70**	**57.99**
	ProFiT-X	**59.94**	57.75	**59.58**	57.86	**57.28**	54.31	57.35	57.35
512	Vanilla-M	64.23	59.38	60.00	60.15	56.90	56.84	56.79	58.34
	ProFiT-M	**73.47**	**69.74**	**70.23**	**70.20**	**63.84**	**64.56**	**66.97**	**67.59**
	Vanilla-X	**77.03**	**71.28**	72.09	**72.46**	**63.43**	**63.79**	66.53	**68.26**
	ProFiT-X	76.94	71.01	**72.29**	71.24	63.19	63.28	**66.61**	67.94
1024	Vanilla-M	74.43	68.44	69.47	70.01	61.95	61.13	64.69	65.95
	ProFiT-M	**81.06**	**74.58**	**76.08**	**76.15**	**66.05**	**66.76**	**70.64**	**71.71**
	Vanilla-X	86.33	**79.23**	80.86	**80.74**	**69.25**	**68.18**	**73.26**	**75.25**
	ProFiT-X	**87.84**	78.94	**81.53**	80.58	67.68	68.01	71.85	74.76
full	Vanilla-M	93.85	84.94	87.11	86.55	73.39	72.44	77.01	80.24
	ProFiT-M	**94.21**	**86.06**	**88.17**	**87.91**	**75.79**	**75.82**	**79.22**	**82.16**
	Vanilla-X	94.33	86.92	88.55	**89.04**	**76.07**	74.71	79.75	82.51
	ProFiT-X	**94.90**	**87.06**	**88.87**	88.86	75.53	**75.40**	**80.63**	**82.73**

Table 10: Few-shot performance on PAWS-X

Shot	Model	en	ar	bg	de	el	es	fr	hi	ru	sw	th	tr	ur	vi	zh	avg.
1	Vanilla-M	33.58	32.97	32.97	33.46	32.70	33.33	33.43	32.44	32.93	32.85	33.12	33.05	32.96	33.00	32.99	33.02
	PROFIT-M	**37.58**	**34.93**	**33.56**	**35.95**	**35.02**	**34.25**	**36.38**	**33.93**	**36.76**	**34.62**	**33.83**	**34.07**	**34.22**	**36.43**	**37.41**	**35.10**
	Vanilla-X	33.73	33.07	32.86	33.51	32.66	33.40	33.54	32.50	33.04	33.15	33.18	33.14	33.00	33.08	33.04	33.08
	PROFIT-X	**39.26**	**34.61**	**34.85**	**36.28**	**36.88**	**33.59**	**34.92**	**39.76**	**34.47**	**36.53**	**36.33**	**36.56**	**37.03**	**37.40**	**36.61**	**36.13**
2	Vanilla-M	34.67	**34.98**	36.21	**36.15**	**35.46**	**36.91**	**36.42**	34.34	35.42	**34.67**	**34.20**	**35.40**	34.04	36.18	35.61	**35.43**
	PROFIT-M	**38.38**	34.85	**34.02**	35.07	35.20	33.44	35.70	**35.63**	**35.65**	34.50	33.78	34.35	**34.67**	**36.57**	**37.12**	35.04
	Vanilla-X	34.84	34.33	35.51	35.62	34.99	**36.25**	35.86	34.14	35.09	34.39	33.95	34.87	33.76	35.55	35.02	34.95
	PROFIT-X	**39.22**	**36.54**	**36.73**	**38.48**	**37.83**	34.21	**37.91**	**38.87**	**35.56**	**37.16**	**38.42**	**38.01**	**37.75**	**38.25**	**36.98**	**37.34**
4	Vanilla-M	37.91	**35.47**	**36.12**	36.20	35.03	**36.22**	36.09	34.60	35.60	**35.01**	**34.35**	**35.49**	**34.49**	36.28	35.74	35.48
	PROFIT-M	**38.04**	35.43	34.64	**36.67**	**36.50**	33.66	**36.63**	**36.07**	**36.83**	34.87	33.42	35.41	34.44	**37.06**	**37.07**	**35.62**
	Vanilla-X	37.55	34.31	35.08	35.11	34.09	**35.06**	34.85	33.74	**34.53**	34.09	33.58	34.39	33.71	35.09	34.56	34.44
	PROFIT-X	**38.79**	**36.03**	**35.23**	**37.49**	**37.36**	33.50	**36.54**	**38.79**	34.21	**37.11**	**37.79**	**36.47**	**37.58**	**37.96**	**36.22**	**36.59**
8	Vanilla-M	**40.83**	**37.39**	**38.56**	**38.69**	**37.77**	**39.25**	**39.06**	36.38	37.72	**37.54**	**36.46**	**38.07**	**36.28**	**38.22**	37.76	**37.80**
	PROFIT-M	38.71	36.59	35.73	37.20	37.33	34.88	38.05	**38.22**	**38.32**	35.37	35.40	36.48	35.99	38.20	**38.93**	36.91
	Vanilla-X	40.84	36.52	37.57	37.97	36.85	**38.50**	**38.35**	35.70	37.00	36.77	35.57	37.33	35.57	37.56	36.95	37.01
	PROFIT-X	**41.58**	**37.81**	**37.61**	**39.74**	**39.06**	35.07	37.65	**39.78**	**37.26**	**38.64**	**40.32**	**38.79**	**38.65**	**40.33**	**38.54**	**38.52**
16	Vanilla-M	42.42	39.56	40.71	40.36	39.63	**41.49**	41.14	37.86	39.60	**38.27**	37.35	38.77	37.44	40.76	40.25	39.51
	PROFIT-M	**44.52**	**42.10**	**41.96**	**40.85**	**42.18**	40.63	**43.98**	**41.17**	**43.10**	36.50	**38.83**	**41.71**	**38.95**	**43.40**	**43.14**	**41.32**
	Vanilla-X	42.65	39.37	40.33	40.09	39.15	**41.12**	40.73	37.72	39.44	38.02	37.34	38.63	37.19	40.73	40.01	39.28
	PROFIT-X	**49.72**	**42.15**	**43.51**	**47.38**	**46.22**	40.19	**44.09**	**45.59**	**43.14**	**44.81**	**46.16**	**45.39**	**44.43**	**47.35**	**45.69**	**44.72**
32	Vanilla-M	46.18	40.39	41.17	41.25	40.39	42.65	41.88	38.69	40.77	**38.29**	38.47	39.62	38.82	41.18	40.89	40.32
	PROFIT-M	**49.02**	**45.64**	**46.01**	**44.64**	**47.57**	**45.00**	**48.32**	**45.06**	**46.37**	38.28	**43.39**	**43.68**	**43.88**	**47.18**	**47.78**	**45.20**
	Vanilla-X	46.11	39.69	40.44	40.57	39.81	42.05	41.28	38.30	40.25	37.71	37.99	39.05	38.17	40.27	40.00	39.68
	PROFIT-X	**52.27**	**46.87**	**48.41**	**49.79**	**49.12**	**45.55**	**48.85**	**48.42**	**48.10**	**45.90**	**49.20**	**47.88**	**46.58**	**49.84**	**48.55**	**48.08**
64	Vanilla-M	52.10	45.26	46.64	48.10	46.32	49.44	48.57	42.71	45.45	39.13	40.24	42.19	42.41	47.23	46.91	45.04
	PROFIT-M	**55.04**	**50.28**	**51.76**	**52.60**	**52.90**	**50.46**	**53.85**	**49.57**	**51.68**	**42.26**	**46.38**	**49.01**	**48.85**	**52.89**	**52.57**	**50.36**
	Vanilla-X	51.86	44.99	46.39	47.86	45.84	48.92	48.47	42.99	45.25	39.04	40.35	42.43	42.51	47.08	46.70	44.92
	PROFIT-X	**59.35**	**50.75**	**53.38**	**55.47**	**55.32**	**50.92**	**55.71**	**53.11**	**52.67**	**51.31**	**53.99**	**52.95**	**51.30**	**55.51**	**54.41**	**53.34**
128	Vanilla-M	58.61	51.91	54.23	54.89	54.32	**56.27**	55.30	49.05	52.87	43.18	46.02	49.56	48.28	54.02	54.06	51.71
	PROFIT-M	**59.12**	**53.87**	**55.09**	**56.44**	**55.33**	55.00	**56.09**	**52.36**	**54.71**	**45.25**	**49.41**	**52.44**	**51.35**	**55.62**	**55.98**	**53.50**
	Vanilla-X	58.27	51.41	53.86	54.61	53.85	55.90	54.89	48.68	52.21	42.87	46.23	49.26	47.89	53.55	53.90	51.36
	PROFIT-X	**64.78**	**56.50**	**60.23**	**60.77**	**60.55**	**59.51**	**61.20**	**57.41**	**59.13**	**55.12**	**58.44**	**58.15**	**55.36**	**60.24**	**59.68**	**58.73**
256	Vanilla-M	61.88	53.54	56.61	57.25	56.20	**58.77**	57.91	51.31	55.45	44.97	46.97	52.75	50.07	56.51	56.76	53.94
	PROFIT-M	**62.30**	**54.82**	**56.96**	**57.92**	**56.48**	58.69	**58.39**	**53.58**	**57.09**	**45.55**	**49.06**	**53.64**	**52.41**	**57.81**	**58.06**	**55.03**
	Vanilla-X	61.68	53.30	56.19	57.01	55.91	58.47	57.74	51.13	55.22	44.86	46.68	52.77	49.79	56.24	56.33	53.69
	PROFIT-X	**66.55**	**58.08**	**62.26**	**62.24**	**61.23**	**62.88**	**63.44**	**58.56**	**60.42**	**54.77**	**59.95**	**59.95**	**56.59**	**62.28**	**61.18**	**60.27**
512	Vanilla-M	64.94	56.75	59.66	60.73	58.53	**61.99**	60.89	53.69	58.94	46.24	48.58	55.50	52.56	59.71	59.89	56.69
	PROFIT-M	**65.39**	**57.36**	**60.18**	**61.03**	**58.95**	61.59	**61.04**	**55.07**	**59.52**	**47.23**	**50.48**	**55.98**	**54.08**	**60.25**	**60.41**	**57.37**
	Vanilla-X	64.92	56.33	59.53	60.47	58.11	61.92	60.59	53.36	58.53	45.92	47.99	55.25	52.15	59.32	59.49	56.35
	PROFIT-X	**70.13**	**61.99**	**66.33**	**65.47**	**64.91**	**67.43**	**66.72**	**60.53**	**64.80**	**57.27**	**63.16**	**63.35**	**58.78**	**65.31**	**64.74**	**63.63**
1024	Vanilla-M	65.90	56.85	59.73	61.10	58.40	**62.73**	**62.07**	54.57	59.38	46.46	48.46	56.19	**54.21**	60.32	60.51	57.21
	PROFIT-M	**66.77**	**57.83**	**59.94**	**61.53**	**59.42**	62.05	61.99	**55.37**	**59.54**	**47.44**	**49.10**	**56.40**	53.91	**60.48**	**60.62**	**57.54**
	Vanilla-X	65.67	56.88	59.61	60.95	57.99	62.47	61.93	54.48	59.30	46.36	48.21	56.01	54.29	60.15	60.25	57.06
	PROFIT-X	**71.51**	**63.04**	**67.62**	**66.26**	**66.27**	**68.64**	**67.72**	**62.02**	**65.86**	**58.12**	**64.33**	**64.41**	**60.46**	**66.36**	**65.50**	**64.76**
full	Vanilla-M	82.57	65.12	68.97	71.40	66.30	74.22	73.68	60.02	68.95	50.24	53.15	62.02	57.96	69.80	68.91	65.05
	PROFIT-M	82.57	**65.55**	**69.47**	**71.57**	**67.43**	**75.10**	**74.57**	**60.57**	**69.55**	**51.13**	**54.58**	**62.64**	**58.04**	**70.74**	**70.08**	**65.79**
	Vanilla-X	84.91	**71.86**	77.78	76.86	75.96	79.25	78.21	69.92	**75.79**	**65.21**	72.02	73.12	66.07	74.71	73.72	73.61
	PROFIT-X	**84.97**	71.81	**77.92**	**77.35**	**76.11**	**79.31**	**78.75**	**70.10**	75.43	65.13	**72.39**	**73.23**	**66.95**	**75.05**	**73.92**	**73.82**

Table 11: Few-shot performance on XNLI

Comparing Pre-Training Schemes for Luxembourgish BERT Models

Cedric Lothritz **Saad Ezzini**
Christoph Purschke **Tegawendé F. Bissyandé** **Jacques Klein**
University of Luxembourg
6, rue Coudenhove-Kalergi
L-1359 Luxembourg
{cedric.lothritz, saad.ezzini,christoph.purschke,tegawende.bissyande,jacques.klein} @uni.lu

Isabella Olariu
Zortify SA
9, rue du Laboratoire
L-1911 Gare Luxembourg
isabella@zortify.com

Andrey Boytsov **Clément Lefebvre** **Anne Goujon**
BGL BNP Paribas
10, rue Edward Steichen
L-2540 Luxembourg
{andrey.boytsov,clement.c.lefebvre,anne.goujon} @bgl.lu

Abstract

Despite the widespread use of pre-trained models in NLP, well-performing pre-trained models for low-resource languages are scarce. To address this issue, we propose two novel BERT models for the Luxembourgish language that improve on the state of the art. We also present an empirical study on both the performance and robustness of the investigated BERT models. We compare the models on a set of downstream NLP tasks and evaluate their robustness against different types of data perturbations. Additionally, we provide novel datasets to evaluate the performance of Luxembourgish language models. Our findings reveal that pre-training a pre-loaded model has a positive effect on both the performance and robustness of fine-tuned models and that using the German GottBERT model yields a higher performance while the multilingual mBERT results in a more robust model. This study provides valuable insights for researchers and practitioners working with low-resource languages and highlights the importance of considering pre-training strategies when building language models.

Keywords: Low-resource languages, Luxembourgish, LuxemBERT, Downstream NLP tasks, Language models, Pre-training, GottBERT, BERT

1 Introduction

The introduction of BERT models in 2018 (Devlin et al., 2019) was a crucial milestone for the NLP community. The ability to fine-tune an already pre-trained BERT model mitigated the need for specialised model architectures for given tasks. Despite the emergence of better-performing architectures in recent years, fine-tuning BERT models continues to be a popular approach for numerous NLP tasks in industrial settings.

While highly performing pre-trained BERT models are readily available for widely spoken languages, they are comparably scarce for low-resource languages due to the amount of data necessary to pre-train adequate models. In fact, we determined that the number of languages for which a pre-trained BERT model is available on Huggingface[1] is less than 150, with many of them supported only through multilingual models such as multilingual BERT (mBERT) (Devlin et al., 2019) and XLM-RoBERTa (Conneau et al., 2019). These multilingual models provide a viable alternative, but monolingual models can outperform them if sufficient pre-training data is available, as shown by Wu and Dredze (2020).

Several factors can influence the quality of a language model (LM), such as the size of the pre-training corpus, which can be increased through data augmentation techniques (Hedderich et al., 2020). The configuration of the model architecture can also be varied to improve performance, as highlighted by Wu and Dredze (2020). Another ap-

[1] https://huggingface.co/models

Proceedings of the 19th Conference on Natural Language Processing (KONVENS 2023), pages 17–27
September 18–22, 2023. ©2023 Association for Computational Linguistics

proach to enhance the performance of a language model is to choose whether to pre-train the LM from scratch or to pre-load the weights from an existing model and continue the pre-training using data from the target language, as discussed in (Muller et al., 2021). These considerations are important when working with low-resource languages as they can greatly impact the quality of the pre-trained models.

In this study, we focus on Luxembourgish, a low-resource language spoken primarily in Luxembourg by nearly 600 000 people worldwide. We investigate the impact of pre-training a pre-loaded LM versus using pre-training from scratch, as well as the impact of pre-loading a monolingual versus a multilingual pre-trained model.

The contributions of this study are threefold: **(a)** We propose two novel BERT models for the Luxembourgish language that improve on the state of the art. These models are trained on a large corpus of Luxembourgish text and are able to capture the unique characteristics of the language. **(b)** We also present an empirical study on both the performance and robustness of the investigated BERT models. This study compares the models on a set of downstream NLP tasks and evaluates their robustness against different types of data perturbations. **(c)** Additionally, we provide novel datasets to evaluate the performance of Luxembourgish language models. These datasets are specifically designed for the Luxembourgish language and are not available in previous studies, which will be useful for future research in this field.

2 Approach

In this section, we describe the creation of the two novel BERT models that we pre-trained for this study: Lb_mBERT and Lb_GottBERT. [2]

2.1 Pre-loaded Models

As mentioned in Section 1, we set out to compare pre-loading a multilingual and a monolingual BERT model. Our models of choice are the multilingual mBERT and the German GottBERT model which we pre-train on a corpus of 12 million sentences.

[2]Our final models are available at https://huggingface.co/lothritz/Lb_mBERT and https://huggingface.co/lothritz/Lb_GottBERT

2.1.1 mBERT

Created by Devlin et al. (2019), mBERT is a multilingual BERT model trained on 104 languages. Specifically, the model was pre-trained on Wikipedia articles, including the Luxembourgish Wikipedia, which contained 59 000 articles. mBERT contains 12 transformer blocks, 768 hidden layers, 12 self-attention blocks, and 110 million trainable parameters, as well as a vocab size of 105 879 WordPiece tokens, 100 of which are unused. Our first model uses mBERT as its starting point and is appropriately named Lb_mBERT. We adapt the vocab file by replacing the unused tokens with the 100 most common ones in our pre-training corpus. We then train the model for 10 epochs on the Masked-Language-Modeling task (MLM) with a masking probability of 15%.

2.1.2 GottBERT

Luxembourgish is a West Germanic language originating from a Moselle Franconian dialect (Gilles, 2022). As such, Luxembourgish and German are closely related. Indeed, both languages are similar in terms of vocabulary and structure (Lothritz et al., 2022). Due to these similarities, we choose the German GottBERT model (Scheible et al., 2020) as a pre-loaded model to create Lb_GottBERT. GottBERT was pre-trained on the German part of the OSCAR corpus (Ortiz Suárez et al., 2020) consisting of nearly 459 million sentences. Its vocab file consists of 52 009 WordPiece tokens. As none of these tokens are unused, we cannot modify the vocab file. Similarly to the training of Lb_mBERT, we pre-train the model for 10 epochs on the MLM task with a masking probability of 15% using the same pre-training corpus.

2.2 Pre-training Corpus

In order to pre-train our models, we use the corpus built by (Lothritz et al., 2022) which consists of 12 million sentences, 6 million of which are written in Luxembourgish. The used corpus includes data from the Luxembourgish Wikipedia, the Luxembourgish news site rtl.lu, and the Leipzig Wortschatz corpus (Goldhahn et al., 2012). The remaining 6 million consist of augmented data resulting from a novel data augmentation scheme based on partial translation. As Luxembourgish is very closely related to the German language in terms of structure and vocabulary, the authors used a German dataset made up of Wikipedia articles that they partially translate to Luxembourgish. Specifically, they used a predetermined set of non-ambiguous and common words to translate a significant portion of their supplementary German data to Luxembourgish.

3 Experimental Setup

In this section, we list our research questions for this study and describe the setup of experiments we perform to answer these questions. For our experiments, we consider six pre-trained language models finetuned on eight NLP tasks: Part-of-Speech (POS) tagging, Named Entity Recognition (NER), Intent Classification (IC), News Classification (NC), Winograd Natural Language Inference (WNLI), Sentence Negation (SN), Sentiment Analysis (SA), and Recognizing Textual Entailment (RTE). Furthermore, when applicable, we apply four perturbation techniques to our test sets: negation, name replacement, location replacement, and synonym replacement.

3.1 Research Questions

We address the following research questions:

RQ1. Which model yields the highest performance on downstream NLP tasks? In this research question, we aim to evaluate and compare the performance of different language models on a set of downstream tasks such as news classification, named entity recognition, part-of-speech tagging, etc. The goal is to identify the model that performs the best across all tasks or a specific set of tasks.

RQ2. How robust are the models against data perturbation? In this research question, we aim to evaluate the robustness of the models against different types of data perturbations, namely: negation, name replacement, location replacement, and synonym replacement. The goal is to understand how well the models can handle these variations in input data and identify the model that is the most robust.

3.2 Baseline Models

In this section, we present the various BERT models we investigated for this study. Most of the models were pre-trained on Luxembourgish data. Table 1 shows an overview of the differences between each model.

3.2.1 mBERT & GottBERT

We use the original versions of both mBERT and GottBERT without additional pre-training as two of our baseline models. This allows us to determine the impact of our pre-training corpus on each respective model. While mBERT was partially trained on Luxembourgish Wikipedia articles, GottBERT was trained exclusively on German data. As such, we expect mBERT to yield better performances on the downstream tasks.

3.2.2 LuxemBERT

(Lothritz et al., 2022) published a Luxembourgish BERT model made from scratch trained on the 12 million sentences described in Section2.2. Its architecture is made up of 12 transformer blocks, 768 hidden layers, 12 self-attention blocks, and 110 million trainable parameters, as well as a vocab size of 30 000 WordPiece tokens. It was trained on the MLM task for 10 epochs with a masking probability of 15%. They found that LuxemBERT improved upon mBERT's performance for numerous tasks. Following that, we expect it to outperform both mBERT and GottBERT in most of our experiments.

3.2.3 DA BERT

DA BERT was created by Olariu et al. (2023) and was trained on the same 6 million Luxembourgish sentences as LuxemBERT. Similarly to LuxemBERT, it was pre-trained from scratch, and has a similar architecture to LuxemBERT: 12 transformer blocks, 768 hidden layers, 12 self-attention blocks, and 110 million trainable parameters. The vocab size is also identical with 30 000 tokens. However, contrary to LuxemBERT, the 6 million remaining sentences were not translated from a different language. Instead, they employed classical data augmentation techniques to create more data. Specifically, they replaced words in the original dataset while preserving the original meaning of the original sentences. The word replacements consisted of synonym replacements, named entity replacements, and modal verb replacements. They found that the performance of their new model is similar to that of LuxemBERT. As such, we also expect its performance in our experiments to be comparable to that of LuxemBERT.

3.3 Downstream Tasks

For this study, we consider eight downstream tasks. In addition to the five tasks introduced in Lothritz et al. (2022) (POS-tagging, Named Entity Recognition, Intent Classification, News Classification, and WNLI), we also investigate Sentence Negation, the

	mBERT	GottBERT	LuxemBERT	DA BERT	Lb_mBERT	Lb_GottBERT
Pre-training	NAP	NAP	from scratch	from scratch	from mBERT	from GottBERT
Authentic Lb Data	No	No	Yes	Yes	Yes	Yes
Translated De Data	No	No	Yes	No	Yes	Yes
Augmented Lb Data	No	No	No	Yes	No	No

Table 1: Differences in pre-training scheme and data for each investigated model. (NAP = no additional pre-training)

Recognizing Textual Entailment task, and Sentiment Analysis, which we describe in the following section.[3]

3.3.1 Part-of-Speech Tagging

Part-of-Speech (POS) tagging task is a classical sequence-to-sequence task. The objective is to categorise each word in a sentence into its correct grammatical class such as noun or verb. This dataset is made up of nearly 5500 sentences from Luxembourgish news articles and words are categorised into 15 different classes (Lothritz et al., 2022).

3.3.2 Named Entity Recognition

Similarly to POS-tagging, Named Entity Recognition (NER) is a common sequence-to-sequence task aimed to detect proper names in text. The raw dataset for this task is the same as the one for POS-tagging, and covers the labels *person*, *geopolitical entity*, *(natural) location*, *organisation*, and *miscellaneous* (Lothritz et al., 2022).

3.3.3 Intent Classification

Intent Classification (IC) is a crucial task for digital assistants and chatbot, concerned with detecting the underlying intent of a user's message. For this study, we use the Banking Client Support dataset introduced in Lothritz et al. (2021). The dataset contains nearly 1000 samples divided into 28 intents for the banking domain.

3.3.4 News Classification

News Classification (NC) is a popular text classification task in NLP. As the name implies, the objective is to categorise news articles into given types of news. This set consists of nearly 10 000 news articles divided into eight labels. (Lothritz et al., 2022)

3.3.5 Winograd Natural Language Inference

Being part of the GLUE benchmark collection (Wang et al., 2018), the Winograd Natural Language Inference (WNLI, Levesque et al., 2012). Given a sentence pair A and B, where A contains at least one pronoun and B replaces the pronoun, the task consists of determining whether or not A entails B. For this study, we use a translated version of the dataset (Lothritz et al., 2022), containing nearly 800 sentence pairs.

3.3.6 Sentence Negation

The Sentence Negation task consists of changing the polarity of a given sentence. Specifically, the objective is to correctly place the word "net"[4] in order to turn the sentence negative. For this task, we only consider sentences that are fewer than 15 words long. The dataset consists of a subset of the Luxembourgish portion of the Leipzig Corpora Collection (Goldhahn et al., 2012)[5], which was not used to pre-train either of our models. We extract all the sentences containing the word "net" and turn them into a labelled dataset accordingly. The resulting training, validation, and test sets contain 33975, 2171, and 10095 sentences, respectively. The word "net" is at position 3 in most sentences (14.52% of the dataset), while it is at position 13 in the fewest cases (0.5%). It is to note, that there are multiple ways to negate sentences in the Luxembourgish language, with slightly different meanings depending on the position of the word "net". As such, a model's prediction may be considered false in our experiments despite producing a correctly negated sentence.

3.3.7 Recognizing Textual Entailment

The Recognizing Textual Entailment (RTE) task was introduced by Haim et al. (2006) and was added to the GLUE benchmark collection (Wang et al., 2018) for evaluating the performance of language models. Given a sentence pair A and B, the objective is to determine whether or not B is entailed by A. As there is currently no Luxembourgish version for this task, we translated the original version to Luxembourgish using the googletrans API.[6] The final dataset contains translation errors,

[3] Our datasets are available at `https://github.com/Trustworthy-Software/LuxemBERT`

[4] The Luxembourgish word for "not"

[5] https://wortschatz.uni-leipzig.de/en/download/Luxembourgish

[6] https://pypi.org/project/googletrans/

but it is serviceable for our experiments as the data is the same for each of our models. However, we would not advise to use this dataset for commercial use without revising the text. The training, validation, and test sets contain 2490, 277, and 801 sentences, respectively. 51% of the sentence pairs are examples for textual entailment while 49% are not.

3.3.8 Sentiment Analysis

Sentiment Analysis is a classic NLP problem consisting of determining whether a given sentence is positive, negative, or neutral. For this study, we use two different datasets: SA1 and SA2. SA1 is a dataset of Luxembourgish user comments collected from the news website RTL[7] that was manually annotated with the labels *positive*, *negative*, and *neutral*. The training, validation and test sets contain 1293, 188, and 367 samples, respectively. 12% of the samples are labelled positive, 34% negative, and 54% are neutral.[8] SA2 is a subset of the SST-2 dataset (Socher et al., 2013) which we automatically translated to Luxembourgish using Google Translate.

Unlike the SA1 dataset, it has binary labels: *positive* and *negative*. SA2's training, validation, and test sets contain 9646, 872, and 2360 samples, respectively. 55% of the samples are labelled *positive* and 45% negative.

3.4 Finetuning Parameters

Devlin et al. (2019) recommends choosing hyperparameters for batch size, learning rate, and number of training epochs from the following ranges: $range_{batch\,size}$={16,32}, $range_{learning\,rate}$={2e-5, 3e-5, 5e-5}, and $range_{epochs}$={1,2,3,4,5}. For the POS, NER, IC, NC, and WNLI tasks, we reuse the same parameters from Lothritz et al. (2022), for the remaining tasks, we perform a grid search using the original LuxemBERT model to find the best-performing configuration of parameters. Table 2 shows the chosen hyperparameters for each task. We finetune each of our models on the same sets of hyperparameters.

3.5 Perturbation Techniques

In order to evaluate the robustness of our models, we investigate three perturbation techniques, some of which are described by Ribeiro et al. (2020): sentence negation, entity replacement, and synonym replacement. For this study, we conduct our experiments as follows: we train our models on unperturbed training and validation sets, and then test them on both the unperturbed and the perturbed test sets, allowing us to determine the robustness of our models to each perturbation technique. Due to the nature of our tasks, we cannot apply each perturbation technique to every test set. Table 3 shows an overview of the techniques we use.

3.5.1 Negation

As described in Section 3.3.6, the aim of sentence negation is to turn a given sentence into a negative. By applying sentence negation to the sentiment analysis, we can change the polarity of sentences, turning positive sentences into negative ones and vice versa. Furthermore, we can apply the technique to RTE by negating one sentence of each *entailment* pair in the test set. This approach will turn an *entailment* sentence pair into a *not_entailment* pair.

3.5.2 Entity Replacement

Entity Replacement describes replacing proper names such as person's or location names in the datasets. Intuitively, changing names should not alter the meaning of sentences in our datasets, so the predictions of the models should remain the same regardless of the test set we use. For this study, we focus on replacing first names as well as location names as they are the most common types of names in our datasets. Specifically, we replace names in each sentence in our test sets by a randomly chosen one from the same list of first names that was used to augment the pre-training data for DA BERT (Olariu et al., 2023). In order to maintain consistency, we ensure that identical names in the datasets are all mapped to the same names during the replacement.

3.5.3 Synonym Replacement

As the name implies, for the synonym replacement perturbation, we replace words in the test set by a randomly selected synonym. Specifically, we replace 0 or 1 synonym in each sentence in each of our test sets. Similarly to entity replacement, this kind of perturbation technique should not change the meaning of a given sentence and thus not modify the prediction of a model. For this, we use the same synonym dictionary that was used to augment the pre-training corpus for DA BERT.

[7] `www.rtl.lu`

[8] We make the dataset available on request

Task	POS	NER	IC	NC	WNLI	SN	RTE	SA1	SA2
batch size	16	16	16	16	16	16	16	16	16
learning rate	5e-5	5e-5	5e-5	2e-5	5e-5	5e-5	5e-5	3e-5	5e-5
# epochs	3	3	5	2	5	4	4	2	2

Table 2: Fine-tuning hyperparameters for each investigated task

PT	POS	NER	IC	NC	WNLI	SN	RTE	SA1	SA2
Negation	✗	✗	✗	✗	✗	✗	✓	✓	✓
Name replacement	✗	✗	✗	✗	✗	✓	✓	✓	✓
Location replacement	✗	✗	✗	✗	✗	✓	✓	✓	✗
Synonym replacement	✗	✗	✗	✗	✗	✓	✓	✓	✓

Table 3: Applicability of the perturbation techniques

4 Experimental Results

In this section, we will present the detailed results from our experiments. Table 4 shows the average performance of each model on each task using the original test sets in terms of F1 score. Table 5 displays the performances on original and perturbed test sets of each model fine-tuned on Sentence Negation, RTE, and Sentiment Analysis.

4.1 RQ1: Which model yields the highest performance on downstream NLP tasks?

In order to answer this question, we refer to the results shown in both Table 4 and Figure 1. Both the simple mBERT and GottBERT models perform poorly compared to the remaining models, which is to be expected. In addition, the GottBERT models fine-tuned for WNLI, SN, and RTE are all naive classifiers that consistently predict *not_entailment* for the WNLI task, position *3* for the SN task, and *not_entailment* for the RTE task. However, GottBERT does outperform each model in the POS-tagging task, and mBERT outperforms every model except for LB_GottBERT in the WNLI task. On the other hand, both the Lb_mBERT and Lb_GottBERT models almost consistently outperform each remaining model, with Lb_GottBERT performing best in four out of nine tasks, and Lb_mBERT performing best in two tasks and second-best in four tasks. The two models that were pre-trained from scratch usually achieve intermediate performances. However, one notable exception is the SA1 task where both outperform Lb_mBERT and Lb_GottBERT with DA BERT significantly outperforming every other model.

4.2 RQ2: How robust are models against data perturbation?

In order to answer this question, we applied the perturbation techniques as described in Section 3.5 to the test sets from three of the investigated tasks: Sentence Negation, RTE, and Sentiment Analysis. For each perturbation technique, we only consider the samples that were affected, omitting the samples that were unchanged during the perturbation process. We then test each fine-tuned model on both the original and the perturbed test sets we generated. We report the differences in performance of each model between the unperturbed and perturbed test sets for SN, RTE, and SA in Table 5.

Overall, we notice that both negation and synonym replacement perturbations have a moderate to high impact on the performance of the models, while name and location replacements have a relatively low impact (cf. Fig. 2, 3, 4, 5)

For the SN task, we notice that both entity perturbation techniques, name replacement and location replacement, generally have a very low impact on the performance of the chosen models. One noticeable outlier is the original LuxemBERT model with an average difference of 1.8 percentage points for name replacement, and 3.7 percentage points for location replacement, showing that fine-tuned LuxemBERT models are somewhat susceptible to this kind of data perturbation. Another outlier is the GottBERT model as there is no difference in performance between the perturbed and unperturbed test sets, but as already mentioned, this particular model always predicts *3*. As such, this score is not meaningful. While the differences are very low for entity replacements, we notice significant differences for synonym replacement, most of which are close to

Task	mBERT	GottBERT	LuxemBERT	DA BERT	Lb_mBERT	Lb_GottBERT
POS	0.886	0.902	0.890	0.887	0.889	0.900
NER	0.689	0.661	0.700	0.708	0.717	0.726
IC	0.460	0.574	0.725	0.717	0.760	0.762
NC	0.900	0.871	0.918	0.900	0.906	0.900
WNLI	0.640	0.780*	0.596	0.544	0.560	0.650
SN	0.804	0.248*	0.859	0.858	0.867	0.883
RTE	0.488	0.512*	0.528	0.551	0.563	0.489
SA1	0.612	0.636	0.666	0.687	0.664	0.651
SA2	0.737	0.697	0.859	0.861	0.868	0.864

Table 4: Results for each task on the original test sets. * denotes naive classifier that always predicts the same class

Perturbation	#samples	mBERT	GottBERT	LuxemBERT	DA BERT	Lb_mBERT	Lb_GottBERT
Sentence Negation							
NR	356	0.1	0.0	1.8	0.6	0.2	0.5
LR	527	0.9	0.0	3.7	1.7	1.1	1.6
SR	6597	13.0	0	14.2	6.9	12.7	13.8
Recognizing Textual Entailment							
Neg	373	100	100	38.2	41.1	2.5	41.6
NR	243	0	0	2.3	2.4	2.4	3.4
LR	363	0	0	2.0	3.4	0.3	5.7
SR	682	0	0	0.2	0.6	0.6	5.1
Sentiment Analysis 1							
Neg	45	8.7	5.1	22.1	32.3	20	19.5
NR	11	4.3	0	1.5	4.3	0	2
LR	24	2.8	2.2	6.3	4	3.1	3.6
SR	276	0.5	0.6	0.9	0.6	1.1	1.2
Sentiment Analysis 2							
Neg	1587	19.6	24.2	27.5	33.1	36.0	33.6
NR	148	0.9	1.0	1.0	1.8	0.8	1.4
SR	1508	1.1	5.3	0.9	2.6	2.2	2.0

Table 5: Difference (in percentage points) of performances between original test sets and perturbed sets (Neg: Negated test set / NR: Test set with name replacement/ LR: Test Set with location replacement/ SR: Test set with synonym replacement)

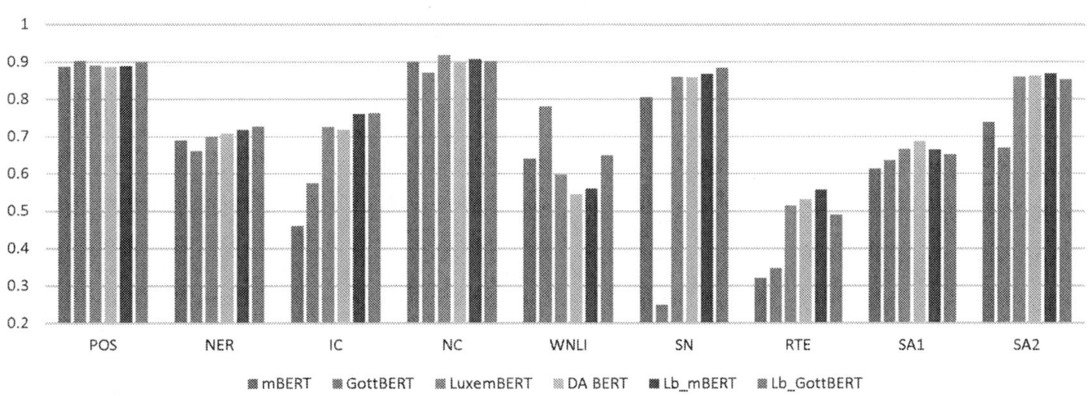

Figure 1: Fine-tuning results of the models on each investigated task

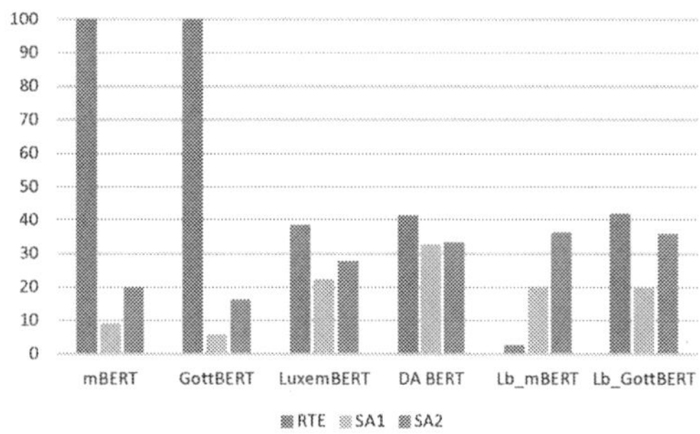

Figure 2: Impact of negation on each model's performance.

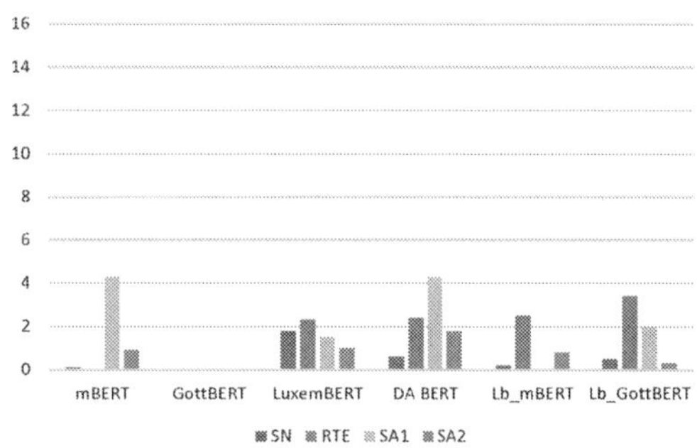

Figure 3: Impact of name replacements on each model's performance.

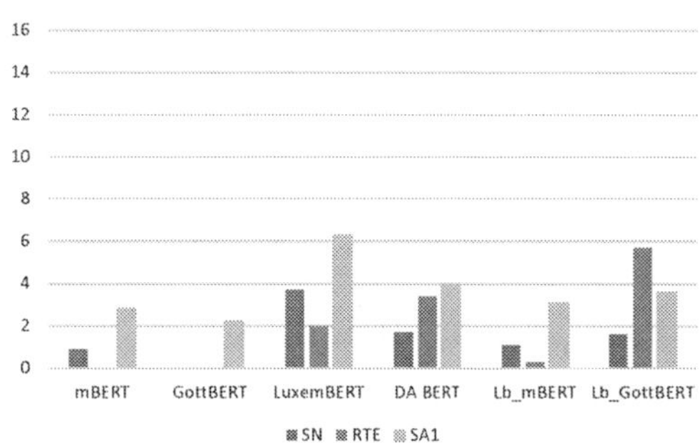

Figure 4: Impact of location replacements on each model's performance.

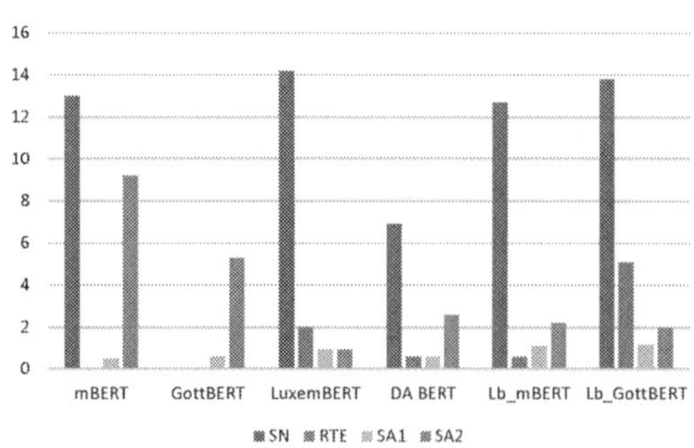

Figure 5: Impact of synonym replacements on each model's performance.

10 percentage points. Once again, the LuxemBERT model shows the highest difference with 14.2 percentage points. DA BERT, which was partially trained on data that was augmented with synonym replacements, shows to be more robust against this kind of data perturbation compared to the remaining models with a difference of only 6.9 percentage points. For the RTE task, we observe that most models with the exception of Lb_GottBERT are fairly robust against the replacement perturbation techniques. On the other hand, they are very susceptible to negation, as only Lb_mBERT's performance is almost unchanged when tested on perturbed data; each remaining model's performance is nearly 40 percentage points lower. We notice a similar trend on the SA2 task, where replacement techniques have only a slight impact on the model performance while negation has a high impact, the difference in performance ranging from nearly 20-35 percentage points depending on the model. Regarding the SA1 task, we observe low, yet mixed results for both entity replacement techniques, but this might be due to the very small sample size of the respective datasets. On the other hand, the impact of sentence negation and synonym replacement is noticeably smaller compared to the SA2 task across all models.

5 Discussion

We show that it is possible to achieve higher performance with the same amount of pre-training data and training time as pre-training from scratch, making our approach both more data- and time-efficient. Overall, both Lb_mBERT and Lb_GottBERT outperform LuxemBERT and DA BERT in almost all tasks. (cf. Table 4) However, while Lb_mBERT is also shown to be highly resistant to data perturbation, it appears that the impact of perturbation on Lb_GottBERT's performance varies depending on the task. On the other hand, both models trained from scratch display worse resistance to data perturbation than Lb_mBERT. As such, we conclude that it is preferable to continue pre-training a pre-existing model on textual data in the target language. According to our experiments, it appears that there is a trade-off between performance and robustness depending on the choice of pre-trained language model. A multilingual model should be chosen if robustness is preferred, while a model for a language that is close to the target language is preferable if the objective is high performance, at least judging by the results from our experiments.

6 Related Works

Wu and Dredze (2020) proposed pairing related languages to train a low-resource language model can result in a performance improvement over a monolingual model. In particular, they combined Latvian and Lithuanian text to create a Latvian BERT model as well as Afrikaans and Dutch text to create an Afrikaans BERT model. Similarly, the Luxembourgish LuxemBERT model (Lothritz et al., 2022) was also trained on bilingual data joining Luxembourgish and German text. However, while those language models are jointly pre-trained on data written in different languages from scratch, for our approach, we pre-train already existing language models on new language data.

Similar to our approach, Muller et al. (2021) continued to pre-train mBERT to various unseen low-resource languages written in different non-Latin scripts and evaluate the performance on three common NLP tasks. Similar to our own experiments, they found that this approach typically leads to models that outperform both the original mBERT and models that were trained from scratch. Our study, however, focuses on a single language that is featured in mBERT. Furthermore, we do not only apply this approach to mBERT, but also to GottBERT to evaluate the performance gain of pre-training a pre-loaded model for a language that is close to the target language.

Ribeiro et al. (2020) introduced CheckList, a tool to semi-automatically create a large number of test cases to determine the robustness of NLP models. Similarly to our study, they consider various types of simple data perturbations to create new test samples. However, their tool is more versatile as it also allows the creation of templates to generate a large number of simple sentences as well as simple additions of phrases that do not change the label of a sample.

7 Threats to Validity

Similar to most experimental studies, there are factors that might threaten the validity of this work when scrutinised.

The first threat is related to the choice of the pre-loaded models, namely mBERT and GottBERT. Both of these models were pre-trained with hyperparameters that slightly differ from the LuxemBERT and DA BERT models, so the improved performance might have been due to confounding variables that we did not control. In particular, the alphabet size and vocabulary size differ significantly as mentioned in Section 2.1. However, we deemed GottBERT and mBERT as appropriate baselines for our study as they are the closest to LuxemBERT and DA BERT in terms of architecture.

Another possible threat concerns some of the downstream tasks we chose to evaluate our models. Specifically, the RTE and SA1 tasks are problematic as they were automatically translated without manually correcting the result. As such, there are numerous translation mistakes present in these datasets which might have influenced the results of our experiments.

8 Conclusion

In this study, we investigated the effects of pre-training pre-loaded language models vs pre-training language models from scratch for building Luxembourgish language models. We evaluated our models in two dimensions: performance and robustness. We conducted our experiments on nine downstream NLP tasks of varying difficulty, and invesitgated the robustness of our models with three perturbation techniques. We found that pre-training a pre-loaded model does indeed have a positive effect on both the performance and robustness of fine-tuned models. In particular, the results from our experiments suggest that using the German GottBERT model yields a higher performance, while the multilingual mBERT results in a more robust model.

9 Acknowledgements

This work was partially supported by the Fonds National de la Recherche (FNR), Luxembourg, under project LUXEMBERT BRIDGES2021/IS/16229163.

10 Limitations

The approach presented in this work was only tested on the Luxembourgish language and using German as an auxiliary language. The approach should be generalisable to other languages, but this might be limited by how similar the auxiliary language is to the target language in terms of structure and vocabulary. We are confident that the approach for continued pre-training is applicable if the target language is either a dialect of or part of the same language family as the language of the preloaded language model. However, the applicability of this approach is unclear for languages that differ significantly from each other.

11 Ethical Considerations

This study involved a pre-training corpus that partially consists of user comments from a news website and chatlogs from a defunct chatroom, both of which originally included usernames (Lothritz et al., 2022). However, this data was anonymised before model training. While we do publish our models that were trained with the same data, we do not publish the pre-training corpus in question. The remaining datasets that we publish are all based on either publicly available textual data dumps or already existing datasets from the GLUE collection, and as such do not violate GDPR guidelines to the best of our knowledge.

References

Alexis Conneau, Kartikay Khandelwal, Naman Goyal, Vishrav Chaudhary, Guillaume Wenzek, Francisco Guzmán, Edouard Grave, Myle Ott, Luke Zettlemoyer, and Veselin Stoyanov. 2019. Unsupervised cross-lingual representation learning at scale. *CoRR*, abs/1911.02116.

Jacob Devlin, Ming-Wei Chang, Kenton Lee, and Kristina Toutanova. 2019. Bert: Pre-training of deep bidirectional transformers for language understanding. In *2019 Conference of the North American Chapter of the ACL: Human Language Technologies*.

Peter Gilles. 2022. Luxembourgish. In *The Oxford Encyclopedia of Germanic Linguistics*.

Dirk Goldhahn, Thomas Eckart, and Uwe Quasthoff. 2012. Building large monolingual dictionaries at the leipzig corpora collection: From 100 to 200 languages. In *Proceedings of the Eighth International Conference on Language Resources and Evaluation (LREC'12)*, pages 759–765.

R Bar Haim, Ido Dagan, Bill Dolan, Lisa Ferro, Danilo Giampiccolo, Bernardo Magnini, and Idan Szpektor. 2006. The second pascal recognising textual entailment challenge. In *Proceedings of the Second PASCAL Challenges Workshop on Recognising Textual Entailment*, volume 7.

Michael A Hedderich, Lukas Lange, Heike Adel, Jannik Strötgen, and Dietrich Klakow. 2020. A survey on recent approaches for natural language processing in low-resource scenarios. *arXiv preprint arXiv:2010.12309*.

Hector Levesque, Ernest Davis, and Leora Morgenstern. 2012. The winograd schema challenge. In *Thirteenth International Conference on the Principles of Knowledge Representation and Reasoning*.

Cedric Lothritz, Kevin Allix, Bertrand Lebichot, Lisa Veiber, Tegawendé F Bissyandé, and Jacques Klein. 2021. Comparing multilingual and multiple monolingual models for intent classification and slot filling. In *International Conference on Applications of Natural Language to Information Systems*, pages 367–375. Springer.

Cedric Lothritz, Bertrand Lebichot, Kevin Allix, Lisa Veiber, Tegawendé Bissyandé, Jacques Klein, Andrey Boytsov, Clément Lefebvre, and Anne Goujon. 2022. Luxembert: Simple and practical data augmentation in language model pre-training for luxembourgish. In *Proceedings of the Language Resources and Evaluation Conference*, pages 5080–5089, Marseille, France. European Language Resources Association.

Benjamin Muller, Antonios Anastasopoulos, Benoît Sagot, and Djamé Seddah. 2021. When being unseen from mbert is just the beginning: Handling new languages with multilingual language models. In *Proceedings of the 2021 Conference of the North American Chapter of the Association for Computational Linguistics: Human Language Technologies*, pages 448–462.

Isabella Olariu, Cedric Lothritz, Tegawendé F. Bissyandé, and Jacques Klein. 2023. Evaluating Data Augmentation Techniques for the Training of Luxembourgish Language Models. In *Proceedings of the 19th Conference on Natural Language Processing (KONVENS 2023)*.

Pedro Javier Ortiz Suárez, Laurent Romary, and Benoît Sagot. 2020. A monolingual approach to contextualized word embeddings for mid-resource languages. In *Proceedings of the 58th Annual Meeting of the Association for Computational Linguistics*, pages 1703–1714, Online. Association for Computational Linguistics.

Marco Tulio Ribeiro, Tongshuang Wu, Carlos Guestrin, and Sameer Singh. 2020. Beyond accuracy: Behavioral testing of nlp models with checklist. In *Proceedings of the 58th Annual Meeting of the Association for Computational Linguistics*, pages 4902–4912.

Raphael Scheible, Fabian Thomczyk, Patric Tippmann, Victor Jaravine, and Martin Boeker. 2020. Gottbert: a pure german language model. *arXiv e-prints*, pages arXiv–2012.

Richard Socher, Alex Perelygin, Jean Wu, Jason Chuang, Christopher D Manning, Andrew Y Ng, and Christopher Potts. 2013. Recursive deep models for semantic compositionality over a sentiment treebank. In *Proceedings of the 2013 conference on empirical methods in natural language processing*, pages 1631–1642.

Alex Wang, Amanpreet Singh, Julian Michael, Felix Hill, Omer Levy, and Samuel Bowman. 2018. Glue: A multi-task benchmark and analysis platform for natural language understanding. In *Proceedings of the 2018 EMNLP Workshop BlackboxNLP: Analyzing and Interpreting Neural Networks for NLP*, pages 353–355.

Shijie Wu and Mark Dredze. 2020. Are all languages created equal in multilingual bert? In *5th Workshop on Representation Learning for NLP*, pages 120–130.

LLpro: A Literary Language Processing Pipeline for German Narrative Texts

Anton Ehrmanntraut and **Leonard Konle** and **Fotis Jannidis**
Julius-Maximilans-Universität Würzburg
{anton.ehrmanntraut, leonard.konle, fotis.jannidis}@uni-wuerzburg.de

Abstract

In this paper, we motivate, describe, and evaluate LLpro[1], a novel NLP pipeline for German with the goal of laying the foundation for computational analysis of literary fiction. Our work is strongly inspired by BookNLP[2], which has a similar goal for English texts and has already shown its relevance through application in various research (e.g. Milli and Bamman, 2016). The pipeline consists of *fundamental NLP tasks* (tokenization, POS tagging, etc.) and *literary tasks* more tailored to narrative texts (e.g. scene segmentation, character recognition, detection of speech, thought, and writing representation, etc.). Building on the work of Ortmann et al. (2019) we present an updated evaluation of the *fundamental NLP tasks* and combine the most appropriate approaches with partially improved models for the *literary tasks* to create a rich representation of narrative fiction.

1 Introduction

'Distant Reading' (Moretti), the computational analysis of large collections of literary texts, has made progress in recent years, but is yet the province of the happy few who have literary expertise and sufficient knowledge about natural language processing and do know how to explore and analyze quantitative data. Especially the NLP part proves to be challenging, because the fast moving research in this field uses very modern techniques which are often hard to apply for someone not close to the rapid developments. At the same time, recent years saw a series of proposals how to extract specific features from literary texts, not only character references but events, scenes, speech renditions and more. The automatic detection of features like these is not part of generic pipelines like spaCy or Stanza. Our goal was to provide a pipeline which covers linguistic tasks like POS tagging, and tasks specific for narrative texts, like scene annotation.

We choose to build this on the basis of spaCy's pipeline framework and to use a Docker image to reduce the complexity of installing the components. The application covers *fundamental NLP tasks*: tokenization, lemmatization normalization, POS tagging morphological analysis and dependency parsing. For performance reasons we decided not to rely on spaCy even for these basic NLP tasks but integrate the best and the fastest solutions available for German texts.

Additionally, we integrate NLP applications that we specifically intend to use for literary analysis, performing the following linguistic tasks: named entity recognition, character mentions detection, coreference resolution, event classification, classification of speech, thought and writing representation, and scene segmentation. In the course of this paper, we will refer to these linguistic tasks as *literary tasks* to contrast them with the usually more simple and more widespread *fundamental tasks*. Concerning the *literary tasks*, we either incorporated published solutions, or improved on them by providing a LLM which has been adapted to the literary domain, or by re-implementing them.

2 Related Work

The NLP pipeline framework spaCy[3] (Honnibal et al., 2023) can be considered the de-facto default Python NLP processing pipeline for German text, also being one of the first to provide an integrated pipeline to process German text at all. The spaCy models were continuously improved, incorporating Transformer-based pipelines since 2021, and thus making state-of-the-art accuracies available in a simple and accessible interface. In the course of this paper, we will refer to version v3.5.2 (April 12, 2023) of spaCy, and to the German models `de_core_news_lg-3.5.0` based on word embeddings and focusing on speed,

[1]https://github.com/cophi-wue/LLpro
[2]https://github.com/booknlp/booknlp
[3]https://spacy.io

Proceedings of the 19th Conference on Natural Language Processing (KONVENS 2023), pages 28–39
September 18–22, 2023. ©2023 Association for Computational Linguistics

and de_dep_news_trf-3.5.0, based on Transformers.

SpaCy's default Transformer-based implementation for German de_dep_news_trf-3.5.0 implements precisely the tasks we denote in this paper as *fundamental NLP tasks*, and hence we will particularly discuss LLpro's performance on these tasks with spaCy and other pipelines. Architecture-wise, the de_dep_news_trf pipeline, like all Transformer-based spaCy pipelines, consists of a single Transformer model to embed each token of the document into a contextualized vector representation, which has been fine-tuned to perform *multiple* tasks, implementing a multi-task learning.

As already sketched, we built upon spaCy's broad and tested APIs for components, pipeline architecture, and data structures, to implement LLpro, profiting from spaCy's easy and flexible extensibility.

While the alternative Python NLP processing toolkit Stanza[4] (Qi et al., 2020) is also designed to perform the *fundamental NLP tasks*, we found Stanza hard to extend to our purposes. First, extensions to Stanza are nontrivial to implement, and secondly, Stanza, by design, focuses on a language-agnostic modeling, building upon the Universal Dependencies formalism. This formalism distinguishes Stanza from other German NLP tools (usually following a German-specific grammar, not UD), which would have caused further difficulties in adapting tools.

The best-known example of the combination of *fundamental NLP tasks* with components specifically targeted at literary texts in one pipeline is BookNLP.[5] Besides the *fundamental NLP tasks*, BookNLP provides NER, coreference resolution, speaker identification, supersense tagging, event tagging and referential gender inference.[6] LLpro covers most of the functionality of BookNLP, only supersense[7] and speaker detection are missing, but also introduces new tasks (scene segmentation, classification of speech, thought and writing representation).

In its current state, BookNLP can only process English language; a further development to a multilingual tool, including support for German, is planned, but not yet available. BookNLP, like LLpro, is built on spaCy infrastructure, so transferring or exchanging modules between pipelines will be facilitated once a German BookNLP version is available.

Finally, the Python NLP pipeline MONAPipe[8] (Dönicke et al., 2022) also extend spaCy to more specialized tasks in the analysis of German literary texts.

While both the MONAPipe and the presented LLpro are intended for the literary texts, the choice of *literary tasks* the respective pipelines perform, are different. As MONAPipe particularly focuses on modes of narration and attribution, it performs a dictionary-based semantic analysis of phrases to enrich a feature set intended to identify the narrative mode 'comment' (in contrast to the narrative modes 'description', 'report' and 'speech'). From the same set of features, MONAPipe attributes each clause to one of 'character', 'author', and/or 'narrator'. (Cf. Weimer et al., 2022; Dönicke et al., 2022) Like Stanza, MONAPipe decided to build upon Universal Dependencies (and in particular trained a new UD-based spaCy parser), since some of its downstream modules require UD parses.

In contrast, LLpro's exclusive components focus around literary characters, and in particular includes a coreference resolution model with state-of-the-art performance, much stronger and more scalable than the one included in MONAPipe, and is the only one of the discussed pipelines that can perform a segmentation into scenes, and can recognize references to literary characters. Furthermore, concerning the *fundamental NLP tasks*, MONAPipe relies on the provided spaCy models, unlike LLpro which provides wrappers for other NLP tools performing *fundamental tasks*. Finally, since MONAPipe is based on spaCy v2.3, it is unable to use the more accurate Transformer-based spaCy models, and can only run the less accurate word-embedding-based models for the *fundamental tasks*.

[4] https://stanfordnlp.github.io/stanza/. We refer to version v1.5.0, March 14, 2023.

[5] https://github.com/booknlp/booknlp; we refer to version v1.0.7, commit 2b42ccdk, December 4, 2021.

[6] Gender inference is a postprocessing step, which maps the usage of pronouns to coreference clusters. Certainly useful, we decided, partly due to a lack of evaluation data, to leave this postprocessing to users

[7] The supersense detection component builds upon WordNet (Fellbaum, 2005; https://wordnet.princeton.edu/). While GermaNet (Hamp and Feldweg, 1997; https://uni-tuebingen.de/en/142806) mirrors WordNet for German, it is still much smaller and differs in its supersense ontology. After a review, we conclude that the direct benefit of the supersenses present in GermaNet, without further refinement, for the analysis of literary texts has yet to be tested more thoroughly.

[8] https://gitlab.gwdg.de/mona/pipy-public. We will refer to version v3.2.

Finally, we want to remark that *locally* executed pipelines (such as spaCy, LLpro, Stanza, or BookNLP) are not the only option to design NLP pipelines. For instance, WebLicht[9] (Hinrichs et al., 2010) follows a service-oriented architecture, chaining together multiple distributed and independet web services, each performing an individual *fundamental* NLP task. These services are hosted online by different providers and not locally, enabling pipeline composition and execution through a browser-based interface. This makes usage far more accessible.

However, in light of the increasing computational effort associated with some tasks (in particular the *literary tasks*), such architecture also has limitations. Extending, e.g., WebLicht's functionality requires independent and reliable hosting of additional services. Moreover, scaling to larger corpora may be challenging as it relies on external providers' compute power, which could have limitations or usage restrictions.

3 Architecture and Pipeline Components

As already outlined, LLpro is built on top of the open-source spaCy (v3.5.2) API using Python. SpaCy provides a programming interface and trained models to individually compose a language processing pipeline for one's use case, building on top of their provided data structures that manages the document, the tokens and the annotations on these objects. Invoked on an input document, spaCy first calls the specified tokenizer that segments the input text into tokens, converting the text to a document object, consisting of all the token objects. Then, in the subsequent steps, the document object is processed by the specified components of the pipeline, each enriching the document object with information that is annotated on the individual token objects, on spans of tokens, or on the entire document.

Now, LLpro's key contribution consists of implementations of pipeline components for the spaCy API, providing wrappers of already existing NLP tools designed to process German text. In particular, LLpro, for one, provides alternative components for the previously mentioned *fundamental tasks* that spaCy (and Stanza) can already do, but with higher accuracy and/or speed. We primarily grounded our choice of tools in the previously mentioned study by Ortmann et al. (2019), selecting the most promising ones.

Secondly, LLpro contributes by implementing new pipeline components that provide access to novel NLP tools that perform specific NLP tasks useful in the field of literary analysis. Table 1 provides an overview of the implemented components, which are discussed below.

Notice, moreover, that while the default pipeline implemented by LLpro can perform all of its tasks without any of spaCy's models or components, the modular structure of spaCy's API allows all components to be replaced or omitted in a custom pipeline, if desired. For instance, instead of the probabilistic parser presented here, it is possible, in a correspondingly custom-programmed pipeline, to switch back to the Transformer-based parser trained by spaCy.

In the remainder of this section, we briefly describe each component LLpro implements.

3.1 Preprocessing and Basic Components

With the **SoMaJoTokenizer** we wrapped the rule-based tokenizer / sentence splitter SoMaJo[10] (Proisl and Uhrig, 2016) as component for spaCy. Additionally, we implemented a simple normalization to correct for historic characters, which otherwise would cause wrong inferences in the successive components. We replace the historic notation of umlauted vowels (superscript E) with contemporary notation (with diaeresis), followed by NFKC Unicode normalization. This has also the effect that long S characters get converted to short S characters. Note that this simple form of normalization does not address for orthographic differences, for instance *selbstthätig*, *seyn* (vs. *selbsttätig*, *sein*).

The **SoMeWeTaTagger** invokes the part-of-speech tagger SoMeWeTa[11] (Proisl, 2018). For LLpro, we use the 'newspaper' model based on the TIGER corpus.[12] Next to the predicted tags (as defined by the TIGER variant of the German STTS tagset, cf. Smith, 2003), the component also provides an automatic table-based conversion[13] to the Universal Dependencies v2 POS tagset (de Marneffe et al., 2021).[14]

[9]https://weblicht.sfs.uni-tuebingen.de/. We want to thank the anonymous reviewer to bring WebLicht to our attention.

[10]https://github.com/tsproisl/SoMaJo

[11]https://github.com/tsproisl/SoMeWeTa

[12]https://corpora.linguistik.uni-erlangen.de/someweta/german_newspaper_2020-05-28.model

[13]https://universaldependencies.org/tagset-conversion/de-stts-uposf.html

[14]See also https://universaldependencies.

Component	Task, Tagset if applicable	Reference(s)	Version
	Fundamental Tasks		
• SoMaJoTokenizer	Tokenization, Normalization, Sentence Splitting	Proisl and Uhrig, 2016	2.2.3
• SoMeWeTaTagger	Part-of-speech tagging; TIGER variant of the STTS tagset	Proisl, 2018	1.8.1; model May 28, 2020
• RNNTagger	Morphological analysis; Universal features inventory	Schmid, 2019	1.3
• RNNLemmatizer	Lemmatization	Schmid, 2019	1.3
• ParZuParser	Dependency Parsing; HDT tagset	Sennrich et al., 2009	Feb 11, 2022
	Literary Tasks		
FLERTNERTagger	Named entity recognition; PER, ORG, MISC, LOC	Schweter and Akbik, 2021	0.12.2
CorefTagger	Coreference Resolution	Schröder et al., 2021	Aug 31, 2021
EventClassifier	Annotates *event types* to verbal phrases; differentiates between *non-event*, *stative* event, *process* event, and *change of state* event	Vauth et al., 2021	0.2
∗ RedewiedergabeTagger	Tagging of German speech, thought and writing representation (STWR); recognizes direct, indirect, reported and free indirect speech cf. Brunner et al., 2020	Schweter and Akbik, 2021	—
∗ CharacterRecognizer	Recognizes references to literary characters cf. Krug et al., 2017	Schweter and Akbik, 2021	—
∗ SceneSegmenter	Segmentation of literary text into *scenes* and *non-scenes*, cf. Zehe et al. (2021a,b)	Kurfalı and Wirén, 2021	—

Table 1: Overview of LLpro's components. Each component marked with • provides a replacement for a spaCy component performing the same task. Each component marked with ∗ has been (re-)implemented and (re-)trained from scratch.

The **RNNTagger** and **RNNLemmatizer** provide a wrapper for the RNNTagger[15] tool (Schmid, 2019) to perform a morphological analysis and lemmatize the tokens. To be consistent with spaCy's API, we convert the output of the tagger into an equivalent form consisting of Universal Dependencies v2 features (de Marneffe et al., 2021).[16]

The **ParZuParser** is a wrapper for the Prolog-based probabilistic dependency parser ParZu[17] (Sennrich et al., 2009; Sennrich and Kunz, 2014). For each token, the component predicts the head token and the respective relation as specified by the grammar of the Hamburg Dependency Treebank (Foth, 2014). Note that this labeling scheme of relations differs from the one used by spaCy's default models, which is trained on a (semi-automatically derived) dataset based on the TIGER corpus/tagset (Smith, 2003). SpaCy's API and subsequent components that build on top of relation labels have been configured accordingly to match the changed labeling scheme.

3.2 Components for Literary Analysis

The following subsection discusses the remainder of LLpro's components, i.e. the *literary NLP tasks*, which particularly perform tasks intended for literary analysis. Since many of the the tasks resp. annotations are not represented in spaCy's data structures, we use the provided "extension attributes" to store the components' results. A full specification of the exposed extension attributes is provided in LLpro's documentation.

In some instances, we (re-)implemented and (re-)trained models to adapt them to our domain. For this, we have domain-adapted the `deepset/gbert-large` BERT model (Chan et al., 2020) with literary texts to obtain `fiction-gbert-large`, which we make available. Details are presented in Sec. A.1 in the Appendix.

The **FLERTNERTagger** invokes the NER tagger FLERT from the Flair[18] framework,

org/u/pos/all.html

[15] https://www.cis.uni-muenchen.de/~schmid/tools/RNNTagger/

[16] See also https://universaldependencies.org/u/feat/all.html

[17] https://github.com/rsennrich/ParZu

[18] https://github.com/flairNLP/flair

which builds upon a BERT-based sequence tagging (Schweter and Akbik, 2021). For LLpro, we use the publicly available Flair model `ner-german-large`.[19] Note that while some models of spaCy include a NER tagger, spaCy misses a Transformer-based one like FLERT. The tagger annotates non-overlapping named entity spans as one of the four CoNLL-03 classes (PER, LOC, ORG, MISC; cf. Tjong Kim Sang and De Meulder, 2003). While the tagger has issues in recognizing *characters* in literary texts (see below), we keep the FLERTNERTagger primarily to recognize locations and organizations.

The **CharacterRecognizer** attempts to resolve a conceptional issue arising with determining mentions of characters in literary texts. In literary texts, character references to an entity appear not only as (1) proper nouns (e.g., *Alice*, *Effi Briest*), but also as (2) nominal phrases, e.g. *gardener, mother, Earl, Lieutenant, idiot, beauty, ...*

While the mention of type (1) are theoretically *named entities* in the sense of an NER tagger, mentions of type (2) are not, therefore not recognized by the FLERTNERTagger. Furthermore, the NER tagger was primarily trained on newspaper articles, implying another domain gap (cf. Krug et al., 2017).

To resolve this, we trained a tagger that recognizes character mention spans of both type (1) and (2), using the DROC corpus (Krug et al., 2017) which annotated character references in German novels, employing the same Transformer-Linear architecture as used in the FLERTNERTagger, fine-tuning our custom BERT model `fiction-gbert-large`. The tagger makes no distinctions between these two types, thus recognizes combined variants such as *Ritterschaftsrätin von Padden* (*knighthood councilor von Padden*).

The **CorefTagger** provides coreference resolution by invoking the neural tagger developed by Schröder et al. (2021).[20] Most importantly, the tool implements an incremental entity-based approach that scales to very long documents such as the literary works we want to process. Also, the model is adapted to our literary domain, as it is fine-tuned and tested on the literary DROC (Krug et al., 2017) dataset. For LLpro, we use the publicly available model `droc_incremental_no_segment_distance`.[21]

The **EventClassifier** invokes a neural sequence classifier developed by Vauth et al. (2021).[22] The authors model the event structure of literary texts using narratological event concepts, and their classifier automatically recognizes these events. In particular, they opt to model events as only occurring in verbal phrases. Their model then categorizes each of the phrases as either 'changes of state', 'process event', 'stative event' or 'non-event'.

To automatically recognize these event types, their proposed classifier automatically extracts verbal phrases from the text using the syntactic structure inferred by a parser (in their case: spaCy's parser), and then classifies phrases using a Transformer-based architecture. For LLpro, we use their publicly available model.[23] We incorporate this tagger by instead re-using the syntactic structure predicted by the previously mentioned ParZu-Parser, and then invoking the Transformer model for classification on the extracted verbal phrases.

The **RedewiedergabeTagger** is a re-implementation of four taggers proposed by Brunner et al. (2021) that use neural representations to recognize four different types of speech, thought and writing representation (STWR) for German texts. The four types of STWR are 'direct', 'indirect', 'free indirect', and 'reported'. They approach this kind of classification by developing four different sequence taggers for each STWR type, each effectively performing a binary classification for each token in the sequence, building on a BiLSTM-CRF architecture on top of a chosen language embedding derived from Transformer models.

For LLpro, we re-implemented these models, and specifically fine-tuned the aforementioned `fiction-gbert-large` on the respective tasks using the same REDEWIEDERGABE corpus. (Brunner et al., 2020) As proposed by Schweter and Akbik (2021), we omit the additional LSTM/CRF and predict the respective STWR type from the token encoding in the final Transformer layer alone, following the Transformer-Linear variant that is also used in the NER tagging of above FLERTNERTagger.

[19] `https://huggingface.co/flair/ner-german-large`

[20] `https://github.com/uhh-lt/neural-coref`

[21] `https://github.com/uhh-lt/neural-coref/releases/tag/konvens`

[22] `https://github.com/uhh-lt/event-classification`

[23] `https://github.com/uhh-lt/event-classification/releases/tag/v0.2`

Pipeline	Tokens	Sents	POS	UPOS	Lemmas	Morph	Deps
spaCy, `de_core_news_lg-3.5`	0.9953	0.9091	0.9465	0.9270	0.9062	0.9149	0.6942
spaCy, `de_dep_news_trf-3.5`	0.9953	0.8936	**0.9635**	0.9320	0.9181	**0.9508**	0.7573
Stanza 1.5	0.9975	0.9784	0.9433	0.9144	0.8778	0.9045	**0.7578**
LLpro	**1.0000**	**1.0000**	0.9458	**0.9610**	**0.9188**	0.9372	0.7425

Table 2: Evaluation of different NLP pipelines on the *fundamental NLP tasks* using the adapted evaluation system by Ortmann et al. (2019) against the gold annotations of the *novelette* text. For columns *Tokens* and *Sents*, metric is F1, comparing the output from raw text input with the gold tokenization/sentencization. In all other columns, metric is accuracy, comparing the output from (gold) pre-tokenized input. Evaluation only run on the novelette text. The column UPOS refers to the universal dependencies POS tags, which are predicted alongside the fine-grained POS tagging in each pipeline.

The **SceneSegmenter** is a re-implementation of a tool by Kurfalı and Wirén (2021) that recognizes contiguous and non-overlapping *scenes* resp. *non-scenes*. In short, a *scene* is "a segment of a text where the story time and the discourse time are more or less equal, the narration focuses on one action and space and character constellations stay the same" (Zehe et al., 2021a), whereas a *non-scene* refers to a non-scenic bridge between scenes like reflections of the narrator or accelerated speed of narration. See the shared task description resp. formal definition (Zehe et al., 2021b,a) for details on scene segmentation task. The model by Kurfalı and Wirén showed best performance in the shared task Track 1 that evaluated on gold annotations in dime novels. The tool adapted the sequential sentence classification system proposed by Cohan et al. (2019) to the scene segmentation task. Similar to the previously mentioned RedewiedergabeTagger, we re-trained the model on our domain-adapted custom BERT model.

We will discuss the results of this re-implementation and re-training of the three preceding components in Section 4.2. Details on the training of each of the models is provided in the Appendix, as well as links to the model weights.

4 Evaluation

Concerning the *fundamental tasks*, we focus on a comparative discussion of LLpro's components with the equivalent components of spaCy and Stanza. For this, firstly, we compare the annotation *accuracies* using human-labeled data provided by Ortmann et al. (2019), and secondly, measure and compare the runtimes of these components to estimate their (computational) *efficiency*.

Concerning the *literary tasks*, we are unable to compare their accuracies with respect to other NLP pipelines, since, in most cases, they are not implemented in any pipeline system. Therefore, we restrict ourselves to a qualitative analysis, discussing the performance of the underlying NLP systems that LLpro's components wrap around. Besides this, we provide quantitative results on the effect of our re-implementing/re-training on the CharacterRecognizer, RedewiedergabeTagger, SceneSegmenter building on the `fiction-gbert-large` model.

4.1 Accuracy on Fundamental Tasks

In order to compare the accuracies of the respective components, we opted to follow the evaluation system developed by Ortmann et al. (2019) that was specifically designed to compare NLP tools performing the NLP tasks tokenization, POS tagging, lemmatization, morphological analysis, and dependency parsing.

The evaluation system consists, in the first part, of five human-labeled documents from different registers. In the second part, the evaluation system consists of a comparison procedure that evaluates a tool's output with the gold label, and in particular, accounts for different naming/annotation schemes between different NLP tools.

For our evaluation, we take over this comparison procedure, but will primarily focus on the one human-labeled *novelette* document (1588 tokens), which was chosen by Ortmann et al. as representative for the literary register. Note that in the original evaluation, pipelines like spaCy were not evaluated as a whole, but only the individual components. For instance, the spaCy dependency parser was provided with (gold) POS annotations as input in the evaluation.

We deviate from this and want to compare the different pipelines in a way that imitates an end-to-end use. To this end, we performed two experiments: first, to compare the different tokenizers, we compare the tokenizers' outputs from raw text with the gold tokenization. Second, to compare all the other downstream components of the components, but controlling for potentially incorrect tokenization, we compare the pipelines' outputs derived from (gold) pre-tokenized input with the gold labels. This means that, e.g., we evaluate how LLpro's parser performs even when given inaccurate POS tagged text from LLpro's POS tagger.

Table 2 gives the evaluation results on the LLpro, spaCy and Stanza pipelines on the *novelette* text. Columns *Tokens*, *Sents* refer to the accuracy on the first experiments; the subsequent columns refer to the second experiment. (See Table 6 in the Appendix for the aggregated results on all five texts.)

Concerning the accuracy of LLpro, we observe that LLpro is competitive with contemporary Stanza and Transformer-based spaCy models, and even slightly outperforming these pipelines in some tasks.

4.2 Accuracy on Literary Tasks

LLpro's components perform the *literary NLP tasks*, either by wrapping around previously developed systems, all of which can be generally considered state of the art in their respective fields, or by running our custom fine-tuned models for the tasks.

Concerning NER tagging, the model used in LLpro's component FLERTNERTagger is published with a reported CoNLL-F1 of 0.92 on the CoNLL-03 German revisited test set. With this high accuracy, we do not expect significant improvements by fine-tuning from our domain-adapted BERT model, and consider the task practically solved for our use-case with this NER tagger. As a comparison, the alternative NER tagger provided by Stanza showed worse performance than Flair's tagger (CoNLL-F1 81.9).

Coreference resolution, as it is done by the CorefTagger by invoking a model by Schröder et al. (2021), is known to be a notoriously hard task. With this background, the (not very impressive-looking) performance of their model on the literary DROC dataset (CoNLL-F1 0.65) can be considered extremely strong. See also the survey and experiments by Dönicke et al. (2022) concerning coreference resolution in German.

The remaining *literary NLP tasks* – event classification, tagging of STWR, tagging of character

Model	Direct	Ind.	Rep.	Fr. Ind.
Brunner et al. (2021)	0.84	0.76	0.58	0.57
RedewiedergabeTagger	0.91	0.79	0.70	0.58

Table 3: Scores on STWR recognition on the held-out test set of the REDEWIEDERGABE corpus. F1 in all cases.

Model	Prec.	Rec.	F1
Track 1			
Kurfalı and Wirén (2021)	0.29	0.51	0.37
SceneSegmenter	0.37	0.44	0.40
Track 2			
Kurfalı and Wirén (2021)	0.14	0.22	0.17
SceneSegmenter	0.32	0.40	0.35

Table 4: Scores on the Shared Task on Scene Segmentation (not publicly released) test set, Tracks 1 (dime novels) and Track 2 (out-of-domain high-brow literature). Results for Kurfalı and Wirén (2021) cited from the task report (Zehe et al., 2021b). Results for our model are reported by the task organizers.

references, and segmentation into scenes – were introduced only very recently, and in all cases, almost no other models appear to approach the respective tasks, making a comparative analysis impossible in most cases. Concerning the component for the first task (EventClassifier), we remark that the classifier designed by Vauth et al. (2021), which LLpro invokes for event classification, should explicitly only be understood as a qualitative indicator: in particular, the tests performed by Vauth et al. to evaluate their model with respect to unseen documents was primarily *visual*, comparing the resulting "narrativity graphs" between predicted event spans and gold-annotated event spans. These graphs can be understood as smoothed time series of "narrativity" assigned to each type of event. In total, the authors observe a sufficient match between the predicted and the gold-derived narrativity graphs, and conclude applicability of their model in corpus analysis.

Concerning the other tasks, we have opted to re-implement and re-train models for each task on our domain-adapted BERT model `fiction-gbert-large`.

For the character recognition (CharacterRecognizer), our simple Transformer-based model resulted in an F1-score of 0.91 on a held-out test dataset from the DROC corpus. With this accuracy, we find this model sufficient for our use-case. Additionally, no other model that performs such tasks is known to us.

Pipeline	Cores 4	8	16	32
spaCy, `de_dep_news_trf-3.5`	62.59	57.18	48.43	36.55
Stanza 1.5	156.4	109.7	55.91	23.04
LLpro, *fundamental tasks* only	151.3	73.00	48.54	20.27
LLpro, all tasks	5.025	3.152	2.959	1.540

Table 5: Number of tokens processed per core in one second, under different intra-op parallelizations.

For the STWR recognition (RedewiedergabeTagger), our fine-tuning was able to increase the models' accuracies on the STWR task, except for the *free indirect* STWR type. See Table 3 for an overview and a comparison to the models by Brunner et al. (2021). Note that the increase is most likely explained by the different model architecture and fine-tuning procedure, which is missing in the original models.

Concerning the scene segmentation, note again that we based our SceneSegmenter on a re-implementation of a sequential sequence classification model by Kurfalı and Wirén (2021), which was the best-performing contribution in the scene segmentation shared task. Our re-implementation directly takes over this architecture and ports it to the contemporary Pytorch/Transformers API (Wolf et al., 2020) with minimal modifications. To evaluate our model, the organizers of the Shared Task on Scene Segmentation (Zehe et al., 2021b) evaluated our model on the test datasets, on both Track 1 (dime novels) and Track 2 (out-of-domain high-brow novels). The fine-tuning was able to increase the model's F1 score by few percentage points in Track 1, with respect to the original model published by Kurfalı and Wirén. See Table 4 for an overview. Also, our model appears to generalize much better to the out-of-domain Track 2. Note that both our model and the one by Kurfalı and Wirén build upon the 'large' variant of the BERT model, hence the difference in performance can be attributed to the domain-adaption of our `fiction-gbert-large` model.

4.3 Computational Efficiency

As we intend to process a large corpus of literary texts with LLpro, we are also interested in their computational efficiency, next to accuracy. In our CPU-only setup with many cores, it is immediately clear that the computational effort required by LLpro will be dominated by the slow Transformer-based components, performing the *literary NLP tasks*. Even with this in consideration, we will briefly discuss our experiments concerning the computational efficiency of our pipeline. In our case, we are particularly interested in *throughput* – the number of tokens we can process per second *and per core*. This delimits our investigation to previous studies, like already mentioned one by Ortmann et al. (2019), that were focused on *latency*, keeping the computational setup fixed.

Table 5 shows the measured throughput of the different pipelines, all restricted to performing the *fundamental tasks* only. In the case of LLpro, we additionally provide the throughput of the full pipeline, including the (computationally much more expensive) *literary tasks*. Measurements were performed by repeated trial runs on Intel Xeon Gold 6148 cores, varying number of cores, and varying length of input documents.

While the results confirm what we already assumed – LLpro with all components is slow in CPU-only setups – we can take away two things from these measurements: first, we see that the tools we use for the *fundamental NLP pipelines* are in some setups much more efficient overall than those (Transformer-based) models of spaCy, while performing equally well accuracy-wise. Second, the experiment indicates that for maximum efficiency of Transformer-based pipelines like LLpro (running all tasks), the appropriate parallelization and partitioning of the available CPU cores still remains an important ingredient, potentially increasing throughput a factor of 3.

5 Conclusion and Future Work

In this report, we present LLpro, a custom spaCy pipeline that provides components for the linguistic and literary analysis of German texts. On the side of linguistic analysis, LLpro provides wrappers to alternative NLP tools that perform tokenization, part-of-speech tagging, morphological analysis, lemmatization, and dependency parsing (*fundamental NLP tasks*). On the side of literary analysis (*literary NLP tasks*), LLpro implements several components that perform novel tasks currently not found in spaCy or other comparable pipelines: coreference resolution, named entity recognition, event classification, tagging of speech, thought and writing representation types, character reference recognition, and segmentation into scenes.

For the first part of components, the *fundamental NLP tasks*, our evaluation shows that our alternative models are, accuracy-wise, competitive with current spaCy, and in some setups, perform their tasks more efficient, particularly when bulk processing many texts. This comparative analysis also continues a research direction started by Ortmann et al. (2019) who evaluated many off-the-shelf NLP tools performing the *fundamental NLP tasks*, effectively giving an update of their evaluation with respect to the contemporary Transformer-based German spaCy model. While spaCy made significant improvement since the last evaluation by Ortmann et al. in 2019, our experiments showed that spaCy (and Stanza) still do not significantly outperform some specialized NLP tools. Furthermore, our analysis broadens the analysis of these NLP tools in terms of their computational efficiency. In total, our evaluation points out that for many simple linguistic NLP tasks, more lightweight models might be a suitable alternative to larger Transformer-based models, being more efficient without sacrificing accuracy.

For the *literary NLP tasks*, LLpro provides an accessible pipeline to perform automatic literary analysis by incorporating specialized Transformer-based models, reaching accuracies that make LLpro a novel basis for quantitative literary analysis on many texts. We can conceive that the outputs of the pipeline can be combined to investigate specific questions, for instance combining the scene segmentation and the character recognizer to carry out a fine-grained variant of a character network analysis. Or, use the coreference resolution, combined with the character recognizer and the parse trees, to collect attributes and adjectives that describe a particular character, or character's actions. LLPro thus provides a a robust basis for the automatic analysis of collections of German fiction.

Limitations

The most obvious limitation of LLpro is the restriction to German language. But since one motivation for this work is the limitation of BookNLP to English, we already consider LLpro as a step towards multilinguality in the analysis of literary texts. This is further highlighted by the plans to extend BookNLP to other languages and the spaCy architecture as the backbone of both systems.

The second restriction refers to the domain for which LLpro can be applied. We focus on narrative texts (novels, short stories, etc.) and thus exclude other literary genres (e.g. plays, poems). Since we offer only a very basal orthographic normalization, a drastic performance loss is to be expected when processing older texts. However, the analysis of large corpora over long periods of time is a central concern of Computational Literary Studies. Therefore normalization is a requirement we need to address in future work. Especially in light of the short novelette text used in our reported experiments, a larger evaluation corpus for all tasks would be mandatory for accurate in-domain evaluation, as well as further experimentation to improve the components.

Thirdly it is plausible that improvements in spaCy's Transformer-based pipeline could significantly outperform our *fundamental* NLP components in the near future, due to its capability to exploit multi-task learning, while relying on a single Transformer model. This Transformer model is fine-tuned to a multitude of NLP tasks, allowing, for one, faster inference as the embedding needs to be computed only once. For another, as soon as better Transformer models for German are released, instant performance gains are to be expected. To address these developments while mitigating the dependence on GPU resources for fast inference, we plan to make LLpro Adapter-based (Pfeiffer et al., 2021; Hu et al., 2021). This should at least drastically reduce the computational effort for the *literary NLP tasks*, ensure SOTA competing performance on *fundamental tasks* and enable more lightweight domain adaptation. Still however, like all NLP pipelines, LLpro faces the challenge of potential tool obsolescence and the need for sustainable maintenance and ongoing development, in order to maintain long-term viability and competitiveness.

Ethics Statement

We do not see any conflict of our work with the principles set out in the ACL Ethics Policy[24]. The

[24]`https://www.aclweb.org/portal/content/acl-code-ethics`

purpose of LLpro is to create a rich representation of literary texts. These texts may contain structural discrimination, which is therefore also present in the output of LLpro. That is not a problem, but an opportunity to systematically uncover and investigate them.

However, such a research perspective requires that the components of the pipeline operate without bias. We are not aware of any anecdotal evidence of biased behavior, but since this has not been systematically investigated for any of the modules, there is at least a possibility that e.g. coreference clusters of female characters are resolved less accurate.

References

Annelen Brunner, Stefan Engelberg, Fotis Jannidis, Ngoc Duyen Tanja Tu, and Lukas Weimer. 2020. Corpus REDEWIEDERGABE. In *Proceedings of the Twelfth Language Resources and Evaluation Conference*, pages 803–812, Marseille, France. European Language Resources Association.

Annelen Brunner, Ngoc Duyen Tanja Tu, Lukas Weimer, and Fotis Jannidis. 2021. To BERT or not to BERT – Comparing contextual embeddings in a deep learning architecture for the automatic recognition of four types of speech, thought and writing representation. In *Proceedings of the 5th Swiss Text Analytics Conference (SwissText) & 16th Conference on Natural Language Processing (KONVENS)*, volume 2624 of *CEUR Workshop Proceedings*, Zurich, Switzerland.

Branden Chan, Stefan Schweter, and Timo Möller. 2020. German's next language model. In *Proceedings of the 28th International Conference on Computational Linguistics*, pages 6788–6796, Barcelona, Spain (Online). International Committee on Computational Linguistics.

Arman Cohan, Iz Beltagy, Daniel King, Bhavana Dalvi, and Dan Weld. 2019. Pretrained language models for sequential sentence classification. In *Proceedings of the 2019 Conference on Empirical Methods in Natural Language Processing and the 9th International Joint Conference on Natural Language Processing (EMNLP-IJCNLP)*, pages 3693–3699, Hong Kong, China. Association for Computational Linguistics.

Marie-Catherine de Marneffe, Christopher D. Manning, Joakim Nivre, and Daniel Zeman. 2021. Universal Dependencies. *Computational Linguistics*, 47(2):255–308.

Tillman Dönicke, Florian Barth, Hanna Varachkina, and Caroline Sporleder. 2022. MONAPipe: Modes of narration and attribution pipeline for German computational literary studies and language analysis in spaCy. In *Proceedings of the 18th Conference on Natural Language Processing (KONVENS 2022)*, pages 8–15, Potsdam, Germany. KONVENS 2022 Organizers.

Tillmann Dönicke, Hanna Varachkina, Anna Mareike Weimer, Luisa Gödeke, Florian Barth, Benjamin Gittel, Anke Holler, and Caroline Sporleder. 2022. Modelling speaker attribution in narrative texts with biased and bias-adjustable neural networks. *Frontiers in Artificial Intelligence*, 4.

Christiane Fellbaum. 2005. Wordnet(s). In Keith Brown, editor, *Encyclopedia of Language and Linguistics*, second edition, pages 665–670. Elsevier.

Kilian A. Foth. 2014. Eine umfassende Constraint-Dependenz-Grammatik des Deutschen. Universität Hamburg.

Suchin Gururangan, Ana Marasović, Swabha Swayamdipta, Kyle Lo, Iz Beltagy, Doug Downey, and Noah A. Smith. 2020. Don't stop pretraining: Adapt language models to domains and tasks. In *Proceedings of the 58th Annual Meeting of the Association for Computational Linguistics*, pages 8342–8360, Online. Association for Computational Linguistics.

Birgit Hamp and Helmut Feldweg. 1997. GermaNet - a lexical-semantic net for German. In *Automatic Information Extraction and Building of Lexical Semantic Resources for NLP Applications*.

Erhard Hinrichs, Marie Hinrichs, and Thomas Zastrow. 2010. WebLicht: Web-based LRT services for German. In *Proceedings of the ACL 2010 System Demonstrations*, pages 25–29, Uppsala, Sweden. Association for Computational Linguistics.

Matthew Honnibal, Ines Montani, Sofie Van Landeghem, and Adriane Boyd. 2023. spaCy: Industrial-strength Natural Language Processing in Python. Supplement to `https://github.com/explosion/spaCy/tree/v3.5.2`.

Edward Hu, Yelong Shen, Phil Wallis, Zeyuan Allen-Zhu, Yuanzhi Li, Lu Wang, and Weizhu Chen. 2021. LoRA: Low-rank adaptation of large language models. ArXiv:2106.09685.

Markus Krug, Lukas Weimer, Isabella Reger, Luisa Macharowsky, Stephan Feldhaus, Frank Puppe, and Fotis Jannidis. 2017. Description of a corpus of character references in German novels – DROC [Deutsches ROman Corpus]. DARIAH-DE Working Papers 27.

Murathan Kurfalı and Mats Wirén. 2021. Breaking the narrative: Scene segmentation through sequential sentence classification. In *Proceedings of the Shared Task on Scene Segmentation*, volume 3001 of *CEUR Workshop Proceedings*, pages 49–53, Düsseldorf, Germany.

Yinhan Liu, Myle Ott, Naman Goyal, Jingfei Du, Mandar Joshi, Danqi Chen, Omer Levy, Mike Lewis, Luke Zettlemoyer, and Veselin Stoyanov. 2019.

RoBERTa: A robustly optimized BERT pretraining approach. ArXiv:1907.11692.

Smitha Milli and David Bamman. 2016. Beyond canonical texts: A computational analysis of fanfiction. In *Proceedings of the 2016 Conference on Empirical Methods in Natural Language Processing*, pages 2048–2053, Austin, Texas. Association for Computational Linguistics.

Katrin Ortmann, Adam Roussel, and Stefanie Dipper. 2019. Evaluating off-the-shelf NLP tools for German. In *Proceedings of the 15th Conference on Natural Language Processing (KONVENS 2019)*, pages 212–222, Erlangen, Germany. German Society for Computational Linguistics & Language Technology.

Jonas Pfeiffer, Aishwarya Kamath, Andreas Rücklé, Kyunghyun Cho, and Iryna Gurevych. 2021. AdapterFusion: Non-destructive task composition for transfer learning. In *Proceedings of the 16th Conference of the European Chapter of the Association for Computational Linguistics: Main Volume*, pages 487–503, Online. Association for Computational Linguistics.

Thomas Proisl. 2018. SoMeWeTa: A part-of-speech tagger for German social media and web texts. In *Proceedings of the Eleventh International Conference on Language Resources and Evaluation (LREC 2018)*, pages 665–670, Miyazaki, Japan. European Language Resources Association ELRA.

Thomas Proisl and Peter Uhrig. 2016. SoMaJo: State-of-the-art tokenization for German web and social media texts. In *Proceedings of the 10th Web as Corpus Workshop*, pages 57–62, Berlin. Association for Computational Linguistics.

Peng Qi, Yuhao Zhang, Yuhui Zhang, Jason Bolton, and Christopher D. Manning. 2020. Stanza: A python natural language processing toolkit for many human languages. In *Proceedings of the 58th Annual Meeting of the Association for Computational Linguistics: System Demonstrations*, pages 101–108, Online. Association for Computational Linguistics.

Helmut Schmid. 2019. Deep learning-based morphological taggers and lemmatizers for annotating historical texts. In *DATeCH, Proceedings of the 3rd International Conference on Digital Access to Textual Cultural Heritage*, pages 133–137, Brussels, Belgium. Association for Computing Machinery.

Fynn Schröder, Hans Ole Hatzel, and Chris Biemann. 2021. Neural end-to-end coreference resolution for German in different domains. In *Proceedings of the 17th Conference on Natural Language Processing (KONVENS 2021)*, pages 170–181, Düsseldorf, Germany. KONVENS 2021 Organizers.

Stefan Schweter and Alan Akbik. 2021. FLERT: Document-level features for named entity recognition. arXiv: 2011.06993.

Rico Sennrich and Beat Kunz. 2014. Zmorge: A German morphological lexicon extracted from Wiktionary. In *Proceedings of the Ninth International Conference on Language Resources and Evaluation (LREC 2014)*, pages 1063–1067, Reykjavik, Iceland. European Language Resources Association (ELRA).

Rico Sennrich, Gerold Schneider, Martin Volk, and Martin Warin. 2009. A new hybrid dependency parser for German. In *Proceedings of the 2009 GSCL Conference*, pages 115–124, Tübingen, Germany.

George Smith. 2003. A brief introduction to the TIGER treebank, version 1. Universität Stuttgart.

Erik F. Tjong Kim Sang and Fien De Meulder. 2003. Introduction to the CoNLL-2003 Shared Task: Language-independent named entity recognition. In *Proceedings of the Seventh Conference on Natural Language Learning at HLT-NAACL 2003*, page 142–147, Edmonton, Canada. Association for Computational Linguistics.

Michael Vauth, Hans Ole Hatzel, Evelyn Gius, and Chris Biemann. 2021. Automated event annotation in literary texts. In *Proceedings of the Conference on Computational Humanities Research 2021*, volume 2989 of *CEUR Workshop Proceedings*, pages 333–345, Amsterdam, the Netherlands.

Anna Mareike Weimer, Florian Barth, Tillmann Dönicke, Luisa Gödeke, Hanna Varachkina, Anke Holler, Caroline Sproleder, and Benjamin Gittel. 2022. The (in-)consistency of literary concepts. Operationalising, annotating and detecting literary comment. *Journal of Computational Literary Studies*, 1(1).

Thomas Wolf, Lysandre Debut, Victor Sanh, Julien Chaumond, Clement Delangue, Anthony Moi, Pierric Cistac, Tim Rault, Remi Louf, Morgan Funtowicz, Joe Davison, Sam Shleifer, Patrick von Platen, Clara Ma, Yacine Jernite, Julien Plu, Canwen Xu, Teven Le Scao, Sylvain Gugger, Mariama Drame, Quentin Lhoest, and Alexander Rush. 2020. Transformers: State-of-the-art natural language processing. In *Proceedings of the 2020 Conference on Empirical Methods in Natural Language Processing: System Demonstrations*, pages 38–45, Online. Association for Computational Linguistics.

Albin Zehe, Leonard Konle, Lea Katharina Dümpelmann, Evelyn Gius, Andreas Hotho, Fotis Jannidis, Lucas Kaufmann, Markus Krug, Frank Puppe, Nils Reiter, Annekea Schreiber, and Nathalie Wiedmer. 2021a. Detecting scenes in fiction: A new segmentation task. In *Proceedings of the 16th Conference of the European Chapter of the Association for Computational Linguistics: Main Volume*, pages 3167–3177, Online. Association for Computational Linguistics.

Albin Zehe, Leonard Konle, Svenja Guhr, Lea Dümpelmann, Evelyn Gius, Andreas Hotho, Fotis Jannidis, Lucas Kaufmann, Markus Krug, Frank

Pipeline	Tokens	Sents	POS	UPOS	Lemmas	Morph	Deps
spaCy, de_core_news_lg-3.5	0.9960	0.9220	0.9407	0.9263	0.9321	0.9084	0.6977
spaCy, de_dep_news_trf-3.5	0.9960	**0.9378**	**0.9563**	0.9343	**0.9409**	**0.9436**	**0.7591**
Stanza 1.5	0.9920	0.8998	0.9390	0.9058	0.9075	0.9050	0.7489
LLpro	**0.9971**	0.8996	0.9406	**0.9563**	**0.9409**	0.9251	0.7444

Table 6: Evaluation of different NLP pipelines on the *fundamental NLP tasks* using the adapted evaluation system by Ortmann et al. (2019) against the gold annotations of the entire evaluation corpus (*wikipedia*, *novelette*, *sermon*, *TED*, *movie*). For columns *Tokens* and *Sents*, metric is F1, comparing the output from raw text input with the gold tokenization/sentencization. In all other columns, metric is accuracy, comparing the output from (gold) pre-tokenized input. Evaluation only run on the novelette text. The column UPOS refers to the universal dependencies POS tags, which are predicted alongside the fine-grained POS tagging in each pipeline.

Puppe, Nils Reiter, and Annekea Schreiber. 2021b. Shared task on scene segmentation @ KONVENS 2021. In *Proceedings of the Shared Task on Scene Segmentation*, volume 3001 of *CEUR Workshop Proceedings*, pages 1–21, Düsseldorf, Germany.

A Appendix

A.1 Model fiction-gbert-large

The foundation of our domain adaptation attempt is the RoBERTa-style (Liu et al., 2019) model deepset/gbert-large published by Chan et al. (2020). It is the best performing German model of its size, only competing with deepset/glectra-large, introduced in the same paper. Following Gururangan et al. (2020) we gathered a collection of in-domain texts and continued the models pre-training task with it. The training is performed over 10 epochs on 2.3 GB of narrative fiction with a learning rate of 1×10^{-4} (linear decrease) and a batch size of 512. The model is available at https://huggingface.co/lkonle/fiction-gbert-large.

A.2 Model droc-character-recognizer

We use the DROC corpus (August 11, 2022) for training. Since the DROC dataset does not define a train/val/test split on its own, we split the documents ourselves, approximating a 80/10/10 split. From the annotated DROC corpus we derive labeled sequences (in BIO format). The precise split and derivation algorithm is provided in the training code included in LLpro. Each input sequence is a concatenation of sentences, maximally filling BERT's input window. Following Flair's training procedure, training of the sequence tagger is performed over 30 epochs with an initial learning rate of 5×10^{-6}, a batch size of 4, annealing the leaning rate by factor 0.5 when micro-F1 on the evaluation set does not increase for three epochs. We take the best overall model with respect to the validation set, and report the results on the held-out test set. The model is available at https://huggingface.co/aehrm/droc-character-recognizer.

A.3 Model redewiedergabe-direct, -indirect, -reported, -freeindirect

We use the identical REDEWIEDERGABE train/val/test split as used for the publication of the original taggers by Brunner et al. (2021).[25] Each binary sequence tagger (one for every STWR type) is identically trained, selected, and evaluated, following the same training procedure as for the droc-character-recognizer. The models are available at https://huggingface.co/aehrm/redewiedergabe-direct, resp. -indirect, -reported, -freeindirect.

A.4 Model stss-scene-segmenter

We use the annotated training data provided by the Shared Task organizers.[26] A single document is held out for validation. We follow the same training procedure as the original model. For the input sequences, we set a threshold of at most 25 sentences per input sequence, and each sentence is truncated to at most 100 tokens. The training is performed over 20 epochs with a learning rate of 5×10^{-6} (linear decrease) and batch size of 4. We take the best overall model with respect to the Shared Task evaluation score on the validation document, and report the results on the held-out test set. The model is available at https://huggingface.co/aehrm/stss-scene-segmenter.

[25] https://github.com/redewiedergabe/corpus/blob/master/resources/docs/data_konvens-paper-2020.md

[26] http://lsx-events.informatik.uni-wuerzburg.de/stss-2021/task.html

Classifying Noun Compounds for Present-Day Compositionality: Contributions of Diachronic Frequency and Productivity Patterns

Maximilian Maurer, Chris Jenkins, Filip Miletić, Sabine Schulte im Walde
Institute for Natural Language Processing, University of Stuttgart
{maximilian-martin.maurer, christopher.jenkins, filip.miletic, schulte}@ims.uni-stuttgart.de

Abstract

We investigate the diachronic evolution of the frequency and productivity of English noun compounds and their constituents relative to their degree of compositionality. We focus on 185 compounds with human compositionality ratings and a range of quantitative information from a large diachronic corpus. We cast our task as binary classification, and show that both diachronic frequency and productivity are useful in determining the present-day degree of compositionality of English noun compounds.

1 Introduction

Multiword expressions such as noun compounds (e.g. *flea market*) are semantically idiosyncratic to some degree, i.e. the meaning of the full expression is not entirely (or even not at all) predictable from the meanings of its constituents (Sag et al., 2002; Baldwin and Kim, 2010). While noun compounds have been extensively explored across research disciplines from synchronic perspectives, this paper provides a novel diachronic approach to predict their present-day compositionality.

More specifically, we investigate the diachronic evolution of the frequency and productivity of English noun compounds and their constituents relative to their degree of compositionality. Our analysis relies on an established gold standard dataset with human compositionality ratings, and a diachronic corpus of English covering approximately two centuries. We hypothesize that distinct frequency and productivity patterns of diachronic evolution can be observed for compounds whose degree of compositionality is high (such as *maple tree*, *prison guard*, *climate change*) vs. low (such as *flea market*, *night owl*, *melting pot*). We cast our task as a binary classification problem, and show that both diachronic frequency and productivity provide useful information in determining the present-day degree of compositionality of English noun compounds.

2 Related work

Existing computational studies have examined noun compounds from a range of perspectives. Common approaches include predicting the meaning of the whole compound (Mitchell and Lapata, 2008; Dima et al., 2019), the semantic relations between a compound's constituents (Girju et al., 2005; Ó Séaghdha, 2007; Dima et al., 2014), and the compound's degree of compositionality, usually framed as an unsupervised ranking task relying on static (Reddy et al., 2011; Schulte im Walde et al., 2013, 2016; Salehi et al., 2014, 2015; Cordeiro et al., 2019; Alipoor and Schulte im Walde, 2020) or contextualized word embeddings (Garcia et al., 2021a,b; Miletic and Schulte im Walde, 2023). A small subset of previous work has also taken into account the distinct linguistic roles and empirical characteristics of compound constituents, showing that compositionality prediction is affected by properties such as frequency, productivity, and ambiguity (Schulte im Walde et al., 2013, 2016; Alipoor and Schulte im Walde, 2020; Miletic and Schulte im Walde, 2023; Schulte im Walde, 2023). However, all of the cited studies adopt a synchronic perspective. As to our knowledge, only two previous approaches applied a diachronic perspective: Dhar et al. (2019) and Dhar and van der Plas (2019) exploited the Google n-gram corpus and information-theoretic as well as cosine distance measures to predict the compositionality of the compounds in Reddy et al. (2011), and to detect novel compounds, respectively.

In this paper, we provide a novel diachronic approach motivated from a linguistic perspective: we expect the present-day degree of compositionality to differ for high- vs. low-frequent compounds and for compounds with high- vs. low-frequent constituents (Lee, 1990; Hamilton et al., 2016, i.a.), as well as for compounds with high- vs. low-productive constituents (Jurafsky et al., 2001;

Proceedings of the 19th Conference on Natural Language Processing (KONVENS 2023), pages 40–51
September 18–22, 2023. ©2023 Association for Computational Linguistics

Hilpert, 2015, i.a.). We further compare the diachronic features against the use of present-day linguistic properties so as to assess the scope of compositionality information recovered through our diachronic approach.

3 Data

3.1 Gold standard of noun compounds

We use the collection of English noun compounds introduced by Cordeiro et al. (2019). It includes an initial set of 90 compounds created by Reddy et al. (2011)[1] and a further 190 compounds annotated by Cordeiro and colleagues using the same rating procedure.[2] Of these, we retain a total of 210 compounds for which both constituents are tagged as nouns in the dataset.

Human annotators were asked to provide compositionality ratings in terms of literality, on a scale from 0 (not at all literal) to 5 (very literal). They provided scores for the interpretation of the whole compound (e.g. *crash course*), as well as for the use of the modifier (*crash*) and the head (*course*) within it. Sample compounds and their ratings are shown in Table 1.

	Compositionality rating		
Compound	Modifier	Head	Compound
guinea pig	0.47 ± 0.72	0.47 ± 0.72	0.24 ± 0.56
flea market	0.38 ± 0.81	4.71 ± 0.84	1.52 ± 1.13
pain killer	4.71 ± 0.64	1.33 ± 1.11	2.05 ± 1.36
health insurance	4.53 ± 0.88	4.83 ± 0.58	4.40 ± 1.17

Table 1: Sample gold standard compounds with compositionality ratings (mean and standard deviation).

3.2 Corpus

As diachronic corpus data for the modeled noun compounds, we rely on the clean version of the Corpus of Historical American English (CCOHA) (Davies, 2012; Alatrash et al., 2020). It contains >400 million words, and ranges from 1810 to 2010. For present-day data, we use ENCOW (Schäfer and Bildhauer, 2012; Schäfer, 2015), a large web corpus that contains ≈9.5 billion tokens. Both corpora are lemmatized, tagged and parsed.

3.3 Empirical diachronic properties

We retrieve the following empirical diachronic properties per decade for our target compounds and their constituents:

- The *frequencies* of the gold standard compounds and their constituents.
- The *productivities* of the constituents of the gold standard compounds, i.e. the number of compounds a constituent appears in: morphological family size (de Jong et al., 2002).

For the latter, we consider a construction to be a relevant (candidate) compound if it is tagged as a sequence of two nouns, neither preceded nor followed by a noun.

4 Experimental setup

To assess whether highly compositional compounds and their constituents exhibit distinct patterns of diachronic evolution of productivity and frequency, we divide the 185 compounds that occur in at least one timeslice in CCOHA into different classes of compositionality. We do that for three types of compositionality ratings: on the level of the whole compound, the modifier, and the head. We cast our task as binary classification of the extremes with maximally different targets regarding their levels of compositionality, thus enforcing a clear picture of distinctiveness.

More specifically, we obtain balanced classes of the 62 least and most compositional compounds, modifiers, and heads ($\frac{1}{3}$ of the targets within each class, leaving out 61 mid-scale items). The compositionality ranges for the sets of least/most compositional compounds are $[0.18, 1.61]$ and $[4.20, 5.00]$, respectively. For the least/most compositional modifiers, the compositionality ranges are $[0.14, 1.76]$ and $[4.56, 5.00]$. For the least/most compositional heads, they are $[0.00, 2.79]$ and $[4.50, 5.00]$.

We conduct experiments for two levels of granularity of timeslices, in order to assess whether temporally finer-grained patterns provide more information related to present-day compositionality, with the potential trade-off of increasing sparsity. In the setup with finer-grained timeslices, we consider decades from the 1830s to the 2000s; in the coarser-grained setup, we combine these decades into 30-year timeslices. Since the sub-corpora of the two earliest decades, the 1810s and 1820s, are considerably smaller than the subsequent ones, we disregard those. Table 2 provides a summary of the sizes of our timeslices in millions of tokens.

[1] http://www.dianamccarthy.co.uk/downloads.html
[2] https://pageperso.lis-lab.fr/carlos.ramisch/?page=downloads/compounds

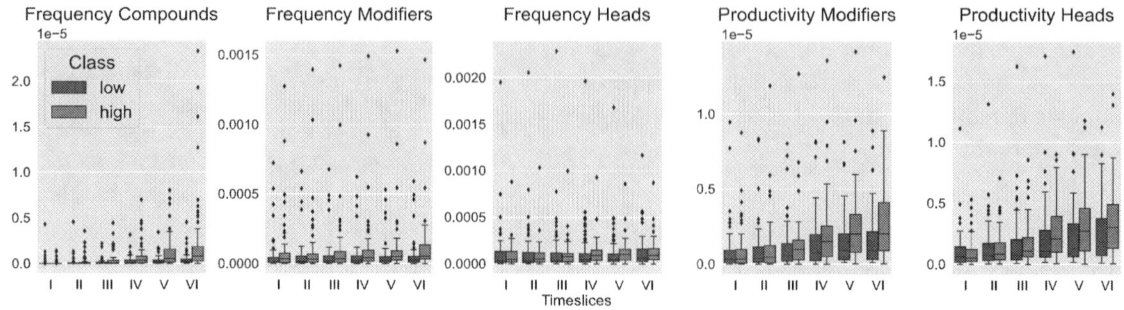

Figure 1: Development of the properties over time per class for the compound compositionality experiment. Timeslices: I: 1830s-1850s, II: 1860s-1880s, III: 1890s-1910s, IV: 1920s-1940s, V: 1950s-1970s, VI: 1980s-2000s.

Timeslice	1830s	1840s	1850s	1860s	1870s	1880s
$Total_{fine}$	16.7	19.4	20.0	20.6	22.6	24.4
$Total_{coarse}$	56.1			67.6		
Timeslice	1890s	1900s	1910s	1920s	1930s	1940s
$Total_{fine}$	24.6	26.7	27.7	31.2	30.1	29.9
$Total_{coarse}$	79.0			91.2		
Timeslice	1950s	1960s	1970s	1980s	1990s	2000s
$Total_{fine}$	30.3	29.6	29.4	31.3	34.6	36.5
$Total_{coarse}$	89.3			100.4		

Table 2: Timeslice sizes for the fine- and coarse-grained timeslices in million tokens.

We assess whether the two compositionality classes for the compounds and for the modifier and head constituents, respectively, have distinct patterns of diachronic evolution in terms of five empirical properties: the compound frequency F_C; the frequency F_M and productivity P_M of the modifier; and the frequency F_H and productivity P_H of the head. For each of the properties, we construct feature vectors $V = [v_1, v_2, \ldots, v_n]$ containing the retrieved values of the respective property across n timeslices. To account for differences in the corpus sizes of the timeslices, each retrieved property value is normalized by the total number of tokens in the respective timeslice. In configurations where we use multiple properties, their feature vectors are concatenated.

Figure 1 outlines the development of each of the empirical properties over the coarse timeslices, for the respective two classes defined for compound-level compositionality; see Appendix C for properties across constituent classes. Appendix E shows to which degree the properties correlate with each other across timeslices. We report Spearman's rank-order correlation coefficient ρ. In most cases the properties do not correlate at all, or just moderately. We find strong correlations only between the frequency and productivity of a constituent within the same timeslice, with an average $\rho = 0.77$ for modifiers and 0.88 for heads.

We conduct experiments using each of the properties individually, using the combination of the frequency of both constituents and the productivity of both constituents (F_{MH} and P_{MH}), the combination of all frequency measures F_{CMH}, and the combination of all features $F_{CMH}P_{MH}$. Other permutations in the following are denoted by combinations of the contained properties (e.g. $P_M F_H$).

In all experimental settings, we use a support vector machine (SVM) as the classifier. To account for data sparsity and overfitting in our results, we evaluate with repeated k-fold cross-validation, using 8 repetitions with different permutations of the compound data and 4 folds per repetition.

Even though our focus is on diachronic evolution, we also compare our approach against a standard static approach, using only synchronic information from (i) the last CCOHA timeslice of either granularity and (ii) present-day information retrieved from ENCOW. For each of the five empirical properties, we order the targets in descending order by that property and assign the positive label[3] to the first N compounds. More specifically, we collect results for all potential class splits, moving from $N = 0$, i.e. no compound is assigned to the positive class, to $N = 124$, i.e. all compounds are assigned to the positive class.

5 Results

The results of our classification experiments are shown in Table 3, which focuses on individual properties as features, as well as combinations of frequency measures, productivity measures, and all five collected properties as features. It further

[3]We refer to the class of highly compositional compounds as the positive class.

	Accuracy					
	Compound		Modifier		Head	
Features	coarse	fine	coarse	fine	coarse	fine
Random	0.500	0.500	0.500	0.500	0.500	0.500
Best last	0.694	0.702	0.710	0.702	0.669	0.637
Best ENCOW	**0.782**		**0.831**		**0.669**	
F_C	***0.663***	***0.665***	0.595	0.600	***0.631***	***0.633***
F_M	0.585	0.597	***0.649***	***0.629***	0.457	0.455
F_H	0.649	0.647	0.519	0.523	0.627	0.617
F_{MH}	0.637	0.643	0.605	0.624	0.592	0.595
F_{CMH}	0.654	0.644	0.594	0.620	0.570	0.576
P_M	0.629	0.626	0.632	0.606	0.457	0.448
P_H	0.571	0.564	0.502	0.472	0.554	0.550
P_{MH}	0.612	0.597	0.610	0.607	0.538	0.518
$F_{CMH}P_{MH}$	0.619	0.634	0.590	0.608	0.568	0.574

Table 3: Classification results for the three experiments per property used as features. We report accuracy for coarse- and fine-grained time slices, as well as the best last coarse- and fine-grained timeslices and the best ENCOW setting. Bold values are the best overall, and bold italic values are the best diachronic settings.

reports the best results for each static synchronic setting. In the coming discussion, we also reference additional combinations of features that are relevant for specific setups. We provide the full results of all permutations of features for each of the experiments in Appendix D. Regarding the static synchronic approach, the effect of positive class size on the compound compositionality experiment is shown in Appendix B.

Overall, we find that all diachronic properties are informative for compound compositionality and that the properties of a given constituent are informative for the compositionality of that constituent (e.g. P_H for head compositionality). The results for combinations of properties indicate that they are informative if they include an informative property. In most cases, however, results for combinations are below those for included properties.

Across the target properties, the best settings of all static synchronic approaches outperform our diachronic setup. This is not especially surprising: our aim is to predict the present-day degree of compositionality, and (near-)present-day data is likely better suited to this task. Moreover, the best synchronic results are systematically obtained using ENCOW data, which is ≈100 times larger than the last coarse CCOHA slice; this suggests that the diachronic approach is hindered by data sparsity. Nevertheless, its performance is well above chance, which confirms that diachronic developments capture distinct patterns with respect to present-day compositionality. Since this issue is the main focus of our work, we limit the remaining discussion of results to our diachronic experiments.

Compound compositionality. All configurations of properties from both granularities of timeslices significantly outperform the random choice baseline ($p < 0.001$).[4] Amongst the individual properties and main combinations summarized in Table 3, F_C performs best, followed by F_{CMH}; this applies both to the fine-grained and the coarse-grained setup. Combinations of properties tend to perform similarly to the most informative property in them. A noteworthy exception is $F_C P_M$, which obtains the best overall result with an accuracy of 0.675 for the coarse-grained and 0.702 for the fine-grained timeslice setup. We hypothesize that this is due to the information of both properties being complementary, as indicated by a weak correlation (average $\rho = 0.30$ per timeslice). Regarding modifier properties, P_M is more informative than F_M. This is flipped for head properties F_H and P_H.

The results do not differ significantly between timeslice granularities, changing in the range of $\pm 1.5\%$. This indicates that the diachronic development of properties retrieved from coarse-grained timeslices is as informative as their counterparts from finer-grained timeslices. We hypothesize that this may be due to two potential reasons. (i) We observe in our data that considerable change in the properties either happens fairly quickly or slowly over time (cf. Section 6). Both are captured to a similar extent in both timeslice granularities. (ii) Despite providing more detailed information, the fine-grained developments may be more susceptible to sparsity and ultimately may not be more informative than the coarse-grained timeslices.

Modifier compositionality. In contrast to the compound compositionality experiment, F_M appears to be most informative for the compositionality of the modifier, followed by P_M. Similarly to the first experiment, combinations of properties are fairly informative, but less so than the most informative property in them. With their results not differing significantly from the random baseline, both F_H and P_H appear to be uninformative for predicting the modifier compositionality class. As expected, we observe that the properties of the modifier are relevant for modifier compositionality, while the properties of the head are not. Similarly to the compound compositionality experiment, results generally do not differ significantly between timeslice granularities for settings with results well above the random baseline. There is a significant

[4]All significance tests were done using the chi-square test.

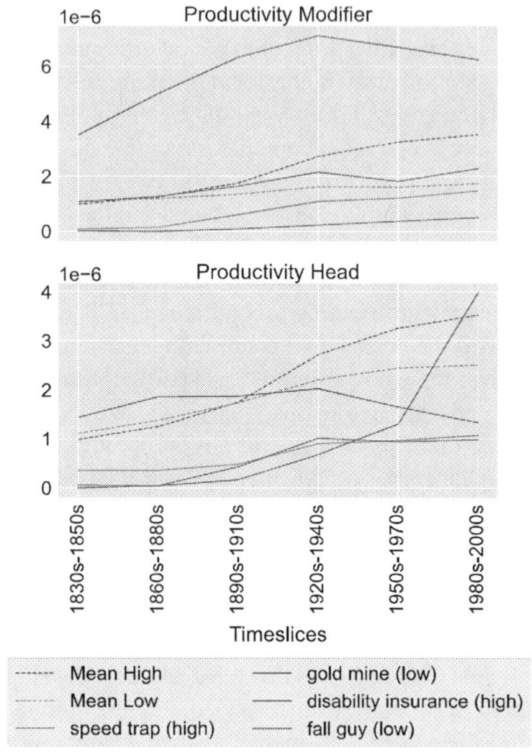

Figure 2: Diachronic development of the productivity of the modifier and of the head for sample compounds. For each example, the compositionality class is indicated in parentheses. Dashed lines indicate the means for the two classes.

difference for the settings P_M and F_{CMH}, but the trends point in opposite directions without an immediately apparent explanation.

Head compositionality. Similarly to the compound compositionality experiment, F_C is the most informative feature. This is in line with the dominant linguistic role of the head in compound structure. The remaining results are overall comparable to the modifier compositionality experiment but flipped: F_H is more informative than P_H, and the results of F_M and P_M are worse than the random baseline. Results do not differ significantly between timeslice granularities.

6 Qualitative analysis

To further assess when the patterns of diachronic development are informative for the classification of present-day compositionality, we inspect where the models fail. We find that, over all the runs, across features and experiments, low-compositionality compounds are misclassified more often than highly compositional ones.

We look more closely into examples from both classes that are misclassified in over 80% of runs in the compound compositionality experiment. Some misclassified compounds of either class exhibit a diachronic evolution profile that clearly differs from the mean trend for their class. For instance, the trend in P_H for *fall guy* (low compositionality) is more similar to the overall trend of the high compositionality class, with a steep increase in later timeslices, while we observe the inverse for *speed trap* (high compositionality), see Figure 2. This, however, does not appear to be the only issue at stake, since profiles of misclassified instances also differ within a class, e.g. for *fall guy* and *gold mine*.

On a more general level, frequently misclassified compounds from both classes exhibit similar patterns in similar ranges for most properties, for instance *speed trap* and *gold mine* (cf. Figure 2 for productivity and Appendix A for frequency evolution). Since the means of both classes are similar to one another across properties, we hypothesize that patterns close to the means or below may be too similar across classes to be informative.

7 Conclusion

We presented experiments aimed at classifying English noun compounds in terms of their present-day degree of compositionality. We proposed a novel diachronic approach, relying on the evolution of frequency and productivity patterns for compounds and their constituents. Both types of features are informative, with our single best diachronic classifier combining the strongest individual variants of frequency and productivity features. The highest performance overall is obtained by a synchronic method based on a much larger present-day corpus, but our diachronic approach is still indicative of distinct compound development profiles relative to their degree of compositionality. This overall demonstrates the relevance of diachronic data in modeling noun compounds, thereby confirming the potential of this under-researched area.

Acknowledgments

The research presented here was supported by the DFG Research Grant SCHU 2580/5-1 (*Computational Models of the Emergence and Diachronic Change of Multi-Word Expression Meanings*).

Limitations

Our experiments were limited to two quantitative properties – frequency and productivity – used to analyze noun compounds in a single language, English. This has potential implications for the generalizability of our results. From a linguistic standpoint, compound properties vary widely across languages. For instance, where English has productive patterns combining two nouns, often in an open (space-separated) compound, German has closed compounds; Romance languages widely rely on N-Prep-N patterns; the structure in many Slavic languages involves patterns of nominal declension; and so forth. The most useful diachronic information for compositionality prediction may vary across these cases. Future work may also investigate the diachronic evolution of other compound properties, such as the degree of ambiguity of the constituents or the semantic relations between them.

Ethical considerations

We do not believe that the research presented in this paper raises ethical concerns. We analyzed the diachronic evolution of a specific type of linguistic structure in English, based on standard aggregate estimates of word usage derived from a large corpus. No personally identifiable or otherwise sensitive information was targeted by our modeling approach. Previously created datasets were used in line with their intended use and licenses.

We acknowledge the fact that the corpus we used contains documents written in American English over the last two centuries. It therefore likely captures biases mirroring the societal inequalities typical of the time in which those texts were produced. However, we do not expect general quantitative properties of a small subset of the vocabulary – on which we relied – to be significantly affected by any potential biases.

References

Reem Alatrash, Dominik Schlechtweg, Jonas Kuhn, and Sabine Schulte im Walde. 2020. CCOHA: Clean corpus of historical American English. In *Proceedings of the Twelfth Language Resources and Evaluation Conference*, pages 6958–6966, Marseille, France. European Language Resources Association.

Pegah Alipoor and Sabine Schulte im Walde. 2020. Variants of vector space reductions for predicting the compositionality of English noun compounds. In *Proceedings of the 12th Conference on Language Resources and Evaluation (LREC 2020)*, pages 4379–4387, Marseille, France. European Language Resources Association.

Timothy Baldwin and Su Nam Kim. 2010. Multiword expressions. In Nitin Indurkhya and Fred J. Damerau, editors, *Handbook of Natural Language Processing*, pages 267–292. CRC Press, Boca Raton, USA.

Silvio Cordeiro, Aline Villavicencio, Marco Idiart, and Carlos Ramisch. 2019. Unsupervised compositionality prediction of nominal compounds. *Computational Linguistics*, 45(1):1–57.

Mark Davies. 2012. Expanding horizons in historical linguistics with the 400-million word Corpus of Historical American English. *Corpora*, 7(2):121–157.

Nicole H. de Jong, Laurie B. Feldman, Robert Schreuder, Michael Pastizzo, and R. Harald Baayen. 2002. The processing and representation of Dutch and English compounds: Peripheral morphological and central orthographic effects. *Brain and Language*, 81:555–567.

Prajit Dhar, Janis Pagel, and Lonneke van der Plas. 2019. Measuring the compositionality of noun-noun compounds over time. In *Proceedings of the 1st International Workshop on Computational Approaches to Historical Language Change*, pages 234–239, Florence, Italy. Association for Computational Linguistics.

Prajit Dhar and Lonneke van der Plas. 2019. Learning to predict novel noun-noun compounds. In *Proceedings of the Joint Workshop on Multiword Expressions and WordNet (MWE-WN 2019)*, pages 30–39, Florence, Italy. Association for Computational Linguistics.

Corina Dima, Daniël de Kok, Neele Witte, and Erhard Hinrichs. 2019. No word is an island—A transformation weighting model for semantic composition. *Transactions of the Association for Computational Linguistics*, 7:437–451.

Corina Dima, Verena Henrich, Erhard Hinrichs, and Christina Hoppermann. 2014. How to tell a schneemann from a milchmann: An annotation scheme for compound-internal relations. In *Proceedings of the Ninth International Conference on Language Resources and Evaluation (LREC'14)*, pages 1194–1201, Reykjavik, Iceland. European Language Resources Association (ELRA).

Marcos Garcia, Tiago Kramer Vieira, Carolina Scarton, Marco Idiart, and Aline Villavicencio. 2021a. Assessing the representations of idiomaticity in vector models with a noun compound dataset labeled at type and token levels. In *Proceedings of the 59th Annual Meeting of the Association for Computational Linguistics and the 11th International Joint Conference on Natural Language Processing (Volume 1: Long Papers)*, pages 2730–2741, Online. Association for Computational Linguistics.

Marcos Garcia, Tiago Kramer Vieira, Carolina Scarton, Marco Idiart, and Aline Villavicencio. 2021b. Probing for idiomaticity in vector space models. In *Proceedings of the 16th Conference of the European Chapter of the Association for Computational Linguistics: Main Volume*, pages 3551–3564, Online. Association for Computational Linguistics.

Roxana Girju, Dan Moldovan, Marta Tatu, and Daniel Antohe. 2005. On the semantics of noun compounds. *Journal of Computer Speech and Language*, 19(4):479–496. Special Issue on Multiword Expressions.

William L. Hamilton, Jure Leskovec, and Dan Jurafsky. 2016. Diachronic word embeddings reveal statistical laws of semantic change. In *Proceedings of the 54th Annual Meeting of the Association for Computational Linguistics*, pages 1489–1501, Berlin, Germany.

Martin Hilpert. 2015. From *hand-carved* to *computer-based*: Noun-participle compounding and the upward strengthening hypothesis. *Cognitive Linguistics*, 26(1):1–36.

Daniel Jurafsky, Alan Bell, Michelle Gregory, and William D. Raymond. 2001. Probabilistic relations between words: Evidence from reduction in lexical production. In Joan Bybee and Paul Hopper, editors, *Frequency and the Emergence of Linguistic Structure*, Typological Studies in Language, pages 229–254. John Benjamins, Amsterdam / Philadelphia.

Christopher J. Lee. 1990. Some hypotheses concerning the evolution of polysemous words. *Journal of Psycholinguistic Research*, 19(4):211–219.

Filip Miletic and Sabine Schulte im Walde. 2023. A systematic search for compound semantics in pretrained BERT architectures. In *Proceedings of the 17th Conference of the European Chapter of the Association for Computational Linguistics*, pages 1499–1512, Dubrovnik, Croatia. Association for Computational Linguistics.

Jeff Mitchell and Mirella Lapata. 2008. Vector-based models of semantic composition. In *Proceedings of ACL-08: HLT*, pages 236–244, Columbus, Ohio. Association for Computational Linguistics.

Diarmuid Ó Séaghdha. 2007. Annotating and learning compound noun semantics. In *Proceedings of the ACL 2007 Student Research Workshop*, pages 73–78, Prague, Czech Republic. Association for Computational Linguistics.

Siva Reddy, Diana McCarthy, and Suresh Manandhar. 2011. An empirical study on compositionality in compound nouns. In *Proceedings of 5th International Joint Conference on Natural Language Processing*, pages 210–218, Chiang Mai, Thailand. Asian Federation of Natural Language Processing.

Ivan A. Sag, Timothy Baldwin, Francis Bond, Ann Copestake, and Dan Flickinger. 2002. Multiword expressions: A pain in the neck for NLP. In *Proceedings of the Conference on Intelligent Text Processing and Computational Linguistics*, Mexico City, Mexico.

Bahar Salehi, Paul Cook, and Timothy Baldwin. 2014. Using distributional similarity of multi-way translations to predict multiword expression compositionality. In *Proceedings of the 14th Conference of the European Chapter of the Association for Computational Linguistics*, pages 472–481, Gothenburg, Sweden. Association for Computational Linguistics.

Bahar Salehi, Paul Cook, and Timothy Baldwin. 2015. A word embedding approach to predicting the compositionality of multiword expressions. In *Proceedings of the 2015 Conference of the North American Chapter of the Association for Computational Linguistics: Human Language Technologies*, pages 977–983, Denver, Colorado. Association for Computational Linguistics.

Roland Schäfer. 2015. Processing and querying large web corpora with the COW14 architecture. In *Proceedings of Challenges in the Management of Large Corpora 3 (CMLC-3)*, Lancaster.

Roland Schäfer and Felix Bildhauer. 2012. Building large corpora from the web using a new efficient tool chain. In *Proceedings of the Eighth International Conference on Language Resources and Evaluation (LREC 2012)*, pages 486–493, Istanbul, Turkey. European Language Resources Association.

Sabine Schulte im Walde. 2023. Collecting and investigating features of compositionality ratings. In Voula Giouli and Verginica Barbu Mititelu, editors, *Multiword Expressions in Lexical Resources. Linguistic, Lexicographic and Computational Perspectives*, Phraseology and Multiword Expressions. Language Science Press, Berlin, Germany.

Sabine Schulte im Walde, Anna Hätty, and Stefan Bott. 2016. The role of modifier and head properties in predicting the compositionality of English and German noun-noun compounds: A vector-space perspective. In *Proceedings of the Fifth Joint Conference on Lexical and Computational Semantics*, pages 148–158, Berlin, Germany. Association for Computational Linguistics.

Sabine Schulte im Walde, Stefan Müller, and Stefan Roller. 2013. Exploring vector space models to predict the compositionality of German noun-noun compounds. In *Second Joint Conference on Lexical and Computational Semantics (*SEM), Volume 1: Proceedings of the Main Conference and the Shared Task: Semantic Textual Similarity*, pages 255–265, Atlanta, Georgia, USA. Association for Computational Linguistics.

A Frequency for target examples over time

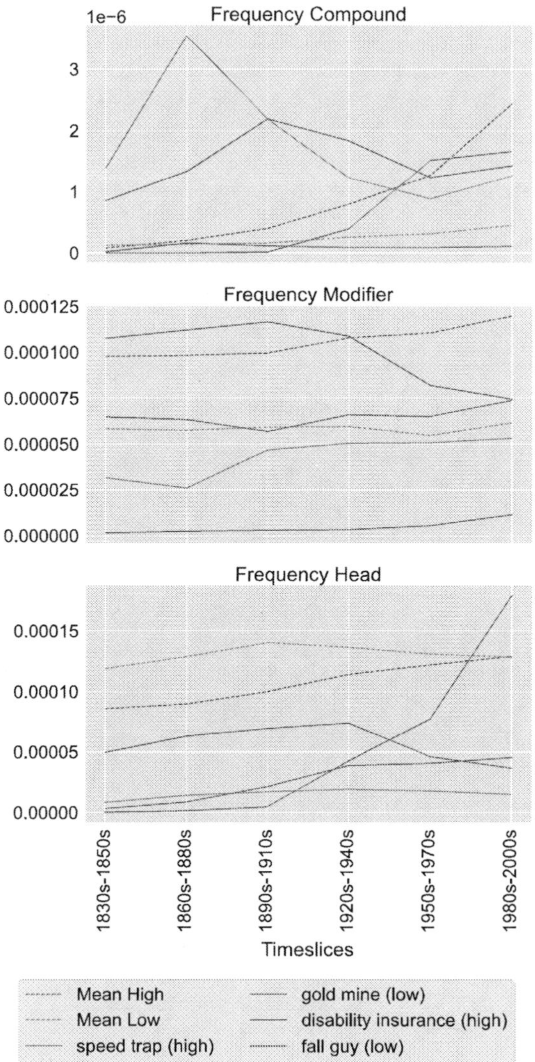

Figure 3: Frequency over time for examples. The class of an example is indicated in parentheses.

B Effect of varying set size in synchronic experiments

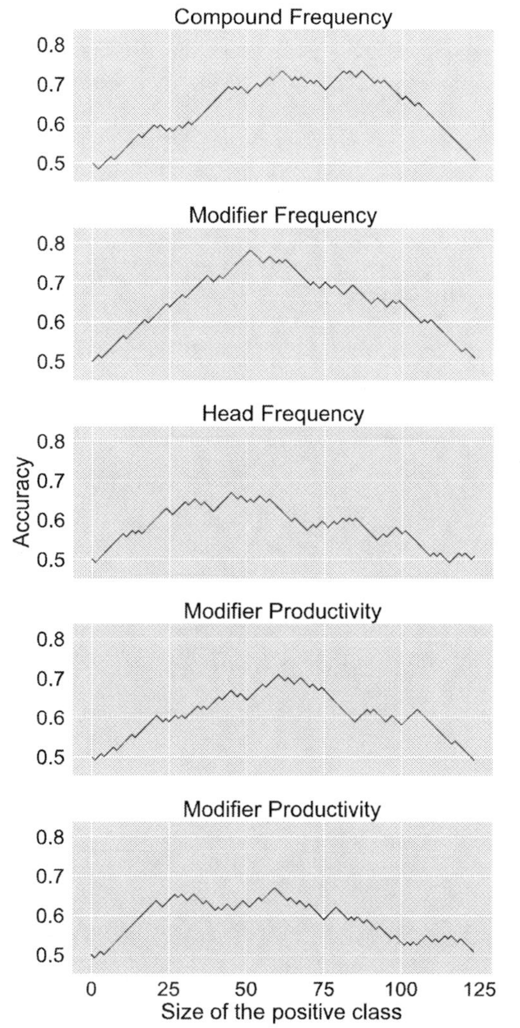

Figure 4: Static compound experiment results per positive class size with ENCOW data.

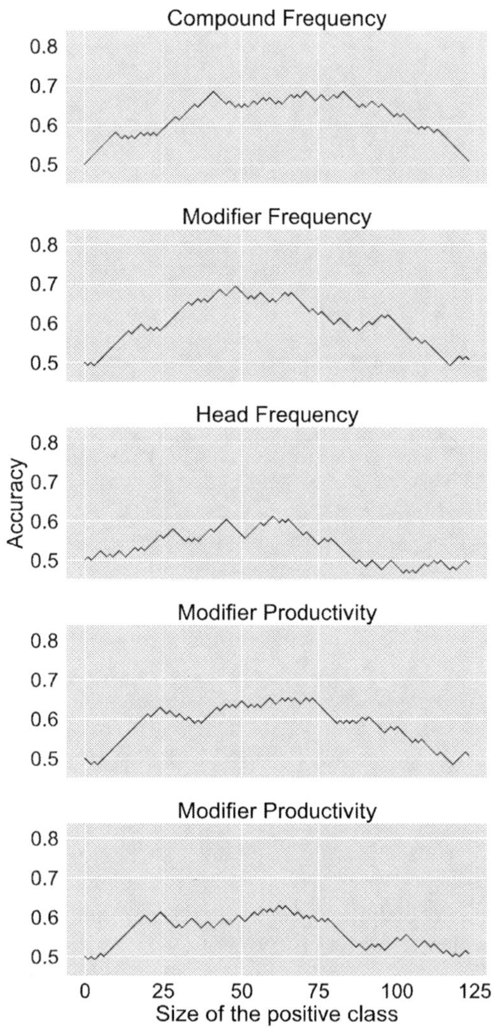

Figure 5: Static compound experiment results per positive class size with the last coarse timeslice.

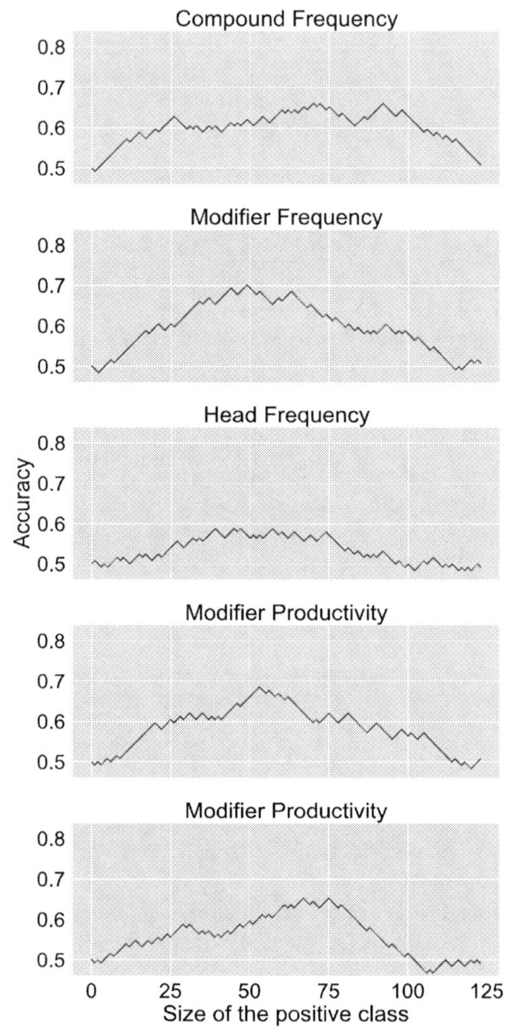

Figure 6: Static compound experiment results per positive class size with the last fine timeslice.

C Development of properties over time

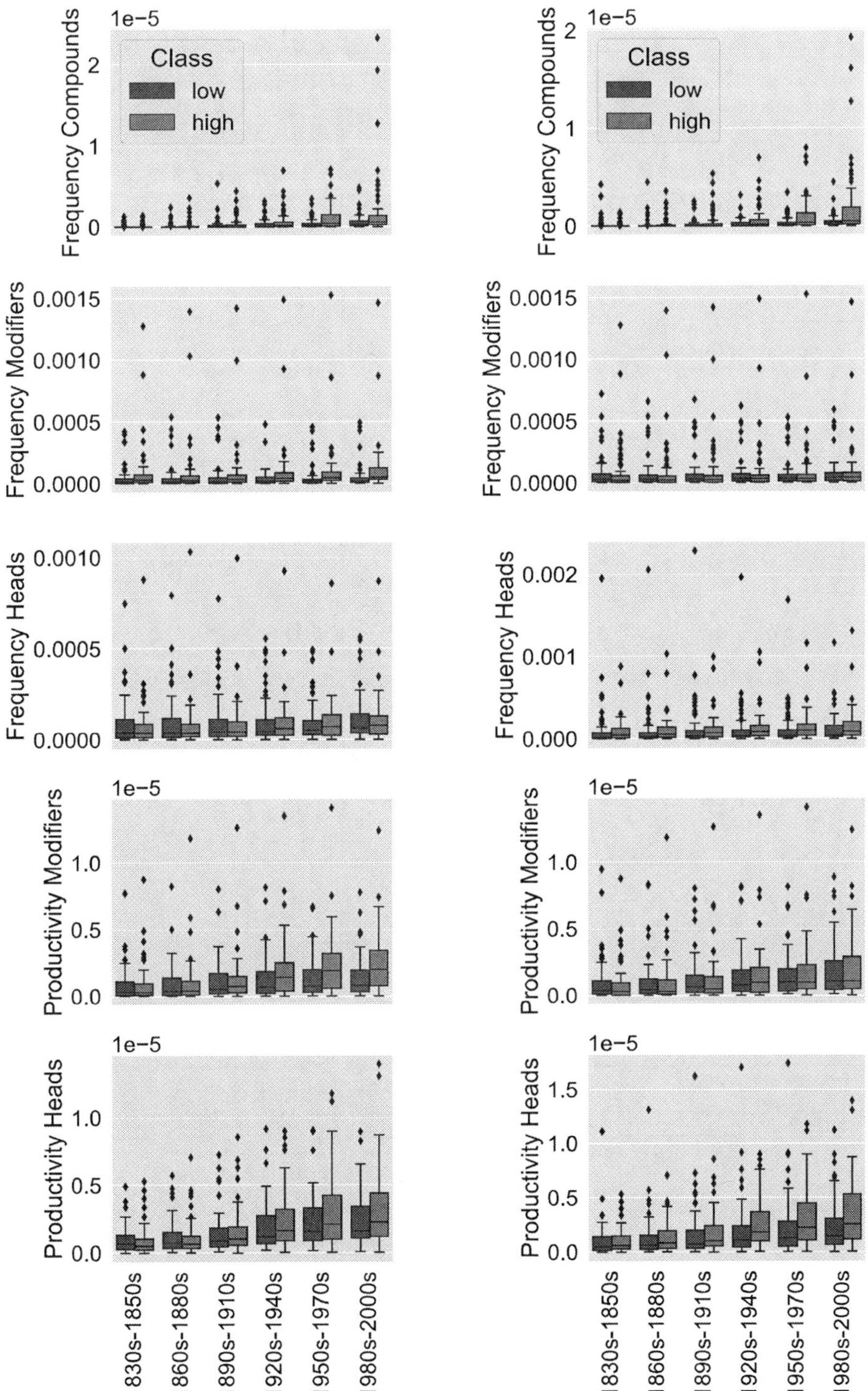

(a) (b)

Figure 7: (a) Development of the properties over time per class for the modifier compositionality experiment. (b) Development of the properties over time per class for the head compositionality experiment.

D Full results

Features	Accuracy					
	Compound		Modifier		Head	
	coarse	fine	coarse	fine	coarse	fine
F_C	0.663	0.665	0.595	0.600	0.631	0.633
F_M	0.585	0.597	0.649	0.629	0.457	0.455
F_H	0.649	0.647	0.519	0.523	0.627	0.617
F_{MH}	0.637	0.643	0.605	0.624	0.592	0.595
F_{CMH}	0.629	0.635	0.594	0.620	0.570	0.576
P_M	0.629	0.626	0.632	0.606	0.457	0.448
P_H	0.571	0.564	0.502	0.472	0.555	0.550
P_{MH}	0.612	0.597	0.610	0.607	0.538	0.518
$F_M P_M$	0.579	0.590	0.638	0.634	0.461	0.457
$F_M P_H$	0.579	0.589	0.639	0.635	0.459	0.456
$F_M P_{MH}$	0.578	0.589	0.637	0.635	0.458	0.455
$F_C P_M$	0.675	0.702	0.651	0.652	0.554	0.558
$F_C P_H$	0.630	0.626	0.575	0.579	0.614	0.615
$F_C P_{MH}$	0.662	0.650	0.614	0.621	0.588	0.590
$F_H P_M$	0.654	0.644	0.500	0.509	0.620	0.613
$F_H P_H$	0.654	0.644	0.504	0.510	0.620	0.614
$F_H P_{MH}$	0.654	0.639	0.497	0.510	0.620	0.612
$F_{MH} P_M$	0.629	0.636	0.595	0.618	0.572	0.577
$F_{MH} P_H$	0.630	0.635	0.594	0.618	0.573	0.577
$F_{MH} P_{MH}$	0.624	0.636	0.588	0.614	0.569	0.570
F_{CM}	0.579	0.590	0.637	0.635	0.458	0.457
$F_{CM} P_M$	0.578	0.590	0.637	0.634	0.458	0.455
$F_{CM} P_H$	0.577	0.589	0.638	0.635	0.457	0.456
$F_{CM} P_{MH}$	0.580	0.590	0.638	0.634	0.457	0.452
F_{CH}	0.651	0.644	0.504	0.509	0.620	0.613
$F_{CH} P_M$	0.654	0.638	0.494	0.510	0.619	0.612
$F_{CH} P_H$	0.655	0.638	0.500	0.509	0.620	0.612
$F_{CH} P_{MH}$	0.654	0.641	0.499	0.501	0.619	0.610
$F_{CMH} P_M$	0.622	0.636	0.589	0.614	0.567	0.570
$F_{CMH} P_H$	0.623	0.637	0.588	0.614	0.568	0.571
$F_{CMH} P_{MH}$	0.619	0.634	0.590	0.608	0.568	0.574

Table 4: Full classification results for the three experiments per property used as features. We report accuracy for properties retrieved from coarse- and fine-grained time slices.

Features	Accuracy														
	Compound					Modifier					Head				
	coarse	fine	c. last	f. last	ENC.	coarse	fine	c. last	f. last	ENC.	coarse	fine	c. last	f. last	ENC.
F_C	0.663	0.665	0.686	0.662	**0.734**	0.595	0.600	0.629	0.637	**0.702**	0.631	0.633	0.669	0.637	**0.669**
F_M	0.585	0.597	0.694	0.702	**0.782**	0.649	0.629	0.710	0.702	**0.831**	0.457	0.455	0.548	0.573	**0.605**
F_H	0.649	0.647	0.613	0.589	**0.669**	0.519	0.523	0.565	0.573	**0.605**	0.627	0.617	0.645	0.621	**0.661**
P_M	0.629	0.626	0.653	0.685	**0.710**	0.632	0.606	0.653	0.661	**0.710**	0.457	0.448	0.540	0.556	**0.573**
P_H	0.571	0.564	0.629	0.653	**0.669**	0.502	0.472	0.556	**0.629**	0.613	0.554	0.550	**0.637**	**0.637**	**0.637**

Table 5: Results per feature including synchronic/last timeslices results. For the experiment using the last timeslices/synchronic data, we report the best result across positive class sizes. Best result per feature and compositionality setting is bolded. Abbreviations: *c. last* = last coarse timeslice, *f. last* = last fine timeslice, *ENC.* = ENCOW.

E Correlations between properties over time

Timeslice	P_M-P_H	P_M-F_M	P_M-F_H	P_M-F_C	P_H-F_M	P_H-F_H	P_H-F_C	F_M-F_H	F_M-F_C	F_H-F_C
1830s-1850s	-0.06	0.79	-0.11	0.34	-0.03	0.89	0.35	0.32	0.18	0.32
1860s-1880s	-0.06	0.78	-0.11	0.44	-0.07	0.90	0.32	0.29	0.31	0.29
1890s-1910s	-0.12	0.79	-0.11	0.41	-0.05	0.90	0.33	0.28	0.36	0.28
1920s-1940s	-0.14	0.80	-0.14	0.37	-0.06	0.90	0.26	0.26	0.30	0.26
1950s-1970s	-0.12	0.78	-0.14	0.27	-0.01	0.89	0.28	0.26	0.26	0.26
1980s-2000s	-0.06	0.79	-0.13	0.19	0.04	0.87	0.26	0.21	0.26	0.21

Table 6: Correlations between properties per coarse-grained timeslice.

Timeslice	P_M-P_H	P_M-F_M	P_M-F_H	P_M-F_C	P_H-F_M	P_H-F_H	P_H-F_C	F_M-F_H	F_M-F_C	F_H-F_C
1830s	-0.03	0.76	-0.09	0.35	-0.03	0.87	0.31	0.27	0.16	0.27
1840s	-0.02	0.75	-0.09	0.33	-0.04	0.87	0.33	0.27	0.18	0.27
1850s	-0.06	0.76	-0.12	0.31	-0.03	0.88	0.29	0.24	0.15	0.24
1860s	-0.02	0.77	-0.10	0.36	-0.05	0.88	0.28	0.24	0.21	0.24
1870s	-0.09	0.77	-0.13	0.36	-0.06	0.89	0.35	0.28	0.24	0.28
1880s	-0.03	0.77	-0.08	0.40	-0.04	0.88	0.35	0.30	0.25	0.30
1890s	-0.08	0.77	-0.09	0.41	-0.03	0.90	0.33	0.28	0.29	0.28
1900s	-0.10	0.77	-0.11	0.30	-0.03	0.90	0.32	0.27	0.26	0.27
1910s	-0.13	0.78	-0.12	0.41	-0.05	0.87	0.31	0.24	0.33	0.24
1920s	-0.13	0.77	-0.14	0.36	-0.06	0.90	0.28	0.21	0.28	0.21
1930s	-0.13	0.81	-0.13	0.39	-0.05	0.89	0.31	0.29	0.31	0.29
1940s	-0.12	0.78	-0.12	0.33	-0.02	0.89	0.27	0.26	0.26	0.26
1950s	-0.13	0.77	-0.14	0.27	-0.04	0.89	0.29	0.26	0.22	0.26
1960s	-0.10	0.77	-0.12	0.29	-0.01	0.88	0.24	0.23	0.27	0.23
1970s	-0.10	0.77	-0.13	0.26	0.00	0.88	0.26	0.25	0.24	0.25
1980s	-0.07	0.77	-0.13	0.21	0.02	0.87	0.31	0.27	0.24	0.27
1990s	-0.06	0.78	-0.11	0.26	0.04	0.87	0.28	0.23	0.29	0.23
2000s	-0.07	0.79	-0.12	0.17	0.02	0.87	0.20	0.16	0.24	0.16

Table 7: Correlations between properties per fine-grained timeslice.

From Qualitative to Quantitative Research: Semi-Automatic Annotation Scaling in the Digital Humanities

Fynn Petersen-Frey* **Tim Fischer*** **Florian Schneider***
Isabel Eiser† **Gertraud Koch†** **Chris Biemann***
*Language Technology Group, Department of Informatics, Universität Hamburg
†Institute for Anthropological Studies in Culture and History, Universität Hamburg
{first.last}@uni-hamburg.de, florian.schneider-1@uni-hamburg.de

Abstract

In today's digital era, massive amounts of data are ubiquitous including discourses in natural language, such as news articles, social media posts or forum threads. The digital humanities aim to qualitatively and quantitatively analyze such data. For interpretive research, it is difficult to benefit from large data. An example is grounded theory, an interpretative method to deal with larger datasets by annotating or coding. However, such approaches are too time-consuming to bridge the gap from qualitative to quantitative analyses. In this work, we propose assistive methods to semi-automatically scale a small number of manual annotations to large corpora. Our approach uses contextualized embeddings of annotated data to find similar occurrences. By interactively providing suggestions learned automatically from user interactions, our method provides a convenient and fast way to annotate large corpora with minimal manual effort. The method finally produces a classifier able to annotate the entire dataset. We performed experiments on multiple tasks and datasets to evaluate our methods demonstrating strong performance. Further, we designed a software for researchers who want to scale their annotation-based research, bridging the gap from qualitative to quantitative results.

1 Introduction

There is a growing interest in the Digital Humanities (DH) to apply Natural Language Processing (NLP) methods to explore textual data and scale textual data analysis. The reason for this is twofold. First, due to the advancing digitization of humanities and cultural studies data, both through retro-digitization and the increase in born digital data, large quantities of data are available that are often infeasible for a single person or team to study. Second, the groundbreaking success of NLP in various disciplines makes it attractive to adapt methods to the DH domain. This is a great opportunity for qualitative DH researchers to benefit from large datasets where in-depth qualitative analysis and annotations cannot be extended to large-scale corpora.

The Digital Humanities often rely on qualitative methodology like grounded theory. Hermeneutic circular processes and theoretical sampling approaches include iterative search, selection, collection, analysis, and interpretation of research data. Grounded theory can be understood as an interactive process where researchers, participants and data construct research together in interaction repeatedly, producing a category system that effectively captures the research problem. It is of great interest to apply the category system to larger datasets for quantitative analysis, but infeasible to do so manually.

Currently, data scientists would need to train a Machine Learning (ML) model requiring large amounts of training data that have to be created by qualified annotators using to-be-developed annotation guidelines. This is time-consuming, costly, requires ML expertise, and is consequently rarely done in the context of DH projects. Thus, new methods combining human and computer actions are needed to enable research on larger datasets and foster further research in the digital humanities as typical ML approaches are no good fit for most projects. Recent studies (Ostheimer et al., 2021; Koch et al., 2022) in the field of human-computer-interaction have shown fruitful incorporation of human decision-making in ML processes and that human-in-the-loop methods can significantly improve ML models. ML-supported annotation needs the human supervision and refinement to offer useful and accurate alternatives in qualitative data analysis. Strengthening the synergy between humans and machines is a promising direction where both sides are profiting: ML-based annotation is improved by human refinements, whereas automation aids iterative processes of human meaning-making and interpretive research by scaling annotations to enable the analysis of vast materials.

Proceedings of the 19th Conference on Natural Language Processing (KONVENS 2023), pages 52–62
September 18–22, 2023. ©2023 Association for Computational Linguistics

This work targets qualitative researchers who annotate textual data to analyse it in-depth and want to increase their efficiency and/or want to leverage large datasets as quantitative grounding for their hypothesises. We propose an ML-based assistive system leveraging current NLP to ease the annotation task and semi-automatically scale annotations from few manual annotations to a fully-annotated corpus. After the user has annotated a few text spans with their categories, representatives for each category are utilised for semantic similarity search to suggest relevant text spans with their context. While the user accepts or discard these suggestions, the system adapts to feedback by updating the category representatives instantly after each verified suggestion. Since verifying suggestions is a much faster task than reading and annotating, users can efficiently annotate their documents. The system automatically fine-tunes models to predict higher-quality suggestions and to apply the learned categories to a large document collection with high accuracy, thereby scaling the annotations.

In this paper, we make several contributions towards a system supporting researchers during and after their qualitative analysis and aids them in scaling their annotations to large corpora: (1) A two-stage method usable without programming or NLP know-how to semi-automatically scale annotations to large-scale corpora by interactively providing adaptive suggestions and employing adapter (Houlsby et al., 2019) technology to automatically annotate large corpora. (2) A user interface for quick batch validation of suggestions while still displaying the most relevant contextual information. (3) An evaluation of our method with a simulated annotation process on multiple large datasets for sentence-level and word-level annotations demonstrating strong scaling capabilities.

2 Related work

Qualitative analyses can be powerfully supported with digital solutions and ML methods addressing annotation, analysis, and interpretation. MAXQDA and ATLAS.ti are two commonly used closed-source, paid solutions for qualitative analysis trying to offer all-in-one-solutions, but include no ML assistance. Prodigy is an annotation software where the workflow is dictated by the active learning (AL) model. Label studio is an annotation platform that offers AL functionalities requiring set-up by connecting external models, thereby making it unsuitable for domain experts. Existing open-source software that offers (semi-)automatic annotation aid in various variations are outlined in the following.

WebAnno (Yimam et al., 2014; Eckart de Castilho et al., 2016) is a web-based tool for fine-grained NLP annotations and includes an automatic method where the system learns from user-provided annotations. However, it requires expert ML knowledge to perform feature engineering and training. The successor INCEpALTION (Klie et al., 2018) can suggest possible labels and includes an AL mode to guide annotators to improve the system by labeling examples providing valuable information to the classifier. Neither WebAnno nor INCEpTION are designed to work on a content-level or on large-scale corpora. CodeAnno (Schneider et al., 2023b) is another WebAnno successor focusing on document-level coding and supports training ML classifiers for this. LabelSleuth (Shnarch et al., 2022) is a software to build binary classifiers by labeling text data using active learning suggestions targeted at domain experts. While it is probably the closest to our application, it only supports binary classification of sentences, unsuitable for multi-class word-level annotations.

Active learning (AL) is a technique to obtain a classifier by soliciting feedback from the user on the most informative sample identified using e.g. uncertainty sampling (Lewis and Gale, 1994) which requires a classifier to output certainty scores. AL is often associated with the Human-in-the-loop (Holzinger, 2016) paradigm where human feedback is integrated in the loop of machine learning development. We see our work as AI-in-the-loop where ML systems assist the workflow of humans who stay in control all the time. Our system assists the user by providing sensible suggestions, but neither disrupts nor dictates their workflow.

Few-shot classification of named entities is a task relevant to our annotation scaling scenario where a classifier is trained to generalize to new classes after observing only a small number of examples. This task was tackled (Fritzler et al., 2019) by using prototypical networks (Snell et al., 2017) which learn a prototype for unseen classes by averaging the representations of the support samples for that class. However, this approach is not made for incrementally increasing samples and it does not scale well with increasing numbers of examples. Our approach utilizes a few-shot classification system based on adapters (Houlsby et al., 2019) to provide a high-quality classifier from few training samples.

Previous work (Remus et al., 2022) evaluated different strategies to find related items in an information retrieval scenario demonstrating that contextualized word embeddings of pre-trained models are suitable to retrieve word-level items such as named entities. They showed a small speedup of manual annotations when annotating similar instead of random items. We build upon these findings and devised a method to scale manual annotations to datasets orders of magnitude larger.

3 Application

In this work, we describe a software for qualitative annotation of text documents that assists users during their annotation process with ML functionality requiring neither programming nor ML knowledge. The assistance comes in two forms: Providing suggestions for semi-automatic annotation and fully automatic annotation to analyse large text collections. Our methods apply to sentence-level (e.g. headlines, arbitrary sentences) and token-level (e.g. named entities) annotations. Document-level annotations are not in the scope of this work. Further, our methods are not intended for a MATTER annotation process (see Pustejovsky and Stubbs (2012)) but for use in hermeneutic contexts where users move back-and-forth between understanding parts of a text and the whole (the so-called 'hermeneutic circle'), continuously build and modify their tagset resp. labels along the way (see Horstmann (2019)).

3.1 Requirements

Throughout our close collaboration between Digital Humanities and Computational Linguistics groups, we identified four essential requirements for our system (method and user interface) to provide the most benefit to the users: (1) *Usable without machine learning knowledge*. This enables all researchers to benefit from the method. (2) *Applicable from small to large-scale document collections containing thousands of documents*. This allows to use the method for a wide range of research questions and datasets. (3) *Instantaneous responses & quick adaptation to the users feedback*. This greatly improves the user experience. (4) *Correction of mistakes*. Users must be able to correct system errors and preventing similar mistakes to achieve their desired outcome which has been found highly important for interactive systems like *new/s/leak* (Wiedemann et al., 2018).

3.2 Workflow

Imagine Alice, a DH researcher working on a climate project, who needs to identify, categorise and quantify different actors and stakeholders involved in the parliamentary discussions about climate change to answer one of her research questions. She downloaded a large collection of all plenary minutes and printed matter of the German Bundestag which is available as open data. Alice creates a new project in the software and adds the crawled documents.

Early guidance She works with the software as always: Finding relevant documents by using the built-in search and filtering methods, reading documents, making spontaneous annotations (possibly creating new classes as necessary in this hermeneutic process) while reading and selecting some documents to annotate in detail. During close reading, the system already suggests and highlights text passages in the current document based on the annotated material if she enabled the feature (see Figure 1, left). Her annotations are quite diverse: Some annotations are named entities coded as actor or stakeholder, possibly hierarchically with fine-grained classes (politician, scientist, activist etc.) while others refer to different entities or entire sentences like public statements. After annotating a handful of documents, she has seen enough different cases of actors and stakeholders.

Semi-automatic annotation scaling She enables the suggestion panel (see Figure 1, right) to explore annotation suggestions in the text collection. The system provides a list of suggestions showing the context of each annotation, i.e. sentence(s) and the document title with a link to the full document in case it's needed for verification. Alice can accept or discard suggestions which are then automatically persisted as annotations in her project.

Fully-automatic annotation for quantitative analysis The system indicates to Alice that enough examples have been labeled and a reliable model is trained to apply her established category system to all documents. She double checks a random selection of these automatic annotations and decides that the quality is high enough for further quantitative analyses. In case she identifies erroneous annotations, she can easily update or remove such cases. The system adapts automatically and potentially fixes similar errors. Alice can iterate and correct the system as often as necessary. To

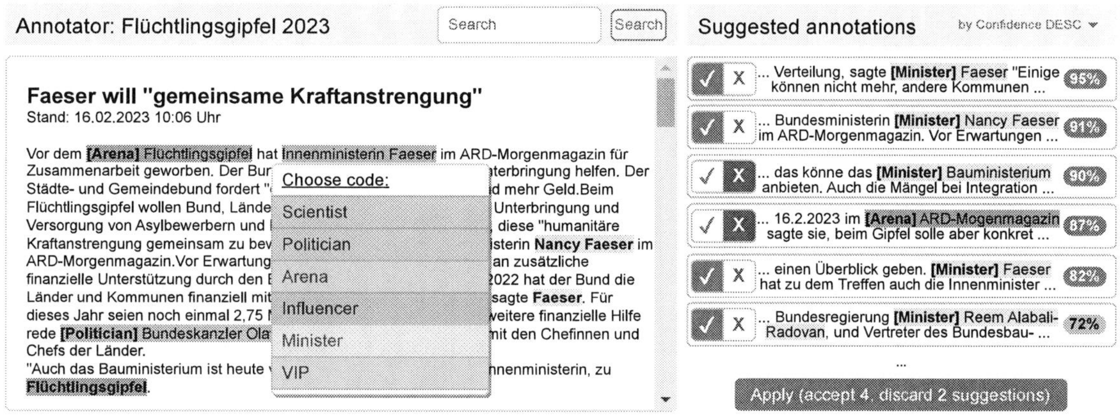

Figure 1: Annotation interface. Left: Document with automatic suggestions enabled. Highlighted texts prefixed with [code] are manually created annotations, other highlights are system suggestions. Right: Batch approving/discarding suggestions to semi-automatically scale annotations.

improve the quality, multiple users can annotate the same documents so Alice can curate annotations. Finally, she retrieves the statistics on the whole corpus (see Figure 2) such as frequency of politicians, scientists etc. or a list of ministers sorted by their frequency in the corpus. By exporting her manual and automatically generated annotations, she can use her favorite analysis and visualization tools to draw further conclusions about her material.

4 Methodology

In this section, we explain our approach to scale few manual annotations with minimal effort to large datasets. First, we perform a one-time process to generate contextualized embeddings for the document collection. Second, we provide interactive suggestions based on contextual embeddings of manual annotations and customized similarity computations. Third, when enough annotations are collected, a classifier is created and applied to the entire dataset. Optionally, the user refines the classifier by correcting aggregated results.

Pre-processing All documents added to the system run through an initial, one-time pre-processing phase: Apache Tika extracts plain text from any document. Sentence-splitting and entity recognition are performed by spaCy (Honnibal et al., 2020). Contextualized embeddings are computed using SBERT (Reimers and Gurevych, 2019) models for sentences, T-NER (Ushio and Camacho-Collados, 2021) for named entities and RoBERTa (Liu et al., 2019) for other structures (see Section 4.1). Multilingual models (e.g. LaBSE (Feng et al., 2022) for sentences, XLM-RoBERTa (Conneau et al., 2020) for tokens) can be used to apply our approach to different languages. The embeddings of each structure are stored in an approximate nearest neighbor (ANN) index like HNSW (Malkov and Yashunin, 2018) or FAISS (Johnson et al., 2021) to enable fast retrieval of similar embeddings for large datasets. The pre-processing is executed automatically in the background before interactive use, satisfying requirements 1–3 (4 is not applicable). Pre-computing contextualized embeddings of sentences and tokens for the document collection enables instantaneous suggestions.

4.1 Interactive, semi-automatic annotation scaling

The system performs the following steps to produce k suggestions for a class c.

Structure selection The system automatically detects which structure fits annotations of class c best by computing and comparing the overlap of annotations with all known structures computed during pre-processing (e.g. sentences, named-entities, noun chunks, single tokens or n-grams). This is a fast database operation (< 10 milliseconds) as only offsets for a few manual annotations need to be compared. The structure s with the highest overlap on average is chosen for the next step.

Candidate retrieval The embeddings of the structures matching each annotation (positive support set, size n) are used to search for the most similar embeddings using cosine similarity in the

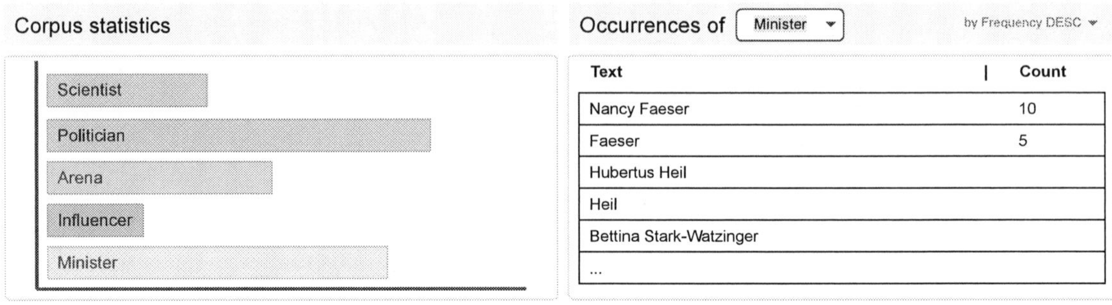

Figure 2: Quantitative analysis interface. Left: Estimation of the frequency of annotated categories in the entire corpus. Right: List of all annotations of a selected category.

ANN index. To do so efficiently, a batch query is performed on the index to retrieve a set of candidates. In total, $N > n$ similar embeddings and their corresponding text spans are retrieved from the ANN index.

Candidate filtering Any already annotated candidates are excluded. The remaining candidates are further filtered by removing a candidate if it is nearest to another sample having a class different than c (negative support set). This *advanced* approach often results in large quality improvements (see Section 5.2 for a comparison). The *naive* approach does not filter using a negative support set. A batch query returning only the most similar item is used to to so efficiently. The remaining candidates are re-ranked by their maximum similarity to any annotated sample of class c. Finally, the top candidates are returned to the user as suggestions.

Reviewing suggestions The user can accept/discard the automatic suggestions batch-wise and accept/discard/edit individual ones. Accepted and edited suggestions are stored as annotations in the database. Rejected suggestions are assigned a hidden 'not-c' class and also stored in the database. The suggestions iteratively improve with every use as more samples of the class c become available as positive support and more samples of other classes become available as negative support.

Requirement check Our method fulfills all requirements (see Section 3.1): Requirement (1) is achieved since no configuration is required. Requirement (2) and (3) are fulfilled as the search in the ANN index scales to billions of embeddings and returns results in a few milliseconds regardless of the collection size. In accordance with requirement (4), users can edit/discard suggestions which automatically affects future suggestions.

4.2 Fully-automatic annotation scaling for quantitative analysis

While the interactive mode allows to quickly annotate hundreds of examples, a real classifier is needed to obtain quantitative results on large datasets. To build a classifier, enough negative samples are required beside the positive samples. If there are fewer negative samples, negative candidates are randomly sampled from all unannotated items (the number of positive samples is usually small compared to all samples). To guard against accidentally choosing a positive sample, candidates are removed if their nearest embedding neighbor is belonging to a positive class. This strategy is more beneficial than selecting negative samples by taking the nearest neighbors of known items as it would not produce a diverse negative support set.

A k-nearest neighbor (KNN) classifier is constructed from the positive and negative support set. To annotate the entire dataset with this classifier, each unannotated structure s is compared to the support set containing all positive and negative samples. This is efficiently done by computing a single matrix multiplication (for cosine similarity) between the support set and all unannotated items. We considered four different strategies to make the final prediction: (1) *Nearest*: The class of the nearest neighbor is chosen as the prediction. (2) *Centroid*: The positive and negative support set are each averaged to centroid embedding. The class of whichever centroid is closer is chosen. This approach is similar to prototypical networks and computationally highly efficient, but often lacks quality. (3) *Majority voting*: The most frequent class within the k nearest neighbors is chosen as the prediction. (4) *Weighted majority voting*: The similarities of each class of the nearest k neighbors are added and the highest is chosen.

This classification is a fast and quickly adaptable approach since no training is required. Applying the classifier on the corpus allows to count how many annotations of a specific class are in the document collection. A list of all potentially annotated text spans can be produced, merged by the same surface text (e.g. all politicians with the same name), and sorted by their frequency. The user can correct the output by assigning a different label to each aggregated group of annotations, thereby immediately improving the KNN classifier to return updated results in less than a second. While a KNN classifier is fast and and adapts quickly, it leaves room for higher-quality predictions. Thus, we experiment with training a stronger classifier in Section 5.3 with few annotated samples.

5 Evaluation

To evaluate our proposed methods, we apply them on fully annotated datasets. This allows us to compare our methods outputs with the correct (as in human created) annotations. We perform three evaluations: (1) We simulate how a user would use the system interactively and evaluate the quality of the automatic suggestions. In this setting, the goal is to find as many annotations of the desired class with the same manual effort (i.e. number of verified suggestions). For named-entity datasets, we directly use the given entity span offsets (instead of first applying an entity detection model). We use the total number of successfully annotated samples as metric. (2) We evaluate the performance of the final KNN-based classifier created after the simulation with the macro F1 score (harmonic mean of precision and recall). (3) We evaluate how many annotated samples are needed to train an even stronger classifier. In these experiments, we train a neural end-to-end classifier with increasing amounts of training data and report the F1 scores.

5.1 Datasets

In this section, we introduce the datasets and data generation processes used in our experiments. An overview of the datasets is provided in Table 1.

OntoNotes5.0 (Weischedel et al., 2013) (ON5) is a well-known named-entity recognition (NER) dataset of 76,714 samples split into 59,924 *train*, 8,262 *test* and 8,528 *validation* samples. Each sample is a sentence in which each word is labeled as one of 18 classes or the other class `O`. We created a custom version of ON5 with the same number of samples and splits as the original dataset but only 12 of the 18 classes. Precisely, we removed `DATE`, `TIME`, `GPE`, `ORG`, `ORDINAL`, and `WORK_OF_ART` from ON5 by replacing the respective tags with the `O` tag. Following (Ding et al., 2021), we merged IOB tags (Ramshaw and Marcus, 1999) into a single tag to ease the few-shot episode data generation.

The MIT Movie Trivia (MITMT) and MIT Restaurant (MITR) datasets[1] are named-entity recognition datasets containing 6,816 *train*, 1,953 *test*, and 1,000 *validation* samples and 6,900 *train*, 1,521 *test*, and 760 *validation* samples. They contain domain-specific named entity classes like *Actor* and *Genre* or *Cuisine* and *Dish*. We created custom versions of the datasets with merged IOB tags, same splits and number of samples containing only classes of at least 1,000 samples. In the custom MITMT, we removed the classes *Award*, *Quote*, *Soundtrack*, *Relationship*, *Origin*, *Opinion* and *Character* and in the custom MITR, we removed *Rating*, *Hours*, and *Price*.

Yahoo! Answers (YA) (Zhang et al., 2015) is a topic classification dataset that includes 4.5 million questions and answers from 10 different categories. We divide the original test set (60,000 items) in half to obtain a validation/test split from which we use the title and its category for our experiments.

5.2 Semi-automatic annotation scaling

We simulate the usage of the system on our custom ON5 and YA dataset with the following strategy. For each of the unseen classes, we randomly select 20 samples (manual annotation) as the initial positive support set from the validation split and iteratively retrieve ten times 20 suggestions that are accepted/rejected with the human-annotated labels from the dataset. Finally, we build a multi-class KNN classifier from the collected samples and classify the test split. We compare the two approaches explained in Section 4.1 to provide suggestions: *Naive* and *advanced* (using a negative support set). For the KNN classifier, we compare four variants nearest neighbor, majority voting ($k = 5$), weighted majority voting ($k = 5$) and centroids. For ON5, we use our named-entity model trained only on 12 out of 18 classes (see Section 5.3 for details) to produce entity embeddings (first token of each entity). To obtain sentence embeddings for YA, we use the pre-trained SBERT model `all-MiniLM-L12-v2`.

[1]see `https://groups.csail.mit.edu/sls/downloads`

Dataset	Type	Size	Classes
OntoNotes 5.0	NER	76,714	CARDINAL, DATE, EVENT, FAC, GPE, LANGUAGE, LAW, LOC, MONEY, NORP, ORDINAL, ORG, PERCENT, PERSON, PRODUCT, QUANTITY, TIME, WORK_OF_ART
MIT Movie Trivia	NER	9,769	Actor, Award, Character, Director, Genre, Opinion, Origin, Plot, Quote, Relationship, Soundtrack, Year
MIT Restaurants	NER	9,181	Amenity, Cuisine, Dish, Hours, Location, Price, Rating, Restaurant_Name
Yahoo! Answers	SC	60,000	Society & Culture, Food & Drink, Cars & Transportation, Education & Reference, Science Mathematics, Business & Finance, News & Events, Computers & Internet, Pets, Politics & Government

Table 1: Overview of the datasets used in the experiments. In the Type column, SC is short for sentence classification.

			(macro) F1 score			
Class	**Approach**	**Samples**	**nearest**	**majority**	**weighted**	**centroid**
OntoNotes5.0						
DATE	naive	161	0.92	**0.93**	**0.93**	0.77
DATE	advanced	190	0.89	0.91	0.90	0.67
WORK_OF_ART	naive	45	0.56	0.61	0.61	0.43
WORK_OF_ART	advanced	89	0.65	**0.71**	**0.71**	0.42
ORDINAL	naive	69	**0.91**	0.90	0.89	0.43
ORDINAL	advanced	148	0.88	0.88	0.88	0.37
GPE	naive	200	0.93	0.94	0.94	0.89
GPE	advanced	200	0.93	0.94	**0.95**	0.89
TIME	naive	27	0.60	0.62	0.62	0.36
TIME	advanced	99	0.60	**0.63**	0.62	0.33
ORG	naive	178	0.86	0.87	0.87	0.87
ORG	advanced	197	**0.89**	**0.89**	**0.89**	**0.89**
all six unseen classes	naive	680	0.83	0.83	0.83	0.65
all six unseen classes	advanced	923	0.83	**0.85**	**0.85**	0.62
Yahoo! Answers						
all ten classes	naive	662	0.50	0.51	0.52	0.53
all ten classes	advanced	1,497	0.56	**0.59**	**0.59**	0.58

Table 2: Annotation simulation & KNN classification results. Samples are the number of correct suggestions.

The results of the experiments are shown in Table 2. While both approaches are able to provide mostly correct suggestions for DATE, GPE and ORG in OntoNotes, the naive approach has a high error rate for the remaining three classes. The advanced approach provides more than twice the samples for the difficult classes (which are rarer and more overlapping, see Figure 3) and reaches an average suggestion precision of 76.9%. On Yahoo! Answers, the advanced approach provides more than twice the number of correct suggestions of the naive approach resulting in an average hit ratio of 75%.

On OntoNotes, the KNN classifier produces very strong F1 scores (≈ 0.9) except for the TIME and WORK_OF_ART classes having the fewest samples. While there is only a small performance difference between nearest and (weighted) majority voting KNN variants, the centroid performs worse by a noticeable margin. The performance on Yahoo! Answers reach scores of 0.59 with the advanced approach widely outperforming a random baseline of 0.1. We attribute this comparatively lower level to fact that the category in the dataset is not only dependent on the title but also the question text which we did not leverage in our experiments.

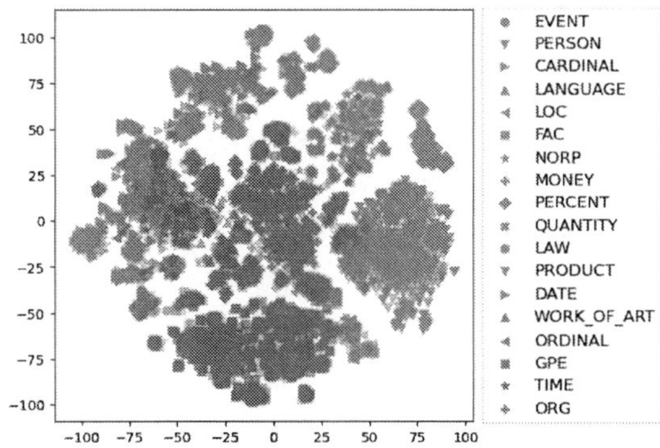

Figure 3: t-SNE Entity embeddings generated on the ON5 test split using our custom trained T-NER model.

We further analyzed the reasons for the behavior of the suggestions and KNN classifier with a visualization of the entity embeddings in Figure 3. Most instances of a class are visually clustered together, even for the the six unseen classes. However, `DATE` and `TIME` are mixed together and explain the lower scores for `TIME` as it is the rarer occurring class. Overall, the visualization shows that the use of embedding similarity metrics for suggestions and classification can work well and should also be able to distinguish between sub-classes as many of the clusters consist of smaller clusters. We also measured the run-time efficiency of our approach: Generating all suggestions and classifying every entity in the test splits for all experiments took only 0.7 seconds in total.

5.3 Few-Shot Transformer Adapter Classifier

With this experiment, we evaluate how many samples are necessary to train a classifier with superior performance to the KNN classifier. The user can instruct the system to (re-)train such a classifier whenever it makes sense, e.g. after annotating a bunch of samples of a new class. A straightforward approach to creating a NER or sentence classifier is to fine-tune a pre-trained large language model (LLM). Due to its numbers of parameters, it would require lots of training samples and be computationally expensive. Since labeled data is scarce in our scenario and a KNN classifier does not need to be trained at all, we train a classifier with as little training data and computational effort as possible. One approach successfully applied in various tasks is training a transformer adapter (Houlsby et al., 2019) using the convenient AdapterHub framework (Pfeiffer et al., 2020). Transformer adapters are a computation- and sample-efficient alternative to full fine-tuning. During training, the LLM's original parameters are frozen, and only the adapter layers are optimized. While different configurations or variants of adapters exist, the parallel configuration (He et al., 2022) outperformed others by a large margin in our preliminary experiments. A new classification head with output dimension equal to the number of classes is trained jointly with the adapter layers.

We used the two setups and the three NER datasets described in Section 5.1 to evaluate how many training samples are required to train an adapter classifier. In the first setup, the ON5 dataset is utilized as follows: We fine-tuned a `roberta-base` model on the train split of the custom ON5 that contains 12 of 18 classes. Next, we injected adapters in the fine-tuned model and trained on episodes containing all 18 classes of ON5. An episode is a set of training samples where every class has between K and $2K$ instances. An episode for $K = 1$ consists of N training samples so that each class is represented at least once and at most twice in all N sentences. In the second setup, we fine-tuned a `roberta-base` model on the train split of the original ON5. Then, we injected adapters and trained on episodes from the customized versions of the MIT Movie Trivia and MIT Restaurant datasets.

In both setups, we trained the adapters with samples of the training split for 5 epochs on episodes for $K \in \{3, 5, 10, 30, 50, 100, 300, 500, 1000\}$ and evaluated on all samples in the test splits. We used the default training hyperparameters from the AdapterHub framework.

As can be observed from the results reported in Figure 4, adapter classifiers demonstrate strong performance (> 0.8 F1) already for small episodes with only 30 to 100 training instances per class. Our adapter models perform similar regardless of the dataset. This further endorses the choice of adapters for robust few-shot NER classifiers. Visible in the left plot in Figure 4 is that adapters are suitable when an existing NER model is extended. The model remembers classes learned in the fine-tuning phase and quickly adapts to new classes.

6 Conclusion

In this work, we proposed and evaluated methods to semi-automatically scale few annotations to large corpora by providing interactive suggestions from adaptable classifiers and developed user interfaces to make our methods usable for domain experts

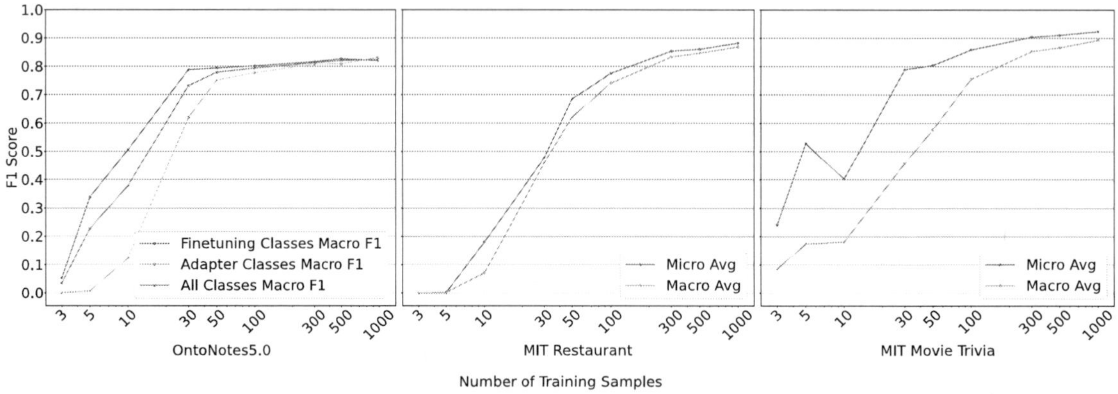

Figure 4: Few-Shot NER performance of transformer adapter classifiers with increasing training data

without programming or NLP skills. Our evaluation on existing datasets shows that these methods can quickly scale annotations with minimal manual effort to large corpora to both obtain quantitative results and aggregated lists enabling a verification of the automated processing. Thus, we see our methods aiding qualitative researchers to bridge the gap to quantitative results and providing quantitative grounding for their hypothesises.

In the future, we want to integrate the developed methods and user interfaces in production-grade code quality into our D-WISE Tool Suite (Schneider et al., 2023a), an open-source web application for digital qualitative discourse analysis in the Digital Humanities. In doing so, we make our developed methods easily accessible to other researchers and plan to further improve the methods by incorporating more feedback. As our methods are also applicable to image or video annotations via object detection, we might explore to adapt them for a good user experience.

Limitations & Ethics Statement

Our work makes NLP models and methods accessible to researchers that could previously not benefit from these advances. Our work targets Digital Humanities researchers and is intended to assist with qualitative discourse analysis. As with any ML-based method, though, it could somehow be misused for other, possibly inappropriate, work. We strongly believe that including and enabling more researchers to benefit from modern ML technology outweighs the potential for misuse.

When using ML models, it is important to understand their limitations and critically reflect on their predictions. ML models often include certain biases that can manifest in various types and forms and are certainly not without error.

Especially the proposed fully-automatic annotation scaling has to be used critically. We developed this method for researchers to easily obtain quantitative insights on the whole dataset, however, the results are most likely not comparable to a careful, manual or semi-automatic analysis of the full material. Instead, they should be understood as an estimation and help to quantitatively verify hypotheses that emerged from the qualitative analysis. We try to mitigate the issues of the fully-automatic annotation scaling by providing confidence scores where applicable, showing aggregated classification results and allowing the user to correct system mistakes. To evaluate the quality of the automatic annotations, a user can manually annotate a random subset and compare this with the automatic results.

We also possibly introduce a bias with our method design and envisioned workflow. While we tried our best to give the user the freedom when and how to use the automated components, we might still restrict a user in their workflow by our design decisions. It is important to note that the workflow was described in a way to best highlight the contributions of this paper. This not the only way to use the described methods. Instead, the proposed methods are intended to be used in addition to established qualitative methods or to augment them, but not to replace them entirely.

Acknowledgement

This work is supported by the D-WISE project, Universität Hamburg, funded by BMBF (grant no. 01UG2124).

References

Alexis Conneau, Kartikay Khandelwal, Naman Goyal, Vishrav Chaudhary, Guillaume Wenzek, Francisco Guzmán, Edouard Grave, Myle Ott, Luke Zettlemoyer, and Veselin Stoyanov. 2020. Unsupervised cross-lingual representation learning at scale. In *Proceedings of the 58th Annual Meeting of the Association for Computational Linguistics*, pages 8440–8451, Online. Association for Computational Linguistics.

Ning Ding, Guangwei Xu, Yulin Chen, Xiaobin Wang, Xu Han, Pengjun Xie, Haitao Zheng, and Zhiyuan Liu. 2021. Few-NERD: A Few-shot Named Entity Recognition Dataset. In *Proceedings of the 59th Annual Meeting of the Association for Computational Linguistics and the 11th International Joint Conference on Natural Language Processing (Volume 1: Long Papers)*, pages 3198–3213, Online.

Richard Eckart de Castilho, Éva Mújdricza-Maydt, Seid Muhie Yimam, Silvana Hartmann, Iryna Gurevych, Anette Frank, and Chris Biemann. 2016. A Web-based Tool for the Integrated Annotation of Semantic and Syntactic Structures. In *Proceedings of the Workshop on Language Technology Resources and Tools for Digital Humanities (LT4DH)*, pages 76–84, Osaka, Japan.

Fangxiaoyu Feng, Yinfei Yang, Daniel Cer, Naveen Arivazhagan, and Wei Wang. 2022. Language-agnostic BERT sentence embedding. In *Proceedings of the 60th Annual Meeting of the Association for Computational Linguistics (Volume 1: Long Papers)*, pages 878–891, Dublin, Ireland. Association for Computational Linguistics.

Alexander Fritzler, Varvara Logacheva, and Maksim Kretov. 2019. Few-shot classification in named entity recognition task. In *Proceedings of the 34th ACM/SIGAPP Symposium on Applied Computing*, pages 993–1000.

Junxian He, Chunting Zhou, Xuezhe Ma, Taylor Berg-Kirkpatrick, and Graham Neubig. 2022. Towards a Unified View of Parameter-Efficient Transfer Learning. In *International Conference on Learning Representations*, Online.

Andreas Holzinger. 2016. Interactive Machine Learning for Health Informatics: When Do We Need the Human-In-the-Loop? *Brain Informatics*, 3(2):119–131.

Matthew Honnibal, Ines Montani, Sofie Van Landeghem, and Adriane Boyd. 2020. spaCy: Industrial-strength Natural Language Processing in Python. `https://spacy.io/`.

Jan Horstmann. 2019. Theory. `https://catma.de/philosophy/theory/`. In *CATMA*. Last accessed: 4 May 2023.

Neil Houlsby, Andrei Giurgiu, Stanislaw Jastrzebski, Bruna Morrone, Quentin De Laroussilhe, Andrea Gesmundo, Mona Attariyan, and Sylvain Gelly. 2019. Parameter-Efficient Transfer Learning for NLP. In *Proceedings of the 36th International Conference on Machine Learning*, volume 97, pages 2790–2799, Long Beach, CA, USA.

J. Johnson, M. Douze, and H. Jegou. 2021. Billion-scale similarity search with gpus. *IEEE Transactions on Big Data*, 7(03):535–547.

Jan-Christoph Klie, Michael Bugert, Beto Boullosa, Richard Eckart de Castilho, and Iryna Gurevych. 2018. The INCEpTION Platform: Machine-Assisted and Knowledge-Oriented Interactive Annotation. In *Proceedings of the 27th International Conference on Computational Linguistics: System Demonstrations*, pages 5–9.

Gertraud Koch, Chris Biemann, Isabel Eiser, Tim Fischer, Florian Schneider, Teresa Stumpf, and Alejandra Tijerina García. 2022. D-WISE Tool Suite for the Sociology of Knowledge Approach to Discourse. In *Culture and Computing*, pages 68–83, Cham.

David D. Lewis and William A. Gale. 1994. A Sequential Algorithm for Training Text Classifiers. In *Proceedings of the 17th Annual International ACM SIGIR Conference on Research and Development in Information Retrieval*, page 3–12, Berlin, Heidelberg.

Yinhan Liu, Myle Ott, Naman Goyal, Jingfei Du, Mandar Joshi, Danqi Chen, Omer Levy, Mike Lewis, Luke Zettlemoyer, and Veselin Stoyanov. 2019. Roberta: A robustly optimized bert pretraining approach. *arXiv preprint arXiv:1907.11692*.

Yu A Malkov and Dmitry A Yashunin. 2018. Efficient and Robust Approximate Nearest Neighbor Search Using Hierarchical Navigable Small World Graphs. *IEEE Transactions on Pattern Analysis and Machine Intelligence*, 42(4):824–836.

Julia Ostheimer, Soumitra Chowdhury, and Sarfraz Iqbal. 2021. An alliance of humans and machines for machine learning: Hybrid intelligent systems and their design principles. *Technology in Society*, 66:101647.

Jonas Pfeiffer, Andreas Rücklé, Clifton Poth, Aishwarya Kamath, Ivan Vulić, Sebastian Ruder, Kyunghyun Cho, and Iryna Gurevych. 2020. AdapterHub: A Framework for Adapting Transformers. In *Proceedings of the 2020 Conference on Empirical Methods in Natural Language Processing: System Demonstrations*, pages 46–54, Online.

James Pustejovsky and Amber Stubbs. 2012. *Natural Language Annotation for Machine Learning: A guide to corpus-building for applications*. " O'Reilly Media, Inc.".

Lance A Ramshaw and Mitchell P Marcus. 1999. Text Chunking Using Transformation-based Learning. *Natural language processing using very large corpora*, pages 157–176.

Nils Reimers and Iryna Gurevych. 2019. Sentence-BERT: Sentence Embeddings using Siamese BERT-Networks. In *Proceedings of the 2019 Conference on Empirical Methods in Natural Language Processing*.

Steffen Remus, Gregor Wiedemann, Saba Anwar, Fynn Petersen-Frey, Seid Muhie Yimam, and Chris Biemann. 2022. More like this: Semantic retrieval with linguistic information. In *Proceedings of the 18th Conference on Natural Language Processing (KONVENS 2022)*, pages 156–166, Potsdam, Germany. KONVENS 2022 Organizers.

Florian Schneider, Tim Fischer, Fynn Petersen-Frey, Isabel Eiser, Gertraud Koch, and Chris Biemann. 2023a. The D-WISE tool suite: Multi-modal machine-learning-powered tools supporting and enhancing digital discourse analysis. In *Proceedings of the 61st Annual Meeting of the Association for Computational Linguistics (Volume 3: System Demonstrations)*, pages 328–335, Toronto, Canada. Association for Computational Linguistics.

Florian Schneider, Seid Muhie Yiman, Fynn Petersen-Frey, Gerret von Nordheim, Katharina Kleinen-von Königslöw, and Chris Biemann. 2023b. CodeAnno: Extending WebAnno with Hierarchical Document Level Annotation and Automation. In *The 17th Conference of the European Chapter of the Association for Computational Linguistics (EACL 2023), System Demonstrations*, Dubrovnik, Croatia.

Eyal Shnarch, Alon Halfon, Ariel Gera, Marina Danilevsky, Yannis Katsis, Leshem Choshen, Martin Santillan Cooper, Dina Epelboim, Zheng Zhang, Dakuo Wang, Lucy Yip, Liat Ein-Dor, Lena Dankin, Ilya Shnayderman, Ranit Aharonov, Yunyao Li, Naftali Liberman, Philip Levin Slesarev, Gwilym Newton, Shila Ofek-Koifman, Noam Slonim, and Yoav Katz. 2022. Label Sleuth: From Unlabeled Text to a Classifier in a Few Hours. In *Proceedings of the 2022 Conference on Empirical Methods in Natural Language Processing: System Demonstrations*.

Jake Snell, Kevin Swersky, and Richard Zemel. 2017. Prototypical Networks for Few-shot Learning. In *Advances in Neural Information Processing Systems*, volume 30.

Asahi Ushio and Jose Camacho-Collados. 2021. T-NER: An all-round python library for transformer-based named entity recognition. In *Proceedings of the 16th Conference of the European Chapter of the Association for Computational Linguistics: System Demonstrations*, pages 53–62, Online. Association for Computational Linguistics.

Ralph Weischedel, Martha Palmer, Mitchell Marcus, Eduard Hovy, Sameer Pradhan, Lance Ramshaw, Nianwen Xue, Ann Taylor, Jeff Kaufman, Michelle Franchini, Mohammed El-Bachouti, Robert Belvin, and Ann Houston. 2013. OntoNotes Release 5.0. *LDC2013T19, Philadelphia, Penn.: Linguistic Data Consortium.*

Gregor Wiedemann, Seid Muhie Yimam, and Chris Biemann. 2018. New/s/leak 2.0 – Multilingual Information Extraction and Visualization for Investigative Journalism. In *Social Informatics*, pages 313–322, Cham.

Seid Muhie Yimam, Chris Biemann, Richard Eckart de Castilho, and Iryna Gurevych. 2014. Automatic annotation suggestions and custom annotation layers in WebAnno. In *Proceedings of 52nd Annual Meeting of the Association for Computational Linguistics: System Demonstrations*, pages 91–96, Baltimore, Maryland. Association for Computational Linguistics.

Xiang Zhang, Junbo Zhao, and Yann LeCun. 2015. Character-level Convolutional Networks for Text Classification. In *Advances in Neural Information Processing Systems*, volume 28, pages 649—-657, Montréal, Canada.

Data and Approaches for German Text simplification – towards an Accessibility-enhanced Communication

Thorben Schomacker, Michael Gille,
Jörg von der Hülls and **Marina Tropmann-Frick**
Hamburg University of Applied Sciences
thorben.schomacker@haw-hamburg.de
michael.gille@haw-hamburg.de
joerg.vonderhuells@haw-hamburg.de
marina.tropmann-frick@haw-hamburg.de

Abstract

This paper examines the current state-of-the-art of German text simplification, focusing on parallel and monolingual German corpora. It reviews neural language models for simplifying German texts and assesses their suitability for legal texts and accessibility requirements. Our findings highlight the need for additional training data and more appropriate approaches that consider the specific linguistic characteristics of German, as well as the importance of the needs and preferences of target groups with cognitive or language impairments. The authors launched the interdisciplinary OPEN-LS [1] project in April 2023 to address these research gaps. The project aims to develop a framework for text formats tailored to individuals with low literacy levels, integrate legal texts, and enhance comprehensibility for those with linguistic or cognitive impairments. It will also explore cost-effective ways to enhance the data with audience-specific illustrations using image-generating AI.

1 Introduction

In German-speaking countries, the majority of the population uses everyday language (Alltagssprache) in their daily affairs, with slight regional variations. However, in written texts, a more standardized vocabulary but with similar complexity (Bredel and Maaß, 2016) is typically preferred. In contrast, 12% of the German population faces challenges in comprehending and utilizing standard language due to reduced literacy (Grotlüschen and Buddeberg, 2020). For more accessible and inclusive communication, this group depends on comprehensibility-enhanced language. Currently, specialized human translators convert standard language texts into simplified versions including easy language, with legal texts posing a particular challenge due to their technical nature and normative subject matter. Technical language texts represent one end of the complexity spectrum and easy language texts the other. This is further amplified by the fact that both text forms are linguistic expressions of constructed languages. To categorize training data effectively, we differentiate between "easy language" (Leichte Sprache) and "simple language" (einfache Sprache). "Easy language" refers to a highly comprehensible and rule-based form of German, whereby "simple language" is used to describe a variety of simplified language versions in the gray area between standard language and easy language (Maaß, 2020). Easy language is roughly equivalent with level A2 of the Common European Framework of Reference for Languages (CEFR). Since public entities in Germany are required by law to translate information and communication texts into an accessible language version (BGG, 2022) the costs of this task burden the public budget. Automated approaches based on machine learning techniques promise to solve many of the challenges of text simplification, including the difficulties caused by technical language. A tool to simplify documents from different domains to a degree that facilitates these texts' comprehensibility for people with language or cognitive disabilities does not only improve understanding of these texts. It is also a key to inclusion and social participation (UN, 2008). This holds especially for domain-specific legal texts that are the starting point for the intralingual translation. In the course of our project we aim to build on existing simplification approaches using NLMs and adjust them with respect to the demands of the application domain. To achieve this objective, two specific aspects must be considered: First, the identification and systematic categorization of training data from the legal domain to build a quality-assured dataset to train a large language model for the domain specific simplification tasks in German. Second, the fine-tuning of an NLM under consideration of target-audience related com-

[1]For more and up-to-date information, please visit our project homepage https://open-ls.entavis.com

Proceedings of the 19th Conference on Natural Language Processing (KONVENS 2023), pages 63–68
September 18–22, 2023. ©2023 Association for Computational Linguistics

prehensibility requirements. After a brief review of related work on German datasets and approaches (Section 2), this paper delivers a systematic assessment of published German datasets and approaches against the backdrop of the requirements of participatory communication of legal texts (Section 3). Finally, we outline the ongoing research project, "OPEN-LS: Open Data for Easy Language", which adopts a more target-group oriented approaches. We also identify and address several gaps in the existing research (Section 4).

2 Related Work

Text simplification can be described as a machine translation task, converting one version of a language to another (Standard → Simple). However, compared to other machine translation tasks, automatic text simplification is a relatively new task. It started with a rule based statistical approach in 2010 (Specia, 2010) on a small parallel Portuguese corpus (roughly 4,500 parallel sentences). The first German simplification corpus was introduced in 2012 (Hancke et al., 2012) and consisted of articles from GEO (similar to National Geographic) and GEOlino (GEO's edition for children). In the initial paper, the corpus was only used for the training of statistical classifiers to predict the reading level of German texts. Their corpus was later improved and enlarged (Weiß and Meurers, 2018). In 2016 the first rule-based automatic text simplification system for German was released (Suter et al., 2016). In 2020 the first parallel corpus for data-driven automatic text simplification for German was published (Säuberli et al., 2020) and a first investigation of the use of a neural machine translation system for this problem in German was conducted. They concluded that the Austrian Press Agency corpus was not large enough to sufficiently train a neural machine translation system that produces both adequate and fluent text simplifications. In a later study, the same neural machine translation architecture was use and further evaluated concerning the levels of simplification which were generated by these models (Spring et al., 2021). In 2021 (Rios et al., 2021) adapted mBART (Liu et al., 2020) with Longformer Attention (Beltagy et al., 2020) and applied it to the task of document-level text simplification. It has been further explored on different domains, recently (Schomacker et al., 2023; Stodden et al., 2023). Furthermore, the first Decoder-only approach for German text simplification has been released (Anschütz et al., 2023).

Automatic simplification of legal documents has only recently, in 2022, emerged (Collantes et al., 2015; Cemri et al., 2022; Manor and Li, 2019; Gallegos and George, 2022; Gille et al., 2023; Kopp et al., 2023). All of these works had to rely on monolingual datasets and state, that the task is still underinvestigated. To this day, there is no dataset with parallel legal documents (standard → simple language). In section 5.1 we will further discuss features and constraints of legal texts.

3 Systematic and accessibility-oriented assessment of dataset landscape

3.1 Parallel Datasets

To find all aligned German text simplification datasets, we focused our Google Scholar search on papers which prioritize German by including the word "German" in the title. Further, we wanted to find textual datasets, so used its synonyms: "dataset", "corpus", "data" or "texts". The task of text simplification can be covered by datasets with "simple" language or which investigate "readability" or text "complexity". So, we concluded on this query: `allintitle: German corpus OR dataset OR data OR texts "Simple" OR "simplification" OR "readability" OR "complexity"`. This resulted in an identification of 14 parallel German datasets or sub-datasets as listed in Table 1. By reading the dataset descriptions in their corresponding publication and checking the underlying data sources, we identified inductively text genres and domains in the dataset. We categorized them in three exclusive genres: 1) Encyclopedic (ENC) texts are summaries of knowledge either general or special to a particular field; 2) Articles (ART), are published nonfiction texts; and 3) Unknown (UNK), are texts, of which its author did not provide sufficient information to be clearly categorized. In addition to the genre, we tagged the datasets with seven domains: 1) Medical, which covers all aspects of human health; 2) Disability, which covers all aspects of the life and interests of people with disabilities; 3) News, are texts about current events without defining a field of interest; 4) Politics, discussing topics about politically viewpoints or activities such as electoral programs of political parties; 5) Government, any information, that is published by public authorities and/or containing administrative and non-partisan legal information; 6) Encyclopedic, collection of texts that could form a reference work without any specific field of interest; 7) Unknown, are texts, of which its author did not provide sufficient information to be clearly categorized. Aligned datasets thematically focused on legal aspects were not identified. We provide an overview of the datasets in Figure 1 by the number of documents. With a percentage of 73% of the documents, News is the largest domain. The more practical and life-oriented categories Government, Disability and Medical are forming together less than 10% of the available data. A significant proportion of 20% of the available simple data is targeted to children. Training machine learning models with children-oriented simple language could lead to a bias. So, this type of data should be used with caution.

3.2 Monolingual Datasets and Sources

To gain a more complete picture of the datasets, we further investigated collections of German easy language, that have no standard language equivalent. Many newspapers or lexicons target children, e.g., "Dein Spiegel" from "Der Spiegel". We decided to only include resources that use simple or easy language and did not research any children-targeted content because children-targeted content does not necessarily mean that it is accessible for the target we defined for simple and easy language. Furthermore, we focused on resources that cover different genres to show the variety of genre currently used in easy language. Many text genres have no published parallel dataset despite the fact, that there are monolingual resources (e.g., narrative texts, legal texts). Similar to the parallel datasets, the majority of texts are news and encyclopedic articles. A comparatively large number of monolingual datasets address the interests of people with disabilities, not least because public authorities in Germany are obliged to communicate in simple and understandable language.

3.3 (Non-)Consideration of Accessibility and Participation in Existing Datasets

For the reasons outlined in Section 1 we focus on two particularly critical dimensions when considering accessibility and participation aspects for the evaluation of existing datasets and approaches: Legal texts and the concrete needs of the addressees.

Legal Texts: Legal language comprises many different types of text such as laws and regulations, court judgements, witness statements, complaints, legal opinions etc. In addition, a large (and increasing) number of legal sub-domains, e.g., constitutional law, criminal law, AI law, exist. All of these different types of texts in the different (sub-)domains share similar linguistic traits, such as the use of legal jargon ('legalese'), formalization, long and complex sentences, a very high degree of intertextuality, mixed authorship (at least to some degree), a wide range of addressees and a unique tension between accuracy and vagueness (Baumann, 2020). In addition, many legal texts are designed to be legally binding and establish rights and obligations. In establishing and organizing legal relationships these texts are fundamentally different from statements of fact that are subject of most intralingual and monolingual corpora. Thus, texts with legal content differ in many respects from texts in standard language. Furthermore, Legal texts fulfill certain text functions (DIN-Normenausschuss Ergonomie, 2023). This text function, e.g. a legal binding, can deviate in the translation into plain language. These deviations should be consciously handled. For these reasons alone, the training of neural language programs for the legal domain must be based on suitable German-language training materials.

Specialized format: We pursue a participatory approach and collaborate with a large service provider and stakeholder of easy language recipients. The largest proportion of people with low literacy are disabled in some form. Most of them have difficulties to read texts, that exceed a half DIN A4 page, even if the text is written in easy language. Translating legal texts to a version that both maintains its meaning and is comprehensible to people with cognitive or language impairments, we need to define a specialized format. We propose the following four-level complexity hierarchy:

1. A summary in easy language of the underlying standard language /legal document, which has a pre-defined maximum length. This text version should be easy to read and understand for people who need low barrier text forms. It also helps the reader to appreciate the central meaning of the underlying document.

2. A longer version in easy language with jump markers that refer the reader to a glossary. This version is especially meant to be digital, so that the reader can access the glossary by a one-click action, that does not disturb the

Name	Doc. Pairs	Simplicity Versions	Genre	Domain	Published		URL
20 Minuten	18305	STD, SIM	ART	News	(Rios et al., 2021)	2021	-
KLEXIKON	2899	CH, AD	ENC	Encyclopedic	(Aumiller and Gertz, 2022)	2022	(Aumiller, 2023)
APA	2472	A2, B1	ART	News	(Säuberli et al., 2020)	2021	-
(apo)	2311	STD, SIM	ART	Medical	(Toborek and Busch, 2023)	2022	(Toborek et al., 2022)
Geo-Geolino	1627	CH, AD	ART	Science	(Hancke et al., 2012)	2022	-
Lexica	1090	CH, AD	ENC	Encyclopedic	(Hewett and Stede, 2021)	2021	(Hewett, 2022)
capito	752	A1, A2, B1	UNK	Unknown	(Rios et al., 2021)	2021	-
Tagesschau / Logo	415	CH, AD	SUB	News	(Weiß and Meurers, 2018)	2018	-
	378	STD, SIM	ART	Unknown	(Battisti et al., 2020)	2020	-
(bra), (mdr), (taz)	377	STD, SIM	ART	News	(Toborek et al., 2022)	2022	(Toborek et al., 2022)
	256	CH, AD	ART	Disability	(Klaper et al., 2013)	2013	-
(koe)	82	STD, SIM	ART	Government	(Toborek et al., 2022)	2022	(Toborek et al., 2022)
(beb), (lmt)	66	STD, SIM	ART	Disability	(Toborek et al., 2022)	2022	(Toborek et al., 2022)
TextComplexityDE	23	STD, SIM	ENC	Encyclopedic	(Seiffe et al., 2022)	2019	(Naderi, 2023)
(soz)	15	STD, SIM	ART	Politics	(Toborek et al., 2022)	2022	(Toborek et al., 2022)

Table 1: All available German parallel text simplification datasets and sub- datasets according to the Google Scholar results by using the query in section 1. For more details about the categorization, please refer to section 3.1. Simplicity Version are Standard Language (STD), any form of simple language (SIM), children-targeted (CH), adult-targeted-language (AD), and A1, A2, B1 are language level from the CEFR.

reading flow.

3. A complete version in easy language that should only reduce the linguistic complexity and not the complexity of content. It aims at conveying most of the (legal) statements of the original document. We assume that this version may be longer than the original text on which it is based.

4. The original text in standard language.

4 Research gaps and planned contributions

We identified and categorized existing resources for simplifying German texts with the aim of a preparatory assessment for the development of an NLM-based approach that supports accessible communication through participation-relevant texts. Our assessment of these intralingual-aligned and monolingual datasets as well as the existing approaches revealed the research gaps. Moreover, we observed that all monolingual datasets use illustrations to improve readability and intelligibility, while none of the parallel datasets do so. All identified datasets have a linear structure without any interactive elements, that could improve the readability. Based on our investigation and analyses in relation to the target group, we identify future areas of research:

1. Identification and investigation of existing texts, which are tailored to the needs of the target group and improve the readability of texts both in monolingual and parallel datasets.

2. Extension of parallel datasets by adding topics, domains and sub-domains, that are relevant for the everyday life of the target group.

3. Addition of any form of illustration to the parallel datasets. By including visual elements, such as images, diagrams, or charts, the dataset becomes more inclusive and accessible to a wider range of users.

4. The transferability of the model to domains and sub-domains (e.g., legal sub-domains) for which it has not been trained.

5. The methodological development of evaluation methods that allow for an assessment that is in line with the objectives and purpose of accessibility, inclusion and participation by incorporating appropriate quantitative and qualitative methods. These evaluation methods may consider factors like readability scores, user feedback, comprehension tests, and other relevant metrics to measure the effectiveness of the model in promoting accessibility, inclusion, and participation.

We want to tackle all five research gaps in the future, so that researchers and developers can enhance the quality and applicability of language models for the target group, making information more accessible and engaging for a broader audience. Our current focus is to make legal texts more accessible in German easy language. Documents from this domain are often pivotal to a self-empowered life. Based on texts in this domain, we aim at designing specialized accessibility-enhanced formats.

Limitations

In this work, we examined the current state-of-the-art of German text simplification. It reviews neural language models for simplifying German texts and assesses their suitability for legal texts and accessibility requirements. The general methodology of this paper is applicable for any domain or language, but only works for the task of text simplification. Furthermore, the review only focuses on German, so no definitive conclusions about the situation for other languages can be made based on this work alone. Additionally, this paper relied on the current draft version of the DIN standard (DIN-Normenausschuss Ergonomie, 2023), the final version and its implications could deviate. Moreover, the DIN standard (DIN-Normenausschuss Ergonomie, 2023) is based on assumptions about its addressees, which we have not questioned further but simply adopted. These assumptions, e.g. include a homogeneity bias. Another limitation would be the limited use for pure information texts or transfers into information texts, i.e. that the target text function (in the sense of DIN) is always an informative one.

Ethics Statement

This paper complies with the ACL Ethics Policy[2]. The research field of this paper can help people to gain access to information by translating and transforming in an accessibility-enhanced way. Our presentation aims at motivating further scientific research and debate.

Acknowledgements

This work is funded by UpdateHamburg (Schomacker), and by Hamburg Call for Transfer (von der Hülls). Furthermore, we thank the anonymous reviewers for their valuable feedback and discussion impulses.

References

Miriam Anschütz, Joshua Oehms, Thomas Wimmer, Bartłomiej Jezierski, and Georg Groh. 2023. Language Models for German Text Simplification: Overcoming Parallel Data Scarcity through Style-specific Pre-training. ArXiv:2305.12908 [cs].

Dennis Aumiller. 2023. Klexikon: A German Dataset for Joint Summarization and Simplification. Original-date: 2022-01-05T09:09:42Z.

Dennis Aumiller and Michael Gertz. 2022. Klexikon: A German Dataset for Joint Summarization and Simplification. In *Proceedings of the 13th Conference on Language Resources and Evaluation (LREC 2022)*, pages 2693–2701.

Alessia Battisti, Dominik Pfütze, Andreas Säuberli, Marek Kostrzewa, and Sarah Ebling. 2020. A Corpus for Automatic Readability Assessment and Text Simplification of German. In *Proceedings of the 12th Language Resources and Evaluation Conference*, pages 3302–3311, Marseille, France. European Language Resources Association.

Antje Baumann. 2020. Rechtstexte als Barrieren – Einige Merkmale der Textsorte "Gesetz" und die Verständlichkeit. In Christiane Maaß and Isabel Rink, editors, *Handbuch Barrierefreie Kommunikation*, 1 edition, volume 3 of *Kommunikation – Partizipation – Inklusion*, pages 679–702. Frank & Timme, Berlin.

Iz Beltagy, Matthew E. Peters, and Arman Cohan. 2020. Longformer: The Long-Document Transformer. ArXiv: 2004.05150.

BGG. 2022. § 11 Disability Equality Act BGG.

Ursula Bredel and Christiane Maaß. 2016. *Leichte Sprache theoretische Grundlagen, Orientierung für die Praxis*. Sprache im Blick. Dudenverlag.

Mert Cemri, Tolga Çukur, and Aykut Koç. 2022. Unsupervised Simplification of Legal Texts. ArXiv:2209.00557 [cs].

Miguel Collantes, Maureen Hipe, and Juan Lorenzo Sorilla. 2015. Simpatico: A Text Simplification System for Senate and House Bills. In *Proceedings of the 11th National Natural Language Processing Research Symposium,*, volume 11, pages 26–32, Manila.

DIN-Normenausschuss Ergonomie. 2023. Empfehlungen für Deutsche Leichte Sprache (DIN SPEC 33429).

Isabel Gallegos and Kaylee George. 2022. The Right to Remain Plain: Summarization and Simplification of Legal Documents.

Michael Gille, Thorben Schomacker, Jörg von der Hülls, and Marina Tropmann-Frick. 2023. Der Einsatz von Neural Language Models für eine barriere-freie Verwaltungskommunikation.

Anke Grotlüschen and Klaus Buddeberg, editors. 2020. *LEO 2018: Leben mit geringer Literalität*. wbv, Bielefeld.

Julia Hancke, Sowmya Vajjala, and Detmar Meurers. 2012. Readability Classification for German using Lexical, Syntactic, and Morphological Features. In *Proceedings of COLING 2012*, pages 1063–1080, Mumbai, India. The COLING 2012 Organizing Committee.

[2]https://www.aclweb.org/portal/content/acl-code-ethics

Freya Hewett. 2022. lexica-corpus. Original-date: 2021-08-13T09:12:24Z.

Freya Hewett and Manfred Stede. 2021. Automatically evaluating the conceptual complexity of German texts. In *Proceedings of the 17th Conference on Natural Language Processing (KONVENS 2021)*, pages 228–234, Düsseldorf, Germany. KONVENS 2021 Organizers.

David Klaper, S. Ebling, and Martin Volk. 2013. Building a German/Simple German Parallel Corpus for Automatic Text Simplification. In *Klaper, David; Ebling, S; Volk, Martin (2013). Building a German/Simple German Parallel Corpus for Automatic Text Simplification. In: The Second Workshop on Predicting and Improving Text Readability for Target Reader Populations (PITR 2013), Sofia, Bulgaria, 8 August 2013.*, pages 11–19, Sofia, Bulgaria. University of Zurich.

Tobias Kopp, Amelie Rempel, Andreas Schmidt, and Miriam Spieß. 2023. Towards machine translation into Easy Language in public administrations: Algorithmic alignment suggestions for building a translation memory. In Silvana Deilen, Silvia Hansen-Schirra, Sergio Hernández Garrido, Christiane Maaß, and Anke Tardel, editors, *Emerging Fields in Easy Language and Accessible Communication Research*, 1 edition, volume 14 of *Easy – Plain – Accessible*, pages 371–406. Frank & Timme.

Yinhan Liu, Jiatao Gu, Naman Goyal, Xian Li, Sergey Edunov, Marjan Ghazvininejad, Mike Lewis, and Luke Zettlemoyer. 2020. Multilingual Denoising Pre-training for Neural Machine Translation. *Transactions of the Association for Computational Linguistics*, 8:726–742. Place: Cambridge, MA Publisher: MIT Press.

Christiane Maaß. 2020. *Easy Language – Plain Language – Easy Language Plus: Balancing Comprehensibility and Acceptability*, 1 edition, volume 3 of *Easy–Plain–Accessible*. Frank & Timme, Berlin. Accepted: 2020-09-28T09:51:54Z.

Laura Manor and Junyi Jessy Li. 2019. Plain English Summarization of Contracts. In *Proceedings of the Natural Legal Language Processing Workshop 2019*, pages 1–11, Minneapolis, Minnesota. Association for Computational Linguistics.

Babak Naderi. 2023. Text Complexity DE. Original-date: 2020-09-30T09:43:40Z.

Annette Rios, Nicolas Spring, Tannon Kew, Marek Kostrzewa, Andreas Säuberli, Mathias Müller, and Sarah Ebling. 2021. A New Dataset and Efficient Baselines for Document-level Text Simplification in German. In *Proceedings of the Third Workshop on New Frontiers in Summarization*, pages 152–161, Online and in Dominican Republic. Association for Computational Linguistics. Tex.ids= riosNewDatasetEfficient2021a.

Thorben Schomacker, Tillmann Dönicke, and Marina Tropmann-Frick. 2023. Exploring Automatic Text Simplification of German Narrative Documents.

Laura Seiffe, Fares Kallel, Sebastian Möller, Babak Naderi, and Roland Roller. 2022. Subjective Text Complexity Assessment for German. In *Proceedings of the Thirteenth Language Resources and Evaluation Conference*, pages 707–714, Marseille, France. European Language Resources Association.

Lucia Specia. 2010. Translating from Complex to Simplified Sentences. In *Computational Processing of the Portuguese Language*, Lecture Notes in Computer Science, pages 30–39, Berlin, Heidelberg. Springer.

Nicolas Spring, Annette Rios, and Sarah Ebling. 2021. Exploring German Multi-Level Text Simplification. In *Proceedings of the International Conference on Recent Advances in Natural Language Processing (RANLP 2021)*, pages 1339–1349, Held Online. INCOMA Ltd.

Regina Stodden, Omar Momen, and Laura Kallmeyer. 2023. DEPLAIN: A German Parallel Corpus with Intralingual Translations into Plain Language for Sentence and Document Simplification. ArXiv:2305.18939 [cs].

Julia Suter, Sarah Ebling, and Martin Volk. 2016. Rule-based Automatic Text Simplification for German. In *Proceedings of the 13th Conference on Natural Language Processing*, pages 279–287.

Andreas Säuberli, Sarah Ebling, and Martin Volk. 2020. Benchmarking Data-driven Automatic Text Simplification for German. In *Proceedings of the 1st Workshop on Tools and Resources to Empower People with REAding DIfficulties (READI)*, pages 41–48, Marseille, France. European Language Resources Association.

Vanessa Toborek and Moritz Busch. 2023. A New Aligned Simple German Corpus. Original-date: 2022-08-22T10:58:53Z.

Vanessa Toborek, Moritz Busch, Malte Boßert, Pascal Welke, and Christian Bauckhage. 2022. A New Aligned Simple German Corpus.

UN. 2008. UN Convention on the Rights of Persons with Disabilities (CRPD).

Zarah Weiß and Detmar Meurers. 2018. Modeling the Readability of German Targeting Adults and Children: An empirically broad analysis and its cross-corpus validation. In *Proceedings of the 27th International Conference on Computational Linguistics*, pages 303–317, Santa Fe, New Mexico, USA. Association for Computational Linguistics.

Steps towards Addressing Text Classification in Low-Resource Languages

Maximilian Weissenbacher
Information Science
University of Regensburg
Maximilian.Weissenbacher@ur.de

Udo Kruschwitz
Information Science
University of Regensburg
Udo.Kruschwitz@ur.de

Abstract

Text classification is an area of NLP in which major improvements have been observed in recent years, primarily via pre-training and fine-tuning of large language models (LLMs). However, low-resource languages still face major challenges. We explore how to address this problem using different text classification tasks across two low-resource languages. Our focus is on adopting multilingual LLMs using data expansion techniques (with and without machine translation). Results indicate that pre-trained, fine-tuned models of the resource-poor language appear more promising than multilingual models, we also find that translating into a resource-poor language is not beneficial in our experimental settings.

1 Introduction

Few languages can be considered resource-rich, the vast majority are not despite a possibly very large pool of speakers. For example, 83 million people speak Marathi (only outnumbered in India by Hindi and Bengali). Malayalam is another Indian language with a sizeable population of speakers (37 million). However, in the context of NLP both languages are considered resource-poor, and more research has been done on more prominent Indian languages like Hindi (Joshi et al., 2016) or Bengali (Patra et al., 2018). In general, resource-poor languages lack annotated training data because there are often no trained linguistic annotators for these languages, and the markets may be too small or premature to invest in such training (Ruder et al., 2019). But many people speak such languages and the amount of textual content on online platforms such as Twitter keeps growing. We adopt both languages as *exemplars* for other low-resource languages. We look at three different classification tasks (sentiment analysis, hate speech detection and claim detection) comparing language-specific fine-tuning with multilingual LLMs. We also look at data expansion by adding training data available from a high-resource language (either with or without first translating into our language of interest). This approach has some similarity with (but is different from) *data augmentation* that focuses on adding synthetic data such as via generating new data samples using autoregressive models (Wullach et al., 2021; Whitfield, 2021). We see our contribution as exploratory work into the problem which offers some interesting insights that can serve as a starting point for more work. To support reproducibility we also make all code available.[1]

2 Related Work

LLMs like BERT (Devlin et al., 2019) have established a new state of the art for text classification tasks, e.g. (Chouikhi et al., 2021; Chan et al., 2020) outperforming traditional ML approaches using Naive Bayes or Support Vector Machines (SVM) (Schmidt et al., 2022; Geetha and Karthika Renuka, 2021). Among a wide range of text classification tasks, sentiment analysis, hate speech detection and claim detection can be seen as typical classification problems (Medhat et al., 2014; Schmidt and Wiegand, 2017; Levy et al., 2014; Konstantinovskiy et al., 2021). However, research is lacking for resource-poor languages. Nevertheless, numerous test collections have been created for low-resource language, e.g. for sentiment analysis (Kulkarni et al., 2021), hate speech detection (Pitenis et al., 2020; Çöltekin, 2020; Mandl et al.,

[1] https://github.com/MaxiWeissenbacher/exploratory_bert_v2/tree/main

Proceedings of the 19th Conference on Natural Language Processing (KONVENS 2023), pages 69–76
September 18–22, 2023. ©2023 Association for Computational Linguistics

2021), and claim detection (Kazemi et al., 2021). Snæbjarnarson et al. 2023 demonstrated that the transfer learning performance of low-resource languages (Faroese in their case) could substantially improve by exploiting data and models of closely-related high-resource languages (other Scandinavian languages). That is a direction we consider promising and we explore how incorporating additional datasets will affect a transformer model. This is an important research topic to establish generalizability and transferability (Mandl et al., 2021; Fortuna et al., 2021).

3 Methodology

We explore **five different approaches**. The first approach focuses on whether **fine-tuned models** of a resource-poor language can perform better than multilingual models like mBERT and XLM-RoBERTa. The second, third, and fourth approach investigate whether it is beneficial if additional data gets **translated into the resource-poor language** and added for training. The fifth approach takes the inverse view: the dataset of the **resource-poor language gets translated into a resource-rich language** (English). After the translation process, fine-tuned English models are used to see if performance increases can be observed.

3.1 Datasets

As the availability of (even high-resource) language resources varies from one task to another we tap into different languages, such as German, Hindi, and English, in addition to the baseline datasets in this work.

Sentiment Analysis. We consider the L3-Cube-MahaSent dataset as our baseline dataset for the sentiment analysis domain, as it is one of the best-known resources in Marathi language. It contains tweets classified as positive, negative, and neutral. It has 12,114 train, 2,250 test, and 1,500 validation examples (Kulkarni et al., 2021). For approaches with data expansion, four additional datasets with the same labels but different annotation guidelines were used (see Appendix A.1) and added:

- GFES Dataset (DE), (Schmidt et al., 2022)
- SB10k Dataset (DE), (Cieliebak et al., 2017)
- Kaggle Covid Dataset (EN), (Miglani, 2020)
- Sentiment Analysis Dataset (HI)

Hate Speech Detection. For this task, the datasets of HASOC2021 Sub-task 1A were used, consisting of datasets in three different languages. The task is a binary classification in which participating systems are required to classify tweets into two classes, namely: Hate or Offensive (HOF) vs. Non-Hate and Non-Offensive (NOT). The Marathi dataset contains 1,874 tweets, the English dataset 3,843 tweets, and the Hindi dataset 4,594 tweets. The annotation quality of this dataset is considered to be reliable (Modha et al., 2021).

Claim Detection. The dataset from Kazemi et al. 2021 was used here. It contains content in high-resource (English, Hindi) and lower-resource (Bengali, Malayalam, Tamil) languages. We used Malayalam as our low-resource baseline language, added texts from the remaining languages and only used texts which were labeled as "Claim" and "No Claim". Therefore a binary classification task was conducted. With this, 4,017 texts remain in the dataset, with 730 texts in Malayalam. Three different annotators worked on this dataset, and the annotation quality is also considered reliable (Kazemi et al., 2021).

3.2 Experimental Setup and Implementation

We use Huggingface for all models and their library "Simpletransformers" (Wolf et al., 2020). We used an "NVIDIA Tesla K80" GPU server to train the different text classification models. All notebooks run on the freely available version of Google Colaboratory (all codebooks in our GitHub repository).

For translating the datasets to Marathi or translating the Marathi datasets to English, the Python library "Googletrans"[2] was used.

The project also investigates how preprocessing the data influences the performance of transformer models. For this, preprocessing steps like removing links, square brackets, punctuation, words containing numbers, and lowercasing the text were used (we also tried over- and undersampling with inconclusive results, so they were not considered further).

We computed Accuracy and weighted F1 if the distribution of the labels is not balanced.

Each model is fine-tuned for three epochs, a train and evaluation batch size of 32, the learning rate of 2e-5, the default epsilon of 1e-8 to find a better minimum for the loss function and Adam

[2]https://pypi.org/project/googletrans/

	Model Name	BASELINE	+ Translation to MR				+ NON-TRANSLATED DATA				+ ALL DATA TRANS-LATED To MR	+ ALL DATA NOT TRANS-LATED To MR
Dataset		L3-Cube-Maha-Sent	+ Kaggle-Covid Data (EN)	+ Kaggle-Tweets (HI)	+ GFES-Tweets (DE)	+ SB10K-Tweets (DE)	+ Kaggle-Covid Data (EN)	+ Kaggle-Tweets (HI)	+ GFES-Tweets (DE)	+ SB10K-Tweets (DE)		
Multilingual Models	mBERT	81.9%	80.9%	81.8%	81.6%	81.7%	82.0%	81.9%	81.9%	81.9%	80.5%	80.6%
	XLM-RoBERTa	83.4%	83.0%	83.0%	83.4%	83.3%	83.5%	83.2%	83.5%	83.6%	82.9%	83.1%
Marathi Models	IndicBERT	84.1%	83.6%	83.7%	84.2%	83.5%						
	MahaBERT	83.8%	82.9%	83.1%	83.5%	83.4%						
	MahaAlBERT	84.0%	83.6%	83.0%	83.6%	83.7%						
	MahaRoBERTa	84.7%	84.4%	84.1%	84.6%	84.3%						

Figure 1: Sentiment Analysis Results (F1 scores)

Model Name	BASELINE	+ TRANSLATION TO MR		+ NON-TRANSLATED DATA		+ ALL DATA TRANSLATED (MR)	+ ALL DATA NOT TRANSLATED
	HASOC 2021	+ EN	+ Hi	+EN	+ Hi		
mBERT	83.7%	85.6%	86.8%	85.8%	87.5%	85.0%	87.2%
XLM-RoBERTa	82.9%	85.5%	85.4%	86.8%	87.4%	85.3%	87.0%
IndicBERT	79.5%	83.2%	85.3%	/	/	/	/
MahaBERT	88.5%	86.6%	88.2%	/	/	/	/
MahaAlBERT	82.7%	83.5%	85.3%	/	/	/	/
MahaRoBERTa	87.7%	86.9%	88.0%	/	/	/	/

Figure 2: Hate Speech Detection Results (F1 scores)

Model Name	BASELINE	+ TRANSLATION TO ML				+ NON TRANSLATED DATA				+ ALL DATA TRANSLATED (ML)	+ ALL DATA NOT TRANSLATED
	Malayalam	+En	+Hi	+Ta	+Bn	+En	+Hi	+Ta	+Bn		
mBERT	82.2%	84.3%	81.8%	83.2%	80.6%	84.1%	83.1%	83.2%	83.8%	84.1%	84.2%
XLM-RoBERTa	73.9%	84.9%	84.1%	83.7%	82.2%	85.1%	83.8%	83.7%	83.1%	85.1%	86.6%

Figure 3: Claim Detection Results (F1 scores)

optimizer for stochastic gradient descent (Tato and Nkambou, 2018).

The models are trained and evaluated in a 5x5 cross-evaluation setting, and the average score over five runs gets reported. For evaluation, we compare against baseline approaches using two-tailed t-tests (with $p < 0.05$).

3.3 Model Selection

In this work we focus on both multilingual and monolingual BERT models, as they count as strong baselines for text classification tasks. The following multilingual models are used (details in Appendix A.2): mBERT-Cased, XLM-RoBERTa. And following monolingual models are used: IndicBERT, MahaBERT, MahaAlBERT, MahaRoBERTa, BERTweet, TimeLMs (Cardiff RoBERTa).

4 Results

4.1 Fine-tuning on resource-poor language

The first approach compares fine-tuned models of a resource-poor language with multilingual models like mBERT and XLM-RoBERTa. It focuses on sentiment analysis and hate speech detection datasets in Marathi. The models are trained on baseline Marathi datasets when no additional data is available. The results (Figures 1 and 2) show that all fine-tuned Marathi models perform better than mBERT and XLM-RoBERTa in sentiment analysis. The best model, MahaRoBERTa, achieves a statistically significant improvement over the best multilingual model. Other Marathi models also exhibit an upward trend in performance, although not statistically significant. MahaRoBERTa with the hyperparameters we have used outperforms the baseline results and results from related studies (Kulkarni et al., 2021; Velankar et al., 2022). For hate speech detection the pattern is slightly different. Here IndicBERT and MahaAlBERT had lower F1 scores. However, the best performing models are still Marathi fine-tuned MahaBERT and MahaRoBERTa, significantly better than the best multilingual model, mBERT. The MahaBERT model would have ranked 6th place for task 1A at the HASOC Subtrack at FIRE 2021 (Mandl et al., 2021).

4.2 Adding translated data

The second approach examines the impact of translating texts into a resource-poor language and adding them for training across three text classification domains. Results show that translating datasets to Marathi slightly decreases F1 for multilingual models in sentiment analysis (see Figure 1 - '+Translation to MR'). However, a slight increase is observed for IndicBERT combined with the translated GFES dataset. In hate speech detection (Figure 2), adding translated English and Hindi datasets benefits both multilingual and Marathi models, except for MahaBERT. The translated Hindi dataset contributes more to F1 improvement. In claim detection (Figure 3) for Malayalam, adding translated English data significantly improves results compared to the baseline model. The approach occasionally helps improve weighted F1-score for datasets in Hindi, Tamil, and Bengali, but not consistently.

4.3 Adding non-translated data

This third approach compares whether it is worth translating the data to a resource-poor language or if the multilingual models perform better if the data is added in its original form. Figure 1 shows the results ("+Non-TRANSLATED DATA"). The Sentiment Analysis approach shows that adding the non-translated data performs slightly better than adding translated data for training. The same pattern can be observed for hate speech detection and the claim detection. However, there is no statistical significance between the translation- and non-translation approaches. This approach has only been done for the multilingual models mBERT and XLM-R, because less accurate results are expected if English or German data is added to fine-tuned-, monolingual Marathi models.

4.4 Adding all datasets combined

For this fourth approach, it was tested to apply all available datasets combined, translated and not

Model Name	BASELINE	TRANSLATION TO EN	
	L3-Cube-MahaSent	+ Preprocessing	+ without Preproccessing
mBERT	81.9%	80.8%	81.8%
XLM-RoBERTa	83.4%	82.2%	83.3%
BerTweet	/	82.8%	83.6%
Cardiff Roberta	/	83.9%	84.0%

Figure 4: Sentiment Analysis (F1 scores)

Model Name	BASELINE	TRANSLATION TO EN	
	HASOC2021	+ Preprocessing	+ without Preproccessing
mBERT	83.7%	80.3%	82.0%
XLM-RoBERTa	82.9%	79.7%	80.4%
BerTweet	/	82.2%	84.3%
Cardiff Roberta	/	83.2%	85.0%

Figure 5: Hate speech Detection (F1 scores)

Model Name	BASELINE	TRANSLATION TO EN	
	Malayalam Claims	+ Preprocessing	+ without Preproccessing
mBERT	82.0%	81.8%	82.1%
XLM-RoBERTa	73.9%	66.9%	73.4%
BerTweet	/	78.8%	82.2%
Cardiff Roberta	/	79.3%	82.5%

Figure 6: Claim Detection results (F1 scores)

translated, for training and if this contributes positively to the model performance. For all three classification domains, the same pattern can be observed. Appending all the non-translated data achieves better results than appending all translated datasets. Compared to the baseline approach of the multilingual models we see significant improvements for hate speech and claim detection classification but not for sentiment analysis.

4.5 Translating to English

The fifth and final approach involved translating resource-poor language datasets into English. This allowed the use of fine-tuned English classification models like BERTweet and TimeLMs (Cardiff Roberta). Results (Figure 4, 5 and 6) show that TimeLMs performed best across all tasks, with statistical significance in sentiment analysis and hate speech detection. Notably, the approach without preprocessing the data performed better than preprocessing before training.

5 Discussion

The first approach (fine-tuning baseline) showed that if fine-tuned models of the resource-poor language are available, it makes sense to use them, as they showed improved results on multilingual models. This is in line with Velankar et al. 2022 who compared mono vs multilingual models for text classification.

For the second approach (where we expanded the dataset by adding translated data), we saw no improvements for the L3-Cube-MahaSent dataset. The dataset is already quite big with more than 12,000 train texts and a balanced distribution of the labels. Adding more data makes the model noisy, as the label distribution is less balanced than the baseline model. For hate speech detection it was beneficial to add translated data. This could be because the HASOC2021 dataset is quite small with 1,874 tweets and more data helps the model make better decisions. Therefore, if researchers only have small datasets available, it might be useful to search for additional datasets, which can be from a different language, and translate them into the target language. This is not guaranteed though, as the claim detection task is in a similar situation with a small amount of data, and adding translations of different datasets did not help.

In general, the third and fourth approaches (expanding by adding non-translated data and expanding by combining all data, respectively) showed the pattern that, for multilingual models, it is better just to append the non-translated data. Reasons for this can be that there is some noise when translating the texts, which sometimes leads to worse model decisions (in line with Ponti et al. 2021). They argued the main limitation of the translation process is that sentences that are possibly not faithful to the original in the target language and/or not grammatical in the source language are fed to the classifier, which degrades its performance (Ponti et al., 2021). The resources for the translation process can therefore be saved.

The fifth and final approach (translating into English to tap into resource-rich resources for fine-tuning) was chosen because it is challenging to preprocess tweets in Marathi or Malayalam due to the different alphabet and there are not many open-source tools available to do so. The idea was to bring those texts to English and use the well-established English preprocessing methods. Clearer results with the preprocessing were expected, but the opposite was the case: The models performed better without preprocessing. This could be because some important information for the model gets removed here. For example, a high volume of punctuation could hint at a bad sentiment, but this information gets lost with preprocessing. Still, the results show the benefit of first translating data to English and then using fine-tuned English models like BERTweet or TimeLMs. For future research this appears to be a promising directions. Overall, the results show that the best performance was achieved by using fine-tuned language-specific models like MahaRoBERTa or MahaBERT.

6 Conclusion

We explored different approaches to enhance the performance of multilingual classification models for low-resource languages, specifically Marathi and Malayalam. Our findings suggest that appending additional datasets in their original form to multilingual models is more effective than translating them to the resource-poor language. Adding extra data is particularly beneficial for small baseline datasets. When the baseline dataset was translated to English without preprocessing, fine-tuned English models outperformed multilingual models. However, the best results were obtained by using fine-tuned models of the resource-poor language. In conclusion, researchers can consider using translation approaches to improve multilingual language models, but if fine-tuned models for the resource-poor language already exist, they tend to yield the best results.

7 Ethical Considerations

Whenever social media data is being processed ethical concerns naturally arise. This is particularly true if the data contains some personal information. We use existing test collections in our work to minimize such problems. In addition to that we operate within the strict framework imposed on any research within our organisation.

Wider issues emerge from the actual classification tasks. The balance between free speech and censorship in hate speech detection is an issue of ongoing debate that also has ethical questions at its heart (Zimmerman et al., 2018). Claim detection also gives rise to such issues (less so sentiment analysis).

8 Limitations

This work also has a number of limitations. First of all, the L3-Cube-MahaSent dataset from Kulkarni et al. 2021 is limited to tweets from political personalities and activists, which may not be representative of the entire Marathi-speaking population. The datasets for the hate speech and claim detection task are relatively small, making it more challenging to ensure that the training data is diverse and representative. It is important to be aware of these limitations and to make efforts to mitigate biases in the model's training and evaluation. Also, low-resource languages often have limited digital footprints, making it difficult to collect sufficient data for training text classification models. Another difficulty that comes with the datasets, especially with the open-source Kaggle datasets, is that it is unclear how the labeling process looked like and what the annotator agreement was. This is indeed important information, as the data quality can have a huge impact on the model performance. One last limitation of this work is that different languages for different NLP-tasks have been chosen as low-resource languages (Marathi and Malayalam), making it hard to generalize the findings. At first, we wanted to use a Marathi dataset for claim detection as well. But to the best of our knowledge, we did not find one and therefore used the Malayalam dataset to see similarities with another language.

Acknowledgments

We would like to thank the anonymous reviewers for their constructive feedback.

References

Branden Chan, Stefan Schweter, and Timo Möller. 2020. German's next language model. *arXiv preprint arXiv:2010.10906*.

Hasna Chouikhi, Hamza Chniter, and Fethi Jarray. 2021. Arabic sentiment analysis using bert model. In *International Conference on Computational Collective Intelligence*, pages 621–632. Springer.

Mark Cieliebak, Jan Milan Deriu, Dominic Egger, and Fatih Uzdilli. 2017. A twitter corpus and benchmark resources for german sentiment analysis. In *5th International Workshop on Natural Language Processing for Social Media, Boston MA, USA, 11 December 2017*, pages 45–51. Association for Computational Linguistics.

Çağrı Çöltekin. 2020. A corpus of turkish offensive language on social media. In *Proceedings of the 12th language resources and evaluation conference*, pages 6174–6184.

Alexis Conneau, Kartikay Khandelwal, Naman Goyal, Vishrav Chaudhary, Guillaume Wenzek, Francisco Guzmán, Edouard Grave, Myle Ott, Luke Zettlemoyer, and Veselin Stoyanov. 2019. Unsupervised cross-lingual representation learning at scale. *arXiv preprint arXiv:1911.02116*.

Jacob Devlin, Ming-Wei Chang, Kenton Lee, and Kristina Toutanova. 2019. BERT: Pre-training of deep bidirectional transformers for language understanding. In *Proceedings of the 2019 Conference of the North American Chapter of the Association for Computational Linguistics: Human Language Technologies, Volume 1 (Long and Short Papers)*, pages 4171–4186, Minneapolis, Minnesota. Association for Computational Linguistics.

Paula Fortuna, Juan Soler-Company, and Leo Wanner. 2021. How well do hate speech, toxicity, abusive and offensive language classification models generalize across datasets? *Information Processing & Management*, 58(3):102524.

M.P. Geetha and D. Karthika Renuka. 2021. Improving the performance of aspect based sentiment analysis using fine-tuned bert base uncased model. *International Journal of Intelligent Networks*, 2:64–69.

Aditya Joshi, Ameya Prabhu, Manish Shrivastava, and Vasudeva Varma. 2016. Towards sub-word level compositions for sentiment analysis of hindi-english code mixed text. In *Proceedings of COLING 2016, the 26th International Conference on Computational Linguistics: Technical Papers*, pages 2482–2491.

Raviraj Joshi. 2022. L3cube-mahacorpus and mahabert: Marathi monolingual corpus, marathi bert language models, and resources. *arXiv preprint arXiv:2202.01159*.

Divyanshu Kakwani, Anoop Kunchukuttan, Satish Golla, NC Gokul, Avik Bhattacharyya, Mitesh M Khapra, and Pratyush Kumar. 2020. Indicnlpsuite: Monolingual corpora, evaluation benchmarks and pre-trained multilingual language models for indian languages. In *Findings of the Association for Computational Linguistics: EMNLP 2020*, pages 4948–4961.

Ashkan Kazemi, Kiran Garimella, Devin Gaffney, and Scott A Hale. 2021. Claim matching beyond english to scale global fact-checking. *arXiv preprint arXiv:2106.00853*.

Lev Konstantinovskiy, Oliver Price, Mevan Babakar, and Arkaitz Zubiaga. 2021. Toward automated factchecking: Developing an annotation schema and benchmark for consistent automated claim detection. *Digital Threats: Research and Practice*, 2(2):1–16.

Atharva Kulkarni, Meet Mandhane, Manali Likhitkar, Gayatri Kshirsagar, and Raviraj Joshi. 2021. L3cubemahasent: A marathi tweet-based sentiment analysis dataset. *arXiv preprint arXiv:2103.11408*.

Ran Levy, Yonatan Bilu, Daniel Hershcovich, Ehud Aharoni, and Noam Slonim. 2014. Context dependent claim detection. In *Proceedings of COLING 2014, the 25th International Conference on Computational Linguistics: Technical Papers*, pages 1489–1500.

Daniel Loureiro, Francesco Barbieri, Leonardo Neves, Luis Espinosa Anke, and Jose Camacho-Collados. 2022. Timelms: Diachronic language models from twitter. *arXiv preprint arXiv:2202.03829*.

Thomas Mandl, Sandip Modha, Gautam Kishore Shahi, Hiren Madhu, Shrey Satapara, Prasenjit Majumder, Johannes Schäfer, Tharindu Ranasinghe, Marcos Zampieri, Durgesh Nandini, et al. 2021. Overview of the hasoc subtrack at fire 2021: Hate speech and offensive content identification in english and indo-aryan languages. *arXiv preprint arXiv:2112.09301*.

Walaa Medhat, Ahmed Hassan, and Hoda Korashy. 2014. Sentiment analysis algorithms and applications: A survey. *Ain Shams engineering journal*, 5(4):1093–1113.

Aman Miglani. 2020. Coronavirus tweets nlp - text classification.

Sandip Modha, Thomas Mandl, Gautam Kishore Shahi, Hiren Madhu, Shrey Satapara, Tharindu Ranasinghe, and Marcos Zampieri. 2021. Overview of the hasoc subtrack at fire 2021: Hate speech and offensive content identification in english and indo-aryan languages and conversational hate speech. In *Forum for Information Retrieval Evaluation*, pages 1–3.

Dat Quoc Nguyen, Thanh Vu, and Anh Tuan Nguyen. 2020. Bertweet: A pre-trained language model for english tweets. *arXiv preprint arXiv:2005.10200*.

Braja Gopal Patra, Dipankar Das, and Amitava Das. 2018. Sentiment analysis of code-mixed indian languages: An overview of sail_code-mixed shared task@ icon-2017. *arXiv preprint arXiv:1803.06745*.

Zeses Pitenis, Marcos Zampieri, and Tharindu Ranasinghe. 2020. Offensive language identification in greek. *arXiv preprint arXiv:2003.07459*.

Edoardo Maria Ponti, Julia Kreutzer, Ivan Vulić, and Siva Reddy. 2021. Modelling latent translations for cross-lingual transfer. *arXiv preprint arXiv:2107.11353*.

Sebastian Ruder, Anders Søgaard, and Ivan Vulić. 2019. Unsupervised cross-lingual representation learning. In *Proceedings of the 57th Annual Meeting of the Association for Computational Linguistics: Tutorial Abstracts*, pages 31–38.

Anna Schmidt and Michael Wiegand. 2017. A survey on hate speech detection using natural language processing. In *Proceedings of the fifth international workshop on natural language processing for social media*, pages 1–10.

Thomas Schmidt, Jakob Fehle, Maximilian Weissenbacher, Jonathan Richter, Philipp Gottschalk, and Christian Wolff. 2022. Sentiment analysis on twitter for the major german parties during the 2021 german federal election. In *Proceedings of the 18th Conference on Natural Language Processing (KONVENS 2022)*, pages 74–87.

Vésteinn Snæbjarnarson, Annika Simonsen, Goran Glavaš, and Ivan Vulić. 2023. Transfer to a low-resource language via close relatives: The case study on faroese. *arXiv preprint arXiv:2304.08823*.

Ange Tato and Roger Nkambou. 2018. Improving adam optimizer. 2018. In *Proceedings of the 6th International Conference on Learning Representations (ICLR 2018 Workshop Track)*.

Abhishek Velankar, Hrushikesh Patil, and Raviraj Joshi. 2022. Mono vs multilingual bert for hate speech detection and text classification: A case study in marathi. In *IAPR Workshop on Artificial Neural Networks in Pattern Recognition*, pages 121–128. Springer.

Dewayne Whitfield. 2021. Using GPT-2 to create synthetic data to improve the prediction performance of NLP machine learning classification models. *CoRR*, abs/2104.10658.

Tomer Wullach, Amir Adler, and Einat Minkov. 2021. Fight fire with fire: Fine-tuning hate detectors using large samples of generated hate speech. In *Findings of the Association for Computational Linguistics: EMNLP 2021, Virtual Event / Punta Cana, Dominican Republic, 16-20 November, 2021*, pages 4699–4705. Association for Computational Linguistics.

Steven Zimmerman, Udo Kruschwitz, and Chris Fox. 2018. Improving hate speech detection with deep learning ensembles. In *Proceedings of the Eleventh International Conference on Language Resources and Evaluation (LREC 2018)*.

A Appendices

A.1 Sentiment Analysis Datasets

- German Federal Election Sentiment Dataset (GFES):
Schmidt et al. provided a German dataset of 2000 annotated tweets of German politicians during the federal election in 2021 (Schmidt et al., 2022). The annotation of the data has been done by students and employees of the University of Regensburg, and the annotation quality counts as reliable.
- SB10k Dataset:
Cieliebak et al. provided a big dataset of 10.000 annotated German tweets for Sentiment Analysis (Cieliebak et al., 2017). Researchers have done annotation, so the annotation quality counts as reliable.
- Kaggle Coronavirus Dataset:
This dataset from Kaggle[3] with 41.000 labeled English tweets was used to see if big, open-source datasets can be used to improve the accuracy of language models. Tweets with the label "Extremely Positive" or "Extremely Negative" were re-labeled as "Positive" and "Negative". There are no insights on how the data was annotated, so the annotation quality counts as questionable.
- Hindi Sentiment Analysis Dataset:
Also, one dataset with an Indian language, Hindi, was used for this project. The dataset consists of 9077 manually labeled tweets in Hindi. Unfortunately, the Kaggle link is no longer available, but as the experiments with this dataset have already been done, the dataset is still included in this work.

A.2 Models used in this work

A.) Multilingual-BERT-Cased (mBERT-Cased)[4]:
mBERT is a transformer-based model, pre-trained on a large corpus of multilingual data (104 languages) in a self-supervised fashion. The mBERT-Cased model is case-sensitive, so it makes a difference, for example, for "Hello World" and "hello world" (Devlin et al., 2019).

B.) XLM-RoBERTa (XLM-R)[5]:
XLM-R is a multilingual version of RoBERTa, pre-trained on 100 languages. Conneau et al. found that this model performs exceptionally well on low-resource languages (Conneau et al., 2019).

C.) IndicBERT[6]:
A multilingual ALBERT model released by Ai4Bharat trained on large-scale corpora. The training languages include 12 major Indian languages. The model has been proven to work better for tasks in Indic language (Kakwani et al., 2020).

D.) MahaBERT[7]:
A multilingual BERT (bert-base-multilingual-cased) model fine-tuned on L3Cube-MahaCorpus and other publicly available Marathi monolingual datasets (Joshi, 2022).

E.) MahaAlBERT[8]:
A monolingual AlBERT model, trained on L3Cube-MahaCorpus and other publicly available Marathi monolingual datasets (Joshi, 2022).

F.) MahaRoBERTa[9]:
A multilingual RoBERTa (xlm-roberta-base) model fine-tuned on L3Cube-MahaCorpus and other publicly available Marathi monolingual datasets (Joshi, 2022).

G.) BERTweet[10]:
A RoBERTa based model pre-trained on 850M English tweets. (Nguyen et al., 2020).

H.) TimeLMs[11]:
A RoBERTa based model pre-trained on English tweets and finetuned for sentiment analysis with the TweetEval benchmark (Loureiro et al., 2022).

[3]https://www.kaggle.com/datasets/datatattle/covid-19-nlp-text-classification?select=Corona_NLP_train.csv
[4]https://huggingface.co/bert-base-multilingual-cased
[5]https://huggingface.co/xlm-roberta-base
[6]https://huggingface.co/ai4bharat/indic-bert
[7]https://huggingface.co/l3cube-pune/marathi-bert
[8]https://huggingface.co/l3cube-pune/marathi-albert-v2
[9]https://huggingface.co/l3cube-pune/marathi-roberta
[10]https://huggingface.co/vinai/bertweet-base
[11]https://huggingface.co/cardiffnlp/twitter-roberta-base-sentiment-latest

Toward a Multilingual Connective Database: Aligning German/French Concessive Connectives

Sophia Rauh[1], Karolina Zaczynska[1], and Peter Bourgonje[1, 2]

[1]Applied CL Discourse Research Lab, Department of Linguistics, University of Potsdam
firstname.lastname@uni-potsdam.de
[2]Language Science and Technology, Saarland University
lastname@coli.uni-saarland.de

Abstract

We report on experiments to align discourse connectives from two language-specific connective lexicons (German and French) by their relation sense. In this case study, we focus on *concessive* connectives, and align them using a parallel corpus. The ultimate goal is to arrive at bi- (or multi-)lingual connective lexicons, that at the same time provide insights on the "semantic space" that connectives cover in different languages.

1 Introduction

A typical way to establish coherence in a text is through the use of *discourse connectives*. Such markers (single words or – potentially discontinuous – phrases) convey a specific relation; *contrast* (e.g., "but"), *contingency* (e.g., "if...then") or *cause* (e.g., "therefore") that links propositions in the text. They can be ambiguous in two ways, and can either signal a discourse relation between two propositions (1) or sentential reading (2).

(1) It would have made a dreadfully ugly child, *but* it makes rather a handsome pig. (Carroll, 1893)

(2) "I beg your pardon?" said the Mouse, frowning, *but* very politely. (Carroll, 1893)

In addition, certain connectives can express multiple senses. In (3), *once* signals a temporal relation, whereas in (4), it signals a conditional relation.

(3) *Once* it gets there, a company can do with it what it wishes. (wsj_0989 (Marcus et al., 1993))

(4) Normally, *once* the underlying investment is suspended from trading, the options on those investments also don't trade. (wsj_1962 (Marcus et al., 1993))

Discourse relations can also be realized implicitly and expressed, for example, by syntactic parallelism, layout, but explicit discourse markers are considered important indicators of coherence relations as explored in various frameworks like Rhetorical Structure Theory (RST) (Mann and Thompson, 1988) and Segmented Discourse Representation Theory (SDRT) (Asher and Lascarides, 2005). After attempts to exhaustively list such markers (Knott and Dale, 1994), specific discourse connective or discourse marker lexicons started to emerge, with the first documented lexicon being for German (Stede and Umbach, 1998), and following ones for French (Roze et al., 2012), Italian (Feltracco et al., 2016), Czech (Mírovský et al., 2016) and several other languages.

Once language-specific lexicons are created and augmented with semantic information, parallels can be drawn based on the *distribution* of relation senses[1] across languages. In addition, since connectives can pose challenges to translators and (L2) language learners, having a layer over language-specific lexicons that aligns entries across languages can be a useful resource. Earlier work in this direction has been carried out by Bourgonje et al. (2017). We use a similar approach, but work on French and German, and base our work on LexConn (Roze et al., 2012), DiMLex (Stede and Umbach, 1998) and a parallel corpus. The main contribution of this paper is to present the results of a case study on aligning French and German connectives that can signal a *concessive* relation. Our code is made publicly available[2].

In Section 2 we summarize related work on connective lexicons. Section 3 explains the corpus and alignment procedure. Section 4 presents the results, and Section 5 sums up our main findings.

[1]Inventories of relation senses for a specific paradigm or theory are, presumably, language-independent.

[2]https://github.com/SophiaRauh/fr_de_connectives_alignment

Proceedings of the 19th Conference on Natural Language Processing (KONVENS 2023), pages 77–84
September 18–22, 2023. ©2023 Association for Computational Linguistics

2 Related Work

Several language-specific lexicons are available online. In addition to the ones mentioned in Section 1, lexicons exist for English (Das et al., 2018), Dutch (Bourgonje et al., 2018), Bangla (Das et al., 2020), Portuguese (Mendes and Lejeune, 2016), Nigerian Pidgin (Marchal et al., 2021) and Turkish (Zeyrek and Başıbüyük, 2019). These lexicons are conveniently bundled on the online platform Connective-Lex[3] (Stede et al., 2019). While this platform already allows multi-lingual comparison of connective groups (grouping by part-of-speech tag or relation sense), with our contribution we aim to expand this multi-lingual aspect to individual connectives.

The lexicons differ slightly with regard to their take on connectives (for example, what syntactic classes to include, and how to encode morphological variation). A comprehensive discussion is offered by (Danlos et al., 2018). We like to note that it is exactly the kind of cross-lingual investigation of connectives we are reporting on in this paper that allows subtle differences to surface, and enables refinement of the understanding and definition of connectives.

3 Method & Data

3.1 Lexicons and Parallel Corpus

Our starting point is the list of entries from DiMLex and LexConn, both of which are available online[4]. We follow Bourgonje et al. (2017) by focussing on concessive connectives for this case study. While the discourse senses of the German connective lexicon are based on the Penn Discourse Treebank (PDTB) (Webber et al., 2019) senses, the French discourse relations are an extended version of SDRT. Both include the relation *concession*, though interestingly, German concessive connectives frequently align with *violation* in French, which is equivalent to the PDTB sense *exception*.

We used the Europarl parallel corpus (Koehn, 2005), as the translations are curated, which avoids the risk of including automatically created low-quality translations. The French part of the corpus consists of 63.2 million tokens and the German part consists of 54.6 million tokens. For the word alignment, our data was tokenized and converted to lower case.

3.2 (Semi-) Automated Word Alignment Procedure

For the word alignment we used eflomal[5], which is based on efmaral (Östling and Tiedemann, 2016). The alignments are saved in "Pharaoh" format, i.e. for the (pre-tokenized) input
`schwarzes Haus || maison noire`
the representation "`0-1 1-0`" is returned, indicating that the first (0-indexed) token in the source is aligned to the second token in the target, and the second token in the source is aligned to the first token in the target. `NULL` alignments are not present in the output.

Once these alignments were calculated for the entire corpus, we used both the German DiMLex connectives and the French LexConn connectives as seed lists to extract the probability that a certain connective is aligned to a word or phrase in the target language.[6] This process is straightforward for single-word connectives. For multi-word (phrasal) connectives, the alignment probabilities are obtained by concatenating the single-word alignments that constitute the phrase. The results were stored in a JSON file and are further processed in a semi-automated way:

1) If contractions of prepositions and articles occur at the end of a phrase, they are replaced with the preposition only, since the articles are not part of the connective. For example, the contracted German word *zur* ("to the") is replaced by *zu* ("to") and the French contraction *aux* ("in the") is substituted with *à* ("in").

2) Since connectives are frequently (sub-)clause initial, hence alignments may include punctuation, punctuation is removed, i.e., "*, weil*" (", because") becomes "*weil*".

3) If tokens were `NULL`-aligned, we included an empty string as alignment, as this influences alignment probabilities. Words that were aligned to punctuation marks were aggregated with the empty string placeholder.

[3] `http://connective-lex.info/` (URLs were all last accessed on 2023-05-06.)

[4] `http://www.linguist.univ-paris-diderot.fr/~croze/`, `https://github.com/discourse-lab/dimlex`

[5] `https://github.com/robertostling/eflomal`

[6] Since the values are extracted from the entire corpus, they are not probabilities, but actual counts converted into floating point values by dividing by the total frequency. We use the term probability throughout the rest of this paper, though, since we interpret this number as the probability that a certain word or phrase in the source language is aligned to a certain word or phrase in the target language.

This slightly modified version of the extracted word alignments was stored in a dictionary, in which we then proceeded to look up connectives from source to target language.

3.3 (Semi-) Manual Filtering

Looking up connectives in our dictionary resulted in several incorrect or irrelevant target words or phrases. Many of these could be discarded in a semi-automated way.

First, for some instances, the alignment probabilities to reasonable candidates were very low. For example, after the above mentioned adjustments, *dabei* ("thereby/at that") aligned to an empty string in 34% of cases, and to *en*, *il*, *à* and *ce* in 7, 5, 3 and 2% of cases, respectively. This might be due to eflomal alignment errors, or could be related to the frequency of sentential instances (e.g., example (2) in Section 1) far outweighing the frequency of discourse reading instances (e.g., example (1) in Section 1) for some connectives.

In (5), for example, *dabei* does not have a connective reading and it is translated with *dans ce processus* ("in this process").

(5) Inwieweit wird das Europäische Parlament <u>*dabei*</u> eine Rolle spielen können?
Dans quelle mesure le Parlement européen pourra-t-il jouer un rôle <u>*dans ce processus*</u>?
To what extent will the European Parliament be able to play a role <u>*in this (process)*</u>?

Using the adjusted alignment probabilities, we filter out all words and phrases below a certain threshold. Due to the concatenation process to arrive at phrase alignment probabilities, we found that working with two different threshold values (one for single word connectives, one for phrasal connectives) worked best. In addition, we use a combination of relative and absolute thresholds. First, all single word connectives with a probability below 2.1%, and all phrasal connectives with a probability below 1.4%, were discarded. Because some very low-frequent connectives can have a relatively high probability, we furthermore discarded connectives below an absolute count in our corpus (20 for single words, 10 for phrases).

Second, results for phrasal connectives were often only partially relevant. For example, for the French connective *alors même que* ("even though"), the German phrase *obwohl die* ("although the") was among the candidates, whereas the relevant German connective would be only *obwohl* ("although"). These only partially relevant alignments could often be filtered out on syntactic grounds, by looking for prepositions, articles and pronouns. In addition, phrasal connectives led to incomplete target phrases. For the French connective *c'est pourquoi* ("that is why"), we found *c'... pourquoi* among the alignments. If we found the complete phrase among the alignment results as well, these incomplete alignments were removed from the list of candidates. Some phrasal connectives truly are discontinuous (e.g., *entweder... oder* ("either... or")), while for others, the connective was not discontinuous but the correct/relevant alignment was just not in the set of results. One example is the 4-token connective *soit dit en passant* ("by the way/incidentally"), for which only *soit dit ... passant* was among our results. This processing of phrasal connectives therefore had to be done in a manual way.

3.4 Augmentation

The combination of semi-automated filtering and manual curation of the results described above mainly deleted irrelevant candidates, and completed some partially correct ones. Since word alignments are extracted from parallel sentences (hence do not go beyond sentence boundary), we constructed sentence tri-grams and also extracted word alignments from those. This procedure lead to further completion of candidates.

Furthermore, this manual augmentation step involved weeding out non-connective, or non-concessive candidates. For example, the concessive connective *entgegen* ("contrary to") was aligned to *contre* ("against"). Looking at the sentences revealed that *entgegen* does not have a connective reading when aligned to *contre*, which is also not a connective.

(6) Das Volk hat das Recht, innerhalb der Grenzen des Gesetzes zu demonstrieren, wenn es das Gefühl hat, dass die Regierung <u>*entgegen*</u> ihrer Interessen handelt.
La population est autorisée à manifester dans les limites de la législation lorsqu'elle estime que le gouvernement agit <u>*contre*</u> ses intérêts.
The population has the right to demonstrate within the limits of the law when it feels that the government is acting <u>*against*</u> its interests.

Some candidates were excluded on these grounds. Finally, other candidates were deleted, modified or completed (for missing particles) based on intuition. After this final curation of the candidates, we arrived at a list of aligned French connectives for the German seed list, and vice versa. We projected the final list of the target language connectives back onto the source once more, to see if we would get any additional results. In principle, this procedure could be repeated until no more new instances are found. Due to the amount of manual labour involved in the process though, we stopped after 3 "turns" (from French to German, back to French, and then back to German again).

4 Results & Discussion

Recall that we start with all connectives that have *concession* as their second-level sense in the PDTB3 Sense Hierarchy. The final alignments are included in Appendix A, Tables 1 and 2, where "-" indicates an empty alignment. The parentheses in the left column contain the absolute occurrence of the connectives in the corpus, whereas those in the right column indicate the relative occurrence of the aligned connectives. To get an overview of the distribution and the degree of ambiguity (i.e., different senses that groups of connectives can express), we include Figures 2 and 3 in Appendix A. The diagrams show which discourse relations align with which based on the connectives of the final alignment. For comparison, the SDRT senses of the French connectives are mapped to PDTB3 senses using the mapping included in Figure 1 in Appendix A.

Since many connectives can express multiple senses, Figures 2 and 3 also include second-level senses other than just *concessive*; we group all connectives by the set of senses they can express. Generally, Figure 3 looks much more straightforward; the set of connectives that can (only) signal concession map to a set in German that also exclusively signals concession, and the ambiguous sets map to each other relatively neatly. Figure 2 is much less straightforward. The set that exclusively signals concession in German maps to a much wider range of senses in French. A case in point is "dennoch", which can only signal *concession*, which is aligned to "néanmoins" and "cependant" (*exception*), "pourtant" (*exception* or *concession*) and "mais" (*contrast* or *exception*). It is interesting to further look into whether particular corpus examples of "dennoch" also carry some aspect of the different senses of the aligned connectives in French. For example, "dennoch" might be relatively ambiguous, as its "semantic space" (for lack of a better description) is covered by several different connectives in French. These semantic spaces could surface through clusters of connectives, which can be explored in this bi-lingual setup. The German connectives "allerdings, dennoch, doch, gleichwohl, jedoch" seem to constitute one potential example of such a cluster, and map to "cependant, néanmoins, pourtant, mais", and "obgleich, obwohl, wenn auch, wenngleich" mostly map to "bien que, même si, alors que". While the PDTB senses are already such clusters in themselves, our approach might lead to a more fine-grained classification or grouping of individual connectives' meanings. Furthermore, interestingly, there seem to be asymmetries in the mapping: The German "aber" frequently maps only to "mais" and "cependant". In reverse, however, "mais" maps to a larger set of German connectives ("aber, sondern, doch, jedoch"). While the reason for some of these asymmetries might just be low frequency, both "aber" and "mais" are fairly common connectives, indicating that this might not just be an artefact of the data we used.

In terms of future work, we plan to include connective disambiguation modules to separate connective instances from their sentential interpretation surface forms. For German, a connective classifier has been developed (Bourgonje and Stede, 2018). To the best of our knowledge, no such (pretrained) classifier is available for French, so for this language, we consider the use of annotation projection (Sluyter-Gäthje et al., 2020).

Furthermore, since the performance of our word aligner is critical for downstream processing, it would also be interesting to evaluate this module in isolation by creating a gold set based on our data.

5 Conclusion

We present work on aligning *concessive* connectives in German and French, using word-alignments extracted from a parallel corpus. Our approach is semi-automated and the code is made available on GitHub. We provide some first insights on how particular relation sense groups are covered by the two languages. In addition to validating the mono-lingual connective lexicons, we hope that this contributes to our ultimate goal of providing insights on how discourse relation senses are covered in different languages through explicit markers (i.e., discourse connectives).

References

Nicholas Asher and Alex Lascarides. 2005. Logics of conversation. In *Studies in Natural Language Processing*.

Peter Bourgonje, Yulia Grishina, and Manfred Stede. 2017. Toward a bilingual lexical database on connectives: Exploiting a German/Italian parallel corpus. In *Proceedings of the Fourth Italian Conference on Computational Linguistics*, Rome, Italy.

Peter Bourgonje, Jet Hoek, Jacqueline Evers-Vermeul, Gisela Redeker, Ted Sanders, and Manfred Stede. 2018. Constructing a Lexicon of Dutch Discourse Connectives. *Computational Linguistics in the Netherlands Journal*, 8:163–175.

Peter Bourgonje and Manfred Stede. 2018. Identifying explicit discourse connectives in German. In *Proceedings of the 19th Annual SIGdial Meeting on Discourse and Dialogue*, pages 327–331, Melbourne, Australia. Association for Computational Linguistics.

Lewis Carroll. 1893. *Alice's adventures in Wonderland*. T. Y. Crowell & co, New York, Boston.

Laurence Danlos, Katerina Rysova, Magdalena Rysova, and Manfred Stede. 2018. Primary and secondary discourse connectives: definitions and lexicons. *Dialogue and Discourse*, 9(1):50–78.

Debopam Das, Tatjana Scheffler, Peter Bourgonje, and Manfred Stede. 2018. Constructing a lexicon of English discourse connectives. In *Proceedings of the 19th Annual SIGdial Meeting on Discourse and Dialogue*, pages 360–365, Melbourne, Australia. Association for Computational Linguistics.

Debopam Das, Manfred Stede, Soumya Sankar Ghosh, and Lahari Chatterjee. 2020. DiMLex-bangla: A lexicon of bangla discourse connectives. In *Proceedings of the 12th International Conference on Language Resources and Evaluation (LREC'20)*, pages 1097–1102, Marseille, France. European Language Resources Association (ELRA).

Anna Feltracco, Elisabetta Jezek, Bernardo Magnini, and Manfred Stede. 2016. Lico: A lexicon of Italian connectives. In *Proceedings of the 3rd Italian Conference on Computational Linguistics (CLiC-it)*, pages 141–145, Napoli, Italy.

Alistair Knott and Robert Dale. 1994. Using linguistic phenomena to motivate a set of coherence relations. *Discourse Processes*, 18:35–62.

Philipp Koehn. 2005. Europarl: A parallel corpus for statistical machine translation. In *Proceedings of Machine Translation Summit X: Papers*, pages 79–86, Phuket, Thailand.

William Mann and Sandra Thompson. 1988. Rhetorical Structure Theory: Towards a functional theory of text organization. *TEXT*, 8:243–281.

Marian Marchal, Merel Scholman, and Vera Demberg. 2021. Semi-automatic discourse annotation in a low-resource language: Developing a connective lexicon for Nigerian Pidgin. In *Proceedings of the 2nd Workshop on Computational Approaches to Discourse*, pages 84–94, Punta Cana, Dominican Republic and Online. Association for Computational Linguistics.

Mitchell P. Marcus, Beatrice Santorini, and Mary Ann Marcinkiewicz. 1993. Building a large annotated corpus of English: The Penn Treebank. *Computational Linguistics*, 19(2):313–330.

Amália Mendes and Pierre Lejeune. 2016. LDM-PT. A Portuguese Lexicon of Discourse Markers. In *Conference Handbook of TextLink – Structuring Discourse in Multilingual Europe Second Action Conference*, pages 89–92, Budapest, Hungary.

Jiří Mírovský, Pavlína Jínová, Magdaléna Rysová, and Lucie Poláková. 2016. Designing CzeDLex – a lexicon of Czech discourse connectives. In *Proceedings of the 30th Pacific Asia Conference on Language, Information and Computation: Posters*, pages 449–457, Seoul, South Korea.

Charlotte Roze, Laurence Danlos, and Philippe Muller. 2012. LEXCONN: A French lexicon of discourse connectives. *Discours. Revue de linguistique, psycholinguistique et informatique*, 10.

Henny Sluyter-Gäthje, Peter Bourgonje, and Manfred Stede. 2020. Shallow discourse parsing for under-resourced languages: Combining machine translation and annotation projection. In *Proceedings of the 12th Language Resources and Evaluation Conference (LREC'20)*, pages 1044–1050, Marseille, France. European Language Resources Association (ELRA).

Manfred Stede, Tatjana Scheffler, and Amalia Mendes. 2019. Connective-lex: A web-based multilingual lexical resource for connectives. *Discours. Revue de linguistique, psycholinguistique et informatique*.

Manfred Stede and Carla Umbach. 1998. DiMLex: A lexicon of discourse markers for text generation and understanding. In *36th Annual Meeting of the Association for Computational Linguistics and 17th International Conference on Computational Linguistics, Volume 2*, pages 1238–1242, Montreal, Quebec, Canada. Association for Computational Linguistics.

Bonnie Webber, Rashmi Prasad, Alan Lee, and Aravind Joshi. 2019. The Penn Discourse Treebank 3.0 Annotation Manual.

Deniz Zeyrek and Kezban Başıbüyük. 2019. TCL - a lexicon of Turkish discourse connectives. In *Proceedings of the First International Workshop on Designing Meaning Representations*, pages 73–81, Florence, Italy. Association for Computational Linguistics.

Robert Östling and Jörg Tiedemann. 2016. Efficient word alignment with markov chain monte carlo. *The Prague Bulletin of Mathematical Linguistics*, 106.

A Appendix

```
{
  "alternation": ["EXPANSION:Disjunction"],
  "background": ["TEMPORAL:Synchronous"],
  "background-inverse": ["TEMPORAL:Asynchronous:Succession"],
  "concession": ["COMPARISON:Concession"],
  "condition": ["CONTINGENCY:Condition"],
  "consequence": ["CONTINGENCY:Condition"],
  "continuation": ["EXPANSION:Conjunction"],
  "contrast": ["COMPARISON:Contrast"],
  "detachment": ["EXPANSION:Exception"],
  "digression": ["EXPANSION:Conjunction"],
  "elaboration": ["EXPANSION:Level-of-detail"],
  "evidence": ["EXPANSION:Conjunction"],
  "explanation": ["EXPANSION:Manner",
                  "EXPANSION:Level-of-detail",
                  "CONTINGENCY:Cause:Reason"],
  "explanation*": ["CONTINGENCY:Cause+belief"],
  "flashback": ["TEMPORAL:Asynchronous:Succession"],
  "goal": ["CONTINGENCY:Purpose"],
  "narration": ["TEMPORAL:Asynchronous:Precedence",
                "EXPANSION:Conjunction"],
  "parallel": ["COMPARISON:Similarity"],
  "rephrasing": ["EXPANSION:Equivalence"],
  "result": ["CONTINGENCY:Cause:Result"],
  "result*": ["CONTINGENCY:Cause:Result+belief",
              "CONTINGENCY:Cause:Result+speechact"],
  "summary": ["EXPANSION:Level-of-detail:Arg2-as-detail"],
  "temploc": ["TEMPORAL"],
  "violation": ["EXPANSION:Exception"]
}
```

Figure 1: SDRT to PDTB Sense Mapping

DE Connective (frequency)	FR Connective(s)
aber (98898)	mais (0.65), - (0.09), cependant (0.04)
abgesehen davon (553)	cela dit (0.06), - (0.05), par ailleurs (0.03), ceci dit (0.02)
allerdings (14935)	cependant (0.18), mais (0.16), - (0.08), néanmoins (0.06), pourtant (0.02)
dennoch (7920)	néanmoins (0.19), cependant (0.13), pourtant (0.09), mais (0.08), - (0.07)
dessen ungeachtet (187)	néanmoins (0.12)
doch (30068)	mais (0.38), - (0.2), cependant (0.03), pourtant (0.03)
gleichwohl (1714)	cependant (0.12), néanmoins (0.12), mais (0.09), - (0.08), pourtant (0.07)
immerhin (1023)	- (0.26), après tout (0.11), pourtant (0.05), quand même (0.03), tout de même (0.02), au moins (0.02)
jedoch (43525)	mais (0.26), cependant (0.16), - (0.09), néanmoins (0.05), pourtant (0.03)
nebenbei gesagt (59)	soit dit en passant (0.24)
nichtsdestotrotz (618)	néanmoins (0.38), cependant (0.09), malgré tout (0.02)
nichtsdestoweniger (213)	néanmoins (0.4)
obgleich (1612)	bien que (0.18), même si (0.15), - (0.09), alors que (0.05), mais (0.05), bien qu' (0.05), même s' (0.03), alors qu' (0.02)
obwohl (10904)	bien que (0.19), même si (0.12), bien qu' (0.06), - (0.06), alors que (0.06), alors qu' (0.03), même s' (0.02)
trotzdem (3585)	néanmoins (0.18), pourtant (0.1), cependant (0.09), - (0.08), mais (0.05), malgré tout (0.04), quand même (0.03)
wenn auch (1849)	même si (0.09), bien que (0.06), - (0.06), mais (0.05), bien qu' (0.03), quoique (0.03), même s' (0.01)
wenngleich (1463)	même si (0.23), bien que (0.15), mais (0.06), - (0.05), même s' (0.05), bien qu' (0.04)

Table 1: German to French Connective Alignments

FR Connective (frequency)	DE Connective(s)
alors même que (542)	während (0.14), obwohl (0.11), - (0.03)
alors qu' (3466)	obwohl (0.14), während (0.12), - (0.09), als (0.03)
alors que (10341)	während (0.22), obwohl (0.09), - (0.07), da (0.03)
après tout (1870)	schließlich (0.3), - (0.09), immerhin (0.08), denn (0.03), doch (0.02), nämlich (0.02)
bien qu' (3413)	obwohl (0.25), - (0.07), obgleich (0.03), zwar (0.02), wenn auch (0.02)
bien que (9678)	obwohl (0.25), - (0.06), obgleich (0.03), wenngleich (0.03)
ceci dit (466)	- (0.14), abgesehen davon (0.03)
cela dit (1163)	- (0.14), allerdings (0.05), aber (0.05), davon abgesehen (0.03), jedoch (0.03), dennoch (0.03), abgesehen davon (0.03), doch (0.02)
cependant (19138)	jedoch (0.36), aber (0.22), allerdings (0.14), - (0.09), doch (0.05), dennoch (0.05)
en dépit du fait que (159)	obwohl (0.17)
mais (142830)	aber (0.46), sondern (0.2), doch (0.09), jedoch (0.08), - (0.07)
malgré le fait qu' (85)	obwohl (0.28)
malgré le fait que (259)	obwohl (0.19)
malgré que (47)	obwohl (0.43)
malgré tout (1145)	trotzdem (0.14), dennoch (0.12), - (0.07), doch (0.05), jedoch (0.03)
même s' (2097)	obwohl (0.13), - (0.05), wenngleich (0.03), wenn auch (0.03), obgleich (0.02)
même si (9593)	obwohl (0.16), wenngleich (0.04), - (0.04), obgleich (0.03), zwar (0.03), wenn auch (0.02)
néanmoins (8521)	doch (0.23), dennoch (0.17), aber (0.16), allerdings (0.11), - (0.09), trotzdem (0.07), doch (0.05), nichtsdestotrotz (0.03), gleichwohl (0.02)
pourtant (5890)	jedoch (0.18), - (0.16), doch (0.14), aber (0.12), dennoch (0.11), allerdings (0.05), trotzdem (0.05), obwohl (0.02)
quand même (1480)	doch (0.15), - (0.13), trotzdem (0.08), dennoch (0.07), immerhin (0.03), auch (0.02)
quoique (413)	- (0.17), obwohl (0.15), aber (0.11), wenngleich (0.07)
soit dit en passant (277)	- (0.05), nebenbei gesagt (0.04)
tout de même (1628)	doch (0.16), - (0.12), immerhin (0.05), dennoch (0.04), trotzdem (0.04)

Table 2: French to German Connective Alignments

Figure 2: Mappings of German to French Connectives

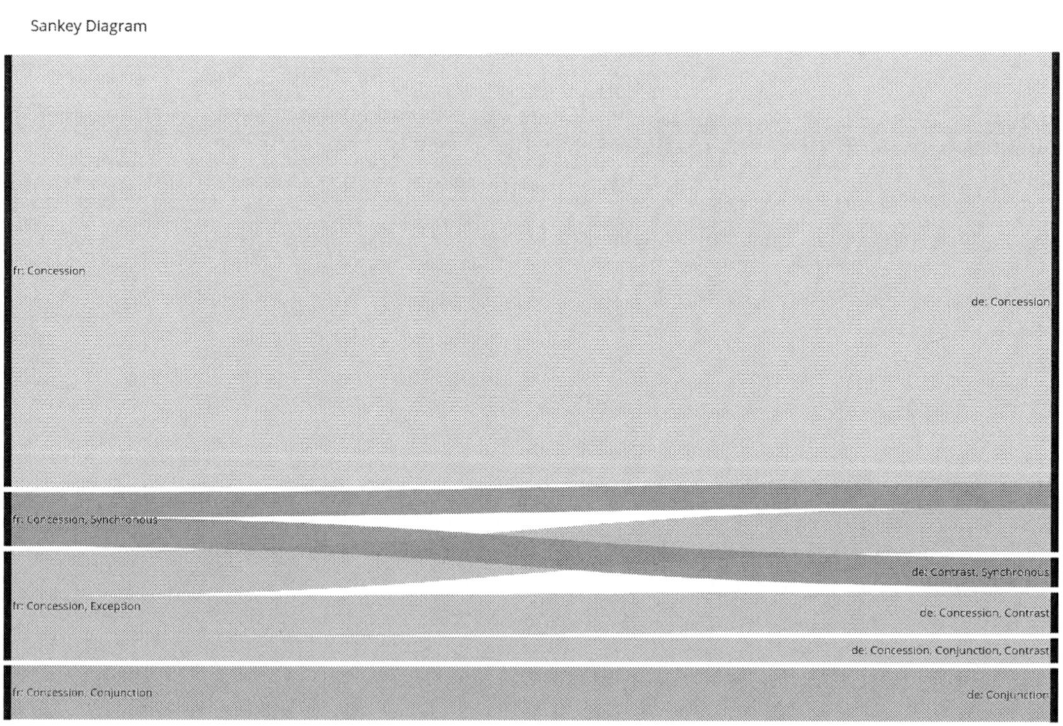

Figure 3: Mappings of French to German Connectives

Factuality Detection using Machine Translation - a Use Case for German Clinical Text

Mohammed Bin Sumait, Aleksandra Gabryszak, Leonhard Hennig and **Roland Roller**
German Research Center for Artificial Intelligence (DFKI)
Speech and Language Technology Lab
{firstname.lastname}@dfki.de

Abstract

Factuality can play an important role when automatically processing clinical text, as it makes a difference if particular symptoms are explicitly not present, possibly present, not mentioned, or affirmed. In most cases, a sufficient number of examples is necessary to handle such phenomena in a supervised machine learning setting. However, as clinical text might contain sensitive information, data cannot be easily shared. In the context of factuality detection, this work presents a simple solution using machine translation to translate English data to German to train a transformer-based factuality detection model.

1 Introduction

Factuality refers to the concept that a speaker can present statements about world events with varying degrees of uncertainty as to whether they happened. Factuality reflects, for instance, if an event is affirmed, negated, or uncertain. In the medical domain, detecting if symptoms or diseases are signaled as present, not present, possibly or doubtfully present, and therefore uncertain is essential. Detecting factuality is challenging since it can be expressed by very different linguistic categories (e.g. verbs, nouns, adjectives, adverbs), plus it must be taken into account how they are embedded in a sentence (Rudinger et al., 2018a). Additionally, linguistic factuality cues can be very domain-specific, so the availability of relevant datasets is essential.

Classical supervised machine learning requires training data, and, at the same time, most existing datasets are published in English. In addition, clinical text contains sensitive patient data, which often makes it difficult to share due to ethical and legal aspects. Although the situation has slowly changed regarding the availability of German clinical text resources (Modersohn et al., 2022), many other languages suffer a similar situation. Conversely, the quality of machine translation has significantly improved in the last decade, also regarding the translation of biomedical text/publications, including clinical case reports (Neves et al., 2022). For this reason, this work explores the usage of machine translation to create (translated) text resources for factuality detection in German clinical text.

Clinical notes are short text documents written by physicians during or shortly after the treatment of a patient. In general, this kind of text contains much valuable information about the current health condition, as well as treatment, of the patient. They differ from biomedical publications and clinical case reports, as notes are often written under time pressure with a high information density, a telegraphic writing style, non-standardized abbreviations, colloquial errors, and misspellings. Therefore, it is unclear if current machine translation systems can handle this text, considering that data might contain sensitive information and should not be shared with a third party outside the hospital.

This work makes the following contributions: 1) We successfully use a local machine translation to train a model for factuality detection on German clinical text. 2) Our model outperforms the only 'competitor' NegEx, and 3) will be published as open access model[1]. Finally, 4) for those interested in NegEx, we release it as a modular PyPI package with a few important fixes[2] and also propose improvement suggestions to the used trigger sets.

2 Methods and Data

The idea of this work is based on the usage of machine translation to generate a German corpus to train a classifier dealing with factuality in clinical text. In the following, we outline the approach, the necessary methods, and the dataset used.

2.1 Factuality Detection

In literature, (medical) factuality detection is often reduced to a simple classification. Given a sentence

[1]https://huggingface.co/binsumait/factual-med-bert-de
[2]https://github.com/DFKI-NLP/pynegex

Proceedings of the 19th Conference on Natural Language Processing (KONVENS 2023), pages 85–92
September 18–22, 2023. ©2023 Association for Computational Linguistics

Factuality	English	German translation
affirmed	Clinically, a <E>severe neuropsychological syndrome</E> was found when the patient was taken over.	Klinisch fand sich bei Übernahme des Patienten in <E>schweres neuropsychologisches Syndrom</E>.
negation	Patient denies <E>headache</E>.	Patient verneint <E>Kopfschmerzen</E>.
possible	Thus, a <E>tumour</E> cannot be ruled out.	Ein <E>Tumor</E> kann daher nicht ausgeschlossen werden.

Table 1: Example sentences with target entities, factuality label, and possible translations.

and an entity, the task is to define the factuality of the entity in the given context. In most cases, the entity of interest is a symptom or medical condition. Most related work targets the three classes **affirmed**, **negated** and **possible**. However, as simple as this sounds, factuality cannot always be easily mapped to those few classes.

One of the most prominent tools to deal with factuality in the medical text is NegEx (Chapman et al., 2001), a rule-based approach with pre-defined regular expressions, so-called triggers, and can detect the three aforementioned factuality classes. It achieves, particularly in the context of negations, quite good results on clinical text. Hedges instead offer more possibilities for how they are described, therefore achieving a much lower performance. Initially, it was developed for English, but over the years, it has also been translated into other languages, such as Spanish or Swedish (Cotik et al., 2016b; Chapman et al., 2013). In addition, many alternative (machine learning) solutions have been published in the last two decades. We refer to the overview by Khandelwal and Sawant (2019) for more details. For German, however, only one negation detection exists, which relies on the NegEx solution and uses a set of translated trigger words (English to German) (Cotik et al., 2016a).

2.2 Data

In the following, we briefly introduce the data used for this work. First, we present i2b2, which has been used for machine translation and to train our model. In addition, we later test our model on additional German data, namely Ex4CDS and NegEx-Ger, and in the appendix also BRONCO150.

The **2010 i2b2/VA** data (Uzuner et al., 2011) consists of English medical text and includes three tasks - extraction of concepts, assertions identification, and relation detection. In this work, we focus on the assertion task. Overall a total of six assertion types were considered, namely present, absent, possible, conditional, hypothetical and not associated with the patient. However, this work focused only on the first three labels, as only those are considered within NegEx. i2b2 data is translated to German to train a German machine learning model.

Ex4CDS (Roller et al., 2022) is a small dataset of physicians' notes containing explanations in the context of clinical decision support. The notes are written in German and include various annotation layers, including factuality. As the data includes multiple factuality labels, we reduced the labels to our three target labels, mapping *possible-future* and *unlikely* to *possible*, and *minor* to *affirmed*. As target entities, we consider only sentences containing *medical-conditions*.

NegEx-Ger is a small dataset consisting of sentences taken from clinical notes and discharge summaries and has been used initially to evaluate the German NegEx version in Cotik et al. (2016a). For our use case, the data has been used for testing, and for this, we merged the sentences of both clinical text types. However, the number of sentences containing the possible label is small (22 for discharge summaries and 4 for clinical notes).

2.3 Translation Approach

For our proposed idea, two aspects need to be considered: First, we aim at a solution that could be applied to sensitive data. Therefore, the machine translation component must run locally. This means we cannot rely on the variety of existing state-of-the-art online approaches. Second, as we define factuality as a classification problem with a given sentence (context) and an entity, our translations need to keep track of the target entity within a sentence. A simple example is given in Table 1, which shows an English sentence with a target entity 'headache' and the label 'negation'. The German translation needs to keep the focus on the target entity.

In this work, we rely on TransIns (Steffen and van Genabith, 2021), an open-source machine translation that can be installed locally. TransIns is built on MarianNMT (Junczys-Dowmunt et al., 2018) framework and enables translating texts with an embedded markup language. Specifically, we translate sentences with tagged entities, as shown in Table 1.

A manual inspection revealed multiple problems

with the translations: In some cases (roughly 40% of the issues), translations were corrupt as they contained cryptic and/or repetitive text sequences that were foreign from the original text. Such noise patterns could partially or entirely affect the target texts' context. Or, in very few cases (only 4%), no translation output could be produced. In the rest of the cases, the markup no longer included the target entity. In any way, such output has been discarded from the data, and we resulted in 18,297 data points (initially 18,397), which we used to train and evaluate our machine learning model.

3 Experiments and Results

We conduct three different experiments - starting with the English i2b2 data, we use Bio+Discharge Summary BERT (Alsentzer et al., 2019) and compare the results to NegEx. Similar experiments have also been conducted in other papers. However, in our case, those results serve as a comparison. Thus, the model is not optimized to achieve the best possible performance. Next, we train German-MedBERT (Shrestha, 2021) on the translated i2b2 data and compare the results to the performance of the German NegEx implementation. Finally, we apply both German factuality approaches to different German medical texts to determine how well the models perform in a more realistic setup.

	NegEx			BERT-based		
Label	Prec	Rec	F1	Prec	Rec	F1
E Affirmed	0.88	0.97	0.93	**0.97**	**0.99**	**0.98**
N Negated	0.89	0.79	0.84	**0.98**	**0.97**	**0.97**
G Possible	0.79	0.04	0.08	**0.85**	**0.64**	**0.73**
G Affirmed	0.84	0.96	0.90	**0.96**	**0.98**	**0.97**
E Negated	0.83	0.65	0.73	**0.95**	**0.93**	**0.94**
R Possible	0.28	0.02	0.04	**0.80**	**0.64**	**0.71**

Table 2: Performance results between NegEx baselines and BERT-based models on the original English i2b2 dataset (upper part) and German translation (lower part).

The results of the first two experiments are presented in Table 2 and show various interesting findings: Firstly, NegEx provides impressive results on the affirmed label, good results for negations, and unsatisfying results for the possible label. Moreover, on both datasets, English and German, the BERT-based model outperforms NegEx, on all scores. Additionally, results on the English dataset are always higher than those on the translated dataset. This might be unsurprising as data quality decreases. Finally, the table shows that BERT-based models show a substantial increase in performance for the possible label.

	NegEx			BERT-based		
Label	Prec	Rec	F1	Prec	Rec	F1
N Affirmed	0.96	0.94	0.95	**0.97**	**0.96**	**0.96**
E Negated	0.93	0.96	0.95	**0.97**	**0.98**	**0.97**
G Possible	0.46	0.50	0.48	**0.50**	0.50	**0.50**
E Affirmed	0.85	0.88	0.86	**0.88**	**0.92**	**0.90**
X Negated	0.66	0.89	0.76	**0.86**	**0.95**	**0.90**
4 Possible	0.50	0.18	0.26	**0.61**	**0.38**	**0.47**

Table 3: Performance results on different German medical text sources, namely the original German NegEx (upper part), and Ex4CDS dataset (lower part).

Table 3 presents the performance of the NegEx and the BERT-based model on two German datasets. In the upper part of the table, the results on NegEx-Ger are presented and the results on Ex4CDS are in the lower part. Similarly, as on the translated i2b2 dataset in Table 2, the machine learning model outperforms NegEx. However, this time the performance gain is not so strong anymore. The NegEx-Ger is small and relatively homogeneous (regarding the variety of negations), and NegEx already performs well on the negations. Therefore the machine learning model achieves only a performance boost of two points in F1. In case of possible, the number of examples might be too small to see the benefit of the ML model.

On Ex4CDS data, NegEx already struggles with *negated* (0.76) and performs low in the case of *possible* (0.26) - although the results are much better in comparison to the results on i2b2 (English and German). Here, the machine learning model leads to a performance boost of 14 points for *negated* and 21 points for *possible*.

4 Analysis and Discussion

Our results indicate that we can successfully apply machine translation to generate a German clinical dataset to train a machine learning model with. Most notably, this model can outperform NegEx, which partially already provides satisfying results. While it is important that a negation detection tool for German clinical text needs to run within a hospital infrastructure, it might be questionable if BERT-based approaches might be the right solution, as it requires much more hardware resources than the simple NegEx solution. This is supported by the results on NegEx-Ger, in which the BERT achieves only a minor performance gain. However, as this data is small and homogeneous, the results on Ex4CDS affirm the usage of machine learning, as we achieve a notable performance gain. Note, information about the frequency of each label in the test data is provided in the appendix. As our BERT model was trained on potential suboptimal translations, we analyse some errors in more detail in the following.

4.1 Linguistic Error Analysis

Our analysis focuses on the prediction errors caused by the translation or by differences in the features of the German and English language. Table 7 contains full-text examples illustrating the issues described below.

In various cases, a factuality cue was completely missing in the translation, or the sense of the cue was not preserved (e.g., *to rule out* was translated with *Vorschriften* instead of *ausschließen*). In those cases, NegEx and BERT labeled the instances wrongly as affirmations.

In other cases, we observe that the factuality cues are outside of the original data's entities but in the translation they are placed within the entity markup. That is often correlated with the prediction changing from negation or possible to affirmation. For example, both NegEx and BERT correctly recognized the negated assertion of the original phrase *did not notice [any blood]*, whereas both German models consider the translation *bemerkte [kein Blut]* as affirmed in which the negation cue (*not / kein*) became part of the entity.

For NegEx, a further problem are missing factuality cues in the trigger list. For example, it systematically does not recognize the cue *verleugnen* (one of the possible translations of the word *deny*, which is included in the English NegEx). Additionally, some problems with factuality cues are specific to the German language and require additional handling: (a) German compounds must be written as one word; unfortunately, German NegEx cannot handle cases when a compound consists of words referring to a medical problem and its negation (e.g. *schmerzfrei / pain free*), since it seems not to recognize a factuality cue if it is not written as a separate phrase, (b) cues with umlauts in text such as *aufgelöst* seem not to be recognized, because the umlauts are encoded as *oe* in the German trigger list, (c) missing possible word orders of factuality phrases (e.g. word order might depend on the embedding syntactic structure; e.g. *wurde ausgeschlossen* vs. *ausgeschlossen wurde* in a main vs. subordinate clause).

5 Related Work

Machine Translation for Cross-lingual Learning MT is a popular approach to address the lack of data in cross-lingual learning (Hu et al., 2020; Yarmohammadi et al., 2021). There are two basic options - translating target language data to a well-resourced source language at inference time and applying a model trained in the source language (Asai et al., 2018; Cui et al., 2019), or translating source language training data to the target language, while also projecting any annotations required for training, and then training a model in the target language (Khalil et al., 2019; Kolluru et al., 2022; Frei and Kramer, 2023). Both approaches depend on the quality of the MT system, with translated data potentially suffering from translation or alignment errors (Aminian et al., 2017; Ozaki et al., 2021). While the quality of machine translation for health-related texts has significantly improved (Neves et al., 2022), using MT in the clinical domain remains underexplored, with very few exceptions (Frei and Kramer, 2023).

Factuality Detection Previous research focused mainly on assigning factuality values to events and often framed this task as a multiclass classification problem over a fixed set of uncertainty categories (Rudinger et al., 2018b; Zerva, 2019; Pouran Ben Veyseh et al., 2019; Qian et al., 2019; Bijl de Vroe et al., 2021; Vasilakes et al., 2022). In the biomedical/clinical domain, Uzuner et al. (2011) present the i2b2 dataset for assertion classification, and Thompson et al. (2011) introduce the Genia-MK corpus, where biomedical relations have been annotated with uncertainty values. van Aken et al. (2021) release factuality annotation of 5000 data points sourced from MIMIC. Kilicoglu et al. (2017) introduce a dataset of PubMed abstracts with seven factuality values, and find that a rule-based model is more effective than a supervised machine learning model on this dataset.

6 Conclusion

This work presented a machine learning-based factuality detection for German clinical text. The model was trained on translated i2b2 data and tested, first on the translations and then on other German datasets and outperformed an existing method for German, NegEx. The simple machine translation approach might interest the Non-English clinical text processing community. The model will be made publicly available.

Ethical Considerations

We use the original datasets "as is". Our translations of i2b2 thus reflect any biases of the original dataset and its construction process, as well as biases of the MT models (e.g., rendering gender-neutral English nouns to gendered nouns in German). We use BERT-based PLMs in our experiments, which were pretrained on a large variety of medical source data. Our models may have inherited biases from these pretraining corpora.

Since medical data is highly sensitive with respect to patient-related information, all datasets used in our work are anonymized. The authors of the original datasets (Uzuner et al., 2011; Roller et al., 2022) have stated various measures that prevent collecting sensitive, patient-related data. Therefore, we rule out the possible risk of sensitive content in the data.

Limitations

A key limitation of this work is the dependence on a machine translation system to get high-quality translations and annotation projections of the source language dataset. Depending on the availability of language resources and the quality of the MT model, the translations we use for training and evaluation may be inaccurate, or be affected by translation noise, possibly leading to overly optimistic estimates of model performance. In addition, since the annotation projection is completely automatic, any alignment errors of the MT system will yield inaccurate instances in the target language.

Acknowledgements

This research was supported by the German Research Foundation (DFG, Deutsche Forschungsgemeinschaft) through the project KEEPHA (442445488) and the German Federal Ministry of Education and Research (BMBF) through the projects KIBATIN (16SV9040) and CORA4NLP (01IW20010).

References

Emily Alsentzer, John R Murphy, Willie Boag, Wei-Hung Weng, Di Jin, Tristan Naumann, and Matthew McDermott. 2019. Publicly available clinical bert embeddings. *arXiv preprint arXiv:1904.03323*.

Maryam Aminian, Mohammad Sadegh Rasooli, and Mona Diab. 2017. Transferring semantic roles using translation and syntactic information. In *Proceedings of the Eighth International Joint Conference on Natural Language Processing (Volume 2: Short Papers)*, pages 13–19, Taipei, Taiwan. Asian Federation of Natural Language Processing.

Akari Asai, Akiko Eriguchi, Kazuma Hashimoto, and Yoshimasa Tsuruoka. 2018. Multilingual extractive reading comprehension by runtime machine translation. *ArXiv*, abs/1809.03275.

Sander Bijl de Vroe, Liane Guillou, Miloš Stanojević, Nick McKenna, and Mark Steedman. 2021. Modality and negation in event extraction. In *Proceedings of the 4th Workshop on Challenges and Applications of Automated Extraction of Socio-political Events from Text (CASE 2021)*, pages 31–42, Online. Association for Computational Linguistics.

Wendy W Chapman, Will Bridewell, Paul Hanbury, Gregory F Cooper, and Bruce G Buchanan. 2001. A simple algorithm for identifying negated findings and diseases in discharge summaries. *Journal of biomedical informatics*, 34(5):301–310.

Wendy W Chapman, Dieter Hilert, Sumithra Velupillai, Maria Kvist, Maria Skeppstedt, Brian E Chapman, Michael Conway, Melissa Tharp, Danielle L Mowery, and Louise Deleger. 2013. Extending the negex lexicon for multiple languages. *Studies in health technology and informatics*, 192:677.

Viviana Cotik, Roland Roller, Feiyu Xu, Hans Uszkoreit, Klemens Budde, and Danilo Schmidt. 2016a. Negation detection in clinical reports written in german. In *Proceedings of the Fifth Workshop on Building and Evaluating Resources for Biomedical Text Mining (BioTxtM2016)*, pages 115–124.

Viviana Cotik, Vanesa Stricker, Jorge Vivaldi, and Horacio Rodríguez Hontoria. 2016b. Syntactic methods for negation detection in radiology reports in spanish. In *Proceedings of the 15th Workshop on Biomedical Natural Language Processing, BioNLP 2016: Berlin, Germany, August 12, 2016*, pages 156–165. Association for Computational Linguistics.

Yiming Cui, Wanxiang Che, Ting Liu, Bing Qin, Shijin Wang, and Guoping Hu. 2019. Cross-lingual machine reading comprehension. In *Proceedings of the 2019 Conference on Empirical Methods in Natural Language Processing and the 9th International Joint Conference on Natural Language Processing (EMNLP-IJCNLP)*, pages 1586–1595, Hong Kong, China. Association for Computational Linguistics.

Johann Frei and Frank Kramer. 2023. German medical named entity recognition model and data set creation using machine translation and word alignment: Algorithm development and validation. *JMIR Form Res*, 7:e39077.

Junjie Hu, Sebastian Ruder, Aditya Siddhant, Graham Neubig, Orhan Firat, and Melvin Johnson. 2020. XTREME: A massively multilingual multi-task benchmark for evaluating cross-lingual generalisation. In *Proceedings of the 37th International*

Conference on Machine Learning, volume 119 of *Proceedings of Machine Learning Research*, pages 4411–4421. PMLR.

Marcin Junczys-Dowmunt, Roman Grundkiewicz, Tomasz Dwojak, Hieu Hoang, Kenneth Heafield, Tom Neckermann, Frank Seide, Ulrich Germann, Alham Fikri Aji, Nikolay Bogoychev, André F. T. Martins, and Alexandra Birch. 2018. Marian: Fast neural machine translation in C++. In *Proceedings of ACL 2018, System Demonstrations*, pages 116–121, Melbourne, Australia. Association for Computational Linguistics.

Talaat Khalil, Kornel Kiełczewski, Georgios Christos Chouliaras, Amina Keldibek, and Maarten Versteegh. 2019. Cross-lingual intent classification in a low resource industrial setting. In *Proceedings of the 2019 Conference on Empirical Methods in Natural Language Processing and the 9th International Joint Conference on Natural Language Processing (EMNLP-IJCNLP)*, pages 6419–6424, Hong Kong, China. Association for Computational Linguistics.

Aditya Khandelwal and Suraj Sawant. 2019. NegBERT: a transfer learning approach for negation detection and scope resolution. *arXiv preprint arXiv:1911.04211*.

Halil Kilicoglu, Graciela Rosemblat, and Thomas C. Rindflesch. 2017. Assigning factuality values to semantic relations extracted from biomedical research literature. *PLoS ONE*, 12.

Madeleine Kittner, Mario Lamping, Damian T Rieke, Julian Götze, Bariya Bajwa, Ivan Jelas, Gina Rüter, Hanjo Hautow, Mario Sänger, Maryam Habibi, et al. 2021. Annotation and initial evaluation of a large annotated german oncological corpus. *JAMIA open*, 4(2):ooab025.

Keshav Kolluru, Muqeeth Mohammed, Shubham Mittal, Soumen Chakrabarti, and Mausam . 2022. Alignment-augmented consistent translation for multilingual open information extraction. In *Proceedings of the 60th Annual Meeting of the Association for Computational Linguistics (Volume 1: Long Papers)*, pages 2502–2517, Dublin, Ireland. Association for Computational Linguistics.

Luise Modersohn, Stefan Schulz, Christina Lohr, and Udo Hahn. 2022. Grascco - the first publicly shareable, multiply-alienated german clinical text corpus. *Studies in health technology and informatics*, 296:66—72.

Mariana Neves, Antonio Jimeno Yepes, Amy Siu, Roland Roller, Philippe Thomas, Maika Vicente Navarro, Lana Yeganova, Dina Wiemann, Giorgio Maria Di Nunzio, Federica Vezzani, Christel Gerardin, Rachel Bawden, Darryl Johan Estrada, Salvador Lima-lopez, Eulalia Farre-maduel, Martin Krallinger, Cristian Grozea, and Aurelie Neveol. 2022. Findings of the WMT 2022 biomedical translation shared task: Monolingual clinical case reports. In *Proceedings of the Seventh Conference on Machine Translation (WMT)*, pages 694–723, Abu Dhabi, United Arab Emirates (Hybrid). Association for Computational Linguistics.

Hiroaki Ozaki, Gaku Morio, Terufumi Morishita, and Toshinori Miyoshi. 2021. Project-then-transfer: Effective two-stage cross-lingual transfer for semantic dependency parsing. In *Proceedings of the 16th Conference of the European Chapter of the Association for Computational Linguistics: Main Volume*, pages 2586–2594, Online. Association for Computational Linguistics.

Amir Pouran Ben Veyseh, Thien Huu Nguyen, and Dejing Dou. 2019. Graph based neural networks for event factuality prediction using syntactic and semantic structures. In *Proceedings of the 57th Annual Meeting of the Association for Computational Linguistics*, pages 4393–4399, Florence, Italy. Association for Computational Linguistics.

Zhong Qian, Peifeng Li, Qiaoming Zhu, and Guodong Zhou. 2019. Document-level event factuality identification via adversarial neural network. In *Proceedings of the 2019 Conference of the North American Chapter of the Association for Computational Linguistics: Human Language Technologies, Volume 1 (Long and Short Papers)*, pages 2799–2809, Minneapolis, Minnesota. Association for Computational Linguistics.

Roland Roller, Aljoscha Burchardt, Nils Feldhus, Laura Seiffe, Klemens Budde, Simon Ronicke, and Bilgin Osmanodja. 2022. An annotated corpus of textual explanations for clinical decision support. In *Proceedings of the Thirteenth Language Resources and Evaluation Conference*, pages 2317–2326.

Rachel Rudinger, Aaron Steven White, and Benjamin Van Durme. 2018a. Neural models of factuality. *CoRR*, abs/1804.02472.

Rachel Rudinger, Aaron Steven White, and Benjamin Van Durme. 2018b. Neural models of factuality. In *Proceedings of the 2018 Conference of the North American Chapter of the Association for Computational Linguistics: Human Language Technologies, Volume 1 (Long Papers)*, pages 731–744, New Orleans, Louisiana. Association for Computational Linguistics.

Manjil Shrestha. 2021. Development of a language model for medical domain. master thesis, Hochschule Rhein-Waal.

Jörg Steffen and Josef van Genabith. 2021. TransIns: Document translation with markup reinsertion. In *Proceedings of the 2021 Conference on Empirical Methods in Natural Language Processing: System Demonstrations*, pages 28–34. Association for Computational Linguistics.

Paul Thompson, Raheel Nawaz, John McNaught, and Sophia Ananiadou. 2011. Enriching a biomedical event corpus with meta-knowledge annotation. *BMC Bioinformatics*, 12:393 – 393.

Özlem Uzuner, Brett R South, Shuying Shen, and Scott L DuVall. 2011. 2010 i2b2/va challenge on concepts, assertions, and relations in clinical text. *Journal of the American Medical Informatics Association*, 18(5):552–556.

Betty van Aken, Ivana Trajanovska, A. Siu, M. Mayrdorfer, Klemens Budde, and Alexander Loeser. 2021. Assertion detection in clinical notes: Medical language models to the rescue? *Proceedings of the Second Workshop on Natural Language Processing for Medical Conversations*.

Jake Vasilakes, Chrysoula Zerva, Makoto Miwa, and Sophia Ananiadou. 2022. Learning disentangled representations of negation and uncertainty. In *Proceedings of the 60th Annual Meeting of the Association for Computational Linguistics (Volume 1: Long Papers)*, pages 8380–8397, Dublin, Ireland. Association for Computational Linguistics.

Mahsa Yarmohammadi, Shijie Wu, Marc Marone, Haoran Xu, Seth Ebner, Guanghui Qin, Yunmo Chen, Jialiang Guo, Craig Harman, Kenton Murray, Aaron Steven White, Mark Dredze, and Benjamin Van Durme. 2021. Everything is all it takes: A multipronged strategy for zero-shot cross-lingual information extraction. In *Proceedings of the 2021 Conference on Empirical Methods in Natural Language Processing*, pages 1950–1967, Online and Punta Cana, Dominican Republic. Association for Computational Linguistics.

Chrysoula Zerva. 2019. *Automatic Identification of Textual Uncertainty*. Ph.D. thesis, University of Manchester.

A Appendix

The main contribution of this short paper was to show that it is possible to develop a machine learning-based factuality detection for non-English, without training examples in the given language - just by using a local machine translation. In addition, we would like to present a small 'bonus' experiment, which did not fit into the main article anymore. More precisely, we wanted to find out how the performance of such a model changes if data in a reasonable size is available for training. The additional experiment is presented in Appendix A.1, followed by some additional text examples for the linguistic error analysis and some further information.

A.1 Additional Experiment

The additional experiment has been conducted with the **BRONCO150** (Kittner et al., 2021) dataset, a relatively large corpus originating from 150 German oncological de-identified discharge summaries and annotated for multiple tasks, including factuality detection. For our experiment, we consider only the target entities *diagnosis*. Similar to Ex4CDS, it has various factuality values, which we mapped to our three target labels, namely *possible future* and *speculation* to *possible*. Note, BRONCO150 contains various fragmented entities (entities split into two to three parts). For our experimental setup, we merged entity fragments and considered only those sentences with not more than 50 characters between the fragments.

The label distribution of the obtained BRONCO150 data and the distribution of the other datasets from the main paper are presented in Table 5.

First, we run the same experiment as presented in Table 3, also on BRONCO150 data. The results using our FactualMedBERT-DE model are presented in Table 4.

	NegEx			BERT-based		
Label	Prec	Rec	F1	Prec	Rec	F1
N Affirmed	0.96	0.94	0.95	**0.97**	**0.96**	**0.96**
E Negated	0.93	0.96	0.95	**0.97**	**0.98**	**0.97**
G Possible	0.46	0.50	0.48	**0.50**	0.50	**0.50**
E Affirmed	0.85	0.88	0.86	**0.88**	**0.92**	**0.90**
X Negated	0.66	0.89	0.76	**0.86**	**0.95**	**0.90**
4 Possible	0.50	0.18	0.26	**0.61**	**0.38**	**0.47**
B Affirmed	0.87	0.96	0.91	**0.88**	**0.97**	**0.92**
R Negated	0.69	0.66	0.68	**0.75**	**0.80**	**0.77**
O Possible	0.68	0.24	0.36	**0.73**	**0.25**	**0.37**

Table 4: Performance results on different German medical text sources, namely the original German NegEx (upper part), the Ex4CDS dataset (middle) and BRONCO150 (lower part).

	Affirmed	Negated	Possible
2010 i2b2/VA	7603	2305	595
Ex4CDS	892	225	179
NegEx-Ger	645	443	26
BRONCO150	3179	331	523

Table 5: Support numbers in the evaluation sets for each processed dataset.

Next, we train two additional models, one on a BRONCO150 training split and a second using the BRONCO150 train together with the translated i2b2 data. Both models were initialized from the same model as that of FactualMedBERT-DE. Table 6 compares our FactualMedBERT-DE against the other two BERT-based models on the different datasets.

Brief discussion: The results show that each model performs best on the data of the same dataset

Model	Label	2010 i2b2/VA Prec	Rec	F1	NegEx-Ger Prec	Rec	F1	Ex4CDS Prec	Rec	F1	BRONCO150 Prec	Rec	F1
FactualMedBERT-DE	Affirmed	0.96	0.98	**0.97**	0.97	0.96	0.96	0.88	0.92	0.90	0.88	0.97	0.92
	Negated	0.95	0.93	**0.94**	0.97	0.98	0.97	0.86	0.95	0.90	0.76	0.79	0.78
	Possible	0.80	0.64	**0.71**	0.50	0.50	0.50	0.61	0.38	0.47	0.68	0.19	0.30
BRONCO150-BERT	Affirmed	0.88	0.95	0.92	0.97	0.92	0.94	0.90	0.90	0.90	0.96	0.96	0.96
	Negated	0.95	0.67	0.79	0.97	0.97	0.97	0.89	0.88	0.88	0.95	0.83	**0.89**
	Possible	0.42	0.47	0.44	0.28	0.65	0.39	0.56	0.59	0.58	0.76	0.84	**0.80**
i2b2+BRONCO150 BERT	Affirmed	0.94	0.98	0.96	0.98	0.95	0.96	0.90	0.94	**0.92**	0.95	0.98	**0.97**
	Negated	0.96	0.91	0.93	0.98	0.97	0.97	0.90	0.91	**0.91**	0.93	0.83	0.88
	Possible	0.82	0.54	0.65	0.39	0.73	**0.51**	0.70	0.54	**0.61**	0.85	0.74	0.79

Table 6: Performance results of three BERT models trained on translated i2b2 (FactualMedBERT-DE), BRONCO150 and 2010 i2b2 + BRONCO150, respectively. The models were evaluated on different German medical text sources, namely our translated i2b2 2010 test set, the German NegEx, the Ex4CDS dataset and BRONCO150 test set. For each dataset, best per-label F1-performances are displayed in **bold**.

Issue	English	German
missing trigger in translation	The patient radiated down her left arm associated with some nausea, no <E> shortness of breath </E>, cough, vomiting, diarrhea.	*Die Patientin strahlte in Verbindung mit Übelkeit, <E> Atemnot, </E> Husten, Erbrechen, Durchfall nach unten.*
incorrect trigger translation	*RULE OUT FOR <E> myocardial infarction </E>*	*VORSCHRIFTEN FÜR <E> den Myokardinfarkt </E>*
trigger in the translation is outside of the entity	*She did not notice <E> any blood / urine / emesis / stool in the bed </E>.*	Sie bemerkte <E> kein Blut / Urin / Erbrechen / Stuhl im Bett. </E>
missing of a possible trigger translation in NegEx-Ger	*Denies <E> fevers </E>, pleuritic chest pain or cough.*	*Verleugnet <E> Fieber, </E> pleuritische Brustschmerzen oder Husten.*
missing of translated compounds of type Entity + trigger in NegEx-Ger	*She was <E> pain </E> free on the day of discharge .*	*Sie war am Tag der Entlassung <E> schmerzfrei. </E>*
missing trigger phrase in NegEx-Ger due to word order	*He then presented to Mass. Mental Health Center where he ruled out for <E> an myocardial infarction </E> by enzymes and electrocardiograms.*	*Er überreichte dann der Messe. Mental Health Center, wo er für <E> einen Myokardinfarkt </E> durch Enzyme und Elektrokardiogramme ausgeschlossen wurde.*
different encoding of umlauts in text and NegEx-Ger	*<E>the hypernatremia</E> fully resolved when he resumed eating on his own and had access to free water .*	*<E>Die Hypernatrimie</E> vollständig aufgeloest, als er wieder essen auf eigene Faust und hatte Zugang zu freien Wasser.*

Table 7: Examples of the potential causes for prediction errors. The analysis focuses on the translation problems and the differences between the German and English language. The tags <E></E> enclose the entities, the factuality triggers are underlined. The original English examples originate from the i2b2 data.

- FactualMedBERT-DE on the translated i2b2 data and BRONCO150-BERT on the BRONCO150 data - this is no surprise. Moreover, the results indicate that the mixed model (i2b2+BRONCO150-BERT) performs generally well on all datasets, therefore might be the model of choice. However, it is important to note, that BRONCO150 has got an unusual label distribution. While *affirmed* is the most frequent label in all datasets, BRONCO has got an unusually high frequency of *possible* labels, which is connected to the way labels were mapped to the three final actuality labels. However, this might influence the actuality classification of other datasets.

A.2 BERT Setup

For BERT, we used epochs number of 3/4 (for English and German BERT, respectively), a batch size of 32, a dropout rate of 0.1, and a learning rate of $1e-5$.

A.3 Examples of Linguistic Error Analysis

Our analysis focuses on the potential sources for false predictions, in particular on causes related to the translation or the differences in the features of the German and English languages. Table 7 presents full-text examples from the original and translated data. For a detailed description of the possible issues see Section 4.1.

Linking Danish Parser Output to a Central Word Repository - From Morphosemantic Disambiguation to Unique Identifiers

Eckhard Bick
Department of Language, Culture, History and Communication
University of Southern Denmark
eckhard.bick@gmail.com

Abstract

This paper describes and evaluates a grammatically informed linking system that assigns unique identifiers (UIDs) from a central word repository (COR) to running Danish text. To do so, the system's algorithm matches the annotation of a morphosyntactic and semantic parser (DanGram) to corresponding information in the word registry, using a scoring method and disambiguated grammatical tags such as lemma, POS, inflection and semantic class. In addition to ordinary words, the linker also assigns UIDs to the parts of compounds and multi-word expressions. For mixed Danish text, the linker assigned correct UIDs to 97.8% of all non-name, non-number words. Linking failures were caused either by parser errors (0.3%) or COR gaps (1.9%) rather than by the matching tool itself (< 0.1%).

1 Introduction

Despite ongoing advances in natural language processing (NLP), integrating different resources remains a recalcitrant problem, not least due to differences in tokenization, lemmatization and tag definitions and granularity. While the latter has been addressed – at least at the morphosyntactic level – by the Universal Dependencies initiative (e.g. Nivre, 2015), resource differences in terms of lexical granularity are often overlooked, even in well-resourced languages. Thus, it is not trivial to which degree differences in etymology, pronunciation and meaning, inflection paradigms or spelling variation should warrant separate lexicon entries or – at the tagger/parser level – different lemmas or sub-categorization. The problem is compounded by the fact that state-of-the-art systems, while getting more and more accurate, still inherit a predefined and unquestioned lemma granularity from their training data, making it difficult to mount a language technology (LT) pipeline with modules created with different training data, or different morphological analyzers. A possible solution is agreeing – for a given language – on a shared lexical inventory of both lemmas and inflected forms, with unique identifiers (UIDs) for each entry. For Danish, the COR word repository (Dideriksen et al., 2022) is such a resource. However, while conceptually sound, the COR registry itself is still only half of (LT) heaven, as long as it isn't aligned with other resources and shared between tools. Notably, taggers, parsers and semantic analyzers need to be able to link their analyses to such a central repository. In this paper, working with output from the DanGram parser[1], we will show how different morphological and semantic tags from a parser pipeline can be used to link a wordform to a unique identifier, handling matching and disambiguation in an integrated fashion.

2 COR

COR (Det Centrale Ordregister) is a new lexical resource that assigns unique IDs to Danish words[2]. The resource is being developed by the Danish Language Council (Dansk Sprognævn[3], DSN) in cooperation with the Danish Society for Language and Literature (DSL[4]) and Copenhagen University's Center for Language Technology (CST[5]). In its first, level-1 edition, COR covers the content of the official Danish spelling dictionary[6]. Each word ID (1a-c) consists of dot-separated parts - a first part for the lemma and a second part for inflection. A third part is reserved for spelling variation[7].

[1] https://visl.sdu.dk/visl/da/parsing/automatic/parse.php

[2] The targeted word classes are the closed and inflecting POS classes, with predictable limitations for proper nouns, numerical expressions, abbreviations and punctuation-based "words" (e.g %, smileys), as well as dialectal and spoken forms.

[3] https://dsn.dk

[4] https://dsl.dk

[5] https://cst.ku.dk/english/

[6] https://dsn.dk/ordboeger/retskrivningsordbogen/

[7] In principle, this includes historical variants and current spelling made obsolete by a future spelling reform

Proceedings of the 19th Conference on Natural Language Processing (KONVENS 2023), pages 93–101
September 18–22, 2023. ©2023 Association for Computational Linguistics

```
1a) COR.37309.200.01 hoste (to cough)
    vb, inf, act
1b) COR.37309.203.01 hoster (coughs)
    vb, pr, act
1c) COR.38283.200.01 hoste (to host)
    vb, inf, act
```

Homographs are regarded as distinct based on surface markers rather than etymology or semantics proper. Thus, distinguishing criteria are part of speech (POS), grammatical gender (2a-b), pronunciation (1c with English [o]) and differences in inflection paradigms, e.g. different plural forms or not allowing a plural at all. Here, traditional etymological or sense distinctions are often captured implicitly rather than explicitly. For instance, the missing plural is typical for +mass (-countable) semantic classes such as substances, liquids and materials. Thus, because the word *træ* ('tree') does not inflect in the plural when meaning 'wood', most Danish tree names have a separate COR entry as a type of wood (3a-b).

```
2a) COR.47455.110.01 brud (bride)
    n, utr , sg, idf
2b) COR.48668.120.01 brud (rupture)
    n, neu, sg, idf
3a) COR.56312.120.01 bøgetræ (beech tree)
    n, neu, sg, idf
3b) COR.59335.120.01 bøgetræ (beech wood)
    n, neu, sg, idf
```

In addition to these implicit semantic distinctions, COR does have a semantic dimension, as it offers short definitions for ambiguous words, illustrating the semantic reach of a given entry. Also, at level 2, external semantic resources can be linked to COR (Nimb et al., 2022), for instance the existing Danish wordnet, DanNet (e.g. Pedersen et al., 2009) or the Danish Framenet[8] (Bick, 2011). However, as will be discussed in more detail in section 4, sense mapping between such resources and a primarily morphological resource like COR is not always a one-to-one mapping, but may involve a many-to-one sense lumping.

3 DanGram

DanGram is a rule-based, modular parsing system, using the Constraint Grammar (CG) formalism (Bick and Didriksen, 2015). For progressive linguistic annotation levels, contextual rules are used to map and disambiguate different types of token-based tags. Input to the morphosyntactic CG is provided by a pattern-based tokenizer and a lexicon-based morphological analyzer. The former establishes multi-word expressions (MWEs) covering e.g. names and complex equivalents to function words. The latter handles inflection, affixation and compound analysis[9]. After morphosyntactic annotation, another CG module assigns dependency relations based on syntactic function tags. At higher levels, extensive semantic lexica are used to support rules for named entity recognition (NER) and word sense disambiguation (WSD), as well as framenet structures and semantic role annotation.

In native format, each token will receive a readings line containing tags for the different annotation levels in space-separated, type-marked fields, or, in export format, as xml attributes. For instance, the lemma field is marked by a [...] bracket, syntactic function by a @-prefix and semantic roles by '§'. Apart from lemma, POS and inflection, the relevant fields for identifying the correct UID in COR are the semantic fields, in angular brackets, e.g. <H...> (human classes), <tool> or <food>, as well as framenet tags of the type <fn:know> or <fn:increase>.

4 ID Linking

4.1 Tag conversion

The linking program described here has a two-way purpose - on the one hand making it possible to enrich DanGram output with lexical information from future resources built around COR (e.g. dictionaries or encyclopedias), and on the other supporting users who want to build text processing applications around COR or to apply their COR-linked ontologies to e.g. news text for information retrieval by using the DanGram parser. The new tool has been implemented as an independent module, to be run after DanGram and working with the output of the parser as is, adding additional COR tags for matchable words. These tags colntain the COR identifier number (UID) as well as the lemma, POS and inflection tags provided by COR for this ID, with the same uppercase, English abbreviations used by DanGram itself, for better comparability. As a default, the inserted tags have the format <UID:lemma:tags>, with dots between tags, e.g. <COR.49032.115.01:lærer:N.UTR.S.DEF.GEN>

[8]https://framenet.dk

[9]For maximal (productive) coverage, the analyzer works with lemmas and morphemes, not a closed fullform list.

for the word *lærerens* ('the teacher's'). If the UID is the only desired information, DanGram tagging can be ignored, and the UID appended to tokens in running text, e.g. ***katten_40150.111 åd_38929.206 musen_74798.111*** (the cat ate the mouse).

In principle, a simple tag filter would allow the Linker to work with other parsers than DanGram, as long as they provide the same type and granularity of tagging. However, while the linker itself is robust enough to work with (filtered) input from other parsers, the quality of the latter would, obviously, have a bearing on the final result. Thus, a lack of tag types, in particular an absence of semantic, compound and MWE analysis, would not break the linker, but negatively affect performance, as would using a parser with a lower tagging accuracy than DanGram for the standard tags (POS/inflection).

It should be noted that even with a correct UID link, parser and COR tags will not necessarily match one-on-one. For instance, POS-mapping may be many-to-one (e.g. 3 DanGram pronoun classes, but only 1 in COR), and DanGram lemmas may have a number extension, superfluous in COR, given the latter's UIDs. Also, DanGram marks "not genitive" as nominative, while COR only specifies the genitive. The automatic linker program has to be robust enough to work in spite of such mismatches.

4.2 The matching algorithm

The basic linking algorithm first looks up each non-number, non-punctuation token in the COR database, acquiring a list of possible UIDs with their respective lemmas and inflection tags. Next, for each UID item on the list, the linker tries to match lemma and tags to equivalent tags found in the DanGram annotation for the word in question, computing a matching score. The reading with the highest score will get its UID selected and linked. In the straight-forward cases, POS and/or inflection will decide the issue. The word form *vise*, for instance, has four readings, and three meanings, in both COR and DanGram (DG), with matching lemma and POS, and a few morphological extra-tags in DanGram: NOM (nominative) and the portmanteau tags nG and nD for under-specified gender and definiteness, respectively[10].

```
4a) COR.30363.200.01, vise, V, INF, AKT
    DG: [vise] V INF AKT ('show')
4b) COR.46620.110.01, vise, N, UTR, S, IDF
    DG: [vise] N UTR S IDF NOM ('tune')
4c) COR.16117.302.01, vis, ADJ, S, DEF
    DG: [vis] ADJ nG S DEF NOM ('wise')
4d) COR.16117.303.01, vis, ADJ, P
    DG: [vis] ADJ nG P nD ('wise')
```

In the case of an adjective singular reading, for instance (e.g *den vise mand* – 'a wise man'), the correct (third) UID will receive 3 points - for lemma, pos and number -, while the adjective plural reading (fourth) will get only 2 points, for lemma and pos. The noun reading (second) will get 1 point, for number, and the verb reading (first) will fail on all tags, scoring 0. The inserted linking tag will then contain the highest-scoring UID and its COR tags.

4.3 Homograph levels and COR adaptation

The case of *vise* ('show', 'tune', 'wise') could be called a level-1 homograph in the sense that its meaning can be resolved by making use of lemma, POS, grammatical gender and inflection only. However, COR also contains about 400 cases of word-forms that are level-2 homographs, with two (or more) meanings that can be differentiated only by resorting to their pronunciation or inflectional paradigm as a whole (cp. section 2). As neither of the latter is marked in writing, but rather a manifestation of what is really a semantic feature (such as plural-less inflection paradigms for +mass nouns), the linker program has to make use of semantic clues provided and contextually disambiguated by the parser[11]. For about half of the level-2 homographs, DanGram itself distinguishes between two (or more) numbered sub-lemmas based on etymology or major meaning differences matching the COR distinction. In these cases, DanGram's semantic tags are simply bound to the individual sub-lemmas, as in the three noun options in the readings cohort for *ret* in (5).

```
(5)
"ret" <aquant> ADV ('rather')
"ret" <jshape> <jappro> ADJ
    ('right', 'straight')
"ret-1" <f-right> <conv>
    ('right [to]', '[the] law')
"ret-2" <food-c-h> N ('dish')
"ret-3" <inst> N ('court')
```

[10] In context, DanGram will specify these through agreement rules, but they still won't match a COR tag.

[11] Pronunciation variation without a difference in meaning (e.g. regional variation) does not lead to different word IDs in COR

```
"rette" <vt> V IMP ('correct!')
```

However, even without a sub-lemma, the remaining COR homographs can be matched, too - because DanGram in these cases assigns (and disambiguates!) the different semantic class tag on the same lemma. This is the case for the adjective *large*, which means 'big' with an English pronunciation (semantic class <jsize>), and 'generous' with a French pronunciation (semantic class <jpsych>), or the verb *hænge* ('hang'), which changes past tense inflection depending on transitivity and meaning. Here, the linker exploits DanGram's framenet tags, distinguishing between the intransitive <fn:spatial_configuration> (past tense *hang*) and the transitive <fn:put_spatial> (past tense *hængte*)[12]. For the linker to be able to use level-2 distinctions, however, they had to be entered into the COR database manually[13]. Thus, the COR version used by our linker program has been "lexicographically" enriched with additional information/tagging[14], adding DanGram sub-lemmas and their semantic classes (6), or just the latter (7), to all level-2 homographs in COR. These will then be matched to DanGram output by the linking algorithm in the same fashion as ordinary tags.

```
6a) COR.56686.110.01,brok-1,<sick>,N...
    ('hernia')
6b) COR.55539.110.01,brok-2,<sem-s>,N...
    ('complaining')
7a) COR.71663.120.01,marsvin,<Aich>,N...
    ('porpoise')
7b) COR.77141.120.01,marsvin,<Azo>,N...
    ('guinea pig')
```

The word ret (5) is an example where a three-way lemma distinction in DanGram has to be matched onto a two-way distinction in COR[15]. In this case, the fused sub-lemmas (*ret-2* and *ret-3*) are not used, because COR's lemma slot is a 1-item slot. Still, the distinction (and the link) will work based on semantic tags alone (8b).

```
8a) COR.43157.110.01,ret-1,
    <f-right><conv><f-cog>, N ...
    ('right [to]','law','[being] right')
8b) COR.43153.110.01,ret,
    <inst><food-c-h>, N ... ('dish')
```

4.4 Multi-part tokens

A special challenge for the linker were multi-part tokens with no equivalent entry in COR. Rather than ignoring such tokens as unlinkable, we opted to perform part-by-part, multiple linking, in order to facilitate NLP tasks such as machine translation, multi-lingual alignment or lemma-driven corpus searches.

For Danish, this issue is of particular importance, as productive compounding is an important aspect of Danish morphology. The process may involve morphological changes for the first part of a compound, such as stemming or the insertion of fuge letters, and a hyphen is only used in special cases. Over 10% of Danish tokens in running text involve compounding or affixation. In our evaluation text (section 5), 1.8% of tokens were words with a live compound analysis and no direct match in COR. An additional 1.4% were words without a COR match, but with a compound lexicon entry in DanGram.

In addition to compounds, tokenization can introduce multi-word expressions (MWEs) by fusing words that syntactically or semantically function as close-knit units. Lexically, an MWE makes sense where its meaning is not transparent from its parts. On the other hand, MWEs create compatibility issues, as there are no authorized closed lists available, and many NLP systems perform tokenization simply by space separation. Therefore, part-by-part linking is useful, as it allows the end user to easily (re)create fully COR-linked "space tokens" by splitting DanGram's MWEs in the Linker's output.

Both DanGram and COR contain closed-class MWEs, but DanGram contains more (table 2), because they help the parser to simplify syntactic

[12] Depending on the semantic type of linked object, prepositions and particles, DanGram distinguishes between nine further framenet meanings for this verb, all of which are grouped into the two COR meanings by the linker in a many-to-one mapping.

[13] It is a matter of interpretation, if this is seen as an enrichment of COR, or as a lookup-filter that is really a part of the linker program. As new words and loan words tend to enter a language with one, well-defined meaning, future level-2 homograph additions to core are unlikely, but they would need to be treated manually, with a linguist selecting those DanGram features necessary to make the homograph distinctions in COR.

[14] This way, for all non-trivial cases (i.e. where POS feature matching is not sufficient), the decision of what constitutes a linking match - and which features to target - has been taken by a linguist. In other words: what is automatic, is not the meaning/definition, but the matching

[15] In principle, DanGram could be used to enrich COR in such cases. However, the two resources are maintained independently and COR has a policy of following the official Danish spelling dictionary and not implementing purely semantic distinctions without pronunciation or paradigmatic support. Therefore, feedback to COR resulting from the work on our DanGram linker has so far only targeted simple errors and inconsistencies in the resource

structure; *i hvert fald* ('in any case'), for instance, is a shared MWE, while *i eftermiddags* ('yesterday afternoon') is DanGram-only. Open-class MWEs are very rare in COR and are limited to a few foreign expressions (e.g. *quiche lorraine*), place names (*Sankt Petersborg*) and first parts of hyphen-compounds (*dag til dag-levering* 'day-to-day delivery'). DanGram, on the other hand, annotates all complex named entities as MWE (e.g. person/company names, institutions and addresses), as well as anatomical expressions, species names and foreign MWE nouns based on pattern matches (e.g. when including English colour words). Because of this discrepancy between DanGram and COR, the linker is set to ignore MWE names without a complete COR match, as well as other "live" (i.e. heuristic, pattern-based) MWEs[16].

For the linker program, we used the same core strategy for matching compounds and MWEs: Failing a full match, the multi-part token is split into its components[17], which are then looked up in COR individually, using a prioritized matching order. COR contains about 8,000 separate UIDs for compound first parts and 75 prefix tags, which will get the highest priority in compound look-ups (COMP for the former, in 9a and 9c, or PREF for the latter). After that, first parts are looked up with the lemma (or sublemma) and POS provided by DanGram (9b). Failing that, or if DanGram only provides "prefix" as POS, they will be looked up as nouns, adjective or without POS, in that order. Second parts are looked up using the inflected fullform stripped of the first part, plus the provided part-lemma (or, in 9c, sublemma). For Danish compounds, the second part inherits POS, inflection tags and semantics from the overall analysis of the word, so ordinary tag scoring (cp. section 4.1) can be used (e.g. P in 9a, DEF in 9b and the <act-d>[18] semantic tag in 9c). For first parts, no separate semantic tag is provided by DanGram, so in a few cases (where there is polysemy but no sublemma), there is a theoretical risk of unresolved ambiguity.

[16]Using DanGram's <heur> tag to block part-by-part matching attempts for these MWEs.

[17]In the absence of a hyphen or space separator, we used DanGram's compound analysis, which provides first and second lemmas (or sublemmas), normalizing first parts as lemmas, independently of their morphological manifestation (cp. fuge-s in 9b and 9c).

[18]The action tag <act-d> represents one of several meanings of brud-2, each linked to another semantic tag and disambiguated by DanGram. In the modified COR entry all options are listed, and a match for any one of them will select *brud-2* ('rupture' etc.) rather than *brud-1* ('bride', 'weasel')

COR link tags for compounds are added to DanGram output in the same fashion as for single words, but with one, consecutively numbered, link tag for each part:

```
9a) havvindmøller  [havvindmølle]
('offshore turbine' - 'sea+windmill')
<1:COR.59371.129.01:hav:N.NEU.#COMP>
<2:COR.88335.112.01:vindmølle:N.UTR.#P.IDF>
<N:hav+vindmølle> <good-compound> <build>
    N UTR #P IDF NOM

9b) nervøsitetsindikatoren
[nervøsitetsindikator]
('fear gauge' - 'nervousness+indicator')
<1:COR.85108.110.01:nervøsitet:N.UTR.S.IDF>
<2:COR.98639.111.01:indikator:N.UTR.S.#DEF>
<N:nervøsitet~s+indikator> <good-compound>
    <ac> N UTR S #DEF NOM

9c) ægteskabsbrud [ægteskabsbrud]
('adultery' - 'marriage+infringement')
<1:COR.43176.129.01:ægteskab:N.NEU.#COMP>
<2:COR.48668.120.01:brud: <f-phys>.
    <event>.#<act-d>.<Lh>.N.NEU.S.IDF>
<N:ægteskab~s+brud-2> #<act-d>
    N NEU S IDF NOM
```

If one or more compound parts do not have a corresponding entry in COR at all (i.e. not even with a different POS), a dummy ID '0' and a dummy tag string 'X' is used instead. For noun or root parts, such gaps are relatively rare, but may occur, if the part in question is itself a compound (10a, *børne|litteratur* – 'child literature') or an MWE (***en=til=en****-programmet* – 'the one-on-one program'). A more serious problem is COR's limited coverage of prefixes (75 entries) and suffixes (6 entries). As long as the missing affix exists as a full-word entry, this will be used as a fall-back, but that is not possible for some otherwise quite productive prefixes like *special-* ('special', 10b) or suffixes like *-mæssig* ('-related', 10c).

```
10a) børnelitteraturfestival [=]
('child literature festival')
<1:COR.0:børnelitteratur:X>
<2:COR.97204.110.01:festival:N.UTR.S.IDF>
<N:børnelitteratur+festival> <occ>
N UTR S IDF NOM

10b) specialgeotekniske [special..nisk]
('specialized geotechnical')
<1:COR.0:special:X>
```

```
<2:COR.22830.302.01:geoteknisk:ADJ.S.DEF>
<F:special+geoteknisk> <jdomain>
ADJ nG P DEF NOM

10c) momsmæssig [momsmæssig]
('VAT-related')
<1:COR.41058.119.01:moms:N.UTR.COMP>
<2:COR.0:mæssig:X>
<N:moms+mæssig><jtype> ADJ UTR S IDF NOM
```

Unless they match as a whole (11a), MWEs are also looked up part by part (11c). But unlike compounds, there is no lemma or POS available for MWE parts, only the individual tokens from the MWE chain. Also, unlike English noun chains, Danish MWEs have a more varied (and un-tagged) internal syntactic structure, so it is unsafe to let the last part inherit POS or other tags from the MWE as a whole. Our matching algorithm has to reflect this lack of (safe) information. Safest are the separate "in-MWE" UID entries listed by COR for some words (270). Although the MWEs themselves are not provided in these "in-MWE" entries, there is no COR ambiguity across MWEs, so if an MWE matches such an entry, it is assumed to be a correct link, even if the string also exists in COR as a full word. The "in-MWE" entry *rette*[19], for instance, can be used for the 2nd part of the MWE *med rette* ('justifiably', literally 'with right'), discarding the verb infinitive reading 'to correct' (11b).

```
11a) frem=for [=] ('rather than')
<COR.04976.930.01:frem=for:MWE>
<complex> PRP

11b) med=rette [=] ('justifiably')
<1:COR.04087.960.01:med:MWE-PART>
<2:COR.04080.960.01:rette:MWE-PART>
<complex> ADV

11c) i=stedet=for [=] ('instead of')
<1:COR.00852.880.01:i:PRP>
<2:COR.44318.121.01:sted:N.NEU.S.DEF>
<3:COR.00093.880.01:for:PRP>
<complex> PRP
```

If no "in-MWE" entry is found, the linker then looks for ordinary entries (11c), beginning with prepositions and articles, followed by other function word classes, and finally the content word classes, nouns first. As an exception, adjective matches are prioritized higher than nouns for first parts, because Danish NP word order places adjectives to the left of nouns. This matching hierarchy correctly handled the typical adverbial MWEs of the type PRP+N+PRP (e.g. *i stedet* for -'instead of'), but failed for about sixty[20] more idiosyncratic closed-class MWEs, where one (or sometimes two) parts were POS-ambiguous and resolved incorrectly, e.g. *om* in the MWE conjunction *om ikke* ('if not'), where the ordinary POS hierarchy would have chosen a preposition reading for om rather than the correct conjunction reading. This was solved by adding a small POS lookup table for problematic closed-class MWEs. The table is used after "in-MWE" matches, but before ordinary POS matches.

5 Evaluation

To evaluate both overall performance and linking accuracy, we generated random excerpts from DSL's general period corpus *Korpus 2010*[21], covering five different text types for lexical diversity: blog, parliament, special interest home page, general news and financial news, with 11,099 raw tokens in all. The texts were annotated with DanGram both morphosyntactically and semantically, i.e. including framenet annotation and word sense disambiguation for nouns and named entities. After DanGram's name and MWE tokenization there were 8,399 parse tokens (incl. 1,112 punctuation tokens).

Tables 1 and 2 show, for each relevant part of speech, the percentage of tokens that could be automatically linked to COR, both for ordinary tokens (table 1) and for multi-word-expressions (table 2). For the closed word classes (PRP, ART, PRON and K) and for adverbs (ADV), coverage was 100% in both cases.

Among the open word classes, verbs had a better coverage (99.6% for full matches) than nouns (97.1%) and adjectives (97.4%). Also, the latter had a greater share of out-of-vocabulary (OOV) compounds, that had to be matched part-by-part, which led to a certain amount of partial matches (first or second part only) . Unmatchable parts were, for instance, prefixes or (***u***|*kontrolleret* 'uncontrolled'), suffixes (*moms*|***mæssig*** – 'VAT-related), names (***Pisa***|***testen*** – 'the Pisa test') or numerical

[19]The form is an archaic dative of the noun *ret* ('right'), that does not exist in modern Danish outside of fixed expressions, and therefore does not have an ordinary inflection entry in COR.

[20]When checking all of DanGram's closed-class MWEs

[21]https://korpus.dsl.dk/resources/details/korpusdk.html

Table 1: Coverage for non-MWE tokens, direct or through compound parts (%)

POS[22]	direct (full)	comp full	comp partial	all full	all partial
N	86.9	10.2	1.8	97.1	98.9
V	99.3	0.4	0.1	99.6	99.7
ADJ	96.9	4.8	1.9	97.4	99.3
ADV	100	-	-	100	-
PROP	25.5	0	2.8	25.5	28.4
PRP	99.9	-	-	99.9	-

parts (*63-årig* '63-year-old), abbreviations (*C20-indekset* – 'the C20 index') or English parts. In a few cases, DanGram provided a 2-way compound split where one of the parts was itself a compound that couldn't be matched (*børne|litteratur||festival* – 'childrens's literature festival'). Finally, proper nouns and numerals had a low coverage simply because COR contains only 700 proper nouns – all place names – and only numerals that are written with letters. Overall coverage for non-punctuation was 97.4%, or 99% when not counting proper nouns.

For closed-class MWEs there was full coverage (table 2), but as DanGram contains more MWEs than COR, only about 1/3 were direct MWE matches (2nd column), the rest were part-by-part matches (3rd column). In absolute terms, the difference is most marked for MWE prepositions, and least marked for MWE adverbs.

Table 2: Coverage for closed-class MWE tokens, as a whole or part-by-part (%)

POS	MWE as a whole (full)	MWE all parts	MWE partial	all full
ADV	45.9	54.1	0	100
PRP	19.6	80.4	0	100
PRON	8.3	91.7	0	100
K	25.0	64.3	0	100
All	35.7	64.3	0	100

Obviously, in addition to coverage, accuracy is important, and because of sense and paradigm ambiguities, and especially for the major word classes, nouns and verbs, a link to a COR entry with the right part-of-speech is not necessarily correct. We therefore checked all links manually for possible errors[23]. Here, a distinction should be made between text-to-COR performance, including DanGram annotation errors propagating as COR-link errors, on the one hand, and linking-only errors on the other, i.e. correct DanGram analyses still leading to a wrong COR entry. The latter type of errors proved to be extremely rare (< 0.1%, first parts in 1 MWE and 1 compound, plus 1 misspelling), but even text-to-COR accuracy was satisfactory, given the fact that linking failures were mostly due to gaps in COR rather than analysis or linking failures (table 3).

Table 3: Text-to-COR - DanGram errors (column 2, rows 2-6), linking errors and COR gaps

Error type	row sums	link match	non-COR class	link error	COR gap
POS error	18:	12	4	1	1
morph error	2:	2			
sem-class error	2:	2			
tokeniz. error	4:	1	3		
comp. error	2:			1	1
link error only				1	
COR error					76
no COR			325		80
Column sums	28	17	332	3	158
% of words	0.3	0.2	4.0	0.0	1.9

4% of all words were outside of COR's scope (numbers, numerical expressions and most proper nouns[24], while 1.9% were COR gaps that could be addressed by improving COR. Of these, about half had no COR entry at all, half were missing an entry for the correct POS, but offered another ID for the word form in question, that could be used as a fall-back[25]. Linking-relevant DanGram errors amounted to only 0.3%, mostly POS errors, but also a few tokenization, inflection and compound analysis errors, as well as two higher-level, semantic subclass errors. A quarter of the DanGram errors concerned non-COR word classes, in

[23]This was carried out as a double-pass inspection, in-house, by one specialist, facilitated by the fact that COR has definition fields for ambiguous entries

[24]DanGram has a high precision for these word classes, and there were only two cross-class false positives, both wrongly tagged PROP - one adjective (that could have been linked) and one noun (not in COR).

[25]This POS gap problem concerned only a few, but frequent word forms. For instance, der was not listed as a relative pronoun, but only as an adverb, and a couple of common adverbs (*sådan* 'this way' and *meget* 'very') were only listed as adjectives.

most of the others (0.2%, i.e. 2/3 of the DanGram errors) the Linker simply ("correctly") assigned a corresponding, wrong UID link. In combination, COR gaps (1.9%), DanGram errors (0.3%) and pure linking errors (< 0.1%) amounted to a text-to-COR failure rate of 2.2%.

6 Conclusion

We have shown how the output of a morphosyntactic and semantic parser with compound analysis (DanGram) can be linked to unique word identifiers by matching annotation tags such as lemma, POS and semantic class with corresponding information in the target resource (COR). In a random text evaluation, 97.8% of all non-number, non-name words could be matched to a correct COR entry. As most of the link failures were not caused by the linking mechanism as such, but by coverage issues, performance should automatically increase with future editions of COR. Parser errors were a smaller issue, and here, too, future improvements should automatically translate into better linking.

Limitations

The good performance of the parser is unlikely to be evenly distributed and likely to be lower if evaluated separately for level-2 homographs only. Given the fact that DanGram uses the same rule-based strategy for both morphosyntax and WSD, alternative methods for this sub-task, in particular word embeddings (Iacobacci et al., 2016), should be compared, possibly by boot-strapping training data with DanGram output. Depending on the applicational uses of COR, it would make sense to add a kind of "encyclopedic" section for proper nouns, for instance by assigning UIDs to (Danish) Wikipedia entries, allowing a more integrated use of the resource in tasks like information extraction. For many applications it would also be extremely useful to link spelling variations and frequent misspellings to the underlying, correct COR entry[26]. Ultimately, of course, it is a design or resource allocation decision whether normalization should be addressed "live" at the parser level, as is the case for DanGram, or whether it (also) should be supported lexically in COR.

[26]For frequent variants, COR's third UID field, reserved for historical spelling changes, could be used for this purpose. For a wider, unsystematic, inventory of spelling errors, linking an external resource would make more sense

Ethics Statement

As it does not use any training or personal data, questionnaires or user logs, this work does not raise any ethical concerns regarding GDPR. As a rule-based system it also does not need much computing power, neither during development nor as a service, making for a very small environmental footprint. In the same vein, no underpaid student or Mechanical Turk labour has been exploited to produce training data.

Acknowledgements

We appreciate the work that has gone into building COR, and are grateful to DSN for making the resource publicly available.

References

Eckhard Bick. 2011. A FrameNet for Danish. In *Proceedings of the 18th Nordic Conference of Computational Linguistics (NODALIDA 2011)*, pages 34–41, Riga, Latvia. Northern European Association for Language Technology (NEALT).

Eckhard Bick and Tino Didriksen. 2015. CG-3 — Beyond Classical Constraint Grammar. In *Proceedings of the 20th Nordic Conference of Computational Linguistics (NODALIDA 2015)*, pages 31–39, Vilnius, Lithuania. Linköping University Electronic Press, Sweden.

Christina Dideriksen, Peter J. Hansen, and Thomas Widmann. 2022. Det Centrale Ordregister. *Nyt fra Sprognævnet*, Oktober 2022.

Ignacio Iacobacci, Mohammad Taher Pilehvar, and Roberto Navigli. 2016. Embeddings for Word Sense Disambiguation: An Evaluation Study. In *Proceedings of the 54th Annual Meeting of the Association for Computational Linguistics (Volume 1: Long Papers)*, pages 897–907, Berlin, Germany. Association for Computational Linguistics.

Sanni Nimb, Bolette S. Pedersen, Nathalie C. Hau Sørensen, Ida Flörke, Sussi Olsen, and Thomas Troelsgaard. 2022. COR-S – den semantiske del af Det Centrale OrdRegister (COR). *Lexico Nordica*, 29:75–97.

Joakim Nivre. 2015. Towards a Universal Grammar for Natural Language Processing. In *Computational Linguistics and Intelligent Text Processing. Lecture Notes in Computer Science*, volume 9041, pages 3–16. Springer, Cham.

Bolette S. Pedersen, Sanni Nimb, Jørg Asmussen, Nicolai Hartvig Sørensen, Lars Trap-Jensen, and Henrik Lorentzen. 2009. DanNet: the challenge of compiling a wordnet for Danish by reusing a monolingual dictionary. In *Language Resources and Evaluation (2009)*, pages 269–299. ELRA.

Automatic Dictionary Generation: Could Brothers Grimm Create a Dictionary with BERT?

Hendryk T. Weiland
Heinrich Heine University Düsseldorf
hendryk.weiland@hhu.de

Maike Behrendt
Heinrich Heine University Düsseldorf
maike.behrendt@hhu.de

Stefan Harmeling
TU Dortmund University
stefan.harmeling@tu-dortmund.de

Abstract

The creation of the most famous German dictionary, also referred to as "Deutsches Wörterbuch" or in English "The German Dictionary", by the two brothers Jacob and Wilhelm Grimm, took more than a lifetime to be finished (1838–1961). In our work we pose the question, if it would be possible for them to create a dictionary using present technology, i.e., language models such as BERT. Starting with the definition of the task of Automatic Dictionary Generation, we propose a method based on contextualized word embeddings and hierarchical clustering to create a dictionary given unannotated text corpora. We justify our design choices by running variants of our method on English texts, where ground truth dictionaries are available. Finally, we apply our approach to Shakespeare's work and automatically generate a dictionary tailored to Shakespearean vocabulary and contexts without human intervention.

1 Introduction

In 1838, the brothers Jacob and Wilhelm Grimm started to create the Deutsches Wörterbuch (Grimm and Grimm, 1854), a comprehensive German dictionary with references for each entry. A *dictionary* is a resource that assigns meanings or translations to words. Words are usually displayed in alphabetical order in their canonical form, called *lemma*, and an explanation of the meaning, called a *gloss*. The first volumes of the famous German dictionary were published in 1852. Brothers Grimm could not finish their work within their lifetime, but different scholars and institutions later succeeded in 1961. The creation took 123 years in total. If the brothers Grimm started their project nowadays, they would likely use state-of-the-art technology like the internet and a pretrained language model like the Bidirectional Encoder Representations from Transformers (BERT) (Devlin et al., 2019) to speed up their work. In our work, we want to examine if the automated generation of a dictionary is possible with state-of-the-art technology and if today's language models could do the extensive work.

In Natural Language Processing (NLP), we have to split sentences into smaller units which we refer to as *tokens*. Tokens are not only written words but also punctuation marks and numbers. To automatically build a dictionary from plain reference texts, we need to find all occurrences of each word and distinguish their sense only from their context, which aligns with Wittgenstein's dictum "the meaning of a word is its use in the language" (Wittgenstein, 1953). Given a fixed set of senses, choosing the correct word sense from that set is defined as the task of *word sense disambiguation* (WSD). As the number of senses for each word appearing in a given text is unknown, we need to separate the senses for each word without any prior knowledge, which is called *word sense induction* (WSI). The class of tokens that have the same meaning is referred to as type. Words with only one meaning are called *monosemous*, while ambiguous words are referred to as *polysemous*.

It has been shown that BERT's contextualized word embeddings hold syntactic and semantic knowledge (Rogers et al., 2021). In addition, they form separable clusters for polysemous words (Wiedemann et al., 2019). We want to utilize these characteristics of contextualized vector representations produced by language models such as BERT and perform word sense induction using a hierarchical clustering method to tackle the task of *automatic dictionary generation* (ADG) from raw text without any further annotations.

Contributions.

1. We define the task of automatic dictionary generation (ADG).

2. We discuss how to evaluate automatically generated dictionaries.

Proceedings of the 19th Conference on Natural Language Processing (KONVENS 2023), pages 102–120
September 18–22, 2023. ©2023 Association for Computational Linguistics

3. We present a simple approach for ADG using a pretrained CharacterBERT (El Boukkouri et al., 2020) model and agglomerative hierarchical clustering (AHC), and apply it to the work of William Shakespeare to create a Shakespearean dictionary.

The remaining paper is structured as follows: in the upcoming section, we discuss related work. We then define the task of ADG and afterward explain our approach to ADG called Grimm's BERT and discuss how we evaluate the model. Section 4 presents our experiments on the task of ADG. To demonstrate the applicability of our ADG pipeline to an interesting real-world text corpus, we apply it to the works of William Shakespeare in order to create a Shakespearean dictionary in Section 5 before giving a conclusion of our work in Section 6. All of our experiments are available on GitHub under: `https://github.com/Weilando/grimm_bert`.

2 Related Work

Among the many possibilities, we choose to use CharacterBERT (El Boukkouri et al., 2020) embeddings to calculate contextualized vector representations of each word in a given text and apply hierarchical clustering to distinguish word types used in a text to create dictionary entries. In the following section we firstly discuss previous approaches to generate dictionaries and secondly look at methods to disambiguate the meaning of words.

Dictionary Generation. The generation of lexical resources such as dictionaries has interested researchers for a long time (Chang et al., 1995). Past work on dictionary generation, also referred to as dictionary construction can be divided into two categories. There have been methods to construct (i) bilingual (Kaji et al., 2008) and (ii) monolingual (Tavast et al., 2020) dictionaries which are either of a general nature or focus on domain-specific terms (Ren et al., 2022). Bilingual dictionaries have been either created by translation (Varga and Yokoyama, 2009), through the use of parallel corpora (McEwan et al., 2002) or by combining two existing dictionaries (Kaji et al., 2008). One challenge all these methods face is the ambiguity of words. To solve it, additional knowledge has been necessary in form of thesauri, WordNet (Nicolas et al., 2021) or statistics given raw text in both languages (Kaji et al., 2008).

Word Sense Induction And Disambiguation. To tackle the task of WSD, there are knowledge-based approaches that utilize linguistic resources like thesauri and supervised (and semi-supervised) approaches that train a classifier on manually labeled training data and possibly unlabeled corpora in addition (Wiedemann et al., 2019). In contrast, we want to solve the task without the use of any annotations or further knowledge as a sub-task of the automatic dictionary generation. For WSD there already have been approaches based on word embeddings. The context-group-discrimination (Schütze, 1998) algorithm, for example, combines context independent word vectors with context vectors that capture information from second-order co-occurrences and clusters. Wiedemann et al. (Wiedemann et al., 2019) investigate the application of the contextualized word embeddings of Flair (Akbik et al., 2018), ELMo (Peters et al., 2018) and an uncased $\text{BERT}_{\text{Large}}$ (Devlin et al., 2019) for WSD. BERT was the only evaluated contextualized embedding that allowed distinguishable clusters and therefore outperformed its competitors (Wiedemann et al., 2019). For the task of WSI many methods apply clustering of some kind of word representation to discriminate the senses of each word in context. A simple clustering approach is k-means, which usually requires to know the number of clusters beforehand (Giulianelli et al., 2020). Other approaches are affinity propagation (Martinc et al., 2020) and agglomerative clustering (Arefyev et al., 2019). For our ADG pipeline we perform WSI with agglomerative clustering and contextualized CharacterBERT embeddings.

3 Automatic Dictionary Generation

Informally, automatic dictionary generation (ADG) is the process of creating a dictionary from raw text, containing a list of senses with reference sentences for each type. While this description appears obvious for common languages like English, there are a couple of choices to make, which we detail next.

More formally, a *text* is given as a sequence of characters, i.e., as a string. The first step is to split the string into a sequence of *tokens*. A trivial choice is to split at whitespace characters. However, many so-called tokenizers split words even further into stem and ending. Punctuation marks and numbers are most often tokens themselves. The second step is to split the sequence of tokens into subsequences called *sentences*. Sentences give context to a token

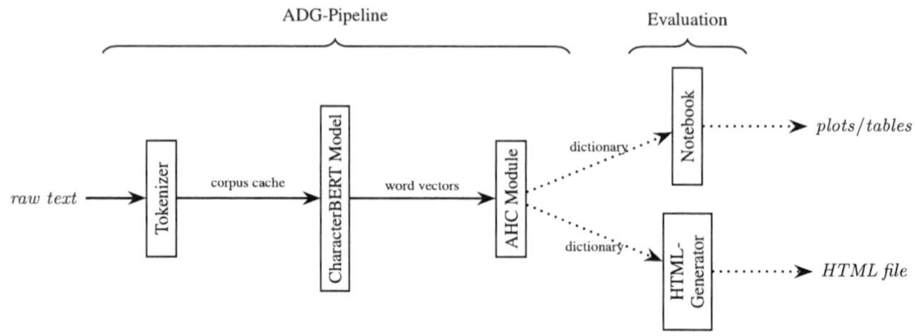

Figure 1: Grimm's BERT: our ADG pipeline implementation. *Solid and dotted arrows indicate obligatory and optional connections, respectively.*

and should be characteristic of the token's sense. Based on these choices, a *dictionary* is a set of one dictionary entry per unique word. Each entry consists of a list of senses, where each sense has a list of reference sentences assigned. Some tokens are possibly excluded from the dictionary, e.g., word endings.

Thus to implement ADG, we have to specify how we define tokens and sentences, since these choices determine what the generated dictionary will contain. For most common languages, the dictionary entries contain an additional human-understandable description called gloss, which we exclude from our pipeline for now. Note that in contrast to WSD, the ADG task does not assume any knowledge about the number of senses a word occurring in a text corpus has. Consequently a step in the ADG pipeline is to perform word sense induction for each word in a text. To solve the task of ADG, we employ contextualized representations of each token that capture semantic and syntactic features. Several studies show that BERT embeddings capture syntactic information (Rogers et al., 2021). Wiedemann et al. (Wiedemann et al., 2019) also compared different contextualized word embeddings for WSD and found that uncased BERT embeddings perform best for this task. Motivated by these results, we use BERT embeddings to tackle the task of ADG.

Algorithm 1: ADG Pipeline

1 Tokenize the input.
2 Generate one contextualized word vector per token.
3 Perform token-wise sense induction clustering the contextualized word vectors.

3.1 Grimm's BERT for ADG.

Next, we propose a method for the ADG task, which we call Grimm's BERT. Figure 1 shows the complete pipeline of our approach. The general steps that are performed for ADG are also written down as Algorithm 1. To give further explanation we next discuss each step separately:

1. Tokenization. $\text{BERT}_{\text{Large}}$ solves the task of WSD better than other contextualized word embeddings (Wiedemann et al., 2019). However, the used WordPiece tokenizer (Wu et al., 2016) cuts words into so-called word pieces. As our dictionary should contain only human-readable words, we decided to use a BERT model that is pretrained using a word level tokenizer. We choose CharacterBERT (El Boukkouri et al., 2020), more precisely $\text{CharacterBERT}_{\text{General}}$ which is a pretrained variant of the uncased $\text{BERT}_{\text{Base}}$ model that uses ELMo's (Peters et al., 2018) word level Character-CNN module instead of WordPiece embeddings.

2. Generate Contextualized Word Embeddings. We calculate one contextualized word vector per token with a pretrained $\text{CharacterBERT}_{\text{General}}$ model, forward the tokenized input and extract the 768 dimensional output from the model's last hidden layer.

3. Token-wise Sense Induction. Each occurring word has at least one word sense. We perform agglomerative hierarchical clustering (AHC) to related word vectors to detect and discriminate different word senses for polysemous words. AHC is a bottom-up method that starts with single objects and successively merges the closest objects to build a binary merge tree. A *linkage criterion* determines the relevant distance between clusters for the process of merging. Average linkage clustering uses the average distance between all pairs of objects in two clusters, complete linkage takes the maximum distances between all objects of two clusters and single linkage uses the minimum distance between all objects of the two sets.

There are several ways to cut the binary merge tree into subtrees to get different clusters. One option is a fixed distance threshold that determines connections to cut and leaves the resulting number of clusters open. Another option is a fixed cluster count that maximizes the linkage criterion but ignores the absolute value of the cut connections. Grimm's BERT builds one dendrogram per unique word using the average linkage criterion with the Euclidean distance as linkage distance. It applies a fixed linkage distance threshold, which is a hyperparameter, to cut the dendrograms into subtrees representing different groups of senses. For our choices of the linkage and cut criterion, we performed extensive experiments presented in the Appendix.

3.2 Evaluation.

While WSD is a classification task, ADG is a clustering problem. The following section discusses how to evaluate an automatically created dictionary for the case where we have ground truth information about the number of word senses. We choose the Adjusted Rand Index (ARI) (Hubert and Arabie, 1985) as an objective evaluation metric to quantify the quality of the resulting clusters. Classical metrics for WSD like the accuracy or the F_1 score are not applicable, as forming clusters of senses can rather be seen as a separation of unnamed senses than a selection from a fixed dictionary.

Let $X = \{X_1, \ldots, X_N\}$ be a set of objects, $Y = \{Y_1, \ldots, Y_K\}$ be a partitioning of X in $K \in 1, \ldots, N$ disjoint sets and m denote a clustering method which describes how to obtain Y from a given X. Then (X, Y, m) describes a clustering problem, and we call Y a clustering. Rand (1971) defines the Rand Index (RI) via

$$\mathrm{RI}(Y, Y') = \frac{\sum_{i<j}^{n} \gamma_{ij}}{\binom{n}{2}} \in [0, \ldots, 1] \qquad (1)$$

where Y' is another clustering and

$$\gamma_{ij} = \begin{cases} 1 & \text{if there exist } k, k' \text{ s.t. both } X_i, X_j \\ & \text{are in both } Y_k \text{ and } Y'_{k'} \\ 1 & \text{if there exist } k, k' \text{ s.t. } X_i \text{ is in both} \\ & Y_k \text{ and } Y'_{k'} \text{ while } X_j \text{ is neither in} \\ & Y_k \text{ or } Y'_{k'} \\ 0 & otherwise \end{cases}$$

with $i, j \in \{1, \ldots, N\}$ and $k, k' \in \{1, \ldots, K\}$. Intuitively, γ_{ij} is true if two objects are together or separate in both clusterings. $\mathrm{RI}(Y, Y') = 1$ indicates identical clusterings, whereas $\mathrm{RI}(Y, Y') = 0$ for two clusterings without any similarities.

Rand (Rand, 1971) defined the Rand Index (RI) to measure the similarity of two clusterings by calculating the agreement between two different partitions. The index considers every pair of the given data points in the obtained and correct clustering and counts how many pairs are in the same clusters and how many are in different clusters. The ARI (Hubert and Arabie, 1985) is the Rand Index, corrected for chance using the hypergeometric distribution. We obtain the ARI with

$$\mathrm{ARI} = \frac{\mathrm{RI} - \mathbb{E}(\mathrm{RI})}{\max(\mathrm{RI}) - \mathbb{E}(\mathrm{RI})} \in [-1, \ldots, 1] \qquad (2)$$

where $\mathbb{E}(\mathrm{RI})$ is the expected value of RI. Please note that $\mathrm{ARI} = 1$ indicates perfectly matched clusterings, $\mathrm{ARI} = 0$ indicates random clusterings regarding the hypergeometric distribution, and $\mathrm{ARI} < 0$ does not have an intuitive interpretation. ARI is symmetric, so $\mathrm{ARI}(Y, Y') = \mathrm{ARI}(Y', Y)$. Only the assignment of objects to the same or different clusters matters, as the score is invariant under the permutation of label names.

As the ARI compares a clustering with some ground truth, we cannot use it to evaluate a dictionary for corpora without any semantic annotations. In that case, we measure the density and separation of clusters using the Silhouette Coefficient (Rousseeuw, 1987) to find a sensible cluster count k for a set of n objects. In our context, objects are tokens and clusters are senses.

The Silhouette Coefficient $s(i)$ for each object i is defined as

$$s(i) = \frac{b(i) - a(i)}{\max\{a(i), b(i)\}} \in [-1, 1], \qquad (3)$$

where $a(i)$ is the average distance inside the cluster and $b(i)$ is the average distance to the closest cluster (Rousseeuw, 1987).

Implementation Details. We transform corpora into lists of sentences, where each sentence is a list of tokens. We save these lists into an archive file to avoid repeated preprocessing steps like tokenization and lower casing. For the actual WSI per token, we apply the implementation of AHC from the machine learning library scikit-learn[1]. We

[1]https://scikit-learn.org/stable/

choose the Euclidean distance between word vectors as affinity and the average linkage criterion (see Table 4 in the Appendix for a comparison of different linkage criteria and Cosine vs Euclidean distance).

4 Experiments

We conduct several experiments to evaluate how well our pipeline works. To numerically measure the performance of our approach, we perform ADG on different annotated corpora and measure the ARI of our obtained clusters.

4.1 Datasets

For the evaluation of our model, we use textual corpora with token-level sense annotations to evaluate the performance of semantic tasks. Please note that many corpora do not contain sense tags for every token, as semantic tagging by hand is a tedious and costly process. So-called all-words corpora contain tags for every token with certain part-of-speech (POS) tags but usually omit closed-class words (Snyder and Palmer, 2004; Moro and Navigli, 2015). Table 1 lists all datasets together with the number of documents, sentences and tokens per corpus and indicates the kind of POS for tokens with semantic tags. Senseval and SemEval are part of WSDEval (Raganato et al., 2017) which is a unified evaluation framework that offers several annotated corpora in the same XML format with sense annotations from WordNet (Miller et al., 1990) version 3.0. Raganato et al. (Raganato et al., 2017) applied the XML schema of the SemEval2013 all-words WSD task (Navigli et al., 2013), removed annotations for auxiliary verbs, semi-automatically updated WordNet senses to version 3.0, lemmatized and POS tagged all tokens to standardize the corpora. Some datasets like Senseval2 and Senseval3 do not contain semantic tags for all words of a POS. Sometimes, multiple sense tags exist in the case of ambiguity or if no suitable WordNet sense was available (Navigli et al., 2013).

4.2 Performance Evaluation of Our Approach

We compare the performance of our approach with two different baselines (see Table 2) to assess its value in practice. The first baseline assigns a distinct sense to each token, called "No Cluster"-baseline. The second baseline assigns all occurrences of the same word to a single sense, called "Single Cluster"-baseline. We perform our ADG pipeline with average linkage and the Euclidean distance (see Table 4 in the Appendix for other options). Table 2 presents our results with linkage distance thresholds, which we optimized within a range of $8 - 16$ (see Appendix A.4). Please note that all ARI scores are slightly better than our baselines (see Table 2), except for the SemEval2013 task for which our best result is equal to the "Single Cluster"-baseline. As a proof of concept, we were able to improve over the baselines with some parameter tuning of the distance threshold.

To study how the ARI scores depend on the distance threshold, we show the distribution of ARI scores in Figure 2 for every dataset for varying distance thresholds. For large distance thresholds, the ARI score matches the "Single Cluster"-baseline, since all occurring tokens end up in a single cluster. Unfortunately, the scores converge to the baseline. However, this might be due to selective annotations in the corpora. Note that for SemEval2007 we can see a peak before reaching the ARI for the "Single Cluster"-baseline, which shows that for that particular dataset, the token embeddings can give meaningful clusterings.

To further analyze the SemEval2007 dataset we show the distribution of the ARI for different linkage criteria in the left panel, together with the "Single Cluster"-baseline and the ARI for different sense counts in the right panel in Figure 3. We see that the exact choice of the linkage criterion is not critical and that for the SemEval2007 corpus the clustering works well for tokens with a single and more than three unique senses. For the other datasets the corresponding plots are in the Figure 7 in the Appendix.

5 ADG for Shakespeare's Works

So far, we defined the ADG task and proposed a simple pipeline to solve it. In the experiments above, we generate contextualized word vectors with a general CharacterBERT model pretrained on the English Wikipedia and the OpenWebText corpus.[2] However, ADG is much more interesting and becomes more complicated if raw text is the only available training resource for the particular language to create a dictionary. In that case we have to pretrain a language model on the exact text that is the input for the complete pipeline. Note that such an approach is also applicable to unannotated

[2]https://skylion007.github.io/OpenWebTextCorpus/

Corpora	Docs.	Sents.	Tokens	Annotations per POS
Senseval2 (Edmonds and Cotton, 2001)	3	242	5,766	ADJ, ADV, NOUN, VERB
Senseval3 (Snyder and Palmer, 2004)	3	352	5,541	ADJ, ADV, NOUN, VERB
SemEval2007 (Pradhan et al., 2007)	3	135	3,201	NOUN, VERB
SemEval2013 (Navigli et al., 2013)	13	306	8,391	NOUN
SemEval2015 (Moro and Navigli, 2015)	4	138	2,604	ADJ, ADV, NOUN, VERB
SemCor (Miller et al., 1993)	352	37,176	802,443	ADJ, ADV, NOUN, VERB

Table 1: Overview of WSDEval Corpora. POS tags are adjectives (ADJ), adverbs (ADV), nouns (NOUN) and verbs (VERB).

Corpus	Dist. Threshold	Unique Senses	No Cluster	Single Cluster	ADG (ours)
SemCor	14.50	54,806	0.0000	0.6521	0.6522
Senseval2	14.00	1,626	0.0000	0.9136	0.9137
Senseval3	10.30	2,144	0.0000	0.8395	0.8671
SemEval2007	9.60	1,685	0.0000	0.7109	0.8632
SemEval2013	15.00	2,376	0.0000	0.9377	0.9377
SemEval2015	10.60	876	0.0000	0.9464	0.9509

Table 2: ARI scores (last three columns) for two baselines "No Cluster" and "Single Cluster" vs our results "ADG (ours)" using Grimm's BERT.

low resource languages.

To investigate this scenario, we apply our method to generate a dictionary for all works of the famous English poet William Shakespeare (1564 – 1616). The vocabulary and grammar from Early Modern English (used in late 15th to mid-to-late 17th century) is different from today's Modern English (used since mid-to-late 17th century). Nevertheless, his works have been widely studied and understood and are readable without too much effort. As the manual creation of appropriate dictionaries is time-consuming and computationally expensive, the results of our automated pipeline (see Algorithm 1) could be a useful starting point for generating such a dictionary.

Training Data. We use an open corpus with sonnets and plays from Shakespeare.[3] For preprocessing, we remove stage directions beginning with "<". We delete all lines that contain only a number, e.g., years of publication or enumerations of sonnets. Additionally, we remove repeated line breaks. The resulting corpus consists of 112,521 sentences with 1,152,400 tokens and 23,547 unique words. It is small compared to typical datasets used to train CharacterBERT, but larger than SemCor (802,443 total tokens, see Table 1).

CharacterBERT Model for Shakespearean English. We train a CharacterBERT model with the original pretraining code[4] and our Shakespeare corpus. The used hyperparameters for pretraining can be found in Table 8 in the Appendix. We also use the LAMB optimizer (You et al., 2019), a layer-wise adaptive large batch optimization technique that works well with attention models like CharacterBERT. Please note that the training process includes two phases. The optimizer works with a higher learning rate and shorter input sequence lengths during the first phase to achieve broadly reasonable weights. The second phase requires fewer update steps and improves the weights with a lower initial learning rate and longer input sequences. Different sequence lengths require adaptions regarding the number of accumulation steps and batch size, as the target batch size and the CharacterBERT model need to fit into the GPU's memory. We perform our ADG pipeline with average linkage and the Euclidean distance, as this setup worked best for most corpora, particularly for the large SemCor. (see Table 4). We run the pipeline with threshold 8.0, 9.0, and 10.0. Table 3 shows that different numbers of senses are found as expected. Since we have no ground truth we arbitrarily choose the threshold 9.0 for the following examples.

Qualitative Evaluation. The raw text from Shakespeare does not provide semantic annotations. So we can not use metrics like the ARI for quantitative evaluation. Instead, we pick examples

[3] https://ocw.mit.edu/ans7870/6/6.006/s08/lecturenotes/files/t8.shakespeare.txt

[4] https://github.com/helboukkouri/character-bert-pretraining

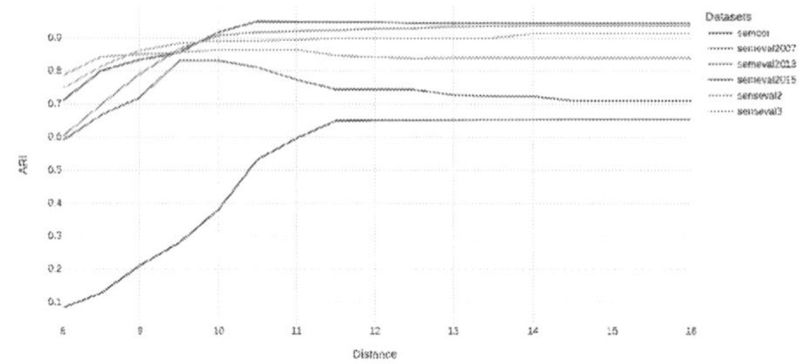

Figure 2: ARI scores for varying linkage distance thresholds.

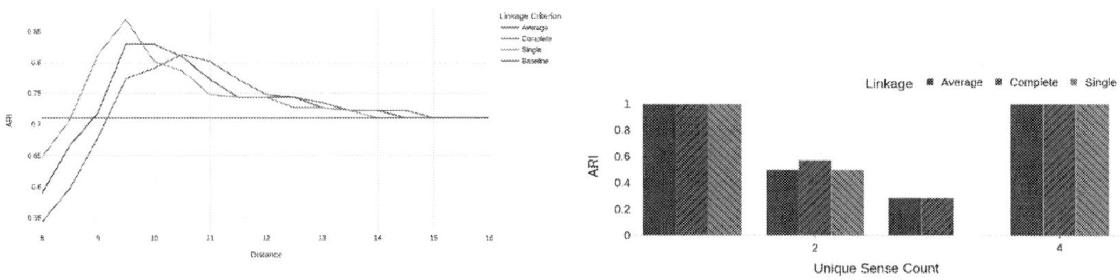

Figure 3: Results only for the SemEval2007 dataset. ARI score for different thresholds and linkage criteria and the "Single Cluster"-baseline (left) and ARI score per sense count and different linkage criteria (right).

Linkage Distance Threshold	8.0	9.0	10.0
Reference Sentences		112,521	
Number Tokens		1,152,400	
Unique Words		23,547	
Unique Senses	52,797	51,070	49,272

Table 3: Number of unique senses for different thresholds in our Shakespeare Dictionary.

from Shakespeare's Words[5], an online glossary, thesaurus, and collection of Shakespeare's works, and compare them with our findings manually. Please note that we present all tokens lowercase and separated with single spaces. The enumerator styles indicate the assigned senses. Our created dictionary offers two different senses for the word *eyed*. Looking at the sentence examples, the first example is an adjective but the second is a verb.

- • *it is the green - eyed monster , which doth mock*
- ◇ *for as you were when first your eye i eyed ,*

Our dictionary correctly lists only one sense for both occurrences of *writer*.

- • *i ' ll haste the writer , and withal*
- • *drive some of them to a non - come . only get the learned writer to*

However, for *wrongful*, we incorrectly get two different senses.

- • *that i despise thee for thy wrongful suit ,*
- ◇ *in wrongful quarrel you have slain your son .*

[5] https://www.shakespeareswords.com

Curiously, words with more reference sentences tend to have outliers. For example, the word *englishman* only has one meaning, however our dictionary assigns eight reference sentences to the same sense but assigns two occurrences to another.

- • *a soul so easy as that englishman ' s . '*
- • *king henry . an englishman ?*
- • *thinking this voice an armed englishman -*
- • *for that my grandsire was an englishman -*
- • *a box of the ear of the englishman , and swore he would pay him*
- • *caius . by gar , then i have as much mockvater as de englishman .*
- • *cassio . is your englishman so expert in his drinking ?*
- • *i do not know that englishman alive*
- ◇ *that any englishman dare give me counsel ?*
- ◇ *where ever englishman durst set his foot .*

The word *major* is an interesting dictionary entry. The first two references form a sense, while the other two occurrences belong to a second cluster. At first glance, the division appears correct since the first sense is a noun, and the second sense is an adjective. However, *major* means "matter" in the first example, but refers to a constellation in the second one. A correct distinction might require background knowledge and logical reasoning. Nevertheless, the entry is almost correct.

- • *fal . i deny your major . if you will deny the sheriff , so ; if not ,*
- • *nativity was under ursa major , so that it follows i am rough and*
- ◇ *the major part of your syllables ; and though i must be content to*

◇ *my major vow lies here , this i ' ll obey .*

In this experiment, the most difficult challenges are the corpus size, which is small for training a language model and large for clustering methods. Contexts in our Shakespeare corpus are often short and incomplete, since we defined a sentence to be limited to a single line, but many sentences extend over several lines. While our generated dictionary tends to list too many senses per word, it also contains valuable groupings and correct entries.

6 Conclusion

In this paper, we examine whether the brothers Grimm could create a dictionary using language models like BERT. To achieve this, we define the ADG task and a first simple approach to automatically generate a dictionary from raw text using a language model and AHC.

At its core, ADG is a clustering problem, and it is possible to evaluate it with ARI scores if sense annotations are available. Thus, (partially) labeled corpora for WSD are suitable for comparing different ADG approaches. Other metrics like the Silhouette Coefficient (see Appendix A.3) measure the cluster quality without any ground truth but usually have strong assumptions and miss some crucial edge cases. In addition, we consider a scenario with texts from Shakespeare's work. We train a CharacterBERT model on it and use our pipeline to generate a customized dictionary. Many dictionary entries are reasonable but sometimes list too many senses per word.

While our first simple approach to ADG does not give perfect results yet, we see great potential for this task and believe that our contribution is a starting point that could be used by linguists who want to create new dictionaries. It might be reasonably assumed that the quality of the resulting clusters of our pipeline will further increase with the continuous improvement of state-of-the-art language models. We assume that with today's technologies, the brothers Grimm would likely have witnessed the completion of their German dictionary during their lifetime.

Limitations

In this work, we defined the task of ADG and proposed one method to solve it. Nevertheless, there are many open questions emphasizing the key challenges and proposing new ideas beyond our experiments.

1. **How can we train language models even for low resource languages?** Our ADG pipeline can be used for low resource languages to build a preliminary dictionary, but requires to pretrain a language model from scratch. As we have seen in our experiments with the works of William Shakespeare, our approach generates reasonable outcomes, but learning language models on small corpora is challenging.
2. **Is there a better way to evaluate automatically generated dictionaries?** The evaluation of dictionaries without any ground truth remains partially open, mainly because the Silhouette coefficient is not applicable to situations where only one cluster exists. Other metrics and techniques to analyze high-dimensional clusters might be useful.
3. **How can we determine the correct number of senses for a word?** We analyze the search range for the linkage thresholds in Appendix A.4. Our experiments show that the optimal threshold is different for every dataset. It is still unclear how the optimal cut criterion can be determined in an unsupervised manner.
4. **How can we find relations between words?** We discuss the detection of relations like synonyms in Appendix A.5 but do not deliver a concrete implementation. The detection of relations like synonyms might be possible using by clustering the centroids and could lead to a reasonable extension of our pipeline.
5. **Can we automatically generate descriptions for the word types?** Generating glosses (aka descriptions) for each extracted sense is a challenging task. Currently we are only able to assign senses to each word in a text, together with references to sentences. In the future it will be interesting to automatically generate short descriptions for each word and each sense respectively and find a meaningful way to evaluate automatically generated glosses.

Our work has shown the potential of ADG, yet some aspects of the approach remain unsolved and for future work. Nevertheless, we believe that ADG can lead to powerful practically useful tools for dictionary generation which will profit from new and more powerful language models and additional input created by the deep learning community.

Ethics Statement

In this paper we propose an approach to automatically generate a dictionary from plain text. Using technology for communication is a great advantage of today's world. Having sentences and whole documents translated in the blink of an eye is beneficial for the communication between humans of all kinds of languages and cultures. The aim of this area of research is to use machines to study languages, potentially also low-resource languages in the context of written text. It is to say that this kind of technology should always have a supporting role and should not be used to make final decisions. Machine learning models always hold the risk of producing biased and incorrect predictions. Our work relies on the use of large language models such as BERT and CharacterBERT. These models are trained on large amounts of data and encode various parts of it. There is a risk that they contain sensitive data, generate false information or are actively misused.

Acknowledgments

Computational infrastructure and support were provided by the Centre for Information and Media Technology at Heinrich Heine University Düsseldorf.[6]

References

Alan Akbik, Duncan Blythe, and Roland Vollgraf. 2018. Contextual string embeddings for sequence labeling. In *Proc. of the 27th Int. Conf. Comput. Ling.*, pages 1638–1649.

Nikolay Arefyev, Boris Sheludko, and Tatiana Aleksashina. 2019. Combining neural language models for word sense induction. In *Analysis of Images, Social Networks and Texts*, pages 105–121, Cham. Springer International Publishing.

Jing-Shin Chang, Yi-Chung Lin, and Keh-Yih Su. 1995. Automatic construction of a Chinese electronic dictionary. In *Third Workshop on Very Large Corpora*.

Kevin Clark, Urvashi Khandelwal, Omer Levy, and Christopher D. Manning. 2019. What does BERT look at? an analysis of BERT's attention. pages 276–286.

Jacob Devlin, Ming-Wei Chang, Kenton Lee, and Kristina Toutanova. 2019. BERT: Pre-training of deep bidirectional transformers for language understanding. In *Proc. of the 2019 Conference of the North American Chapter of the Assoc. Comput. Linguist.*, pages 4171–4186.

Philip Edmonds and Scott Cotton. 2001. SENSEVAL-2: Overview. In *Proceedings of SENSEVAL-2 Second International Workshop on Evaluating Word Sense Disambiguation Systems*, pages 1–5, Toulouse, France. Association for Computational Linguistics.

Hicham El Boukkouri, Olivier Ferret, Thomas Lavergne, Hiroshi Noji, Pierre Zweigenbaum, and Jun'ichi Tsujii. 2020. CharacterBERT: Reconciling ELMo and BERT for word-level open-vocabulary representations from characters. In *Proceedings of the 28th International Conference on Computational Linguistics*, pages 6903–6915, Barcelona, Spain (Online). International Committee on Computational Linguistics.

Mario Giulianelli, Marco Del Tredici, and Raquel Fernández. 2020. Analysing lexical semantic change with contextualised word representations. In *Proceedings of the 58th Annual Meeting of the Association for Computational Linguistics*, pages 3960–3973, Online. Association for Computational Linguistics.

Jacob Grimm and Wilhelm Grimm. 1854. *Deutsches Wörterbuch*, volume 2. S. Hirzel.

Lawrence Hubert and Phipps Arabie. 1985. Comparing partitions. *Journal of classification*, 2(1):193–218.

Ganesh Jawahar, Benoît Sagot, and Djamé Seddah. 2019. What does BERT learn about the structure of language? In *Proc. of the 57th Annual Meeting of the Assoc. Comput. Linguist.*, pages 3651–3657.

Hiroyuki Kaji, Shin'ichi Tamamura, and Dashtseren Erdenebat. 2008. Automatic construction of a Japanese-Chinese dictionary via English. In *Proceedings of the Sixth International Conference on Language Resources and Evaluation (LREC'08)*, Marrakech, Morocco. European Language Resources Association (ELRA).

Matej Martinc, Syrielle Montariol, Elaine Zosa, and Lidia Pivovarova. 2020. Capturing evolution in word usage: Just add more clusters? In *Companion Proceedings of the Web Conference 2020*, WWW '20, page 343–349, New York, NY, USA. Association for Computing Machinery.

Craig J. A. McEwan, Iadh Ounis, and Ian Ruthven. 2002. Building bilingual dictionaries from parallel web documents. In *Proceedings of the 24th BCS-IRSG European Colloquium on IR Research: Advances in Information Retrieval*, page 303–323, Berlin, Heidelberg. Springer-Verlag.

George A. Miller, Richard Beckwith, Christiane Fellbaum, Derek Gross, and Katherine J. Miller. 1990. Introduction to WordNet: An On-line Lexical Database. *International Journal of Lexicography*, 3(4):235–244.

[6]https://wiki.hhu.de/display/HPC/Wissenschaftliches+Hochleistungs-Rechnen+am+ZIM

George A. Miller, Claudia Leacock, Randee Tengi, and Ross T. Bunker. 1993. A semantic concordance. In *Proceedings of the Workshop on Human Language Technology*, HLT '93, page 303–308, USA. Association for Computational Linguistics.

Andrea Moro and Roberto Navigli. 2015. SemEval-2015 task 13: Multilingual all-words sense disambiguation and entity linking. In *Proceedings of the 9th International Workshop on Semantic Evaluation (SemEval 2015)*, pages 288–297, Denver, Colorado. Association for Computational Linguistics.

Roberto Navigli, David Jurgens, and Daniele Vannella. 2013. SemEval-2013 task 12: Multilingual word sense disambiguation. In *Second Joint Conference on Lexical and Computational Semantics (*SEM), Volume 2: Proceedings of the Seventh International Workshop on Semantic Evaluation (SemEval 2013)*, pages 222–231, Atlanta, Georgia, USA. Association for Computational Linguistics.

Gandalf Nicolas, Xuechunzi Bai, and Susan T Fiske. 2021. Comprehensive stereotype content dictionaries using a semi-automated method. *European journal of social psychology*, 51(1):178–196.

Karl Pearson. 1901. Liii. on lines and planes of closest fit to systems of points in space. *The London, Edinburgh, and Dublin philosophical magazine and journal of science*, 2(11):559–572.

Matthew E. Peters, Mark Neumann, Mohit Iyyer, Matt Gardner, Christopher Clark, Kenton Lee, and Luke Zettlemoyer. 2018. Deep contextualized word representations. In *Proceedings of the 2018 Conference of the North American Chapter of the Association for Computational Linguistics: Human Language Technologies, Volume 1 (Long Papers)*, pages 2227–2237, New Orleans, Louisiana. Association for Computational Linguistics.

Sameer Pradhan, Edward Loper, Dmitriy Dligach, and Martha Palmer. 2007. SemEval-2007 task-17: English lexical sample, SRL and all words. In *Proceedings of the Fourth International Workshop on Semantic Evaluations (SemEval-2007)*, pages 87–92, Prague, Czech Republic. Association for Computational Linguistics.

Alessandro Raganato, Jose Camacho-Collados, and Roberto Navigli. 2017. Word sense disambiguation: A unified evaluation framework and empirical comparison. In *Proceedings of the 15th Conference of the European Chapter of the Association for Computational Linguistics: Volume 1, Long Papers*, pages 99–110, Valencia, Spain. Association for Computational Linguistics.

William M. Rand. 1971. Objective criteria for the evaluation of clustering methods. *Journal of the American Statistical Association*, 66(336):846–850.

Wei Ren, Hengwei Zhang, and Ming Chen. 2022. A method of domain dictionary construction for electric vehicles disassembly. *Entropy*, 24(3).

Anna Rogers, Olga Kovaleva, and Anna Rumshisky. 2021. A Primer in BERTology: What We Know About How BERT Works. *Transactions of the Association for Computational Linguistics*, 8:842–866.

Peter J. Rousseeuw. 1987. Silhouettes: A graphical aid to the interpretation and validation of cluster analysis. *Journal of Computational and Applied Mathematics*, 20:53–65.

Hinrich Schütze. 1998. Automatic word sense discrimination. *Computational Linguistics*, 24(1):97–123.

Benjamin Snyder and Martha Palmer. 2004. The English all-words task. In *Proceedings of SENSEVAL-3, the Third International Workshop on the Evaluation of Systems for the Semantic Analysis of Text*, pages 41–43, Barcelona, Spain. Association for Computational Linguistics.

Arvi Tavast, Kristina Koppel, Margit Langemets, and Jelena Kallas. 2020. Towards the Superdictionary: Layers, Tools and Unidirectional Meaning Relations. pages 215–223.

István Varga and Shoichi Yokoyama. 2009. Bilingual dictionary generation for low-resourced language pairs. In *Proceedings of the 2009 Conference on Empirical Methods in Natural Language Processing*, pages 862–870, Singapore. Association for Computational Linguistics.

Gregor Wiedemann, Steffen Remus, Avi Chawla, and Chris Biemann. 2019. Does bert make any sense? interpretable word sense disambiguation with contextualized embeddings. In *Proceedings of the 15th Conference on Natural Language Processing (KONVENS 2019): Long Papers*, pages 161–170, Erlangen, Germany. German Society for Computational Linguistics & Language Technology.

Ludwig Wittgenstein. 1953. *Philosophical Investigations*. Wiley-Blackwell, New York, NY, USA.

Yonghui Wu, Mike Schuster, Zhifeng Chen, Quoc V Le, Mohammad Norouzi, Wolfgang Macherey, Maxim Krikun, Yuan Cao, Qin Gao, Klaus Macherey, et al. 2016. Google's neural machine translation system: Bridging the gap between human and machine translation. *arXiv preprint arXiv:1609.08144v2*.

David Yenicelik, Florian Schmidt, and Yannic Kilcher. 2020. How does BERT capture semantics? a closer look at polysemous words. In *Proceedings of the Third BlackboxNLP Workshop on Analyzing and Interpreting Neural Networks for NLP*, pages 156–162, Online. Association for Computational Linguistics.

Yang You, Jing Li, Sashank Reddi, Jonathan Hseu, Sanjiv Kumar, Srinadh Bhojanapalli, Xiaodan Song, James Demmel, Kurt Keutzer, and Cho-Jui Hsieh. 2019. Large batch optimization for deep learning: Training bert in 76 minutes. *arXiv preprint arXiv:1904.00962v5*.

A Appendix

Our design choices for the ADG pipeline are based on extensive experiments that we conducted. These are described in the following sections. Namely, we compare different linkage criteria and metrics for clustering.

A.1 ARI for Clusterings with Different Affinities and Linkage Criteria

As the geometry of clusters in the embedding space is not trivial, we empirically search for the best linkage criterion with the WSDEval corpora. Therefore, we perform AHC with average linkage, complete linkage and single linkage and aid it with the true number of clusters it should find. More precisely, we cluster the word vectors for each distinct, sense annotated token based on all corresponding word vectors and the total, unique number of its annotated senses. We compute the ARI to measure the quality of the clustering and omit generated senses.

While the cosine distance measures angles between vectors, the Euclidean distance compares their lengths. Even if we usually use the cosine distance for NLP tasks, we also set both affinities side by side.

Table 4 presents the ARIs for sense clusterings with different affinities and linkage criteria and underline indicates the best performance for each corpus. All runs but for SemCor with complete linkage outperform our baselines from Table 4, indicating that our pipeline extracts meaningful word senses. Average linkage works best for SemCor, Senseval2, Senseval3 and SemEval2013. Complete linkage yields the highest ARI for SemEval2007 and SemEval2015. Often, the three criteria perform similarly well and SemCor is the only corpus for which complete linkage works significantly worse than the other two criteria. SemCor contains not only far more tokens and sense annotations but also some words with a higher disambiguity with up to 57 unique senses, whereas the other corpora only hold words with at most 5 unique senses.

We expect marginally better results for the Euclidean distance $\mathsf{D}_{\text{Euc}}(A, B)$ with $A, B \in \mathbb{R}^d$ and $d \in \mathbb{N}_{>0}$, because the cosine distance $\mathsf{D}_{\cos}(A, B)$ is equivalent to the Euclidean distance of normalized vectors. By expansion, it holds

$$
\begin{aligned}
\mathsf{D}^2_{\text{Euc}}(A - B) &= (A - B) \cdot (A - B) \\
&= \mathsf{D}^2_{\text{Euc}}(A) + \mathsf{D}^2_{\text{Euc}}(B) - 2(A \cdot B).
\end{aligned}
$$

With normalized vectors $\mathsf{D}^2_{\text{Euc}}(A) = \mathsf{D}^2_{\text{Euc}}(B) = 1$, this term is equal to $2(1 - \cos(A, B))$ and therefore $\mathsf{D}_{\cos}(A, B) = \frac{\mathsf{D}^2_{\text{Euc}}(A,B)}{2}$.

However, the Euclidean distance usually produces slightly stronger results, but yields the same ARI as the cosine distance for SemEval2013 and SemEval2015 with average linkage, Senseval3 and SemEval2013 with complete linkage and SemEval2013 with single linkage. Senseval2 with single linkage is the only setup for which the cosine distance moderately outperforms the Euclidean distance. This experiment suggests a setup with the Euclidean distance and average linkage. Possible explanations for the results are rounding errors and word vectors that are not exactly normalized to length one.

Please note that Yenicelik et al. (2020) investigate the organization of BERT's word vectors for polysemous words. More precisely, they use the semantic annotations in SemCor (Miller et al., 1993) to analyze the separability and clusterability of the 768 dimensional output of BERT's last layer.

They perform a dimensionality reduction via principal component analysis (PCA) (Pearson, 1901) and predict a semantic class per token with a linear classifier (Yenicelik et al., 2020). They interpret its accuracy as a measure of linear separability. Results for frequently occurring words show that individual semantic classes are reasonably linearly separable and contextual word embeddings form closed semantic regions (Yenicelik et al., 2020).

For clusterability, they apply several clustering algorithms on word vectors for sampled words from SemCor and the news.2007.corpus[7] and measure the quality of the resulting clusters with the *ARI* (Rand, 1971; Hubert and Arabie, 1985) (Yenicelik et al., 2020). No clustering method was able to distinguish between multiple semantic classes on a satisfying level (Yenicelik et al., 2020). For several words, resulting clusters differ not only in meanings but also in other linguistic properties like sentiment (Yenicelik et al., 2020). BERT's word embeddings form closed but overlapping semantic regions (Yenicelik et al., 2020).

We perform the analysis on the whole SemCor corpus with AHC and without PCA. In contrast, Yenicelik et al. (2020) use more complex clustering methods and sample polysemous words.

[7] `https://www.statmt.org/wmt14/training-monolingual-news-crawl/`

Corpus	Average Linkage Cosine	Average Linkage Euclidean	Complete Linkage Cosine	Complete Linkage Euclidean	Single Linkage Cosine	Single Linkage Euclidean
Semcor	0.6615	0.6627	0.4899	0.4958	0.6561	0.6558
Senseval2	0.9594	0.9596	0.9553	0.9558	0.9541	0.9540
Senseval3	0.9322	0.9326	0.9280		0.9261	0.9287
SemEval2007	0.9457	0.9612	0.9687	0.9844	0.9457	0.9612
SemEval2013	0.9700		0.9632		0.9694	
SemEval2015	0.9712		0.9723	0.9734	0.9711	0.9681

Table 4: ARI for Clusterings with Different Affinities and Linkage Criteria using known sense counts. Underline indicates the best result per corpus. Joined cells indicate identical ARIs for both affinities. We ignore all tokens with generated senses.

A.2 Sense-Count-Level ARI for Clusterings with Different Linkage Criteria

While Table 4 presents the overall performance of our approach with one ARI per corpus, Figure 4 shows bar plots with one average ARI per unique sense count. We analyze the dictionaries from Table 4 and completely omit tokens with generated senses in our plots again.

The results for monosemous words are almost perfect for all corpora and linkage criteria, because we provide the true number as we generate these dictionaries (see Section A.1). For polysemous words, the average ARI is usually smaller but clearly positive, indicating clusterings that are better than random choice. Especially for larger corpora like SemCor or SemEval2013, the drop is more evident. Please note that the total number of words per bar usually decreases with higher unique sense counts.

A.3 Sense-Count-Level Silhouette Coefficient for Clusterings with Different Linkage Criteria

Now we calculate one average Silhouette coefficient per sense count for the dictionaries from Table 4 to investigate the quality of sense clusterings. Please note that the score requires $2 \leq k \leq n-1$ with the sense count k and token count n (Rousseeuw, 1987). Thus, we omit all annotated tokens that do not fulfil the condition and cannot provide any measurements for $n = 1$. Similar to Figure 4, the significance of the bars decreases with higher unique sense counts. As the SemEval corpora provide very few polysemous words, their plots are less representative.

The cluster quality decreases with increasing sense counts, starting at a score of approximately 0.15 for $n = 2$ and approaching values near 0.1 for most configurations and corpora. Average and complete linkage usually yield similar scores, whereas single linkage often performs worse and even gets some negative scores for SemCor.

A.4 Linkage Distances at the Cut

The sensible prediction of sense counts per word is problematic due to the fact that we need to evaluate multiple clusterings per word and do not have any reliable information for single senses. Choosing one linkage distance threshold above which we do not merge any clusters avoids the choice of a suitable number of senses and requires only one clustering per word. Therefore, we investigate the linkage distances at the last cuts that occur during our clusterings with known sense counts (see Table A.1).

As the linkage criterion optimizes a certain distance between clusters, there are $n - 1$ distances for n samples. AHC is a bottom-up approach that starts with clusters that contain only one sample and successively builds a binary merge tree. We investigate the exact linkage distance at the tree node that marks the last merge. If all linkage distances differ, we can generate the same clustering by setting the distance threshold to the exact distance at the last merge and add a small number. In cases with no available distance, for example, if we merge all samples into one cluster, we pick the closest obtainable distance in the tree. For words with a single occurrence, we do not consider any distances.

Table 5 and Table 6 show the averages and standard deviations of the Euclidean and cosine linkage distances at the last performed merge in the merge tree. Again, we analyze the dictionaries from Table A.1 and only consider tokens with known senses. The averages are fairly similar for all corpora and the standard deviations are rather small. Our results for SemEval2015 are clearly the worst due to lower averages and higher standard deviations, possibly because it contains comparatively few samples.

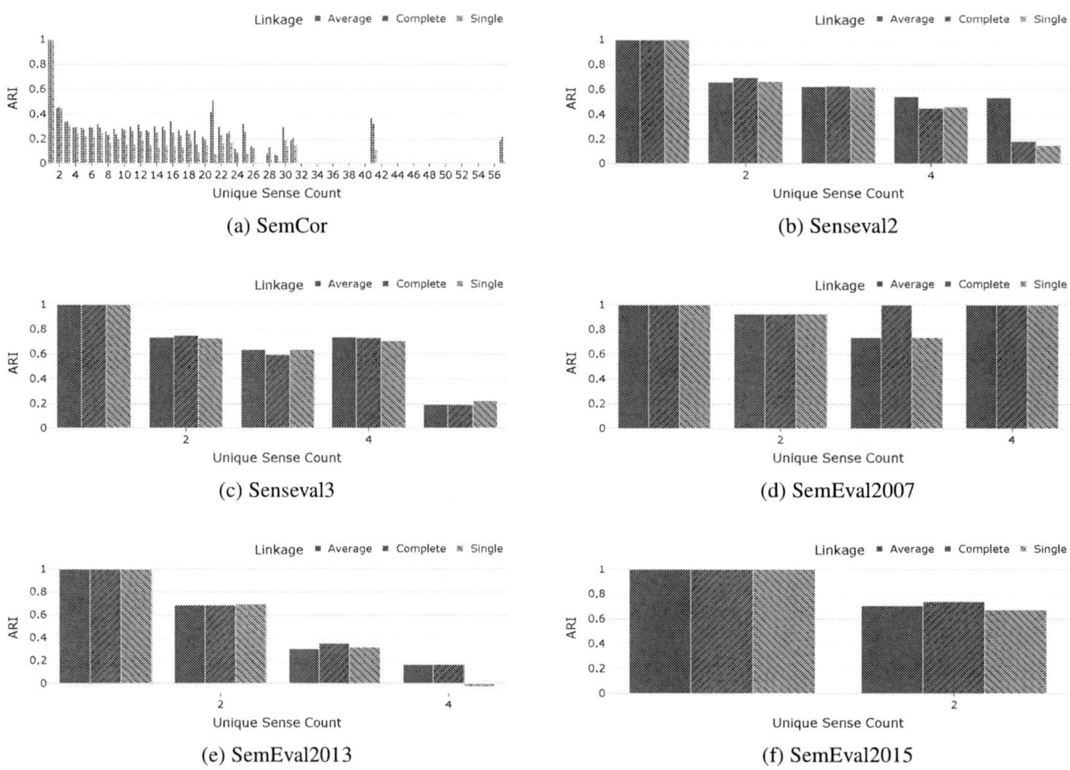

(a) SemCor (b) Senseval2 (c) Senseval3 (d) SemEval2007 (e) SemEval2013 (f) SemEval2015

Figure 4: Sense-Count-Level ARI for Clusterings with Different Linkage Criteria using known sense counts and the Euclidean distance as affinity. Each bar plot shows the average ARI for all words that have the same number of true unique senses and no generated senses. We analyze the dictionaries from Section A.1.

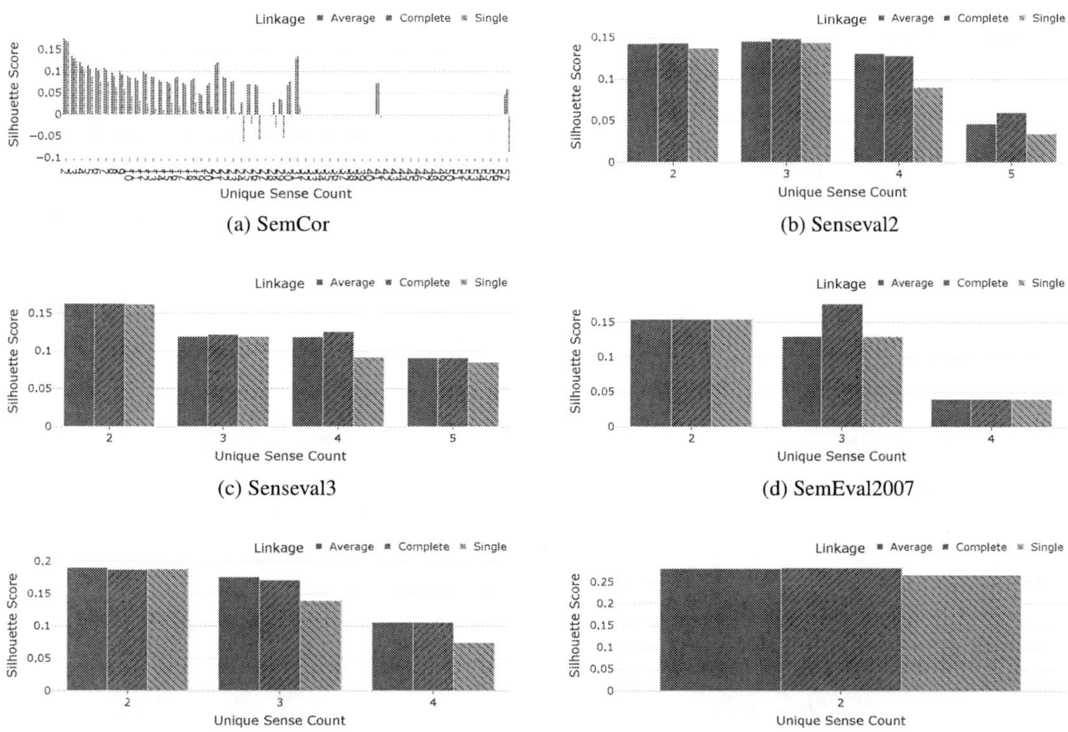

(a) SemCor (b) Senseval2 (c) Senseval3 (d) SemEval2007 (e) SemEval2013 (f) SemEval2015

Figure 5: Sense-Count-Level Silhouette Coefficient for Clusterings with Different Linkage Criteria *using known sense counts and the Euclidean distance as affinity. Each bar plot shows the average Silhouette Score for all words that have the same number of true unique senses and no generated senses. We analyze the dictionaries from Section A.1.*

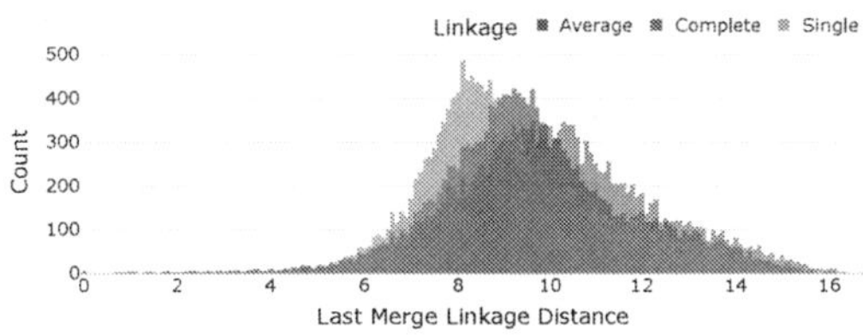

(a) SemCor

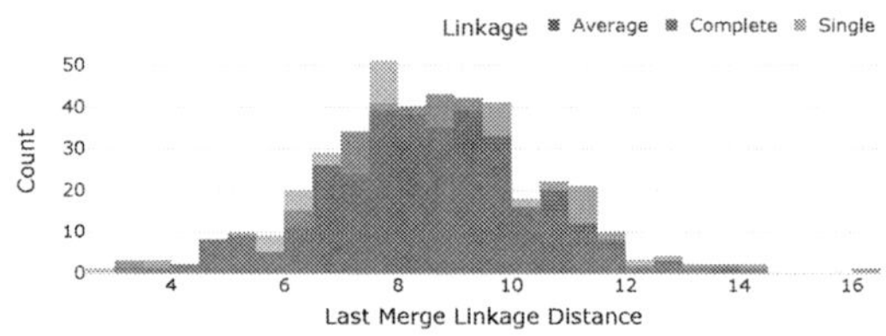

(b) Senseval2

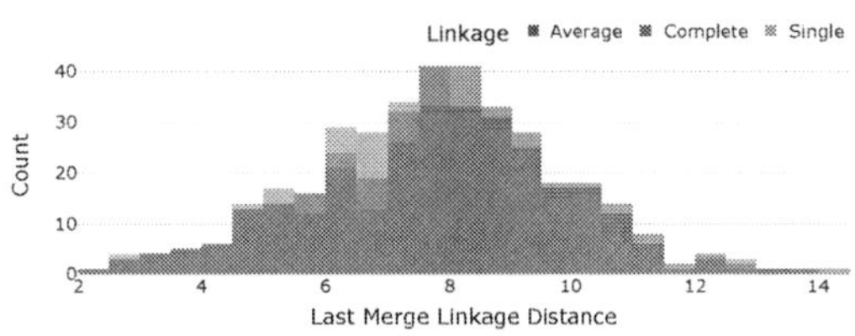

(c) Senseval3

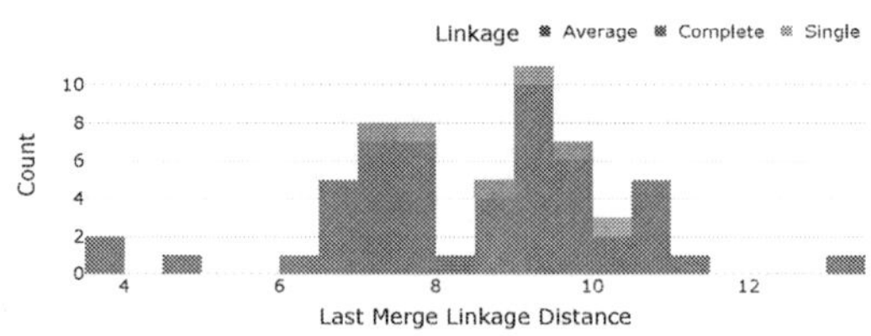

(d) SemEval2007

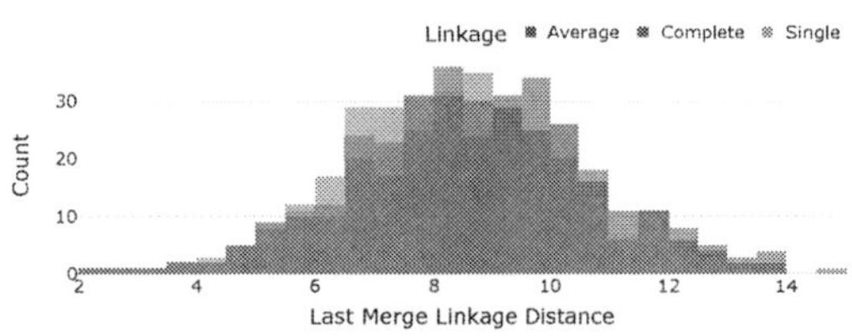

(e) SemEval2013

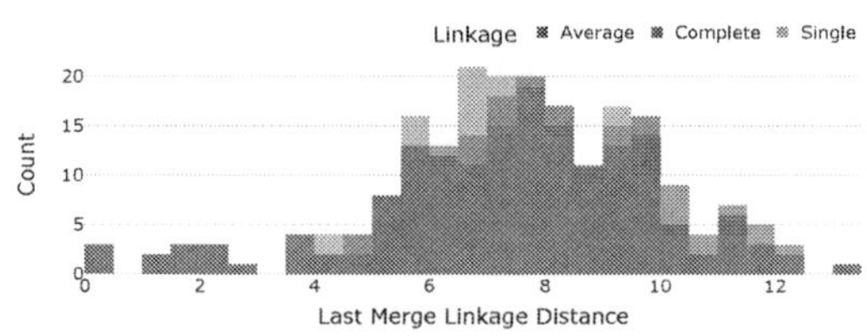

(f) SemEval2015

Figure 6: Euclidean Linkage Distances at the Last Merge using known sense counts. Each histogram shows frequencies for all words that have no generated senses. We analyze the dictionaries from Section A.1.

Corpus	Average Linkage Avg.	Average Linkage Std.	Complete Linkage Avg.	Complete Linkage Std.	Single Linkage Avg.	Single Linkage Std.
SemCor	9.6395	2.0394	10.0726	2.1631	9.1755	2.0249
Senseval2	8.4796	1.8256	8.7032	1.9295	8.2633	1.7940
Senseval3	7.7612	2.0223	7.9206	2.0855	7.5898	2.0015
SemEval2007	8.5086	1.7495	8.5396	1.7577	8.4842	1.7464
SemEval2013	8.5505	2.0034	8.7958	2.1140	8.3034	1.9379
SemEval2015	7.4175	2.4254	7.6239	2.5386	7.2192	2.3627

Table 5: Average and Standard Deviation of Euclidean Linkage Distances at the Last Merge using known sense counts. We analyze the dictionaries from Section A.1 and ignore tokens with generated senses or only one occurrence.

Corpus	Average Linkage Avg.	Average Linkage Std.	Complete Linkage Avg.	Complete Linkage Std.	Single Linkage Avg.	Single Linkage Std.
SemCor	0.3624	0.1469	0.3960	0.1610	0.3285	0.1423
Senseval2	0.2900	0.1198	0.3060	0.1304	0.2753	0.1156
Senseval3	0.2464	0.1183	0.2566	0.1234	0.2358	0.1165
SemEval2007	0.2928	0.1156	0.2947	0.1161	0.2912	0.1152
SemEval2013	0.2946	0.1297	0.3125	0.1410	0.2771	0.1224
SemEval2015	0.2357	0.1306	0.2497	0.1404	0.2229	0.1257

Table 6: Average and Standard Deviation of Cosine Linkage Distances at the Last Merge using known sense counts. We analyze the dictionaries from Section A.1 and consider all words with at least two occurrences and no generated senses.

Figure 6 exhibits histograms for Euclidean linkage distances at the cut corresponding to Table 5. Considering the averages and standard deviations of linkage distances in combination with their distributions from the histograms, we propose that most last merges occur near a Euclidean linkage distance of about $8.5 - 9.0$ with a standard deviation of about 1.7. This observation holds for most examined corpora and even accross different linkage criteria. Due to the sample size of SemCor, the related results are most representative and suggest a bell curve with said parameters. Therefore, a linkage distance threshold slightly above the maximum of the bell curves should yield a reasonable dictionary. The similarities in our experiments suggest that $8.0 - 9.5$ is a reasonable initial search space in hyperparameter optimization.

Table 7 offers the averages and standard deviations of the Euclidean linkage distances at the successor of the last merge in the tree. We need to cut the tree between the last performed merge and its successor to obtain the same clustering. The latter distances are significantly higher than those from Table 7 and the standard deviations indicate minor overlaps of both distributions. These results indicate clear gaps and further suggest the existence of a reasonable linkage distance threshold.

A.5 Relation Detection

Often, terms and names consist of more than one token, for example, the "White House". We could use syntactic knowledge to find related words in the sentences. For instance, the contextualized word embedding BERT encodes some syntactic rules (Clark et al., 2019; Jawahar et al., 2019). In contrast, there are syntactic correlations between different words, e.g., for the combination of an auxiliary verb and its participle like "has finished". Some approaches mitigate such problems with semantic knowledge about existing entities and phrases. Inflections help determine syntax and context in a sentence. Usually, only one entry per infinitive exists in resources like dictionaries. Mapping inflected forms to their infinitives is challenging and may require prior knowledge. We need to pick a distance criterion to separate clusters of word vectors. The criterion could be a fixed threshold or a relative factor for distances. Some methods might depend on more sophisticated geometric criteria or estimate the number of clusters or objects. Its choice might depend on the given corpus.

Similar contexts yield word vectors close in the embedding space, so similar word vectors for different words might indicate synonyms. In contrast, word vectors that point in the opposite direction might reveal antonyms.

However, performing clustering methods on all

Corpus	Average Linkage Avg.	Average Linkage Std.	Complete Linkage Avg.	Complete Linkage Std.	Single Linkage Avg.	Single Linkage Std.
SemCor	10.1048	2.0594	10.6219	2.1876	9.5731	2.0454
Senseval2	8.7927	1.7905	9.0681	1.9032	8.5312	1.7627
Senseval3	8.0880	2.1119	8.2969	2.2062	7.8749	2.0615
SemEval2007	8.8758	2.0199	8.9492	2.0532	8.7969	1.9871
SemEval2013	8.7354	2.0456	9.0253	2.1949	8.4543	1.9713
SemEval2015	7.7537	2.3858	8.0112	2.5202	7.5166	2.3156

Table 7: Average and Standard Deviation of Euclidean Linkage Distances after the Last Merge using known sense counts. We analyze the dictionaries from Section A.1 and ignore tokens with generated senses or only one occurrence.

words is more computationally expensive. Clustering the centroids of sense clusters might also reveal related words. In this setting, the definition of negative concepts like antonyms is less obvious. We could measure the strength of the relation between two clusters via the distance between their centroids. The closer any two centroids are, the stronger their relation is and vice versa. We could choose thresholds or ranges to define certain concepts like synonyms and antonyms.

A.6 ARI scores for different linkage distance thresholds

In Figure 7 we show the details for every dataset on the distribution of the ARI score next to the "Single Cluster"-baseline. As described before, for large thresholds the ARI converges to the ARI of our "Single Cluster"-baseline. For both the Senseval3 and the SemEval2007 corpus a clear peak before converging to the baseline. To gain further insights why our method works better for some corpora than for others, an analysis of the corpora and the tagged annotations is necessary.

A.7 Details on Creating Shakespearean Dictionary

Table 8 shows all hyperparameters we used to pretrain CharacterBERT for creating a Shakespearean dictionary.

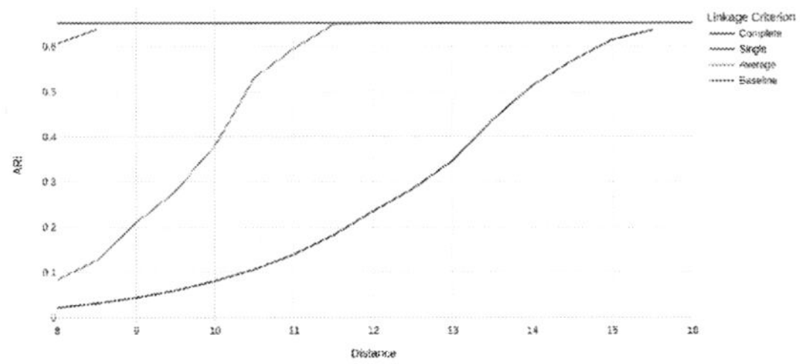

(a) SemCor

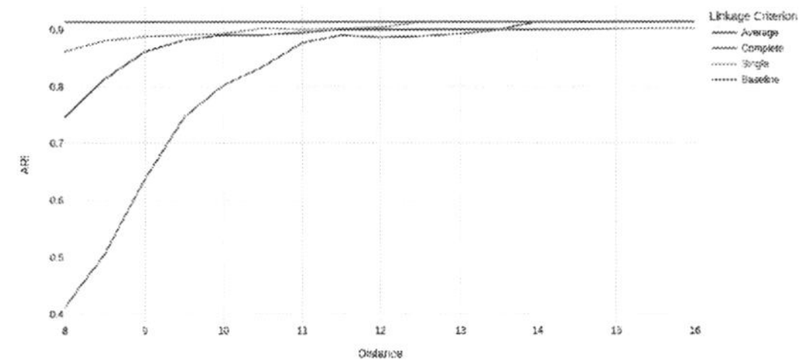

(b) Senseval2

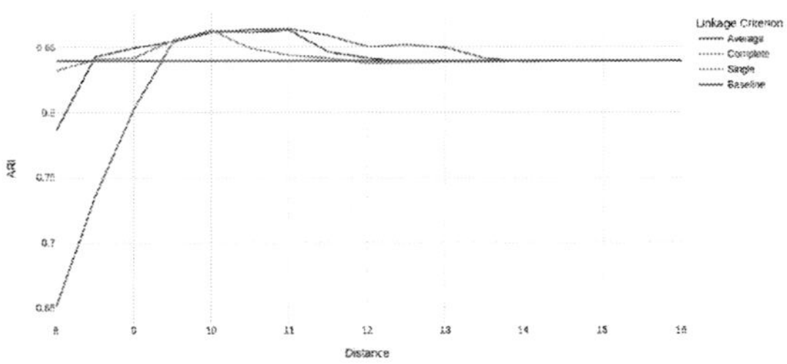

(c) Senseval3

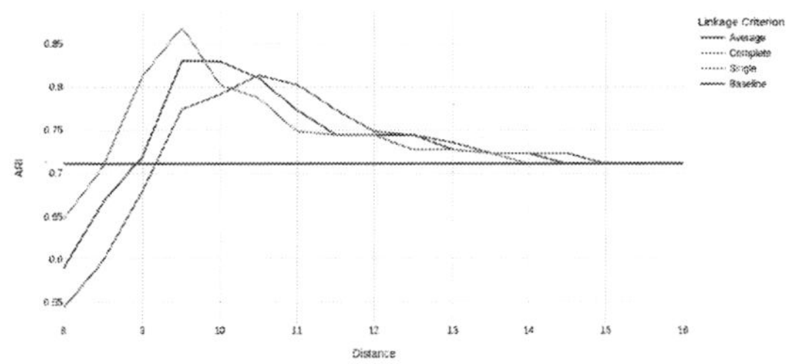

(d) SemEval2007

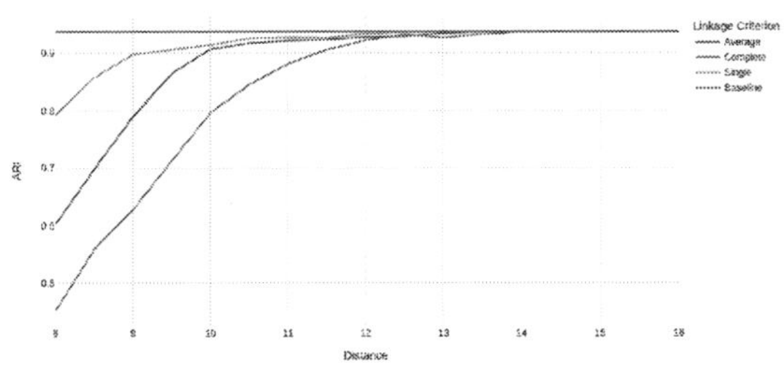

(e) SemEval2013

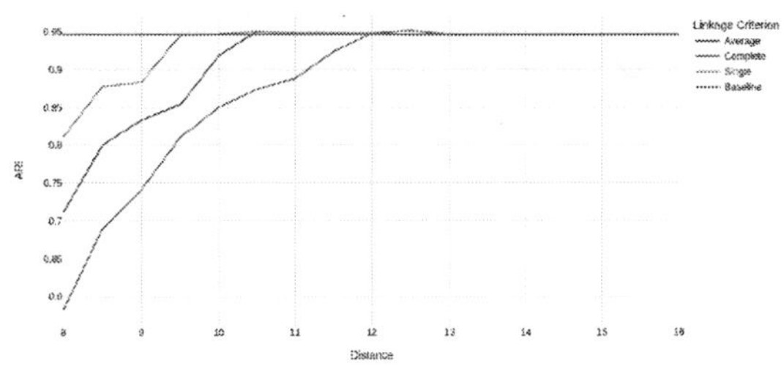

(f) SemEval2015

Figure 7: Linkage distance thresholds per dataset

Hyperparameter	Phase 1	Phase 2
Learning Rate	6×10^{-3}	4×10^{-3}
Warm-Up Proportion	0.2843	0.128
Warm-Up Rate	0.01	
Weight Decay	0.01	
Target Batch Size	$2,048$	
Accumulation Steps	256	$1,024$
Total Batch Size	8	2
Update Steps	$1,800$	800
Max. Input Sequence Size	128	512
Max. Masked Tokens per Input	20	80

Table 8: Hyper-Parameters for Training CharacterBERT on Shakespeare's Works, based on the hyper-parameters for the general CharacterBERT model (El Boukkouri et al., 2020).

Towards Ukrainian WordNet: Incorporation of an Existing Thesaurus in the Domain of Physics

Melanie Siegel and **Maksym Vakulenko** and **Jonathan Baum**
Darmstadt University of Applied Sciences

Abstract

In this paper, we represent the first version of the Ukrainian wordnet – Ukrajinet 1.0. It contains 3,360 sets of full synonyms in the field of physics, consisting of 8,700 words. This knowledge base will help incorporate the Ukrainian language into multilingual scenarios of Natural Language Processing that need information about lexical-semantic relations.

1 Introduction

Information about words and their meanings is traditionally stored in dictionaries. With the increasing importance of automatic processing of language, a need for machine-readable dictionaries arose. In this context, wordnets emerged to store lexical information in a format that can be used by language processing systems. A wordnet (WN) is a lexical database of semantic relations between words in a given language. The basis of wordnets are synsets: groups of synonyms in the language that stand for the concepts of meaning. The first wordnet was created for the English language at Princeton University (also known as Princeton WordNet, (Fellbaum, 1998)). As the usefulness of wordnets as lexical resources for a wide variety of language technology applications became clear, the Princeton WordNet (PWN) was expanded and wordnets in other languages were created. The Open Multilingual Wordnet (OMW) is an open-source project created with the goal of facilitating the use of wordnets in multiple languages with open source license (Bond and Foster, 2013). The OMW has the added benefit of connecting equivalent synsets in different languages (Bond et al., 2016). This connection is created by an Interlingual Index called "ILI". The English version of the OMW (Open English WordNet, OEWN) is basically a copy of the PWN, with some improvements and additions, most notably the addition of an interlingual index for each synset (McCrae et al., 2019); (McCrae et al., 2020). Many of the OMW wordnets in other languages were developed using existing translations in the Natural Language Toolkit (NLTK). These translations were extracted and packaged into new wordnets. Consequently, the corresponding synsets in the resulting wordnets were linked using the ILI. Goodman and Bond (2021) developed the Wordnet Python library that can be used to access the OMW project wordnets in Python. The OEWN is distributed in electronic form as part of the NLTK, among others, and can be used with a corresponding Python library. NLTK provides translations for synsets into different languages, although these translations are incomplete. This means that not every synset in English has an equivalent translation in another language. There are also wordnets in other languages that were developed independently of OMW, such as GermaNet (Hamp et al., 1997). Many of these wordnets contain high-quality data that is resource- and time-consuming to create manually. As a result, some of these wordnets are commercially licensed and not free to use (nor are they part of NLTK, for example).

Ukrainian is a language with still few linguistic resources that is not yet contained in OMW. Therefore, an initiative has been launched to create an open-source Ukrainian wordnet (Ukrajinet, Ukrainian pronunciation [ʊːkrəːjiːːnət]), which is being developed as part of the OMW project. The Ukrainian wordnet, Ukrajinet, will help incorporate the Ukrainian language into multilingual scenarios of Natural Language Processing that need information about lexical-semantic relations. This paper presents the first version and demonstrates how this resource will be expanded.

We will present the related work and show, how other wordnets have been developed and how the development of Ukrajinet fits into it. We outline the process of developing the first version of Ukrajinet and show how we applied existing methods. Fi-

Proceedings of the 19th Conference on Natural Language Processing (KONVENS 2023), pages 121–126
September 18–22, 2023. ©2023 Association for Computational Linguistics

nally, we discuss the initial results and demonstrate how we will proceed.

2 Related Work

In the Open Multilingual Wordnet initiative (OMW, Bond and Paik, 2012; Bond et al., 2015), wordnets for several languages were developed and linked with each other.

Vossen (1998, p11) describes two basic approaches to developing new wordnet resources: In the first case (*expand*), existing PWN synsets of other languages are taken, and lexical entries are added for the specific language. In the second case (*merge*), language-specific resources are built and then linked to the PWN.

An example of *expand* is the Japanese wordnet (Isahara et al., 2008). It is based on translations of PWN to Japanese. The Japanese wordnet is not built fully automatically: most translations are manually checked. The authors found that there are differences between concept structures in English and Japanese, such that several synsets could not be translated. Other examples of *expand* include the Finnish (Lindén and Carlson, 2010) and the French (Sagot and Fišer, 2008) wordnets.

The Russian wordnet (Alexeyevsky and Temchenko, 2016) is an example of the *merge* approach. It is based on a monolingual dictionary and the word definitions in these. The idea is that definitions contain hypernyms of the defined words, often in the form of WORD:HYPERNYM ..., and that this information can be used to set up hierarchical structures in the wordnet. Other examples of *merge* with partly different ideas are the Polish Wordnet (Derwojedowa et al., 2008), the Norwegian Wordnet (Fjeld and Nygaard, 2009), the Danish Wordnet (Pedersen et al., 2009), and the Turkish Wordnet (Bakay et al., 2021).

There were previous attempts to create Ukrainian wordnets that, however, did not result in the release of an open Ukrainian wordnet. In particular, (Kuljchycjkyj et al., 2010) state that their earlier attempts to apply an expansion method to Ukrainian failed. The authors claim that in the next attempt, having used frequency dictionaries, they created the fragment of a wordnet-like dictionary of the Ukrainian language, in which 194 noun synsets were implemented, being connected by hypo-/hyperonymy links (183 examples), antonymy (14 examples), as well as additionally meronymy/holonymy connections (over 150 cases). However, the project was not continued, and the results were not made publicly available.

(Anisimov et al., 2013) report the main results of a project aimed to create the Ukrainian lexical-semantic knowledge base UkrWordNet (UWN), describing tools and results. The authors claim that they automatically created more than 82,000 noun synsets and have about 145,000 nouns in the lexicon. However, this wordnet cannot be accessed.

Nykonenko et al. (2013) describe a correction tool designed to create and modify the Ukrainian linguistic ontology in the UWN. However, the site of the mentioned project UWN (`http://lingvoworks.org.ua/`) is not accessible any more.

Thus, we may conclude that despite some efforts and announced results, a Ukrainian wordnet as part of the OMW effort under an open source license is still not available and remains an open field for research.

3 Method and Material

For Ukrajinet, we decided to use the same approach as for the (Siegel and Bond, 2021; Bergh and Siegel, 2023) wordnet. So, the approach of the Ukrajinet initiative is *merge*. We use an existing synonym dictionary and several methods to link the synsets to OMW. The methods from the development of the (Siegel and Bond, 2021; Bergh and Siegel, 2023) wordnet are reused for Ukrajinet.

The first version of the open Ukrainian wordnet, Ukrajinet 1.0, was created on a basis of a dictionary of physical synonymous terms (Vakulenko and Vakulenko, 2017).

As in other languages, the establishment of an ontology for the Ukrainian lexical information necessitates proper accounting of ambiguities resulting from homonymy and polysemy. These lexical semantic relations prevalently occur within the same syntactic category (Part of Speech, POS) but can also arise across different POS, e.g.

мати 'mother' (noun) – мати 'have' (verb)

In most cases, such ambiguities are not parallel to English ones, which results in difficulties in translation and linking Ukrajinet to OMW. For example, the Ukrainian term вал has three main meanings corresponding to different English terms: 1. (tech.) 'shaft'; 2. 'barrage'; 3. (arch.) 'torus'. In addition, Ukrainian verbal nouns stemming from the same verb, bear subtle semantic differences that cannot be reflected in other languages (Vakulenko and Vakulenko, 2017).

4 Process of Creating Ukrajinet

Basic information on the wordnet idea can be found in (Fellbaum, 1998) and (Kunze and Lemnitzer, 2010), among others. The data structure of wordnets in OMW is an XML structure (which can be converted to a JSON format). A lexeme has a "LexEntry" with a unique ID, information about the written form, syntactic category, and meanings, with links to associated concepts.

The dictionary of physical terms that we use as a basis for Ukrajinet was not created primarily for NLP purposes. It is in Microsoft Word © format and has entries such as[1]

будова
будова атомного ядра, структура атомного ядра
/+/ збудова атомного ядра

Therefore, the first step was to convert the dictionary entries into a machine-readable format. Then, existing methods could be used to compile this information into the OMW XML format (section 4.1). Furthermore, the information is extended with POS (section 4.2) and multilingual indexing information (section 4.3).

4.1 From the Dictionary of Physical Synonym Terms to Synsets

We extracted only the synonym information from the dictionary and ignored (for the time being) other information, such as subdomains (optics, molecular physics, quantum mechanics, etc.). This information will be added in future work. The output of the preprocessing was a file of synsets, with each synset on one line. An example of such a synset is:

аглютинація;склеювання;грудкування (agglutination, adhesion, clumping)

The target of the transfer process of this synset is to have three lexical entries and a synset entry. The format is described in Bond et al. (2016). We start with the synset and its basic information[2]:

```
<Synset id="ukrajinet-30-n" ili="i36192" partOfSpeech="n">
<Definition> міцне з'єднання між собою (strong connection between each other) </Definition>
</Synset>
```

The synset has a unique synset ID, a link to the interlingual wordnet IDs in "ili", a POS, and a definition. Further, it has relations to other synsets that we ignore for the moment.

4.2 Adding POS Information

The next task is to find information about the syntactic category (Part-of-Speech, POS). One option for the part-of-speech tagging of Ukrainian words is to use a tool such as VESUM[3]. However, a noticeable part of our terms is not present in VESUM, such as the words "видим ('antinode'), вогкомір ('psychrometer'), замичник ('relay'), іскриш ('pyrites'), etc. This is due to the fact that we have many very specific terms in the field of physics. Given this, we used the following heuristic approach, which showed better results.

As the dictionary contains only verbs and nouns (with rare exceptions), we recognize verbs by their endings. If a word ends with one of the verbal endings, then it is a verb in the infinitive form (with rare exceptions for " ти "), otherwise a noun:

- ти
- тися
- тись

As with other wordnets, we have some cases of multiword expressions. An example is ставати більшим (to grow larger). We use the POS of the first word in the expression, as these are (in this dictionary) mostly consisting of verb + adjective (POS V) or noun + noun (POS N). We manually checked and corrected the cases where a synset contained words with different assigned POS's.

A further task is to generate the lexical entries for the words, sharing the synset sense. This is what is aimed for:

```
<LexicalEntry id="w76">
<Lemma writtenForm=" аглютинація "4
partOfSpeech="n"/>
<Sense id="w76_30-n" synset="ukrajinet-30-n"/>
</LexicalEntry>
```

[1] structure, structure of the atomic nucleus, construction of a nuclear core

[2] The English translation is not part of the synset; the translation is given here only for better understanding

[3] https://github.com/brown-uk/nlp_uk

[4] agglutination

```
<LexicalEntry id="w77">
<Lemma writtenForm=" склеювання "5
partOfSpeech="n"/>
<Sense id="w77_30-n" synset="ukrajinet-30-n"/>
</LexicalEntry>

<LexicalEntry id="w78">
<Lemma writtenForm=" грудкування "6
partOfSpeech="n"/>
<Sense id="w78_30-n" synset="ukrajinet-30-n"/>
</LexicalEntry>
```

The lexical entries in a synset belong to one sense with the same synset ID. Further senses for lexical entries come from other synsets in the dictionary. Each lexical entry has a unique word ID, a lemma, and a part of speech (POS).

A validation process is implemented to ensure correctness of the wordnet. It checks for XML correctness, duplicate lexical entries (that are only allowed for homonyms), consistency of POS in LexEntries, synsets, duplicate ilis, synsets without words, words without synsets, and others.

4.3 Linking the Synsets with the Open Multilingual Wordnet

In order to create a useful resource in the OMW context, it is necessary to link the Ukrainian synsets by adding an interlingual index in "ili". We used the translation table that we had created for another wordnet (Bergh and Siegel, 2023). It contains the words and definitions for each English synset in OEWN. The idea behind using the definitions with the words is that these provide some context for the translation, such that lexical ambiguity is reduced. For our example above, we get:

i36192 bonding: fastening firmly together

The obtained list was automatically translated into Ukrainian through the DeepL tool and post-processed by a linguist to render precise meaning. Then we searched for the Ukrainian terms in our dictionary. Hence, we found the rows in the following form:

i36192 bonding: fastening firmly together
аглютинація;склеювання;грудкування

[5]adhesion

[6]clumping

In the non-ambiguous cases in which an ILI could be assigned exactly to one synset, we were able to transfer these words and definitions directly to Ukrajinet. We used the words and definitions from WordNet corresponding to those of Ukrajinet where 571 synsets were connected. We have also adopted the Ukrainian translation of the definition in these cases.

The ambiguous cases, where either one ILI is assigned to more than one synsets or a synset got more than one ILI assigned, are currently checked manually.

4.4 Results

So far, we have the first version of Ukrajinet with 8,700 lexical entries organized in 3,360 synsets, all in the physical domain. 571 of these synsets are connected to OMW via the ILI. We use a validation script for Ukrajinet that is based on the OMW validation, before submitting the wordnet to Github. Ukrajinet is released via GitHub, under a (CC-BY-SA 4.0)[7] license at `https://github.com/hdaSprachtechnologie/ukrajinet`. This can then be loaded directly into the WN Python library (Goodman and Bond, 2021), which allows easy use: either on its own or linked to other wordnets through the Collaborative Interlingual Index (CILI).

5 Discussion and Future Plans

We presented in this paper the process of creating the first version of the Ukrainian wordnet, Ukrajinet 1.0, which synsets and lexical entries in the field of physics.

It was possible to reuse methods that were developed for the creation of the German Wordnet OdeNet (Siegel and Bond, 2021) and therefore prove that this is an efficient way to create a wordnet for a new language.

Ukrajinet 1.0 is a starting point for future elaboration of this resource.

We are currently checking ambiguous translations, such that most of the terms in Ukrajinet 1.0 can be linked to OMW. Wordnets contain relations between synsets, such as hypernym, meronym, or antonym relations. Some relations are available in the dictionary that we use as the basis for our wordnet. Others can be taken over from OEWN, in cases where we have the ILI connection. Defini-

[7]`https://creativecommons.org/licenses/by-sa/4.0/`

tions for the terms in the domain of physics will be taken from the "Explanatory dictionary in physics" (Vakulenko and Vakulenko, 2008).

We have so far ignored information in the physics dictionary that we plan to include in the future: information about hierarchical relations and information about subdomains of physics.

Once the information for the terms we now have in Ukrajinet 1.0 is complete, we can begin to *expand* the wordnet. Various sources of information come into question for this: We can use the existing translation table to add general terms translated from OEWN to Ukrajinet. This will be done following the method described by (Bergh and Siegel, 2023). The domain information can be used to fine-tune the synsets. Further, we can look at the Wiktionary database of Ukrainian lemmata. We can also include the information in an academic dictionary of Ukrainian words, such as (Burjachok et al., 2001).

It is also planned to provide a Latinized version of Ukrajinet, Romanized according to the Ukrainian national standard 9112:2021[8] that yields isomorphic transliteration of Ukrainian texts (Vakulenko, 2022).

We are currently developing a user interface for manual work on Ukrajinet - corrections, edits, and additions.

Ukrajinet will be used in various multilingual scenarios of NLP requiring Ukrainian semantic and lexical resources, such as multilingual information retrieval, text analysis and comparison, machine translation, etc.

Limitations

The work described is work in progress. The results are promising, but not yet complete.

Acknowledgements

The described work was supported by Darmstadt University of Applied Sciences and the Hessian Ministry of Science and Art.

References

Daniil Alexeyevsky and Anastasiya V. Temchenko. 2016. WSD in monolingual dictionaries for Russian WordNet. In *Proceedings of the Eighth Global WordNet Conference*, Bucharest, Romania.

Anatoly Anisimov, Oleksandr Marchenko, Andrey Nikonenko, Elena Porkhun, and Volodymyr Taranukha. 2013. Ukrainian wordnet: creation and filling. In *Flexible Query Answering Systems: 10th International Conference, FQAS 2013, Granada, Spain, September 18-20, 2013. Proceedings 10*, pages 649–660. Springer. In Ukrainian.

Özge Bakay, Özlem Ergelen, Elif Sarmış, Selin Yıldırım, Bilge Nas Arıcan, Atilla Kocabalcıoğlu, Merve Özçelik, Ezgi Sanıyar, Oğuzhan Kuyrukçu, Begüm Avar, et al. 2021. Turkish wordnet KeNet. In *Proceedings of the 11th Global Wordnet Conference*, pages 166–174.

Johann Bergh and Melanie Siegel. 2023. Connecting multilingual wordnets: Strategies for improving ILI classification in OdeNet. In *Proceedings of the Global Wordnet Conference*, Donostia, Spain.

Francis Bond, Luis Morgado Da Costa, and Tuan Anh Le. 2015. Imi—a multilingual semantic annotation environment. *Proceedings of ACL-IJCNLP 2015 System Demonstrations*, pages 7–12.

Francis Bond and Ryan Foster. 2013. Linking and extending an open multilingual wordnet. In *Proceedings of the 51st Annual Meeting of the Association for Computational Linguistics*, pages 1352–1362, Sofia.

Francis Bond and Kyonghee Paik. 2012. A survey of wordnets and their licenses. *Small*, 8(4):5.

Francis Bond, Piek Vossen, John P McCrae, and Christiane Fellbaum. 2016. CILI: The Collaborative Interlingual Index. In *Proceedings of the Global WordNet Conference*, volume 2016.

Andrij Burjachok, Andrij Ghnatjuk, Serghij Gholovashchuk, Ghalyna Ghorjushyna, Nina Lozova, Natalija Meljnyk, Oljgha Nechytajlo, Lidija Rodnina, Valentyna Taranenko, and Oleksandr Frydrak. 2001. *Slovnyk synonimiv ukrajinsjkoji movy: V dvokh tomakh (A dictionary of Ukrainian synonyms: In two volumes).* Naukova dumka, Kyjiv. In Ukrainian.

Magdalena Derwojedowa, Maciej Piasecki, Stanislaw Szpakowicz, Magdalena Zawislawska, and Bartosz Broda. 2008. Words, concepts and relations in the construction of Polish WordNet. *Proceedings of GWC 2008*, pages 162–177.

Christiane Fellbaum, editor. 1998. *WordNet: An Electronic Lexical Database*. MIT Press, Cambridge, MA.

Ruth Vatvedt Fjeld and Lars Nygaard. 2009. Nornet-a monolingual wordnet of modern norwegian. In *NODALIDA 2009 workshop: WordNets and other Lexical Semantic Resources-between Lexical Semantics, Lexicography, Terminology and Formal Ontologies*, volume 7, pages 13–16.

Michael Wayne Goodman and Francis Bond. 2021. Intrinsically interlingual: The Wn Python library for wordnets. In *11th International Global Wordnet Conference (GWC2021)*.

[8] http://online.budstandart.com/ru/catalog/doc-page.html?id_doc=95601

Birgit Hamp, Helmut Feldweg, et al. 1997. GermaNet-a lexical-semantic net for German. In *Proceedings of ACL workshop Automatic Information Extraction and Building of Lexical Semantic Resources for NLP Applications*, pages 9–15.

Hitoshi Isahara, Francis Bond, Kiyotaka Uchimoto, Masao Utiyama, and Kyoko Kanzaki. 2008. Development of the Japanese wordnet. In *Sixth International conference on Language Resources and Evaluation (LREC 2008)*, Marrakech.

I.M. Kuljchycjkyj, A.B. Romanjuk, and K.B. Khariv. 2010. Rozroblennja wordnetpodibnogho slovnyka ukrajinsjkoji movy (development of a wordnetlike dictionary for the ukrainian language). *Visnyk Nacionaljnogho universytetu Ljvivsjka politekhnika. Informacijni systemy ta merezhi*, 673:306–318. In Ukrainian.

Claudia Kunze and Lothar Lemnitzer. 2010. Lexical-semantic and conceptual relations in germanet. *Lexical-semantic relations: Theoretical and practical perspectives*, pages 163–183.

Krister Lindén and Lauri Carlson. 2010. Finnwordnet – finnish wordnet by translation. *LexicoNordica – Nordic Journal of Lexicography*, 17:119–140.

John Philip McCrae, Alexandre Rademaker, Francis Bond, Ewa Rudnicka, and Christiane Fellbaum. 2019. English wordnet 2019–an open-source wordnet for english. In *Proceedings of the 10th Global WordNet Conference*, pages 245–252.

John Philip McCrae, Alexandre Rademaker, Ewa Rudnicka, and Francis Bond. 2020. English wordnet 2020: Improving and extending a wordnet for english using an open-source methodology. In *proceedings of the LREC 2020 workshop on multimodal WordNets (MMW2020)*, pages 14–19.

A.O. Nykonenko, E.V. Lyman, K.S.and Zabelin, and B.O. Rybachok. 2013. Uwn: Ontocorrector as a tool for ukrainian language linguistic ontology creation. *Shtuchnyj intelekt*, 4. In Ukrainian.

Bolette Sandford Pedersen, Sanni Nimb, Jørg Asmussen, Nicolai Hartvig Sørensen, Lars Trap-Jensen, and Henrik Lorentzen. 2009. Dannet: the challenge of compiling a wordnet for Danish by reusing a monolingual dictionary. *Language resources and evaluation*, 43:269–299.

Benoît Sagot and Darja Fišer. 2008. Building a free French wordnet from multilingual resources. In *OntoLex*.

Melanie Siegel and Francis Bond. 2021. Compiling a German wordnet from other resources. In *11th International Global Wordnet Conference (GWC2021)*.

M. O Vakulenko and O. V Vakulenko. 2008. Tlumachnyj slovnyk iz fizyky [explanatory dictionary on physics]. *Kyjiv: VPC Kyjivsjkyj universytet.*

Maksym Vakulenko. 2022. Deep contextual disambiguation of homonyms and polysemants. *Digital Scholarship in the Humanities.*

Maksym O. Vakulenko and Olegh V. Vakulenko. 2017. *Tlumachnyj slovnyk iz fizyky: [6644 statti] (Explanatory dictionary on physics: [6644 articles]).* Naukova dumka, Kyjiv. In Ukrainian.

Piek Vossen, editor. 1998. *Euro WordNet*. Kluwer.

Pointer Networks: A Unified Approach to Extracting German Opinions

Julia Wunderle and **Jan Pfister** and **Andreas Hotho**
Julius-Maximilians-Universität Würzburg
Computer Science Chair X: Data Science
{lastname}@informatik.uni-wuerzburg.de

Abstract

Transformer-based pointer networks currently represent the state of the art for English aspect-based sentiment analysis. Inspired by their performance in extracting structured sentiment information from text, we aim to transfer this success to the German language. For evaluation we use the GermEval shared task on "Aspect-based Sentiment in Social Media Customer Feedback", as it consists of four subtasks: (A) Relevance Classification, (B) Document-level Polarity, (C) Aspect-level Polarity, and (D) Opinion Target Extraction (Wojatzki et al., 2017). We follow the intuition of the English approach by training a single model to solve all related subtasks at once. Therefore, the subtasks are formulated as a single unified index generation problem, enabling the model to solve all four subtasks simultaneously. We find that solving all four subtasks at once only has a minimal impact on the overall performance of our model. Consequently, we closely match or outperform all previous approaches despite them training subtask-specific models.

1 Introduction

Explicit customer feedback is an extremely valuable source for understanding the needs of customers and improving products and services accordingly, while being available in a large amount on the Internet in unstructured form. It is necessary to be able to aggregate and analyze the feedback in a comprehensive way, to understand the wide variety of opinions and sentiments expressed. Ideally, the feedback has to be extracted in a fine-grained but easily understandable way. The main interests are, of course, voiced opinions and their aspects that determine whether and why exactly, e.g. a review is positive or negative. Consequently, to break down a long review to its core information, tuples of opinion terms and their associated sentiment have to be extracted. This structured span-based extraction process, called "Opinion Extraction", can easily be solved by pointer networks. Specifically, BARTABSA (Yan et al., 2021) is a sequence-to-sequence pointer model, which predicts a sequence of class tokens and pointers to token indices of the input text. Current research developments related to pointer networks and aspect-based sentiment analysis do include multilingual approaches (R et al., 2022; Pfister et al., 2022) but notably until now not German. Thus, the research gap arises on how recent advances in structured sentiment prediction can be leveraged for German Opinion Extraction. Despite this gap, for German evaluation there exists a comparably large data set introduced by the GermEval 2017 Task that contains customer feedback about "Deutsche Bahn". To this end, four subtasks were formulated and, while all are related to the analysis of customer feedback, each subtask focuses on a different level of information classification and extraction. In order of increasing complexity, the formulated tasks are (A) Relevance Classification, (B) Document-level Polarity, (C) Aspect-level Polarity (D) Opinion Target Extraction (Wojatzki et al., 2017). Thus, to solve all tasks successfully, a model needs to not only classify the entire document itself but also extract and label all relevant spans correctly. In contrast to existing approaches, we leverage a pointer network to solve all of these subtasks with the same model simultaneously, which we find to sometimes even increase performance over a model specialized on a subset of the tasks. In summary our main contributions are: (i) Formulating all GermEval 2017 subtasks as a single unified index generation problem, (ii) thereby introducing document-level classes next to sentiment spans to the BARTABSA approach. (iii) Extensively evaluating various German-capable transformer encoder-decoder basemodels on this German language task. (iv) We show that our model outperforms or closely matches all previously existing approaches while solving all tasks at once.

Proceedings of the 19th Conference on Natural Language Processing (KONVENS 2023), pages 127–138
September 18–22, 2023. ©2023 Association for Computational Linguistics

Figure 1: Exemplary input sentence for aspect-based sentiment analysis, annotated with aspects, opinions and sentiments (Yan et al., 2021).

2 Preliminaries & Related Work

2.1 Seq2Seq-Transformers

Transformer models consisting of an encoder and decoder are commonly referred to as *Seq2Seq* models, as the encoder generates an intermediate representation of the input sequence using which the decoder then generates the output sequence. In our experiments, we compare different Seq2Seq models with each other.

First, *BART* was pretrained as a denoising autoencoder (Lewis et al., 2020). Here denoising refers to the training process, in which a noised/-masked text sequence is given as input and the model is trained to reproduce the original sequence as output. The model is applicable to a wide range of tasks such as sequence classification, token classification, sequence generation, or machine translation. We also explore a BART model fine-tuned on the MNLI task as inspired by R et al. (2022) and one fine-tuned on the German MLSUM dataset (Scialom et al., 2020). Furthermore, we use *mBART50* which was trained in translating between 50 languages, including German (Tang et al., 2020). Lastly, *M2M-100* is a Many-to-Many multilingual Seq2Seq model trained on sentence pairs to translate between any pair of 100 languages, including German (Fan et al., 2020).

2.2 Aspect-Based Sentiment Analysis

The goal of *Aspect-based Sentiment Analysis (ABSA)* is, given a sentence containing expressed opinions, to extract explicitly voiced opinions, each consisting of an aspect term, its opinion term and corresponding sentiment polarity (see Figure 1 for example). Thereby, the aspect terms are the target to which the opinion terms refer, and thus express the polarity of the sentiment.

This task consists of two types of subtasks: extraction and classification. Here extraction refers to extracting and annotating the span of terms (a_1, a_2, o_1, o_2 in Figure 1), while classification describes the prediction of characteristics of this relationship, e.g. sentiment polarities (s_1, s_2).

2.3 BARTABSA Pointer Network

The BARTABSA pointer framework introduced by Yan et al. (2021) proposes a unified solution to solve various predefined ABSA subtasks. This comes with a substantial performance gain over comparable well-performing baselines, including BERT-based approaches. To achieve this, they reformulate all subtasks as a unified generative task, meaning that every subtask is defined as a sequence of pointers to indices in the source sequence and sentiment class tokens. To predict pointers to indices of the source sequence, they implement a pointer network, which uses BART as a backbone. Unlike a regular transformer, pointer networks do not output a probability distribution over a vocabulary of fixed size, but instead a distribution over tokens of the input sequence.

The model works by first generating an input representation $H^e \in \mathbb{R}^{n \times d}$ from its encoder. Here, d denotes the embedding size and n the number of tokens in the input sequence. This H^e is used by the decoder to autoregressively generate the target sequence. In every timestep, it takes H^e and previously generated tokens $Y_{<t}$ as input and returns a vector $H^d \in \mathbb{R}^d$. To obtain a token probability distribution P^X over the input sequence, the following calculations are performed: Both - the input sequence X, and the list of class tokens C - get embedded by the token embedding layer of the model, resulting in the embedding vectors $E^X \in \mathbb{R}^{n \times d}$ and $E^C \in \mathbb{R}^{l \times d}$, where l denotes the number of class tokens in the vocabulary. Next, a weighted average is calculated between the encoder output H^e and the embedded input sequence E^X, to obtain a new representation $\bar{H}^e \in \mathbb{R}^{n \times d}$.

$$\bar{H}^e = \alpha \text{MLP}(H^e) + (1 - \alpha) E^X \quad (1)$$

Before calculating this weighted average, H^e gets processed by a multilayer perceptron (MLP). Finally, the pointer distribution over the input tokens $P^X \in \mathbb{R}^{n+l}$ is calculated, by the softmax over the concatenation of $\bar{H}^e$ and E^C times H^d.

$$P^X = \text{Softmax}([\bar{H}^e \parallel E^C] H^d) \quad (2)$$

In order to use the list of previous predictions $Y_{<t}$ as autoregressive input, all pointers are replaced by their respective token they are pointing to from the input sequence before feeding them to the decoder.

2.4 GermEval 2017: Aspect-Based Sentiment in Social Media Customer Feedback

The GermEval 2017 task is a shared task on analyzing customer reviews and news related to "Deutsche Bahn" and provides an annotated data set of 26 209 documents for training and evaluation. The shared task consists of four subtasks to be tackled individually (Wojatzki et al., 2017).

(A) Relevance Classification: The goal of this subtask is to classify a document as relevant (true) or irrelevant (false) for Deutsche Bahn.

(B) Document-Level Polarity: This subtask is about concluding whether the entire customer review is overall positive, neutral, or negative.

(C) Aspect-Level Polarity: Subtask C involves the identification of all categories mentioned in the document and their associated polarity.

(D) Opinion Target Extraction: The goal of subtask D is to identify the exact term(s) in the document matching the categories and their polarity from subtask C. Each term is predicted as a span in the document, and a single span can be associated to multiple categories.

2.5 Data Set

The provided data was collected using web scraping with a list of query terms, from May 2015 to June 2016, thus covering various seasonal and everyday problems such as holidays or strikes (Wojatzki et al., 2017).

In the following, we take a close look at the training data and list common properties that we found. In general, the data is divided into two main categories: irrelevant and relevant to the topic of "Deutsche Bahn". Irrelevant documents do not contain annotated opinions and the sentiment is always set to "neutral". Relevant data can be further split into two subcategories: Some documents contain clearly expressed opinions, which are annotated accordingly, while others are topically relevant but do not contain any concrete opinions. In the latter case, the opinion term, represented by a span in the source document, is set to "NULL". Thus the data can be divided into the following three types: 1. irrelevant 2. relevant without annotated opinion spans 3. relevant with annotated opinion spans.

The GermEval subtasks C and D require classifying the opinion terms according to suitable categories. In total, there are 20 main categories and up to 54 subcategories used to categorize the opinion terms. For the purpose of the shared task, it is sufficient to predict the correct main categories, as the subcategories are not taken into account. Notably, a single opinion term can be associated with multiple categories (opinions 2 and 3 in Figure 2).

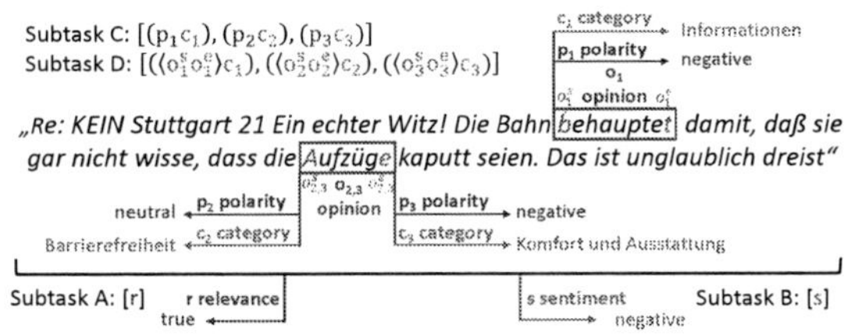

Figure 2: Example document containing labels for all four subtasks and our sequential encoding for each.

3 Methodology

Inspired by the performance of pointer networks in English aspect-based sentiment, we adapt and extend the BARTABSA framework (2021) aiming to solve the four subtasks introduced previously (Section 2.4) - at once and in German.

3.1 Formulating the Subtasks as a Single Sequence-to-Sequence Task

In order to predict all subtasks at once, the output sequence of our model needs to take into account all spans and labels required to extract the four subtasks. If we are able to model all four subtasks as a single sequence, we can consequently train a model to predict this sequence. This sequential representation has to be unambiguous, so that the output of the model is always correctly interpretable. In the following, we define our prediction targets as a sequence consisting of index pointers and class tokens, as shown in Figure 2 and Table 1.

Document-Level Classification

The first two subtasks are document-level classification tasks, which are represented by the first two rows in Table 1. The output for both tasks can be modeled by only a single special token, each specifying the class the document belongs to. For subtask A we define $r \in \{\text{true}, \text{false}\}$ as the relevance class token, indicating whether the document is relevant to the topic of "Deutsche Bahn" or not, while for subtask B we define $s \in \{\text{positive}, \text{negative}, \text{neutral}\}$ as the sentiment class token, indicating the overall sentiment of the entire input document.

Table 1: Representation of the target sequences required to solve all four GermEval subtasks first individually and then together. Here i represents the ith category and opinion span present and | depicts the separator token.

Task	Target Sequence Representation
A	$[r]$
B	$[s]$
C	$[c_1, p_1 \mid \dots \mid c_i, p_i \mid \dots]$
D	$[o_1^s, o_1^e, c_1 \mid \dots \mid o_i^s, o_i^e, c_i \mid \dots]$
Comb.	$[r, s \mid o_1^s, o_1^e, c_1, p_1 \mid \dots \mid o_i^s, o_i^e, c_i, p_i \mid \dots]$

Category & Span Prediction

For subtask C a combination of two classes has to be predicted: a category implicitly or explicitly rated in the input document and additionally the expressed sentiment for each category. Therefore, we define $c \in \{\text{Allgemein}, \text{Zugfahrt}, \text{Ticketkauf}, \dots\}$ as the category and $p \in \{\text{positive}, \text{negative}, \text{neutral}\}$ as the class token associated with the category. A document can contain several different opinions, consequently a category-polarity pair has to be predicted for each mentioned category. We enumerate and predict these pairs in the order they occur in the text input, which is why we introduce i representing the ith pair, associated to the ith mentioned category. For subtask D, in addition to the category c and polarity p the matching opinion term o has to be predicted, where applicable. Therefore, we introduce pointer indices corresponding to the start and end index of the target opinion term in the source sequence, which we indicate with o using superscript to mark the start^s and end^e index token. Again, i represents the ith term, and again we encode the opinion terms in the order in which they appear in the text. It is important to note that a single opinion span can be associated with multiple categories and polarities (see Figure 2).

Finally, to solve all four subtasks at once, we string together the four target sequences into one by concatenating subtasks A and B, while interleaving the matching parts of subtasks C and D (Table 1). In doing so, we must carefully consider the data types we identified in Section 2.5. We distinguish between these three mentioned kinds of data types in the process, to achieve a natural encoding for all data points. In the following, we lay out the three encodings for the different data types ordered by increasing complexity.

Document irrelevant to "Deutsche Bahn"

{"text": "RT @DLR_next: Ach ja: Sie dürfen jetzt das Alu-Hütchen wieder absetzen. Zu unserer eigenen Überraschung hatten wir die Asteroiden-Bahn korr", "relevance": "false", "sentiment": "neutral"}

Data points labeled as not relevant for the topic of "Deutsche Bahn" are characterized by their target for subtask A being "not relevant" and sentiment for subtask B being "neutral". Furthermore, these data points do not contain annotated categories, polarities, or opinion terms for tasks C and D. Consequently, the target sequence contains the following information: relevance and sentiment, which gets encoded as two tokens: [BOS, false, neutral, SEP, EOS].

Document relevant but without Opinion Terms

{"text": "@DB_Bahn Gibts denn ne Ersatzfahrt oder so?!", "relevance": "true", "sentiment": "neutral", "opinions": [{"category": "Allgemein", "polarity": "neutral"}]}

Next we address data points which are relevant and thus have categories and polarities annotated but do not contain opinion terms. We extend our existing encoding scheme by appending a list of categories and polarity tuples to the target sequence: [BOS, true, neutral, SEP, Allgemein, neutral, SEP, EOS]. The sequence now contains the information: relevance, sentiment, category and polarity.

Document relevant and contains Opinion Terms

{"text": "Juhu Weichen Störung! Ich liebe die Bahn... Nicht -.-", "relevance": "true", "sentiment": "negative", "opinions": [{ "category": "Allgemein", "polarity": "negative"}, {"category": "Unregelmässigkeiten", "polarity": "negative", "from": 1, "to": 2, "term": ["Weichen", "Störung"]}]}

Finally, we add the ability to encode the spans that represent opinion terms in our target sequence. As indicated in Table 1, one document can be annotated with multiple categories or opinion terms (spans). These spans are associated with the category we implemented above, and consequently we concatenate these to their respective category. The sequence thus has to contain the document's relevance and sentiment as well as a list of $\text{opinion}_{\text{start}}$, $\text{opinion}_{\text{end}}$, category and polarity. For above example we define this target sequence: [BOS, true, negative, SEP, Allgemein, negative, SEP, 1, 2, Unregelmässigkeiten, negative, SEP, EOS]. Following the BARTABSA encoding, we first predict the span and the associated category afterwards.

3.2 Pointer Network

Architecturally we keep the model introduced in BARTABSA (Section 2.3) unchanged. To enable it to predict our previously defined target sequence, we need to extend the special token vocabulary of our model, as the task at hand includes document-level classes as well as 20 categories, all of which need to be predicted by our model. The vocabulary has to contain the following special tokens: (i) BOS, EOS, PAD, SEP (ii) two tokens for document relevance: true, false (iii) three tokens for sentiment and category polarity: positive, negative, neutral (iv) 20 tokens for the categories (Allgemein, Zugfahrt, Ticketkauf, etc.). At every decoding step, the pointer network either predicts a pointer to a token index of the source sequence, or a class special token. Conceptionally, these special tokens are assigned to the lowest available ids, so the first 29 tokens (4+2+3+20) are special tokens. Predictions larger than this offset are interpreted as pointers to indices of tokens in the source sequence. The target sequence is created by converting all tokens to ids and then adding this constant offset of 29 to all index pointers to the source sequence. Thus our previous example of [BOS, true, negative, SEP, Allgemein, negative, SEP, 1, 2, Unregelmässigkeiten, negative, SEP, EOS] becomes [0, 4, 7, 3, 9, 7, 3, 30, 31, 14, 7, 3, 2]. The model is then trained to predict this sequence of special tokens and indices for each input document. Of course, before converting the predicted index pointers back to spans, this constant offset is subtracted again.

3.3 Handling Encoding Issues

Inputs longer than the model's context size are truncated such that during evaluation twenty data points of the synchronic test set and eleven of the diachronic test set could not be encoded in its entirety. During evaluation we set fallback defaults of relevance=true for subtask A and sentiment=neutral for subtask B for data points, where the model fails to predict either of these tasks. Both values are the respective majority classes in the training set. This is necessary to evaluate our results, as the original evaluation binary provided by the task hosts cannot handle missing values. For subtasks C and D, no fallback predictions are required or set.

4 Experiments

4.1 Data Set

To assess the robustness of the participating systems, two test sets were introduced. In addition to the "synchronic test set" (Test_{syn}), a "diachronic test set" (Test_{dia}) is provided, consisting of documents from a different time frame: November 2016 to January 2017 (Wojatzki et al., 2017). In total, the data set consists of 26 209 German messages across all splits (Train: 19 432 (of which 3231 irrelevant for "Deutsche Bahn"), Dev: 2369, Test_{syn}: 2566, Test_{dia}: 1842), annotated with the document id, relevance, and sentiment, as well as the opinion terms including exact spans, its sentiment, and category.

4.2 Evaluation & Metric

For evaluation, we use the original GermEval evaluation script, which compares the predicted results considering the micro-averaged F_1-score (Wojatzki et al., 2017). For subtasks A and B the F_1-score is reported, while for subtask C, the task hosts distinguish two types of metrics: (C1) Only the category has to match the ground truth. (C2) In addition to the category, the polarity must be predicted correctly. Furthermore, for subtask D also two types of results are differentiated: (D1) Exact result: The "from" and "to" tags have to exactly match the ground truth. (D2) Overlap result: The "from" and "to" tags can deviate from the ground truth by +/- 1 at the word level. We report our performance for all task metrics.

4.3 Hyperparameter Search

In order to improve the performance of our model, we perform an extensive training hyperparameter search. This includes exploring various ways to encode our targets, hoping to gain a better understanding of how the models performance is influenced by the different parameters. To gain a better understanding of how well each base model works for this German task, we perform a grid search, examining the hyperparameters listed in Table 8, resulting in 300 combinations of parameters. This enables us to find the best working model for German by comparing the performance of all available models against each other, while also finding the best hyperparameter combination for each of them. For batch size, epochs, and learning rate, we decide to search and analyze parameters close to the values proposed by Yan et al. (2021) and keep AdamW.

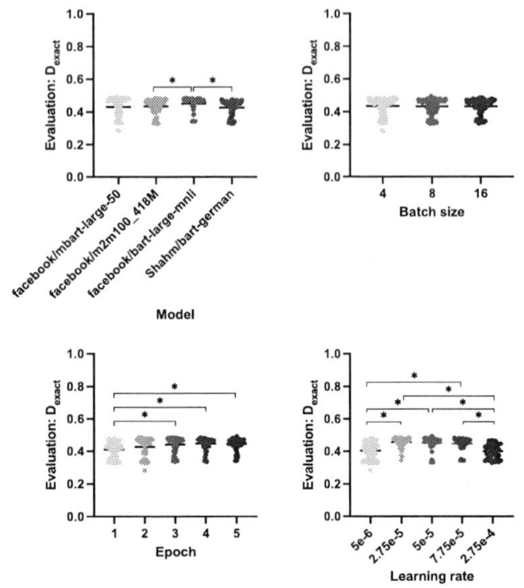

Figure 3: Results for subtask D1, aggregated for each hyperparameter configuration. The hyperparameters are listed on the x-axis and the results for D1 on the y-axis.

5 Evaluation and Results

First we evaluate the findings of our hyperparameter search, before we analyze the impact of different prediction orders. Afterwards, we compare our performance against previous approaches.

5.1 Hyperparameter Study

We systematically evaluate the impact of each hyperparameter on the overall performance of our approach. To identify statistically significant differences between hyperparameter combinations, we performed the Kruskal-Wallis test (Corder and Foreman, 2014) and corrected for multiple comparisons using post hoc Dunn's test (Dunn, 1964). Large learning rates can result in training instabilities for some hyperparameter combinations, so the exploration of the largest learning rate (5e-4) was canceled early after no valid run could be conducted. Thus, we do not have paired data points for all learning rates.

To this end, we consider $p < 0.05$ as a statistically significant difference and mark it with an $*$ in Figure 3 and Appendix A. We use a black line to represent the average values. In Figure 3 we representatively plot the performance on the validation set for subtask D1. The results for the other subtasks are similar, and their plots can be found in Appendix A. To prevent overfitting and ensure that the test set remains independent for unbiased model evaluation, the hyperparameter study is performed using the validation split.

Hyperparameter: Base Model Figure 3 illustrates that the choice of the base model can have a significant impact on the overall performance. Here, we refer to the evaluated base models by their HuggingFace identifier. We find that "facebook/bart-large-mnli" performs best, achieving significantly better results than "facebook/m2m100_418M" and "Shahm/bart-german". The difference between "facebook/bart-large-mnli" and "facebook/mbart-large-50" is minimal.

Hyperparameter: Batch Size Noticeably, the batch size has a smaller effect on the performance of the model and does not show significant differences between the different configurations.

Hyperparameter: Epochs Inspecting the number of epochs shows that training just one epoch is, as expected, statistically worse than training for three, four, or five epochs. Nevertheless, increasing the number of epochs to more than two does result in slight but not significant improvements.

Hyperparameter: Learning Rate Regarding the learning rate a clear performance deterioration can be observed starting from a learning rate of 7.75e-5 and becomes significantly worse when the learning rate increases further. The learning rate suggested by Yan et al. (2021) of 5e-5 also achieves statistically significant better results than 5e-6. We consequently identify a learning rate of 5e-5 to be the best option over all tasks.

Selected Hyperparameters After conducting this hyperparameter search, we select the configuration that ranks best across the most subtasks on the validation split. In doing so, we identify "facebook/mbart-large-50" as the best model with a learning rate of 5e-5, when training for 5 epochs with a batch size of 8. As listed in Table 9 we find that this configuration is among the top-3 combinations for subtasks C and D for both metrics each. Therefore this configuration will be used for all following analyses.

5.2 Performance on Subtasks C and D

In order to train the model to solve all subtasks at once, we have to consider all data points in the training set. In particular, this includes training on a large number of data points that are irrelevant

Table 2: Comparison of results achieved when predicting all subtasks, versus only subtasks C and D. Furthermore different permutations for subtasks C and D are evaluated. First column matches Section 3.

Ordering	r, s, o^s, o^e, c, p	o^s, o^e, c, p	o^s, o^e, p, c	c, p, o^s, o^e	p, c, o^s, o^e
C1	.657	.676	.688	**.695**	.693
C2	.543	.559	.556	.569	**.581**
D1	.476	.489	.468	.494	**.500**
D2	.500	.512	.490	.519	**.523**

Table 3: Comparison of results on the validation set for all subtasks using the best hyperparameter combination and only changing the order of the target sequence

Ordering	r, s, o^s, o^e, c, p	s, r, o^s, o^e, c, p	s, r, p, c, o^s, o^e	r, s, p, c, o^s, o^e	p, c, o^s, o^e, s, r	p, c, o^s, o^e, r, s
A	.958	.954	**.959**	**.959**	.955	.957
B	.813	.823	**.827**	.822	.824	.823
C1	.657	.662	.677	.677	.673	**.684**
C2	.543	.554	.560	**.563**	.559	.562
D1	.476	.487	.486	.490	**.498**	.497
D2	.500	.507	.510	.509	.518	**.522**

for subtasks B, C and D, as these data points are only required for subtask A (Section 4.1). As all previous approaches train separate models for each subtask, this leads us to investigate how the performance of our model changes, when dropping all irrelevant data points from the training set and training only on the two closely related and most complex tasks: subtasks C and D. Table 2 lists the results achieved, while training our model only on subtasks C and D in the first section. Comparing the first two columns, it is noticeable that leaving out subtasks A and B slightly improves the performance on subtasks C and D, although the impact on subtask C seems to be slightly larger. We deduce that additionally predicting subtasks A and B, and thus even training on a significant amount of off-topic data, does not impact performance strongly.

Table 4: Comparison of existing approaches for subtask A. Best in **bold**, second underlined.

Team Subtask A	**Test$_{syn}$**	**Test$_{dia}$**
Wojatzki et al.	0.852	0.868
Sayyed et al.	0.903	0.906
Hövelmann and Friedrich	0.899	0.897
Aßenmacher et al.	**0.957**	**0.948**
Our (A,B,C&D)	0.953	0.943

5.3 Order of Prediction

In preliminary experiments, we found slight differences in performance when changing the order of the target sequence introduced in Section 3. Therefore, we systematically evaluate the impact of this order and list the results for different prediction orders of subtasks C and D in Table 2. We find that our proposed order in Section 3 overall, scores rather low among all possible permutations and that moving the predictions for subtask C in front of subtask D slightly improves the results.

Consequently, in Table 3 we take the best prediction order for subtasks C and D and analyze it in combination with different permutations of subtasks A and B. We find that the overall differences are small, but predicting subtasks A and B last (p, c, o^s, o^e, r, s) achieves the best results considering the mean over all subtasks. Thus, this is the prediction order we fix for further evaluation.

5.4 Results on the Test Set

Previous analyses were conducted on the validation split, while the following comparisons against existing approaches are carried out on the test set. We also examined the impact of different seeds on the performance, to get insights into robustness and reproducibility (Table 10). Notably, in Section 5.1 we selected a combination that performs better on subtasks C and D than on A and B.

(A) Relevance Classification:

For subtask A (Table 4), our approach outperforms all original participants and the system provided by the organizers (Sayyed et al., 2017; Hövelmann and Friedrich, 2017; Wojatzki et al., 2017). With the recent approach by Aßenmacher et al. (2021) achieving the best results, our model comes second. Our model predicts all four subtasks at once while remaining competitive with Aßenmacher et al. who trained a separate model for each subtask.

Table 5: Comparison of existing approaches for subtask B. Best in **bold**, second best underlined.

Team Subtask B	$\textbf{Test}_{syn}$	$\textbf{Test}_{dia}$
Wojatzki et al.	0.667	0.694
Naderalvojoud et al.	0.749	0.736
Hövelmann and Friedrich	0.748	0.742
Aßenmacher et al.	<u>0.807</u>	<u>0.800</u>
Our (A,B,C&D)	**0.815**	**0.811**

Table 6: Comparison of existing approaches for subtask C. Best in **bold**, second best underlined.

Team Subtask C	$\textbf{C1}_{syn}$	$\textbf{C2}_{syn}$	$\textbf{C1}_{dia}$	$\textbf{C2}_{dia}$
Wojatzki et al.	0.481	0.322	0.495	0.389
Lee et al.	0.482	0.354	-	-
Mishra et al.	0.421	0.349	0.460	0.401
Aßenmacher et al.	0.761	0.655	0.791	0.689
↪ reevaluated	<u>0.614</u>	<u>0.475</u>	<u>0.649</u>	<u>0.493</u>
Our (C&D)	0.624	**0.514**	**0.657**	**0.553**
Our (A,B,C&D)	**0.632**	0.510	0.634	0.535

(B) Document-Level Polarity:

For subtask B (Table 5) our model not only outperforms all original participants (Wojatzki et al., 2017; Naderalvojoud et al., 2017; Hövelmann and Friedrich, 2017) but also the newer approach by Aßenmacher et al. (2021) while solving all subtasks at once. Again, the newer LLM-based approaches clearly perform better than previous models.

(C) Aspect-Level Polarity:

For subtask C (Table 6), our approach again outperforms all original participants (Wojatzki et al., 2017; Lee et al., 2017; Mishra et al., 2017). While Aßenmacher et al. (2021) report better results for subtask C, it should be noted that their scores are calculated using a custom reimplementation of the evaluation metric. Consequently, we reevaluated their outputs using the original GermEval metric and achieved different results for subtask C, as we detail in Appendix C.1. We assume that this discrepancy results from different calculations of the average (micro vs. macro). Nevertheless, we list both values in Table 6, the result of their custom metric in gray, and the result we calculated using the original metric in black. We report the results achieved by the best model trained from each: Table 2 and 3. Our model trained only on subtasks C and D outperforms all other previous approaches for all reported results, including our model trained on all subtasks in three out of four cases. Nevertheless, we find that our model trained on all subtasks is able to outperform our model, which specializes in subtasks C and D once, and even outperforms all previous approaches in three out of four cases.

Table 7: Comparison of existing approaches subtask D. Best in **bold**, second best underlined.

Team Subtask D	$\textbf{D1}_{syn}$	$\textbf{D2}_{syn}$	$\textbf{D1}_{dia}$	$\textbf{D2}_{dia}$
Wojatzki et al.	0.170	0.237	0.216	0.271
Mishra et al.	<u>0.220</u>	0.221	<u>0.281</u>	<u>0.282</u>
Lee et al.	0.203	<u>0.348</u>	-	-
Aßenmacher et al.	0.515	0.523	0.518	0.533
Our (C&D)	0.404	0.430	0.442	0.471
Our (A,B,C&D)	**0.415**	**0.440**	**0.448**	**0.479**

(D) Opinion Target Extraction:

For subtask D (Table 7), our approach again comfortably outperforms all previous approaches (Wojatzki et al., 2017; Lee et al., 2017; Mishra et al., 2017). Despite close contact with the authors of Aßenmacher et al. (2021), we were unable to generate reportable results for their approach using the original evaluation script, as we assume that their approach suffers from a preprocessing bug (C.2). Interestingly, again we find that our model trained on all subtasks is able to outperform our model trained only on subtasks C and D, verifying our intuition of training a single model for all subtasks.

6 Conclusion

In this work, we proposed the first approach that is able to solve all four subtasks of the GermEval 2017 shared task simultaneously. To achieve this goal, we used a pointer network to sequentially predict a single, unified target sequence that encodes all subtasks. We conducted an extensive hyperparameter search and thoroughly evaluated different configurations and orders of prediction. In doing so, we find that predicting all subtasks at once does not negatively impact the overall performance of our model and on the test set can even result in a performance increase, verifying our strategy of unifying all subtasks. Consequently, although our model solves all subtasks at once, it outperforms or closely matches all previous approaches on both test sets. For all subtasks we find that our results on the synchronic and dedicated diachronic test sets are very similar, indicating robustness.

7 Limitations

Certain limitations of our approach should be considered. Our approach to a large degree assumes that not only multilingual base models, but even English-only base models are effectively applicable to the German language. This may not translate well to more niche, specialized, or low-resource languages or domains. Nevertheless, the assumption only comes into play as to our knowledge there is no specifically German trained BART model available. Unifying various subtasks on a data set might not always improve performance, but investigating transferability of this paradigm to other similar (German) tasks consisting of related subtasks seems worthwhile and promising.

8 Ethical Considerations

We acknowledge the potential concern about large-scale analysis of user content posted online. We argue that this issue applies only to a lesser extent to our approach, since the source of the content is mainly social networks, microblogs, news sites, and QA sites, which are explicitly written to be public. Furthermore, the only metadata available are the URLs such that the identities of the participants are not disclosed, as no personally identifiable data are collected. The data set utilized had previously already been collected, analyzed, and published.

Acknowledgements

This work is partially supported by the MOTIV research project funded by the Bavarian Research Institute for Digital Transformation (bidt), an institute of the Bavarian Academy of Sciences and Humanities. The authors are responsible for the content of this publication.

References

Matthias Aßenmacher, Alessandra Corvonato, and Christian Heumann. 2021. Re-evaluating germeval17 using german pre-trained language models. *CoRR*, abs/2102.12330.

Gregory W. Corder and Dale I. Foreman. 2014. *Nonparametric statistics: a step-by-step approach*, second edition edition. Wiley, Hoboken, New Jersey.

Olive Jean Dunn. 1964. Multiple Comparisons Using Rank Sums. *Technometrics*, 6(3):241–252.

Angela Fan, Shruti Bhosale, Holger Schwenk, Zhiyi Ma, Ahmed El-Kishky, Siddharth Goyal, Mandeep Baines, Onur Celebi, Guillaume Wenzek, Vishrav Chaudhary, Naman Goyal, Tom Birch, Vitaliy Liptchinsky, Sergey Edunov, Edouard Grave, Michael Auli, and Armand Joulin. 2020. Beyond English-Centric Multilingual Machine Translation. ArXiv:2010.11125 [cs].

Leonard Hövelmann and Christoph M. Friedrich. 2017. Fasttext and Gradient Boosted Trees at GermEval-2017 on Relevance Classification and Document-level Polarity. In *Proceedings of the GermEval 2017 – Shared Task on Aspect-based Sentiment in Social Media Customer Feedback*, pages 30–35, Berlin, Germany.

Ji-Ung Lee, Steffen Eger, Johannes Daxenberger, and Iryna Gurevych. 2017. UKP TU-DA at GermEval 2017: Deep learning for Aspect Based Sentiment Detection. In *Proceedings of the GermEval 2017 – Shared Task on Aspect-based Sentiment in Social Media Customer Feedback*, pages 22–29, Berlin, Germany.

Mike Lewis, Yinhan Liu, Naman Goyal, Marjan Ghazvininejad, Abdelrahman Mohamed, Omer Levy, Veselin Stoyanov, and Luke Zettlemoyer. 2020. BART: Denoising sequence-to-sequence pre-training for natural language generation, translation, and comprehension. In *Proceedings of the 58th Annual Meeting of the Association for Computational Linguistics*, pages 7871–7880, Online. Association for Computational Linguistics.

Pruthwik Mishra, Vandan Mujadia, and Soujanya Lanka. 2017. GermEval 2017 : Sequence based Models for Customer Feedback Analysis. In *Proceedings of the GermEval 2017 – Shared Task on Aspect-based Sentiment in Social Media Customer Feedback*, pages 36–42, Berlin, Germany.

Behzad Naderalvojoud, Behrang Qasemizadeh, and Laura Kallmeyer. 2017. HU-HHU at GermEval-2017 Sub-task B: Lexicon-Based Deep Learning for Contextual Sentiment Analysis. In *Proceedings of the GermEval 2017 – Shared Task on Aspect-based Sentiment in Social Media Customer Feedback*, pages 18–21, Berlin, Germany.

Jan Pfister, Sebastian Wankerl, and Andreas Hotho. 2022. SenPoi at SemEval-2022 task 10: Point me to your opinion, SenPoi. In *Proceedings of the 16th International Workshop on Semantic Evaluation (SemEval-2022)*, pages 1313–1323, Seattle, United States. Association for Computational Linguistics.

Raghav R, Adarsh Vemali, and Rajdeep Mukherjee. 2022. ETMS@IITKGP at SemEval-2022 task 10: Structured sentiment analysis using a generative approach. In *Proceedings of the 16th International Workshop on Semantic Evaluation (SemEval-2022)*, pages 1373–1381, Seattle, United States. Association for Computational Linguistics.

Zeeshan Ali Sayyed, Daniel Dakota, and Sandra Kübler. 2017. IDS IUCL: Investigating Feature Selection and Oversampling for GermEval2017. In *Proceedings of*

Table 8: Configuration search space for our hyperparameter optimization conducted.

Parameter	Values
Model	facebook/bart-large-mnli, facebook/mbart-large-50, Shahm/bart-german, facebook/m2m100_418M
Batch Size	4, 8, 16
Epochs	1, 2, 3, 4, 5
Learning Rate	5e-6, 2.75e-5, 5e-5, 7.75e-05, 2.75e-04, 5e-4

the GermEval 2017 – Shared Task on Aspect-based Sentiment in Social Media Customer Feedback, pages 43–48, Berlin, Germany.

Thomas Scialom, Paul-Alexis Dray, Sylvain Lamprier, Benjamin Piwowarski, and Jacopo Staiano. 2020. MLSUM: The multilingual summarization corpus. In *Proceedings of the 2020 Conference on Empirical Methods in Natural Language Processing (EMNLP)*, pages 8051–8067, Online. Association for Computational Linguistics.

Yuqing Tang, Chau Tran, Xian Li, Peng-Jen Chen, Naman Goyal, Vishrav Chaudhary, Jiatao Gu, and Angela Fan. 2020. Multilingual translation with extensible multilingual pretraining and finetuning.

Michael Wojatzki, Eugen Ruppert, Sarah Holschneider, Torsten Zesch, and Chris Biemann. 2017. GermEval 2017: Shared Task on Aspect-based Sentiment in Social Media Customer Feedback. In *Proceedings of the GermEval 2017 – Shared Task on Aspect-based Sentiment in Social Media Customer Feedback*, pages 1–12, Berlin, Germany.

Hang Yan, Junqi Dai, Tuo Ji, Xipeng Qiu, and Zheng Zhang. 2021. A unified generative framework for aspect-based sentiment analysis. In *Proceedings of the 59th Annual Meeting of the Association for Computational Linguistics and the 11th International Joint Conference on Natural Language Processing (Volume 1: Long Papers)*, pages 2416–2429, Online. Association for Computational Linguistics.

A Hyperparameter Analysis

A.1 Parameter Range

In Table 8 we depict the range of explored hyperparameters, as described in Section 5.1. Since training runs for the largest learning rate (5e-4) resulted in training instabilities, the exploration of this learning rate was canceled early after no valid run could be conducted.

Table 9: Ranking of the selected hyperparameter combination across all subtasks.

	A	B	C1	C2	D1	D2
Rank	34	22	3	3	1	1

A.2 Ranking across Subtasks

As described in Section 5.1 we select the combination "facebook/mbart-large-50" as the best model with a learning rate of 5e-5, when training for 5 epochs and a batch size of 8. Table 9 lists the ranking of this selected hyperparameter configuration across all subtasks relative to all combinations of hyperparameters explored.

A.3 Results per Subtask

In the following we show the hyperparameter search results for subtasks A, B, C1, C2 and D2 on the validation set (Figures 4 to 8). As before, we consider $p < 0.05$ as statistically significant difference and mark it with an $*$. Black lines are again used to represent the average values. Overall, we find very similar results to subtask D1 (Section 5.1 and figure 3).

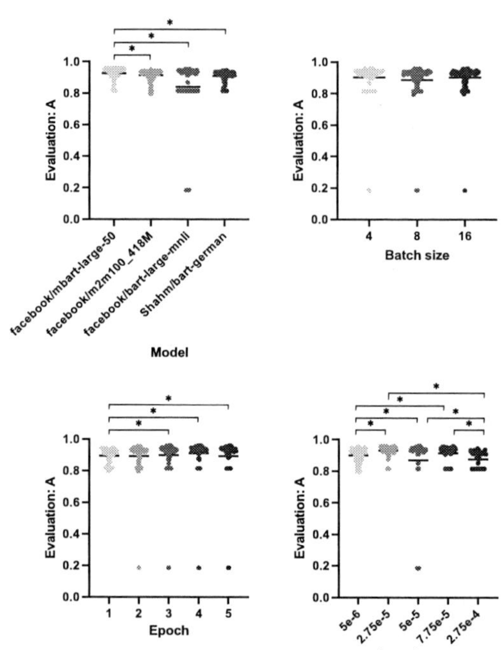

Figure 4: Results for subtask A, aggregated for each hyperparameter configuration. The hyperparameters are listed on the x-axis and the results for D1 on the y-axis.

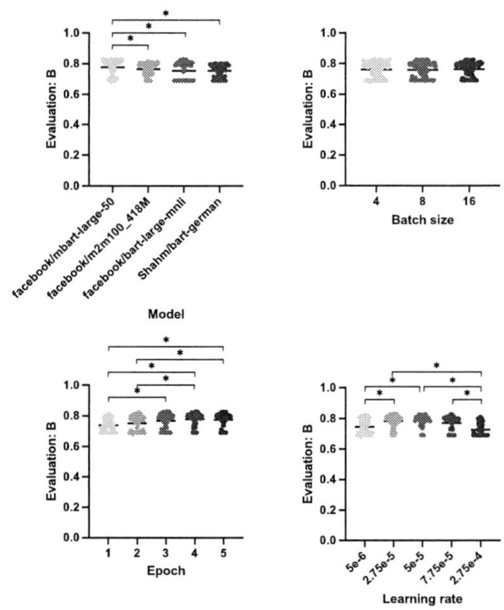

Figure 5: Results for subtask B, aggregated for each hyperparameter configuration. The hyperparameters are listed on the x-axis and the results for D1 on the y-axis.

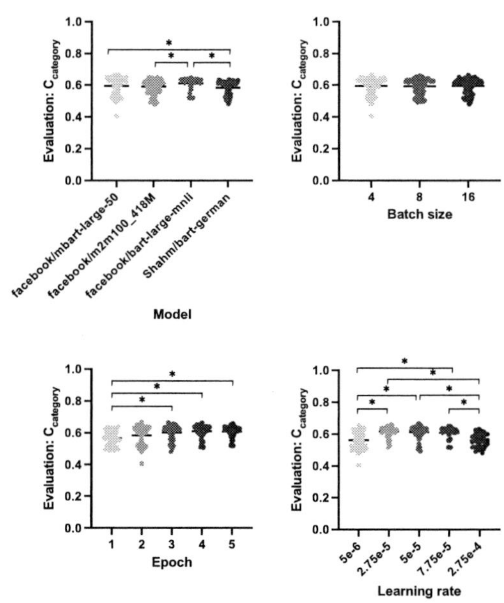

Figure 6: Results for subtask C1, aggregated for each hyperparameter configuration. The hyperparameters are listed on the x-axis and the results for D1 on the y-axis.

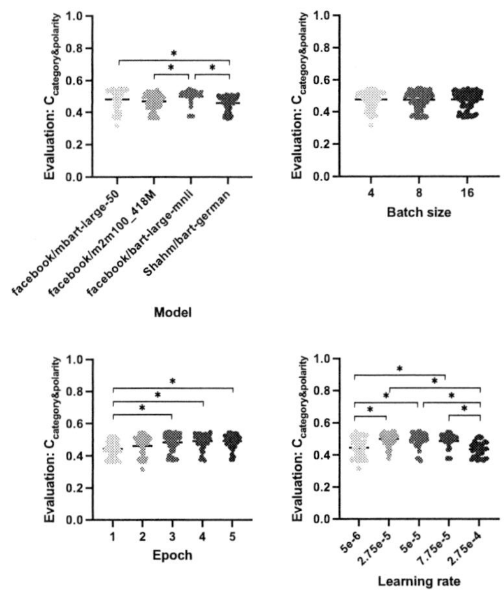

Figure 7: Results for subtask C2, aggregated for each hyperparameter configuration. The hyperparameters are listed on the x-axis and the results for D1 on the y-axis.

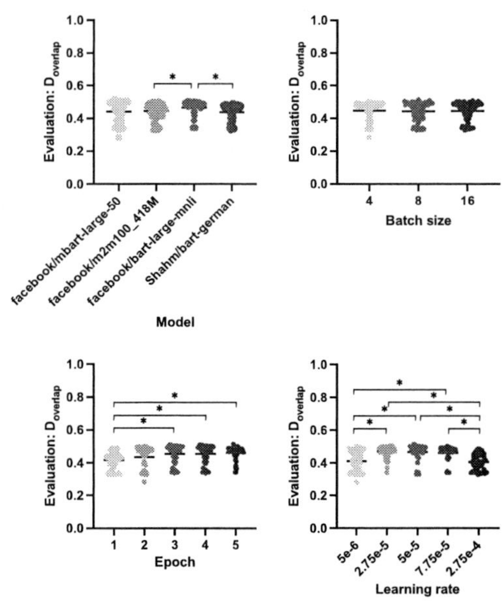

Figure 8: Results for subtask D2, aggregated for each hyperparameter configuration. The hyperparameters are listed on the x-axis and the results for D1 on the y-axis.

Table 10: Achieved results on the Test_{syn} set using different seeds. $\overline{x}$ denotes the average and σ the standard deviation. Both are computed per subtask.

Seed	A	B	C1	C2	D1	D2
1	0.940	0.807	0.594	0.485	0.371	0.388
2	0.954	0.832	0.635	0.525	0.419	0.443
3	0.951	0.829	0.633	0.527	0.418	0.444
4	0.942	0.816	0.618	0.507	0.407	0.430
5	0.948	0.821	0.633	0.516	0.413	0.436
42	0.953	0.815	0.632	0.510	0.415	0.440
$\overline{x}$	0.948	0.820	0.624	0.512	0.407	0.430
σ	0.006	0.009	0.016	0.015	0.018	0.021

B Seeds

When conducting the hyperparameter optimization we used the seed 42 for all runs. To illustrate how robust our results are to changes in random initialization, we additionally examined five more seeds in Table 10. It should be mentioned that, overall, the results are stable across different seeds. In our experiment, only seed value 1 can be viewed as an outlier, as it performs comparably poor.

C Analyzing Aßenmacher et al. (2021)

During the reevaluation of Aßenmacher et al. (2021), we found two performance differences when comparing their custom reimplementation of the metric with the original metric. All analyzes are based on the results generated using their repository: `https://github.com/ac74/reevaluating_germeval2017`. In the following we detail our analysis.

C.1 Subtask C

We reran subtask C and recorded the outputs obtained. During this run, according to the costum metric, the model achieved a performance close to their reported results. However, when we converted these results to the challenge XML format and evaluated it using the original GermEval binaries for easier comparison, we obtained the results, which we report in Table 6. We suspect different usages of micro vs. macro averaging to be the issue, but did not further investigate any possible differences between the metrics.

C.2 Subtask D

When inspecting the results obtained for subtask D, we observed that some spans in the input document are duplicated. This makes it hard to convert these predicted word-level span annotations to the original XML format, as the input string to be predicted gets changed during preprocessing. We show this using a truncated example: *"AZ Muenchen : Technischer Defekt: Störung am Isartor: S- Bahn-Stammstrecke dicht: Ein technischer Defekt[. . .]"*, which is annotated in the groundtruth with the opinion terms "Technischer Defekt" twice, as well as the terms "Störung" and "Bahn-Stammstrecke". During preprocessing this sample is transformed to the following input document: *"az muenchen : technischer defekt technischer defekt : storung am isartor : s - bahn - stammstrecke : storung am isartor : s - bahn - stammstrecke dicht : ein technischer defekt[. . .]"*, duplicating "technischer defekt" as well as "storung am isator: s-bahn-stammstrecke" in the process. Notably, these duplications seem to be connected to the groundtruth opinion spans. Thus, the annotations for the ground-truth label seem to leak into the model input, as spans that have to be annotated multiple times seem to be fed in multiple times. Due to this presumed bug in the data preprocessing, we are unable to reliably convert the model outputs to processable inputs for the original metric.

Exploring Automatic Text Simplification of German Narrative Documents

Thorben Schomacker
Hamburg Univ. of Applied Sciences
thorben.schomacker@haw-hamburg.de

Tillmann Dönicke
Univ. of Göttingen
tillmann.doenicke@uni-goettingen.de

Marina Tropmann-Frick
Hamburg Univ. of Applied Sciences
marina.tropmann-frick@haw-hamburg.de

Abstract

In this paper, we apply transformer-based Natural Language Generation (NLG) techniques to the problem of text simplification. Currently, there are only a few German datasets available for text simplification, even fewer with larger and aligned documents, and not a single one with narrative texts. In this paper, we explore to which degree modern NLG techniques can be applied to German narrative text simplifications. We use Longformer attention and a pre-trained mBART model. Our findings indicate that the existing approaches for German are not able to solve the task properly. We conclude on a few directions for future research to address this problem.

1 Introduction

1.1 Motivation

With the rise of the internet, it has become convenient and often free to access an abundance of texts. However, not all people who have access can fully read and understand the texts, even though they speak the language that the text is written in. Most often this problem originates in the complex nature of the texts. Text simplification can help to overcome this barrier.

Narrative forms are one of the primary ways humans create meaning (Felluga, 2011). Narrative texts, then, make an important contribution to how we describe and shape our environment. Simple language also contributes to involving as many people as possible in this process. Providing narrative texts in a Simple Language (*Einfache Sprache*) version, enables a large audience to read them. So, we present the first approach for the automatic text simplification of German narrative texts.

1.2 Related Works

Automatic text simplification started in 2010 (Specia, 2010) as statistical machine translation to the rule-based automatic text simplification task, using a Portuguese corpus (4500 parallel sentences). The first German text simplification dataset was created by (Hancke et al., 2012) to train a readability classifier. The dataset consisted of unaligned articles from one adult-targeting and one child-targeting journal, and was later improved and enlarged by (Weiß and Meurers, 2018), which added unaligned transcripts from one adult-targeting and one child-targeting German TV news show. Similarly, (Aumiller and Gertz, 2022) published a German document-aligned dataset with lexicon articles for adults and for children. The first sentence-aligned German simplification dataset was published in 2013 (Klaper et al., 2013) with 270 articles from five different websites, mainly of organizations that support people with disabilities. In 2016 the first (rule-based) automatic text simplification system for German was released (Suter et al., 2016). The first parallel corpus for data-driven automatic text simplification for German was introduced by (Säuberli et al., 2020). The corpus contains 3616 sentence pairs from news articles. They additionally were the first to use transformer models for German text simplification and found out that their corpus was not large enough to train them. (Battisti et al., 2020) collected a larger corpus with 378 text pairs, mostly from websites of governments, specialized institutions, and non-profit organizations. (Rios et al., 2021) investigated the usage of an adapted mBART (Liu et al., 2020) version with Longformer attention (Beltagy et al., 2020) on Swiss newspaper articles. These results have been further improved with a sentence-based approach (Ebling et al., 2022). Most recently, the first detailed surveys about German text simplification have been released (Anschütz et al., 2023; Stodden et al., 2023; Schomacker et al., 2023).

Proceedings of the 19th Conference on Natural Language Processing (KONVENS 2023), pages 139–148
September 18–22, 2023. ©2023 Association for Computational Linguistics

2 Methods

Longformer mBART Our goal was to train a document-level text generation model with a larger context (> 510 input tokens; exceeding most transformer-based models). Longformer is the only model to our knowledge, which could extend the context on a pre-trained transformer model. We searched on huggingface.co and filtered for text2text-generation models (8551), German (225), > 5000 downloads (30), and that they can perform a German-to-German translation task. This leaves only *facebook/mbart-large-50* and *facebook/mbart-large-cc25*, both introduced in (Liu et al., 2020). We decided to take *facebook/mbart-large-cc25* since it has been trained on fewer languages (25; in the CC25 dataset extracted from (Wenzek et al., 2020; Conneau et al., 2020)) in comparison to *facebook/mbart-large-50* (50). Because we reasoned that the greater the relative proportion of German in pre-training, the better. Our situation is very similar to (Rios et al., 2021), so we base our methods on their approaches. mBART uses a specific input format consisting of the sentence and a language-tag. We additionally created two tags: `de_OR` and `de_SI` for Standard German and Simple German, respectively. Both of them are derived from the original German tag `de_DE` (fifth-largest proportion in CC25) and only modified during our fine-tuning process. Similar to (Rios et al., 2021), we applied the Longformer conversion to the mBART model with a maximum input length of 1024 and 512 as the attention window size.

Domain Adaptation By using domain adaptation, we aim to enrich the vocabulary with previously unseen words and adapt the existing embeddings to the narrative text domain and the historical environment of the texts. After we created the longmbart-model we started the domain adaptation process. We downloaded all documents from TextGrid (textgrid.de) in the category "prose" and randomly sampled 60 documents. In a next step, we sentence-split the documents using spaCy (spacy.io), shuffled them and masked 15% of the words. We used these masked and unmasked sentence-pairs for a single epoch training of the model. Both sides of the pair are tagged with the `de_DE` tag. We used a learning rate of $3e{-}10$, an attention window size of 512 during the conversion, a maximum input and output length of 70, and a batch size of 8.

Fine-Tuning We fine-tune our model on document-aligned German narrative texts, using three sources for Standard Language data: 1) gutenberg.org, 2) projekt-gutenberg.org, and 3) textgridrep.org. We selected *Die Bremer Stadtmusikanten* (`mils-stadtmusikanten`), *Der seltsame Fall von Dr Jekyll und Mr Hyde* (`eb-hyde`) and *Der Schimmelreiter* (`pv-schimmelreiter`) as development set because their amount of words is close to the average amount of all samples in the fine-tuning dataset and they originate from different sources. For the same reasons, we selected *Des Teufels rußiger Bruder* (`mils-bruder`), *Der Graf von Monte Christo* (`eb-christo`) and *Der Sandmann* (`pv-sandmann`) for testing. We used four sources for Simple Language texts: 1) einfachebuecher.de (eb), 2) kindermannverlag.de (kv), and 3) passanten-verlag.de (pv), which consist of classic novels, as well as 4) the *Märchen in Leichter Sprache* 'Fairy Tales in Simple Language' from ndr.de (`mils`). The links to the Standard Language and Simple Language version can be found in Table 2 in the appendix. The `mils` samples include the complete text, while for the novels we use only the excerpts provided in the form of free reading samples (usually the first chapter of the text). We manually cut in the end of the Standard Language version to match the extent of the Simple Language version.

Hyperparameter Setup Following (Rios et al., 2021), we set the attention mode (Beltagy et al., 2020) to sliding chunks (with overlap) and the attention window size to 512. Since our dataset is rather small, we turn gradient accumulation (`accumulate_grad_batches`) off. We use the Adam optimizer and optimize the learning rate with the PyTorch Lightning `LearningRateFinder` between $3e{-}20$ and $3e{-}1$. For Decoding we use beam search (size = 4).

3 Analysis and Evaluation

3.1 Analysis

We manually compared the three generated output sequences of our test texts to the Standard Language version and the Simple Language version. In summary, we found that 1) the model copies the input text to a very high degree without any modifications, 2) in cases where the model discarded parts of the inputs, it did not recognize the importance of the sequence, such as spelled-out antecedents for pronouns, and 3) it truncates rather randomly and without any semantic reason.

For reasons of space, we only discuss *Der Sandmann* in the appendix (section B), on which we can show all the phenomena we want to discuss.

3.2 Evaluation Measures

3.2.1 BERTscore, BLEU and ROUGE

BERTscore (Zhang et al., 2020) is currently the recommended (Alva-Manchego et al., 2021) way of comparing (generated) text simplification candidates and the (gold) references. It is a soft metric that yields high correlations with human judgments (Alva-Manchego et al., 2021). We select *google/mt5-base* as the underlying model, since it is the best performing model with Max Length > 1022, German support, and a compatible transformers version (Zhang, 2020) (*google/mt5-xl* and *google/mt5-large* did not fit our hardware resources). Following (Alva-Manchego et al., 2021) we use the BERTscore to determine the early stopping point during fine-tuning. We additionally employed two n-gram based approaches, BLEU (Papineni et al., 2002) and ROUGE (Lin, 2004), because they are the most commonly used metrics for text generation.

3.2.2 Entropy

We use two flavors of Shannon entropy as a characterization, or measurement, of redundancy. In the basic implementation, we calculate the bag-of-words (BOW) entropy: $H(W) = \sum_{w \in W} \frac{count(w)}{n} \cdot -\log_2 \left(\frac{count(w)}{n}\right)$, where w is a word in the bag of words W, $count(w)$ is the frequency of w in W, n is the total size of W, and $H(W)$ is the text-level entropy.

In addition, we calculate the shortest-unique-prefix (SUP) entropy (Kontoyiannisy, 1997), by calculating the length of the shortest prefix starting at x_i that does not appear starting anywhere in the previous i tokens $x_0, x_1, \ldots, x_{i-1}$. This prefix-length l_i can be thought of as the length of the next unique substring after the past up to position $(i-1)$ has been encoded. In other words, this metric measures the surprise value of a substring. The SUP entropy is calculated as: $\hat{H}_N = \left[\frac{1}{N}\sum_{i=1}^{N}\frac{l_i}{log(i+1)}\right]^{-1}$ with $N < M$, where M is the largest possible index (= the sequence length $+1$). (Kontoyiannisy, 1997) do not elaborate on how N should be chosen, so we set it to $\lfloor \frac{M}{2} \rfloor$.

In both cases, we use spaCy to tokenize the generated output. We consider all tokens including punctuation marks and lowercase them.

3.3 Results and Discussion

We analyze the model's performance via two kinds of metrics: similarity-based (BERTscore, BLEU and ROUGE) and entropy-based (SUP and BOW). Table 1 shows that the model without fine-tuning and domain adaptation performs the best both in terms of entropy and similarity. A single epoch of fine-tuning seems not to affect the models' performance, but fine-tuning it for 11 epochs worsens it drastically. Similarly, domain adaption without and with 1 epoch of fine-tuning drops below all non-domain-adapted models. Both domain adaptation set-ups (50 and 100 documents) perform the same, so the number of domain adaptation documents seems to have no effect on the performance. Interestingly, with more fine-tuning (11 epochs) the SUP entropy is improved, while the BERTscore-similarity further drops.

The model without domain adaptation and without fine-tuning performed the best and the more we trained the model, the more frequently individual text elements are repeated—first individual clauses, then words, and in the end only characters. These are results that no longer represent meaningful texts, let alone a high-quality text simplification. We did not manage to definitively conclude on reasons why both fine-tuning and domain adaptation do not outperform the pre-trained model. We assume that the main reason could be so-called catastrophic forgetting, which can occur in all scenarios where machine learning models are trained on a sequence of tasks and the accuracy on earlier tasks drops significantly. The model in our experiments was previously trained on inter-language translation (from one language to another) and we fine-tune it on intra-language translation (from one version of a language to another version of the same language). So, domain adaptation, being an intra-language task, differs from the original mBART task. The model's general text generation capability dropped after fine-tuning and domain adaptation. (Ramasesh et al., 2021) demonstrate that forgetting is concentrated at the higher model layers and argue that it should be mitigated there. In their set-up, these layers change significantly and erase earlier task subspaces through sequential training of multiple tasks. All the mitigation methods they in-

Domain Adapt.	BERTscore$_{F1}$	ROUGE-l_{F1}	BLEU	SUP	BOW	Fine Tuning ♣	lr
-	**0.682**	**0.127**	**1.43**	**1.000**	**6.685**	0	-
-	0.682	0.127	1.43	1.000	6.685	1	7.8e-20
-	0.318	0	0	340.000	0.003	11 (100;10)	8.1e-07
50 texts	0.301	0	0	123.666	0.038	1	3e-10 ♠
50 texts	0.301	0	0	123.666	0.038	0	-
100 texts	0.301	0	0	123.666	0.038	0	-
100 texts	0.301	0	0	123.666	0.038	1	3e-10 ♠
100 texts	0.298	0	0	49.666	0.0441	11 (100;10)	3e-10 ♠

Table 1: Average performance of our models on the test texts. ♣ : Best epochs with max epochs (and early stopping patience, if used, in parenthesis). ♠ : The lr auto was unable to find an optimal learning rate; so we use a predefined value.

vestigate stabilize higher layer representations, but vary on whether they enforce more feature reuse, or store tasks in orthogonal subspaces. There are several other possible reasons for this behavior and opportunities to improve the models' performance. In the following section, we give an outlook on possible ways of adjustment.

4 Conclusion and Future Work

In this paper, we apply existing transformer-based methods to generate text simplifications on document level. Furthermore, we investigate the usage of fine-tuning and domain adaptation.

Our work contributes to the field of automatic German text simplifications. This field is understudied, and future works that want to build on top of our and other previous works' findings could research the following areas:

Catastrophic Forgetting (Yu et al., 2021) investigate catastrophic forgetting and speculate that their second phase of pre-training results in some form of catastrophic forgetting for the pre-trained model, which could have hurt the adaptation performance. They recommend to use RecAdam (Chen et al., 2020), which mitigated the problem in their abstractive text summarization study.

Repetition Problem (Fan et al., 2018) show that maximization-based approaches (such as beam search) tend to produce text that contains undesirable repetitions, and stochastic methods tend to produce text that is semantically inconsistent with the given prefix. We use beam search in our approach and experience a significant increase of repetition during training. (Xu et al., 2022) divide approaches for mitigating repetition into 1) training-based (Welleck et al., 2020; Lin et al., 2021; Xu et al., 2022) and decoding-based (See et al., 2017; Fan et al., 2018; Holtzman et al., 2020) approaches. Recently, two new decoding approaches, Nucleus (Holtzman et al., 2020) and Contrastive Search (Su and Collier, 2022), have shown promising results in terms of reducing repetition and improving the overall quality of generated text. Future work could apply these newer decoding methods to the task of document-level text simplification. However, although there is an increasing number of mitigating techniques, the causes of the repetition problem are still under-investigated.

Entropy Entropy metrics provide additional and very inexpensive guidance on the quality of generated text simplification. They can show very well to what degree the repetition problem is present in the text generation model. We encourage future research in similar tasks to measure entropy in their works.

Masking Strategies We only use the commonly used token masking strategy for BART. (Lewis et al., 2019) describes other strategies, that can be used in the future as well.

Controllability and Learning Strategies (Erdem et al., 2022, p. 1165–1168) name a few resources where adding metadata, such as named entities or parts of speech, to the input can be used as an advanced learning strategy to improve results and offer more controllability over the output. We do not add any metadata and observed in Section 3 that our model is not able to properly recognize named entities. Inserting corresponding metadata could potentially improve the performance in this regard.

Unify Designations Designations of people are interchangeably used in Standard Language. A good example is the father in *Der Sandmann*, who is mostly addressed as *Vater* ("father") but also as *Papa* ("dad") by his children and as *Herr* ("master"), as in *Herr des Hauses* ("man of the house"), by his house staff. All these words mean the same and are referring to the same person. Unifying them could help.

Limitations

The work we described in this paper investigates the automatic simplification of narrative documents in German. Our Methodology is focussed on document-level simplification and is only transferable to a limited extent to simplification that works on sentence-level or other linguistic levels. Additionally, our approach as well as the future research areas are generally applicable to document-level simplification in a broad variety of languages. The choice of quantitative evaluation can be applied to any text simplification task, with structural and linguistic limitations. The qualitative evaluation highly considers the narrative nature of our data, so it is transferable to the simplification of narrative texts in any form but hardly applicable to other text genres.

The data we used is targeted towards different audiences, children and/or people with a lower literacy. Furthermore, some are written in easy language (*Leichte Sprache*) and others in the broader category simple language (*Einfache Sprache*). Future researchers are advised to carefully check the data sources and evaluate to which degree the data can be used for the intended purpose. Due to copyright restrictions, we are only able to provide public URLs to the data, and cannot provide the data directly.

Ethics Statement

We state that our work complies with the ACL Ethics Policy.[1] Our work investigates the automatic simplification of narrative documents in German. Providing simplified versions of texts positively contributes to the inclusion of people with cognitive disabilities and lower literacy into a growing number of aspects of society. Automatically generated simplifications offer a lower cost point compared to their human-made equivalents. On the one hand, this increases the number of people that can afford to read these text, on the other hand, it can endanger the future job prospects of human translators, which specialized in simplifying texts.

Acknowledgments

We would like to thank the Norddeutscher Rundfunk (NDR) for allowing us to use the "Märchen in Leichter Sprache" [2] and make them available to a scientific audience.

[1] https://www.aclweb.org/portal/content/acl-code-ethics

[2] https://www.ndr.de/fernsehen/barrierefreie_angebote/leichte_sprache/Maerchen-in-Leichter-Sprache,maerchenleichtesprache100.html

References

Fernando Alva-Manchego, Carolina Scarton, and Lucia Specia. 2021. The (Un)Suitability of Automatic Evaluation Metrics for Text Simplification. *Computational Linguistics*, 47(4):861–889.

Miriam Anschütz, Joshua Oehms, Thomas Wimmer, Bartłomiej Jezierski, and Georg Groh. 2023. Language Models for German Text Simplification: Overcoming Parallel Data Scarcity through Style-specific Pre-training. ArXiv:2305.12908 [cs].

Dennis Aumiller and Michael Gertz. 2022. Klexikon: A German Dataset for Joint Summarization and Simplification. In *Proceedings of the 13th Conference on Language Resources and Evaluation (LREC 2022)*, pages 2693–2701.

Alessia Battisti, Dominik Pfütze, Andreas Säuberli, Marek Kostrzewa, and Sarah Ebling. 2020. A Corpus for Automatic Readability Assessment and Text Simplification of German. In *Proceedings of the 12th Language Resources and Evaluation Conference*, pages 3302–3311, Marseille, France. European Language Resources Association.

Iz Beltagy, Matthew E. Peters, and Arman Cohan. 2020. Longformer: The Long-Document Transformer. ArXiv: 2004.05150.

Sanyuan Chen, Yutai Hou, Yiming Cui, Wanxiang Che, Ting Liu, and Xiangzhan Yu. 2020. Recall and Learn: Fine-tuning Deep Pretrained Language Models with Less Forgetting. In *Proceedings of the 2020 Conference on Empirical Methods in Natural Language Processing (EMNLP)*, pages 7870–7881, Online. Association for Computational Linguistics.

Alexis Conneau, Kartikay Khandelwal, Naman Goyal, Vishrav Chaudhary, Guillaume Wenzek, Francisco Guzmán, Edouard Grave, Myle Ott, Luke Zettlemoyer, and Veselin Stoyanov. 2020. Unsupervised Cross-lingual Representation Learning at Scale. In *Proceedings of the 58th Annual Meeting of the Association for Computational Linguistics*, pages 8440–8451, Online. Association for Computational Linguistics.

Sarah Ebling, Alessia Battisti, Marek Kostrzewa, Dominik Pfütze, Annette Rios, Andreas Säuberli, and Nicolas Spring. 2022. Automatic Text Simplification for German. *Frontiers in Communication*, 7:706718. Publisher: Frontiers Research Foundation.

Erkut Erdem, Menekse Kuyu, Semih Yagcioglu, Anette Frank, Letitia Parcalabescu, Barbara Plank, Andrii Babii, Oleksii Turuta, Aykut Erdem, Iacer Calixto, Elena Lloret, Elena-Simona Apostol, Ciprian-Octavian Truică, Branislava Šandrih, Sanda Martinčić-Ipšić, Gábor Berend, Albert Gatt, and Grăzina Korvel. 2022. Neural Natural Language Generation: A Survey on Multilinguality, Multimodality, Controllability and Learning. *Journal of Artificial Intelligence Research*, 73:1131–1207.

Angela Fan, Mike Lewis, and Yann Dauphin. 2018. Hierarchical Neural Story Generation. In *Proceedings of the 56th Annual Meeting of the Association for Computational Linguistics (Volume 1: Long Papers)*, pages 889–898, Melbourne, Australia. Association for Computational Linguistics.

Dino Felluga. 2011. General Introduction to Narratology.

Julia Hancke, Sowmya Vajjala, and Detmar Meurers. 2012. Readability Classification for German using Lexical, Syntactic, and Morphological Features. In *Proceedings of COLING 2012*, pages 1063–1080, Mumbai, India. The COLING 2012 Organizing Committee.

Ari Holtzman, Jan Buys, Li Du, Maxwell Forbes, and Yejin Choi. 2020. The Curious Case of Neural Text Degeneration. In *International Conference on Learning Representations*, pages 1–16.

David Klaper, S. Ebling, and Martin Volk. 2013. Building a German/Simple German Parallel Corpus for Automatic Text Simplification. In *Klaper, David; Ebling, S; Volk, Martin (2013). Building a German/Simple German Parallel Corpus for Automatic Text Simplification. In: The Second Workshop on Predicting and Improving Text Readability for Target Reader Populations (PITR 2013), Sofia, Bulgaria, 8 August 2013.*, pages 11–19, Sofia, Bulgaria. University of Zurich.

I Kontoyiannisy. 1997. The Complexity and Entropy of Literary Styles. Technical report.

Mike Lewis, Yinhan Liu, Naman Goyal, Marjan Ghazvininejad, Abdelrahman Mohamed, Omer Levy, Ves Stoyanov, and Luke Zettlemoyer. 2019. BART: Denoising Sequence-to-Sequence Pre-training for Natural Language Generation, Translation, and Comprehension.

Chin-Yew Lin. 2004. ROUGE: A Package for Automatic Evaluation of Summaries. In *Text Summarization Branches Out*, pages 74–81, Barcelona, Spain. Association for Computational Linguistics.

Xiang Lin, Simeng Han, and Shafiq Joty. 2021. Straight to the Gradient: Learning to Use Novel Tokens for Neural Text Generation. In *Proceedings of the 38th International Conference on Machine Learning*, pages 6642–6653. PMLR. ISSN: 2640-3498.

Yinhan Liu, Jiatao Gu, Naman Goyal, Xian Li, Sergey Edunov, Marjan Ghazvininejad, Mike Lewis, and Luke Zettlemoyer. 2020. Multilingual Denoising Pre-training for Neural Machine Translation. *Transactions of the Association for Computational Linguistics*, 8:726–742. Place: Cambridge, MA Publisher: MIT Press.

Kishore Papineni, Salim Roukos, Todd Ward, and Wei-Jing Zhu. 2002. Bleu: a Method for Automatic Evaluation of Machine Translation. In *Proceedings of the 40th Annual Meeting of the Association for Computational Linguistics*, pages 311–318, Philadelphia, Pennsylvania, USA. Association for Computational Linguistics.

Vinay Venkatesh Ramasesh, Ethan Dyer, and Maithra Raghu. 2021. Anatomy of Catastrophic Forgetting: Hidden Representations and Task Semantics. In *Proceedings of Conference on Learning Representations*, pages 1–31. International Conference on Learning Representations.

Annette Rios, Nicolas Spring, Tannon Kew, Marek Kostrzewa, Andreas Säuberli, Mathias Müller, and Sarah Ebling. 2021. A New Dataset and Efficient Baselines for Document-level Text Simplification in German. In *Proceedings of the Third Workshop on New Frontiers in Summarization*, pages 152–161, Online and in Dominican Republic. Association for Computational Linguistics. Tex.ids= riosNewDatasetEfficient2021a.

Thorben Schomacker, Michael Gille, Marina Tropmann-Frick, and Jörg von der Hülls. 2023. Data and Approaches for German Text Simplification - Next Steps toward an Accessibility-enhanced Communication.

Abigail See, Peter J. Liu, and Christopher D. Manning. 2017. Get To The Point: Summarization with Pointer-Generator Networks. In *Proceedings of the 55th Annual Meeting of the Association for Computational Linguistics (Volume 1: Long Papers)*, pages 1073–1083, Vancouver, Canada. Association for Computational Linguistics.

Lucia Specia. 2010. Translating from Complex to Simplified Sentences. In *Computational Processing of the Portuguese Language*, Lecture Notes in Computer Science, pages 30–39, Berlin, Heidelberg. Springer.

Regina Stodden, Omar Momen, and Laura Kallmeyer. 2023. DEPLAIN: A German Parallel Corpus with Intralingual Translations into Plain Language for Sentence and Document Simplification. ArXiv:2305.18939 [cs].

Yixuan Su and Nigel Collier. 2022. Contrastive Search Is What You Need For Neural Text Generation. ArXiv:2210.14140 [cs].

Julia Suter, Sarah Ebling, and Martin Volk. 2016. Rule-based Automatic Text Simplification for German. In *Proceedings of the 13th Conference on Natural Language Processing*, pages 279–287.

Andreas Säuberli, Sarah Ebling, and Martin Volk. 2020. Benchmarking Data-driven Automatic Text Simplification for German. In *Proceedings of the 1st Workshop on Tools and Resources to Empower People with REAding DIfficulties (READI)*, pages 41–48, Marseille, France. European Language Resources Association.

Zarah Weiß and Detmar Meurers. 2018. Modeling the Readability of German Targeting Adults and Children: An empirically broad analysis and its cross-corpus validation. In *Proceedings of the 27th International Conference on Computational Linguistics*, pages 303–317, Santa Fe, New Mexico, USA. Association for Computational Linguistics.

Sean Welleck, Ilia Kulikov, Stephen Roller, Emily Dinan, Kyunghyun Cho, and Jason Weston. 2020. Neural Text Generation With Unlikelihood Training. In *International Conference on Learning Representations*, pages 1–18. International Conference on Learning Representations.

Guillaume Wenzek, Marie-Anne Lachaux, Alexis Conneau, Vishrav Chaudhary, Francisco Guzmán, Armand Joulin, and Edouard Grave. 2020. CCNet: Extracting High Quality Monolingual Datasets from Web Crawl Data. In *Proceedings of the 12th Conference on Language Resources and Evaluation (LREC 2020)*, page 10.

Jin Xu, Xiaojiang Liu, Jianhao Yan, Deng Cai, Huayang Li, and Jian Li. 2022. Learning to Break the Loop: Analyzing and Mitigating Repetitions for Neural Text Generation. In *Proceedings of the 36th Conference on Neural Information Processing Systems*, pages 1–36. 36th Conference on Neural Information Processing Systems. ArXiv:2206.02369 [cs].

Tiezheng Yu, Zihan Liu, and Pascale Fung. 2021. AdaptSum: Towards Low-Resource Domain Adaptation for Abstractive Summarization. In *Proceedings of the 2021 Conference of the North American Chapter of the Association for Computational Linguistics: Human Language Technologies*, pages 5892–5904, Online. Association for Computational Linguistics.

Tianyi Zhang. 2020. BERTScore Default Layer Performance on WMT16 (last accessed: 2022-09-26).

Tianyi Zhang, Varsha Kishore, Felix Wu, Kilian Q. Weinberger, and Yoav Artzi. 2020. BERTScore: Evaluating Text Generation with BERT. ArXiv:1904.09675 [cs].

A Code

Our code is available on GitHub:

Pre-Processing of the Fine-Tuning Dataset based on Projekt Gutenberg, Gutenberg, and PDF-Reading Samples Texts:
github.com/tschomacker/aligned-narrative-documents

Pre-Processing of the Domain Adapation based on Textgrid Texts:
github.com/tschomacker/textgrid-domain-adaptation-dataset

Machine Learning Architecture and Implementation:
github.com/tschomacker/longmbart

B Analysis of *Der Sandmann*

The output of the model is shown in Figure 1. From line 1 to 18, the complete text is equivalent to the Standard Language input. After *Franz Moor den Daniel* (line 19) the model inserts multiple passages that occur previously in the text, e.g. three times *unglückseligen Krämers gar feindlich auf mich wirken muß* ("I can't help but think that the unfortunate grocer must have a hostile effect on me") in line 23.

Furthermore, the model changes facts in the text, e.g. in line 26 supper is served at seven o'clock, while in the Standard Language version lunch is served at the same time. The reference Simple Language version from Passanten Verlag completely discards the facts about dinner and supper, boiling this passage down to a brief introduction of the father and mentioning that he was busy with his work and that he told fascinating stories to his kids. Another aspect of line 26 is that the model output does not mention the father. This is the first introduction of this character in the story, so the model discarded an important character from this text passage. Furthermore, although the model does not fully remove the father from the text, it only refers to him via pronouns: *Er mochte mit seinem Dienst* ("He might be with his work") (line 27) refers to the father by the pronoun *Er* ("He"), despite the fact that the character was never introduced or referred to before. For a reader who has only access to the model's output, it is impossible to understand who *Er* ("He") is. A clean or complete removal of a character would show some simplification capability, even if it was an important character. In this case, it was an incomplete removal of an arguably important character.

Most of the repeated sentences do not contain information that is important to follow the story. In this respect, there is actually no need to transfer them into the simplification, let alone repeat them. Especially sentences like *So ist es in der Tat* ("So it is indeed"), are only a linguistic emphasis and arguably add linguistic complexity without additional content. If we assume that repeated sentences are perceived as important by the model [3], the model correctly recognizes an importance only in one case, namely the first mention of the barometer seller Coppolla (one of the main characters in the story) and the narrator's fear of him in lines 26–28, *unglückseligen Krämers gar feindlich auf mich wirken muß* ("unfortunate grocer must have a hostile effect on me").

[3] Profound hypothesis on the causes of repetition are sparse. We base our conjecture on the results of Xu et al. (2022), assuming a correlation between initial probability and repetition rate. If a text fragment occurs more often in the course of the document, it is more likely to be repeated. Therefore, we would say that *unglückseligen Krämers* ("unfortunate grocer") has a high initial probability for the model. In this respect, it is information that should be repeated more frequently in the text and can therefore be considered as important.

Ofel an LotharGewiß seid Ihr alle voll Unruhe, daß ich so lange - lange nicht geschrieben. Mutter zürnt wohl, und Clara mag glauben, ich lebe hier in Saus und Braus und vergesse mein holdes Engelsbild, so tief mir in Herz und Sinn eingeprägt, ganz und gar. - Dem ist aber nicht so; täglich und stündlich gedenke ich Eurer aller und in süßen Träumen geht meines holden Clärchens freundliche Gestalt vorüber und lächelt mich mit ihren hellen Augen so anmutig an, wie sie wohl pflegte, wenn ich zu Euch hineintrat. - Ach wie vermochte ich denn Euch zu schreiben, in der zerrissenen Stimmung des Geistes, die mir bisher alle Gedanken verstörte! - Etwas Entsetzliches ist in mein Leben getreten! - Dunkle Ahnungen eines gräßlichen mir drohenden Geschicks breiten sich wie schwarze Wolkenschatten über mich aus, undurchdringlich jedem freundlichen Sonnenstrahl. - Nun soll ich Dir sagen, was mir widerfuhr. Ich muß es, das sehe ich ein, aber nur es denkend, lacht es wie toll aus mir heraus. - Ach mein herzlieber Lothar! wie fange ich es denn an, Dich nur einigermaßen empfinden zu lassen, daß das, was mir vor einigen Tagen geschah, denn wirklich mein Leben so feindlich zerstören konnte! Wärst Du nur hier, so könntest Du selbst schauen; aber jetzt hältst Du mich gewiß für einen aberwitzigen Geisterseher. - Kurz und gut, das Entsetzliche, was mir geschah, dessen tödlichen Eindruck zu vermeiden ich mich vergebens bemühe, besteht in nichts anderm, als daß vor einigen Tagen, nämlich am 30. Oktober mittags um 12 Uhr, ein Wetterglashändler in meine Stube trat und mir seine Ware anbot. Ich kaufte nichts und drohte, ihn die Treppe herabzuwerfen, worauf er aber von selbst fortging.Du ahnest, daß nur ganz eigne, tief in mein Leben eingreifende Beziehungen diesem Vorfall Bedeutung geben können, ja, daß wohl die Person jenes unglückseligen Krämers gar feindlich auf mich wirken muß. So ist es in der Tat. Mit aller Kraft fasse ich mich zusammen, um ruhig und geduldig Dir aus meiner frühern Jugendzeit so viel zu erzählen, daß Deinem regen Sinn alles klar und deutlich in leuchtenden Bildern aufgehen wird. Indem ich anfangen will, höre ich Dich lachen und Clara sagen: 'Das sind ja rechte Kindereien!' - Lacht, ich bitte Euch, lacht mich recht herzlich aus! - ich bitt Euch sehr! - Aber Gott im Himmel! die Haare sträuben sich mir und es ist, als flehe ich Euch an, mich auszulachen, in wahnsinniger Verzweiflung, wie Franz Moor den Daniel. So ist es in der Tat. Mit aller Kraft fasse ich Euch aus meiner frühern Jugendzeit so viel zu erzählen, daß Deinem regen Sinn alles klar und deutlich in leuchtenden Bildern aufgehen wird. Indem ich anfangen will, höre ich Dich lachen und Clara sagen: 'Das sind ja rechte Kindereien!' - Lacht, ich bitte Euch, lacht mich recht herzlich aus! - es ist, als flehe ich Euch an, mich auszulachen, in wahnsinniger Verzweiflung, wie Franz Moor den Daniel. So ist es in der Tat. So ist es in der Tat . Mit aller Kraft fasse ich Euch aus meiner frühern Jugendzeit so viel zu erzählen, daß Deinem unglückseligen Krämers gar feindlich auf mich wirken muß , ja, daß wohl die Person jenes unglückseligen Krämers gar feindlich auf mich wirken muß, ja, daß wohl die Person jenes unglückseligen Krämers gar feindlich auf mich wirken muß. So ist in der Tat. So ist es in der Tat. - Nun fort zur Sache!Außer dem Mit aller dem Mittagsessen, das alter Sitte gemäß schon um sieben Uhr aufgetragen wurde , das alter Sitte gemäß schon um sieben Uhr aufgetragen wurde. Er mochte mit seinem Dienst . Er mochte mit seinem Dienst viel beschäftigt sein. Nach dem Abendessen. Er mochte mit seinem Dienst viel beschäftigt sein. Nach dem Abendessen, das alter Sitte gemäß, das alter Sitte gemäß, das alter Sitte gemäß, das alter Sitte gemäß von uns um sieben Uhr aufgetragen. Nach dem Abendessen, daß er aber von selbst fortging, daß er aber von selbst fortging.

Figure 1: Generated output of our best performing model, with "Der Sandmann" by E. T. A. Hoffmann as input. We did not change the format of the besides adding highlights and line numbers. The yellow highlights point the reader towards text passages, which showcase our model's shortcomings, which we discuss in Section B. For more information on the of the text, please refer to Table 2.

C Additional Tables

Full Title	Source-ID	Published	Source Texts (Standard and Simple)
Die Abenteuer von Tom Sawyer	eb-sawyer	English (1876)	gutenberg.org/ebooks/30165 einfachebuecher.de/Die-Abenteuer-von-Tom-Sawyer/978-3-947185-33-7
Moby Dick	eb-moby	English (1851)	projekt-gutenberg.org/melville/mobydick/ einfachebuecher.de/Moby-Dick/978-3-944668-86-4
Der Graf von Monte Christo	eb-christo	French (1846)	projekt-gutenberg.org/dumasalt/montchr1/ einfachebuecher.de/Der-Graf-von-Monte-Christo/978-3-944668-53-6
Die Abenteuer von Huckleberry Finn	eb-huckleberry	English (1885)	gutenberg.org/ebooks/64482 einfachebuecher.de/Die-Abenteuer-von-Huckleberry-Finn/978-3-947185-34-4
Der seltsame Fall von Dr Jekyll und Mr Hyde	eb-hyde	English (1886)	projekt-gutenberg.org/stevenso/jekyhyde/ einfachebuecher.de/Der-seltsame-Fall-von-Dr-Jekyll-und-Mr-Hyde/978-3-944668-54-3
In 80 Tagen um die Welt	eb-welt	French (1873)	projekt-gutenberg.org/verne/80tage/ einfachebuecher.de/In-80-Tagen-um-die-Welt/978-3-944668-32-1
Aus Kinderzeiten (in *Diesseits*)	eb-hesse	German (1907)	gutenberg.org/ebooks/47818 einfachebuecher.de/Erzaehlungen-von-Hermann-Hesse/978-3-944668-85-7
Sherlock Holmes. Das gesprenkelte Band	eb-band	English (1892)	projekt-gutenberg.org/doyle/getupfte/chap002.html einfachebuecher.de/Sherlock-Holmes.-Das-gesprenkelte-Band/978-3-944668-36-9
Sherlock Holmes. Das Zeichen der Vier	eb-vier	English (1890)	projekt-gutenberg.org/doyle/zeichen4/ einfachebuecher.de/Sherlock-Holmes.-Das-Zeichen-der-Vier/978-3-944668-39-0
20.000 Meilen unter dem Meer	eb-meer	French (1870)	projekt-gutenberg.org/verne/zwanzig1/ einfachebuecher.de/20.000-Meilen-unter-dem-Meer/978-3-947185-56-6
Die Verwandlung	eb-verwandlung	German (1912)	gutenberg.org/ebooks/22367 einfachebuecher.de/Die-Verwandlung/978-3-947185-99-3
Wolfsblut	pv-wolfsblut	English (1906)	projekt-gutenberg.org/london/wolfsblu/ passanten-verlag.de/lesen/#wolfsblut
Der Schimmelreiter	pv-schimmelreiter	German (1888)	projekt-gutenberg.org/storm/schimmel/ passanten-verlag.de/lesen/#schimmelreiter
Undine	pv-undine	French (1811)	projekt-gutenberg.org/fouque/undine/ passanten-verlag.de/lesen/#undine
Hiob	pv-hiob	German (1930)	projekt-gutenberg.org/roth/hiob/ passanten-verlag.de/lesen/#hiob
Der Sandmann	pv-sandmann	German (1816)	gutenberg.org/ebooks/6341 passanten-verlag.de/lesen/#sandmann
Weiße Nächte	pv-naechte	Russian (1848)	projekt-gutenberg.org/dostojew/novellen/chap01.html passanten-verlag.de/lesen/#naechte
Der glückliche Prinz	pv-prinz	English (1888)	projekt-gutenberg.org/wilde/maerche1/chap001.html passanten-verlag.de/lesen/#prinz3
Der Sandmann	kv-sandmann	German (1816)	gutenberg.org/ebooks/6341 kindermannverlag.de/produkt/der-sandmann/
Der Schimmelreiter	kv-schimmelreiter	German (1888)	projekt-gutenberg.org/storm/schimmel/ kindermannverlag.de/produkt/der-schimmelreiter/
Kinder- und Hausmärchen - Brüder Grimm	All mils-documents	German (1858)	projekt-gutenberg.org/grimm/khmaerch/ ndr.de/fernsehen/barrierefreie_angebote/leichte_sprache/Maerchen-in-Leichter-Sprache, maerchenleichtesprache100.html

Table 2: All documents in our corpus from `einfachebuecher.de` (eb) which are classified as "Klassiker" (classic novel) (snapshot from 07/14/2022), and Passanten Verlag (pv) (snapshot from 07/14/2022), Kindermann Verlag (kv) (snapshot from 07/14/2022) and *Märchen in Leichter Sprache* (`mils`) (snapshot from 07/14/2022).

Are idioms surprising?

J. Nathanael Philipp
Serbski Institut
August-Bebel-Straße 82
03046 Cottbus
Leipzig University
Augustusplatz 10
04109 Leipzig
nathanael@philipp.land

Michael Richter
Erik Daas
Leipzig University
Augustusplatz 10
04109 Leipzig
mprrichter@gmail.com
erik.daas.uni@outlook.de

Max Kölbl
Osaka University
1-5 Yamadaoka, Suita
565-0871 Osaka
max.w.koelbl@gmail.com

Abstract

This study focuses on the identification of English Idiomatic Expressions (IE) using an information theoretic model. In the focus are verb-noun constructions only. We notice significant differences in semantic surprisal and information density between IE-data and literals-data. Surprisingly, surprisal and information density in the IE-data and in a large reference data set do not differ significantly, while, in contrast, we observe significant differences between literals and a large reference data set.

1 Introduction

The aim of this study is the identification of English Idiomatic Expressions (IE) with an information theoretic model (Shannon, 1948). We focus solely on verb-noun constructions (VNC) such as *kick the bucket*, *make scene*, *blow whistle* or *take heart*. As in a study from Peng et al. (2018), we look at VNC which can be used either idiomatically or literally. In this study, we restrict ourselves to IE in English because we had manually annotated data available in which sentences are labelled as "idiomatic" or as "literal". We assume that the amount of information in general and the *Flow of Information* (FoI) in IE and literals differ from each other. We operationalise FoI as information density (see below subsection *Information Density*). Information density is calculated from the change of information over time in linguistic units such as sentences and utterances. The principle of *Uniform Information Density* in language production postulates the smallest possible information changes in a linguistic unit (preferably no steep information peaks and no deep information troughs) in order not to threaten the processing of the message by the receiver (Levy and Jaeger, 2007).

In this study, we utilise contextualised information that is *surprisal* (Tribus, 1961; Hale, 2001; Hale et al., 2015; Levy, 2008)[1]. Surprisal represents the amount of certainty / uncertainty, i.e., it measures the deviation between what the language processor expects to occur and what actually occurs in a linguistic unit. We expect that idioms will cause a different amount of surprisal (over time) than literals do because we assume that literal meaning is the expected case, while IE is a deviation from that and will provide surprisal. That is, the information jumps in the sentence should be more pronounced with IE than with literals. In particular, we use *semantic surprisal* as the feature of words since it is derived from the topics in the environment of the target word, and to this end, we employ the *Topic Context Model* (TCM) (Kölbl et al., 2020, 2021; Philipp et al., 2022). TCM indicates how surprising a word is given its distribution in topics and given the distribution of topics in its environment, which can for instance be a document or the entire corpus. We motivate the use of the TCM to distinguish IE and literals by the assumption that the distributions of topics in either case differ which will cause significant differences in surprisal.

IE are far less subject to the principle of compositionality than literal expressions (Espinal and Mateu, 2019; Nunberg et al., 1994). IE are stable linguistic constructions, mostly with specific syntax as in *loose face* or *blow whistle*, a feature referred to as *(In)flexibility* (Espinal and Mateu, 2019; Nunberg et al., 1994). This feature also means the impermeability of IE, i.e., grammatical transformations, extractions and insertions lead to ungrammaticality. To understand an IE touches on conventional-

[1]For empirical evidence of surprisal, see i. a. (DeLong et al., 2005; Bentum, 2021)

Proceedings of the 19th Conference on Natural Language Processing (KONVENS 2023), pages 149–154
September 18–22, 2023. ©2023 Association for Computational Linguistics

ity in language, since its meaning has evolved through specific language usage and convention. Espinal and Mateu (2019) emphasise that *[t]he meaning of IE involves metaphors, hyperboles, and other kinds of cognitive figure.*

2 Selected work on automatic detection of idiomatic expressions

To the best of our knowledge there is no work on IE within the framework of information theory. However, the following two studies described take the approach that is also taken in the present study, that the occurrence of IE is a semantic deviation from the expected. Peng et al. (2018) report an unsupervised classification of IE that is based on topic detection. The authors show that words that are highly relevant in the main topic of the discourse are not very likely to occur in IE, that is, IE are semantically distinct from the main topic of the discourse. In their point of departure, Peng et al. (2018) follow an earlier study by (Feldman and Peng, 2013) in which the authors state that IE are semantic outliers in a given context. This approach is also pursued in Zeng and Bhat (2021) where a BiLSTM-neural network is employed for the prediction of a token as idiom or literal. Basis are static and contextualised embeddings. To the former, additional information such as PoS-tags is added, and the enriched static embeddings are further combined with the contextualised embeddings. If a contextualized representation is semantically compatible with its context, is classified as literal, else it is an idiom. In both studies, IE classification is successful which is indicated by high precision, recall and accuracy values.

3 Dataset, concepts and technique of analysis

The dataset in the recent study comprises 1,997 sentences that are labelled as idioms and 535 sentences labelled as literals.[2] The sentences have been extracted from *British National Corpus* (BNC) and, in addition, from COCA, COHA and GloWbE[3] and served as data basis in Peng et al. (2018). For the determination of a VNC as IE or as a literal expression, Peng et al. (2018) used the list in Cook et al. (2008); Fazly et al. (2009). Peng et al. (2018) treated idiomacity as a binary and explicitly not as a gradual property (Pradhan et al., 2018), and this dichotomy is maintained in the present study.

3.1 Topic Context Model

TCM (Kölbl et al., 2020, 2021; Philipp et al., 2022) is an extended topic model, since it outputs surprisal based on genuine topic models. In this study, we employ *Latent Dirichlet Allocation* (Blei et al., 2003) (LDA).

TCM is built within the framework of *Surprisal Theory* (Hale, 2001; Jaeger and Levy, 2007). It calculates semantic surprisal of a word w given the distribution of topics its non-local environment, for instance a corpus, or in its local environments, for instance documents and paragraphs. Surprisal is defined as the negative log-conditional probability of w, as given in Formula 1.

$$surprisal = \log_2 P(w|\text{CONTEXT}) \quad (1)$$

We define the context as a topic calculated by LDA and calculate the average surprisal for each word, see Formula 2, where n is the number of topics of the LDA. We fixed this at 100 topics. The calculation is given in Formula 2.

$$\overline{surprisal}(w_d) = -\frac{1}{n}\sum_{i=1}^{n}\log_2 P(w_d|t_i) \quad (2)$$

The term $P(w_d|t_i)$ is the probability of a word w_d given a topic t_i in a document d, which is calculated according to Formula 3. $c_d(w)$ is the frequency of a word w given a document d, $|d|$ is the total number of words in the document d, WT is the normalized word topic distribution of the LDA[4], and $P(t_i|d)$ is probability of a topic t in a document d given by the LDA.

[2]The data were made available for us by Jing Peng and Anna Feldman.

[3]http://corpus.byu.edu, https://github.com/bondfeld/BNC_idioms

[4]model.components_ / model.components_.sum(axis=1)[:, np.newaxis] as suggested by https://scikit-learn.org/stable/modules/generated/sklearn.decomposition.LatentDirichletAllocation.html

$$P(w_d|t_i) = \frac{c_d(w_d)}{|d|} WT_{w_d,t_i} P(t_i|d) \quad (3)$$

We trained the LDA on a compilation of an English news corpus (from 2020) and an English Wikipedia (from 2016) corpus, with with 1M sentences each. Both corpora are taken from the *Wortschatz Leipzig* (Goldhahn et al., 2012)[5]. This compilation of two corpora forms the reference data set.

3.2 Information Density

We compare the flow of information in IE and literals utilising the concept of information density.

Formula 4 defines *local Uniform Information Density* (Collins, 2014) (UID, also termed *wordwise* Information density (Scheffler et al., 2023)) as the average of the squared change in surprisal from word-to-word in sentences. In Formula 4, it is not distinguished between increases and decreases in surprisal.

$$UID_{LOCAL} = -\frac{1}{n}\sum_{i=1}^{n}(id_i - id_{i-1})^2 \quad (4)$$

UID_{LOCAL} is per definition negative (Jain et al., 2018), and therefore a UID_{LOCAL} value close to zero indicates a high uniformity of the information density distribution. A high UID value is close to zero and thus expresses, on average, small changes in surprisal in the flow of information in sentences.

4 Results

First, we run *Welch* tests (Welch, 1938) to check whether there are significant mean differences between the data for surprisal. A Welch test does not assume homogeneity of variances in the dataset that are compared. The sizes of the data sets vary considerably: the News-Wikipedia data set comprises 41, 284, 165 surprisal values, the IE set hat 48, 500, and the data set with literals has 11, 655 surprisal values. We observe significant differences of means between IE ($M = 30.26$, $SD = 8.12$) and literals ($M = 30.10$, $SD = 8.19$), i.e., $t = 2.19$, $p = .029$ and between the News and Wikipedia-training and reference data set ($M = 30.25$, $SD = 7.94$) and literals, i.e., $t = 2.23$ $p = 0.025$. Not significant is the difference of means between the News and Wikipedia data set and IE ($t = -0.40$, $p = 0.69$). Despite of a number significant mean differences as described above, the effect sizes that we determined by *Cohen'sd* (Cohen and Cohen, 1988) are consistently small in these cases. That is to say, idiomacity has not a strong effect on the information density: *Cohen's d* for the pair IE and literals yields .022, and for the pair News-Wikipedia and IE it yields .021.

[5]https://wortschatz.uni-leipzig.de/de

Figure 1 depicts the distribution of the UID_{LOCAL}-values in complete sentences. Values close to zero represent small surprisal jumps in sentences. The x-axis gives the UID_{LOCAL}-values, the y-axis gives the normalised relative frequency of each value, and the area under each curve should be 1.

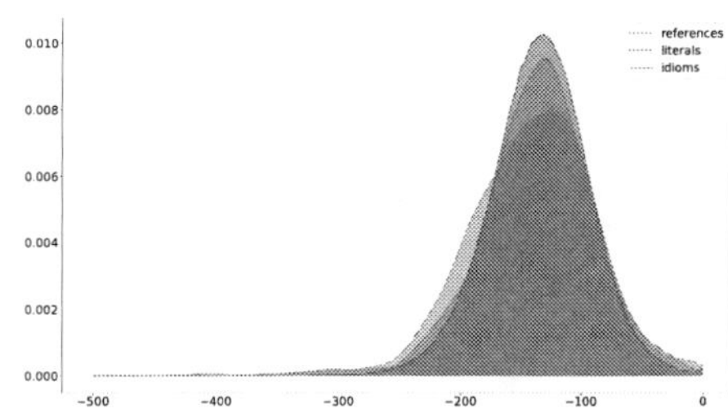

Figure 1: The density of the average surprisal change per word (UID) and **sentence** in the datasets. The x-axis depicts the average surprisal change, the y-axis depicts normalised frequencies of UID-values.

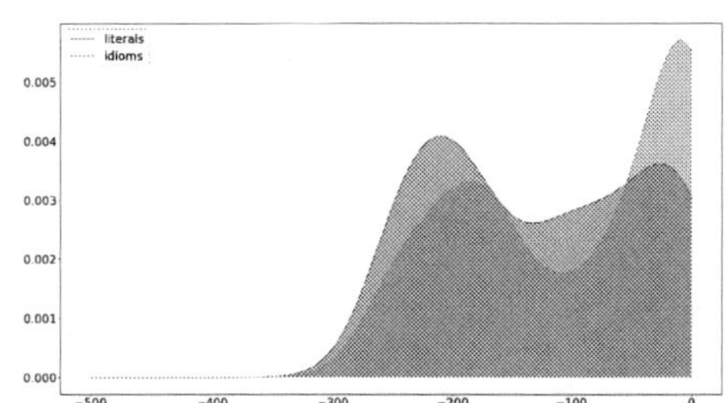

Figure 2: The density of the average surprisal change per word (UID) and **VNC** in the datasets. The x-axis depicts the average surprisal change, the y-axis depicts normalised frequencies of UID-values.

The plots show that the distribution of the IE data takes the middle position between the distributions of the news wiki data and the literals. The News-Wikipedia training set forms the steepest peak and the most even distribution. In contrast, a strongly flattened peak and a distribution that buys out more to the left and right can be observed in the literals, while the IE data set occupies the middle position. As a next step, we focus solely on the VNC in IE and Literals data, in particular on the VNC-list of 12 constructions in Peng et al. (2018). The resulting data sets comprise 793 (IE, $M = 30.40$, $SD = 7.61$) and 637 (literals $M = 31.22$, $SD = 8.07$) surprisal values. A Welch test discloses a significant difference $t = -1.955$, $p-value = 0.05$. Cohen's d is now higher than in the comparisons above, that is .104. The corresponding UID_{LOCAL} density plots are given in Figure 2. The density peak of IE is closer to 0 than the one of the literals whose density is evenly distributed, indicating that information jumps tend to be smaller in IE.

5 Conclusion and discussion

Our study provides first evidence for differences in surprisal between IE and literals. This is reflected in the differences average level of the surprisal values and also in the flow of information (flow of surprisal), the determination of which we operationalised through the measurement of information density (UID_{LOCAL}). We conclude therefore that semantic surprisal from our TCM is a discriminating feature that distinguishes IE from literals. Our study is comparable with the precursor study (Philipp et al.): Here, surprisal was derived from POS tags and thematic roles which did not result in any differences between IE and literal expressions.[6]

Our study has the same point of departure as (Peng et al., 2018): we as well assumed that IE are deviations from the semantically expected, and so it seemed to be plausible to predict that sentences with IE deviate stronger than literals from the reference set w.r.t. the total amount of surprisal and the sentential information density.

However, this is not what we observe: surprisingly IE and the reference dataset exhibit smaller differences in surprisal and UID_{LOCAL}, respectively, than literals and the reference dataset do. Even with significant mean differences, there is only a low effect strength of surprisal. We attribute this outcomes to the fact that surprisal and information density over the entire sentence lengths are compared, i.e., we used a *global measure*, so to speak. It is all the more remarkable, however, that between IE and literals differences nevertheless emerge. In contrast, the *local measure*, which we applied solely to VNC within sentences, increases the effect size of surprisal considerably which underlines the classificatory power of the surprisal feature.

The observation that IE and the reference dataset hardly differ in terms of surprisal and information density indicates that the reference-set has a certain idiomatic character. Our assumption that IE are semantic outliers given a reference dataset has thus to be revised, rather we conclude that the reference dataset seems to have a considerable amount of IE. One important question for future research is whether this conclusion could be generalised: Does language in general tend to be more idiomatic or literal?

Limitations

The News and Wikipedia corpora are only composed of single sentences. However, the TCM is designed to calculate semantic surprisal of words from large extra-sentential contexts, which the corpora do not offer. Future work should thus be based on longer, coherent texts and documents when calculating the surprisal in order to make full use of the possibilities of the TCM. The results could thus become more valid, to which larger corpora as data base will also contribute, especially in the case of literals. In addition, it would be desirable if the study could be extended to other languages and thus take on a comparative character. However, this requires annotated corpora in order to train classification models, which is a desideratum for the future.

[6]The comparison with the results in (Feldman and Peng, 2013) and (Peng et al., 2018) who took a completely different approach is hard because the evaluation measures there differ from ours.

References

Martijn Bentum. 2021. *Listening with great expectations: A study of predictive natural speech processing.* Ph.D. thesis, [Sl]:[Sn].

David M. Blei, Andrew Y. Ng, and Michael I. Jordan. 2003. Latent dirichlet allocation. *Journal of machine Learning research*, 3(Jan):993–1022.

Jacob Cohen and Jacob Willem Cohen. 1988. *Statistical power analysis for the behavioral sciences*, 2. ed. edition. Erlbaum, Hillsdale, NJ [u.a.]. Literaturverz. S. 553 - 558.

Michael Xavier Collins. 2014. Information density and dependency length as complementary cognitive models. *Journal of psycholinguistic research*, 43(5):651–681.

Paul Cook, Afsaneh Fazly, and Suzanne Stevenson. 2008. The vnc-tokens dataset. In *Proceedings of the LREC Workshop Towards a Shared Task for Multiword Expressions (MWE 2008)*, pages 19–22. Citeseer.

Katherine A DeLong, Thomas P Urbach, and Marta Kutas. 2005. Probabilistic word preactivation during language comprehension inferred from electrical brain activity. *Nature neuroscience*, 8(8):1117–1121.

M Teresa Espinal and Jaume Mateu. 2019. Idioms and phraseology. In *Oxford Research Encyclopedia of Linguistics.*

Afsaneh Fazly, Paul Cook, and Suzanne Stevenson. 2009. Unsupervised type and token identification of idiomatic expressions. *Computational Linguistics*, 35(1):61–103.

Anna Feldman and Jing Peng. 2013. Automatic detection of idiomatic clauses. In *Computational Linguistics and Intelligent Text Processing: 14th International Conference, CICLing 2013, Samos, Greece, March 24-30, 2013, Proceedings, Part I 14*, pages 435–446. Springer.

Dirk Goldhahn, Thomas Eckart, Uwe Quasthoff, et al. 2012. Building large monolingual dictionaries at the leipzig corpora collection: From 100 to 200 languages. In *LREC*, volume 29, pages 31–43.

John Hale. 2001. A probabilistic earley parser as a psycholinguistic model. In *Proceedings of the second meeting of the North American Chapter of the Association for Computational Linguistics on Language technologies*, pages 1–8. Association for Computational Linguistics.

John Hale, David Lutz, Wen-Ming Luh, and Jonathan Brennan. 2015. Modeling fmri time courses with linguistic structure at various grain sizes. In *Proceedings of the 6th workshop on cognitive modeling and computational linguistics*, pages 89–97.

T Florian Jaeger and Roger P Levy. 2007. Speakers optimize information density through syntactic reduction. In *Advances in neural information processing systems*, pages 849–856.

Ayush Jain, Vishal Singh, Sidharth Ranjan, Rajakrishnan Rajkumar, and Sumeet Agarwal. 2018. Uniform information density effects on syntactic choice in hindi. In *Proceedings of the Workshop on Linguistic Complexity and Natural Language Processing*, pages 38–48.

Max Kölbl, Yuki Kyogoku, J. Nathanael Philipp, Michael Richter, Clemens Rietdorf, and Tariq Yousef. 2020. Keyword Extraction in German: Information-theory vs. Deep Learning. In *Proceedings of the 12th International Conference on Agents and Artificial Intelligence - Volume 1: NLPinAI,*, pages 459–464. INSTICC, SciTePress.

Max Kölbl, Yuki Kyogoku, J. Nathanael Philipp, Michael Richter, Clemens Rietdorf, and Tariq Yousef. 2021. The semantic level of shannon information: Are highly informative words good keywords? a study on german. In Roussanka Loukanova, editor, *Natural Language Processing in Artificial Intelligence - NLPinAI 2020*, volume 939 of *Studies in Computational Intelligence (SCI)*, pages 139–161. Springer International Publishing.

Roger Levy. 2008. Expectation-based syntactic comprehension. *Cognition*, 106(3):1126–1177.

Roger Levy and T Florian Jaeger. 2007. Speakers optimize information density through syntactic reduction. *Advances in neural information processing systems*, 19:849.

Geoffrey Nunberg, Ivan A Sag, and Thomas Wasow. 1994. Idioms. *Language*, 70(3):491–538.

Jing Peng, Anna Feldman, and Ekaterina Vylomova. 2018. Classifying idiomatic and literal expressions using topic models and intensity of emotions. *arXiv preprint arXiv:1802.09961.*

J. Nathanael Philipp, Max Kölbl, Erik Daas, Yuki Kyogoku, and Michael Richter. Perplexed by idioms. (in press).

J. Nathanael Philipp, Max Kölbl, Yuki Kyogoku, Tariq Yousef, and Michael Richter. 2022. One step beyond: Keyword extraction in german utilising surprisal from topic contexts. In *Intelligent Computing*, pages 774–786, Cham. Springer International Publishing.

Manali Pradhan, Jing Peng, Anna Feldman, and Bianca Wright. 2018. Idioms: Humans or machines, it's all about context. In *Computational Linguistics and Intelligent Text Processing: 18th International Conference, CICLing 2017, Budapest, Hungary, April 17–23, 2017, Revised Selected Papers, Part I 18*, pages 291–304. Springer.

Tatjana Scheffler, Michael Richter, and Roeland van Hout. 2023. Tracing and classifying german intensifiers via information theory. *Language Sciences*, 96:101535.

Claude Elwood Shannon. 1948. A mathematical theory of communication. *The Bell system technical journal*, 27(3):379–423.

Myron Tribus. 1961. Information theory as the basis for thermostatics and thermodynamics.

Bernard L Welch. 1938. The significance of the difference between two means when the population variances are unequal. *Biometrika*, 29(3/4):350–362.

Ziheng Zeng and Suma Bhat. 2021. Idiomatic expression identification using semantic compatibility. *Transactions of the Association for Computational Linguistics*, 9:1546–1562.

Answer Candidate Type Selection: Text-to-Text Language Model for Closed Book Question Answering Meets Knowledge Graphs

Mikhail Salnikov[1], **Maria Lysyuk**[1], **Pavel Braslavski**[3],
Anton Razzhigaev[1,2], **Valentin Malykh**[4], **Alexander Panchenko**[1,2]
[1]Skolkovo Institute of Science and Technology, [2]Artificial Intelligence Research Institute,
[3]Ural Federal University, [4]ISP RAS Research Center for Trusted Artificial Intelligence
{m.salnikov,a.panchenko}@skol.tech

Abstract

Pre-trained Text-to-Text Language Models (LMs), such as T5 or BART yield promising results in the Knowledge Graph Question Answering (KGQA) task. However, the capacity of the models is limited and the quality decreases for questions with less popular entities. In this paper, we present a novel approach which works on top of the pre-trained Text-to-Text QA system to address this issue. Our simple yet effective method performs filtering and re-ranking of generated candidates based on their types derived from Wikidata `instance_of` property. This study demonstrates the efficacy of our proposed methodology across three distinct one-hop KGQA datasets. Additionally, our approach yields results comparable to other existing specialized KGQA methods. In essence, this research endeavors to investigate the integration of closed-book Text-to-Text QA models and KGQA.

1 Introduction

Information stored in Knowledge Graphs (KG), such as Wikidata (Vrandecic and Krötzsch, 2014), for general domain or some specific knowledge graphs, e.g. for the medical domain (Huang et al., 2021), can be used to answer questions in natural language. Knowledge Graph Question Answering (KGQA) methods provide not a simple string as an answer, but instead an entity a KG.

Pre-trained Text-to-Text LMs, such as T5 (Raffel et al., 2019) or BART (Lewis et al., 2020), showed promising results on Question Answering (QA). Besides, recent studies have demonstrated the potential of Text-to-Text models to address Knowledge Graph Question Answering problems (Roberts et al., 2020; Sen et al., 2022).

While fine-tuning a Text-to-Text LM can significantly improve its performance, there are cases where questions cannot be answered without access to a knowledge graph, especially in case of less popular entities (Mallen et al., 2022): not all required knowledge can be "packed" into parameters of a neural model. However, even in such cases, Text-to-Text models can generate plausible answers that often belong to the *same type* as the correct answer. For example, Text-to-Text answers to the question "What is the place of birth of Philipp Apian?" are not correct (e.g., T5 model produced "Neuilly-sur-Seine" or "Freiburg im Breisgau" as answers), but these wrong candidates are of the correct type. Namely, the correct type "city" can be derived from the list of generated answers and used to perform a local KG search around the question entity "Philipp Apian" to derive the correct answer "Ingolstadt". Motivated by these observations, this study presents a method for answer type prediction utilizing the output of pre-trained Text-to-Text language models.

The contributions of our study are as follows: (1) A simple yet effective approach for improving generative KGQA using candidate answer type selection method based on `instance_of` properties aggregated from diversified beamsearch. (2) An open implementation of the method that is easily applicable to pre-trained generative models.[1]

2 Related Work

Traditional KGQA methods can be classified into two categories: retrieval-based and semantic parsing. Retrieval-based methods involve vectorizing the textual question and projecting it into a graph-based vector space containing candidate entities (Huang et al., 2019; Razzhigaev et al., 2023). Semantic parsing approaches generate formal question representations (e.g., SPARQL queries) to query a KG for the answer. Retrieval-based approaches rely on computationally expensive similarity searches using vector indices of millions of candidate entities. Semantic parsing requires maintaining a graph database capable of process-

[1]https://github.com/s-nlp/act

Proceedings of the 19th Conference on Natural Language Processing (KONVENS 2023), pages 155–164
September 18–22, 2023. ©2023 Association for Computational Linguistics

ing SPARQL queries.

Recently, to address these shortcomings of existing methods, a third wave of approaches emerged based on pre-trained Text-to-Text LMs such as T5 (Raffel et al., 2019) or BART (Lewis et al., 2020). Given a question, these models generate a label of the answer that can be directly linked to the entity in a KG. These models are more computationally convenient and they are described below.

The *Text-To-Text Transfer Transformer (T5)* (Raffel et al., 2019) is effective for question answering, as demonstrated by Roberts et al. (2020), or as part of a retrieval pipeline (Izacard and Grave, 2021). Furthermore, it has been shown that training T5 with Salient Span Masking (SSM) improves the model's performance on QA task. T5-ssm involves tuning T5 as a language model, masking *entities* instead of random tokens. T5-ssm-nq is a variant of the T5-ssm that is additionally fine-tuned on the NaturalQuestions (NQ) (Kwiatkowski et al., 2019) dataset. *BART*, a Text-to-Text model trained as a denoising autoencoder (Lewis et al., 2020), can also be applied to KGQA task (Cao et al., 2022).

3 Answer Candidate Type Selection

This section presents our proposed approach, Answer Candidate Type (ACT) Selection. We propose a universal approach to selecting the correct answer in the KGQA task by using any pre-trained sequence-to-sequence (seq2seq) model (in our cases a Text-to-Text Language Model) to generate answer candidates and to infer the type of expected answer. The answer candidate type selection pipeline shown in Figures 1 and 2 consists of four parts: the Text-to-Text model for candidate generation, Answer Type Extractor, Entity Linker, and the Candidate Scorer.

3.1 Initial Answer Candidate List Generation

To increase the diversity of the generated results, we use Diverse Beam Search (Vijayakumar et al., 2016) to generate an initial list of answer candidates C. It often leads to a better exploration of the search space by ensuring that alternative answers are considered. We define the types of entities using the Wikidata property `instance_of` (P31). Note that an entity can be of multiple types. Finally, the initial list of answer candidates is used in the Answer Candidate Typing and the Candidate Scorer with the mined candidates.

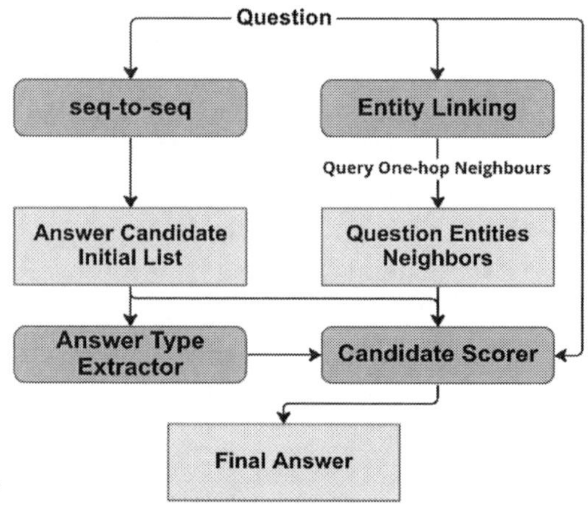

Figure 1: Answer Candidate Type (ACT) Selection.

3.2 Answer Candidate Typing

We rank all types by their frequency in the initial list of answer candidates. After that, we merge the top-K most frequent types and similar types to the final list T. Types similarity is calculated as a cosine similarity between Sentence-BERT (Reimers and Gurevych, 2019) embeddings of respective labels. The final types are defined as the ones where similarity is greater than a threshold.

A similar aggregation method using hypernyms (also known as "is-a" or "instance-of" relations) was used in the past to label clusters of words senses in distributional models (Biemann and Riedl, 2013; Panchenko et al., 2017): distributionally similar words share common hypernym and "top" common hypernyms are surprisingly good labels for sense clusters. The analogy in our method is that Text-to-Text models appear to produce a list of distributionally similar candidates.

3.3 Entity Linking

To enrich the list of candidates, we add all one-hop neighbours of the entities found in the question. For that we use the fine-tuned spaCy Named Entity Recognition (NER)[2] and the mGENRE (Cao et al., 2021) entity linking model.

3.4 Candidates Scorer

Finally, we calculate four scores for each answer candidate and rank them based on the weighted sum of the scores. The scores are as follows:

(1) Type score represents the size of the intersection between the set of types extracted from the

[2]`https://spacy.io`. More details about fine-tuning of the NER can be found in Appendix A.

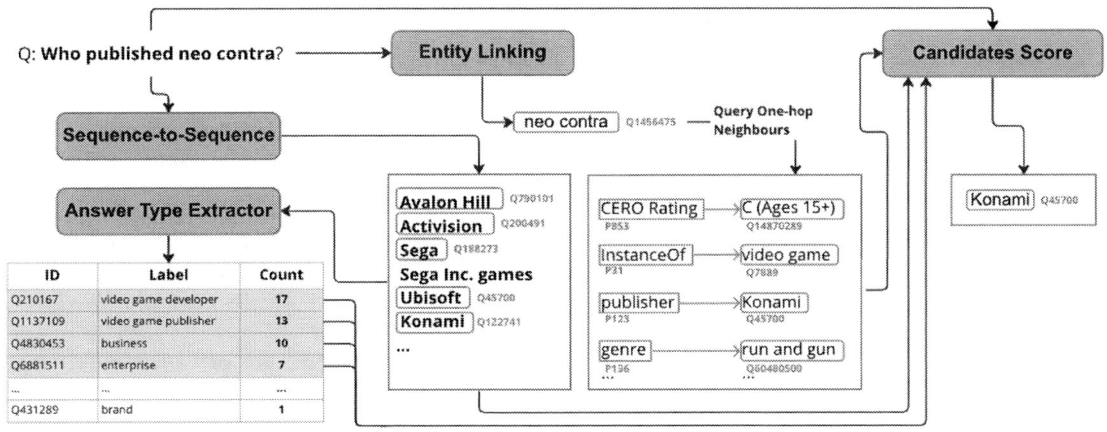

Figure 2: An example of the proposed Answer Candidate Type (ACT) Selection result.

answer candidates and the selected answer types. It is weighted by the number of selected answer types:

$$S_{\text{type}} = \frac{|\text{Candidates' Types} \cap T|}{|T|}.$$

(2) Forward one-hop neighbors score $S_{\text{neighbour}}$ is assigned 1 if the candidate is among the neighbors of the question entities, and 0 otherwise.

(3) Text-to-Text answer candidate score is determined by the rank of the candidate in the initial list C generated by the Text-to-Text model divided by the size of the list:

$$S_{\text{t2t}} = \frac{C.index(\text{Candidate})}{|C|}.$$

(4) Question-Property Similarity score S_{property} measures the cosine similarity between the embeddings of the relevant property and the entire question. We employ Sentence-BERT (Reimers and Gurevych, 2019) to encode the question, following a similar approach used for the Answer Candidate Type module.

The four scores are calculated for each entity and then are combined to generate a final score that determines the entity's ranking. The answer with the highest weighted sum of scores in the candidate list is selected as the final answer:

$$S_{\text{final}} = S_{\text{type}} + S_{\text{neighbour}} + S_{\text{t2t}} + S_{\text{property}}.$$

4 Experiments

We fine-tuned the Text-to-Text and spaCy NER models by using the entire training part of the respective datasets and fitting the model for eight epochs. The initial answer candidate lists were generated using Diverse Beam Search with 200 beams and a diversity penalty of 0.1. The Answer Candidate Typing module utilized the top-3 types and a similarity threshold of 0.6.

4.1 Data

We evaluate the ACT Selection on three Wikidata datasets containing one-hop questions. *SimpleQuestions-Wikidata (SQWD)* (Diefenbach et al., 2017) is a mapping of SimpleQuestions (Bordes et al., 2015) to Wikidata containing 21,957 questions. *RuBQ* (Korablinov and Braslavski, 2020; Rybin et al., 2021) is a KGQA dataset that contains 2,910 Russian questions of different types along with their English translations. *Mintaka* (Sen et al., 2022) is a multilingual KGQA dataset composed of 20,000 questions of different types. For our experiments we took only *generic* questions, whose entities are one hop away from the answers' entities in Wikidata, which resulted in 1,757 English questions.

4.2 Evaluation

We hypothesize that even if a closed-book QA text-to-text model returns an incorrect answer, the odds are that it is of the correct type.

The present study involves the extraction of answer types from Text-to-Text generated answers, followed by a comparison with the ground-truth answer types in the SQWD dataset. Our experimental findings demonstrate that the fine-tuned T5-Large-SSM model equipped with the ACT Selection can accurately predict the correct answer type in **94%** of the cases, while only **61%** of the candidate answers share the same type as the correct answer.

Model	SQWD	RuBQ en
QAnswer	33.31	32.30
KEQA TransE PTBG	**48.89**	33.80
ChatGPT	15.32	36.53
T5-Large-ssm (fine-tuned)	23.66	21.44
Ours: T5-Large-ssm (fine-tuned)	47.42	26.02
T5-11b-ssm-nq (zero-shot)	10.94	33.38
Ours: T5-11b-ssm-nq (zero-shot)	38.51	**38.31**

Table 1: Comparsion of the ACT Selection with KGQA baselines in terms of Hit@1 for SimpleQuestion-Wikidata (SQWD) with T5-Large-ssm fine-tuned on its training part and T5-11b-ssm-nq in zero-shot mode.

These results have provided an impetus to leverage this information to facilitate question-answering.

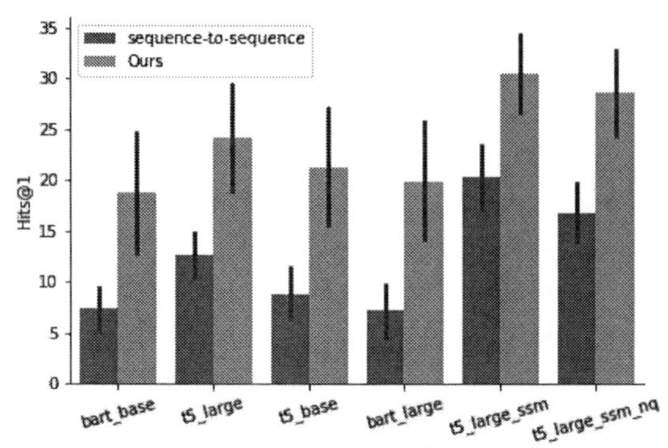

Figure 3: Average Hit@1 scores for the tuned models on SQWD, RuBQ, and Mintaka datasets from Table 2.

We evaluate the performance of two commonly used architecture types, T5 and BART. The proposed approach consistently improves the results of the Text-to-Text models on various datasets, as illustrated in Figure 3. We compare the mean Hit@1 scores of the tuned Text-to-Text models with the aforementioned datasets. Text-to-Text models were fine-tuned on the train splits of SQWD and the full train split of Mintaka datasets, and subsequently evaluated on the test splits of SQWD, RuBQ, and Mintaka using both tuned versions of the models.

As demonstrated in Table 2, the proposed approach consistently enhances the quality of KGQA tasks across various Text-to-Text models. Furthermore, we conducted experiments to verify that the proposed method can be employed with the Text-to-Text models in a zero-shot learning manner, without any fine-tuning. The benefits of the approach, in terms of quality improvement, are more noticeable when applied to smaller models. For example, the T5-large model, with its 737 million parameters, when paired with ACT Selection, delivers comparable performance to the T5-11b model, which has 11 billion parameters.

In line with expectations, larger models generally yield superior results. Notably, T5 models using the suggested method outperformed BART models. Moreover, across all tested T5 and BART models, implementing the ACT Selection markedly enhanced the performance of the foundational Text-to-Text model.

Table 1 showcases performance comparison between our suggested method and prominent KGQA systems, namely QAnswer (Diefenbach et al., 2020), KEQA (Huang et al., 2019), and chatGPT.[3] QAnswer is a multilingual rule-based system that tranforms the question into a SPARQL query. KEQA utilizes TransE embeddings of 200 dimensions, trained on Wikidata using the Pytorch-BigGraph (PTBG) framework (Lerer et al., 2019). ChatGPT is a conversational model that was launched in late 2022 and has received worldwide acclaim. Further details about evaluating ChatGPT and other generative models through entity-linked predictions can be found in appendix B. The tabulated data reveals that our approach delivers outcomes commensurate with those of state-of-the-art (SOTA) systems.

4.3 Ablation Study

We conducted an ablation study (cf. Table 3) to investigate the effects of the proposed scores on the candidate set collection process. Our main goal was to confirm that incorporating type information enhances candidate selection. We observed that methods relying solely on scores (such as Question-Property Similarity score) were not as effective as the ACT Selection approach.

Furthermore, we examined the necessity of initial candidates generated by the Text-to-Text model and whether restricting to question entity neighbors was sufficient. This investigation aimed to determine the added value of initial candidates in the selection process.

4.4 Error Analysis

We showed above that the ACT Selection approach fixed errors produced by the Text-to-Text LMs. We evaluate this approach using a subset of questions and predictions from the T5-Large-SSM model for the SQWD dataset. Our focus is on questions

[3] https://openai.com/blog/chatgpt

	SimpleQuestions-Wikidata			*RuBQ (English)*			*Mintaka (one-hop, English)*		
Tuned on →	**Zero-shot**	**SQWD**	**Mintaka**	**Zero-shot**	**SQWD**	**Mintaka**	**Zero-shot**	**SQWD**	**Mintaka**
BART-base	0	16.54	7.08	0	5.93	3.72	0	2.06	9.12
Ours	30.38	**42.60**	30.70	9.50	11.65	**11.72**	4.70	5.88	**10.29**
BART-large	0	16.97	3.02	0	4.07	4.86	0	1.76	12.65
Ours	30.42	**42.64**	31.39	9.50	12.15	**12.79**	4.41	5.29	**15.29**
T5-base	0	21.26	6.19	0	6.22	6.93	0	4.41	8.24
Ours	30.47	**43.13**	34.60	9.44	14.44	**16.58**	4.71	8.53	**10.59**
T5-large	0	22.36	9.43	0	11.15	12.15	0	7.06	14.41
Ours	29.88	**43.05**	36.89	9.44	18.94	**20.51**	4.71	10.00	**15.88**
T5-large-ssm	0.57	23.66	5.92	0.42	21.44	23.87	0.50	19.71	27.65
Ours	23.39	**47.42**	36.54	9.72	26.02	**27.88**	6.76	18.53	**28.24**
T5-large-ssm-nq	5.12	22.52	4.34	18.87	17.80	19.23	17.65	14.12	23.24
Ours	35.09	**43.88**	36.39	**27.52**	25.38	26.38	22.94	14.12	**25.59**
T5-11b-ssm	1.81	—	—	14.09	—	—	20.88	—	—
Ours	**25.84**	—	—	**20.94**	—	—	**24.71**	—	—
T5-11b-ssm-nq	10.94	—	—	33.38	—	—	41.76	—	—
Ours	**38.51**	—	—	**38.31**	—	—	**45.00**	—	—

Table 2: Evaluation results on three one-hop KGQA datasets (Hit@1 scores): comparing Text-To-Text Language Model with and without our proposed ACT Selection approach in zero-shot (without tuning for QA) or tuned on SQWD or Mintaka.

	Type score	Forward one-hop neighbours score	Text-to-Text LM candidates score	Question-Property Similarity score	All scores
Only initial candidates generated by Text-to-Text	2.51	31.73	27.04	31.82	35.89
Only question neighbours candidates	5.07	4.84	4.52	29.86	30.06
Full answer candidates set	2.81	5.46	27.04	30.75	**47.42**

Table 3: Ablation study of ACT Selection. Reporting Hit@1 at SQWD for T5-large-ssm fine-tuned on SQWD.

where the model's top-1 prediction was incorrect, but the ACT Selection approach extracted the correct answer.

The Text-to-Text model generated the correct answer in only 58.4% of questions in the chosen subset. However, our Entity Linking module was able to correctly extract 99.11% of question entities for this subset. The extraction of additional candidates from the question entity neighbors played a critical role in finding the correct answer.

5 Conclusion

We introduced a method for question answering over knowledge graph based on post-processing of beam-search outputs of a Text-to-Text model. Namely, a simple aggregation of KG "instance-of" relations is used to derive a likely type of the answer. This simple technique consistently improves performance of various Text-to-Text LMs favorably comparing to both specialized KGQA methods and ChatGPT with a carefully selected prompt and entity linked output on three distinct English one-hop KGQA datasets.

Our method may be also used to directly perform answer typing. In principle, it can be straightforwardly adapted to multilingual setup, but also multi-hop questions. We find it promising to use the method with larger pre-trained models to further boost performance as our current experiments show that the a quality growth as the model size increased.

6 Limitations

The main limitation of the current study is that the approach was only tested for one-hop questions. In principle, one can, however, sample candidates from graph from arbitrary subgraphs, e.g. second-order ego-networks of entity found in question. At the same time, improvements shown in this paper may not nessesarily generalize to such setting and need to be tested.

Another limitation is using diverse beam search, which is a computationally more expensive process as it requires larger beam sizes, usually.

Finally, requesting KG data can be a bottleneck if one is using a public SPARQL endpoint with query limits. This limitation can be alleviated by using an in-house private copy of a KG.

7 Ethical Considerations

Large pre-trained Text-to-Text models such as those used in our work are trained on datasets which may contain biased opinions. Therefore, QA/KGQA systems built on top of such models may transitively reflect such biases potentially generating stereotyped answers to the questions. As a consequence, it is recommended in production, not research settings, to use a special version of debiased pre-trained neural models and/or other technologies for the alleviation of the undesired biases of LLMs.

References

Chris Biemann and Martin Riedl. 2013. Text: now in 2d! A framework for lexical expansion with contextual similarity. *J. Lang. Model.*, 1(1):55–95.

Antoine Bordes, Nicolas Usunier, Sumit Chopra, and Jason Weston. 2015. Large-scale simple question answering with memory networks. *CoRR*, abs/1506.02075.

Nicola De Cao, Ledell Wu, Kashyap Popat, Mikel Artetxe, Naman Goyal, Mikhail Plekhanov, Luke Zettlemoyer, Nicola Cancedda, Sebastian Riedel, and Fabio Petroni. 2021. Multilingual autoregressive entity linking. *CoRR*, abs/2103.12528.

Shulin Cao, Jiaxin Shi, Liangming Pan, Lunyiu Nie, Yutong Xiang, Lei Hou, Juanzi Li, Bin He, and Hanwang Zhang. 2022. KQA Pro: A large diagnostic dataset for complex question answering over knowledge base. In *ACL'22*.

Dennis Diefenbach, Andreas Both, Kamal Singh, and Pierre Maret. 2020. Towards a question answering system over the semantic web. *Semantic Web*, 11(3):421–439.

Dennis Diefenbach, Thomas Pellissier Tanon, Kamal Deep Singh, and Pierre Maret. 2017. Question answering benchmarks for wikidata. In *Proceedings of the ISWC 2017 Posters & Demonstrations and Industry Tracks co-located with 16th International Semantic Web Conference (ISWC 2017), Vienna, Austria, October 23rd - to - 25th, 2017.*

Xiao Huang, Jingyuan Zhang, Dingcheng Li, and Ping Li. 2019. Knowledge graph embedding based question answering. In *Proceedings of the Twelfth ACM International Conference on Web Search and Data Mining, WSDM 2019, Melbourne, VIC, Australia, February 11-15, 2019*, pages 105–113. ACM.

Xiaofeng Huang, Jixin Zhang, Zisang Xu, Lu Ou, and Jianbin Tong. 2021. A knowledge graph based question answering method for medical domain. *PeerJ Computer Science*, 7:e667.

Gautier Izacard and Edouard Grave. 2021. Leveraging passage retrieval with generative models for open domain question answering. In *Proceedings of the 16th Conference of the European Chapter of the Association for Computational Linguistics: Main Volume, EACL 2021, Online, April 19 - 23, 2021*, pages 874–880. Association for Computational Linguistics.

Vladislav Korablinov and Pavel Braslavski. 2020. Rubq: A russian dataset for question answering over wikidata. In *The Semantic Web - ISWC 2020 - 19th International Semantic Web Conference, Athens, Greece, November 2-6, 2020, Proceedings, Part II*, volume 12507 of *Lecture Notes in Computer Science*, pages 97–110. Springer.

Tom Kwiatkowski, Jennimaria Palomaki, Olivia Redfield, Michael Collins, Ankur Parikh, Chris Alberti, Danielle Epstein, Illia Polosukhin, Jacob Devlin, Kenton Lee, et al. 2019. Natural questions: a benchmark for question answering research. *Transactions of the Association for Computational Linguistics*, 7:453–466.

Adam Lerer, Ledell Wu, Jiajun Shen, Timothée Lacroix, Luca Wehrstedt, Abhijit Bose, and Alex Peysakhovich. 2019. Pytorch-biggraph: A large scale graph embedding system. In *Proceedings of Machine Learning and Systems 2019, MLSys 2019, Stanford, CA, USA, March 31 - April 2, 2019*. mlsys.org.

Mike Lewis, Yinhan Liu, Naman Goyal, Marjan Ghazvininejad, Abdelrahman Mohamed, Omer Levy, Veselin Stoyanov, and Luke Zettlemoyer. 2020. BART: denoising sequence-to-sequence pre-training for natural language generation, translation, and comprehension. In *Proceedings of the 58th Annual Meeting of the Association for Computational Linguistics, ACL 2020, Online, July 5-10, 2020*, pages 7871–7880. Association for Computational Linguistics.

Alex Mallen, Akari Asai, Victor Zhong, Rajarshi Das, Hannaneh Hajishirzi, and Daniel Khashabi. 2022. When not to trust language models: Investigating effectiveness and limitations of parametric and non-parametric memories. *CoRR*, abs/2212.10511.

Alexander Panchenko, Eugen Ruppert, Stefano Faralli, Simone Paolo Ponzetto, and Chris Biemann. 2017. Unsupervised does not mean uninterpretable: The case for word sense induction and disambiguation. In *Proceedings of the 15th Conference of the European Chapter of the Association for Computational Linguistics: Volume 1, Long Papers*, pages 86–98, Valencia, Spain. Association for Computational Linguistics.

Colin Raffel, Noam Shazeer, Adam Roberts, Katherine Lee, Sharan Narang, Michael Matena, Yanqi Zhou,

Wei Li, and Peter J. Liu. 2019. Exploring the limits of transfer learning with a unified text-to-text transformer. *CoRR*, abs/1910.10683.

Anton Razzhigaev, Mikhail Salnikov, Valentin Malykh, Pavel Braslavski, and Alexander Panchenko. 2023. A system for answering simple questions in multiple languages. In *Proceedings of the 61st Annual Meeting of the Association for Computational Linguistics (Volume 3: System Demonstrations)*, pages 524–537, Toronto, Canada. Association for Computational Linguistics.

Nils Reimers and Iryna Gurevych. 2019. Sentence-bert: Sentence embeddings using siamese bert-networks. In *Proceedings of the 2019 Conference on Empirical Methods in Natural Language Processing and the 9th International Joint Conference on Natural Language Processing, EMNLP-IJCNLP 2019, Hong Kong, China, November 3-7, 2019*, pages 3980–3990. Association for Computational Linguistics.

Adam Roberts, Colin Raffel, and Noam Shazeer. 2020. How much knowledge can you pack into the parameters of a language model? In *Proceedings of the 2020 Conference on Empirical Methods in Natural Language Processing, EMNLP 2020, Online, November 16-20, 2020*, pages 5418–5426. Association for Computational Linguistics.

Ivan Rybin, Vladislav Korablinov, Pavel Efimov, and Pavel Braslavski. 2021. Rubq 2.0: An innovated russian question answering dataset. In *The Semantic Web - 18th International Conference, ESWC 2021, Virtual Event, June 6-10, 2021, Proceedings*, volume 12731 of *Lecture Notes in Computer Science*, pages 532–547. Springer.

Priyanka Sen, Alham Fikri Aji, and Amir Saffari. 2022. Mintaka: A complex, natural, and multilingual dataset for end-to-end question answering. In *Proceedings of the 29th International Conference on Computational Linguistics*, pages 1604–1619, Gyeongju, Republic of Korea. International Committee on Computational Linguistics.

Sowmya Vajjala and Ramya Balasubramaniam. 2022. What do we really know about state of the art ner? In *Proceedings of the Thirteenth Language Resources and Evaluation Conference, LREC 2022, Marseille, France, 20-25 June 2022*, pages 5983–5993. European Language Resources Association.

Ashwin K. Vijayakumar, Michael Cogswell, Ramprasaath R. Selvaraju, Qing Sun, Stefan Lee, David J. Crandall, and Dhruv Batra. 2016. Diverse beam search: Decoding diverse solutions from neural sequence models. *CoRR*, abs/1610.02424.

Denny Vrandecic and Markus Krötzsch. 2014. Wikidata: a free collaborative knowledgebase. *Commun. ACM*, 57(10):78–85.

A Named Entity Recognition

According to the recent review of SOTA NER (Vajjala and Balasubramaniam, 2022), top-3 approaches were chosen: spaCy[4], Stanza[5] and SparkNLP[6]. Pre-rained NERs showed very poor quality ranging from 64% to 88% of missing cases for the SQWD data set. Among them, spaCy was the best; therefore, the standard spaCy configuration[7] was chosen for further fine-tuning. This pipeline requires two main pre-processing steps. First, the span of the entity should be fed into the algorithm. This span is predefined for Mintaka. However, for SQWD and RuBQ only Wikidata IDs of the entities are presented. Therefore, it was necessary first to define labels of the entities and all corresponding redirects. Next, these labels should have been found in the initial sentence for the span detection. Since for some of the entities there was no direct match in the sentence, the fuzzy search[8] was started. Second, spaCy requires the tag of the entity label (e.g., PERSON for Elon Musk , ORG for Tesla - the so-called BIO type tagging) for training, but in the initial data this label is missing. PERSON tag was chosen as the one for all cases. Additional experiments with partial data tagging (defining exact tag for each entity) were not successful.

B Evaluation generative models on KGQA problem

To link predicted answers with entities, we utilized the full-text search engine provided by the Wikidata API[9]. For answers generated by ChatGPT, we performed an additional step of removing the trailing dot at the end of the prediction (e.g., changing 'Yes.' to 'Yes'). For RuBQ dataset we just checked that predicted entity is one of the possible answers.

For predicting answers in the KGQA style, we experimented with different prompts for ChatGPT. Specifically, we used the prompt 'Answer as briefly as possible without additional information.' for evaluating the SQWD dataset and 'Answer as briefly as possible. The answer should be 'Yes', 'No' or a number if I am asking for a quantity of something, if possible, otherwise just a few words.'

[4]https://spacy.io

[5]https://stanfordnlp.github.io/stanza/

[6]https://nlp.johnsnowlabs.com

[7]https://spacy.io/usage/training/

[8]https://pypi.org/project/fuzzywuzzy/

[9]https://www.wikidata.org/w/api.php

for the RuBQ dataset.

C Examples

In this section, we include figures that illustrate examples of the working pipeline. Figure 2 presents the pipeline for the question "Who published neo contra?" The Text-to-Text model generates a set of answer candidates, such as "Avalon Hill," "Activision," and "Sega." These candidates are used to extract the type information, such as "video game developer." This type information is then employed in the Candidate Score module to rerank the final set of candidates, ultimately identifying the correct answer as "Konami."

Additionally, in Figures 4, 5, and 6, we provide additional examples that demonstrate the extraction of types and the calculation of scores within the pipeline.

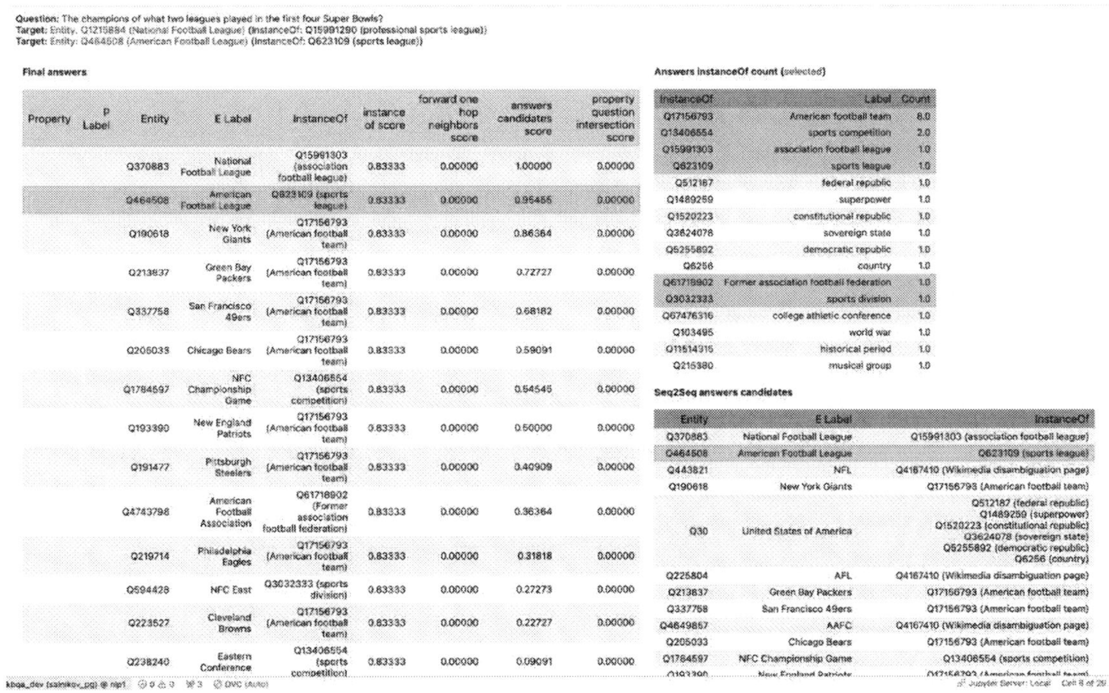

Question: The champions of what two leagues played in the first four Super Bowls?
Target: Entity. Q1215884 (National Football League) (InstanceOf: Q15991290 (professional sports league))
Target: Entity: Q464508 (American Football League) (InstanceOf: Q623109 (sports league))

Final answers

Property	P Label	Entity	E Label	InstanceOf	instance of score	forward one hop neighbors score	answers candidates score	property question intersection score
		Q370883	National Football League	Q15991303 (association football league)	0.83333	0.00000	1.00000	0.00000
		Q464508	American Football League	Q623109 (sports league)	0.83333	0.00000	0.95455	0.00000
		Q190618	New York Giants	Q17156793 (American football team)	0.83333	0.00000	0.86364	0.00000
		Q213837	Green Bay Packers	Q17156793 (American football team)	0.83333	0.00000	0.72727	0.00000
		Q337758	San Francisco 49ers	Q17156793 (American football team)	0.83333	0.00000	0.68182	0.00000
		Q205033	Chicago Bears	Q17156793 (American football team)	0.83333	0.00000	0.59091	0.00000
		Q1784597	NFC Championship Game	Q13406554 (sports competition)	0.83333	0.00000	0.54545	0.00000
		Q193390	New England Patriots	Q17156793 (American football team)	0.83333	0.00000	0.50000	0.00000
		Q191477	Pittsburgh Steelers	Q17156793 (American football team)	0.83333	0.00000	0.40909	0.00000
		Q4743798	American Football Association	Q61718902 (Former association football federation)	0.83333	0.00000	0.36364	0.00000
		Q219714	Philadelphia Eagles	Q17156793 (American football team)	0.83333	0.00000	0.31818	0.00000
		Q594428	NFC East	Q3032333 (sports division)	0.83333	0.00000	0.27273	0.00000
		Q223527	Cleveland Browns	Q17156793 (American football team)	0.83333	0.00000	0.22727	0.00000
		Q238240	Eastern Conference	Q13406554 (sports competition)	0.83333	0.00000	0.09091	0.00000

Answers instanceOf count (selected)

InstanceOf	Label	Count
Q17156793	American football team	8.0
Q13406554	sports competition	2.0
Q15991303	association football league	1.0
Q623109	sports league	1.0
Q512187	federal republic	1.0
Q1489259	superpower	1.0
Q1520223	constitutional republic	1.0
Q3624078	sovereign state	1.0
Q5255892	democratic republic	1.0
Q6256	country	1.0
Q61718902	Former association football federation	1.0
Q3032333	sports division	1.0
Q67476316	college athletic conference	1.0
Q103495	world war	1.0
Q11514315	historical period	1.0
Q215380	musical group	1.0

Seq2Seq answers candidates

Entity	E Label	InstanceOf
Q370883	National Football League	Q15991303 (association football league)
Q464508	American Football League	Q623109 (sports league)
Q443821	NFL	Q4167410 (Wikimedia disambiguation page)
Q190618	New York Giants	Q17156793 (American football team)
Q30	United States of America	Q512187 (federal republic) Q1489259 (superpower) Q1520223 (constitutional republic) Q3624078 (sovereign state) Q5255892 (democratic republic) Q6256 (country)
Q225804	AFL	Q4167410 (Wikimedia disambiguation page)
Q213837	Green Bay Packers	Q17156793 (American football team)
Q337758	San Francisco 49ers	Q17156793 (American football team)
Q4849857	AAFC	Q4167410 (Wikimedia disambiguation page)
Q205033	Chicago Bears	Q17156793 (American football team)
Q1784597	NFC Championship Game	Q13406554 (sports competition)

Figure 4: Example question: The champions of what two leagues played in the first four Super Bowls?

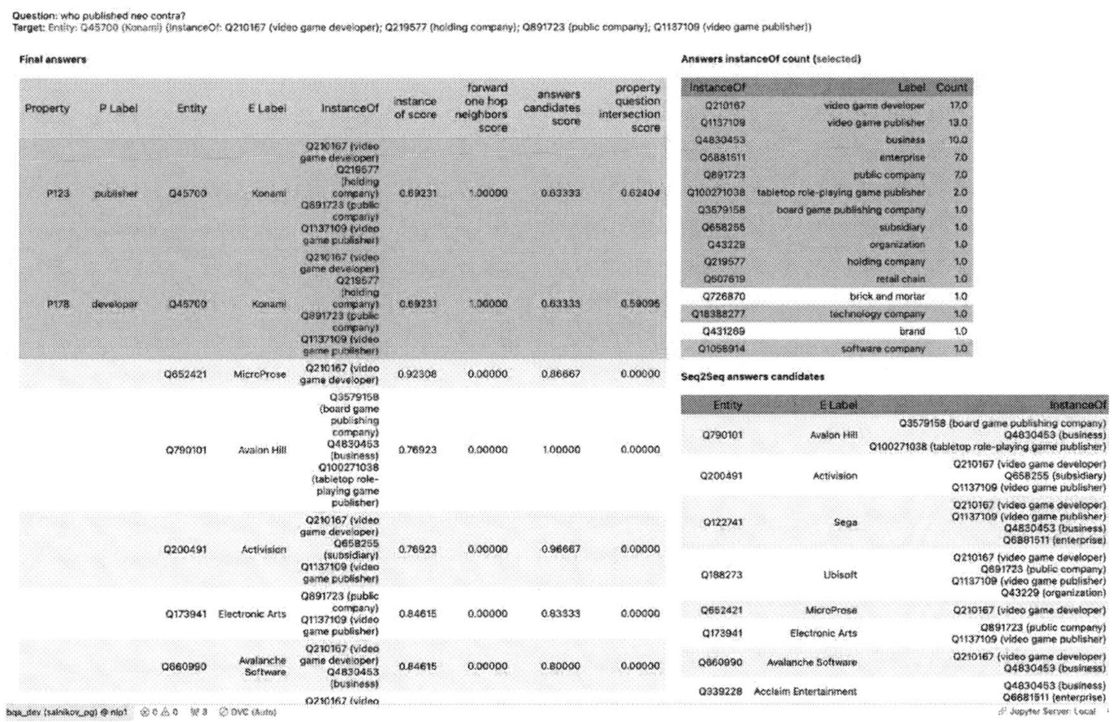

Question: who published neo contra?
Target: Entity: Q45700 (Konami) (InstanceOf: Q210167 (video game developer); Q219577 (holding company); Q891723 (public company); Q1137109 (video game publisher))

Final answers

Property	P Label	Entity	E Label	InstanceOf	instance of score	forward one hop neighbors score	answers candidates score	property question intersection score
P123	publisher	Q45700	Konami	Q210167 (video game developer) Q219577 (holding company) Q891723 (public company) Q1137109 (video game publisher)	0.69231	1.00000	0.63333	0.62404
P178	developer	Q45700	Konami	Q210167 (video game developer) Q219577 (holding company) Q891723 (public company) Q1137109 (video game publisher)	0.69231	1.00000	0.63333	0.59096
		Q652421	MicroProse	Q210167 (video game developer)	0.92308	0.00000	0.86667	0.00000
		Q790101	Avalon Hill	Q3579158 (board game publishing company) Q4830453 (business) Q100271038 (tabletop role-playing game publisher)	0.76923	0.00000	1.00000	0.00000
		Q200491	Activision	Q210167 (video game developer) Q658255 (subsidiary) Q1137109 (video game publisher)	0.76923	0.00000	0.96667	0.00000
		Q173941	Electronic Arts	Q891723 (public company) Q1137109 (video game publisher)	0.84615	0.00000	0.83333	0.00000
		Q660990	Avalanche Software	Q210167 (video game developer) Q4830453 (business)	0.84615	0.00000	0.80000	0.00000

Answers instanceOf count (selected)

InstanceOf	Label	Count
Q210167	video game developer	17.0
Q1137109	video game publisher	13.0
Q4830453	business	10.0
Q6881511	enterprise	7.0
Q891723	public company	7.0
Q100271038	tabletop role-playing game publisher	2.0
Q3579158	board game publishing company	1.0
Q658255	subsidiary	1.0
Q43229	organization	1.0
Q219577	holding company	1.0
Q507619	retail chain	1.0
Q726870	brick and mortar	1.0
Q18388277	technology company	1.0
Q431289	brand	1.0
Q1058914	software company	1.0

Seq2Seq answers candidates

Entity	E Label	InstanceOf
Q790101	Avalon Hill	Q3579158 (board game publishing company) Q4830453 (business) Q100271038 (tabletop role-playing game publisher)
Q200491	Activision	Q210167 (video game developer) Q658255 (subsidiary) Q1137109 (video game publisher)
Q122741	Sega	Q210167 (video game developer) Q1137109 (video game publisher) Q4830453 (business) Q6881511 (enterprise)
Q188273	Ubisoft	Q210167 (video game developer) Q891723 (public company) Q1137109 (video game publisher) Q43229 (organization)
Q652421	MicroProse	Q210167 (video game developer)
Q173941	Electronic Arts	Q891723 (public company) Q1137109 (video game publisher)
Q660990	Avalanche Software	Q210167 (video game developer) Q4830453 (business)
Q339228	Acclaim Entertainment	Q4830453 (business) Q6881511 (enterprise)

Figure 5: Example question: Who published neo contra?

Question: what is the place of birth of sam edwards??
Target: Entity: Q23051 (Swansea) (InstanceOf: Q1549591 (big city); Q515 (city))

Final answers

Property	P Label	Entity	E Label	InstanceOf	instance of score	forward one hop neighbors score	answers candidates score	property question intersection score
P19	place of birth	Q23051	Swansea	Q1549591 (big city) Q515 (city)	0.93333	1.00000	0.00000	0.72962
P19	place of birth	Q219656	Macon	Q62049 (county seat) Q486972 (human settlement) Q1093829 (city in the United States) Q1549591 (big city) Q3301053 (consolidated city-county) Q76514543 (municipality of Georgia)	0.93333	1.00000	0.00000	0.72962
P20	place of death	Q1012665	Durango	Q62049 (county seat) Q1093829 (city in the United States)	0.96667	1.00000	0.00000	0.35553
P937	work location	Q350	Cambridge	Q1187811 (college town) Q1357964 (county town) Q1549591 (big city) Q515 (city)	0.93333	1.00000	0.00000	0.38336
P20	place of death	Q350	Cambridge	Q1187811 (college town) Q1357964 (county town) Q1549591 (big city) Q515 (city)	0.93333	1.00000	0.00000	0.35553
		Q126269	Wolverhampton	Q515 (city)	0.96667	0.00000	0.96923	0.00000
		Q205679	London Borough of Hackney	Q211690 (London borough) Q7897276 (unparished	0.93333	0.00000	1.00000	0.00000

Answers instanceOf count (selected)

InstanceOf	Label	Count
Q1549591	big city	16.0
Q515	city	13.0
Q7897276	unparished area	12.0
Q3957	town	12.0
Q1093829	city in the United States	11.0
Q18511725	market town	8.0
Q211690	London borough	4.0
Q1115575	civil parish	4.0
Q1637706	million city	4.0
Q62049	county seat	4.0
Q1357964	county town	3.0
Q188509	suburb	3.0
Q174844	megacity	2.0
Q200250	metropolis	2.0
Q208511	global city	2.0
Q2264924	port settlement	2.0
Q5119	capital city	2.0
Q13218391	charter city	2.0
Q2154459	New England town	2.0
Q748198	gay village	2.0
Q2755753	area of London	2.0
Q1074523	planned community	1.0
Q10270157	new town	1.0
Q15063611	city in the state of New York	1.0
Q51929311	largest city	1.0
Q15210668	lower-tier municipality	1.0
Q44551483	city in Newfoundland and Labrador	1.0
Q15221310	second-class city	1.0
Q6489113	large burgh	1.0
Q50330360	second largest city	1.0
Q745456	business cluster	1.0
Q106646149	Climate emergency declarations in New Zealand	1.0
Q3184121	municipality of Brazil	1.0
Q2974552	city in New Jersey	1.0

bqa_dev (salnikov_pg) @ nlp1 ⊗ 0 ⚠ 0 3 DVC (Auto)

Figure 6: Example question: What is the place of birth of Sam Edwards?

HS-EMO: Analyzing Emotions in Hate Speech

Johannes Schäfer and **Elina Kistner**
Institute for Information Science and Natural Language Processing
University of Hildesheim
Hildesheim, Germany
{johannes.schaefer,kistner}@uni-hildesheim.de

Abstract

This paper investigates the interplay between hate speech and emotions in social media postings with the goal of modeling both phenomena jointly. We present a bottom-up analysis and introduce an English text corpus with fine-grained annotations for both phenomena, in which we analyze possible correlations. Our results show that only some of the categories representing negative emotions correlate with hate speech classes, while others, such as sadness, do not. With our dataset, we explore methods for using partially annotated data to learn both classifications jointly in an experiment with a transformer-based neural network model. Our results suggest that using a hate speech dataset with emotion labels is more useful than standard multi-task learning with multiple separate datasets. We make our annotation and the code of our experiments publicly available.[1]

1 Introduction

Hate speech[2] remains a persisting issue in social media. This includes offensive language (Wiegand et al., 2018; Struß et al., 2019; Mandl et al., 2021) and toxicity (Borkan et al., 2019) which are of interest for regulation and thus motivate automatic detection approaches. Methods have to consider a variety of features to capture the complex phenomenon. A survey on general approaches for hate speech detection is given by Schmidt and Wiegand (2017). Recently, mainly transformer-based pretrained language models (e.g. BERT by Devlin et al., 2019) have shown the most promising results (e.g. in Caselli et al., 2021; Magnossão de Paula et al., 2022). Typically, the focus in natural language processing research is on fine-tuning using a specialized dataset and on model development. In this paper, we propose to broaden the scope of analysis to include knowledge from the related field of emotions.

The underlying emotions in posts on social media are often studied based on datasets, e.g. Bostan and Klinger (2018) discuss several corpora annotated for emotion categories. These include emotions such as anger, disgust, sadness, joy, fear and surprise. Although hate can be considered a type of emotion, the interplay of the different emotions with hate speech content has not been precisely identified. Alorainy et al. (2018) find hate speech messages from suspended user accounts are often associated with negative emotions such as disgust, fear and sadness. This motivates using emotion analysis as features for hate speech detection, e.g. as shown by Martins et al. (2018), Markov et al. (2021), Chiril et al. (2022) and Rana and Jha (2022). Madukwe et al. (2021) use an emotion lexicon to generate a weighted emotion embedding vector as additional features that prove beneficial for hate speech classification.

To take emotions in hate speech even more into account, both phenomena can be learned in a joint model (Rajamanickam et al., 2020; Awal et al., 2021). Plaza-del Arco et al. (2021) present a multitask learning system which includes a classifier for emotion detection as well as a classifier for hate speech and offensive language detection. They use a shared encoder which is trained sequentially with batches from a different dataset for each classification task.

In this paper, we investigate whether such a multi-task learning approach benefits further from using a single dataset that contains annotations for both phenomena. To this end, we perform a bottom-up analysis of emotions in hate speech posts and create an annotated dataset that can be used for joint classification. Our contributions include (i) a corpus annotated both for four hate speech and offensive language categories as well as for six

[1] https://github.com/Johannes-Schaefer/HS-EMO

[2] Warning: This paper contains examples of hate speech and offensive language. These examples are taken from social media corpora and do not represent the opinion of the authors.

Proceedings of the 19th Conference on Natural Language Processing (KONVENS 2023), pages 165–173
September 18–22, 2023. ©2023 Association for Computational Linguistics

	anger	*disgust*	*sadness*	*joy*	*fear*	*surprise*	*?*	*_*	total
TEC	1,555 (7 %)	761 (4 %)	3,830 (18 %)	8,239 (39 %)	2,814 (13 %)	3,848 (18 %)	-	-	21,047 (100 %)
HS-EMO	352 (35 %)	172 (17 %)	158 (16 %)	113 (11 %)	79 (8 %)	62 (6 %)	37 (4 %)	27 (3 %)	1,000 (100 %)

Table 1: Emotion label distribution in our HS-EMO corpus in comparison to the TEC corpus. The percentages refer to the proportions in each data set, i.e. they are relative values for the respective row of the table.

emotion categories, and (ii) a preliminary experiment to explore methods for learning the phenomena jointly by leveraging emotion analysis in hate speech detection.

The remainder of this paper is structured as follows. In Section 2, we outline our annotation procedure that we use for our dataset, which is presented in Section 3, where we also discuss salient observations. Section 4 presents the experiments on our dataset for joint modeling of hate speech and emotions. Finally, we conclude in Section 5.

2 Annotation

Since the phenomenon of hate speech is rarer than individual emotion categories, we begin our analysis with a dataset that has already been annotated for fine-grained categories relevant to the detection of hate speech. Here we use HASOC in the version from 2021 (Mandl et al., 2021) which contains Hate and Offensive (HOF) content collected from Twitter during the Covid-19 pandemic. This dataset comprises 3,843 English text messages of hate speech (HATE, 683 cases), offensive language (OFFN, 622 cases) and profane content (PRFN, 1,196 cases) as well as other/neutral content (NONE, 1,342 cases).

To analyze these data for the underlying emotions, we annotate a stratified sample of 1,000 instances with six different emotions (joy, anger, disgust, fear, sadness, surprise) on the basis of the categories by Ekman (1988). Additionally, we annotate the label *"?"* in cases where the classification is not clear and the label "_" in cases where no emotion is apparent from the message content. Emotions were classified according to the presumed emotional state of the author of the analyzed message. The annotation was performed by one annotator. To gain a better understanding of the annotation of Twitter data for emotions, the annotator trained on the Hashtag Emotion Corpus (TEC, Mohammad, 2012).

Challenges were presented by cases in which multiple emotions could be detected in a tweet, i.e., when the author presumably felt two different emotions. In such cases, the stronger emotion was determined by guessing which emotion triggered the writing of the message. While in total we annotate six different emotions, we also consider subclasses to ease the annotation. These include, for example:

- Joy: affection, goodwill, zest, pride, hope, acceptance, excitement, relief, passion, caring.
- Anger: irritability, jealousy, rage, frustration.
- Disgust: torment, shame, contempt.
- Fear: nervousness, threat, uncertainty, anxiety, panic, shock.
- Sadness: suffering, regret, displeasure, embarrassment, sympathy, depression.
- Surprise: unexpectedness, astonishment, confusion, unpreparedness.

We provide examples for the annotation of different emotions found in this dataset in Appendix A.

3 HS-EMO Corpus

Our corpus is a sample of instances from the HASOC corpus which we annotate for emotion categories as described above. In total our annotated dataset HS-EMO comprises 1,000 messages where approximately 65% are to be considered hateful or offensive. Table 1 illustrates the distribution of emotions which we identified in this data in comparison to the distribution in the TEC dataset. We observe a more skewed distribution in our data towards negative emotions (especially *anger* and *disgust*) while more positive emotions are less frequent.

We now analyze the correlation of the different emotions with the annotated hate speech categories (see Table 2 and Table 3). Table 2 shows the distributions for the binary categories HOF vs. NONE. Here we observe an even stronger skewed distribution for the HOF class towards the negative emotions *anger* and *disgust*. Out of the instances annotated as HOF, approximately 64% (278 and

	anger	*disgust*	*sadness*	*joy*	*fear*	*surprise*	*?*	_	total
HOF	278 (43 %)	139 (21 %)	47 (7 %)	78 (12 %)	30 (5 %)	40 (6 %)	20 (3 %)	16 (2 %)	648 (100 %)
NONE	74 (21 %)	33 (9 %)	111 (32 %)	35 (10 %)	49 (14 %)	22 (6 %)	17 (5 %)	11 (3 %)	352 (100 %)

Table 2: Emotion and coarse-grained HOF/NONE label correlation in our corpus HS-EMO. The percentages refer to the proportions for each of the labels HOF/NONE, i.e. they are relative values for the respective row of the table. The total counts for each emotion are displayed in Table 1 (row HS-EMO).

	anger	*disgust*	*sadness*	*joy*	*fear*	*surprise*	*?*	_	total
PRFN	136 (44 %)	33 (11 %)	14 (5 %)	65 (21 %)	8 (3 %)	26 (8 %)	16 (5 %)	11 (4 %)	309 (100 %)
OFFN	75 (46 %)	48 (29 %)	9 (5 %)	11 (7 %)	9 (5 %)	7 (4 %)	1 (1 %)	4 (2 %)	164 (100 %)
HATE	67 (38 %)	58 (33 %)	24 (14 %)	2 (1 %)	13 (7 %)	7 (4 %)	3 (2 %)	1 (1 %)	175 (100 %)

Table 3: Emotion and fine-grained HOF label correlation in our corpus HS-EMO. The percentages refer to the proportions for each label PRFN/OFFN/HATE, i.e. they are relative values for the respective row of the table. The total counts for each emotion are displayed in Table 2 (row HOF).

139 instances) fall into one of these two emotion categories. Interestingly, the other negative category *sadness* does not correlate with HOF. Only 7% (47 instances) of HOF cases occur with the emotion *sadness*, while *sadness* was annotated for 32% (111 instances) of non-HOF cases. We find this to be the case, since such examples often contain only sad sympathy for the misfortunes of others and tend not to be offensive or hateful. We support these findings by discussing the HOF content for these emotion categories using selected examples displayed in Table 4. Examples #1 through #4 are HOF cases with the emotions *anger* or *disgust*. These texts mostly report negative feelings on the government or political situation. Here we find expressions in which the blame is assigned to someone. Actions of certain people or groups are despised and they are attacked for it. This blaming is rarely found in examples with *sadness*. For example, consider examples #5 through #7, in which the authors are more reflective. The expressions are not necessarily directed towards a person, but rather refer to an event or the general situation, which is not expressed as hate speech.

As a deeper analysis, we further consider the distribution of emotion categories in the fine-grained hate speech classes. In Table 3, the tweets annotated with emotions are divided into the three HOF categories (PRFN, OFFN and HATE). Out of the 352 tweets annotated with *anger* (cf. Table 1), 278 contain HOF (cf. Table 2) and of these 136 are PRFN, i.e. almost half of the HOF tweets labeled as *anger* contain just vulgar language without targeting a particular person or group. However, for the emotion label *disgust* we observe a correlation with the more severe hate speech categories (HATE and OFFN). For the emotion label *surprise*, 40 out of a total of 62 tweets are marked with HOF and of these only seven examples are considered to be severe HATE (most of them instead belong to the PRFN class). Similarly, for the emotion label *joy* with a total of 113 examples, 78 are marked as HOF with most of them belonging to the PRFN class. Interestingly, for this emotion label *joy* we even find two cases which involve HATE. We now take a closer look at the texts that contain some of these surprising findings.

The most unexpected cases are probably the two examples which are both annotated for *joy* und HATE. These texts of these messages are as follows:

- "@USER I don't think so I am a stupid and never tell others stupid bcoz it is their Ignorance. But still I stand with #Resign_PM_Modi #ResignModi #resign_modi"
- "This time I am with you! Bloody #China spreading #chinesevirus! URL"

Both examples can be seen as instances where the

#	Text	Emotion	HOF
1	"#CommunistVirus is wreaking havoc in india. Not a single liberal is blaming their Beijing Masters. Hypocrites. #ChineseVirus"	*anger*	yes
2	"Wow. Massive asshole timing. Fuck this guy forever. He must be popular with the Trumpers. URL"	*anger*	yes
3	"What a bunch of absolute fucking idiots in #india #IndiaCovidCrisis. Brainless morons wonder why they have a "crisis" (this is goa, sent by an Armenian living there for months) @USER @USER @USER"	*disgust*	yes
4	"Such a pathetic government who keeps denying that there is no shortage of oxygen....shameless characters to go immediately #AndhBhakt #BjpDestroyedIndia @USER @USER #ResignModi"	*disgust*	yes
5	"I have coworkers whose family and friends are sick and dying in India. Other offshore coworkers are sick themselves. Praying the international community does the right thing to help India. Yes, India's Covid crisis hurts everyone. #PrayForIndia #IndiaCovidCrisis URL"	*sadness*	no
6	"#COVID19 After 70 years of independence we failed to deliver Oxigen, medical facilities and vaccination to us. #IndiaCovidCrisis"	*sadness*	no
7	"We aren't opposing BJP, we're only criticizing them because we don't want to loss lives of Hindus in Bengal violence .. #SpinelessBJP #isupportmodi #Modi #BJP #Shamemamatabannerjee #tmcgoons #ShameOnMamata #ArrestMamata #BengalBurning #BengalViolence #TMCTerror URL"	*sadness*	no

Table 4: Examples of anger/disgust HOF cases in comparison to sadness non-HOF cases as text instances from our corpus (HS-EMO). Username mentions and URLs have been anonymized.

author seems to be joyful out of an enthusiastic group sentiment, but that collectively fuels hatred.

In addition, we report another example from the HATE category where, unexpectedly, no emotion was detected:

- "Now, the "poorly paid, but professional, criminals" i.e. "gutter worms" from BJP IT Cell - which is India's No. 1 #FakeNews factory - have got another picture to trend by using these following hashtags: #BengalBurning #BengalViolence #ShameOnMamata #ArrestMamata URL"

4 Experiments

We now use our data sample annotated for both emotion and hate speech to assess whether this joint annotation can be beneficial for modeling both phenomena jointly. To test different methods for learning to recognize hate speech while possibly considering emotion analysis, we implement a neural network approach. We encode text messages using the transformer-based pre-trained language model BERT (Devlin et al., 2019) and perform the classification for each task in a separate linear layer on top of the pooled encoder output. Further details and hyperparameters are described in Appendix B.

4.1 Experimental Setups

We train the shared encoder in any setup and the classifiers only for the respective tasks available given the used dataset. All our models are trained on the HASOC data to optimize the hate speech classification component (training data *HS*). Additionally, we implement optional training steps to incorporate emotion analysis in different ways as follows. We use the TEC corpus as additional source material to train the emotion classifier alternately with the hate speech classifier (standard multi-task learning (MTL) on separate datasets, training data *HS&Emo*). We also allow for training on our dataset to train both classifiers simultaneously via joint classification (training data *HSEmo*). The combination of these training steps results in four overall approaches which we investigate:

- *HS* as a first baseline for hate speech detection without emotion analysis.
- *HS & Emo* as a second baseline with standard MTL on two separate datasets.
- *HS & Emo & HSEmo* as extension of the second baseline including joint MTL on our dataset.
- *HS & HSEmo* as extension of the first baseline including joint MTL on our dataset.

For each of those we investigate coarse-grained (binary) as well as fine-grained (four classes) hate speech detection.

4.2 Results

The performance results of our optimized models are displayed in Table 6 for the coarse-grained (binary) hate speech detection and in Table 5 for the fine-grained (four classes) hate speech detection. For the different models, we respectively report the class-based F1 score values as well as the macro-averaged F1 score value for hate speech

Training Data	$F1_{NONE}$	$F1_{PRFN}$	$F1_{OFFN}$	$F1_{HATE}$	macro-avg F1
HS	.7018	**.7827**	**.5121**	.5438	**.6351**
HS & Emo	.7100	.7143	.4054	.5436	.5933
HS & Emo & HSEmo	**.7169**	.7522	.4823	.5620	.6283
HS & HSEmo	.7154	.7315	.4509	**.5655**	.6158

Table 5: Fine grained hate speech detection performance of best models trained on different data.

Training Data	$F1_{HOF}$	$F1_{NONE}$	macro-avg F1
HS	.7277	**.8535**	**.7906**
HS & Emo	.7293	.8326	.7810
HS & Emo & HSEmo	**.7340**	.8459	.7900
HS & HSEmo	.7147	.8299	.7723

Table 6: Coarse grained hate speech detection performance of best models trained on different data.

detection on the HASOC 2021 test dataset (Mandl et al., 2021). Detailed results of different runs including hyperparameter optimization are given in Appendix C.

We briefly compare our best results to the performances of the top systems according to the leaderboards from the HASOC 2021 shared task which are available online.[3] The best observed performance of all our models on test data is 0.8187 macro-average F1 for coarse-grained hate speech detection (see Appendix C, Table 8) and 0.6486 macro-average F1 for fine-grained hate speech detection (see Appendix C, Table 9). These runs would place us fourth for coarse-grained detection and third for fine-grained detection, only about 1% and 2% behind the top systems. Thus, we assume that our general approach is competitive, while the hyperparameter optimization of our basic model remains quite simple.

When incorporating emotion classification, the overall results (i.e. the macro-average F1 scores of the optimized models displayed in Table 6 and in Table 5) show that this does not improve the hate speech detection performance (the *HS* approach performs best). However, in the MTL setups, the approaches including joint multi-task learning (*HS & Emo & HSEmo* and *HS & HSEmo*) mostly outperform the standard MTL approach (*HS & Emo*).

5 Conclusion

In total, we present a corpus of 1,000 messages with emotion labels containing also hate speech and offensive language. Our bottom-up analysis of the occurrence of emotions in hate speech shows that, as expected, there is a correlation between certain negative emotions such as disgust and severe hate speech classes. However, we also identified other negative emotions that mostly do not correlate with hate speech, such as sadness. In some cases, we even found that the authors presumably felt positive emotions such as joy in hateful messages.

Our experiments with this preliminary dataset show the benefit of a joint annotation in comparison to standard multi-task learning with multiple datasets. However, since we have only annotated a sample of the hate speech data so far, further research is needed to use such data to improve hate speech detection. Future work has to consider a fair comparison with a fully annotated dataset for joint learning. Further attempts for optimization should consider assigning variable weights to the auxiliary task when the main goal is to improve hate speech detection.

Ethical Considerations

Limitations. Our analysis of the correlation of hate speech and emotions is based on an emotion annotation by only one single annotator. While we extensively discussed difficult cases beforehand and the annotation was carefully done, we currently cannot evaluate the quality of this annotation. In addition, the annotator was indecisive about the emotion in about 4% of the instances. Future plans are to include a second annotation by another annotator.

The dataset used for our analysis and experiment is rather small and contains a topic bias towards Covid-19 in India in particular. This limits the generalizability of our results.

Reproducibility. We use datasets with annotations for hate speech and emotions. All of these datasets are freely available for research use. We use these data for their intended use, to develop detection systems. Since we research hate speech, the datasets have not been filtered or anonymized for offensive language.

[3] `https://hasocfire.github.io/hasoc/2021/results.html`

We publish our program code for maximum transparency. The described models and predictions of labels can be reproduced with this code. For training we randomly split the dataset into specific portions. Additionally, we provide a script to reproduce the random split used in our experiments to benefit future research. We report relevant information for the used artifacts and refer to the original publications for further documentation. We believe that these descriptions make our approach reproducible.

References

Wafa Alorainy, Pete Burnap, Han Liu, Amir Javed, and Matthew L Williams. 2018. Suspended accounts: A source of tweets with disgust and anger emotions for augmenting hate speech data sample. In *2018 International Conference on Machine Learning and Cybernetics (ICMLC)*, volume 2, pages 581–586. IEEE.

Md Rabiul Awal, Rui Cao, Roy Ka-Wei Lee, and Sandra Mitrović. 2021. AngryBERT: Joint Learning Target and Emotion for Hate Speech Detection. In *Advances in Knowledge Discovery and Data Mining*, pages 701–713, Cham. Springer International Publishing.

Daniel Borkan, Lucas Dixon, Jeffrey Sorensen, Nithum Thain, and Lucy Vasserman. 2019. Nuanced metrics for measuring unintended bias with real data for text classification. In *Companion proceedings of the 2019 world wide web conference*, pages 491–500.

Laura-Ana-Maria Bostan and Roman Klinger. 2018. An analysis of annotated corpora for emotion classification in text. In *Proceedings of the 27th International Conference on Computational Linguistics*, pages 2104–2119, Santa Fe, New Mexico, USA. Association for Computational Linguistics.

Tommaso Caselli, Valerio Basile, Jelena Mitrović, and Michael Granitzer. 2021. HateBERT: Retraining BERT for abusive language detection in English. In *Proceedings of the 5th Workshop on Online Abuse and Harms (WOAH 2021)*, pages 17–25, Online. Association for Computational Linguistics.

Patricia Chiril, Endang Wahyu Pamungkas, Farah Benamara, Véronique Moriceau, and Viviana Patti. 2022. Emotionally informed hate speech detection: a multi-target perspective. *Cognitive Computation 14*, pages 322–352.

Jacob Devlin, Ming-Wei Chang, Kenton Lee, and Kristina Toutanova. 2019. BERT: Pre-training of Deep Bidirectional Transformers for Language Understanding. In *Proceedings of the 2019 Conference of the North American Chapter of the Association for Computational Linguistics: Human Language Technologies, Volume 1 (Long and Short Papers)*, pages 4171–4186.

Paul Ekman. 1988. Gesichtsausdruck und Gefühl: 20 Jahre Forschung von Paul Ekman. *Innovative Psychotherapie und Humanwissenschaften*, 38.

Kosisochukwu Judith Madukwe, Xiaoying Gao, and Bing Xue. 2021. What emotion is hate? incorporating emotion information into the hate speech detection task. In *PRICAI 2021: Trends in Artificial Intelligence*, pages 273–286, Cham. Springer International Publishing.

Angel Felipe Magnossão de Paula, Paolo Rosso, Imene Bensalem, and Wajdi Zaghouani. 2022. UPV at the Arabic hate speech 2022 shared task: Offensive language and hate speech detection using transformers and ensemble models. In *Proceedinsg of the 5th Workshop on Open-Source Arabic Corpora and Processing Tools with Shared Tasks on Qur'an QA and Fine-Grained Hate Speech Detection*, pages 181–185, Marseille, France. European Language Resources Association.

Thomas Mandl, Sandip Modha, Gautam Kishore Shahi, Hiren Madhu, Shrey Satapara, Prasenjit Majumder, Johannes Schäfer, Tharindu Ranasinghe, Marcos Zampieri, Durgesh Nandini, and Amit Kumar Jaiswal. 2021. Overview of the HASOC Subtrack at FIRE 2021: Hate Speech and Offensive Content Identification in English and Indo-Aryan Languages. In *Working Notes of FIRE 2021 - Forum for Information Retrieval Evaluation*, pages 1–19, India. CEUR Workshop Proceedings.

Ilia Markov, Nikola Ljubešić, Darja Fišer, and Walter Daelemans. 2021. Exploring stylometric and emotion-based features for multilingual cross-domain hate speech detection. In *Proceedings of the Eleventh Workshop on Computational Approaches to Subjectivity, Sentiment and Social Media Analysis*, pages 149–159, Online. Association for Computational Linguistics.

Ricardo Martins, Marco Gomes, José João Almeida, Paulo Novais, and Pedro Henriques. 2018. Hate speech classification in social media using emotional analysis. In *2018 7th Brazilian Conference on Intelligent Systems (BRACIS)*, pages 61–66.

Saif Mohammad. 2012. #emotional tweets. In **SEM 2012: The First Joint Conference on Lexical and Computational Semantics – Volume 1: Proceedings of the main conference and the shared task, and Volume 2: Proceedings of the Sixth International Workshop on Semantic Evaluation (SemEval 2012)*, pages 246–255, Montréal, Canada. Association for Computational Linguistics.

Flor Miriam Plaza-del Arco, Sercan Halat, Sebastian Padó, and Roman Klinger. 2021. Multi-Task Learning with Sentiment, Emotion, and Target Detection to Recognize Hate Speech and Offensive Language. *In Working Notes of FIRE 2021 – Forum for Information Retrieval Evaluation, December 13-17, 2021, India.*

Santhosh Rajamanickam, Pushkar Mishra, Helen Yannakoudakis, and Ekaterina Shutova. 2020. Joint modelling of emotion and abusive language detection. In *Proceedings of the 58th Annual Meeting of the Association for Computational Linguistics*, pages 4270–4279, Online. Association for Computational Linguistics.

Aneri Rana and Sonali Jha. 2022. Emotion based hate speech detection using multimodal learning. *arXiv preprint arXiv:2202.06218*.

Anna Schmidt and Michael Wiegand. 2017. A Survey on Hate Speech Detection using Natural Language Processing. In *Proceedings of the Fifth International Workshop on Natural Language Processing for Social Media (SocialNLP@EACL 2017)*, pages 1–10, Valencia, Spanien.

Julia Struß, Melanie Siegel, Josef Ruppenhofer, Michael Wiegand, and Manfred Klenner. 2019. Overview of GermEval Task 2, 2019 Shared Task on the Identification of Offensive Language. In *Proceedings of the 15th Conference on Natural Language Processing (KONVENS 2019)*, pages 354–365, Erlangen, Deutschland. German Society for Computational Linguistics & Language Technology.

Michael Wiegand, Melanie Siegel, and Josef Ruppenhofer. 2018. Overview of the GermEval 2018 Shared Task on the Identification of Offensive Language. In *Proceedings of GermEval 2018, 14th Conference on Natural Language Processing (KONVENS 2018)*, pages 1–10, Wien, Österreich. Österreichische Akademie der Wissenschaften.

A Examples from HS-EMO

Table 7 enumerates examples of Twitter text messages from the HASOC 2021 dataset (Mandl et al., 2021) which we annotate for emotion labels and collect in the HS-EMO corpus.

General Examples for the Emotion Categories. #1 is an example for the emotion category *joy*. The writer of this tweet was presumably happy about something. In the tweet, the person was waiting for something and now they are excited that it is the time of "Babs".

#2 is an example for the emotion category *anger*. The author of this message is probably frustrated, angry and annoyed. The writer compares his actions to the actions of someone else. He uses a swear word calling the other person a "shitbag" in an expression of anger presumably over an unfair treatment.

#3 is an example for the emotion category *disgust*. Here the writer probably feels shame for his country and its people. They are disgusted by the behavior of the people. They feel shame for something and are contemptuous towards someone.

#4 is an example for the emotion category *fear*. This person may be afraid as they see only cruelty around them and no help. They list everything that frightens them and ask for help. The words "dying", "begging", "clueless", "lies" in this context may be alarming and are an indicator for the emotion fear.

#5 is an example for the emotion category *surprise*. Here the writer is confused by the actions of a certain group.

#6 is an example for the emotion category *sadness*. The writer of this message is saddened by the situation in India. They suffer with their fellow human beings. Words such as "hurting me", "hope", "god save us" may be indicators of sadness.

#7 and #8 are examples where no emotion could be detected. From these tweets it is impossible to tell the emotional state of the author without additional context. Are they pleased, disappointed or angry? This distinction is not evident from the content of the message alone.

Borderline Cases. Potentially ambiguous cases were mostly between the emotion categories *disgust* vs. *anger*, *anger* vs. *sadness* and *disgust* vs. *sadness*. The stronger emotion was selected when multiple emotions could be detected. The main goal was to identify which one was the guiding motivation for writing the tweet.

Example #9 is annotated it with *sadness*, however, it could also be *disgust*. The writer is presumably sad and at the same time ashamed of his government. However, they probably wrote this tweet out of sadness. Thus, this emotion is stronger in this example.

Example #10 is annotated with *anger* while at first glance it could also be *disgust*. However, the anger the person feels seems to be stronger and ultimately the reason for writing the message.

B Hyperparameters

We pad/truncate instances to the length of 103 tokens. We determined this value by the 99th percentile of instance lengths in the HASOC 2021 dataset.

In all our experiments we use a batch size of 8 and apply a dropout (probability 0.2) to the output of the encoder. For optimization we use the Adam optimizer with default parameters.

We reserve 10% of the HASOC 2021 data as validation dataset to determine an optimal early

#	Text	Emotion
1	"@USER @USER Because karma is a bitch. Babs' time had finally come. The Wanker. #LGRW"	*joy*
2	"@USER Here's hoping. That little shitbag gets arrested. I got arrested for "threatening" when I didn't even make a direct threat, and our law system is furbar if crap like this keeps sliding."	*anger*
3	"@USER @USER @USER You guys make me sick to the core!!!! Is that really your concern right now, formation of alliance, when the entire country is on its knees!!! I guess news of dead bodies pilling up, people dropping dead on the st"	*disgust*
4	"People are dying, left to go begging for basic medical resources. No ventilators. No O2. Delayed/No Response from Centre. State govts clueless due lack of aid from Centre. Lies. Cover ups. Please, for the countrys sake, #ResginModi & let someone more competent do the job. URL"	*fear*
5	"What the heck the bjp is doing... destroying people life? #ResignPMmodi #BjpDestroyedIndia #BJP #prayaraj"	*surprise*
6	"@USER Just tired of all these deaths hurting me from inside hope good days will come back :(may god save us all #COVIDSecond #COVIDSecondWAVE #COVID119India #COVID19 #OxygenEmergency #IndiaFightsCorona #IndiaFightsCOVID19 #CovidVaccine #Covid19IndiaHelp #COVIDSecondWaveInIndia #indianeedoxygen"	*sadness*
7	"@USER Did you get the old bastard 1 or the young gun 1"	_
8	"@USER @USER We need Ethan Winters to say it too"	_
9	"I feel devastated for India and deeply ashamed of our Government'a attitude and actions. #IndiaCovidCrisis URL"	*sadness*
10	"I am ashamed that I was blind supporter of @USER Your People are dying , Gang Raped and You are doing this Shit ? #SpinelessBJP #spinelessmodi #MamtaisTerrorist #BengalViolence #BengalBurning"	*anger*

Table 7: Examples of annotated text instances from our corpus (HS-EMO). Username mentions and URLs have been anonymized.

stopping epoch (patience 3, minimum delta 0.005) with a maximum of 10 training epochs. To be able to use the same data split when training on our dataset (which is a sample from the HASOC 2021 data), we ensure that the validation data is sampled from the HASOC 2021 data instances which are not included in our dataset. The remaining 90% of the HASOC 2021 data is used for training (training data *HS*).

We run hyperparameter optimization by selecting the best learning rate based on validation dataset performance. We test the following ten different values for the learning rate: $1e{-}7$, $2.5e{-}7$, $5e{-}7$, $7.5e{-}7$, $1e{-}6$, $2.5e{-}6$, $5e{-}6$, $7.5e{-}6$, $1e{-}5$, $2.5e{-}5$.

C Detailed Experimental Results

Table 8 shows the performance of the different approaches for different learning rate values at coarse grained hate speech and emotion classification. Table 9 shows the performance of the different approaches for different learning rates at fine grained hate speech and emotion classification. In both tables we report the performance of the different models on the validation dataset which has been used for early stopping and learning rate optimization (test data: Val HS) as well as the performance on the HASOC 2021 (Mandl et al., 2021) test dataset (test data: Test HS). The best macro-averaged F1 scores for hate speech detection on the validation dataset are underlined for each training data setup (best learning rate value). The last column in each of the two tables shows the macro-averaged F1 score for emotion classification on our dataset (test data: HS-EMO). Note that for some runs (training data: HSEmo) this dataset is also used during training.

Training Data	Epochs	lr	Val HS F1$_{HOF}$	Val HS F1$_{NONE}$	Val HS macro-avg F1$_{HS}$	Test HS F1$_{HOF}$	Test HS F1$_{NONE}$	Test HS macro-avg F1$_{HS}$	HS-EMO F1$_{Emo}$
HS	10	1e-07	.6200	.7120	.6660	.6416	.7109	.6762	–
HS	10	2.5e-07	.6800	.7990	.7400	.6788	.7967	.7377	–
HS	8	5e-07	.7200	.8540	.7870	.7119	.8443	.7781	–
HS	7	7.5e-07	.7340	.8680	.8010	.7221	.8551	.7886	–
HS	7	1e-06	.7290	.8660	.7980	.7213	.8517	.7865	–
HS	2	2.5e-06	.7090	.8570	.7830	.6987	.8443	.7715	–
HS	2	5e-06	.7540	.8750	.8140	.7277	.8535	.7906	–
HS	1	7.5e-06	.7370	.8610	.7990	.7329	.8462	.7896	–
HS	1	1e-05	.7430	.8590	.8010	.7707	.8667	.8187	–
HS	1	2.5e-05	.7540	.8560	.8050	.7623	.8486	.8054	–
HS & Emo	3	1e-07	.4950	.6350	.5650	.5019	.6416	.5717	.0649
HS & Emo	10	2.5e-07	.6140	.6870	.6510	.6341	.6939	.6640	.0759
HS & Emo	8	5e-07	.6560	.8260	.7410	.6565	.8095	.7330	.1163
HS & Emo	9	7.5e-07	.7170	.8510	.7840	.7078	.8352	.7715	.1742
HS & Emo	8	1e-06	.7090	.8570	.7830	.6861	.8323	.7592	.1802
HS & Emo	3	2.5e-06	.6800	.8490	.7650	.6818	.8459	.7639	.1449
HS & Emo	4	5e-06	.7140	.8580	.7860	.7435	.8646	.8041	.2104
HS & Emo	3	7.5e-06	.7100	.8650	.7870	.7315	.8634	.7974	.1916
HS & Emo	2	1e-05	.7330	.8470	.7900	.7293	.8326	.7810	.1923
HS & Emo	3	2.5e-05	.7130	.8640	.7880	.7146	.8517	.7832	.2279
HS & Emo & HSEmo	3	1e-07	.3790	.6480	.5140	.3671	.6399	.5035	.0606
HS & Emo & HSEmo	10	2.5e-07	.6490	.7810	.7150	.6524	.7674	.7099	.3482
HS & Emo & HSEmo	10	5e-07	.7210	.8500	.7860	.6881	.8214	.7547	.4280
HS & Emo & HSEmo	5	7.5e-07	.7070	.8330	.7700	.7226	.8290	.7758	.4483
HS & Emo & HSEmo	5	1e-06	.7130	.8430	.7780	.7164	.8283	.7723	.5602
HS & Emo & HSEmo	2	2.5e-06	.7090	.8320	.7710	.7238	.8223	.7731	.4256
HS & Emo & HSEmo	3	5e-06	.7700	.8760	.8230	.7340	.8459	.7900	.8291
HS & Emo & HSEmo	4	7.5e-06	.7290	.8540	.7910	.7227	.8330	.7779	.9824
HS & Emo & HSEmo	2	1e-05	.7390	.8610	.8000	.7360	.8310	.7835	.8824
HS & Emo & HSEmo	3	2.5e-05	.7490	.8670	.8080	.7109	.8380	.7744	.9871
HS & HSEmo	9	1e-07	.5880	.5960	.5920	.5991	.5726	.5858	.1359
HS & HSEmo	10	2.5e-07	.6300	.7780	.7040	.6387	.7679	.7033	.2889
HS & HSEmo	9	5e-07	.7460	.8520	.7990	.7044	.8196	.7620	.5469
HS & HSEmo	9	7.5e-07	.7570	.8670	.8120	.7147	.8299	.7723	.6352
HS & HSEmo	8	1e-06	.7380	.8480	.7930	.7209	.8225	.7717	.7001
HS & HSEmo	2	2.5e-06	.7440	.8560	.8000	.7193	.8313	.7753	.6710
HS & HSEmo	3	5e-06	.7380	.8670	.8030	.7194	.8486	.7840	.8977
HS & HSEmo	1	7.5e-06	.7280	.8690	.7990	.7208	.8555	.7881	.6214
HS & HSEmo	1	1e-05	.7360	.8580	.7970	.7458	.8517	.7987	.6431
HS & HSEmo	1	2.5e-05	.7400	.8510	.7950	.7325	.8282	.7804	.8524

Table 8: Coarse grained (binary) hate speech and emotion classification performance.

Training Data	Epochs	lr	Val HS F1$_{NONE}$	Val HS F1$_{PRFN}$	Val HS F1$_{OFFN}$	Val HS F1$_{HATE}$	Val HS macro-avg F1$_{HS}$	Test HS F1$_{NONE}$	Test HS F1$_{PRFN}$	Test HS F1$_{OFFN}$	Test HS F1$_{HATE}$	Test HS macro-avg F1$_{HS}$	HS-EMO F1$_{Emo}$
HS	9	1e-07	.1930	.7040	.0430	.4640	.3510	.1856	.6965	.0153	.4190	.3291	–
HS	10	2.5e-07	.5590	.7480	.0770	.5230	.4770	.4986	.7566	.0957	.5114	.4656	–
HS	10	5e-07	.5410	.7470	.3690	.5060	.5410	.5544	.7553	.2073	.4955	.5031	–
HS	10	7.5e-07	.6940	.7750	.5540	.5920	.6530	.6473	.7532	.3973	.5325	.5826	–
HS	10	1e-06	.7040	.7760	.5360	.5520	.6420	.7079	.7798	.5012	.5455	.6336	–
HS	8	2.5e-06	.7370	.7680	.5470	.6420	.6730	.7182	.7539	.4822	.5343	.6221	–
HS	4	5e-06	.7690	.7750	.5690	.5830	.6740	.7091	.7598	.4849	.5475	.6253	–
HS	2	7.5e-06	.7510	.7700	.5670	.6470	.6840	.7018	.7827	.5121	.5438	.6351	–
HS	3	1e-05	.7360	.7410	.5560	.6170	.6620	.7307	.7582	.5246	.5808	.6486	–
HS	4	2.5e-05	.7450	.7660	.5650	.6460	.6800	.7119	.7503	.4452	.5285	.6090	–
HS & Emo	10	1e-07	.5630	.7160	.3970	.0900	.4420	.5685	.7193	.2373	.1254	.4126	.1063
HS & Emo	9	2.5e-07	.5480	.7610	.0450	.4460	.4500	.5072	.7625	.0199	.4603	.4375	.0637
HS & Emo	10	5e-07	.5780	.7670	.1430	.5510	.5100	.5452	.7634	.1185	.5131	.4851	.1416
HS & Emo	9	7.5e-07	.6470	.7660	.3260	.5470	.5710	.6062	.7668	.2890	.4970	.5397	.1114
HS & Emo	7	1e-06	.6580	.7700	.4690	.5690	.6170	.6131	.7664	.3021	.4960	.5444	.0694
HS & Emo	9	2.5e-06	.7420	.7570	.5100	.5940	.6510	.7086	.7378	.4467	.5666	.6149	.1574
HS & Emo	4	5e-06	.7200	.7920	.5690	.6480	.6820	.7036	.7665	.5149	.5750	.6400	.0958
HS & Emo	3	7.5e-06	.7270	.7720	.5760	.5690	.6610	.7256	.7748	.4692	.5639	.6334	.1511
HS & Emo	2	1e-05	.7000	.7810	.5270	.6220	.6580	.7057	.7690	.4847	.5726	.6330	.1363
HS & Emo	3	2.5e-05	.7840	.7500	.5790	.6330	.6870	.7100	.7143	.4054	.5436	.5933	.1555
HS & Emo & HSEmo	9	1e-07	.2210	.7190	.0100	.4530	.3510	.2927	.7238	.0591	.4600	.3839	.1069
HS & Emo & HSEmo	10	2.5e-07	.5790	.7670	.1020	.5030	.4880	.5419	.7342	.0648	.4925	.4584	.1813
HS & Emo & HSEmo	10	5e-07	.7130	.7650	.3690	.5810	.6070	.6553	.7577	.3446	.5171	.5687	.5139
HS & Emo & HSEmo	10	7.5e-07	.6940	.7470	.4300	.5920	.6160	.6943	.7665	.3765	.5521	.5974	.6320
HS & Emo & HSEmo	5	1e-06	.6840	.7570	.5040	.5890	.6330	.6561	.7537	.3259	.5348	.5676	.3449
HS & Emo & HSEmo	8	2.5e-06	.7360	.7320	.5300	.5920	.6470	.7053	.7116	.3187	.5191	.5637	.7907
HS & Emo & HSEmo	4	5e-06	.7110	.7280	.5710	.6540	.6660	.7174	.7000	.3910	.5420	.5876	.8134
HS & Emo & HSEmo	2	7.5e-06	.7460	.7430	.5470	.5930	.6570	.7027	.7306	.4346	.5223	.5975	.7409
HS & Emo & HSEmo	2	1e-05	.7500	.7710	.5670	.6270	.6790	.7169	.7522	.4823	.5620	.6283	.8000
HS & Emo & HSEmo	2	2.5e-05	.7420	.7630	.5550	.5830	.6610	.7242	.7412	.4256	.5407	.6079	.9574
HS & HSEmo	10	1e-07	.4780	.7320	.2190	.4950	.4810	.4394	.7023	.1885	.4098	.4350	.1426
HS & HSEmo	10	2.5e-07	.6320	.7560	.3060	.5380	.5580	.6065	.7525	.2582	.4861	.5259	.2588
HS & HSEmo	10	5e-07	.6060	.7690	.4300	.5700	.5940	.5977	.7735	.2856	.4745	.5328	.3308
HS & HSEmo	6	7.5e-07	.7040	.7630	.5170	.6110	.6490	.6667	.7384	.3404	.5230	.5671	.3567
HS & HSEmo	10	1e-06	.7130	.7690	.4660	.5770	.6310	.6777	.7320	.4072	.5125	.5824	.5114
HS & HSEmo	3	2.5e-06	.7350	.7520	.5260	.5870	.6500	.6987	.7413	.4319	.5501	.6055	.4416
HS & HSEmo	4	5e-06	.7560	.7440	.5840	.6280	.6780	.7154	.7315	.4509	.5655	.6158	.8005
HS & HSEmo	2	7.5e-06	.7230	.7080	.5670	.6620	.6650	.7022	.7322	.3357	.5444	.5787	.6371
HS & HSEmo	3	1e-05	.7620	.7210	.5860	.6280	.6740	.7308	.7241	.3772	.5751	.6018	.9246
HS & HSEmo	2	2.5e-05	.7050	.7540	.5980	.5970	.6640	.7093	.7256	.3492	.5547	.5847	.9521

Table 9: Fine grained hate speech and emotion classification performance.

Evaluating Data Augmentation Techniques for the Training of Luxembourgish Language Models

Isabella Olariu[†⋆], **Cedric Lothritz**[⋆], **Tegawendé F. Bissyandé**[⋆], **Jacques Klein**[⋆]
[†] Zortify S.A.
[†] 9, Rue du Laboratoire, L-1911 Gare Luxembourg
[⋆]University of Luxembourg
[⋆]6, Rue Coudenhove-Kalergi, L-1359 Luxembourg
isabella@zortify.com
{cedric.lothritz, tegawende.bissyande, jacques.klein}@uni.lu

Abstract

Training large language models is challenging when data availability is limited, as it is the case for low-resource languages. We investigate different data augmentation techniques for the training of models on Luxembourgish, a low-resource language. We leverage various word substitution methods for artificially increasing textual data: synonym replacements, entity replacements and modal verbs replacements. We present DA BERT and LuxemBERT-v2, two BERT models for the Luxembourgish language. We evaluate our models on several downstream tasks and conduct an ablation study to assess the impact of each replacement method. Our work provides valuable insights and highlights the importance of finding solutions to training models in low-resource settings.

1 Introduction

Neural network models are data-hungry, making them challenging to exploit when resources are scarce. The development of Natural Language Processing (NLP) tools for low-resource languages is, however, important since a large number of people around the world predominantly speak a language that can be classified as under-resourced due to its shortage in available data (Feng et al., 2021). Therefore, the research community is looking for ways to get extra data for training models targeting low-resource languages. Data augmentation is a common practical way of generating synthetic data by slightly altering existing data.

Luxembourgish, the national language of Luxembourg, is an example of a low-resource language, in a country that is known as being multilingual: in addition to Luxembourgish, German, French, English, Portuguese and Italian are widely spoken among its citizens. Only about 430 000 citizens (Eberhard et al., 2022) speak Luxembourgish as their native language. Given the limited number of speakers, textual data in Luxembourgish is not abundant. LuxemBERT is an existing language model for Luxembourgish and was developed by Lothritz et al. (2022) for use cases mainly targeted to the financial technology (FinTech) domain. To address the limitation of insufficient data, the authors develop a novel data augmentation technique leveraging automatic translation of common words from a closely related language.

In this study, we investigate the effectiveness of data augmentation techniques other than the one used by Lothritz et al. (2022). We use synonym, entity, and modal verb replacements to create new data for building Luxembourgish language models.

We explore the following research questions:

RQ1: What impact on the model's performance can we observe when we modify its input data through data augmentation techniques?

RQ2: Which data augmentation technique has the highest impact on our model's performance?

The contributions of this paper are threefold: **(i)** we contribute to the community with new pre-trained models for Luxembourgish; **(ii)** we provide insights on the effectiveness of existing data augmentation techniques for low-resource language modeling; **(iii)** we assess, from a different perspective, the relevance of the data augmentation proposed in LuxemBERT by discussing the added value of traditional data augmentation techniques.

2 Related Work

One of the most common choices of language models for many low-resource languages is mBERT (Pires et al., 2019; Wu and Dredze, 2020), a multilingual BERT model (Devlin et al., 2019). mBERT was trained on 104 languages, one of which is Luxembourgish. Even though mBERT includes a range of low-resource languages, Wu and Dredze (2020) do not recommend using it as the only option for low-resource languages. It was trained solely on Wikipedia articles, therefore its ability to

Proceedings of the 19th Conference on Natural Language Processing (KONVENS 2023), pages 174–179
September 18–22, 2023. ©2023 Association for Computational Linguistics

learn and understand a language decreases notably the smaller the Wikipedia size of the respective language is.

LuxemBERT is a recent Luxembourgish BERT model (Lothritz et al., 2022). The authors implement a data augmentation technique based on partial translation to train this model. They augment the training data by incorporating text data from an auxiliary language, German, which is structurally closely related to Luxembourgish. Specifically, they translate a subset of common and unambiguous German function words (e.g. pronouns, determiners, prepositions) to Luxembourgish.

There are several other data augmentation techniques that prove to be useful when working with limited data (Hedderich et al., 2021; Xu et al., 2019). The idea is that because there is not enough data for low-resource languages, the existing data has to be leveraged as efficiently as possible through various augmentation techniques which makes it possible to generate more data without collecting additional samples. Hedderich et al. (2021) differentiate between approaches performed on a word or sentence level. They suggest replacing words with synonyms and named entities of the same type on a token level. On a sentence level, they propose using back-translation to create more diverse sentences. This approach translates a sentence in a source language to a sentence in a target language, before translating it back to the source language (Sennrich et al., 2016). Pellicer et al. (2023) propose paraphrasing as an efficient strategy to add lexical diversity while retaining the original meaning. Negation is another approach that creates new sentences by reversing the meaning of the original ones (Tarasov, 2020).

3 The Data

Pre-Training Data. This dataset was used in the pre-training corpus of LuxemBERT (Lothritz et al., 2022), which consists of a total of 12 million sentences, out of which six million are Luxembourgish and six million are partially translated German sentences. It was collected from different sources including news articles, chatrooms, user comments posted on Radio Television Luxembourg (RTL),[1] a Luxembourgish news station website, and the Luxembourgish Wikipedia. Lothritz et al. (2022) provide further details on the breakdown of the pre-training corpus.

[1]https://www.rtl.lu/

Data for Data Augmentation. We use the existing six million Luxembourgish sentences from LuxemBERT to create the same number of new (augmented) sentences. Furthermore, to perform word substitutions via synonym, entity, and modal verb replacements, for our data augmentation task we collect additional data from the Luxembourgish Online Dictionary[2] consisting of Luxembourgish modal verbs, first names, surnames and locations (e.g. countries, cities, etc.). We also create a dictionary consisting of Luxembourgish words and corresponding synonyms.[3]

Data Augmentation Scheme. Our data augmentation scheme is applied to the six million Luxembourgish sentences that LuxemBERT was trained on and checks for each word whether that word is in one of our lists or dictionary. If there is a match with words from the original data, we replace those matches with random words from the corresponding lists.

The systematic substitution of words from LuxemBERT's training data with words from our lists allows us to obtain new sentences containing different words without considerably changing the meaning of the original sentences. Following these steps, we create six million new Luxembourgish sentences, for a total of 12 million, the same number of sentences used for LuxemBERT.

4 Experimental Setup

In this section, we introduce our novel models and the baselines we compare them against, describe the training and fine-tuning specifications and formulate the set of experiments consisting of five downstream tasks to evaluate our models on.

4.1 Models

As mentioned in Section 1, we compare two new BERT models to LuxemBERT to assess the impact of our data augmentation scheme. We describe our two models, DA BERT and LuxemBERT-v2, which we trained using an augmented dataset.

DA BERT: Data Augmented BERT is a model which we build and pre-train completely from scratch using the data obtained through our data augmentation scheme. The configuration specifications are the same as for Lothritz et al. (2022) and are as follows: a vocabulary size of 30 000, 12

[2]https://lod.lu/

[3]Data available at https://github.com/iolariu/Data-Augmentation

attention heads, 12 hidden layers, and maximum sequence length of 512.[4]

LuxemBERT-v2: This model is also trained with augmented data. We do not pre-train this model from scratch, but continue pre-training LuxemBERT by adding more data. To the original 12 million Luxembourgish sentences, we add our new 6 million augmented sentences to obtain a final dataset of 18 million sentences.

4.2 Training Parameters

To configure our DA BERT and LuxemBERT-v2 models, we re-use the same parameters as LuxemBERT (Lothritz et al., 2022) originating from the BERT-base model (Devlin et al., 2019): 12 Transformer blocks, 768 hidden layers, 12 self-attention blocks, and a total of 110 million trainable parameters. We choose a tailored alphabet size of 120 characters as for LuxemBERT to take into account the Luxembourgish alphabet by restricting the characters to letters used in the Luxembourgish language.

We pre-train our model on the Masked Language Modeling task and leave out Next Sentence Prediction due to the largely unordered nature of our dataset. We pre-train our model for 10 epochs using a masking probability of 15%.

4.3 Baselines

We examine two baseline models for comparison purposes: mBERT and the original LuxemBERT.

mBERT: The multilingual BERT model was trained on a mixture of high- and low-resource languages. Luxembourgish is one of the included languages and this part was trained on the Luxembourgish Wikipedia data, which contained 59 000 articles at the time of release of the model. The architecture consists of 12 Transformer blocks, 768 hidden layers, 12 self-attention blocks, and 110 million trainable parameters (Devlin et al., 2019).

LuxemBERT: We consider LuxemBERT as another baseline model, which is one of the currently existing BERT-based models for the Luxembourgish language. LuxemBERT and DA BERT use the same configurations in terms of model architecture, training parameters, and dataset size.

[4]Models available at `https://huggingface.co/iolariu/DA_BERT` and `https://huggingface.co/iolariu/LuxemBERT-v2`

4.4 Downstream Tasks

To evaluate the performance of our language models, we fine-tune them on the same five downstream tasks as in Lothritz et al. (2022).

POS Tagging. This sequence labelling task consists of assigning to each word in a given sequence of words a specific grammatical class (Jurafsky and Martin, 2008). We use the dataset provided by Lothritz et al. (2022), which consists of 450 Luxembourgish news articles and 5500 sentences. It is labelled with 15 POS tags including verbs, pronouns, adjectives, and adverbs.

Named Entity Recognition. This sequence-to-sequence task extracts key information in a given piece of text. It assigns a label to each word in a sentence by locating and classifying proper names in the sentence. We use the same dataset as for POS tagging,for which we have five labels: person, organisation, location, geopolitical entity, and miscellaneous.

Intent Classification.[5] Sometimes also referred to as intent recognition, this task tries to find an author's intention given an extract of text, where the labels of the intents are determined in advance. We use the Banking Client Support dataset created by Lothritz et al. (2021), which consists of 28 intents associated to various banking requests, such as checking bank account balances, opening and closing bank accounts, or ordering a new credit card.

News Classification. This task consists of correctly classifying news articles into various topics such as politics or sports. The dataset was created by Lothritz et al. (2022) and consists of 10 052 Luxembourgish news articles, which can be classified into eight topics.

Winograd Natural Language Inference. This task consists of a pair of texts A and B, where text A contains one or several pronouns and text B contains a substring of text A, where the pronoun in text B is replaced by either a word or a name. The label is 1 if the pronoun was replaced with the correct token from text A, or 0 otherwise. We use the original WNLI dataset (Levesque et al., 2012) translated into Luxembourgish by Lothritz et al. (2022).

[5]We distinguish between IC a and IC b, where we use all labels for IC a, but leave out trivial intents (e.g. *greeting, thanking, goodbyes*) for IC b.

Fine-tuning Parameters. To allow for a fair comparison, we choose the values of the fine-tuning hyperparameters identical to those used for LuxemBERT. Details for the chosen values can be found in Lothritz et al. (2022).

5 Experimental Results

In this section, we present the results from our experiments across six downstream tasks and address the research questions introduced in Section 1. For each task, we fine-tune the pre-trained models over five runs and take the average of the performance of each run as our final evaluation measure. The F1 scores for each model on each task are reported in Table 1.

5.1 RQ1: What impact on the model's performance can we observe when we modify its input data through data augmentation techniques?

Table 1 shows the results of the fine-tuned models. We observe an improvement in performance of our data-augmented DA BERT and LuxemBERT-v2 models on certain downstream tasks. DA BERT outperforms all models on NER and IC b tasks. For IC a, it outperforms mBERT as well as LuxemBERT-v2. For NC, the performance of mBERT, DA BERT, and LuxemBERT-v2 are equivalent; all of them perform just slightly worse than LuxemBERT. For POS tagging, LuxemBERT-v2 reaches the same performance as LuxemBERT, outperforming both mBERT and DA BERT. Furthermore, LuxemBERT-v2 outperforms mBERT on NER, IC a, and IC b. Finally, on WNLI which can be considered as the hardest task, LuxemBERT-v2 outperforms DA BERT, but none of the models perform better than mBERT on that task.

5.2 RQ2: Which data augmentation technique has the highest impact on our model's performance?

We perform an ablation study to answer this research question which allows us to identify the effects of individual augmentation techniques. We compare the difference between applying only synonym replacements or entity replacements to the data. For this purpose, we pre-train two smaller models that we compare against a baseline model described below.

BASELINE-BERT This is a smaller BERT model that is trained only on the Luxembourgish Wikipedia data, which consists of half a million sentences. We use this model as a baseline to compare two same-sized models against for which we separately perform synonym and entity replacements.

BERT-SYNS This model is trained on a synonym-augmented Luxembourgish Wikipedia data. We generate a total of 465 070 sentences to double the corpus size compared to the one of BASELINE-BERT.

BERT-ENTS This model is also only trained on Wikipedia data, this time augmented with entity replacements. For the dataset for this model, we generate 494 241 new sentences.

As shown in Table 2, BERT-ENTS outperforms BASELINE-BERT and BERT-SYNS on four out of six downstream tasks. In contrast, BERT-SYNS outperforms BASELINE-BERT and BERT-ENTS only on one task, suggesting a tendency towards using entity replacements for better outcomes.

6 Discussion

Overall, we believe that data augmentation for our Luxembourgish language models is beneficial despite the mixed conslusions of results. DA BERT and LuxemBERT-v2 consistenly outperform mBERT on most tasks except WNLI. This could be because mBERT lacks training on augmented text data and relies merely on Wikipedia articles for each language. Low-resource languages with small Wikipedia articles perform significantly worse with mBERT. DA BERT and LuxemBERT-v2 perform better due to various data augmentation techniques, which provide more training data.

Nevertheless, mBERT performs best in the challenging WNLI task. Training data for this task is relatively small, potentially hindering the learning ability of DA BERT and LuxemBERT-v2. LuxemBERT also fails to outperform mBERT on this task. We suppose that more training examples or considering some task-specific architectural modifications could help better capture the information required for WNLI.

Lastly, inconsistent findings from our ablation study suggest that several factors could influence why a certain technique is more suitable for a specific task. For instance, entity replacements seem to help NER, whereas other techniques might fall short on properly understanding context or lack in entity diversity for that task.

Models	POS	NER	IC a	IC b	NC	WNLI
mBERT	88.6 ± 0.1	68.9 ± 1.0	46.0 ± 5.6	48.3 ± 9.4	90.0 ± 0.5	$\mathbf{57.3 \pm 0.0}$
LuxemBERT	89.0 ± 0.1	70.0 ± 0.8	$\mathbf{72.5 \pm 1.1}$	70.9 ± 1.8	$\mathbf{91.8 \pm 0.2}$	54.6 ± 1.6
LuxemBERT-v2	$\mathbf{89.0 \pm 0.0}$	69.4 ± 0.0	67.6 ± 2.5	68.0 ± 1.0	90.0 ± 2.2	55.0 ± 0.0
DA BERT	88.7 ± 0.0	$\mathbf{70.8 \pm 0.0}$	71.7 ± 2.0	$\mathbf{73.8 \pm 2.2}$	90.0 ± 2.8	52.0 ± 0.0

Table 1: Comparison of results of our fine-tuned models on downstream tasks.

Models	POS	NER	IC a	IC b	NC	WNLI
BASELINE-BERT	88.0 ± 0.0	59.4 ± 0.0	56.9 ± 5.2	55.8 ± 3.8	85.7 ± 0.0	51.8 ± 0.0
BERT-SYNS	$\mathbf{88.0 \pm 0.0}$	61.8 ± 0.0	55.8 ± 2.4	55.4 ± 0.9	$\mathbf{87.8 \pm 2.2}$	50.0 ± 0.0
BERT-ENTS	87.0 ± 0.0	$\mathbf{62.0 \pm 0.0}$	$\mathbf{57.2 \pm 2.3}$	$\mathbf{59.6 \pm 1.5}$	84.8 ± 3.3	$\mathbf{54.0 \pm 0.0}$

Table 2: Ablation study results on downstream tasks.

7 Conclusion

In this paper we investigate the effectiveness of data augmentation techniques for low-resource language modeling, focusing on Luxembourgish. We compare two new BERT models, DA BERT and LuxemBERT-v2, to LuxemBERT and mBERT as baselines. Results show that data augmentation can improve the performance of models on certain downstream tasks and that one approach is more effective than another depending on the task.

While this study focused on synonym, entity, and modal verb replacements, we would like to see future work investigate additional techniques such as paraphrasing, back-translation or negation. We would also suggest gathering more diverse and representative data for Luxembourgish as well as exploring different model architectures such as Generative Pre-Trained Transformer (GPT; (Radford et al., 2018)) or RoBERTa (Liu et al., 2019) that are designed to capture the semantics and context of words.

8 Limitations

We argue that our study has some limitations. The choice of not training LuxemBERT-v2 from scratch due to time constraints might have affected its rather average performance compared to our expectations. We assume that during the continued pre-training of LuxemBERT, the model might have overfitted to the added portion of the data or forgotten what it had learned before.

We take into account that the slightly higher number of sentences for BERT-ENTS might result in favouring the entity replacement technique over synonym replacements.

Lastly, our study is limited to the BERT architecture. There is a risk that after data augmentation the meaning of sentences might change and that the data is not true anymore, especially after replacing entities. Using data augmentation with other models such GPT (Radford et al., 2018) could be risky as these generative models rely solely on the provided data to learn linguistic and commonsense reasoning.

9 Ethical Considerations

For this study, we trained our models on a text corpus that includes comments on news articles and chats from a chatroom. While this data originally included usernames, they were anonymised in order to comply with data privacy laws (Lothritz et al., 2022). Furthermore, we do not publish this text corpus, merely the models that were pre-trained using the corpus.

10 Acknowledgements

This work was partially supported by the Fonds National de la Recherche (FNR), Luxembourg, under project LUXEMBERT BRIDGES2021/IS/16229163.

References

Jacob Devlin, Ming-Wei Chang, Kenton Lee, and Kristina Toutanova. 2019. BERT: Pre-training of deep bidirectional transformers for language understanding. In *Proceedings of the 2019 Conference of the North American Chapter of the Association for*

Computational Linguistics: Human Language Technologies, Volume 1 (Long and Short Papers), pages 4171–4186, Minneapolis, Minnesota. Association for Computational Linguistics.

David Eberhard, Gary F Simons, and Charles D Fenning. 2022. *Ethnologue: Languages of Africa and Europe*. SIL International Publications.

Steven Y. Feng, Varun Gangal, Jason Wei, Sarath Chandar, Soroush Vosoughi, Teruko Mitamura, and Eduard Hovy. 2021. A survey of data augmentation approaches for NLP. In *Findings of the Association for Computational Linguistics: ACL-IJCNLP 2021*, pages 968–988, Online. Association for Computational Linguistics.

Michael A. Hedderich, Lukas Lange, Heike Adel, Jannik Strötgen, and Dietrich Klakow. 2021. A survey on recent approaches for natural language processing in low-resource scenarios. In *Proceedings of the 2021 Conference of the North American Chapter of the Association for Computational Linguistics: Human Language Technologies*, pages 2545–2568, Online. Association for Computational Linguistics.

Daniel Jurafsky and James Martin. 2008. *Speech and Language Processing: An Introduction to Natural Language Processing, Computational Linguistics, and Speech Recognition*, volume 2.

Hector Levesque, Ernest Davis, and Leora Morgenstern. 2012. The winograd schema challenge. In *Thirteenth International Conference on the Principles of Knowledge Representation and Reasoning*.

Yinhan Liu, Myle Ott, Naman Goyal, Jingfei Du, Mandar Joshi, Danqi Chen, Omer Levy, Mike Lewis, Luke Zettlemoyer, and Veselin Stoyanov. 2019. Roberta: A robustly optimized bert pretraining approach. *arXiv preprint arXiv:1907.11692*.

Cedric Lothritz, Kevin Allix, Bertrand Lebichot, Lisa Veiber, Tegawendé F Bissyandé, and Jacques Klein. 2021. Comparing multilingual and multiple monolingual models for intent classification and slot filling. In *International Conference on Applications of Natural Language to Information Systems*, pages 367–375. Springer.

Cedric Lothritz, Bertrand Lebichot, Kevin Allix, Lisa Veiber, Tegawende Bissyande, Jacques Klein, Andrey Boytsov, Clément Lefebvre, and Anne Goujon. 2022. LuxemBERT: Simple and practical data augmentation in language model pre-training for Luxembourgish. In *Proceedings of the Thirteenth Language Resources and Evaluation Conference*, pages 5080–5089, Marseille, France. European Language Resources Association.

Lucas Francisco Amaral Orosco Pellicer, Taynan Maier Ferreira, and Anna Helena Reali Costa. 2023. Data augmentation techniques in natural language processing. *Applied Soft Computing*, 132:109803.

Telmo Pires, Eva Schlinger, and Dan Garrette. 2019. How multilingual is multilingual bert? In *Proceedings of the 57th Annual Meeting of the Association for Computational Linguistics*, pages 4996–5001.

Alec Radford, Karthik Narasimhan, Tim Salimans, Ilya Sutskever, et al. 2018. Improving language understanding by generative pre-training. OpenAI.

Rico Sennrich, Barry Haddow, and Alexandra Birch. 2016. Improving neural machine translation models with monolingual data. In *Proceedings of the 54th Annual Meeting of the Association for Computational Linguistics (Volume 1: Long Papers)*, pages 86–96, Berlin, Germany. Association for Computational Linguistics.

Alexey Tarasov. 2020. Towards reversal-based textual data augmentation for NLI problems with opposable classes. In *Proceedings of the First Workshop on Natural Language Interfaces*, pages 11–19, Online. Association for Computational Linguistics.

Shijie Wu and Mark Dredze. 2020. Are all languages created equal in multilingual BERT? In *Proceedings of the 5th Workshop on Representation Learning for NLP*, pages 120–130, Online. Association for Computational Linguistics.

Nuo Xu, Yinqiao Li, Chen Xu, Yanyang Li, Bei Li, Tong Xiao, and Jingbo Zhu. 2019. Analysis of back-translation methods for low-resource neural machine translation. In *Natural Language Processing and Chinese Computing: 8th CCF International Conference, NLPCC 2019, Dunhuang, China, October 9–14, 2019, Proceedings, Part II*, page 466–475, Berlin, Heidelberg. Springer-Verlag.

Information Type Classification with Contrastive Task-Specialized Sentence Encoders

Philipp Seeberger, Tobias Bocklet, Korbinian Riedhammer
Technische Hochschule Nürnberg
{firstname.lastname}@th-nuernberg.de

Abstract

User-generated information content has become an important information source in crisis situations. However, classification models suffer from noise and event-related biases which still poses a challenging task and requires sophisticated task-adaptation. To address these challenges, we propose the use of contrastive task-specialized sentence encoders for downstream classification. We apply the task-specialization on the CRISISLEX, HUMAID, and TRECIS information type classification tasks and show performance gains w.r.t. F_1 score. Furthermore, we analyse the cross-corpus and cross-lingual capabilities for two German event relevancy classification datasets.

1 Introduction

User-generated information content on social media has become an important information source in crisis and emergency situations (Reuter et al., 2018). Social media posts immediately provide details about ongoing developments, first-party observations, and other information which would be missed with traditional sources (e.g., official news) (Sakaki et al., 2010). Access to this information content is thereby crucial for situational awareness in order to support official institutions, government organisations, and relief providers (Kruspe et al., 2021).

However, processing this noisy high-volume social media streams is challenging and requires sophisticated methods for automatic reliable detection of information content. To tackle this challenge, recent work has focused on binary, multi-class, and multi-label information type classification approaches (Alam et al., 2018, 2021b; Buntain et al., 2021). For instance, important information categories cover missing and injured people, damaged infrastructure, etc.

Another challenge is the nature of data prevalent in social media and microblogging platforms. For example, a large portion of noisy user-generated texts inherit properties such as a limited number of words, less contextual information, hashtags, and noise (e.g., misspellings, emojis) (Wiegmann et al., 2020; Zahera et al., 2021). Furthermore, event-related biases and entities prevent models from generalizing to unseen disaster events and therefore degrade in performance (Zhang et al., 2021a; Seeberger and Riedhammer, 2022).

These challenges motivates the use of efficient and effective approaches for adapting classifiers to the noisy text domain and the different information type tasks. Recently, contrastive fine-tuning mechanisms attracted research efforts for few-shot and task-specialization settings by adapting language models and sentence encoders (SE) for downstream classification (Vulić et al., 2021; Tunstall et al., 2022; Su et al., 2022). Following this approach, we aim to analyse the contrastive task-specialization in the field of information type classification.

Contributions Our main contributions are as follows: **1)** We introduce the contrastive task-specialization method for information type classification. **2)** We analyse the cross-corpus capabilities of the task-specialized models. **3)** We empirically show the cross-lingual and cross-task transfer capabilities for two German disaster datasets.

2 Method

As discussed in section 1, we follow previous work (Vulić et al., 2021) and aim to fulfill the requirement of effective adaptation by **1)** quickly bootstrapping a general-purpose SE for new domains and tasks via contrastive learning, and **2)** training a classifier on top of the fixed SE.

2.1 Contrastive Task-Specialization

The main idea is to follow the specialization of a general-purpose SE which is pre-trained on a large corpus of sentence pairs. Specializing a universal

Proceedings of the 19th Conference on Natural Language Processing (KONVENS 2023), pages 180–186
September 18–22, 2023. ©2023 Association for Computational Linguistics

SE to particular tasks has been proven effective in prior work for multi-class and multi-label scenarios via further fine-tuning by a contrastive loss (Vulić et al., 2021; Zhang et al., 2021b; Vulić et al., 2022). In this way, we can utilize available annotations to achieve task-adaptation to create more accurate encodings for the downstream classification.

Positive and Negative Pairs For the creation of sentence pairs, we follow prior efficient contrastive and few-shot approaches by implicitly leveraging the information type ids to create positive and negative learning examples (Tunstall et al., 2022). Therefore, we use the sentence pair creation scheme proposed by SETFIT[1] and construct the positive set Pos and negative set Neg by applying n iterations of sentence pair generations. For the multi-label task, we follow (Vulić et al., 2022) by sampling a positive sentence for each label in the label set of sentence s_i.

Contrastive Loss As contrastive loss, we opt for the Online Contrastive Loss (OCL) (Reimers and Gurevych, 2019; Vulić et al., 2022). This online version of contrastive loss operates with hard in-batch negative pairs and hard in-batch positive pairs and yields the final task-specialized SE. The constrastive learning should attract similar sentences together and push dissimilar sentences apart.

2.2 MLP Classification

A standard approach for classification based on SE's is the Multi Layer Perceptron (MLP) which is stacked on top of a fixed SE. This is much more lightweight than fine-tuning the entire SE but still achieves comparable performance in low-resource settings. We train a MLP classifier composed of a single hidden layer with non-linearity. For the multi-class and multi-label classifier, we use the standard cross-entropy and binary cross-entropy loss, respectively. A threshold θ determines the final classification for the multi-label task by only classifying information types with probability scores $\geq \theta$.

3 Experimental Setup

3.1 Datasets

We experiment with three TWITTER datasets, covering **1)** multi-class and multi-label classification, **2)** different information type ontologies, and **3)** numerous diverse event types composed of natural disasters and human-made disasters.

CRISISLEX The T26 variant of CRISISLEX (Olteanu et al., 2015) includes labeled tweets for 26 crisis events, annotated with seven information types including the category NOT RELATED. This set reflects a wide variety of events about emergencies with approximately 1,000 tweets per individual event. As preprocessing step, we removed tweets with the label NOT APPLICABLE as these contain issues such as "not readable" for the annotator (Olteanu et al., 2015). This task represents a multi-class classification problem.

HUMAID This collection contains data about 19 events with dataset sizes ranging from approximately 570 to 9500 tweets (Alam et al., 2021a). HUMAID covers eleven categories ranging from NOT HUMANITARIAN to INURED OR DEAD PEOPLE which captures fine-grained information about disasters. We ignore posts with the labels CAN'T JUDGE and MISSING OR FOUND PEOPLE as the latter case is only available for four events. Similar to CRISISLEX, this task is about multi-class classification.

TRECIS TREC Incident Streams is a multi-label classification task composed of over 70 events with annotations for 25 information types (Buntain et al., 2021). The sample ranges are from 90 to 5900 tweets and highly vary across events in terms of tweets and label distribution. Furthermore, the collection also covers the large-scale public-health event COVID whereby we only focus on general crisis events. For our experiments, we drop COVID events and select the top-30 events with the highest number of posts as events with a few posts only cover a small subset of relevant information types.

Data Splits For within-corpus classification, we evaluate each method with 5-fold cross-validation (5-fold CV) with disjoint events. Due to the high cost of task-specific annotations, we additionally focus on low-data scenarios for bootstrapping SE's. Therefore, we conduct experiments in the two data configurations **1)** *Low* and **2)** *High*. For the *High*-setup, we use the training and test splits provided by the 5-fold CV method. Then, in the *low*-setup, we randomly sample 10 posts for each information type and event in order to construct the low-

[1]Tunstall et al. (2022) introduced SETFIT as an efficient and prompt-free framework for few-shot classification and fine-tunes sentence transformers in a contrastive manner.

resource training sets. Throughout all experiments, the test splits remain the same.

3.2 Models and Hyperparameters

For our evaluation, we use MPNET_{LM}[2] (Song et al., 2020) as language model and MPNET_{SE}[3] as SE variant, transformed by a standard contrastive dual-encoder framework. MPNET_{LM} comprises 12 transformer layers with hidden size $h_T = 768$ and prior work has trained MPNET_{SE} with approximately one billion sentence pairs.

Baseline As baseline, we additionally conduct full end-to-end fine-tuning of the MPNET_{LM} model with a MLP classification head which we denote as MPNET_{LM}+FFT. Following suggested settings (Wang et al., 2021; Alam et al., 2021b; Seeberger and Riedhammer, 2022), we train the baseline models for 15 epochs with the optimizer AdamW, learning rate $2e-5$, weight decay 0.01, batch size 32, and evaluate the best checkpoint selected by a validation set.

Contrastive Task-Specialization In terms of CTS fine-tuning with OCL, we adopt a similar setup. The learning rate of AdamW is set to $2e-5$, weight decay to 0.01, and batch size to 64. For the *High*- and *Low*-setup, we construct sentence pairs with $n = 1$ and $n = 5$, respectively. We fine-tune the models on the sentence pairs for 3 epochs with the warmup ratio of 0.05 and cosine decay.

Classification The classifier consists of a MLP architecture with one hidden layer of size 512 with ReLU as non-linear activation function. We train the classifier for 30 epochs with the opimizer AdamW, learning rate $1e-3$, weight decay 0.01, dropout 0.4, and batch size 32. For multi-label classification, we use the threshold θ of 0.3. We select the best classifier based on a validation split sampled from the training set with the ratio of 0.1.

3.3 Evaluation

For all experiments, we report the micro-averaged and macro-averaged F_1 scores across events. In the *High*-setup, all reported results are averaged across the five folds. For the *Low*-setup, we additionally conduct three runs with random seeds in order to reach more stable results with respect to few-shot sampling.

4 Results and Discussion

The main results are summarized in Table 1, while further cross-corpus and cross-lingual experiments are shown in Table 2 and Table 3. In the following, we discuss the results and findings.

Contrastive Task-Specialization The results in Table 1 reveal that performance gains for the multiclass-classification are achieved via CTS. These performance boosts are across all *Low*- and *High*-setups with respect to the CRISISLEX and HUMAID datasets. With focus on the low-resource setup, we additionally experience significant improvements over the full fine-tuning baseline. In comparison, the gap between MPNET_{SE} and MPNET_{SE}+CTS is consistently higher than the counterpart MPNET_{LM} and MPNET_{SE} which suggests the effectiveness of CTS. However, there are no substantial performance gains or even a decrease for the TRECIS multi-label task. This finding is contrary to the results in the domain of multi-label intent detection (Vulić et al., 2022). We hypothesize the cause are differences in semantic concepts across events and annotations (Seeberger and Riedhammer, 2022). More sophisticated sentence pair sampling techniques, hard-negative mining or the usage of high level information types may tackle these shortcomings.

Cross-Corpus With cross-corpus evaluation we aim to analyze other important aspects of CTS fine-tuning. We hypothesize that similar information type ontologies lead to better classification performances by transfering the fine-tuned knowledge about semantically similar information types. Therefore, we trained the SE's on the source corpus and only trained the MLP classifier with the fixed SE on the target corpus. The results in Table 2 indicate an improvement for the datasets CRISISLEX and HUMAID which share similar information type ontologies. However, the knowledge transfer for TRECIS does not maintain improvements or even leads to worse results. We believe the reason for this observation is two-fold. Firstly, the results of Table 1 suggest that the obtained embedding representations are less semantically discriminative than the pre-trained language model for multi-label classification. This may result into a worse cross-corpus knowledge transfer. Secondly, the information type ontologies of CRISISLEX and HUMAID differ from TRECIS. While CRISISLEX and HUMAID share most of the information types, the

[2] `microsoft/mpnet-base`

[3] `sentence-transformers/all-mpnet-base-v2`

	CrisisLex		HumAID		TrecIS	
Variant	**Low**	**High**	**Low**	**High**	**Low**	**High**
MPNET$_{LM}$+FFT	$\underline{54.5}_{5.0}$ / $\underline{46.7}_{5.7}$	$\underline{62.9}_{4.9}$ / $\mathbf{55.0}_{3.6}$	$\underline{63.6}_{4.0}$ / $\underline{57.6}_{3.6}$	$\mathbf{73.2}_{2.8}$ / $\underline{66.3}_{3.6}$	$18.1_{1.2}$ / $14.3_{0.5}$	$29.1_{2.1}$ / $22.8_{2.6}$
MPNET$_{LM}$	$49.9^{*}_{4.7}$ / $42.9^{*}_{5.4}$	$56.7^{*}_{5.9}$ / $48.6^{*}_{5.4}$	$56.4^{*}_{4.3}$ / $52.2^{*}_{3.3}$	$64.2^{*}_{5.8}$ / $59.5^{*}_{4.5}$	$\mathbf{32.9}^{*}_{3.0}$ / $\underline{25.2}^{*}_{3.1}$	$\mathbf{30.4}^{*}_{2.4}$ / $\mathbf{23.1}_{3.3}$
MPNET$_{SE}$	$51.7^{*}_{4.0}$ / $44.1^{*}_{4.8}$	$56.7^{*}_{5.6}$ / $49.0^{*}_{5.8}$	$58.4^{*}_{4.4}$ / $53.1^{*}_{2.6}$	$65.6^{*}_{4.1}$ / $60.1^{*}_{3.2}$	$32.1^{*}_{2.2}$ / $24.3^{*}_{3.7}$	$\underline{30.1}_{2.3}$ / $\underline{22.9}_{3.6}$
MPNET$_{SE}$+CTS	$\mathbf{56.6}^{*}_{4.9}$ / $\mathbf{49.2}^{*}_{5.5}$	$\mathbf{63.0}_{5.4}$ / $\underline{54.3}_{5.7}$	$\mathbf{66.7}^{*}_{3.1}$ / $\mathbf{60.6}^{*}_{3.0}$	$\underline{72.7}^{*}_{2.9}$ / $\mathbf{67.4}_{3.7}$	$\underline{32.7}^{*}_{3.1}$ / $\mathbf{25.3}^{*}_{2.8}$	$29.4_{3.0}$ / $22.6_{3.1}$

Table 1: Overall results for event micro-averaged F_1 (x100%) and macro-averaged F_1 (x100%) scores with standard deviations. **Bold** numbers indicate the best performance whereas underlined numbers denote the second best performance in each column. Results with * are significantly different from MPNET$_{LM}$+FFT (p-value < 0.05).

ontology of TrecIS differs with fine-grained information types such as New Sub Event, EmergingThreats, and Factoid.

Cross-Lingual In the cross-lingual setup, we aim to analyse the adaptation to the German language. However, we are not aware of any German datasets which cover crisis events and information types. Therefore, we adopt the German BASF Explosion (Habdank et al., 2017) and German Floods (Reuter et al., 2015) datasets which represent binary classification tasks about relevancy. We train a classifier on the entire CrisisLex corpus and map the information type prediction NOT RELATED to the irrelevant class and all other categories to the relevant class. Here, we assume that the SE considers irrelevant and relevant clusters in the embedding space which can boost the relevancy classification. Furthermore, we compare the multilingual variant of MPNET$_{SE}$[4] and the translation[5] to English tweets. We summarize the findings in Table 3 whereby Random corresponds to a randomized classifier. As expected, the comparison of the Random baseline and the MLP classifiers validates the task transfer to the binary classification. Importantly, we experience the effectiveness of CTS in the cross-task transfer by comparing the language model and CTS fine-tuned SE's. The performance improvements with the multilingual variant of MPNET$_{SE}$+CTS further demonstrates the capabilities of fine-tuning in the multi-lingual setting. However, the translated posts outperform the multilingual model in all English model variants. This is an indication of catastrophic forgetting which occurs during training with only English task data. The lack of multi-lingual data in the domain of information type classification is still a challenge.

	Target Corpus		
	CrisisLex	**HumAID**	**TrecIS**
CrisisLex	-	$63.7_{3.8}$ (3.6↑)	$22.9_{2.5}$ (0.0)
HumAID	$50.4_{5.9}$ (1.4↑)	-	$21.9_{2.2}$ (1.0↓)
TrecIS	$45.8_{4.1}$ (3.2↓)	$56.5_{2.0}$ (0.4↑)	-

Table 2: High-data results of cross-corpus transfer with MPNET$_{SE}$+CTS. For the results, we report the event macro-averaged F_1 (x100%) score with standard deviations. The numbers and arrows in brackets indicate absolute improvements (↑) or degradations (↓) in comparison to MPNET$_{SE}$.

Language	**DE**	**DE → EN**
Random	42.2	-
MPNET$_{LM}$	48.8	$\underline{54.6}$
MPNET$_{SE}$+CTS	50.1	**55.1**
MPNET$_{SE}$+ML+CTS	53.4	54.1

Table 3: Results of cross-lingual transfer with MPNET variants trained on CrisisLex. For the results, we report the event macro-averaged F_1 (x100%) score. The column DE → EN indicates the translation to the English language. The symbol +ML represents the multilingual variant of MPNET which is further trained with CTS.

5 Conclusion

In this work, we investigated the contrastive task-specialization of SE's for the information type classification. The transformation of universal SE's into task-specialized models demonstrates performance gains especially in low-resource setups. Furthermore, we demonstrate the first results and opportunities in cross-corpus, cross-lingual, and cross-task transfer in the focused crisis domain. There are multiple avenues for future research that can improve different aspects with respect to information type classification. Research directions may include but are not limited to: **1)** data augmentation techniques, **2)** retrieval-augmented classification, and **3)** hierarchical contrastive learning.

[4] `sentence-transformers/paraphrase-multilingual-mpnet-base-v2`

[5] `Helsinki-NLP/opus-mt-en-de`

Ethical Considerations

Open Source Intelligence (OSINT) has become a significant role for various authorities and NGOs for advancing struggles in global health, human rights, and crisis management (Bernard et al., 2018; Evangelista et al., 2021; Kaufhold, 2021). Following the view of OSINT as a tool, our work pursues the goal to support relief government agencies, organizations, and other stakeholders during ongoing and evolving disaster events. We argue that Natural Language Processing techniques for OSINT and disaster response can have a positive impact on comprehensive situational awareness and in decision-making processes such as coordination of particular services. For example, NLP for social media can enrich the information with the public as co-producers (Li et al., 2018). In contrast, relying on noisy user-generated content as an information source runs the risk of introducing mis- and disinformation. This can cause adverse effects on downstream processing and requires strategies and particular care before the deployment. Furthermore, data privacy issues may arise due to the inherited properties of user-based data. Various anonymization processes should be taken into account for identifying and neutralizing sensitive references (Medlock, 2006).

Limitations

We believe there is much room for improving the contrastive task-specialization method with respect to the multi-class, multi-label, and noisy user-generated text setup. We tested only one variant of language models without considering different transformer encoder sizes or specialized Twitter-based pre-trained models. Furthermore, we did not conduct experiments for a variety of loss functions which may be expanded to triplet loss, cosine similarity, supervised contrastive loss, and the hierarchical variants for higher level information types. We relied for the cross-lingual analysis only on the German language datasets and only conducted experiments for relevancy classification which poses a simplification of information type classification. Future research should consider multi-lingual information type datasets and tasks to comprehensively validate the cross-lingual and cross-task setups in the crisis-related domain. As highlighted in section 5, sophisticated data augmentation methods can further improve the overall classification results but still poses a major challenge for noisy user-generated content. Lastly, recent advanced in the area of instruction-based Large Language Model's (LLM's) should be considered for future research.

Acknowledgements

The authors acknowledge the financial support by the Federal Ministry of Education and Research of Germany in the project ISAKI (project number 13N15572).

References

Firoj Alam, Ferda Ofli, and Muhammad Imran. 2018. Crisismmd: Multimodal twitter datasets from natural disasters. In *Proceedings of the 12th International AAAI Conference on Web and Social Media (ICWSM)*.

Firoj Alam, Umair Qazi, Muhammad Imran, and Ferda Ofli. 2021a. Humaid: Human-annotated disaster incidents data from twitter with deep learning benchmarks. *Proceedings of the International AAAI Conference on Web and Social Media*, 15(1):933–942.

Firoj Alam, Hassan Sajjad, Muhammad Imran, and Ferda Ofli. 2021b. Crisisbench: Benchmarking crisis-related social media datasets for humanitarian information processing. In *15th International Conference on Web and Social Media (ICWSM)*.

Rose Bernard, G. Bowsher, C. Milner, P. Boyle, P. Patel, and R. Sullivan. 2018. Intelligence and global health: assessing the role of open source and social media intelligence analysis in infectious disease outbreaks. *Journal of Public Health*, 26(5):509–514.

Cody L. Buntain, Richard McCreadie, and Ian Soboroff. 2021. Incident Streams 2020: TREC-IS in the Time of COVID-19. In *ISCRAM 2021: 18th International Conference on Information Systems for Crisis Response and Management*.

João Rafael Gonçalves Evangelista, Renato José Sassi, Márcio Romero, and Domingos Napolitano. 2021. Systematic Literature Review to Investigate the Application of Open Source Intelligence (OSINT) with Artificial Intelligence. *Journal of Applied Security Research*, 16(3):345–369. Publisher: Routledge _eprint: https://doi.org/10.1080/19361610.2020.1761737.

Matthias Habdank, Nikolai Rodehutskors, and Rainer Koch. 2017. Relevancy assessment of tweets using supervised learning techniques: Mining emergency related tweets for automated relevancy classification. In *2017 4th International conference on information and communication technologies for disaster management (ICT-DM)*, pages 1–8. IEEE.

Marc-André Kaufhold. 2021. *Information Refinement Technologies for Crisis Informatics: User Expectations and Design Principles for Social Media and Mo-*

bile Apps. Springer Fachmedien Wiesbaden, Wiesbaden.

Anna Kruspe, Jens Kersten, and Friederike Klan. 2021. Review article: Detection of actionable tweets in crisis events. *Natural Hazards and Earth System Sciences*, 21(6):1825–1845.

Lifang Li, Qingpeng Zhang, Jun Tian, and Haolin Wang. 2018. Characterizing information propagation patterns in emergencies: A case study with Yiliang Earthquake. *International Journal of Information Management*, 38(1):34–41.

Ben Medlock. 2006. An introduction to NLP-based textual anonymisation. In *Proceedings of the Fifth International Conference on Language Resources and Evaluation (LREC'06)*, Genoa, Italy. European Language Resources Association (ELRA).

Alexandra Olteanu, Sarah Vieweg, and Carlos Castillo. 2015. What to expect when the unexpected happens: Social media communications across crises. In *Proceedings of the 18th ACM Conference on Computer Supported Cooperative Work amp; Social Computing*, CSCW '15, page 994–1009, New York, NY, USA. Association for Computing Machinery.

Nils Reimers and Iryna Gurevych. 2019. Sentence-BERT: Sentence embeddings using Siamese BERT-networks. In *Proceedings of the 2019 Conference on Empirical Methods in Natural Language Processing and the 9th International Joint Conference on Natural Language Processing (EMNLP-IJCNLP)*, pages 3982–3992, Hong Kong, China. Association for Computational Linguistics.

Christian Reuter, Amanda Lee Hughes, and Marc-André Kaufhold. 2018. Social Media in Crisis Management: An Evaluation and Analysis of Crisis Informatics Research. *International Journal of Human–Computer Interaction*, 34(4):280–294.

Christian Reuter, Thomas Ludwig, Marc-André Kaufhold, and Volkmar Pipek. 2015. Xhelp: Design of a cross-platform social-media application to support volunteer moderators in disasters. In *Proceedings of the 33rd Annual ACM Conference on Human Factors in Computing Systems*, CHI '15, page 4093–4102, New York, NY, USA. Association for Computing Machinery.

Takeshi Sakaki, Makoto Okazaki, and Yutaka Matsuo. 2010. Earthquake shakes twitter users: Real-time event detection by social sensors. In *Proceedings of the 19th International Conference on World Wide Web*, WWW '10, page 851–860, New York, NY, USA. Association for Computing Machinery.

Philipp Seeberger and Korbinian Riedhammer. 2022. Enhancing crisis-related tweet classification with entity-masked language modeling and multi-task learning. In *Proceedings of the Second Workshop on NLP for Positive Impact (NLP4PI)*, pages 70–78, Abu Dhabi, United Arab Emirates (Hybrid). Association for Computational Linguistics.

Kaitao Song, Xu Tan, Tao Qin, Jianfeng Lu, and Tie-Yan Liu. 2020. Mpnet: Masked and permuted pre-training for language understanding. In *Advances in Neural Information Processing Systems*, volume 33, pages 16857–16867. Curran Associates, Inc.

Xi'ao Su, Ran Wang, and Xinyu Dai. 2022. Contrastive learning-enhanced nearest neighbor mechanism for multi-label text classification. In *Proceedings of the 60th Annual Meeting of the Association for Computational Linguistics (Volume 2: Short Papers)*, pages 672–679, Dublin, Ireland. Association for Computational Linguistics.

Lewis Tunstall, Nils Reimers, Unso Eun Seo Jo, Luke Bates, Daniel Korat, Moshe Wasserblat, and Oren Pereg. 2022. Efficient few-shot learning without prompts.

Ivan Vulić, Iñigo Casanueva, Georgios Spithourakis, Avishek Mondal, Tsung-Hsien Wen, and Paweł Budzianowski. 2022. Multi-label intent detection via contrastive task specialization of sentence encoders. In *Proceedings of the 2022 Conference on Empirical Methods in Natural Language Processing*, pages 7544–7559, Abu Dhabi, United Arab Emirates. Association for Computational Linguistics.

Ivan Vulić, Pei-Hao Su, Samuel Coope, Daniela Gerz, Paweł Budzianowski, Iñigo Casanueva, Nikola Mrkšić, and Tsung-Hsien Wen. 2021. ConvFiT: Conversational fine-tuning of pretrained language models. In *Proceedings of the 2021 Conference on Empirical Methods in Natural Language Processing*, pages 1151–1168, Online and Punta Cana, Dominican Republic. Association for Computational Linguistics.

Congcong Wang, Paul Nulty, and David Lillis. 2021. Transformer-based Multi-task Learning for Disaster Tweet Categorisation. In *ISCRAM 2021: 18th International Conference on Information Systems for Crisis Response and Management*.

Matti Wiegmann, Jens Kersten, Friederike Klan, Martin Potthast, and Benno Stein. 2020. Analysis of Detection Models for Disaster-Related Tweets. In *ISCRAM 2020: 17th International Conference on Information Systems for Crisis Response and Management*.

Hamada M. Zahera, Rricha Jalota, Mohamed Ahmed Sherif, and Axel-Cyrille Ngonga Ngomo. 2021. I-aid: Identifying actionable information from disaster-related tweets. *IEEE Access*, 9:118861–118870.

Hongming Zhang, Haoyu Wang, and Dan Roth. 2021a. Zero-shot Label-aware Event Trigger and Argument Classification. In *Findings of the Association for Computational Linguistics: ACL-IJCNLP 2021*, pages 1331–1340, Online. Association for Computational Linguistics.

Jianguo Zhang, Trung Bui, Seunghyun Yoon, Xiang Chen, Zhiwei Liu, Congying Xia, Quan Hung Tran, Walter Chang, and Philip Yu. 2021b. Few-shot intent detection via contrastive pre-training and fine-tuning.

In *Proceedings of the 2021 Conference on Empirical Methods in Natural Language Processing*, pages 1906–1912, Online and Punta Cana, Dominican Republic. Association for Computational Linguistics.

German Text Embedding Clustering Benchmark

Silvan Wehrli[1] **Bert Arnrich**[2] **Christopher Irrgang**[1]

[1]Centre for Artificial Intelligence in Public Health Research (ZKI-PH)
Robert Koch Institute, Berlin, Germany
{WehrliS,IrrgangC}@rki.de

[2]Digital Health - Connected Healthcare
Hasso Plattner Institute, University of Potsdam, Germany
Bert.Arnrich@hpi.de

Abstract

This work introduces a benchmark assessing the performance of clustering German text embeddings in different domains. This benchmark is driven by the increasing use of clustering neural text embeddings in tasks that require the grouping of texts (such as topic modeling) and the need for German resources in existing benchmarks. We provide an initial analysis for a range of pre-trained mono- and multilingual models evaluated on the outcome of different clustering algorithms. Results include strong performing mono- and multilingual models. Reducing the dimensions of embeddings can further improve clustering. Additionally, we conduct experiments with continued pre-training for German BERT models to estimate the benefits of this additional training. Our experiments suggest that significant performance improvements are possible for short text. All code and datasets are publicly available.

1 Introduction

Clustering is increasingly used in tasks requiring to group semantically similar text pieces. This includes, for instance, data selection (Aharoni and Goldberg, 2020), data exploration (Voigt et al., 2022), and neural topic modeling (Zhao et al., 2021). One approach for this kind of topic modeling is BERTopic (Grootendorst, 2022), which, in principle, uses generic clustering algorithms for text embeddings to find latent topics in text corpora. This is in stark contrast to more traditional topic modeling techniques using Latent Dirichlet Allocation (Blei et al., 2003) or Non-Negative Matrix Factorization (Févotte and Idier, 2011) and representing text as simple bag-of-words. The shift to embedding-based approaches is driven by the continuous development of neural language models, successfully used in natural language understanding (NLU) tasks such as semantic textual similarity (Reimers and Gurevych, 2019; Gao et al., 2021) or retrieval and reranking (Huang et al., 2020; Yates et al., 2021). The availability of plug-and-play frameworks for the computation of vector representation only fosters this trend. One such framework is Sentence Transformers (Reimers and Gurevych, 2019), which is used by BERTopic. It provides an extensive collection of pre-trained transformer models and techniques to fine-tune models for similarity-focused language tasks.

Benchmarks help to understand the usefulness of these easily available language models, allowing to compare existing and newly developed models for language tasks of interest. The Massive Text Embedding Benchmark (MTEB, Muennighoff et al., 2023) provides such a benchmark for a wide range of embedding-based tasks (e.g., classification, clustering, or reranking) and datasets from different domains (e.g., online reviews, scientific publications, or social media). MTEB includes a wider range of tasks and focuses on more recent language models than other benchmarks (such as SentEval (Conneau and Kiela, 2018)). MTEB, offering an easy-to-use API, invites the evaluation of models and submissions to a publicly accessible leaderboard.[1]

However, MTEB only considers the English language for the evaluation of clustering. The inclusion of non-English data is important, as the performance of multilingual models may not equal their monolingual counterparts (Rust et al., 2021), and as a means to evaluate the potentially strong cross-lingual transfer capability of multilingual models

[1]https://huggingface.co/spaces/mteb/leaderboard

Proceedings of the 19th Conference on Natural Language Processing (KONVENS 2023), pages 187–201
September 18–22, 2023. ©2023 Association for Computational Linguistics

(e.g., Huang et al., 2019). This work addresses this limitation by providing benchmark datasets and results for German. What is more, MTEB evaluates clustering performance on a single clustering algorithm. This is a suitable approach for such a broad benchmark as it simplifies the evaluation in terms of computational and content-related complexity. From a practical point of view, and specifically for clustering, the evaluation of different algorithms is helpful. Building on the MTEB API, we provide code and evaluation results for a broader range of clustering algorithms.

Finally, we conduct experiments with continued pre-training. The idea of this additional training is to adapt language models, typically trained on large and heterogeneous data collections, to the data of a specific domain or task, and has been shown to improve performance on downstream tasks (e.g., Howard and Ruder, 2018; Lee et al., 2019; Gururangan et al., 2020). We analyze the benefit of such adaptive training for clustering within this work. All code and datasets are publicly available.[2]

2 Datasets

2.1 MTEB Clustering

Data sources The MTEB clustering benchmark covers a range of topical domains and writing styles using data from different sources: arXiv, bioRxic, and medRxiv for scientific publications (e.g., economics or medicine), Reddit for informal social media, Stack Exchange for topical online discussions (such as code), and the 20 Newsgroup dataset (Buitinck et al., 2013).

Text length MTEB contains two datasets for each data source: A sentence-to-sentence (S2S) dataset compares short texts, and a paragraph-to-paragraph (P2P) dataset compares relatively longer texts. For instance, in the case of arXiv, the S2S dataset only contains publication titles, and the P2P dataset contains the concatenation of titles and abstracts. The two datasets provide models with different amounts of information.

Metric The evaluation is based on the V-measure (Rosenberg and Hirschberg, 2007). Given a ground truth, the V-measure outputs a score between 0 and 1, measuring homogeneity (clusters contain only one class) and completeness (clusters contain all class samples). MTEB uses topical categories derived from the data, such as the scientific discipline of a publication or newsgroup, as the ground truth.

Data selection Lastly, datasets in the MTEB clustering benchmark comprise up to 30 random samples of varying size and with a number of different classes drawn from all samples of a data source (splits).

2.2 German Additions

We follow MTEB's design for German datasets, aiming to simulate a wide range of real-world scenarios by including different domains, text lengths, and clustering complexities (Subsection 2.1). Compared to English, fewer German open-source datasets seem to exist, which are suitable for this work. Furthermore, some of the open-source datasets in MTEB are generally less relevant for a German benchmark as they contain little to no German content. This includes, for instance, arXiv and Stack Exchange, both mostly English-only data sources.[3] We have identified three openly available German data sources relevant to this benchmark. In the following, we discuss these data sources and the constructed benchmark datasets in more detail (see Table 1 for a summary).[4]

Blurbs As a first data source, we use data from the GermEval 2019 shared task on hierarchical blurbs classification (Remus et al., 2019). This data consists of German book metadata, including titles, blurbs (short, promotional descriptions of books), and genres. Even though blurbs are not part of MTEB, the data is well-suited: it is open source and contains topical texts of different lengths (titles, blurbs). What is more, three levels of genres express different levels of detail. The most general genres, for instance, include *Sachbuch* (non-fiction) or *Literatur und Unterhaltung* (literature and entertainment). Secondary and tertiary genres are increasingly specific (e.g., *Fantasy* (fantasy) and *Historische Fantasy* (historical fantasy)). We use this information to evaluate a model's ability to cluster at different granularity (i.e., the ground truth). We build two datasets, one

[2]`https://github.com/ClimSocAna/tecb-de`. Additionally, the datasets are officially part of the MTEB library, and results are available in the MTEB leaderboard.

[3]There are only around 600 submissions on arXiv (following best practices for search) at the time of writing (`https://info.arxiv.org/help/faq/multilang.html`). Similarly, Stack Exchange content is almost exclusively in English: `https://meta.stackexchange.com/questions/13676/do-posts-have-to-be-in-english-on-stack-exchange`

[4]We provide the scripts used to create these datasets in the Hugging Face repositories linked in our GitHub repository.

Name	Target	Unique Samples	Splits	Size (per split)	Classes (per split)	Avg. chars (per sample)
BlurbsClusteringS2S	book titles	17,726	28	177 to 16,425	4 to 93	23
BlurbsClusteringP2P	blurbs (title and blurb)	18,084	28	177 to 16,425	4 to 93	664
TenKGnadClusteringS2S	news article titles	10,267	9	1,436 to 9,962	9	51
TenKGnadClusteringP2P	news article texts (title and text)	10,275	9	1,436 to 9,962	9	2,648
RedditClusteringS2S	submission titles	40,181	10	9,288 to 26,221	10 to 50	52
RedditClusteringP2P	submission descriptions (title and text)	40,305	10	9,288 to 26,221	10 to 50	902

Table 1: Summary of the German benchmark datasets for evaluating the clustering performance of neural language models. Numbers for *Avg. chars* are rounded.

that only includes book titles (BlurbClusteringS2S) and one that includes the concatentation of titles and blurbs (BlurbsClusteringP2P). The design is based on MTEB's arXiv-based clustering tasks, which use arXiv's two-level categorization (e.g., math and numerical analysis) to simulate cluster granularity.

More concretely, we create 10 splits (subsamples) that consider only the broadest category (coarse clustering) and, similarly, 10 splits that consider the second-level genre (fine-grained clustering across all top-level genres). We randomly selected between 10 and 100 percent of the available data for each split. Lastly, we create eight splits by splitting the data based on the top-level genre and considering the second-level genre (fine-grained clustering within a genre).[5]

> *Der Krieg der Trolle (4)*
>
> *Im Land zwischen den Bergen ist die Zeit des Friedens vorbei. Krieg liegt in der Luft, und dann taucht auch noch ein tödlich verwundeter Zwerg im südlichen Hochland von Wlachkis auf – Ereignisse, die wie ein dunkler Schatten auf dem Land liegen. [...]*

Example for a book title and blurb from the main category *Literatur & Unterhaltung* respectively *Fantasy* and *Abenteuer-Fantasy* (second level).

News articles As a second source, we use data from the One Million Posts Corpus (Schabus et al., 2017), inspired by the 10kGNAD dataset[6]. 10kGNAD extracts news article information from the One Million Posts Corpus, which consists of annotated user comments (including the corresponding news articles) posted to an Austrian newspaper website. There are nine news categories such as *Wissenschaft* (science) or *Web*, and we use these categories as ground truth for the evaluation. We build two datasets: TenKGnadClusteringS2S, only using article titles, and TenKGnadClusteringP2P dataset, using the whole article texts. We follow MTEB's TwentyNewsgroupsClustering (consisting of news article titles and newsgroups) data selection strategy and draw 10 random samples of varying sizes (selecting at least 10% of all data).

> *Stoke holt Shaqiri von Inter*
>
> *Arnautovic-Klub zahlt Rekordsumme für Schweizer*
>
> *Stoke-on-Trent/Mailand – Xherdan Shaqiri wechselt von Inter Mailand zu Stoke City und wird damit Teamkollege von Marko Arnautovic. [...]*

Example of a news article consisting of the title, the subheadline and the article text from the *Sport* news section.

Reddit We use data from Reddit as a third data source which we retrieved from the official Reddit API[7]. More precisely, we have collected popular (i.e., hot and top) submissions to 80 German Subreddits such as *r/Bundesliga*, *r/Finanzen*, or

[5] We only consider samples with one top-level and up to two second-level genres. If a sample has two second-level genres, we select the less frequent one (assuming it is more descriptive) to make the label selection less ambiguous.

[6] https://tblock.github.io/10kGNAD

[7] https://www.reddit.com/dev/api

r/reisende.[8] We do not disclose the raw data. Instead, we provide the submission ids and scripts to reproduce the datasets in our GitHub repository. Additionally, Figure 3 in the appendix summarizes the collected data. Our approach is motivated by data privacy and sharing considerations, as discussed in detail in the Ethics Statement.

In any case, we construct two datasets from the collected data: SubredditClusteringS2S, which only considers the submission titles, and SubredditClusteringP2P, which combines submission titles and texts. Subreddits We follow the data selection used for MTEB's Reddit-based datasets and build 10 splits with submissions from 10 to 50 randomly selected Subreddits.

> *Wieviel "Trinkgeld" für Lieferdienste?*
>
> *Wie viel gebt ihr - sofern ihr Lieferdienste wie Lieferando etc. nutzt - den Fahrern Trinkgeld? Richtet ihr euch nach der 10% Faustregel in der Gastro?*

Example for a submission consisting of the title and text to the German Subbredit *r/Finanzen*.

3 Evaluation Setup

3.1 Models

We select a range of transformer-based models (Vaswani et al., 2017) based on their ability to process German text, architecture, and pre-training methods.[9] For all models, similar to MTEB, we use the mean of a model's output embeddings as text embedding (mean-pooling).

Monolingual models We include the monolingual GBERT and GELECTRA models (Chan et al., 2020), both based on the BERT (Devlin et al., 2019) architecture. GBERT uses whole word masking (WWM) for pre-training[10], while GELECTRA uses the ELECTRA pre-training method (Clark et al., 2020), which aims to improve computational efficiency. The models are pre-trained on the German part of OSCAR (Ortiz Suárez et al., 2019), a set of monolingual corpora based on Common Crawl (Wenzek et al., 2020), which is a repository for multilingual web crawl data. Additionally, the pre-training data includes, in smaller parts, dumps from Wikipedia and text from a range of domains such as court decisions, movie subtitles, speeches, or books. GottBERT (Scheible et al., 2020) presents another BERT-flavoured German language model. It is trained on the German part of OSCAR. It uses the RoBERTa pre-training setup (Liu et al., 2019), aiming to optimize the training setup (e.g., hyperparameter values) of the original BERT setup (Devlin et al., 2019).

Multilingual models We choose competitive multilingual models based on the MTEB leaderboard. This includes two pre-trained English models (MiniLM-L12-v2-ml, MPNet-base-v2-ml) fine-tuned using multilingual knowledge distillation (Reimers and Gurevych, 2020). Another model, USE-CMLM-ml, uses an adapted masked language modeling technique for training (Yang et al., 2021). SRoBERTa-cross, a Hugging Face community model, is based on the small variant of XLM-RoBERTa, a RoBERTa model trained on data in over 100 languages from Common Crawl, and then fine-tuned for German-English sentence similarity. We also use Sentence-T5 (ST5) encoders (Ni et al., 2022). These models are based on the multilingual general-purpose T5 encoder-decoder model (Raffel et al., 2020) and fine-tuned on a large English dataset for sentence similarity. All of these models use training techniques designed to improve short text representations. Therefore, we also select XLM-RoBERTa-large as a more general-purpose multilingual model. It uses the masking technique from BERT (Devlin et al., 2019) for pre-training.

3.2 Clustering

Algorithms Like MTEB, we use Minibatch k-Means (Buitinck et al., 2013) and V-measure as an evaluation metric. Additionally, we perform analyses for Agglomerative Clustering (Buitinck et al., 2013), DBSTREAM (Montiel et al., 2021), and HDBSCAN (McInnes et al., 2017). We select these algorithms based on their ease of use (e.g., pip-ready package), popularity, and abilities: Agglomerative Clustering is distance-based, similar to Minibatch k-Means. However, it may be more suited for modeling clusters of varying shapes and sizes. HDBSCAN, a density-based clustering algorithm, is used per default by the increas-

[8] A Subreddit is a topic-specific forum on Reddit, and a submission is a post to a Subreddit. We select active German Subreddit based on desk research and filter for German submissions if Subreddits also contain non-German submissions.

[9] Table 4 in the appendix lists the repositories of all models.

[10] The originally proposed BERT architecture (Devlin et al., 2019) masks subword tokens during pre-training. The authors introduced whole word masking after the publication: `https://github.com/google-research/bert/commit/0fce55`.

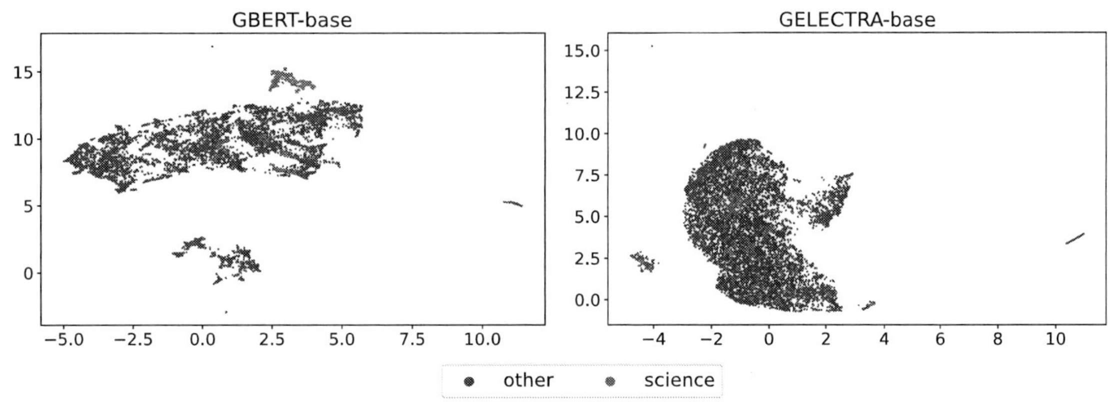

Figure 1: Word embeddings of all texts from the TenkGnadClusteringP2P dataset reduced to two dimensions with UMAP. Texts belonging to the news category *Wissenschaft* (science) are highlighted by color and size.

ingly popular BERTopic. Lastly, DBSTREAM is a density-based algorithm for evolving data streams. In principle, DBSTREAM could cluster documents for real-time analysis (e.g., news monitoring). We use default parameters for all algorithms, focusing on the out-of-the-box performance. DBSTREAM does not support setting the number of clusters. In all other cases, we provide clustering models with this information (similar to MTEB).

Dimensionality reduction We also experiment with dimensionality reduction to cluster lower dimensional data, motivated by the curse of dimensionality (Beyer et al., 1999; Aggarwal et al., 2001). We reduce the embedding vectors to two dimensions for every language model using PCA (Buitinck et al., 2013), a standard technique and UMAP (McInnes et al., 2018), which BERTopic suggests.

3.3 Adaptive Pre-training

We conduct experiments with adaptive pre-training separately for each dataset described in Subsection 2.2. In general, we assume an application scenario, where clustering is used to unsupervisingly analyze an ongoing text-based information feed, e.g., Twitter. Here, the focus lies not on the extrapolation capability towards new unseen data but on a consistent clustering of the entire text body. Thus, we use the evaluation data simultaneously as training data. This setup allows us to draw real-world conclusions, whether continued pre-training as an additional step before clustering can reliably improve clustering outcomes. We experiment with two pre-training techniques and evaluate them through V-measure. Firstly, we train with the general-purpose WWM technique (similar to GBERT). Given the relatively small training datasets, we follow the parameter setup for task-adaptive pre-training suggested in Gururangan et al. (2020). We also experiment with the Transformers and Sequential Denoising Auto-Encoder (TSDAE) method (Wang et al., 2021), a state-of-the-art unsupervised training method for improving sentence embeddings, and we use the suggested parameter setup by the authors.

We use GBERT for these experiments. GBERT perform competitively (as discussed in Section 4), and we are interested in the potential improvements for such strong models. What is more, GBERT uses the general-purpose WWM for pre-training, allowing it to evaluate the effect of the more task-specific TSDAE training. Generally, we want to provide some intuition for the potential use of these training methods specifically for clustering.

4 Results and Discussion

4.1 Baseline: Minibatch k-Means

Monolingual models GBERT models perform better than the other monolingual GELECTRA and GottBERT models, as shown in Table 2. GBERT-large ranks second best of all evaluated models. All models perform relatively better on P2P datasets compared to the S2S counterparts. This is an intuitive result, considering that models are presented with more information in these tasks. The weak performance of the GELECTRA models is surprising, given the strong results on downstream tasks reported in Chan et al. (2020). Figure 1 provides some visual intuition for this performance lack. For the news articles from the TenKGnadClusteringP2P dataset, GELECTRA produces more

Model	Blurbs S2S	Blurbs P2P	TenkGnad S2S	TenkGnad P2P	Reddit S2S	Reddit P2P	Avg.
GBERT-base	11.27	35.36	24.23	37.16	28.57	35.30	28.65
GBERT-large	13.38	39.30	**34.97**	41.69	34.47	44.61	34.74
GELECTRA-base	7.74	10.06	4.11	9.02	6.59	7.73	7.54
GELECTRA-large	7.57	13.96	3.91	11.49	7.59	10.54	9.18
GottBERT	8.37	34.49	9.34	33.66	16.07	19.46	20.23
MiniLM-L12-v2-ml	14.33	32.46	22.26	36.13	33.34	44.59	30.52
MPNet-base-v2-ml	15.81	34.38	22.00	35.96	36.39	48.43	32.16
SRoBERTa-cross	12.69	30.82	10.94	23.50	27.98	33.01	23.16
USE-CMLM-ml	15.24	29.63	25.64	37.10	33.62	49.70	31.82
ST5-base	11.57	30.59	18.11	**44.88**	31.99	45.80	30.49
ST5-xxl	**15.94**	**39.91**	19.69	43.43	**38.54**	**55.90**	**35.57**
XLM-RoBERTa-large	7.29	29.84	6.16	32.46	10.19	23.50	18.24

Table 2: V-measure scores for the benchmark results of all evaluated models using the Minibatch k-Means algorithm. Results are multiplied by 100 and rounded to two decimals. **Bold** numbers indicate best column-wise result.

Algorithm	Blurbs S2S	Blurbs P2P	TenKGnad S2S	TenKGnad P2P	Reddit S2S	Reddit P2P	Avg.
Minibatch k-Means	11.77	30.07	16.78	32.21	25.44	34.88	25.19
PCA-reduced embeddings	*9.40*	*23.50*	*11.41*	*20.56*	*11.95*	*16.10*	*15.49*
UMAP-reduced embeddings	*12.65*	*29.58*	*21.76*	*39.73*	*28.56*	*41.28*	*28.93*
Agglomerative Clustering	12.45	30.40	17.25	34.18	25.74	35.86	25.98
PCA-reduced embeddings	*9.33*	*23.30*	*11.03*	*20.24*	*11.89*	*16.67*	*15.41*
UMAP-reduced embeddings	*12.72*	*32.88*	*21.45*	*39.94*	*28.65*	*41.50*	***29.52***
HDBSCAN	n/a						n/a
PCA-reduced embeddings	*9.68*	*13.12*	*7.08*	*10.60*	*14.58*	*16.83*	*11.98*
UMAP-reduced embeddings	*14.98*	*22.51*	*14.46*	*27.95*	*24.19*	*30.61*	*22.45*
DBSTREAM	n/a						n/a
PCA-reduced embeddings	*6.41*	*14.19*	*7.79*	*12.46*	*8.38*	*10.68*	*9.99*
UMAP-reduced embeddings	*12.93*	*31.41*	*22.56*	*38.27*	*28.61*	*36.59*	*28.40*

Table 3: Average V-measure score of all evaluated models using different clustering algorithms and reduced embeddings as input (in *italic*). Results are multiplied by 100 and rounded to two decimals. The **bold** number indicates the best overall result and underlined results the best result per clustering algorithm.

evenly-spread embeddings than GBERT, and embeddings belonging to the same topic (such as science) tend to be more spread. GottBERT lies in the middle between the GELECTRA and GBERT models. The gap to GBERT models is likely caused by GottBERT's smaller and less diverse training data. As discussed in Subsection 3.1, GBERT models contain training data that is more similar to the characteristics of the evaluation datasets (e.g., books and shorter text sequences such as movie subtitles).

Multilingual models Apart from SRoBERTa-cross and XLM-RoBERTA-large, multilingual models perform competitively with scores close to the monolignual GBERT-base and GBERT-large. ST5-xxl is the best-performing model overall, scoring best on five out of six datasets (Table 2). Moreover, the scaled ST5-xxl model (4.8B parameters) shows clear performance gains compared to its base variant (ST5-base, 110M parameters). ST5 models' fine-tuning data includes Reddit data, which may explain the strong performance on German Reddit datasets, i.e., a robust cross-lingual transfer. The relatively weak results for XLM-RoBERTa-large are likely caused by less diverse training data and more general pre-training compared to the other multilingual models. The performance of SRoBERTa-cross, based on the smaller version of the XLM-RoBERTA-large model and fine-tuned for sentence similarity, also points in this direction, performing better on five out of six datasets than XLM-RoBERTA-large.

4.2 Beyond k-Means

Table 3 reports the average V-measure score of all evaluated models for different clustering algorithms. We do not report results for DBSTREAM and HDBSCAN for non-reduced embeddings, as we observed very poor computational performance for high-dimensional data during our experiments. In any case, results for Minibatch k-Means and Agglomerative Clustering suggest possibly better performance with reduced embeddings: Using UMAP-reduced embeddings improves the Minibatch k-Means and Agglomerative Clustering scores, on average, by around +13-15% (compared to not using any reduction at all). What is more, clustering in low dimensions may benefit the explainability of models as it allows to visually analyze results (e.g., Figure 1). However, this does not hold for clustering with PCA-reduced embeddings, which show the worst results by far. This limits its use for text-based clustering.

Overall, and based on the results for clustering with UMAP-reduced embeddings, Minibatch k-Means and Agglomerative Clustering perform very similarly. DBSTREAM performs slightly worse on average, caused by relatively weaker results for P2P datasets.[11] HDBSCAN performs worst on five out of six datasets. We suspect the weaker results for HDBSCAN are caused by its sensitivity to classifying data points as noise. In our experiments, we observe that in some cases, more than 30% of the data is labeled as noise. A different configuration for HDBSCAN would likely improve results. However, the usefulness of such sensitive algorithms may also depend on the use case (e.g., whether any text data is considered as noise).

4.3 Adaptive Pre-training with GBERT

The evaluation for GBERT-base and adaptive pre-training with WWM and TSDAE, reported in Figure 2, shows clear performance improvements for all benchmark datasets.[12] The improvements on the S2S datasets are considerably more significant for both pre-training methods: After around one epoch of TSDAE training, V-measures improve by around +31% on average. After around 10 epochs of WWM training, V-measures improve by around +30% on average. For P2P datasets, the improvements are relatively smaller, and models profit from more extended WWM training (average improvement of around +15% after 30 epochs). The benefit of TSDAE training seems less clear, requiring more extended training to compensate for initial performance drops and different training times to reach maximum improvements. Overall, and based on the results for 10 epochs of WWM training (Table 5), GBERT-base converges to the performance of the larger GBERT-large (33.70 vs. 34.74) and ranks second best out of all models for all S2S dataset. We suspect the more significant improvements on smaller text sequences (S2S) are likely caused by the fact that GBERT models are generally pre-trained on much longer sequences (maximum of 512 subword tokens per sample), considering that S2S samples are, on average, only around up to 50 characters long (Table 1). This may also explain why the improvements for P2P datasets are relatively minor, as these texts more closely resemble the pre-training data of the unadopted GBERT (in terms of text length).

We performed similar experiments for GBERT-large, as shown in Figure 4 in the appendix. In most cases, and for both pre-training methods, the performance decreases significantly (e.g., TenKGnadClusteringS2S with TSDAE) or stays relatively unchanged (e.g., TenKGnadClusteringS2S with WWM). The training stability seems low as different training with different seeds may result in different performances (see also Table 5). We suspect the relatively low batch sizes (256 for WWM and eight for TSDAE compared to 2,048 for GBERT-large's previous pre-training) lead to these training instabilities, as parameter updates are too aggressive. The parameter setups we used are based on experiments with BERT models similar to GBERT-base in terms of parameters (Gururangan et al., 2020; Wang et al., 2021). Our results suggest that these setups are unsuitable for larger models.

5 Conclusion

This work introduces German benchmark datasets for the evaluation of embedding-based clustering, building on the monolingual clustering benchmark from Massive Text Embedding Benchmark (MTEB). We introduce six datasets from three sources (blurbs, news articles, and Reddit). Additionally, we evaluate the out-of-the-box performance of different clustering algorithms and show that UMAP-reduced embeddings improve cluster-

[11] Shortly before the final submission, we found a small bug in the DBSTREAM implementation we used: `https://github.com/online-ml/river/issues/1265`. However, we do not expect a significant influence on the overall results.

[12] We provide exact numbers in Table 5 in the appendix.

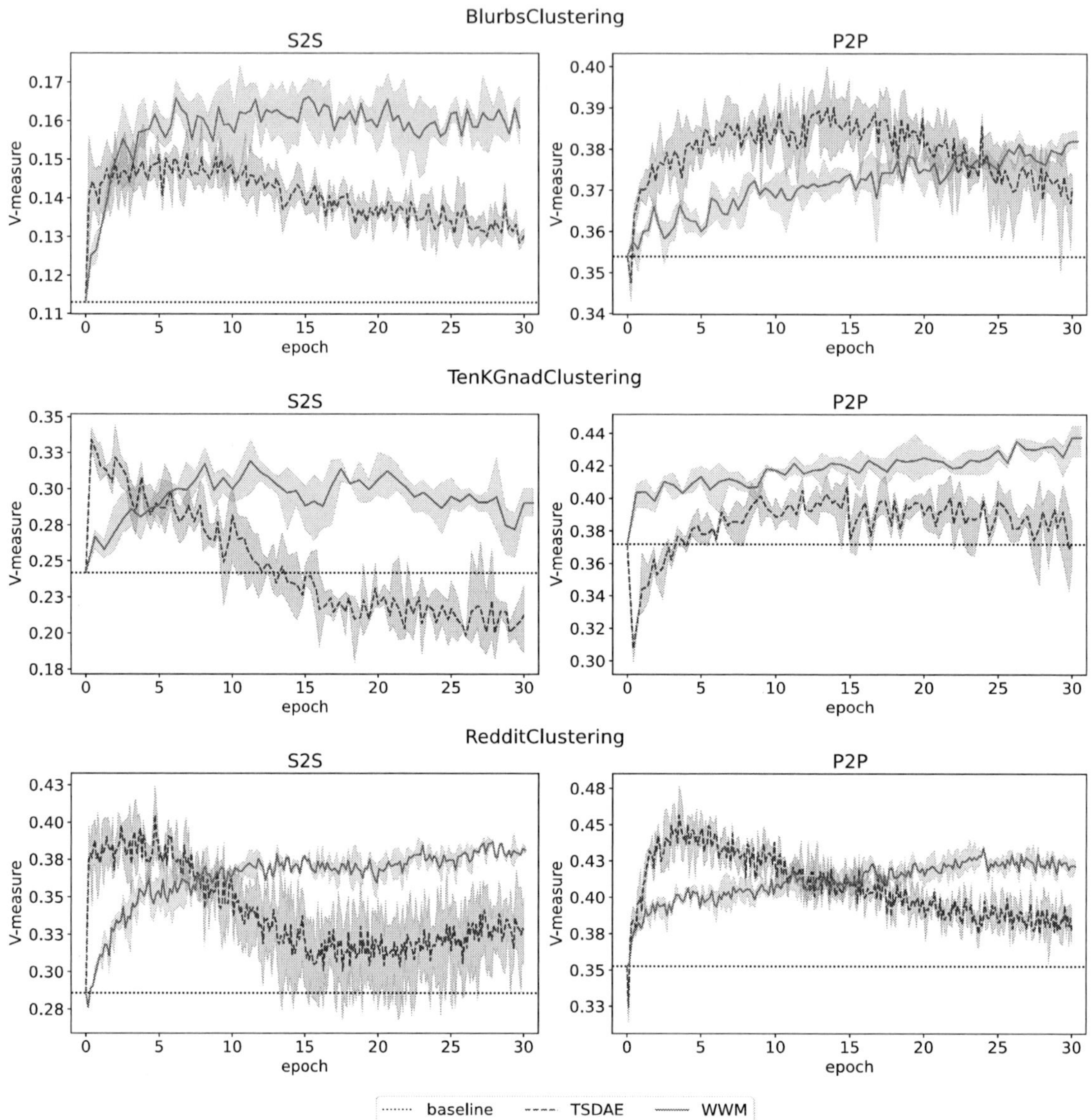

Figure 2: Change of the V-measure score with continued pre-training for GBERT-base comparing WWM and TSDAE pre-training methods for Minibatch k-Means clustering. Lines represent the average of three model runs with different seeds, and filled areas indicate minimum and maximum V-measure scores. *baseline* indicates results without additional pre-training.

ing outcomes and simplify the visual analysis simultaneously.

In total, we evaluate 12 language models. Results are mixed as there are both strong (GBERT-large, ST5-xxl) and weak (GELECTRA-base, XLM-RoBERTa-large) monolingual and multilingual models (Table 2). The selected models cover a wide range of different pre-training data, model sizes, and pre-training methods. A thorough investigation of how these factors influence clustering outcomes could build on this work.

Lastly, we experiment with adaptive pre-training for GBERT models. We show that for GBERT-base, TSDAE and WWM pre-training drastically improves the performance for short texts and relatively modestly for longer texts. Results for the larger GBERT model are inconsistent and only show improvements in one case, which we suspect is caused by a too aggressive hyperparameter configuration. This leaves room for future experimentation, which would ideally include larger datasets.

Limitations

Diversity of datasets Compared to the MTEB clustering benchmark, our proposed German benchmark is less diverse. For instance, it does not contain formal writing (e.g., scientific papers). Moreover, the proposed datasets are relatively small with a maximum split size of around 26k samples (Table 1). Real-world applications may involve larger data (possibly hundreds of thousands of data samples) with a high degree of semantic variability (e.g., hundreds of topics), forcing models to perform extremely fine-grained clustering.

Pre-training experiments Given the relatively small training datasets, our experiments do not allow us to conclude the possible benefits of more extensive data. In the case of larger available data, longer pre-training might be beneficial. Furthermore, the experiments focus on monolingual BERT-based model architecture. Benefits of continued pre-training may differ for, e.g., multilingual models or pre-trained models with smaller pre-training datasets (such as GottBERT).

Beneficial model properties As discussed in Section 4, some models perform very differently, although trained on similar data. From a practical point of view, a more thorough analysis of performance-increasing factors would be helpful (i.e., model size and architecture, pre-training method, and training data). Moreover, it would also be interesting to better understand how models assess the similarity of text. This could affect how well models are suited for specific clustering tasks (e.g., how models deal with words with specific grammatical functions or unseen words).

Large language models The rise of generative large language models (LLMs), such as GPT-4 (OpenAI, 2023), and primarily open-source models, such as LLaMA (Touvron et al., 2023), are not represented in this work. While the benefit of generative models for NLU may not yet be fully understood, preliminary work suggests strong performance (e.g., Neelakantan et al., 2022; Muennighoff, 2022). However, this work focuses on well-established models and training techniques that can be easily used with decent resources (e.g., a single GPU) and thus benefit the open-source community the most.

Ethics Statement

We acknowledge the ACL Code of Ethics[13] as an essential instrument in ensuring that research in computer science serves the public good. In the context of this work, we want to discuss our approach to share user-owned social media data responsibly. Social media has become an integral part of everyday life and an important data source in many research fields. For instance, social media can be used to address information voids during health emergencies (Boender et al., 2023). Consequently, the use of social media data in NLU research and applications has increased, rendering the inclusion of such data in this benchmark (i.e., Reddit) essential.

We use Reddit data for this benchmark for comparability (to MTEB) and because Reddit has open API access (meaning that any interested user can reproduce the published results). In fact, Reddit data is also available in large amounts without registration to the Reddit services: The Pushshift dataset (Baumgartner et al., 2020) has been collecting any public Reddit data for over a decade, providing the collected data to anyone and without any form of authentication. We believe this is a problematic approach as the data is distributed without requiring parties to accept the Reddit API terms of use. Specifically, and as per the current terms, Reddit data is owned by Reddit users (and not the platform itself), allowing users to delete accounts and content.[14] Specifically, the General Data Protection Regulation (GDPR), applicable to member states of the European Union (EU), mandates the right of the deletion of personal data ("the right to be forgotten").[15] Deliberately sharing user-owned data to anonymous parties makes it practically impossible for users to invoke their rights. Instead, data should only be obtained through the official Reddit API, which can be used to obtain and update Reddit data. Therefore, we do not disclose the raw data and instead, only share data identifiers and advise interested researchers to use the official channels.

[13] https://www.aclweb.org/portal/content/acl-code-ethics

[14] Reddit recently updated the API terms, which became effective on June 19, 2023 (https://www.redditinc.com/policies/data-api-terms). The updated terms define a less permissive use of Reddit data for artificial intelligence applications, and interested researchers should carefully consider these terms. This work was performed under the old, more permissive API terms.

[15] https://gdpr.eu/right-to-be-forgotten

References

Charu C. Aggarwal, Alexander Hinneburg, and Daniel A. Keim. 2001. On the surprising behavior of distance metrics in high dimensional space. In *Database Theory — ICDT 2001*, pages 420–434, Berlin, Heidelberg. Springer Berlin Heidelberg.

Roee Aharoni and Yoav Goldberg. 2020. Unsupervised domain clusters in pretrained language models. In *Proceedings of the 58th Annual Meeting of the Association for Computational Linguistics*, pages 7747–7763, Online. Association for Computational Linguistics.

Jason Baumgartner, Savvas Zannettou, Brian Keegan, Megan Squire, and Jeremy Blackburn. 2020. The pushshift reddit dataset. *Proceedings of the International AAAI Conference on Web and Social Media*, 14(1):830–839.

Kevin Beyer, Jonathan Goldstein, Raghu Ramakrishnan, and Uri Shaft. 1999. When is "nearest neighbor" meaningful? In *Database Theory — ICDT'99*, pages 217–235, Berlin, Heidelberg. Springer Berlin Heidelberg.

David M. Blei, Andrew Y. Ng, and Michael I. Jordan. 2003. Latent dirichlet allocation. *J. Mach. Learn. Res.*, 3:993–1022.

T Sonia Boender, Paula Helene Schneider, Claudia Houareau, Silvan Wehrli, Tina D Purnat, Atsuyoshi Ishizumi, Elisabeth Wilhelm, Christopher Voegeli, Lothar Wieler, and Christina Leuker. 2023. Establishing infodemic management in germany: a framework for social listening and integrated analysis to report infodemic insights at the national public health institute. *JMIR Infodemiology*.

Lars Buitinck, Gilles Louppe, Mathieu Blondel, Fabian Pedregosa, Andreas Mueller, Olivier Grisel, Vlad Niculae, Peter Prettenhofer, Alexandre Gramfort, Jaques Grobler, Robert Layton, Jake VanderPlas, Arnaud Joly, Brian Holt, and Gaël Varoquaux. 2013. API design for machine learning software: experiences from the scikit-learn project. In *ECML PKDD Workshop: Languages for Data Mining and Machine Learning*, pages 108–122.

Branden Chan, Stefan Schweter, and Timo Möller. 2020. German's next language model. In *Proceedings of the 28th International Conference on Computational Linguistics*, pages 6788–6796, Barcelona, Spain (Online). International Committee on Computational Linguistics.

Kevin Clark, Minh-Thang Luong, Quoc V. Le, and Christopher D. Manning. 2020. Electra: Pre-training text encoders as discriminators rather than generators. In *International Conference on Learning Representations*.

Alexis Conneau and Douwe Kiela. 2018. SentEval: An evaluation toolkit for universal sentence representations. In *Proceedings of the Eleventh International Conference on Language Resources and Evaluation (LREC 2018)*, Miyazaki, Japan. European Language Resources Association (ELRA).

Jacob Devlin, Ming-Wei Chang, Kenton Lee, and Kristina Toutanova. 2019. BERT: Pre-training of deep bidirectional transformers for language understanding. In *Proceedings of the 2019 Conference of the North American Chapter of the Association for Computational Linguistics: Human Language Technologies, Volume 1 (Long and Short Papers)*, pages 4171–4186, Minneapolis, Minnesota. Association for Computational Linguistics.

Cédric Févotte and Jérôme Idier. 2011. Algorithms for nonnegative matrix factorization with the β-divergence. *Neural Computation*, 23(9):2421–2456.

Tianyu Gao, Xingcheng Yao, and Danqi Chen. 2021. SimCSE: Simple contrastive learning of sentence embeddings. In *Proceedings of the 2021 Conference on Empirical Methods in Natural Language Processing*, pages 6894–6910, Online and Punta Cana, Dominican Republic. Association for Computational Linguistics.

Maarten Grootendorst. 2022. Bertopic: Neural topic modeling with a class-based tf-idf procedure. *arXiv preprint arXiv:2203.05794*.

Suchin Gururangan, Ana Marasović, Swabha Swayamdipta, Kyle Lo, Iz Beltagy, Doug Downey, and Noah A. Smith. 2020. Don't stop pretraining: Adapt language models to domains and tasks. In *Proceedings of the 58th Annual Meeting of the Association for Computational Linguistics*, pages 8342–8360, Online. Association for Computational Linguistics.

Jeremy Howard and Sebastian Ruder. 2018. Universal language model fine-tuning for text classification. In *Proceedings of the 56th Annual Meeting of the Association for Computational Linguistics (Volume 1: Long Papers)*, pages 328–339, Melbourne, Australia. Association for Computational Linguistics.

Haoyang Huang, Yaobo Liang, Nan Duan, Ming Gong, Linjun Shou, Daxin Jiang, and Ming Zhou. 2019. Unicoder: A universal language encoder by pre-training with multiple cross-lingual tasks. In *Proceedings of the 2019 Conference on Empirical Methods in Natural Language Processing and the 9th International Joint Conference on Natural Language Processing (EMNLP-IJCNLP)*, pages 2485–2494, Hong Kong, China. Association for Computational Linguistics.

Jui-Ting Huang, Ashish Sharma, Shuying Sun, Li Xia, David Zhang, Philip Pronin, Janani Padmanabhan, Giuseppe Ottaviano, and Linjun Yang. 2020. Embedding-based retrieval in facebook search. In *Proceedings of the 26th ACM SIGKDD International Conference on Knowledge Discovery & Data Mining*, KDD '20, page 2553–2561, New York, NY, USA. Association for Computing Machinery.

Jinhyuk Lee, Wonjin Yoon, Sungdong Kim, Donghyeon Kim, Sunkyu Kim, Chan Ho So, and Jaewoo Kang. 2019. BioBERT: a pre-trained biomedical language representation model for biomedical text mining. *Bioinformatics*, 36(4):1234–1240.

Yinhan Liu, Myle Ott, Naman Goyal, Jingfei Du, Mandar Joshi, Danqi Chen, Omer Levy, Mike Lewis, Luke Zettlemoyer, and Veselin Stoyanov. 2019. Roberta: A robustly optimized bert pretraining approach. *arXiv preprint arXiv:1907.11692*.

Leland McInnes, John Healy, and Steve Astels. 2017. hdbscan: Hierarchical density based clustering. *The Journal of Open Source Software*, 2(11):205.

Leland McInnes, John Healy, Nathaniel Saul, and Lukas Grossberger. 2018. Umap: Uniform manifold approximation and projection. *The Journal of Open Source Software*, 3(29):861.

Jacob Montiel, Max Halford, Saulo Martiello Mastelini, Geoffrey Bolmier, Raphael Sourty, Robin Vaysse, Adil Zouitine, Heitor Murilo Gomes, Jesse Read, Talel Abdessalem, and Albert Bifet. 2021. River: Machine learning for streaming data in python. *J. Mach. Learn. Res.*, 22(1).

Niklas Muennighoff. 2022. Sgpt: Gpt sentence embeddings for semantic search. *arXiv preprint arXiv:2202.08904*.

Niklas Muennighoff, Nouamane Tazi, Loic Magne, and Nils Reimers. 2023. MTEB: Massive text embedding benchmark. In *Proceedings of the 17th Conference of the European Chapter of the Association for Computational Linguistics*, pages 2014–2037, Dubrovnik, Croatia. Association for Computational Linguistics.

Arvind Neelakantan, Tao Xu, Raul Puri, Alec Radford, Jesse Michael Han, Jerry Tworek, Qiming Yuan, Nikolas Tezak, Jong Wook Kim, Chris Hallacy, et al. 2022. Text and code embeddings by contrastive pretraining. *arXiv preprint arXiv:2201.10005*.

Jianmo Ni, Gustavo Hernandez Abrego, Noah Constant, Ji Ma, Keith Hall, Daniel Cer, and Yinfei Yang. 2022. Sentence-t5: Scalable sentence encoders from pretrained text-to-text models. In *Findings of the Association for Computational Linguistics: ACL 2022*, pages 1864–1874, Dublin, Ireland. Association for Computational Linguistics.

OpenAI. 2023. Gpt-4 technical report. *arXiv preprint arXiv:2303.08774*.

Pedro Javier Ortiz Suárez, Benoît Sagot, and Laurent Romary. 2019. Asynchronous Pipeline for Processing Huge Corpora on Medium to Low Resource Infrastructures. In *7th Workshop on the Challenges in the Management of Large Corpora (CMLC-7)*, Cardiff, United Kingdom. Leibniz-Institut für Deutsche Sprache.

Colin Raffel, Noam Shazeer, Adam Roberts, Katherine Lee, Sharan Narang, Michael Matena, Yanqi Zhou, Wei Li, and Peter J. Liu. 2020. Exploring the limits of transfer learning with a unified text-to-text transformer. *J. Mach. Learn. Res.*, 21(1).

Nils Reimers and Iryna Gurevych. 2019. Sentence-BERT: Sentence embeddings using Siamese BERT-networks. In *Proceedings of the 2019 Conference on Empirical Methods in Natural Language Processing and the 9th International Joint Conference on Natural Language Processing (EMNLP-IJCNLP)*, pages 3982–3992, Hong Kong, China. Association for Computational Linguistics.

Nils Reimers and Iryna Gurevych. 2020. Making monolingual sentence embeddings multilingual using knowledge distillation. In *Proceedings of the 2020 Conference on Empirical Methods in Natural Language Processing (EMNLP)*, pages 4512–4525, Online. Association for Computational Linguistics.

Steffen Remus, Rami Aly, and Chris Biemann. 2019. Germeval 2019 task 1: Hierarchical classification of blurbs. In *Proceedings of the 15th Conference on Natural Language Processing (KONVENS 2019)*, pages 280–292, Erlangen, Germany. German Society for Computational Linguistics & Language Technology.

Andrew Rosenberg and Julia Hirschberg. 2007. V-measure: A conditional entropy-based external cluster evaluation measure. In *Proceedings of the 2007 Joint Conference on Empirical Methods in Natural Language Processing and Computational Natural Language Learning (EMNLP-CoNLL)*, pages 410–420, Prague, Czech Republic. Association for Computational Linguistics.

Phillip Rust, Jonas Pfeiffer, Ivan Vulić, Sebastian Ruder, and Iryna Gurevych. 2021. How good is your tokenizer? on the monolingual performance of multilingual language models. In *Proceedings of the 59th Annual Meeting of the Association for Computational Linguistics and the 11th International Joint Conference on Natural Language Processing (Volume 1: Long Papers)*, pages 3118–3135, Online. Association for Computational Linguistics.

Dietmar Schabus, Marcin Skowron, and Martin Trapp. 2017. One million posts: A data set of german online discussions. In *Proceedings of the 40th International ACM SIGIR Conference on Research and Development in Information Retrieval (SIGIR)*, pages 1241–1244, Tokyo, Japan.

Raphael Scheible, Fabian Thomczyk, Patric Tippmann, Victor Jaravine, and Martin Boeker. 2020. Gottbert: a pure german language model. *arXiv preprint arXiv:2012.02110*.

Hugo Touvron, Thibaut Lavril, Gautier Izacard, Xavier Martinet, Marie-Anne Lachaux, Timothée Lacroix, Baptiste Rozière, Naman Goyal, Eric Hambro, Faisal Azhar, Aurelien Rodriguez, Armand Joulin, Edouard

Grave, and Guillaume Lample. 2023. Llama: Open and efficient foundation language models.

Ashish Vaswani, Noam Shazeer, Niki Parmar, Jakob Uszkoreit, Llion Jones, Aidan N Gomez, Ł ukasz Kaiser, and Illia Polosukhin. 2017. Attention is all you need. In *Advances in Neural Information Processing Systems*, volume 30. Curran Associates, Inc.

Henrik Voigt, Monique Meuschke, Sina Zarrieß, and Kai Lawonn. 2022. KeywordScape: Visual document exploration using contextualized keyword embeddings. In *Proceedings of the 2022 Conference on Empirical Methods in Natural Language Processing: System Demonstrations*, pages 137–147, Abu Dhabi, UAE. Association for Computational Linguistics.

Kexin Wang, Nils Reimers, and Iryna Gurevych. 2021. TSDAE: Using transformer-based sequential denoising auto-encoderfor unsupervised sentence embedding learning. In *Findings of the Association for Computational Linguistics: EMNLP 2021*, pages 671–688, Punta Cana, Dominican Republic. Association for Computational Linguistics.

Guillaume Wenzek, Marie-Anne Lachaux, Alexis Conneau, Vishrav Chaudhary, Francisco Guzmán, Armand Joulin, and Edouard Grave. 2020. CCNet: Extracting high quality monolingual datasets from web crawl data. In *Proceedings of the Twelfth Language Resources and Evaluation Conference*, pages 4003–4012, Marseille, France. European Language Resources Association.

Ziyi Yang, Yinfei Yang, Daniel Cer, Jax Law, and Eric Darve. 2021. Universal sentence representation learning with conditional masked language model. In *Proceedings of the 2021 Conference on Empirical Methods in Natural Language Processing*, pages 6216–6228, Online and Punta Cana, Dominican Republic. Association for Computational Linguistics.

Andrew Yates, Rodrigo Nogueira, and Jimmy Lin. 2021. Pretrained transformers for text ranking: BERT and beyond. In *Proceedings of the 2021 Conference of the North American Chapter of the Association for Computational Linguistics: Human Language Technologies: Tutorials*, pages 1–4, Online. Association for Computational Linguistics.

He Zhao, Dinh Phung, Viet Huynh, Yuan Jin, Lan Du, and Wray Buntine. 2021. Topic modelling meets deep neural networks: A survey. In *Proceedings of the Thirtieth International Joint Conference on Artificial Intelligence, IJCAI-21*, page 4713–4720. International Joint Conferences on Artificial Intelligence Organization. Survey Track.

A Additional Results

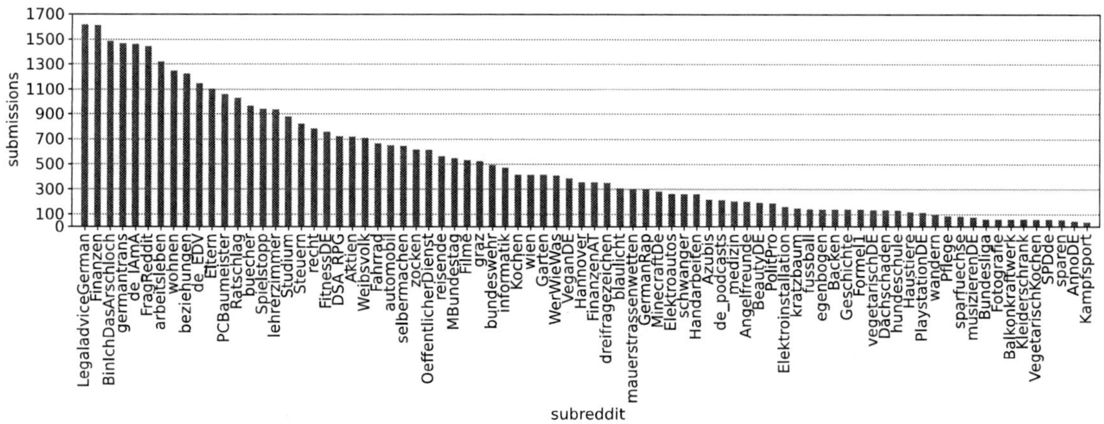

Figure 3: Distribution of German Reddit dataset used for RedditClusteringS2S and RedditClusteringP2P.

Model	Hugging Face Repository
GBERT-base	https://huggingface.co/deepset/gbert-base
GBERT-large	https://huggingface.co/deepset/gbert-large
GELECTRA-base	https://huggingface.co/deepset/gelectra-base
GELECTRA-large	https://huggingface.co/deepset/gelectra-large
GottBERT	https://huggingface.co/uklfr/gottbert-base
MiniLM-L12-v2-ml	https://huggingface.co/sentence-transformers/paraphrase-multilingual-MiniLM-L12-v2
MPNet-base-v2-ml	https://huggingface.co/sentence-transformers/paraphrase-multilingual-mpnet-base-v2
SRoBERTa-cross	https://huggingface.co/T-Systems-onsite/cross-en-de-roberta-sentence-transformer
USE-CMLM-ml	https://huggingface.co/sentence-transformers/use-cmlm-multilingual
ST5-base	https://huggingface.co/sentence-transformers/sentence-t5-base
ST5-xxl	https://huggingface.co/sentence-transformers/sentence-t5-xxl
XLM-RoBERTa-large	https://huggingface.co/xlm-roberta-large

Table 4: Hugging Face repositories for all evaluated language models.

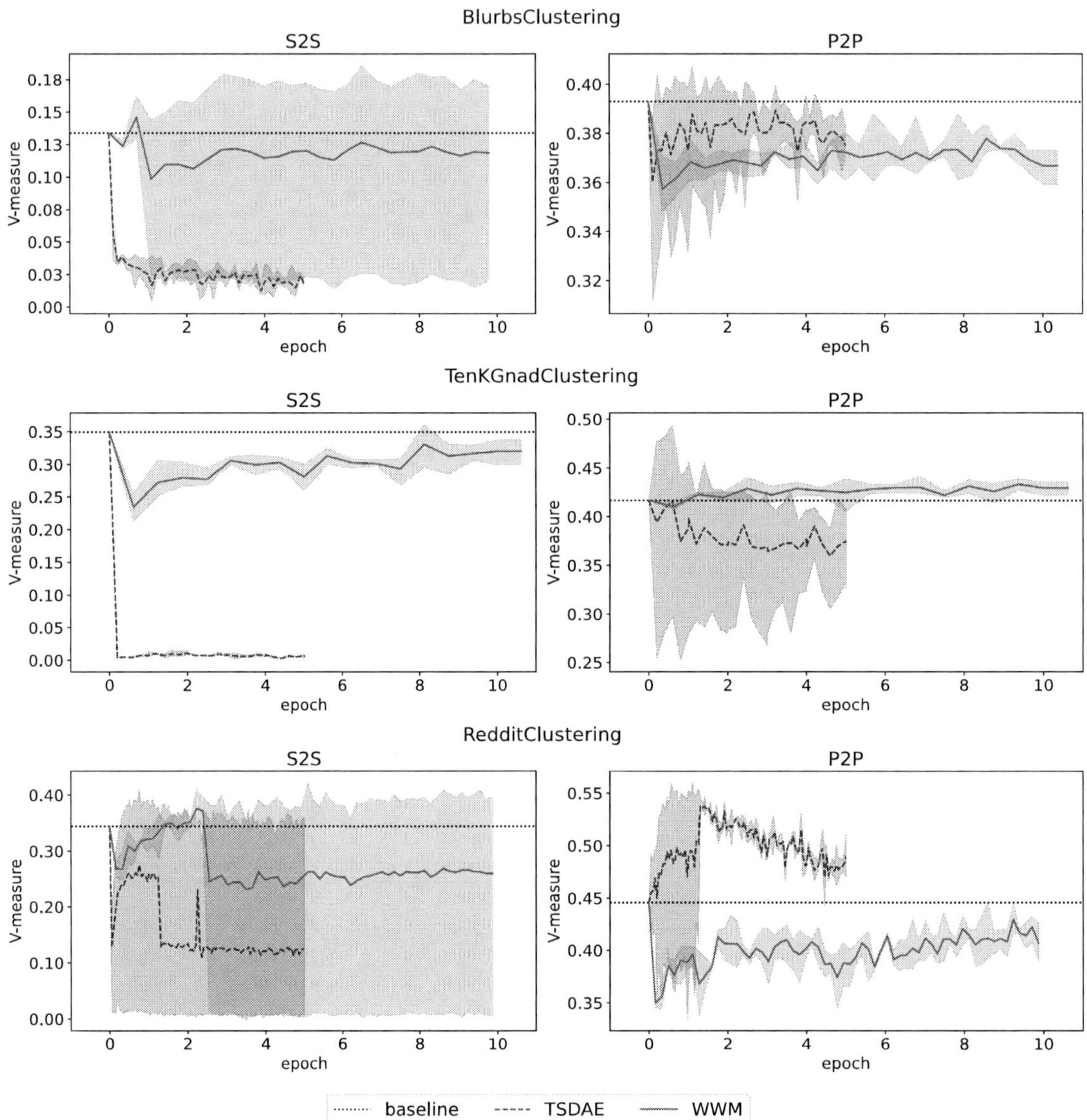

Figure 4: Change of the V-measure score with continued pre-training for GBERT-large comparing WWM and TSDAE pre-training methods for Minibatch k-Means clustering. Lines represent the average of three model runs with different seeds, and filled areas indicate minimum and maximum V-measure scores. *baseline* indicates results without additional pre-training.

	Method	Blurbs						TenKGnad						Reddit							
		S2S			P2P			S2S			P2P			S2S			P2P				
		SD	Avg.	Δ	SD	Avg.	Δ	SD	Avg.	D	SD	Avg.	Δ	SD	Avg.	Δ	SD	Avg.	Δ	**Avg.**	Δ
base	TSDAE (1)	0.46	14.37	+3.10	0.29	37.08	+1.72	1.40	32.87	+8.64	0.79	34.73	-2.43	0.42	37.29	+8.72	0.33	39.03	+3.73	32.56	+3.91
	WWM (10)	0.80	15.71	+4.44	0.41	36.83	+1.47	1.12	30.81	+6.58	0.27	41.47	+4.31	0.53	36.48	+7.91	0.87	40.90	+5.60	33.70	+5.05
	WWM (30)		n/a		0.18	38.20	+2.84		n/a		0.85	43.77	+6.61		n/a		0.25	42.16	+6.86	41.38	+12.73
large	TSDAE (1)	0.87	2.57	-10.81	1.35	38.48	-0.82	0.36	0.82	-34.15	7.47	35.60	-6.09	17.63	25.90	-8.57	8.65	48.89	+4.28	25.38	-9.36
	WWM (10)	6.98	11.89	-1.49	0.57	36.70	-2.60	1.60	32.07	-2.90	0.58	42.98	+1.29	17.99	26.04	-8.43	1.53	40.74	-3.87	31.74	-3.00

Table 5: V-measure scores for GBERT-base (**base**) and GBERT-large (**large**) with continued pre-training for TSDAE and WWM methods. Evaluated is based on Minibatch k-Means clustering, and reported V-measure scores are multiplied by 100. Results are multiplied by 100 and rounded to two decimals. Numbers in brackets denote the number of epochs. *Avg.* represents the average of three training runs with different seeds and *SD* the standard deviation of V-measures. Δ reports the absolute difference to the baseline, i.e., the model results without additional pre-training.

Aspect-Based Sentiment Analysis as a Multi-Label Classification Task on the Domain of German Hotel Reviews

Jakob Fehle
Media Informatics Group
University of Regensburg
Regensburg, Germany
jakob.fehle@ur.de

Leonie Münster
Media Informatics Group
University of Regensburg
Regensburg, Germany
leonie.muenster@stud.uni-regensburg.de

Thomas Schmidt
Media Informatics Group
University of Regensburg
Regensburg, Germany
thomas.schmidt@ur.de

Christian Wolff
Media Informatics Group
University of Regensburg
Regensburg, Germany
christian.wolff@ur.de

Abstract

Aspect-Based Sentiment Analysis (ABSA) plays a crucial role in understanding fine-grained customer feedback, particularly in domains like hospitality where specific aspects of service often influence overall satisfaction. However, non-English languages such as German face a scarcity of readily available corpora and evaluated methods for ABSA, making it a challenging problem. This paper addresses this gap by utilizing BERT-based transformer models, known for their exceptional performance in context-sensitive natural language processing tasks, to perform ABSA in a multi-label classification setting. We demonstrate our approach on a novel dataset of German hotel reviews that we have collected and annotated from *TripAdvisor*, thus contributing a new resource to the field and proving the effectiveness of our methodology. With achieving a micro f1-score of up to 0.91 for aspect category classification and 0.81 for end-to-end ABSA, our approach aligns with the performance of similar methods on other German-language datasets and surpasses performance achieved on English-language datasets in the hotel domain.

1 Introduction

Sentiment analysis deals with the classification of attitudes, opinions, and sentiments and typically focuses on the three classes positive, neutral, and negative. The ever-increasing integration and presence of social media and the internet in everyday life is generating a huge amount of user-generated data that favors the use of sentiment analysis. As a result, it is nowadays used in various fields and domains, such as the analysis of political discourse (Xia et al., 2021; Schmidt et al., 2022), digital humanities (Schmidt and Burghardt, 2018; Schmidt et al., 2020), healthcare natural language processing (Moßburger et al., 2020), in improving products and services (Xu et al., 2019), and in the financial sector to predict stock market movement (Sousa et al., 2019). In recent years, sentiment analysis has also expanded its application areas to non-text-based media such as images and videos, e.g., in human-computer interaction (Halbhuber et al., 2019; Ortloff et al., 2019) or film analysis (Schmidt et al., 2021c; El-Keilany et al., 2022).

Assigning a positive or negative label to entirely positive or negative texts is usually straightforward. However, analyzing texts that contain a mixture of different sentiments in a single sentence or text quickly becomes a challenge. This is particularly the case when it is not about general trends or developments but about precise statements concerning different aspects or characteristics of products or services, where a rough estimate of sentiment is insufficient. For over a decade, Aspect Based Sentiment Analysis (ABSA) has gained popularity to solve this problem, whereby instead of determining an overall sentiment for a sentence or a document, the sentiment is determined in relation to individual aspects or entities occurring in the text, such as the battery life of a smartphone or the friendliness of a service employee (Liu et al., 2005).

As in other research fields of natural language processing (NLP), there is a clear imbalance in sentiment analysis in terms of available resources and evaluated techniques when looking at differ-

Proceedings of the 19th Conference on Natural Language Processing (KONVENS 2023), pages 202–218
September 18–22, 2023. ©2023 Association for Computational Linguistics

ent languages and domains. While research has progressed a lot during recent years in the English language domain, the field of ABSA in German is still relatively unexplored. To our knowledge, only a small number of ready-to-use corpora exist and only a few methods have been evaluated (Fehle et al., 2021; Chebolu et al., 2022). Moreover, corpora that are needed for the training of aspect-based machine learning approaches or for the evaluation of ABSA methods are not compatible with corpora that can be used as resources for general sentiment analysis approaches that determine sentiment only at the document or sentence level. Since annotation of training data for ABSA usually involves working at the phrase or word level to establish complex relationships between phrases describing the aspect and phrases containing the sentiment, the annotation process is often highly time-consuming and difficult. To counteract this, there are approaches that handle datasets that have not been annotated manually or only in a less complex way (Chang et al., 2019; Kastrati et al., 2020). One promising example is the definition of ABSA as a multi-label classification problem (Tao and Fang, 2020; Jin et al., 2020). In this case, the classifiers are trained with texts annotated with aspects and polarities, albeit at the sentence level rather than the phrase level, thus decreasing complexity. The annotation contains information about the aspect occurring in the text as well as its assigned sentiment, but no information about where the aspect occurs or by which exact phrase it is composed. This approach has already achieved good results in the German language (Aßenmacher et al., 2021). Building on prior research, this work explores the potential of applying the multi-label classification method for ABSA to a different domain. Given the promising results this approach has yielded in the realm of customer reviews in context of public transportation (Aßenmacher et al., 2021), this work determines its effectiveness and the expected classification results when applied to other areas and domains for which ABSA is a relevant tool for extracting fine-grained opinions from user-generated content. For this purpose, a new corpus was created on a domain that is widely discussed in the English language (Akhtar et al., 2017; Abro et al., 2020), but to our knowledge has not yet been addressed in the German language: Online reviews of hotels and their services.

The contributions of this paper are as follows: (1) the creation of a dataset for ABSA in the domain of hotel reviews in the German language, (2) an evaluation of multiple pre-trained transformer-based models for ABSA as a multi-label classification task on hotel reviews in German and (3) a discussion about the performance of transformer-based models for ABSA at different tasks and various levels of annotation complexity.

2 Related Work

Over the last decade, ABSA has experienced significant growth through different shared task workshops, such as the SemEval Shared Tasks for the English language from 2014 to 2016 (Pontiki et al., 2014, 2015, 2016), stimulating the development of various methods addressing the three fundamental subtasks in aspect-based sentiment analysis: aspect term extraction, aspect category classification, and aspect sentiment classification. These tasks utilized datasets compiled from two domains: restaurant and laptop reviews. With each iteration of the SemEval Shared Task, the size of the dataset and the complexity of the annotations increased. Initially, only the specific aspect word, its aspect category, and the corresponding polarity were annotated. Later, however, the aspects were divided into entities/main aspect categories and attributes/sub-aspect categories (these terms are often used interchangeably), thus increasing the complexity of the datasets due to a large number of possible combinations between main and subcategories. Even after these workshops, the datasets continue to be used as a benchmark resource for the evaluation of new-found ABSA approaches (Brauwers and Frasincar, 2022; Nazir et al., 2020).

These datasets are far from being the only ones available in the English language. In particular, since the first SemEval workshop on ABSA in 2014, the number of accessible datasets for the English language has significantly increased, covering various domains with different levels of annotation complexity, such as hotel reviews (Yin et al., 2017), financial microblogs (Maia et al., 2018), and Amazon product reviews (Liu et al., 2015).

Approaches to determining aspect-based sentiment are diverse and have evolved over time. While earlier methods primarily relied on rules, word frequencies, or lexicon-based techniques and tackled only sub-tasks to the ABSA problem, contemporary approaches emphasize neural networks and deep learning and try to solve ABSA as a one-in-all/end-to-end solution (Chen et al., 2022; Yan et al., 2021). Since their introduction in 2017, pre-trained transformer models have, together with deep learning neural networks, been recognized as state-of-the-art in the field. Nowadays, approaches achieve accuracy and f1-scores of over 80 % for subtasks of ABSA or complete ABSA solutions on various corpora. Notably, some transformer-based architectures attain scores exceeding 90 % on specific datasets (Brauwers and Frasincar, 2022; Do et al., 2019).

In the hotel domain, methods usually only deal with subtasks of ABSA. For that, star ratings of the review or individual aspects on rating portals (e.g. *Tripadvisor*) are often used to derive the polarity of individual reviews and aspects and to gain a ground truth dataset. Chang et al. (2019) builds on this method and classifies the individual aspect categories by using support vector machines and convolution tree kernels with good success on eight classes (macro f1-score: 0.80). Tran et al. (2019) uses the combination of a BiLSTM-CRF model for the extraction of aspect phrases and their polarity and LDA topic modeling for aspect category classification to capture the aspect category and the associated sentiment from hotel reviews and achieves a micro f1-score of 0.873 for the extraction of aspect phrases and their polarity and an accuracy of 0.800 for the determination of the associated aspect category. Qiang et al. (2020) tackled the aggregation of aspect-sentiment information and used a Multi-Attention-Network BiLSTM to capture the fine-grained statements regarding individual aspects in hotel reviews in order to infer the overall sentiment of a review and achieved a micro f1-score of 0.798 on a custom generated dataset.

In German, the largest available dataset was published as part of the GermEval Shared Task Workshop in 2017, which contains more than 26,000 annotations consisting of entity-attribute-polarity tuples related to the German transportation service provider *Deutsche Bahn* (Wojatzki et al., 2017). However, the dataset was evaluated only based on main aspects and their corresponding polarities, with the category of attributes being omitted.

Other datasets in German language include the SCARE corpus, consisting of 1,760 Google Play Store reviews with 2,487 aspect-polarity annotations (Sänger et al., 2016); the USAGE corpus, comprising 611 Amazon reviews with more than 5,000 aspect-polarity annotations (Klinger and Cimiano, 2014); the PotTS dataset, made of 7,992 Twitter messages on political topics with annotations for sentiment targets and their sentiment phrases (Sidarenka, 2016); a corpus in the domain of German historical plays consisting of around 6,500 sentiment/emotion and 12,000 source and target annotations (Schmidt et al., 2021a,b); and the TDDL corpus, consisting of 4,521 tweets about the "Tage der deutschsprachigen Literatur" (Engl.: "Days of German Literature") with 8,264 main aspect-attribute-polarity annotations (De Greve et al., 2021). As with the English-language datasets, these German datasets also vary in quality and have been annotated using different levels of complexity and granularity in their annotation schemes.

ABSA approaches have been evaluated on German-language datasets only to a limited extent. While earlier approaches were mainly based on classical machine learning like conditional random fields or neural networks with pre-trained word-embeddings, more recent methods focus on recent advances in NLP like deep learning and pre-trained transformer architectures (Sänger et al., 2016; Schmitt et al., 2018; Akhtar et al., 2019). Aßenmacher et al. (2021) were able to significantly improve the performance for classifying aspects and their polarities on the GermEval dataset. They achieved this by treating ABSA as a multi-label classification problem and employed a BERT-transformer model instead of the CNN+FastText model used by Schmitt et al. (2018). This led to a significant improvement of the model's accuracy with a rise of micro-averaged f1-scores from 0.54 and 0.44 to 0.78 and 0.67 for aspect and aspect-polarity classification respectively. De Greve et al. (2021) also addressed the subtasks of aspect-term classification and aspect-sentiment classification using a BERT architecture. They achieved macro and weighted F1 scores of 0.69 and 0.83 for the classification of the six main aspects on the TDDL dataset, as well as macro and weighted f1-scores of 0.54 and 0.73 for the classification of all 48 combinations of main and sub-aspects while using the gold annotations of the aspect terms as input. The authors were also able to achieve a macro f1-score of 0.72 for aspect-polarity classification by implementing a context window of five words before and after the aspect phrase.

3 Methods

3.1 Creation of a Dataset of German Hotel Reviews

3.1.1 Dataset Generation

The foundation of the dataset are 1,512 user reviews about a selection of hotels in the city of Regensburg (situated in the south of Germany) in German language. The reviews were acquired with the web scraping application Parsehub[1] from the site *TripAdvisor*.[2] The selection process focused on five mid-class hotels, chosen specifically for their substantial number of user reviews and diverse proximity to the city center. In this way, we were able to capture a range of perspectives related to the location of the hotels. Furthermore, attention was paid to ensure that the selected hotels had comparable features (e.g. restaurants and parking) to facilitate consistent topics across the user reviews.

In order to annotate the dataset with aspects and polarities contained at the sentence level, the 1,512 user reviews were split into sentences with the online sentence splitter tool TextConverter.[3] Subsequently, we manually inspected the splits and made any necessary corrections, in case the user's statement was otherwise no longer comprehensible.[4] This results in a dataset of 21,182 sentences. For the annotation process, the dataset was divided into chunks of 200 units and randomly distributed to the participants. This resulted in a subset of 5,000 sentences, with each sentence annotated by two different annotators as part of the annotation study.

3.1.2 Data Annotation

The goal of the study was the annotation of three-part tuples consisting of an aspect, an attribute or sub-aspect (a specific facet of an aspect), and the associated polarity, following the approach of previous work (Pontiki et al., 2015, 2016; Wojatzki et al., 2017). The aspect (e.g. hotel) and the attribute (e.g. price) are combined to form the aspect category pair. For the determination of the aspect categories of our dataset, the four predefined rating categories of each *TripAdvisor* review - location (Ger.: Lage), price (Ger.: Preis), cleanliness (Ger.: Sauberkeit), and service (Ger.: Service) - were taken into account, as we assumed that, at least to some extent, these categories were used by the users as reference for their written reviews. Furthermore, we also took into account findings from related work in the same domain, in which additional aspects and attributes such as ambience (ger. Ambiente), restaurant (Ger.: Restaurant), rooms (Ger.: Zimmer), general (Ger.: Haupt) and quality (Ger.: Qualität) were used (Abro et al., 2020; Chang et al., 2019). On the basis of this information, the five aspects hotel (Ger.: Hotel), food & drink (Ger.: Essen & Trinken), location, service, and rooms were selected for annotation. General, price, quietness (Ger.: Ruhe), cleanliness, and style (Ger.: Style) were selected as attributes, which could be annotated in different combinations with the main aspects. The annotation of the polarity of the aspects was carried out using the three classes positive, neutral, and negative. All possible annotations of aspects and attributes can be seen in Table 1, furthermore all possible combinations of aspect categories are depicted in Table 5 in the appendix. It was possible to annotate one or more tuples of entities, attributes, and polarities per sentence. If no aspect could be identified in the sentence, it was also possible to skip the sentence and omit it from the annotation.

Category	Possible Class Labels
Aspect	Hotel, Location, Food & Drinks, Service, Rooms
Attribute	General, Price, Quietness, Cleanliness, Style
Polarity	Positive, Neutral, Negative

Table 1: All possible class labels of the annotation.

The annotation was carried out in the web tool INCEpTION (Klie et al., 2018) which is a more advanced version of its predecessor WebAnno (Yimam et al., 2014). All study participants received detailed annotation guidelines with an explanation of the background of the study, an introduction to the topic, a list of all possible combinations of aspects and attributes with example annotations, and an introduction on how to operate the annotation tool INCEpTION. The selection of the different aspects, attributes, and polarities was predetermined by the annotation tool in order to prevent incorrect annotations. The annotation study was carried

[1] https://www.parsehub.com/

[2] https://www.tripadvisor.de/

[3] https://textconverter.com/

[4] In rare cases, the manual correction resulted in a sample comprising up to two sentences. However, for ease of understanding, we refer to one sample as a sentence in the remainder of the text.

Aspect	Count	Percentage
Hotel	1,477	26.3 %
Rooms	1,457	25.9 %
Location	963	17.1 %
Service	907	16.2 %
Food & Drinks	813	14.5 %

Attribute	Count	Percentage
General	3,326	59.2 %
Style	1,201	21.4 %
Cleanliness	405	7.2 %
Price	396	7.1 %
Quietness	289	5.1 %

Polarity	Count	Percentage
Positive	4,032	71.8 %
Neutral	957	17.0 %
Negative	628	11.2 %

Table 2: Amount of samples per aspect, attribute, and polarity class, ordered by the respective portions.

out by 27 students, with each participant annotating a subset of either 200 or 400 sentences. Each sentence was annotated by two annotators. The agreement between the annotators is visualized in Table 6 in the appendix. Due to the possibility of assigning none, one or more aspects to a sentence, Krippendorff's α[5] is a suitable metric for agreement. The metric is calculated using the masi distance (Passonneau, 2006). The agreement can be examined at different levels of complexity: (1) an isolated view on the aspects, (2) the combination of either aspects and attributes or (3) aspects and polarities, and (4) all metrics together - the aspects, attributes as well as their polarities. If only the aspects are considered, the average agreement of the annotators is 0.61, if the attributes are included, the average value drops to 0.48 and if the whole tuple is considered, the average agreement goes down to 0.43. If the complexity of the attribute is removed from the tuple and only the aspect and its polarity are considered, the average agreement is 0.54. These agreement values are considered to be of moderate agreement (Hayes and Krippendorff, 2007; Landis and Koch, 1977).

Subsequently, to increase the quality of the dataset, all 5,000 sentences were manually curated. First, all the annotations were approved where both annotators assigned the same aspect tuple. If sentences were annotated by only one annotator, it was decided individually whether to accept or discard the annotation. For sentences with different annotations in terms of entity, attribute or polarity, it was individually decided which annotation should be classified as correct or not.

3.1.3 Dataset Characteristics

After curation, the dataset consists of 4,254 sentences (746 sentences did not contain clearly discernible aspects) and 5,617 annotations of aspect tuples (see Figure 2 in the appendix for an excerpt of the dataset). Table 2 contains the frequency distribution of the dataset at the level of the aspects, attributes, and polarities in an isolated view. The frequencies of the aspects are slightly unbalanced, with the most frequent aspect "hotel" occurring almost twice as often as the least frequent aspect "food & drinks". The distributions for the attributes, as well as the polarities, are strongly unbalanced. Thus, about 59 % of all attributes are assigned to the general class, while the three least represented attributes cleanliness, price, and quietness take up less than 20 % of the total amount. A similar picture emerges for the polarities. Thus, almost 72 % of all labels are assigned to the polarity positive, while the classes neutral and negative are only represented with around 17 % and 11 % respectively. The distributions for different combinations of aspects, attributes, and polarities in the data set are also strongly unbalanced (see Figure 1 and additionally Tables 7, 8 and 9 in the appendix). The frequency distributions for the combinations of multiple classes are depicted in Figure 1. For example, for the aspect-polarity combinations, 1/3 of the most frequently occurring combinations account for more than 2/3 of the total dataset; this value is significantly higher for the aspect-attribute combinations with about 83 % and is still topped off by the aspect-attribute-polarity combinations, where 1/3 of all combinations account for more than 87 % of all samples in the dataset.

3.2 Dataset Evaluation with Pre-Trained Transformer-Models

3.2.1 Data Preprocessing

In multi-label classification, one or more classes are assigned to each sample, which requires remodeling the dataset structure. For each class, each sample is given a binary truth value about whether the class is present in the sample or not, resulting in a one-hot-encoded sequence. The number of classes is determined by the level of annotation granularity. For instance, classifying only the aspects results in 5 classes, considering both aspects and attributes leads to 18 classes, and incorporating aspects, attributes, and polarity results in 54 classes. It is

[5]https://pypi.org/project/krippendorff/

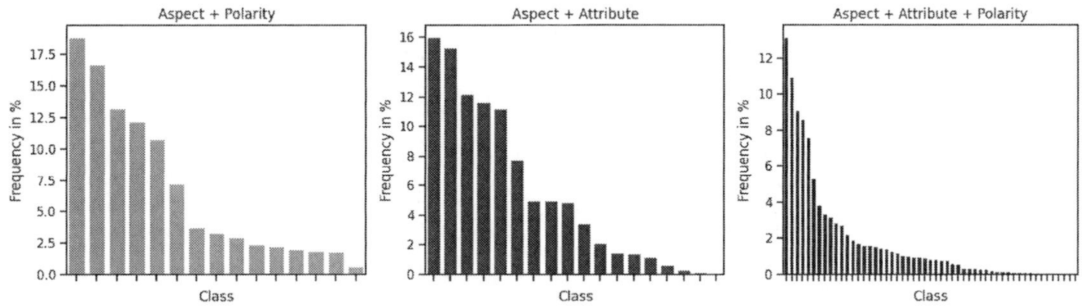

Figure 1: Frequency distributions for all combinations of classes.

important to note that out of these 54 classes, one class, namely "Food & Drinks#Quietness:Neutral" did not occur in the dataset and was therefore unintentionally omitted during the annotation process. However, through the conversion into a binary statement regarding the occurrence of a class, a maximum of one occurrence of the same class/same combination of classes can be included. Thus, the information of identical classes occurring several times in the same sequence is considered as one.

As an example, the class labels of the sentence "The service staff was very nice, but I think the location of the hotel is inconvenient." are depicted in Table 3. Here, the aspect "Location" was annotated as negative and the aspect "Service" was annotated as positive, resulting in the one-hot-encoded labeling sequence [0,0,1,0,0,0,0,0,0,1,0,0,0,0,0] which serves as input for our classifier.

3.2.2 Metrics

In a multi-label classification setting commonly used metrics are hamming loss, accuracy, precision, recall, and f1-score (Zhang and Zhou, 2013; Tsoumakas and Katakis, 2007).

Similar to the metrics used in SemEval 2014, 2015, and 2016, and GermEval 2017 Shared Tasks, we use a micro-averaged f1-score as the primary evaluation metric. However, since the balancing of the created dataset tends to be skewed depending on the level of detail of the annotation, we also provide a macro f1-score, averaged over the individual class f1-scores. Thus, this value also takes into account the prediction performance of the underrepresented classes.

3.2.3 Evaluation Procedure

We tested three different pre-trained BERT transformer models publicly available: (1) one of the largest transformer-based BERT language models for German, *gbert-large* by *Deepset* (Chan et al., 2020), and two of the best-performing BERT-based models in similar studies, (2) *bert-base-german-uncased* by DBMDZ[6] and (3) the comparatively lightweight model *distilbert-base-german-cased* (Sanh et al., 2019), pre-trained on the same dataset as (2).[7] All models were acquired via the *Hugging Face* platform and implemented using the Python libraries *Pytorch* (Paszke et al., 2019) and *Transformers* (Wolf et al., 2020). Evaluation metrics were calculated using *scikit-learn* (Pedregosa et al., 2011).

For increased validity, the dataset was cross-evaluated with stratified 4-split kfold, alternating 3 parts of the dataset for training and one part of the dataset for evaluation. Each model was evaluated based on four different tasks, split into two categories of subtasks of ABSA: (1) aspect category classification and (2) aspect sentiment classification. For each subtask, we evaluated on different

[6]Munic Digitalization Centre Digital Library team at the Bavarian State Library, see `https://github.com/dbmdz`.

[7]In text further referenced as *deepset-gbert-large*, *dbmdz-bert-base* and *distilbert-base*.

Aspect-Polarity-Combinations

Hotel			Location			Food & Drinks			Service			Rooms		
Pos	Neut	Neg	Pos	Neut	Neg	Pos	Neut	Neg	Pos	Neut	Neg	Pos	Neut	Neg
0	0	1	0	0	0	0	0	0	1	0	0	0	0	0

Table 3: Example labels of the input for the model of an aspect polarity classification. A '1' means that this class occurs in the text, a '0' the opposite.

sets of data, once with information about attributes and once without. Thus, both subtasks differ in complexity of the ground truth data used: classification of the aspect class, classification of the aspect class and its associated polarity, and both in combination with the attribute class. This resulted in classification tasks with 5 and 18 classes for task 1 and 15 and 53 classes for task 2.

Training was done using an AdamW-optimizer (Loshchilov and Hutter, 2017) and a binary cross entropy loss function with sigmoid activation, which is mandatory for multi-label classification. Since finding the right hyperparameters is a crucial component in every deep learning-based classification task, we performed systematic hyperparameter tuning for 20 trials per evaluation run with *Optuna* (Akiba et al., 2019) while trying to minimize the value of hamming loss with a *Tree-structured Parzen Estimator (TPE)*. The pre-selection of hyperparameters is based on Devlin et al. (2019) and own pre-experiments:

- Learning rate $\in [2e-5, 5e-5]$
- Batch size $\in \{8, 16, 32\}$
- Number of epochs $\in \{2, 3, 4\}$

Hyperparameter optimization showed that for 11 out of the 12 runs the best configuration comprised a batch size of 8 and 3 or 4 epochs. The only exception was the aspect class determination by *deepset-gbert-large*, which achieved the best result with a batch size of 32. It's worth noting that all models struggled significantly with classifying the aspect-attribute-polarity tuple when using a batch size of 32, frequently failing to predict any class. Regarding the learning rate, no clear trend is discernible, although often the best results were achieved with values just at the specified minimum or maximum, which indicates that the actual optimum of the parameter might lie outside the limits we had defined.

The training and evaluation were done on a workstation setup with an Intel Xeon W-2275 CPU, 128 GB of Ram, and 2x NVIDIA RTX A5000 GPUs.

4 Results

The evaluation results for all four subtasks are depicted in Table 4, divided in subtasks and models. In addition, we also included values obtained by Aßenmacher et al. (2021) which implemented multi-label classification with BERT on the GermEval 2017 dataset.[8]

4.1 Evaluation of Aspect Category Classification

The three BERT models for classifying aspects and aspects & attributes differ only slightly in terms of performance. In predicting the five aspect classes, *deepset-gbert-large* performs best with micro and macro f1-scores of 0.906 and 0.910, placing it about one percentage point ahead of both *dbmdz-bert-base* and *distilbert-base*. Further analysis showed that for the best performing model *deepset-gbert-large* the individual classes could be predicted almost equally well with an f1-score of approximately 0.92, the only outlier being the aspect "Hotel" with 0.86. Furthermore, when the attribute classes are included, *deepset-gbert-large* also performed best in the classification of the 18 aspect combinations, achieving micro and macro f1 scores of 0.797 and 0.542, but this time by a margin of between about 2 and 6 percentage points over the other models. Upon further analysis of the individual aspect-attribute class combinations, it's obvious that the prediction performance of all models correlates with the frequency of occurrence of the class

[8]The GermEval dataset was published along with two datasets for evaluation, each collected at different points in time. When referring to the results of the GermEval dataset throughout this paper, we report the average of both eval datasets.

Language Model	Aspect		Aspect + Attribute		Aspect + Polarity		Aspect + Attribute + Polarity	
	F1 Micro	F1 Macro	F1 Micro	F1 Macro	F1 Micro	F1 Macro	F1 Micro	F1 Macro
deepset-gbert-large	**0.906**	**0.910**	**0.797**	**0.542**	**0.809**	**0.659**	**0.651**	**0.173**
dbmdz-bert-base-german-uncased	0.891	0.895	0.774	0.504	0.779	0.599	0.592	0.119
distilbert-base-german-cased	0.880	0.886	0.744	0.432	0.741	0.490	0.561	0.107
Multi-label BERT on GermEval2017 (Aßenmacher et al., 2021)	0.776		0.776		0.672		0.672	

Table 4: Results for the 4 subtasks of the evaluation. Best values are depicted in bold.

samples. In terms of the *deepset-gbert-large* model, this means that the four least frequently occurring classes are not detected by the model, while the four most frequently occurring classes are among the top 5 predicted classes in terms of classification results.

4.2 Evaluation of Aspect Sentiment Classification

The classification of aspects in combination with polarity gives a similar picture as in chapter 4.1. Again, *deepset-gbert-large* achieves the best results both with and without consideration of the attribute class. Thus, *deepset-gbert-large* achieves micro f1- and macro f1-scores of 0.809 and 0.659 for the classification of the 15 classes from aspect & polarity. The model obtains relatively good classification results for most of the 15 individual classes, up to an f1-score of 0.931. However, once more, the performance drops off with the decrease in frequency of the class in the dataset, whereby the rarest combination "Service - Neutral" with only 36 occurrences cannot be predicted at all. Aspects related to positive polarity labels are recognized best, followed by negative and eventually neutral polarity labels.

Taking the attribute category into account, thus predicting the whole aspect-attribute-polarity tuple, *deepset-gbert-large* achieves a micro f1-score of 0.651 and is, therefore, at least five percentage points ahead of the other models. Since *deepset-gbert-large* can only make a correct prediction for 17 of the total 53 classes, the macro f1-score drops significantly, down to 0.173. The model almost completely fails to recognize combinations with the neutral polarity class, while aspects & attributes in combination with the positive polarity class work best.

5 Discussion

5.1 Aspect Category and Aspect Sentiment Classification

In this work, we investigated the adaptation of ABSA as a multi-label classification for the domain of hotel reviews and compared its performance in the context of previous methods. However, comparing values between corpora and approaches should be done with caution, given the considerable disparities in the origin, quality, depth, and size of the datasets that most approaches rely on. Based on the fact that *deepset-gbert-large* was pre-trained on ten times the amount of raw data and at the same time has more than three times as many parameters and more than twice as many layers as the other two models, it is plausible that this model also achieves the best classification results. Nevertheless, the results in some categories (e. g. aspect classification) are sufficiently close to each other that it can be considered that the significantly smaller model size and the much faster fine-tuning phase could outweigh the disadvantages in classification accuracy (see Table 10 for model parameters and Table 11 for training times).

With regard to the subtask of aspect category classification, the best transformer model we evaluated, *deepset-gbert-large*, achieves micro and macro f1-scores of 0.906 and 0.910 for the classification of the 5 aspect classes, outperforming values achieved in the domain of English hotel reviews, such as Andono et al. (2022) with a micro f1-score of 0.89 on 5 aspects, Chang et al. (2019) with a macro f1-score of 0.80 on 8 aspect categories or Afzaal et al. (2019) with 0.85 on an unknown number of aspects, and in the domain of social media comments about German literary prize winners with a macro f1-score 0.79 on 7 aspects (De Greve et al., 2021).

In terms of the end-to-end approach which combines aspect category classification and aspect sentiment classification, all tested BERT models delivered convincing results. Among them, the highest f1-scores were obtained by *deepset-gbert-large* with micro- and macro-averages of 0.809 and 0.651 on aspects and their polarities. Our results surpass those achieved in comparable settings, such as the results reported by Tran et al. (2019) and Afzaal et al. (2019) on the domain of hotel reviews in the English language. Notably, the approach by Tran et al. (2019) achieved an f1-score of 0.873 for aspect term extraction and binary polarity classification, as well as an accuracy of 0.80 for aspect category classification, while Afzaal et al. (2019) managed to achieve f1-scores of 0.85 and 0.91 for aspect category and aspect sentiment classification, respectively. However, two key considerations highlight the differences between their works and ours: (1) Their approach relied exclusively on binary polarity labels, which inherently simplified the sentiment analysis process compared to our approach and (2) they concatenated both subtasks, which could potentially compound error propagation throughout their pipeline and, thus, lower the overall classification performance. In contrast, our approach produced superior results while combining both subtasks, likely due to the individual strengths of transfer-learning and our chosen BERT models.

However, it must be noted that our results have shown that the classification performance can decrease significantly when additional aspect classes are added, which is in line with results obtained in current research (Aßenmacher et al., 2021). Therefore the number of classified aspects can be decisive for a comparison between different methods and datasets.

Additionally, our results for the aspect classification subtask on 18 aspect categories (micro f1-score: 0.797) are slightly better than the results achieved by Aßenmacher et al. (2021) on 20 aspect categories (micro f1-score: 0.776), which followed the same approach as we did, a (BERT-based) multi-label classification, but on a German dataset of user ratings (GermEval 2017). If polarity is taken into account for the end-to-end overall ABSA solution, here again, *deepset-gbert-large* achieves comparable classification results with a micro f1-score of 0.651 on 53 classes (aspect-attribute-polarity combinations) to Aßenmacher et al. (2021) on the GermEval corpus with an f1-score of 0.672 on 60 classes by their best-performing model *dbmdz-bert-base*. Although the classification results for the aspect-polarity classification case are slightly worse than the results obtained on GermEval 2017 by Aßenmacher et al. (2021), *deepset-gbert-large* performs better than *dbmdz-bert-base* in the direct comparison on the domain of hotel reviews, suggesting that the performance difference may not be due to the model itself, but to the underlying language-specific differences of the domain or the dataset. Nevertheless, it can be observed with both approaches on both domains that the classification of strongly under-represented classes is significantly worse than that of frequently occurring classes. This suggests that this is not a domain-specific problem, but could be due to the implementation of our approach or the underlying datasets, which needs to be taken into account when developing future multi-label classification approaches.

In summarization, our results allow the conclusion that (BERT-based) multi-label classification is a valid method for aspect classification and end-to-end ABSA on domains other than user ratings on social media, and should be extended to other domains as it is already the case for the English language (Kumar et al., 2019).

5.2 Limitations & Ethical Considerations

As the selection of the right dataset is an essential component for any classification task, the quality of its (manual) annotations may also reflect on the classification results of machine learning approaches. The agreement of the participants regarding the annotation of the dataset of this work indicates a low to moderate agreement. Considering the fact that a large number of combinations of different classes can be annotated in ABSA, this is usually presented as an acceptable result (Moreno-Ortiz et al., 2019), even though it is reasonable that a lower level of agreement and thus a debatable lower quality of the dataset is likely to affect the classification performance of the methods applied to it (Mozetič et al., 2016). Since Krippendorff's α varies considerably between individual annotator-pairings (see Table 6 in the appendix), it is possible that demographic characteristics, such as previous experience with annotation studies or the subject of the sentiment analysis, could have an influence on the quality of the annotations. However, the imbalance of the annotated classes does not seem to be a rare phenomenon and often occurs in context of ABSA in connection with user reviews in general or reviews from the hotel domain or *Tripadvisor* in particular (Risch et al., 2021; Tran et al., 2019; Pontiki et al., 2015).

The process of gathering our dataset followed strict privacy guidelines to protect the rights of users. The primary aim was to extract reviews or texts, while carefully avoiding the collection of personalized data that could potentially identify individual users or specific user groups. By doing so, we aimed to mitigate the risk of drawing unwarranted or ethically questionable conclusions from our analyses. Additionally, any direct references to individuals or hotels were systematically anonymized. This was done to prevent indirect identification of individuals or establishments.

The dataset and its annotations are available upon request from the authors, to ensure that the dataset is used responsibly and for academic purposes only, thus, respecting the original intent of the data collection. The Python code for the implementation of this evaluation and the documentation about the evaluation process is accessible via

GitHub.[9]

Despite our thorough data collection and anonymization procedures, some inherent limitations and ethical considerations persist. Our dataset may not capture the full spectrum of user sentiment due to potential bias in review writing, as those who write reviews may only represent a certain subset of the population. The ability to transfer knowledge about semantics and characteristics of reviews across different rating platforms cannot be guaranteed either. This inherent bias may be unintentionally perpetuated by BERT-based models used in our ABSA, despite their general effectiveness in NLP. In addition, our dataset was composed of reviews in German, which may include the bias of different language characteristics that might not be transferable to other languages.

5.3 Future Work

Our work provides valuable insight into the implementation and expected performance of a multi-label classification approach for detecting aspect categories and their associated polarities in reviews about the hotel industry. Importantly, we demonstrate that this methodology can be applied beyond social media to other domains in the German language. However, several potential directions for future work emerge from this study.

Foremost, we want to improve our dataset both in terms of size and annotation quality. Increasing the number of sentences in the dataset will provide a more robust representation of reviews, while a refined curation process ensures higher accuracy of labels. Currently, our dataset exhibits class imbalance, which presents challenges to the ABSA methods applied and can distort classification performance, particularly for underrepresented aspect categories.

From a methodological perspective, despite our results outperforming comparable ABSA approaches in both German and English languages, there is still room for improvement. We observed that the classification performance for severely underrepresented classes tends to decline significantly. To mitigate this, future efforts could involve optimizing training data balance via class weighting or subsampling, coupled with a more thorough hyperparameter tuning process.

Furthermore, we see great potential in further investigating the performance of large language models in the scenario of zero- or few-shot learning in the context of ABSA, which has already yielded remarkable results in the field of (aspect-based) sentiment analysis (Zhang et al., 2023; Qin et al., 2023).

[9] https://github.com/JakobFehle/absa-hotel-reviews

References

Sindhu Abro, Sarang Shaikh, Rizwan Ali Abro, Sana Fatima Soomro, and Hafiz Mehmood Malik. 2020. Aspect based sentimental analysis of hotel reviews: A comparative study. *Sukkur IBA Journal of Computing and Mathematical Sciences*, 4(1):11–20.

Muhammad Afzaal, Muhammad Usman, and Alvis Fong. 2019. Tourism mobile app with aspect-based sentiment classification framework for tourist reviews. *IEEE Transactions on Consumer Electronics*, 65(2):233–242.

Md Shad Akhtar, Abhishek Kumar, Asif Ekbal, Chris Biemann, and Pushpak Bhattacharyya. 2019. Language-agnostic model for aspect-based sentiment analysis. In *Proceedings of the 13th International Conference on Computational Semantics-Long Papers*, pages 154–164.

Nadeem Akhtar, Nashez Zubair, Abhishek Kumar, and Tameem Ahmad. 2017. Aspect based sentiment oriented summarization of hotel reviews. *Procedia computer science*, 115:563–571.

Takuya Akiba, Shotaro Sano, Toshihiko Yanase, Takeru Ohta, and Masanori Koyama. 2019. Optuna: A next-generation hyperparameter optimization framework. In *Proceedings of the 25th ACM SIGKDD international conference on knowledge discovery & data mining*, pages 2623–2631.

Pulung Nurtantio Andono, Sunardi, Raden Arief Nugroho, and Budi Harjo. 2022. Aspect-based sentiment analysis for hotel review using lda, semantic similarity, and bert. *International Journal of Intelligent Engineering and Systems*, 15.

Matthias Aßenmacher, Alessandra Corvonato, and Christian Heumann. 2021. Re-evaluating germeval17 using german pre-trained language models. *arXiv preprint arXiv:2102.12330*.

Gianni Brauwers and Flavius Frasincar. 2022. A survey on aspect-based sentiment classification. *ACM Computing Surveys*, 55(4):1–37.

Branden Chan, Stefan Schweter, and Timo Möller. 2020. German's next language model. *arXiv preprint arXiv:2010.10906*.

Yung-Chun Chang, Chih-Hao Ku, and Chun-Hung Chen. 2019. Social media analytics: Extracting and visualizing hilton hotel ratings and reviews from tripadvisor. *International Journal of Information Management*, 48:263–279.

Siva Uday Sampreeth Chebolu, Franck Dernoncourt, Nedim Lipka, and Thamar Solorio. 2022. Survey of aspect-based sentiment analysis datasets. *arXiv preprint arXiv:2204.05232*.

Hao Chen, Zepeng Zhai, Fangxiang Feng, Ruifan Li, and Xiaojie Wang. 2022. Enhanced multi-channel graph convolutional network for aspect sentiment triplet extraction. In *Proceedings of the 60th Annual Meeting of the Association for Computational Linguistics (Volume 1: Long Papers)*, pages 2974–2985.

Lore De Greve, Pranaydeep Singh, Cynthia Van Hee, Els Lefever, and Gunther Martens. 2021. Aspect-based sentiment analysis for german: analyzing'talk of literature'surrounding literary prizes on social media. *Computational Linguistics in the Netherlands Journal*, 11:85–104.

Jacob Devlin, Ming-Wei Chang, Kenton Lee, and Kristina Toutanova. 2019. BERT: Pre-training of deep bidirectional transformers for language understanding. In *Proceedings of the 2019 Conference of the North American Chapter of the Association for Computational Linguistics: Human Language Technologies, Volume 1 (Long and Short Papers)*, pages 4171–4186, Minneapolis, Minnesota. Association for Computational Linguistics.

Hai Ha Do, Penatiyana WC Prasad, Angelika Maag, and Abeer Alsadoon. 2019. Deep learning for aspect-based sentiment analysis: a comparative review. *Expert systems with applications*, 118:272–299.

Alina El-Keilany, Thomas Schmidt, and Christian Wolff. 2022. Distant Viewing of the Harry Potter Movies via Computer Vision. In *Proceedings of the 6th Digital Humanities in the Nordic and Baltic Countries Conference (DHNB 2022).*, pages 33–49, Uppsala, Sweden.

Jakob Fehle, Thomas Schmidt, and Christian Wolff. 2021. Lexicon-based sentiment analysis in German: Systematic evaluation of resources and preprocessing techniques. In *Proceedings of the 17th Conference on Natural Language Processing (KONVENS 2021)*, pages 86–103, Düsseldorf, Germany. KONVENS 2021 Organizers.

David Halbhuber, Jakob Fehle, Alexander Kalus, Konstantin Seitz, Martin Kocur, Thomas Schmidt, and Christian Wolff. 2019. The mood game-how to use the player's affective state in a shoot'em up avoiding frustration and boredom. In *Proceedings of Mensch Und Computer 2019*, pages 867–870.

Andrew F Hayes and Klaus Krippendorff. 2007. Answering the call for a standard reliability measure for coding data. *Communication methods and measures*, 1(1):77–89.

Zeyi Jin, Xin Lai, and Jingjig Cao. 2020. Multi-label sentiment analysis base on bert with modified tf-idf. In *2020 IEEE International Symposium on Product Compliance Engineering-Asia (ISPCE-CN)*, pages 1–6. IEEE.

Zenun Kastrati, Ali Shariq Imran, and Arianit Kurti. 2020. Weakly supervised framework for aspect-based sentiment analysis on students' reviews of moocs. *IEEE Access*, 8:106799–106810.

Jan-Christoph Klie, Michael Bugert, Beto Boullosa, Richard Eckart de Castilho, and Iryna Gurevych. 2018. The inception platform: Machine-assisted and knowledge-oriented interactive annotation. In *Proceedings of the 27th International Conference on Computational Linguistics: System Demonstrations*, pages 5–9. Association for Computational Linguistics. Veranstaltungstitel: The 27th International Conference on Computational Linguistics (COLING 2018).

Roman Klinger and Philipp Cimiano. 2014. The usage review corpus for fine-grained, multi-lingual opinion analysis. In *Proceedings of the Ninth International Conference on Language Resources and Evaluation (LREC'14)*. Citeseer.

J Ashok Kumar, S Abirami, and Tina Esther Trueman. 2019. Multilabel aspect-based sentiment classification for abilify drug user review. In *2019 11th International Conference on Advanced Computing (ICoAC)*, pages 376–380. IEEE.

J Richard Landis and Gary G Koch. 1977. The measurement of observer agreement for categorical data. *biometrics*, pages 159–174.

Bing Liu, Minqing Hu, and Junsheng Cheng. 2005. Opinion observer: analyzing and comparing opinions on the web. In *Proceedings of the 14th international conference on World Wide Web*, pages 342–351.

Qian Liu, Zhiqiang Gao, Bing Liu, and Yuanlin Zhang. 2015. Automated rule selection for aspect extraction in opinion mining. In *Twenty-Fourth international joint conference on artificial intelligence*.

Ilya Loshchilov and Frank Hutter. 2017. Decoupled weight decay regularization. *arXiv preprint arXiv:1711.05101*.

Macedo Maia, Siegfried Handschuh, André Freitas, Brian Davis, Ross McDermott, Manel Zarrouk, and Alexandra Balahur. 2018. Www'18 open challenge: Financial opinion mining and question answering. In *Companion Proceedings of the The Web Conference 2018*, WWW '18, page 1941–1942, Republic and Canton of Geneva, CHE. International World Wide Web Conferences Steering Committee.

Antonio Moreno-Ortiz, Soluna Salles-Bernal, and Aroa Orrequia-Barea. 2019. Design and validation of annotation schemas for aspect-based sentiment analysis in the tourism sector. *Information Technology & Tourism*, 21:535–557.

Igor Mozetič, Miha Grčar, and Jasmina Smailović. 2016. Multilingual twitter sentiment classification: The role of human annotators. *PloS one*, 11(5):e0155036.

Luis Moßburger, Felix Wende, Kay Brinkmann, and Thomas Schmidt. 2020. Exploring Online Depression Forums via Text Mining: A Comparison of Reddit and a Curated Online Forum. In *Proceedings of the Fifth Social Media Mining for Health Applications Workshop & Shared Task*, pages 70–81, Barcelona, Spain (Online). Association for Computational Linguistics.

Ambreen Nazir, Yuan Rao, Lianwei Wu, and Ling Sun. 2020. Issues and challenges of aspect-based sentiment analysis: A comprehensive survey. *IEEE Transactions on Affective Computing*, 13(2):845–863.

Anna-Marie Ortloff, Lydia Güntner, Maximiliane Windl, Thomas Schmidt, Martin Kocur, and Christian Wolff. 2019. Sentibooks: Enhancing audiobooks via affective computing and smart light bulbs. In *Proceedings of Mensch Und Computer 2019*, MuC'19, page 863–866, New York, NY, USA. Association for Computing Machinery.

Rebecca Passonneau. 2006. Measuring agreement on set-valued items (MASI) for semantic and pragmatic annotation. In *Proceedings of the Fifth International Conference on Language Resources and Evaluation (LREC'06)*, Genoa, Italy. European Language Resources Association (ELRA).

Adam Paszke, Sam Gross, Francisco Massa, Adam Lerer, James Bradbury, Gregory Chanan, Trevor Killeen, Zeming Lin, Natalia Gimelshein, Luca Antiga, et al. 2019. Pytorch: An imperative style, high-performance deep learning library. *Advances in neural information processing systems*, 32.

F. Pedregosa, G. Varoquaux, A. Gramfort, V. Michel, B. Thirion, O. Grisel, M. Blondel, P. Prettenhofer, R. Weiss, V. Dubourg, J. Vanderplas, A. Passos, D. Cournapeau, M. Brucher, M. Perrot, and E. Duchesnay. 2011. Scikit-learn: Machine learning in Python. *Journal of Machine Learning Research*, 12:2825–2830.

Maria Pontiki, Dimitrios Galanis, Harris Papageorgiou, Suresh Manandhar, and Ion Androutsopoulos. 2015. Semeval-2015 task 12: Aspect based sentiment analysis. In *Proceedings of the 9th international workshop on semantic evaluation (SemEval 2015)*, pages 486–495.

Maria Pontiki, Dimitris Galanis, Haris Papageorgiou, Ion Androutsopoulos, Suresh Manandhar, Mohammed AL-Smadi, Mahmoud Al-Ayyoub, Yanyan Zhao, Bing Qin, Orphée De Clercq, et al. 2016. Semeval-2016 task 5: Aspect based sentiment analysis. In *ProWorkshop on Semantic Evaluation (SemEval-2016)*, pages 19–30. Association for Computational Linguistics.

Maria Pontiki, Dimitris Galanis, John Pavlopoulos, Harris Papageorgiou, Ion Androutsopoulos, and Suresh Manandhar. 2014. SemEval-2014 task 4: Aspect based sentiment analysis. In *Proceedings of the 8th International Workshop on Semantic Evaluation (SemEval 2014)*, pages 27–35, Dublin, Ireland. Association for Computational Linguistics.

Yao Qiang, Xin Li, and Dongxiao Zhu. 2020. Toward tag-free aspect based sentiment analysis: A multiple attention network approach. In *2020 International Joint Conference on Neural Networks (IJCNN)*, pages 1–8. IEEE.

Chengwei Qin, Aston Zhang, Zhuosheng Zhang, Jiaao Chen, Michihiro Yasunaga, and Diyi Yang. 2023. Is ChatGPT a General-Purpose natural language processing task solver?

Julian Risch, Anke Stoll, Lena Wilms, and Michael Wiegand, editors. 2021. *Proceedings of the GermEval 2021 Shared Task on the Identification of Toxic, Engaging, and Fact-Claiming Comments*. Association for Computational Linguistics, Duesseldorf, Germany.

Mario Sänger, Ulf Leser, Steffen Kemmerer, Peter Adolphs, and Roman Klinger. 2016. Scare—the sentiment corpus of app reviews with fine-grained annotations in german. In *Proceedings of the Tenth International Conference on Language Resources and Evaluation (LREC'16)*, pages 1114–1121.

Victor Sanh, Lysandre Debut, Julien Chaumond, and Thomas Wolf. 2019. Distilbert, a distilled version of bert: smaller, faster, cheaper and lighter. *arXiv preprint arXiv:1910.01108*.

Thomas Schmidt and Manuel Burghardt. 2018. An Evaluation of Lexicon-based Sentiment Analysis Techniques for the Plays of Gotthold Ephraim Lessing. In *Proceedings of the Second Joint SIGHUM Workshop on Computational Linguistics for Cultural Heritage, Social Sciences, Humanities and Literature*, pages 139–149, Santa Fe, New Mexico. Association for Computational Linguistics.

Thomas Schmidt, Katrin Dennerlein, and Christian Wolff. 2021a. Towards a Corpus of Historical German Plays with Emotion Annotations. In *3rd Conference on Language, Data and Knowledge (LDK 2021)*, volume 93 of *Open Access Series in Informatics (OASIcs)*, pages 9:1–9:11, Dagstuhl, Germany. Schloss Dagstuhl – Leibniz-Zentrum für Informatik. ISSN: 2190-6807.

Thomas Schmidt, Katrin Dennerlein, and Christian Wolff. 2021b. Using Deep Learning for Emotion Analysis of 18th and 19th Century German Plays. In Manuel Burghardt, Lisa Dieckmann, Timo Steyer, Peer Trilcke, Niels-Oliver Walkowski, Joëlle Weis, and Ulrike Wuttke, editors, *Fabrikation von Erkenntnis: Experimente in den Digital Humanities*. Melusina Press, Esch-sur-Alzette, Luxembourg.

Thomas Schmidt, Alina El-Keilany, Johannes Eger, and Sarah Kurek. 2021c. Exploring Computer Vision for Film Analysis: A Case Study for Five Canonical

Movies. In *2nd International Conference of the European Association for Digital Humanities (EADH 2021)*, Krasnoyarsk, Russia.

Thomas Schmidt, Jakob Fehle, Maximilian Weissenbacher, Jonathan Richter, Philipp Gottschalk, and Christian Wolff. 2022. Sentiment analysis on twitter for the major german parties during the 2021 german federal election. In *Proceedings of the 18th Conference on Natural Language Processing (KONVENS 2022)*, pages 74–87.

Thomas Schmidt, Florian Kaindl, and Christian Wolff. 2020. Distant reading of religious online communities: A case study for three religious forums on reddit. In *Proceedings of the Digital Humanities in the Nordic Countries 5th Conference (DHN 2020)*, pages 157–172, Riga, Latvia.

Martin Schmitt, Simon Steinheber, Konrad Schreiber, and Benjamin Roth. 2018. Joint aspect and polarity classification for aspect-based sentiment analysis with end-to-end neural networks. *arXiv preprint arXiv:1808.09238*.

Uladzimir Sidarenka. 2016. Potts: the potsdam twitter sentiment corpus. In *Proceedings of the Tenth International Conference on Language Resources and Evaluation (LREC'16)*, pages 1133–1141.

Matheus Gomes Sousa, Kenzo Sakiyama, Lucas de Souza Rodrigues, Pedro Henrique Moraes, Eraldo Rezende Fernandes, and Edson Takashi Matsubara. 2019. Bert for stock market sentiment analysis. In *2019 IEEE 31st International Conference on Tools with Artificial Intelligence (ICTAI)*, pages 1597–1601.

Jie Tao and Xing Fang. 2020. Toward multi-label sentiment analysis: a transfer learning based approach. *Journal of Big Data*, 7:1–26.

Thang Tran, Hung Ba, and Van-Nam Huynh. 2019. Measuring hotel review sentiment: An aspect-based sentiment analysis approach. In *Integrated Uncertainty in Knowledge Modelling and Decision Making: 7th International Symposium, IUKM 2019, Nara, Japan, March 27–29, 2019, Proceedings 7*, pages 393–405. Springer.

Grigorios Tsoumakas and Ioannis Katakis. 2007. Multi-label classification: An overview. *International Journal of Data Warehousing and Mining (IJDWM)*, 3(3):1–13.

Michael Wojatzki, Eugen Ruppert, Sarah Holschneider, Torsten Zesch, and Chris Biemann. 2017. Germeval 2017: Shared task on aspect-based sentiment in social media customer feedback. *Proceedings of the GermEval*, pages 1–12.

Thomas Wolf, Lysandre Debut, Victor Sanh, Julien Chaumond, Clement Delangue, Anthony Moi, Pierric Cistac, Tim Rault, Rémi Louf, Morgan Funtowicz, et al. 2020. Transformers: State-of-the-art natural language processing. In *Proceedings of the 2020 conference on empirical methods in natural language processing: system demonstrations*, pages 38–45.

Ethan Xia, Han Yue, and Hongfu Liu. 2021. Tweet sentiment analysis of the 2020 us presidential election. In *Companion proceedings of the web conference 2021*, pages 367–371.

Hu Xu, Bing Liu, Lei Shu, and Philip S Yu. 2019. Bert post-training for review reading comprehension and aspect-based sentiment analysis. *arXiv preprint arXiv:1904.02232*.

Hang Yan, Junqi Dai, Xipeng Qiu, Zheng Zhang, et al. 2021. A unified generative framework for aspect-based sentiment analysis. *arXiv preprint arXiv:2106.04300*.

Seid Muhie Yimam, Chris Biemann, Richard Eckart de Castilho, and Iryna Gurevych. 2014. Automatic annotation suggestions and custom annotation layers in webanno. In *Proceedings of 52nd Annual Meeting of the Association for Computational Linguistics: System Demonstrations*, pages 91–96.

Yichun Yin, Yangqiu Song, and Ming Zhang. 2017. Document-level multi-aspect sentiment classification as machine comprehension. In *Proceedings of the 2017 conference on empirical methods in natural language processing*, pages 2044–2054.

Min-Ling Zhang and Zhi-Hua Zhou. 2013. A review on multi-label learning algorithms. *IEEE transactions on knowledge and data engineering*, 26(8):1819–1837.

Wenxuan Zhang, Yue Deng, Bing Liu, Sinno Jialin Pan, and Lidong Bing. 2023. Sentiment analysis in the era of large language models: A reality check.

A Appendix

A.1 Possible Combinations for Aspects and Attributes

Aspect	Sub-Aspect/Attribute
Food & Drinks	General (Universal Assessments)
	Price (Restaurant, Bar, Minibar)
	Style (Food Options, Extras)
	Quietness (Loudness in the Dining Area, Privacy)
Hotel	General (Universal Assessments)
	Price (Spa, Wellness, Fitness, Parking)
	Cleanliness
	Style (Furniture, Products, Convenience)
Location	General (Universal Assessments)
	Quietness (Traffic Noise)
	Price (Public Transport, Taxi)
Service	General (Universal Assessments, Friendliness, Helpfullness)
	Cleanliness
Rooms	General (Universal Assessments)
	Price (Stay)
	Quietness (Sleep, Noise)
	Cleanliness
	Style (Furniture, Size, Comfort)

Table 5: All possible combinations of aspects and their attributes.

A.2 Annotators Agreement for the Dataset Annotation

Ann. 1	Ann. 2	Size	Asp	Asp + Attr	Asp + Pol	Asp + Attr + Pol
2	9	200	0.74	0.59	0.66	0.53
4	7	400	0.76	0.61	0.66	0.53
3	13	400	0.72	0.52	0.65	0.49
15	17	400	0.65	0.56	0.62	0.54
5	18	400	0.63	0.5	0.60	0.48
24	25	400	0.66	0.51	0.58	0.47
14	16	400	0.62	0.49	0.56	0.45
8	10	400	0.66	0.55	0.55	0.46
1	20	400	0.58	0.46	0.54	0.43
11	23	400	0.61	0.51	0.52	0.44
12	21	200	0.54	0.42	0.47	0.35
6	22	200	0.55	0.39	0.4	0.29
26	27	400	0.46	0.36	0.37	0.28
2	19	400	0.29	0.25	0.27	0.22
Total/Mean	14	5000	0.61	0.48	0.54	0.43

Table 6: Krippendorf's α values with different levels of granularity for the 14 annotator pairings, sorted by α values of aspect-polarity combinations.

A.3 Dataset Excerpt

```
<documents>

    ...

    <document id="159">
        <opinions>
            <opinion category="SERVICE#HAUPT" polarity="positiv" />
        </opinions>
        <text>Der Service war sehr nett und es hat alles unkompliziert funktioniert</text>
    </document>
    <document id="160">
        <opinions>
            <opinion category="ZIMMER#STYLE" polarity="positiv" />
            <opinion category="ZIMMER#SAUBERKEIT" polarity="positiv" />
        </opinions>
        <text>Das Zimmer war schön eingerichtet, modern und sauber</text>
    </document>

        ...

</documents>
```

Figure 2: Example snippet of the dataset with two entries.

A.4 Class Frequencies for Aspect-Attribute Combinations

Aspect#Attribute	Count	Percentage
Service#General	901	16.0 %
Location#General	861	15.3 %
Rooms#Style	684	12.2 %
Food&Drinks#General	654	11.6 %
Hotel#General	629	11.2 %
...	...	...
Food&Drinks#Price	69	1.2 %
Rooms#Price	37	0.7 %
Location#Price	18	0.3 %
Food&Drinks#Quietness	10	0.2 %
Service#Cleanliness	6	0.1 %

Table 7: Amount of samples per aspect-attribute combination.

A.5 Class Frequencies for Aspect-Polarity Combinations

Aspect + Polarity	Count	Percentage
Hotel - Positive	1,062	18.9 %
Rooms - Positive	937	16.7 %
Service - Positive	743	13.2 %
Location - Positive	685	12.2 %
Food & Drinks - Positive	605	10.8 %
Rooms - Negative	405	7.2 %
Hotel - Negative	209	3.7 %
Hotel - Neutral	186	3.3 %
Location - Neutral	166	3.0 %
Rooms - Neutral	135	2.4 %
Service - Negative	128	2.3 %
Location - Negative	112	2.0 %
Food & Drinks - Neutral	105	1.9 %
Food & Drinks - Negative	103	1.8 %
Service - Neutral	36	0.6 %

Table 8: Amount of samples per aspect-polarity combination.

A.6 Class Frequencies for Aspect-Attribute-Polarity Combinations

Aspect#Attribute:Polarity	Count	Percentage
Service#General:Positive	740	13.1 %
Location#General:Positive	615	10.9 %
Food&Drinks#General:Positive	513	9.1 %
Hotel#General:Positive	485	8.6 %
Rooms#Style:Positive	428	7.6 %
...	...	...
Food&Drinks#Quietness:Positive	3	<0.1 %
Service#Cleanliness:Positive	3	<0.1 %
Service#Cleanliness:Neural	2	<0.1 %
Location#Price:Negative	1	<0.1 %
Service#Cleanliness:Negative	1	<0.1 %

Table 9: Amount of samples per aspect-attribute-polarity tuple.

A.7 Model Parameters and Characteristics of the Pre-Trained BERT models

Model	Parameters	Layers	Attention Heads	Training Data	Hidden States
deepset-gbert-large	335 M	24	16	161 GB	768
dbmdz-bert-base-german-uncased	110 M	12	12	16 GB	768
distilbert-base-german-cased	66 M	12	12	16 GB	1024

Table 10: Model parameters and characteristics for each of the 3 pre-trained BERT models.

A.8 Hyperparameter Configurations for the Best Runs

Task	Language Model	Learning Rate	Batch Size	Epochs	Runtime
Aspect	deepset-gbert-large	2.01 E-05	32	4	3 m 53 s
	dbmdz-bert-base-german-uncased	3.90 E-05	8	4	4 m 00 s
	distilbert-base-german-cased	5.00 E-05	8	3	1 m 51 s
Aspect + Attribute	deepset-gbert-large	2.06 E-05	8	4	10 m 07 s
	dbmdz-bert-base-german-uncased	2.82 E-05	8	3	3 m 04 s
	distilbert-base-german-cased	4.83 E-05	8	3	1 m 51 s
Aspect + Polarity	deepset-gbert-large	3.50 E-05	8	3	7 m 36 s
	dbmdz-bert-base-german-uncased	4.66 E-05	8	4	3 m 56 s
	distilbert-base-german-cased	3.97 E-05	8	4	2 m 26 s
Aspect + Attribute + Polarity	deepset-gbert-large	2.28 E-05	8	4	10 m 07 s
	dbmdz-bert-base-german-uncased	4.42 E-05	8	4	3 m 58 s
	distilbert-base-german-cased	4.99 E-05	8	3	1 m 51 s

Table 11: Best hyperparameter configuration for each model per task. Average runtime is given for a single train-eval run.

Political claim identification and categorization in a multilingual setting: First experiments

Urs Zaberer and **Sebastian Padó** and **Gabriella Lapesa**
Institut für Maschinelle Sprachverarbeitung
University of Stuttgart, Germany
{urs.zaberer,sebastian.pado,gabriella.lapesa}@ims.uni-stuttgart.de

Abstract

The identification and classification of political claims is an important step in the analysis of political newspaper reports; however, resources for this task are few and far between. This paper explores different strategies for the cross-lingual projection of political claims analysis. We conduct experiments on a German dataset, DebateNet2.0, covering the policy debate sparked by the 2015 refugee crisis. Our evaluation involves two tasks (claim identification and categorization), three languages (German, English, and French) and two methods (machine translation – the best method in our experiments – and multilingual embeddings).

1 Introduction

The identification of political claims in news is a core step in the analysis of policy debates. *Discourse networks*, whose nodes correspond to claims and the actors who advance them, provide a rich source of information on phenomena such as formation of coalitions (who agrees with whom), shift in salience due to external events (e.g., migration waves making the issues of refugee accommodation more central in a debate), emergence of leadership, and polarization of a discourse (Leifeld and Haunss, 2012; Koopmans and Statham, 1999; Hajer, 1993).

Political claims are defined as demands, proposals or criticism that are *supported* or *opposed* by an *actor* (a person or a group of persons). Political claims generally form a call to action: they refer to something that should (or should not) be done in a policy domain (e.g., assigning empty flats to refugees). Thus, political claims are related to, but add a new perspective on, the Argument Mining question of what claims are, and what are the best strategies for modeling them across domains (Daxenberger et al., 2017; Schaefer et al., 2022).

The potential and challenges of the NLP support to political claim analysis have been thoroughly explored in the recent years in a monolingual setting (Chen et al., 2020; Dayanik et al., 2022); however, there are very few resources available in multilingual or crosslingual settings. Thus, there is little work on the comparison of policy debates in different countries, either completely automatic, or semi-automatic (supporting the inductive development of annotation guidelines in a new language).

This paper reports on cross-lingual pilot experiments on two tasks (claim identification and categorization), comparing two well known approaches to cross-lingual transfer in NLP in general, and argument mining in particular: machine translation and multilingual embeddings (Eger et al., 2018; Toledo-Ronen et al., 2020). We first work with a reference dataset for the German migration policy debate (Blokker et al., 2023), and on its projection to English and French, before moving on to a newly annotated English test set on the same topic. Machine Translation turns out to be the best cross-lingual projection strategy.

2 Experimental Setting

2.1 Tasks

This work focusses on two constituent tasks of political claim analysis (Padó et al., 2019). Our first task is **claim identification**, performed as a binary classification task at the sentence level. Our second task is **claim categorization**, phrased as a multi-label classification task at the sentence level.[1]

2.2 Data

We carry out two experiments. In the first one, we use a German corpus, DebateNet, which we automatically translate into English and French: this represents a cross-lingual transfer within the same media outlet. In the second experiment, we transfer our DebateNet models to an original English dataset based on the *Guardian* newspaper.

[1] For our evaluation in the claim categorization task, we consider all claims in the manually annotated gold standard.

Proceedings of the 19th Conference on Natural Language Processing (KONVENS 2023), pages 219–228
September 18–22, 2023. ©2023 Association for Computational Linguistics

DebateNet 2.0. Blokker et al. (2023) is a dataset[2] targeting the German public debate on migration policies in the context of the 2015 so-called 'refugee crisis'. It is based on 700 articles from the German quality newspaper *die Tageszeitung (taz)* with a total of 16402 sentences.

Political claims are annotated as textual spans, and each claim span is associated with at least one of 110 categories drawn from a theory-based codebook (annotation guidelines). Around 15% of sentences are annotated to contain a claim span. In total, the dataset contains 3442 claim spans corresponding to 4417 claim labels (i.e., each claim span is associated with an average of 1.3 claim categories). Annotations are first proposed by pairs of students of political science, with an inter-coder reliability is $\kappa = 0.59$ (Padó et al., 2019), and then accepted, rejected or merged by domain experts. We randomly split DebateNet into a training, development, and test set with a ratio of 80:10:10.

Crucially for our experiments, the 110 fine-grained categories are organized into 8 top-level categories which encode general domains of the migration policy field. In the claim categorization experiments in this paper we focus on the 8 top-level categories. Table 5 in the Appendix shows them with the percentage of claims annotated for each category and illustrative examples.

Guardian test set To compare German news translated into English to actual UK news, we collected an English-language test set of 36 articles from the British quality newspaper Guardian, extracted from the World News section and published in 2015. To make our test set as compatible as possible with *DebateNet2.0*, we look at the five months most represented in *DebateNet2.0* and within each month sample from articles written in the seven-day spans with the highest frequency of articles in *DebateNet2.0*. Articles were further filtered by keywords (*migrant, refugee, asylum, Germany, Syria, Afghanistan* and their morphological and syntactic variants) and by the mention of the most salient political actors (politician and parties).

The Guardian test set was manually annotated by a native speaker, a MSc-level student in Computational Linguistics, based on the *DebateNet2.0* guidelines. Claims were identified and assigned to one of the 8 top-level categories described in the previous section. Across the 36 articles with 1347 sentences, the test set contains 82 claim spans which correspond to 101 claim categories (mean of 1.2 categories per span).[3] Refer to Table 5 in the Appendix for the distribution of claim categories.

2.3 Methods

2.3.1 Projection methods

With the German DebateNet2.0 as our starting point, and the goal of testing the feasibility of cross-lingual projection to English and French (as target languages), we compare the two most established projection methods (Eger et al., 2018; Toledo-Ronen et al., 2020): machine translation (to make the modeling task monolingual) and multilingual embeddings (to let the model bridge the language gap implicitly). This yields three experimental conditions:

Translate-train: We machine-translate the German training data into the target languages and fine-tune a monolingual target-language model on it, to be evaluated on the target-language test data.[4]

Translate-test: We machine-translate the test data into German (as described above) and apply a monolingual German model fine-tuned on the original German data to it. For the DebateNet experiments in Section 3.1, we can only simulate this setting, as we do not have genuine foreign-language test data. We simulate it with a back-translation: first, we machine-translate the German DebateNet test set into the target language (EN/FR); then we translate the simulated EN/FR test sets back into German. It is only on the Guardian test set (Section 4) that we can fully evaluate our models in the translate-test configuration.

Multilingual: We employ multilingual embeddings, fine-tune them on the original German data, and apply the resulting classifier on the target language test data, exploiting the model's internal alignment of the source and target languages.

For both claim identification and classification, we re-implement standard Transformer-based models from the literature (Dayanik and Padó, 2020). We use BERT as well as its German, French and multilingual versions. Details on the classifier setups for both tasks follow below.

[2] http://hdl.handle.net/11022/ 1007-0000-0007-DB07-B

[3] 30 claims, albeit identified by our annotator, could not be classified in any categories of the codebook.

[4] We uses the DeepL translator via its web interface on a free trial of the "advanced" plan as of August 2022.

2.3.2 Claim identification

Translate-train: For English, we select the uncased model (`bert-base-uncased`) based on its performance on the development set, and we set learning rate to 5e-5 and warm-up steps to 30. The same configuration is used for the German monolingual baseline. For French, we select the base version of CamemBERT, `camembert-base`, with a learning rate of 4e-5 with 30 warm-up steps.

Translate-test: we employ a German BERT model, `bert-base-german-cased`, fine-tuned on the original German dataset. The hyperparameters are the same as for English translate-train.

Multilingual: Based on performance on the development set, we select the cased variant of the multilingual BERT from the Huggingface transformer library, `bert-base-multilingual-cased`. Training this model requires a lower learning rate of 2.5e-5 and correspondingly more epochs.

2.3.3 Claim categorization

Translate-train: For the English model, we assess both the cased and uncased versions. Since the uncased one (`bert-base-uncased`) again performs slightly better, we select it and use a learning rate of 5e-5. Experiments on the corresponding development sets establishes 25 warm-up steps as a reasonable choice for all configurations in Task 2. The French model – the same as for the claim identification task – requires a learning rate of 4e-5.

Translate-test: We employ `bert-base-german-cased` with a learning rate of 4e-5. The same model is also used for the monolingual German baseline model.

Multilingual: Based on performance on the development set, we select `bert-base-multilingual-uncased` with a low learning rate of 3e-5 and correspondingly more epochs.

3 Experiment 1: Within-outlet cross-lingual transfer

3.1 Claim Identification on DebateNet

The left-hand side of Table 1 shows results for the first main experiment, comparing the translate-train, translate-test, and the multilingual embedding approaches to claim identification to a monolingual baseline.[5] For comparison, we also run

Setup	Train	Test	Id	Cat
BL (mono)	de	de	56.2	**70.5**
Translate-train	en	en	**57.3**	67.8
Translate-train	fr	fr	**57.4**	69.7
Translate-test	de	de-en	55.8	69.5
Translate-test	de	de-fr	58.3	69.8
Multilingual	de	en	45.8	50.3
Multilingual	de	fr	51.1	51.0
Multilingual†	de	de-en	52.0	60.0
Multilingual†	en	de	55.4	64.1

Table 1: DebateNet test set results: F1 scores (positive class for claim identification (ID), macro average for claim categorization (Cat)). BL (mono): monolingual baseline.

the translate-train and translate-test approaches on the multilingual model (multilingual:en:de and multilingual:de:de-en). The language labels de-en and de-fr stand for German data translated into EN or FR and back-translated into German.

The main contrast of this set of experiments is the one between the translate-train approach and the multilingual embeddings approach with respect to their performance on the target languages (EN/FR). For both target languages, the translate-train approach outperforms the monolingual baseline and the multilingual embedding approach. We ascribe this (small) performance gain to the higher quality of the embeddings available for the target languages: The monolingual English model, `bert-base`, is trained on a much larger corpus (English Wikipedia and BookCorpus) than `bert-base-german`, which is only trained on the significantly smaller German Wikipedia. The French model's training corpus is also over ten times larger than the German one. This also means the translation process, albeit not perfect, has not degraded the claim "signal" in the training data.

This point is also supported by the results for the "simulated" translate-test approach, which (cf. Section 2.3) can be considered a test of translation quality. Since the performance is in line with the monolingual baseline (de-en) or even slightly superior to it (de-fr)[6], the claim signal is preserved

[5] Unless indicated by a dagger †, reported values for all conditions are the averages of two runs to reduce variance.

[6] The exact reason for the improved performance in the de-fr setup is to be further investigated. Given that we consider the translate-test setup in DebateNet as a translation quality check, the result is not highlighted in bold even if higher than

	Target: yes	Target: no
Predicted: yes	71	39
Predicted: no	75	822

Table 2: Claim identification (DebateNet) confusion matrix of the best model for English (translate-train)

through the back-translation process.

In contrast, the multilingual embeddings perform poorly, below the monolingual baseline. The bottom part of Table 1 shows additional experiments we carried out to better understand this result. We find that a monolingual setup with multilingual embeddings (DE-DE) still performs below the monolingual baseline, but the performance gap is narrower than for the cross-lingual setups (DE-EN and DE-FR). Reverting the direction of the mapping, contrasting the performance of English-German (55.6) vs. German-English (45.8), again speaks in favor of the German representations being the weak point – the training data for the English-German multilingual embeddings setup is the same as that of the translate-train approach.

The confusion matrix for the best cross-lingual model for English (translate-train), Table 2, shows many fewer false negatives than false positives (i.e., a high precision). Regarding application to the (semi-)automatic extraction of discourse networks, this outcome is complementary to the high-recall approach applied by Haunss et al. (2020) to the German annotation in DebateNet, but lends itself to high-precision human-in-the-loop approaches like the one proposed by Ein-Dor et al. (2019) for argument mining.

Error Analysis. The misclassified instances provide some more insight into the model. For instance, we might expect the word "fordern" ("demand", "call for") to frequently appear in claims and therefore lead the model to make a positive prediction. Indeed, in the misclassified instances of the German-French translate-test model, forms of the word "fordern" or "Forderung" are 13 times more likely to be FP than FN even though there are almost twice as many FNs. We can therefore conclude that this word influences the model in the expected way. We bolster these observations with more formal methods: using saliency-based analysis (Simonyan et al., 2014) we can assign each token a relevance for the model's prediction. The results partially confirm this: the token "fordert" gets scores above 0.9 throughout. However, other forms, like the infinitive, receive lower scores, presumably because the 3rd person singular is more highly associated with concrete claiming situations.

translate-train.

Saliency scores are highly correlated between models and between languages. E.g., the sentence "Der bayerische Ministerpräsident Horst Seehofer begrüßte die Pläne" and its corresponding English version 'Bavaria's prime minister Horst Seehofer welcomed the plans.', are both labeled as claims. In both cases, the highest saliency is assigned to "Pläne"/"plans". A systematic comparison of scores among models is however complicated by the differences in tokenizations among embedding models. Alternatively, we can compare instances misclassified by different models. Here, we observe large overlap. On one test run, the multilingual German-French model misclassified 122 out of 1007 test instances, while the monolingual English model misclassified 120 instances. These instances have an overlap of 58% (random assignment, should result in 12% overlap). This suggests that the models struggle with the same instances. A first qualitative inspection at such "difficult" instances has ruled out the impact of proper names, length of sentences as well as the type of involved actors; further analysis in this direction is required.

3.2 Claim Categorization on DebateNet

The right-hand side of Table 1 shows the results for the claim categorization task (F1 macro over all classes; Tables 6–9 in the Appendix provide per-category results). Unsurprisingly, this fine-grained task is more challenging for cross-lingual transfer. None of the experimental configurations beats the monolingual baseline. As in claim id, translate-train outperforms multilingual embeddings.

Error analysis. Inspection of sentences shows that many misclassifications arise from misleading local lexical material in the sentences. For example, "Die SPD findet dies könnte die Integration unterstützen" ("The Social Democratic party believes this could support integration") includes the word 'integration' which is a strong cue for the claim category 'integration', which the model predicts. However, the correct category is 'residency', as becomes clear from the broader context of the article. Another example is: "Die sollen ja auch in der Gesellschaft ankommen" ("They must arrive

Setup	Train	Test	Id	Cat
translate-train	en	en	**25.5**	51.0
translate-test	de	de-en	20.6	**53.4**
multilingual	de	en	20.0	39.0

Table 3: Guardian test set results for claim identification (Id, F1 of positive class) and claim categorization (Cat, macro F1)

in society after all"), with misleading cue 'society' indicating claim category 'society' and gold category 'integration'. A saliency analysis, as before, confirmed this pattern: the "red herring" cues consistently receive the highest saliency scores in the sentences. Notably, the error pattern persists in the case of literal translations, but disppears when the translation changes the wording ('mit Sicherheit' – "with security/certainty" $\rightarrow$ 'certainly').

4 Experiment 2: Cross-outlet cross-lingual transfer

Results on the Guardian test set are shown in Table 3. For claim identification, the translate-train approach outperforms the other approaches, confirming the trend seen on the DebateNet data. For claim categorization, translate-test outperforms translate-train and multilingual embeddings. Both of these results are in line with our findings in Exp. 1.

For both tasks, we see a substantial decrease of performance on the Guardian data (-30 points for claim identification, -15 points for claim categorization). Since our previous experiment also used English data, this difference cannot be due to cross-lingual differences, but rather to differences between the two outlets, taz and the Guardian. Indeed, we see that a British newspaper is likely to report differently on German domestic affairs than a German newspaper, which leads to differences in claim form and substance: They tend to focus on the internationally most visible actors and report claims on a more coarse-grained level. They also overreport the claim categories most relevant for the British readership: claims migration control account for 22% of all claims in DebateNet but for 34% in the Guardian. In contrast, domestic (German) residency issues make up 14% of the DebateNet claims but only 2% of the Guardian claims. See Table 5 in the Appendix for a detailed breakdown and example claims.

	Target: yes	Target: no
Predicted: yes	29	147
Predicted: no	83	1088

Table 4: Claim identification (Guardian): confusion matrix of the best model for English (translate-train)

Thus, even if the Guardian claims might be structurally easier to recognize, the cross-outlet differences in claim distribution make transferring model representations from DebateNet to the Guardian hard. The confusion matrix for claim identification in Table 4 shows a low-precision scenario, in contrast to the high precision of the cross-lingual within-DebateNet setup.

It is interesting to note that claim identification suffers much more (-30 points) than claim categorization (-15 points), indicating that the model of claim topics survives the transfer to another outlet better than the model of what constitutes a claim.

5 Conclusion

This paper explores different strategies for the cross-lingual projection of political claims analysis from German into English and French. Our experiments establish the potential of machine translation for both claim identification and categorization, setting the stage for further investigations on the factors affecting projection performance and on the applicability of cross-lingual transfer for similar analyses. Multilingual embeddings yielded worse results, in line with previous analyses arguing that they attempt to solve a harder (since more open-ended) task than Machine Translation (Pires et al., 2019; Barnes and Klinger, 2019). We find that the language is not the only relevant dimension, though: in fact, the differences in presentation between German and British articles on German affairs go substantially beyond the language gap (Vu et al., 2019).

Acknowledgements

This study was partially funded by Deutsche Forschungsgemeinschaft (DFG) through MARDY (Modeling Argumentation Dynamics) within SPP RATIO and by Bundesministerium für Bildung und Forschung (BMBF) through E-DELIB (Powering up e-deliberation: towards AI-supported moderation). We are grateful to Brandon Sorensen, who annotated the Guardian test set.

Limitations

Our main experiment was limited to German, English, and French, three typologically very similar languages. Generalization to more distant languages is presumably harder, but was outside the scope of our study. Our Guardian test set is very small (albeit not significantly smaller than out-of-domain gold sets often gathered for validation purposes), and annotating it was challenging due to the need to apply a codebook developed for the German debate to an English source. We are currently working on improving the size and quality of our test set.

While our experiments are reassuring as regards translation quality, we cannot exclude that translation biases may have been introduced in the data. We are also aware that DeepL is not the only option for automatic translation; evaluating different translation methods, however, falls outside the scope of this work.

Ethical Considerations

At the level of datasets and annotations, we employed an existing dataset (DebateNet2.0). Our own annotation contribution (the Guardian test set) was based on publicly available data; moreover, the annotation task was carried out following best practices. The Guardian test set is available upon request.

At the modeling level, we use previously defined models that are publicly available; in this sense, our contribution does not raise new ethical questions (e.g. in terms of misuse potential). To the contrary, our focus is on understanding how these models transfer across languages and what biases can potentially arise in this transfer, as shown by our focus on error analysis.

References

Jeremy Barnes and Roman Klinger. 2019. Embedding projection for targeted cross-lingual sentiment: Model comparisons and a real-world study. *Journal of Artificial Intelligence Research*, 66:691–742.

Nico Blokker, Andre Blessing, Erenay Dayanik, Jonas Kuhn, Sebastian Padó, and Gabriella Lapesa. 2023. Between welcome culture and border fence: The European refugee crisis in German newspaper reports. *Language Resources and Evaluation*, 57:121–153.

Wei-Fan Chen, Khalid Al Khatib, Benno Stein, and Henning Wachsmuth. 2020. Detecting media bias in news articles using Gaussian bias distributions. In *Findings of the Association for Computational Linguistics: EMNLP 2020*, pages 4290–4300, Online. Association for Computational Linguistics.

Johannes Daxenberger, Steffen Eger, Ivan Habernal, Christian Stab, and Iryna Gurevych. 2017. What is the essence of a claim? cross-domain claim identification. In *Proceedings of the 2017 Conference on Empirical Methods in Natural Language Processing*, pages 2055–2066, Copenhagen, Denmark. Association for Computational Linguistics.

Erenay Dayanik, Andre Blessing, Nico Blokker, Sebastian Haunss, Jonas Kuhn, Gabriella Lapesa, and Sebastian Pado. 2022. Improving neural political statement classification with class hierarchical information. In *Findings of the Association for Computational Linguistics: ACL 2022*, pages 2367–2382, Dublin, Ireland. Association for Computational Linguistics.

Erenay Dayanik and Sebastian Padó. 2020. Masking actor information leads to fairer political claims detection. In *Proceedings of the 58th Annual Meeting of the Association for Computational Linguistics*, pages 4385–4391, Online. Association for Computational Linguistics.

Steffen Eger, Johannes Daxenberger, Christian Stab, and Iryna Gurevych. 2018. Cross-lingual argumentation mining: Machine translation (and a bit of projection) is all you need! In *Proceedings of the 27th International Conference on Computational Linguistics*, pages 831–844, Santa Fe, New Mexico, USA. Association for Computational Linguistics.

Liat Ein-Dor, Eyal Shnarch, Lena Dankin, Alon Halfon, Benjamin Sznajder, Ariel Gera, Carlos Alzate, Martin Gleize, Leshem Choshen, Yufang Hou, Yonatan Bilu, Ranit Aharonov, and Noam Slonim. 2019. Corpus wide argument mining - a working solution. In *AAAI Conference on Artificial Intelligence*.

Maarten A Hajer. 1993. Discourse Coalitions and the Institutionalization of Practice: The Case of Acid Rain in Britain. In *The Argumentative Turn in Policy Analysis and Planning*, pages 43–76. Duke University Press.

Sebastian Haunss, Jonas Kuhn, Sebastian Pado, Andre Blessing, Nico Blokker, Erenay Dayanik, and Gabriella Lapesa. 2020. Integrating manual and automatic annotation for the creation of discourse network data sets. *Politics and Governance*, 8(2).

Ruud Koopmans and Paul Statham. 1999. Political Claims Analysis: Integrating Protest Event And Political Discourse Approaches. *Mobilization*, 4(2):203–221.

Philip Leifeld and Sebastian Haunss. 2012. Political Discourse Networks and the Conflict over Software Patents in Europe. *European Journal of Political Research*, 51(3):382–409.

Sebastian Padó, Andre Blessing, Nico Blokker, Erenay Dayanik, Sebastian Haunss, and Jonas Kuhn. 2019. Who sides with whom? towards computational construction of discourse networks for political debates. In *Proceedings of the 57th Annual Meeting of the Association for Computational Linguistics*, pages 2841–2847, Florence, Italy. Association for Computational Linguistics.

Telmo Pires, Eva Schlinger, and Dan Garrette. 2019. How multilingual is multilingual BERT? In *Proceedings of the 57th Annual Meeting of the Association for Computational Linguistics*, pages 4996–5001, Florence, Italy. Association for Computational Linguistics.

Robin Schaefer, René Knaebel, and Manfred Stede. 2022. On selecting training corpora for cross-domain claim detection. In *Proceedings of the 9th Workshop on Argument Mining*, pages 181–186, Online and in Gyeongju, Republic of Korea. International Conference on Computational Linguistics.

Karen Simonyan, Andrea Vedaldi, and Andrew Zisserman. 2014. Deep inside convolutional networks: Visualising image classification models and saliency maps. In *2nd International Conference on Learning Representations, ICLR 2014, Banff, AB, Canada, April 14-16, 2014, Workshop Track Proceedings*.

Orith Toledo-Ronen, Matan Orbach, Yonatan Bilu, Artem Spector, and Noam Slonim. 2020. Multilingual argument mining: Datasets and analysis. In *Findings of the Association for Computational Linguistics: EMNLP 2020*, pages 303–317, Online. Association for Computational Linguistics.

Hong Tien Vu, Yuchen Liu, and Duc Vinh Tran. 2019. Nationalizing a global phenomenon: A study of how the press in 45 countries and territories portrays climate change. *Global Environmental Change*, 58:101942.

A Appendix

A.1 Datasets: quantitative details and comparison

Class	Label	%DN	%G	Examples
C1	Controlling Migration	22	34	*DN*: A fixed resettlement programme is needed, with binding annual admission quotas. *G*: Angela Merkel stressed the need for a fairer distribution of refugees across the EU
C2	Residency	14	2	*DN*: These urgent procedures shall be carried out in special reception facilities. *G*: We have to find suitable accommodation for all of them.
C3	Integration	9	3	*DN*: The CDU insists on an integration obligation for migrants. *G*: Michael Fuchs called on the government to set up language courses and to send job centre employees to assess newcomers
C4	Domestic Security	3	8	*DN*: The head of the police union, RainerWendt, has called for a "ban mile around refugee shelters". *G*: We should not hand over our streets to hollow rallying cries
C5	Foreign Policy	16	11	*DN*: The current problems with the refugees must nevertheless be solved at European and international level, she said. *G*: Tomas de Maizière said pressure should be applied to rejectionist nations such as Hungary, Slowakia and the Czech Republic.
C6	Economy + Labour Market	3	7	*DN*: A condition for waiving such proof, however, must be that collective bargaining conditions or a minimum wage apply in order to prevent dirty competition to the detriment of all employees. *G*: Folkerts-Landau said the influx of refugees has the potential not just to invigorate our economy but to protect prosperity for the future generations
C7	Society	17	21	*DN*: And Reinhard Marx, chairman of the Catholic Bishops' Conference, criticized the strict separation between war refugees and economic refugees. *G*: As chancellor, I come to the defense of Muslims, most of whom are upright, constitutionally loyal citizens
C8	Procedures	15	14	*DN*: The federal government is planning a new law to speed up asylum procedures. *G*: Gerd Mueller called on Tuesday for the EU to appoint a European Refugees commissioner and said it had to treat the problem with more urgency

Table 5: Claim categories: class, labels, distribution (percentage of total claims), and example claim in DebateNet2.0 (DN) (manually translated into English) and Guardian test set (G).

A.2 Per-category Results

Class	#instances in test	Precision	Recall	F1 score
C1 (Controlling Migration)	35	0.67	0.83	0.74
C2 (Residency)	2	0.66	0.74	0.70
C3 (Integration)	3	0.66	0.60	0.63
C4 (Domestic Security)	8	0.50	0.44	0.47
C5 (Foreign policy)	11	0.87	0.76	0.81
C6 (Economy)	7	0.88	0.50	0.64
C7 (Society)	21	0.70	0.67	0.69
C8 (Procedures)	14	0.75	0.70	0.72
micro avg		0.71	0.71	0.71
macro avg		0.71	0.66	0.67

Table 6: Claim categorization: precision, recall and F1 values for the different classes, translate-train French

Class	#instances in test	Precision	Recall	F1 score
C1 (Controlling Migration)	35	0.66	0.74	0.70
C2 (Residency)	2	0.68	0.70	0.69
C3 (Integration)	3	0.72	0.51	0.60
C4 (Domestic Security)	8	0.40	0.33	0.36
C5 (Foreign policy)	11	0.85	0.65	0.73
C6 (Economy)	7	0.80	0.57	0.67
C7 (Society)	21	0.77	0.56	0.65
C8 (Procedures)	14	0.76	0.58	0.66
micro avg		0.71	0.62	0.67
macro avg		0.70	0.58	0.63

Table 7: Claim categorization: precision, recall and F1 values for the different classes, translate-train English

Class	#instances in test	Precision	Recall	F1 score
C1 (Controlling Migration)	35	0.76	0.71	0.73
C2 (Residency)	2	0.76	0.69	0.72
C3 (Integration)	3	0.72	0.58	0.64
C4 (Domestic Security)	8	0.40	0.33	0.36
C5 (Foreign policy)	11	0.86	0.65	0.74
C6 (Economy)	7	0.83	0.36	0.50
C7 (Society)	21	0.86	0.56	0.68
C8 (Procedures)	14	0.73	0.61	0.66
micro avg		0.76	0.62	0.68
macro avg		0.74	0.56	0.63

Table 8: Claim categorization: precision, recall and F1 values for the different classes, German baseline

Class	#instances in test	Precision	Recall	F1 score
C1 (Controlling Migration)	35	0.74	0.78	0.76
C2 (Residency)	2	0.69	0.84	0.76
C3 (Integration)	3	0.72	0.62	0.67
C4 (Domestic Security)	8	0.48	0.61	0.54
C5 (Foreign policy)	11	0.81	0.81	0.81
C6 (Economy)	7	0.70	0.50	0.58
C7 (Society)	21	0.72	0.66	0.69
C8 (Procedures)	14	0.70	0.68	0.69
micro avg		0.72	0.73	0.72
macro avg		0.70	0.69	0.69

Table 9: Claim categorization: precision, recall and F1 values for the different classes. Model: best cross-lingual model (translate-test)

Class	Precision	Recall	F1 score
C1 (Controlling Migration)	0.66	0.66	0.66
C2 (Residency)	0.25	0.50	0.33
C3 (Integration)	0.50	0.67	0.57
C4 (Domestic Security)	1.00	0.25	0.40
C5 (Foreign policy)	0.45	0.82	0.58
C6 (Economy)	0.50	0.29	0.36
C7 (Society)	0.76	0.76	0.76
C8 (Procedures)	0.57	0.29	0.38
micro avg	0.61	0.58	0.60
macro avg	0.59	0.53	0.51

Table 10: Claim categorization: precision, recall and F1 values for the different classes on Guardian dataset. Model: translate-test

Policy Domain Prediction from Party Manifestos with Adapters and Knowledge Enhanced Transformers

Hsiao-Chu Yu **Ines Rehbein** **Simone Paolo Ponzetto**
Data and Web Science Group
University of Mannheim
hsiao-chu.yu@students.uni-mannheim.de, {rehbein,ponzetto}@uni-mannheim.de

Abstract

Recent work has shown the potential of knowledge injection into transformer-based pre-trained language models for improving model performance for a number of NLI benchmark tasks. Motivated by this success, we test the potential of knowledge injection for an application in the political domain and study whether we can improve results for policy domain prediction, that is, for predicting fine-grained policy topics and stance for party manifestos. We experiment with three types of knowledge, namely (1) domain-specific knowledge via continued pre-training on in-domain data, (2) lexical semantic knowledge, and (3) factual knowledge about named entities. In our experiments, we use adapter modules as a parameter-efficient way for knowledge injection into transformers. Our results show a consistent positive effect for domain adaptation via continued pre-training and small improvements when replacing full model training with a task-specific adapter. The injected knowledge, however, only yields minor improvements over full training and fails to outperform the task-specific adapter without external knowledge, raising the question which type of knowledge is needed to solve this task.

1 Introduction

Identifying policy domains in political text such as parliamentary speeches or party manifestos is an important ingredient for many analyses in political science. This type of information is crucial for studying party competition and voting behaviour or for investigating agenda setting and framing, and for many other research questions in the field. Many research projects have thus addressed this problem, either by creating annotated data sets for manual and automated analyses (Baumgartner et al., 2006; Bevan, 2019; Volkens et al., 2019b) or by developing systems for policy domain prediction (Subramanian et al., 2017; Glavaš et al., 2017; Abercrombie et al., 2019; Koh et al., 2021). This task, however, is quite challenging, due to the large number of fine-grained topic labels in the respective coding schemes. For many of these labels, only a small number of annotated instances exist in the training set. Furthermore, as this type of annotation has been adopted in different research projects and across countries and time, the annotations themselves include inconsistencies, as the defined classes might have been interpreted differently by the coders, depending on their background, situational context and training.

One way to address (at least part of) this problem is to enrich the models with external information, in order to make them more robust to inconsistencies in the data and to provide more information especially for the infrequent labels. A number of studies have looked into this problem, with promising results. Previous work has demonstrated improvements for various natural language understanding tasks by incorporating general human knowledge presented in knowledge bases (Zhang et al., 2019; Sun et al., 2019; Peters et al., 2019; Lauscher et al., 2020b) and by adapting pre-trained language models (PLMs) to specific domains (Lee et al., 2020; Beltagy et al., 2019; Gururangan et al., 2020). However, these approaches are resource intensive as they typically require either re-training the entire model from scratch (Lauscher et al., 2020b) or tuning pre-trained parameters (Zhang et al., 2019) on auxiliary pre-training tasks.

To alleviate these problems, researchers have turned to the lightweight adapter architecture (Houlsby et al., 2019; Pfeiffer et al., 2021) for knowledge integration. The *adapter module* (or simply *adapter*) is a set of parameters inserted into the original transformer layers in the pre-trained model. Unlike the standard fine-tuning of BERT-based models where the entire model is updated, the adapter-based tuning only updates the newly inserted adapter parameters when the model is tuned on downstream tasks, while the underlying pre-

Proceedings of the 19th Conference on Natural Language Processing (KONVENS 2023), pages 229–244
September 18–22, 2023. ©2023 Association for Computational Linguistics

trained model is frozen. This approach makes model tuning more efficient, due to the smaller size of parameters that need to be trained. In addition to its efficiency, several studies have demonstrated the effectiveness of adapters for knowledge injection into BERT-based models (Hung et al., 2022; Meng et al., 2021; Lauscher et al., 2020a).

Building upon this body of work, we use the adapter-based approach to incorporate multiple knowledge sources into multilingual RoBERTa (XLM-R) (Conneau et al., 2020). Different from past studies that mostly focused on integrating single knowledge sources, we enrich the pre-trained language model with multiple types of knowledge: (i) domain knowledge, (ii) lexical semantic knowledge (such as word synonyms) and (iii) factual knowledge about named entities (e.g., Angela Merkel is a politician). The main research questions addressed in this paper are:

RQ1 How does external knowledge, such as domain knowledge and structured knowledge from knowledge bases, impact the language model's capability to understand natural language in the political science domain?

RQ2 Can we use adapters to inject this knowledge into a pre-trained language model in a more parameter-efficient manner?

The paper is structured as follows. In Section 2, we outline related work on topic and policy prediction in the political domain and review recent studies that incorporate adapters into PLMs. Section 3 presents our approach for adapter-based knowledge injection, and Section 4 discusses our results for predicting policy domains from party manifestos, using adapters and external domain and world knowledge. In Section 5, we conclude and outline future work.

2 Related Work

2.1 Predicting Manifesto Policy Domains

Many studies in the context of computational political text analysis have focused on topic or policy issue prediction, using dedicated datasets created within the Comparative Agenda Project (Baumgartner et al., 2006; Bevan, 2019) or the Comparative Manifesto Project (CMP) (Mikhaylov et al., 2012; Werner et al., 2014). In our work, we use the Manifesto Corpus from the CMP which includes a large collection of party manifestos from over 50 countries. Each document in the corpus has been segmented into "quasi-sentences" (mostly clauses) and has been manually categorized into eight coarse-grained policy domains (see Table 1). Those main classes are further subdivided into a set of 57 fine-grained policy goals and issues that also encode the author's stance towards a specific policy issue (positive/negative), as illustrated in Example 2.1.

Label	Policy Domain	% of quasi-sentences
1	External Relations	6.6
2	Freedom & Democracy	4.7
3	Political System	10.6
4	Economy	24.9
5	Welfare & Quality of Life	30.9
6	Fabric of Society	11.2
7	Social Groups	10.0
0	Not Categorized	1.1

Table 1: Distribution of major policy domains in the manifesto dataset of Koh et al. (2021).

Ex. 2.1

"We view the diversity of our nation not as a liability, but rather as a shared strength and source of pride"

Main topic: FABRIC OF SOCIETY
Minor topic: MULTICULTURALISM → POSITIVE

2.2 Introducing domain-specific knowledge into PLMs

Transfer learning based on large, pre-trained language models (PLMs) has shown to improve model performance of transformer-based architectures for a wide range of NLP tasks (Devlin et al., 2019; Liu et al., 2019). The model is trained on large amounts of text, using self-supervision, which provides the model with information about language structure and the meaning of words in context. Exploiting this generic knowledge to specific downstream tasks reduces the amount of training data needed for each task. However, many domains require the model to understand specialised vocabulary terms and information that the model cannot learn from generic corpora such as Wikipedia. Below, we describe a number of techniques that have been proposed to address this shortcoming.

Domain adaptation Many studies have demonstrated that continued pre-training of PLMs on domain-specific corpora before fine-tuning them for the final task can improve model performance of transformer-based models. BioBERT (Lee et al., 2020) and ClinicalBERT (Alsentzer et al., 2019) both adopted the continual pre-training framework. Other work has skipped pre-training on generic text collections and, instead, pre-trained domain-specific models from scratch (Beltagy et al., 2019; Gu et al., 2022). In our work, we use PolSciBERT, a PLM that has been adapted to the political domain through continual pre-training.

External knowledge injection Numerous studies have shown that integrating knowledge graphs into BERT-based models is beneficial for natural language understanding tasks (Sun et al., 2019; Zhang et al., 2019; Peters et al., 2019; Lauscher et al., 2020b; Peinelt et al., 2021). These studies mainly focused on two types of knowledge: facts about entities and linguistic knowledge. Zhang et al. (2019) aligned named entities in the Wikipedia corpora with entities in the knowledge base Wikidata (Vrandečić and Krötzsch, 2014) and trained the model, ERNIE, to learn the alignment, based on an *entity alignment masking objective*. Sun et al. (2019) proposed Baidu-ERNIE, which was pre-trained via knowledge masking strategies. Specifically, the authors used entity-level and phrase-level masking techniques on Chinese Wikipedia and in-house text collections in their masked language model pre-training. Peters et al. (2019) utilized the multi-head attention mechanism to fuse knowledge from multiple knowledge bases, while Peinelt et al. (2021) adopted the gating mechanism to combine linguistic embeddings and contextual embeddings from BERT. Lauscher et al. (2020b) effectively introduced word-level semantic similarity information into BERT via additional pre-training by predicting semantic relations in a knowledge graph.

Building on this line of work, we propose to enrich PolSciBERT with (1) lexical semantic information and (2) knowledge about named entities.

Adapter-based architectures Most of the work described above involves re-training the entire model with additional pre-training objectives which, due to the large number of parameters, is computationally expensive and might suffer from catastrophic forgetting (McCloskey and Cohen, 1989). To alleviate this problem, adapters have been proposed as an alternative strategy for downstream fine-tuning (Rebuffi et al., 2017; Houlsby et al., 2019; Pfeiffer et al., 2020a). Unlike the standard fine-tuning approach, adapter-based tuning does not require re-training the entire model. Instead, it injects a lightweight task-specific adapter layer in each transformer layer. During fine-tuning, these newly added adapter layers are trained along with the final classification layer, while the original pre-trained parameters are frozen. Fixing the original pre-trained model makes it easier to share its parameters across several different tasks. In addition, the adapter layer typically has a much smaller number of parameters than the original pre-trained model, making adapter-based fine-tuning much more efficient.

A number of studies have leveraged the adapter-based approach and demonstrated its potential not only for domain adaptation (Lu et al., 2021; Hung et al., 2022; Meng et al., 2021), but also for integrating structured knowledge bases into transformer-based models (Wang et al., 2021; Lauscher et al., 2020a). Inspired by these studies, this work focuses on incorporating knowledge bases into PolSciBERT using adapters, to investigate whether semantic similarity and/or entity knowledge can also be beneficial for NLP tasks in the political domain. We compare different methods for combining multiple adapters, namely adapter stacking (Pfeiffer et al., 2020b) and adapter fusion (Pfeiffer et al., 2021).

3 Training Knowledge Adapters

To introduce knowledge into PolSciBERT, we pre-train a number of specialized adapters, each of which encodes a certain type of knowledge. These pre-trained modular adapters allow us to transfer knowledge from external sources into our model. We first describe our base model, PolSciBERT, and then explain the training procedure of the adapters.

All models are implemented in PyTorch, using the HuggingFace Transformers library (Wolf et al., 2020)[1] and the adapter-transformer library from AdapterHub (Pfeiffer et al., 2020a).[2]

3.1 PolSciBERT

PolSciBERT is based on the multilingual XLM-R model (Conneau et al., 2020) and was further pre-trained in a multilingual setting with full fine-tuning. Specifically, the pre-training corpus is a collection of parliamentary speeches in 5 languages, German, English, Spanish, French and Italian, including debates from the European parliament (Koehn, 2005) and transcripts from parlia-

[1]v4.17.0. `https://huggingface.co/transformers`.

[2]v3.0.0. `https://docs.adapterhub.ml`.

mentary meetings (Rauh and Schwalbach, 2020; MIT Election Data and Science Lab, 2017).[3] Starting with the pre-trained XLM-R, we continued pre-training of PolSciBERT on the political text corpus, using the masked language modelling (MLM) objective.

3.2 Corpora for knowledge injection

We explore two publicly available datasets to acquire different types of knowledge: ConceptNet (Speer et al., 2017) for semantic (dis)similarity and the KELM corpus (Agarwal et al., 2021) for factual information about entities.

ConceptNet (Speer et al., 2017) is a large multilingual knowledge base which encodes commonsense knowledge, such as the *causes* of an event (e.g., exercise causes sweat) or the *synonyms* of a word. It integrates multiple knowledge sources, including Wiktionary and a subset of DBPedia (Lehmann et al., 2012). The latest version (ConceptNet 5.7) comprises 34 million edges and supports hundreds of languages. ConceptNet has been used in NLP research to incorporate external knowledge into large language models (Camacho-Collados et al., 2017; Zhong et al., 2019; Lauscher et al., 2020a; Yasunaga et al., 2021).

Since we are interested in enriching PolSciBERT with semantic similarity and dissimilarity information, we extract edges from the knowledge graph for three types of lexical relations (*IsA*, *Synonym* and *Antonym* relations) and 5 languages (DE, EN, IT, FR, ES) as training data for our knowledge adapters. For each relation type, we extract all word pairs connected by this relation. Then we perform a simple clean-up and split the data into training (85%) and test set (15%) for adapter training. We only keep word pairs where both words exist in each of the 5 languages and remove duplicates from the data. We also remove triplets whose entities contain numbers or have a word length of ≤ 1 character. Note that the triplets can be cross-lingual (e.g., <*Synonym*, énorme (FR), enorme (IT)>).

To train the CN-SIMILARITY adapter, we merge the *IsA* and *Synonym* relation triplets into one training and test set since they both encode information on semantic similarity. This results in 1.3 million training instances for CN-SIMILARITY. The CN-ANTONYM adapter was trained solely on

	Task	Train Size	Test Size
CN-SIMILARITY	TCL	1,317,027	232,417
CN-ANTONYM	TCL	30,501	5,383
KELM-ADAP	MLM	13,284,213	2,344,273

Table 2: Summary of adapter training tasks and data (TCL: triple classification; MLM: masked language modelling).

triplets from the *Antonym* relation, which comprises 30,000 training instances.

KELM In addition to word or phrase level semantic information, factual knowledge about named entities has also proven to improve the performance of pre-trained language models (Zhang et al., 2019; Sun et al., 2019). Thus, we utilize the Corpus for Knowledge-Enhanced Language Model pre-training (KELM) (Agarwal et al., 2021) to inject factual knowledge into PolSciBERT. The KELM corpus is a synthetic corpus generated by a T5 model (Raffel et al., 2020). The model has been fine-tuned on aligned data from English Wikidata (Vrandečić and Krötzsch, 2014) and Wikipedia by training the model to convert the Wikidata triples to natural text (Agarwal et al., 2021).

The raw dataset[4] includes more than 15 million instances. Each instance is a `JSON` object with three fields: (1) a list of triples where each triple is in the format `[head entity, relation, tail entity]`, (2) the serialized triple sequence which is concatenated by the list of triples and input to the T5 model, and (3) the generated text output of the T5 model. For an example, refer to Figure 1 in the Appendix. The average length of the generated sentences in the KELM corpus is 15.2 tokens.

To create the dataset for training the KELM adapter (KELM-ADAP), we extract the generated text (the `gen_sentence` field) from each instance in the raw dataset and split the resulting dataset into training set (85%) and test set (15%). The training (test) set includes about 13 million (2 million) sentences, as summarized in Table 2.

3.3 Adapter Training

For all our experiments, we adopt the adapter architecture proposed in Pfeiffer et al. (2021). That is, we insert a single adapter with a bottleneck hidden size M after the feed-forward sub-layer in the transformer layer (Vaswani et al., 2017).

[3] For a detailed list of datasets and information on preprocessing and pre-training, please refer to §A in the Appendix.

[4] Downloaded from `https://github.com/google-research-datasets/KELM-corpus` on April 23, 2022.

CN-SYNONYM **and** CN-ANTONYM The ConceptNet adapters aim at enriching PolSciBERT with semantic similarity and dissimilarity information. To learn this type of knowledge, we follow Lauscher et al. (2020b) and train the adapter in a relation classification task where we input a word pair from our data and predict whether a CN-SYNONYM (CN-ANTONYM) relation holds between the two words.

The negative samples needed for training have been created, using an approach similar to Yao et al. (2019). For each relation, a triple from the data is corrupted by replacing either its head h or its tail t (but not both) by a randomly selected entity h' or t' from the dataset. We make sure that the new, corrupted triple does not appear in the dataset, to avoid inserting false negatives. This way, we create k corrupted triples for k true triples, resulting in $2k$ triples in total. The set of negative samples can be presented as

$$\begin{aligned} D_R^- = &\{(h', r, t) | r \in R \wedge h' \in E \wedge h' \neq h \wedge (h', r, t) \notin D_R^+\} \\ &\cup \{(h, r, t') | r \in R \wedge t' \in E \wedge t' \neq t \wedge (h, r, t') \notin D_R^+\}, \end{aligned}$$

where E is the set of all entities in a semantic relation R, and D_C^+ is the set of positive triples for the semantic relation R.

Similar to previous work (Yao et al., 2019; Lauscher et al., 2020b), we model a word pair (h, t) as a sequence pair to perform the relation classification task. Specifically, each word pair (h, t) in a semantic relation,[5] including both positive and negative examples, is turned into a sequence pair that starts with the <s> token and is separated by the </s> token. For illustration, the true word pair in the *Similarity* relation <color blind, farbenblind> is transformed into

```
[s] _color _blind  [/s][/s] _far ben blind [/s]
```

The relation classification task can thus be modeled as a standard sequence pair classification task for transformer models (Devlin et al., 2019; Liu et al., 2019; Conneau et al., 2020). The last output hidden state of the `[s]` token is used for prediction. For a true positive instance, the correct label is 1, and 0 for the generated negative examples.

KELM-ADAP For the KELM adapter, we seek to encode facts about named entities in the world. To achieve this goal, we train the adapter with the masked language modeling objective (MLM) (Devlin et al., 2019; Lauscher et al., 2020a; Lu et al., 2021) on the KELM dataset described above. We follow the standard MLM procedure to randomly mask 15% of the tokens in each input sequence and use the last hidden state of the masked token for prediction.[6]

4 Experiments

We now want to test our knowledge adapters on the task of predicting policy positions in political manifestos.

Baselines As baselines, we use multilingual RoBERTa (XLM-R) (Conneau et al., 2020) and PolSciBERT, our multilingual in-domain RoBERTa model, to assess whether domain-specific knowledge improves model performance **(RQ1)** and whether the effect of inserting additional lexical and/or factual knowledge in the model can further improve results **(RQ2)**.

4.1 Predicting Manifesto Policy Domains

The Manifesto Project Database (Volkens et al., 2019a) has been widely used in political text analysis (Laver et al., 2003; Abercrombie et al., 2019; Menini et al., 2017; Glavaš et al., 2017; Koh et al., 2021).[7] It comprises a large collection of party manifestos from over 50 countries. The text in the party manifestos has been segmented into "quasi-sentences" (similar to clauses). Each quasi-sentence contains exactly one unique statement (Werner et al., 2021) and has been categorized into one of 57 fine-grained classes reflecting the most relevant policy goal and issue preference for this statement. These 57 policy goals and issues are grouped into 8 coarse-grained policy domains. Thus, each quasi-sentence in the dataset has a coarse-grained policy domain label (the "major label") and a fine-grained label capturing the policy goal and issue (the "minor label"). For illustration, see Example 2.1.[8]

To compare our results with related work, we evaluate our models on the dataset of Koh et al. (2021) which includes a subset of the manifesto corpus (version 2019) (Volkens et al., 2019a,c) consisting of all English manifestos.[9] Koh et al. (2021) split this subset into training, validation and test

[5] *Synonym* and *IsA* for CN-SYNONYM; *Antonym* for CN-ANTONYM

[6] For training details and hyperparameters, see §B in the Appendix.

[7] https://manifesto-project.wzb.eu/

[8] For more information, schema please refer to the codebook of the Manifesto Project (Volkens et al., 2019b,d)

[9] Note that there are two versions *2019a* and *2019b*, but the authors did not specify which version they used.

	Major topics	Minor topics
Number of labels	8	57
Number of quasi-sent.		
Total	99,279	99,279
Train (0.70)	69,499	69,499
Validation (0.15)	14,887	14,887
Test (0.15)	14,893	14,893

Table 3: Number of labels and examples in the final manifesto dataset

sets with a ratio of 70/15/15. We first remove examples with empty text fields from the data, and then follow the same split to evaluate our models. The final dataset includes 99,279 quasi-sentences (see Table 3).

Following Koh et al. (2021), we perform the quasi-sentence classification task for both major and minor topics. We model the task as a text classification problem and use the last hidden state of the [S] token as a pooled representation of the input sequence to predict labels and compute the loss. During evaluation, we noticed some preprocessing problems in the dataset, specifically missing tokens at the end of most quasi-sentences. We therefore tried to recreate the dataset with complete quasi-sentences and report results for both datasets (see Appendix, C for a more detailed description of the problem and information on the recreated dataset).

4.2 Experimental setup

To investigate the effectiveness of knowledge injection via adapters, we experiment with three different model setups for our semantic similarity knowledge adapters (CN-SIMILARITY) and the factual knowledge adapter KELM-ADAP, following previous work in this area (Lauscher et al., 2021; Pfeiffer et al., 2020b, 2021):

- **Adapter full fine-tuning** inserts one single pre-trained knowledge adapter into PolSciBERT and tunes the entire model, including the PolSciBERT parameters and the inserted adapter. That is, the model is initialized with the pre-trained parameters and updated during fine-tuning on the downstream task.

- **AdapterStack** utilizes the AdapterStack architecture (Pfeiffer et al., 2020b) and stacks adapters –the pre-trained knowledge adapter(s) and a randomly initialized task adapter on top– and only tunes the task adapter during fine-tuning while PolSciBERT and all knowledge adapters are frozen. This setup differs from *Adapter full fine-tuning* in that the model learns the task-specific information separately, which might be better at preserving the in-domain information encoded in PolSciBERT and the knowledge encoded in the pre-trained adapters (Lauscher et al., 2021).

- **AdapterFusion** (Pfeiffer et al., 2021) combines multiple pre-trained knowledge adapters and a pre-trained task adapter, using a randomly initialized fusion layer. Similar to the attention mechanism (Vaswani et al., 2017), the fusion layer learns to weight the different pre-trained adapters for the downstream task. During downstream fine-tuning, PolSciBERT and all adapters are frozen, only the parameters in the fusion layer are updated.

For all three setups, the final task-specific prediction head is randomly initialized. Additional task adapters are pre-trained for the *AdapterFusion* (Pfeiffer et al., 2021) setup. Specifically, we follow the standard single task training for adapters (Pfeiffer et al., 2021; Houlsby et al., 2019), in which randomly initialized task adapters are inserted into PolSciBERT and fine-tuned on the downstream task while PolSciBERT is kept frozen. For training details, also see Appendix B.1 and B.2.

4.3 Results

Table 4 reports results for major and minor topics on our dataset. Results for the original dataset from Koh et al. (2021) are included in the Appendix.

4.4 Baseline Results

Our baseline models (XLM-R, PolSciBERT) outperform the BERT-GRU and BERT-CNN models of Koh et al. (2021) by 2-3% Micro-F1 for the major topics and by around 5% Micro-F1 for minor topics (see Appendix, Table 8). For Macro-F1, the improvements are more profound, with around 10% for the fine-grained minor topics.

When training the same models on our new dataset (without missing tokens), we observe a slight increase in results across most settings, with one noteworthy exception. For Macro-F1 on the minor topics, results on the corrupted training (and test) data were higher (around 5% for PolSciBERT, from 36% to 31%). We will look into this issue in §4.7.

Model Setup		Major Topics Micro-F1	Major Topics Macro-F1	Minor Topics Micro-F1	Minor Topics Macro-F1
Baselines (w/o adapters)	XLM-R	$62.3_{(0.2)}$	$51.0_{(0.3)}$	$49.1_{(0.4)}$	$32.8_{(1.2)}$
	PolSciBERT	$64.6_{(0.6)}$	$53.4_{(0.8)}$	$50.8_{(0.3)}$	$31.2_{(2.2)}$
(with adapter)	PolSciBERT + task adapter	$65.0{*}_{(\mathbf{0.1})}$	$\mathbf{54.5}_{(0.4)}$	$\mathbf{51.8}{*}_{(\mathbf{0.3})}$	$\mathbf{36.5}_{(0.2)}$
CN-SYNONYM	Full	$62.6_{(0.8)}$	$52.5_{(0.9)}$	$49.6_{(0.7)}$	$35.0_{(0.8)}$
	AdapterStack	$64.1_{(0.8)}$	$53.3_{(0.8)}$	$51.3_{(0.6)}$	$35.5_{(1.2)}$
	AdapterFusion	$65.0_{(0.5)}$	$54.3_{(0.2)}$	$51.7{*}_{(\mathbf{0.3})}$	$36.0_{(0.5)}$
KELM-ADAP	Full	$62.5_{(0.7)}$	$53.3_{(0.4)}$	$50.0_{(0.6)}$	$34.3_{(1.9)}$
	AdapterStack	$64.8_{(0.3)}$	$54.1_{(0.3)}$	$51.5{*}_{(\mathbf{0.3})}$	$36.0_{(0.4)}$
	AdapterFusion	$64.7_{(0.2)}$	$54.0_{(0.2)}$	$\mathbf{51.8}{*}_{(\mathbf{0.2})}$	$36.2_{(0.5)}$
CN-SYNONYM & KELM-ADAP	AdapterStack	$63.8_{(0.2)}$	$52.9_{(0.3)}$	$51.2_{(0.2)}$	$35.4_{(0.6)}$
	AdapterFusion	$\mathbf{65.2}{*}_{(\mathbf{0.4})}$	$54.4_{(0.3)}$	$51.6{*}_{(\mathbf{0.2})}$	$36.2_{(0.8)}$
Experiments including antonym relations					
CN-SYNONYM & CN-ANTONYM	AdapterStack	$61.8_{(1.0)}$	$50.6_{(1.3)}$	$51.3{*}_{(\mathbf{0.5})}$	$35.7_{(0.6)}$
	AdapterFusion	$65.0_{(0.5)}$	$54.2_{(0.4)}$	$51.7{*}_{(\mathbf{0.3})}$	$36.4_{(0.3)}$
CN-SYNONYM & CN-ANTONYM & KELM-ADAP	AdapterStack	$62.1_{(0.5)}$	$51.0_{(0.8)}$	$50.9_{(0.5)}$	$34.9_{(1.0)}$
	AdapterFusion	$65.1{*}_{(\mathbf{0.2})}$	$\mathbf{54.5}_{(0.2)}$	$51.5{*}_{(\mathbf{0.1})}$	$34.7_{(2.5)}$

Table 4: Test set results of the manifesto quasi-sentence domain classification (Major topics). The first column specifies the model setup, including the knowledge adapter(s) and the fine-tuning strategy applied. All evaluation metrics reported for our model setups were averaged over 5 random initializations. The number in the parenthesis indicates the standard deviation of the 5 runs. Micro-F1 results marked with $*$ are significantly better than the PolSciBERT baseline w/o adapters (Cochran's Q with $p <= .001$).

4.5 Domain Adaptation

We observe an increase in results of around 2% (major topics) for PolSciBERT, compared to the vanilla XLM-R. For the minor topics, results are mixed, with improvements in the same range for Micro-F1 while Macro-F1 decreases, probably caused by a high number of infrequent topics. Our results show that domain adaptation through continuous pre-training on in-domain data from the political domain has a positive effect (**RQ1**). When replacing full finetuning with a task adapter, we see further improvements especially for the minor topics. In addition, the task adapter seems more robust (increase in standard deviation). Next, we look into the performance of the knowledge adapters.

4.6 Knowledge Adapters

Full fine-tuning vs. freezing the LM parameters In general, PolSciBERT equipped with a single knowledge adapter, either CN-SIMILARITY or KELM-ADAP, brings performance benefits across different fine-tuning strategies compared to PolSciBERT without any adapters. When comparing results for AdapterStack and AdapterFusion with full fine-tuning, we see that for all settings it is beneficial to freeze the LM parameters as well as the knowledge adapter parameters and update only the weights for the task-specific adapter and (for AdapterFusion) the fusion layer.

Stacking vs. Fusion Our second observation concerns the performance of AdapterStack versus AdapterFusion. When inserting only one knowledge adapter, AdapterFusion works better or on par with AdapterStack. However, when combining multiple knowledge adapters, adapter fusion substantially outperforms stacking and yields improvements in the range of 3-4% for the major topics. This shows that letting the model learn the weights for the different adapters is beneficial. Overall, however, the knowledge adapters do not outperform the task-specific adapter.

Micro-F1 vs. Macro-F1 For the fine-grained minor topics, we observe more significant improvements for Macro-F1 than for the Micro-F1 metric. This implies that the improvements we gain from adapter training are mostly driven by improvements for the rare labels in the dataset. That is, the adapters seem to be mostly helpful for sparse data (i.e., topics with few instances). This observation is interesting, as it shows that the adapters seem to have learned additional information that our in-domain PolSciBERT has not yet learned (as evidenced by the lower Macro-F1 of PolSciBERT, compared to the vanilla XLM-R model).

Type of knowledge adapters When comparing the different types of knowledge that we inserted, we do not see any crucial differences between the entity-based knowledge and the semantic similarity adapters. Both types of information yield similarly small improvements. This raises some doubts whether the information we inserted is crucial to solve our task. We will come back to this question in §4.7.

Lessons learned Our results show that freezing the LM parameters and training only the weights of the adapter(s) can outperform full fine-tuning, at least in our setup. This provides more evidence that adapters are a good way to prevent "catastrophic forgetting" (Kirkpatrick et al., 2017; Lauscher et al., 2021).

	Model Setup	F1 (Major) Mic.	F1 (Major) Mac.	F1 (Minor) Mic.	F1 (Minor) Mac.
English	XLM-R	62.3	51.0	49.1	31.8
	PolSciBERT	64.6	53.4	50.8	31.2
	PolSciB+Adap	**65.0**	**54.5**	**51.8**	**36.5**
	CN-SYN AdaptFus	**65.0**	54.3	51.7	36.0
	KELM AdaptFus	64.7	54.0	**51.8**	36.2
German	XLM-R	51.5	41.8	35.7	22.5
	PolSciBERT	**56.8**	48.0	41.4	24.6
	PolSciB+Adap	56.3	47.9	**41.5**	**27.6**
	CN-SYN AdaptFus	56.5	47.3	40.2	26.8
	KELM AdaptFus	56.5	**48.8**	**41.8**	25.8

Table 5: Results for English (from Tab. 4) and zero-shot results for German manifestos.

4.7 Error Analysis

We will now look into some open questions mentioned above. First, we would like to know why Macro-F1 for PolSciBERT for the minor classes decreased (as compared to the vanilla XLM-R model) when training on the new dataset while, at the same time, Micro-F1 for PolSciBERT increased. This was in contrast to the results on the original dataset of Koh et al. (2021) where both, Micro and Macro-F1 for PolSciBERT were around 2% higher than the ones for the generic XLM-R. When looking into the data, we found that PolSciBERT trained on the newly created dataset does not predict labels for 14 out of the 57 classes. Those classes are the ones with few training (and test) instances only and the underlying reason for the different behaviour of the two models lies in the way the data was sampled. Koh et al. (2021) decided to create a training set where the different classes are equally distributed over the train/dev/test sets. In contrast to this approach, we did not distribute sentences from the same file over train, dev and test but selected 33 unseen manifestos and put all sentences from those documents in the test set. This results in a slightly less balanced, but more realistic test case. We assume that, as a result of our sampling decision, the model had more difficulties to predict the low-frequency classes which resulted in a lower Macro-F1 but higher accuracies for most other predicted classes.

4.8 Zero-shot experiments for German

In our final experiment, we test our multilingual model on German data in a zero-shot setup where we predict policy domains and preferences in a new, unseen language. We apply our model that has been fine-tuned exclusively on English data to German manifestos that have been annotated within the same framework.[10] We are interested to see (i) how well the model does without any task-specific German training data and (ii) which of the different methods (if any) is able to improve results over the baseline.

Our results for German show a decrease of more than 10% for the vanilla XLM-R for major topics (62.4% vs. 51.5% Macro-F1) and around 15-20% for the minor topics. The in-domain PolSciBERT is able to improve results for major and minor topics by around 5% (Micro-F1). However, as seen for English, none of the knowledge adapters is able to obtain further significant improvements over the best model trained without external knowledge, again questioning whether the information that we injected in the model is needed for solving the task at hand. The adapters, however, provide competitive results without the need to retrain the full model.

5 Conclusions

Inspired by previous work on enhancing transformer-based LMs with domain knowledge, common-sense knowledge and semantic similarity information, we tested the impact of knowledge injection for the task of policy domain prediction from party manifestos. Our results showed that (a) in-domain pre-training can yield substantial improvements (PolSciBERT vs. vanilla XLM-R); (b) freezing the LM parameters and training task-specific adapters can yield comparable or better results, compared to full model finetuning; and (c) adapter fusion is especially important when integrating more than one adapter in the model.

[10]Our test set includes German manifestos from 1998 – 2021 (88,694 quasi-sentences), downloaded from `https://manifesto-project.wzb.eu` (see Table 3 in the Appendix).

6 Limitations

While our results showed the effectiveness of adapters as a parameter-efficient alternative to full fine-tuning, our attempts to improve model performance based on the injection of external knowledge were not successful. This, however, does not prove that knowledge injection for the task at hand is not feasible. More thorough testing of different types of knowledge is needed to answer the question whether knowledge injection can improve results for policy domain prediction from party manifestos.

7 Ethical Considerations

While the task of policy domain prediction from party manifestos has attracted a lot of attention especially in the political sciences and in the field of Text-as-Data, it is clear that the results so far are not yet good enough for applications in the real world. We thus advise researchers not to use the output of our system for political text analyses without any manual post-correction.

Acknowledgements

The work presented in this paper is partly funded by the German Research Foundation (DFG) under the UNCOVER project (PO 3536/3-1 and 1900/7-1).

References

Gavin Abercrombie, Federico Nanni, Riza Batista-Navarro, and Simone Paolo Ponzetto. 2019. Policy preference detection in parliamentary debate motions. In *Proceedings of the 23rd Conference on Computational Natural Language Learning (CoNLL)*, pages 249–259, Hong Kong, China. Association for Computational Linguistics.

Oshin Agarwal, Heming Ge, Siamak Shakeri, and Rami Al-Rfou. 2021. Knowledge Graph Based Synthetic Corpus Generation for Knowledge-Enhanced Language Model Pre-training. In *Proceedings of the 2021 Conference of the North American Chapter of the Association for Computational Linguistics: Human Language Technologies*, pages 3554–3565, Online. Association for Computational Linguistics.

Emily Alsentzer, John Murphy, William Boag, Wei-Hung Weng, Di Jindi, Tristan Naumann, and Matthew McDermott. 2019. Publicly Available Clinical BERT Embeddings. In *Proceedings of the 2nd Clinical Natural Language Processing Workshop*, pages 72–78, Minneapolis, Minnesota, USA. Association for Computational Linguistics.

Adrien Barbaresi. 2018. A corpus of German political speeches from the 21st century. In *Proceedings of the Eleventh International Conference on Language Resources and Evaluation (LREC 2018)*, pages 792–797, Paris, France. European Language Resources Association (ELRA).

Frank R. Baumgartner, Christoffer Green-Pedersen, and Bryan D. Jones. 2006. Comparative studies of policy agendas. *Journal of European Public Policy*, 13(7):959–974.

Iz Beltagy, Kyle Lo, and Arman Cohan. 2019. SciBERT: A pretrained language model for scientific text. In *Proceedings of the 2019 Conference on Empirical Methods in Natural Language Processing and the 9th International Joint Conference on Natural Language Processing (EMNLP-IJCNLP)*, pages 3615–3620, Hong Kong, China. Association for Computational Linguistics.

Shaun Bevan. 2019. Gone Fishing: The Creation of the Comparative Agendas Project Master Codebook. In *Comparative Policy Agendas: Theory, Tools, Data*. Oxford University Press.

Andreas Blaette. 2017. GermaParl. Corpus of Plenary Protocols of the German Bundestag. TEI files.

Jose Camacho-Collados, Mohammad Taher Pilehvar, Nigel Collier, and Roberto Navigli. 2017. SemEval-2017 Task 2: Multilingual and Cross-lingual Semantic Word Similarity. In *Proceedings of the 11th International Workshop on Semantic Evaluation (SemEval-2017)*, pages 15–26, Vancouver, Canada. Association for Computational Linguistics.

Alexis Conneau, Kartikay Khandelwal, Naman Goyal, Vishrav Chaudhary, Guillaume Wenzek, Francisco Guzmán, Edouard Grave, Myle Ott, Luke Zettlemoyer, and Veselin Stoyanov. 2020. Unsupervised cross-lingual representation learning at scale. In *Proceedings of the 58th Annual Meeting of the Association for Computational Linguistics*, pages 8440–8451, Online. Association for Computational Linguistics.

Jacob Devlin, Ming-Wei Chang, Kenton Lee, and Kristina Toutanova. 2019. BERT: Pre-training of deep bidirectional transformers for language understanding. In *Proceedings of the 2019 Conference of the North American Chapter of the Association for Computational Linguistics: Human Language Technologies, Volume 1 (Long and Short Papers)*, pages 4171–4186, Minneapolis, Minnesota. Association for Computational Linguistics.

Goran Glavaš, Federico Nanni, and Simone Paolo Ponzetto. 2017. Cross-lingual classification of topics in political texts. In *Proceedings of the Second Workshop on NLP and Computational Social Science*, pages 42–46, Vancouver, Canada. Association for Computational Linguistics.

Yu Gu, Robert Tinn, Hao Cheng, Michael Lucas, Naoto Usuyama, Xiaodong Liu, Tristan Naumann, Jianfeng Gao, and Hoifung Poon. 2022. Domain-Specific Language Model Pretraining for Biomedical Natural Language Processing. *ACM Transactions on Computing for Healthcare*, 3(1):1–23.

Suchin Gururangan, Ana Marasović, Swabha Swayamdipta, Kyle Lo, Iz Beltagy, Doug Downey, and Noah A. Smith. 2020. Don't stop pretraining: Adapt language models to domains and tasks. In *Proceedings of the 58th Annual Meeting of the Association for Computational Linguistics*, pages 8342–8360, Online. Association for Computational Linguistics.

Neil Houlsby, Andrei Giurgiu, Stanislaw Jastrzebski, Bruna Morrone, Quentin De Laroussilhe, Andrea Gesmundo, Mona Attariyan, and Sylvain Gelly. 2019. Parameter-efficient transfer learning for NLP. In *International Conference on Machine Learning*, pages 2790–2799. PMLR.

Chia-Chien Hung, Anne Lauscher, Simone Ponzetto, and Goran Glavaš. 2022. DS-TOD: Efficient Domain Specialization for Task-Oriented Dialog. In *Findings of the Association for Computational Linguistics: ACL 2022*, pages 891–904, Dublin, Ireland. Association for Computational Linguistics.

James Kirkpatrick, Razvan Pascanu, Neil Rabinowitz, Joel Veness, Guillaume Desjardins, Andrei A. Rusu, Kieran Milan, John Quan, Tiago Ramalho, Agnieszka Grabska-Barwinska, Demis Hassabis, Claudia Clopath, Dharshan Kumaran, and Raia Hadsell. 2017. Overcoming catastrophic forgetting in neural networks. *Proceedings of the National Academy of Sciences*, 114(13):3521–3526.

Philipp Koehn. 2005. Europarl: A parallel corpus for statistical machine translation. In *Proceedings of Machine Translation Summit X: Papers*, pages 79–86, Phuket, Thailand.

Allison Koh, Daniel Kai Sheng Boey, and Hannah Béchara. 2021. Predicting policy domains from party manifestos with BERT and convolutional neural networks. In *Proceedings of the 1st Workshop on Computational Linguistics for Political Text Analysis (CPSS-2021)*, pages 67–77, Düsseldorf, Germany.

Anne Lauscher, Tobias Lueken, and Goran Glavaš. 2021. Sustainable Modular Debiasing of Language Models. In *Findings of the Association for Computational Linguistics: EMNLP 2021*, pages 4782–4797, Punta Cana, Dominican Republic. Association for Computational Linguistics.

Anne Lauscher, Olga Majewska, Leonardo FR Ribeiro, Iryna Gurevych, Nikolai Rozanov, and Goran Glavaš. 2020a. Common sense or world knowledge? Investigating adapter-based knowledge injection into pretrained transformers. In *Proceedings of Deep Learning Inside Out (DeeLIO): The First Workshop on Knowledge Extraction and Integration for Deep Learning Architectures*, pages 43–49, Online. Association for Computational Linguistics.

Anne Lauscher, Ivan Vulić, Edoardo Maria Ponti, Anna Korhonen, and Goran Glavaš. 2020b. Specializing unsupervised pretraining models for word-Level semantic similarity. In *Proceedings of the 28th International Conference on Computational Linguistics*, pages 1371–1383, Barcelona, Spain (Online). International Committee on Computational Linguistics.

Michael Laver, Kenneth Benoit, and John Garry. 2003. Extracting policy positions from political texts using words as data. *American political science review*, 97(2):311–331.

Jinhyuk Lee, Wonjin Yoon, Sungdong Kim, Donghyeon Kim, Sunkyu Kim, Chan Ho So, and Jaewoo Kang. 2020. BioBERT: a pre-trained biomedical language representation model for biomedical text mining. *Bioinformatics*, 36(4):1234–1240.

Jens Lehmann, Robert Isele, Max Jakob, Anja Jentzsch, Dimitris Kontokostas, Pablo N. Mendes, Sebastian Hellmann, Mohamed Morsey, Patrick van Kleef, Sören Auer, and Christian. Bizer. 2012. Dbpedia–A large-scale, multilingual knowledge base extracted from wikipedia. *Semantic Web*.

Yinhan Liu, Myle Ott, Naman Goyal, Jingfei Du, Mandar Joshi, Danqi Chen, Omer Levy, Mike Lewis, Luke Zettlemoyer, and Veselin Stoyanov. 2019. RoBERTa: A robustly optimized BERT pretraining approach. *arXiv preprint arXiv:1907.11692*.

Ilya Loshchilov and Frank Hutter. 2019. Decoupled Weight Decay Regularization. In *International Conference on Learning Representations*.

Qiuhao Lu, Dejing Dou, and Thien Huu Nguyen. 2021. Parameter-Efficient Domain Knowledge Integration from Multiple Sources for Biomedical Pre-trained Language Models. In *Findings of the Association for Computational Linguistics: EMNLP 2021*, pages 3855–3865, Punta Cana, Dominican Republic. Association for Computational Linguistics.

Michael McCloskey and Neal J. Cohen. 1989. Catastrophic Interference in Connectionist Networks: The Sequential Learning Problem. In *Psychology of Learning and Motivation*, volume 24, pages 109–165. Academic Press.

Zaiqiao Meng, Fangyu Liu, Thomas Clark, Ehsan Shareghi, and Nigel Collier. 2021. Mixture-of-Partitions: Infusing Large Biomedical Knowledge Graphs into BERT. In *Proceedings of the 2021 Conference on Empirical Methods in Natural Language Processing*, pages 4672–4681, Online and Punta Cana, Dominican Republic. Association for Computational Linguistics.

Stefano Menini, Federico Nanni, Simone Paolo Ponzetto, and Sara Tonelli. 2017. Topic-Based Agreement and Disagreement in US Electoral Manifestos. In *Proceedings of the 2017 Conference on Empirical Methods in Natural Language Processing*, pages 2938–2944, Copenhagen, Denmark. Association for Computational Linguistics.

Slava Mikhaylov, Michael Laver, and Kenneth R. Benoit. 2012. Coder reliability and misclassification in the human coding of party manifestos. *Political Analysis*, 20(1):78–91.

MIT Election Data and Science Lab. 2017. U.S. House 1976–2020.

Nicole Peinelt, Marek Rei, and Maria Liakata. 2021. GiBERT: Enhancing BERT with Linguistic Information using a Lightweight Gated Injection Method. In *Findings of the Association for Computational Linguistics: EMNLP 2021*, pages 2322–2336, Punta Cana, Dominican Republic. Association for Computational Linguistics.

Matthew E. Peters, Mark Neumann, Robert Logan, Roy Schwartz, Vidur Joshi, Sameer Singh, and Noah A. Smith. 2019. Knowledge enhanced contextual word representations. In *Proceedings of the 2019 Conference on Empirical Methods in Natural Language Processing and the 9th International Joint Conference on Natural Language Processing (EMNLP-IJCNLP)*, pages 43–54, Hong Kong, China. Association for Computational Linguistics.

Jonas Pfeiffer, Aishwarya Kamath, Andreas Rücklé, Kyunghyun Cho, and Iryna Gurevych. 2021. AdapterFusion: Non-destructive task composition for transfer learning. In *Proceedings of the 16th Conference of the European Chapter of the Association for Computational Linguistics: Main Volume*, pages 487–503, Online. Association for Computational Linguistics.

Jonas Pfeiffer, Andreas Rücklé, Clifton Poth, Aishwarya Kamath, Ivan Vulić, Sebastian Ruder, Kyunghyun Cho, and Iryna Gurevych. 2020a. AdapterHub: A framework for adapting transformers. In *Proceedings of the 2020 Conference on Empirical Methods in Natural Language Processing: System Demonstrations*, pages 46–54, Online. Association for Computational Linguistics.

Jonas Pfeiffer, Ivan Vulić, Iryna Gurevych, and Sebastian Ruder. 2020b. MAD-X: An Adapter-Based Framework for Multi-Task Cross-Lingual Transfer. In *Proceedings of the 2020 Conference on Empirical Methods in Natural Language Processing (EMNLP)*, pages 7654–7673, Online. Association for Computational Linguistics.

Colin Raffel, Noam Shazeer, Adam Roberts, Katherine Lee, Sharan Narang, Michael Matena, Yanqi Zhou, Wei Li, and Peter J. Liu. 2020. Exploring the limits of transfer learning with a unified text-to-text transformer. *Journal of Machine Learning Research*, 21(140):1–67.

Christian Rauh and Jan Schwalbach. 2020. The ParlSpeech V2 data set: Full-text corpora of 6.3 million parliamentary speeches in the key legislative chambers of nine representative democracies.

Sylvestre-Alvise Rebuffi, Hakan Bilen, and Andrea Vedaldi. 2017. Learning Multiple Visual Domains with Residual Adapters. In *Proceedings of the 31st International Conference on Neural Information Processing Systems*, NIPS'17, page 506–516, Long Beach, California, USA.

Robyn Speer, Joshua Chin, and Catherine Havasi. 2017. ConceptNet 5.5: An open multilingual graph of general knowledge. In *Proceedings of the Thirty-First AAAI Conference on Artificial Intelligence*, AAAI'17, page 4444–4451. AAAI Press.

Shivashankar Subramanian, Trevor Cohn, Timothy Baldwin, and Julian Brooke. 2017. Joint sentence-document model for manifesto text analysis. In *Proceedings of the Australasian Language Technology Association Workshop, ALTA 2017, Brisbane, Australia, December 6-8, 2017*, pages 25–33.

Yu Sun, Shuohuan Wang, Yukun Li, Shikun Feng, Xuyi Chen, Han Zhang, Xin Tian, Danxiang Zhu, Hao Tian, and Hua Wu. 2019. ERNIE: Enhanced representation through knowledge integration. *arXiv preprint arXiv:1904.09223*.

Naomi Truan. 2019. Parliamentary Debates on Europe at the Assemblée nationale (2002-2012) [Corpus].

Ashish Vaswani, Noam Shazeer, Niki Parmar, Jakob Uszkoreit, Llion Jones, Aidan N. Gomez, Łukasz Kaiser, and Illia Polosukhin. 2017. Attention is all you need. In *Proceedings of the 31st International Conference on Neural Information Processing Systems*, NIPS'17, page 6000–6010, Red Hook, NY, USA. Curran Associates Inc.

Andrea Volkens, Werner Krause, Pola Lehmann, Theres Matthieß, Nicolas Merz, Sven Regel, and Bernhard Weßels. 2019a. The Manifesto Data Collection. Manifesto Project (MRG/CMP/MARPOR). Version 2019a.

Andrea Volkens, Werner Krause, Pola Lehmann, Theres Matthieß, Nicolas Merz, Sven Regel, and Bernhard Weßels. 2019b. The Manifesto Project Dataset - Codebook. Manifesto Project (MRG/CMP/MARPOR). Version 2019a.

Andrea Volkens, Werner Krause, Pola Lehmann, Theres Matthieß, Nicolas Merz, Sven Regel, and Bernhard Weßels. 2019c. The Manifesto Data Collection. Manifesto Project (MRG/CMP/MARPOR). Version 2019b.

Andrea Volkens, Werner Krause, Pola Lehmann, Theres Matthieß, Nicolas Merz, Sven Regel, and Bernhard Weßels. 2019d. The Manifesto Project Dataset - Codebook. Manifesto Project (MRG/CMP/MARPOR). Version 2019b.

Denny Vrandečić and Markus Krötzsch. 2014. Wikidata: A Free Collaborative Knowledgebase. *Communications of the ACM*, 57(10):78–85.

Ruize Wang, Duyu Tang, Nan Duan, Zhongyu Wei, Xuanjing Huang, Jianshu Ji, Guihong Cao, Daxin Jiang, and Ming Zhou. 2021. K-Adapter: Infusing knowledge into pre-trained models with adapters. In *Findings of the Association for Computational Linguistics: ACL-IJCNLP 2021*, pages 1405–1418, Online. Association for Computational Linguistics.

Annika Werner, Onawa Lacewell, and Andrea Volkens. 2014. *Manifesto Coding Instructions: 5th fully revised edition*. Manifesto Project.

Annika Werner, Onawa Lacewell, Andrea Volkens, Theres Matthieß, Lisa Zehnter, and Leila van Rinsum. 2021. Manifesto Coding Instructions. 5th rerevised edition.

Thomas Wolf, Lysandre Debut, Victor Sanh, Julien Chaumond, Clement Delangue, Anthony Moi, Pierric Cistac, Tim Rault, Rémi Louf, Morgan Funtowicz, Joe Davison, Sam Shleifer, Patrick von Platen, Clara Ma, Yacine Jernite, Julien Plu, Canwen Xu, Teven Le Scao, Sylvain Gugger, Mariama Drame, Quentin Lhoest, and Alexander M. Rush. 2020. Transformers: State-of-the-Art Natural Language Processing. In *Proceedings of the 2020 Conference on Empirical Methods in Natural Language Processing: System Demonstrations*, pages 38–45, Online. Association for Computational Linguistics.

Liang Yao, Chengsheng Mao, and Yuan Luo. 2019. KG-BERT: BERT for knowledge graph completion. *arXiv preprint arXiv:1909.03193*.

Michihiro Yasunaga, Hongyu Ren, Antoine Bosselut, Percy Liang, and Jure Leskovec. 2021. QA-GNN: Reasoning with Language Models and Knowledge Graphs for Question Answering. In *Proceedings of the 2021 Conference of the North American Chapter of the Association for Computational Linguistics (NAACL): Human Language Technologies*, pages 535–546. Association for Computational Linguistics.

Zhengyan Zhang, Xu Han, Zhiyuan Liu, Xin Jiang, Maosong Sun, and Qun Liu. 2019. ERNIE: Enhanced language representation with informative entities. In *Proceedings of the 57th Annual Meeting of the Association for Computational Linguistics*, pages 1441–1451, Florence, Italy. Association for Computational Linguistics.

Peixiang Zhong, Di Wang, and Chunyan Miao. 2019. Knowledge-Enriched Transformer for Emotion Detection in Textual Conversations. In *Proceedings of the 2019 Conference on Empirical Methods in Natural Language Processing and the 9th International Joint Conference on Natural Language Processing (EMNLP-IJCNLP)*, pages 165–176, Hong Kong, China. Association for Computational Linguistics.

Supplementary Material

A PolSciBERT

We list the collection of corpora utilized for pre-training PolSciBERT in Table 6. The raw texts have been split into sentences using Spacy (Version 2.3.1. `https://spacy.io`). Sentences without any lower-case Latin characters have been removed from the data.

A.1 Hyperparameters for PolSciBERT pre-training

The pre-training of PolSciBERT was continued on the political text corpus, using a batch size of 16. Note that the gradient accumulation step was set to be 4, meaning model weights were updated once every 4 batches. The learning rate was $5e-05$. A new checkpoint was saved every 50,000 steps. We use the checkpoint at the 5950000-th step as our base model.

A.2 The KELM Corpus

```
{
  "triples": [
    ["Valentin Lavigne", "member of sports team", "FC Lorient"],
    ["Valentin Lavigne", "FC Lorient", "start time", "01 January 2014"],
    ["Valentin Lavigne", "FC Lorient", "end time", "01 January 2016"]
   ],
  "serialized_triples":
    "Valentin Lavigne member of sports team FC Lorient, FC Lorient"
    "end time 01 January 2016, FC Lorient start time 01 January 2014.",
  "gen_sentence":
    "Valentin Lavigne played for FC Lorient between 2014 and 2016."
}
```

Figure 1: An example instance in the KELM corpus

Language	Name	Time Period	# Tokens	Link
German	GermanParl (Blaette, 2017)	1996 - 2016	77,661,778	https://github.com/PolMine/GermaParlTEI
	Europarl-de (Koehn, 2005)	1996 - 2011	46,747,617	https://opus.nlpl.eu/Europarl-v3.php
	Austrian Nationalrat (Rauh and Schwalbach, 2020)	2003 - 2018	56,687,818	https://dataverse.harvard.edu/dataset.xhtml?persistentId=doi:10.7910/DVN/L4OAKN
	Bundestag	2017 - 2020	11,542,765	https://www.bundestag.de/services/opendata
	Bundestag Barbaresi (Barbaresi, 2018)	1982 - 2017	11,257,316	https://politische-reden.eu
English	Europarl-en (Koehn, 2005)	1996 - 2011	48,984,323	https://opus.nlpl.eu/Europarl-v3.php
	NZ House of Representatives (Rauh and Schwalbach, 2020)	1996 - 2016	135,135,640	https://dataverse.harvard.edu/dataset.xhtml?persistentId=doi:10.7910/DVN/L4OAKN
	UK House of Commons (Rauh and Schwalbach, 2020)	1989 - 2019	361,921,136	https://dataverse.harvard.edu/dataset.xhtml?persistentId=doi:10.7910/DVN/L4OAKN
	US Congressional Record (MIT Election Data and Science Lab, 2017)	1989 - 2010	439,913,096	https://www.bundestag.de/services/opendata
Spanish	Europarl-es (Koehn, 2005)	1996 - 2011	54,617,946	https://opus.nlpl.eu/Europarl-v3.php
	Congreso de los Disputados (Rauh and Schwalbach, 2020)	1996 - 2018	66,395,968	https://dataverse.harvard.edu/dataset.xhtml?persistentId=doi:10.7910/DVN/L4OAKN
French	Europarl-fr (Koehn, 2005)	1996 - 2011	54,956,800	https://opus.nlpl.eu/Europarl-v3.php
	Assemblee Nationale (Truan, 2019)	2002 - 2012	113,765	https://www.ortolang.fr/market/corpora/fr-parl/5
	TAPS Assemblée Nationale	2017 - 2020	30,415,252	https://data.assemblee-nationale.fr/travaux-parlementaires/debats
Italian	Europarl-it (Koehn, 2005)	1996 - 2011	50,488,760	https://opus.nlpl.eu/Europarl-v3.php
	Camera	2008 - 2020	68,419,585	https://www.camera.it

Table 6: Source and links to the pre-trained corpora for PolSciBERT

B Training Details

B.1 Baseline models

We perform downstream fine-tuning for all model setups with a batch size of 16 and a linear learning rate decay and use AdamW (Loshchilov and Hutter, 2019) as optimizer. The learning rate is $5e^{-5}$ for the baseline models and adapter full fine-tuning. The maximum number of epochs is 30, with early stopping and a patience of 5, meaning the model will stop training if the evaluation results on the development set stop improving for 5 consecutive epochs.

B.2 Adapters

The training arguments and configurations for the adapters are presented in Table 7. Following the settings in Pfeiffer et al. (2021), all adapters are trained with a learning rate of $1e - 4$ with linear learning rate decay. The warm-up ratio is 0.1. We train adapters for different batch sized and number of epochs, depending on the size of the training data. For CN-SIMILARITY and CN-ANTONYM, we perform early stopping based on the accuracy on the test set: If the accuracy stops improving for 5 consecutive evaluation steps, the training is stopped. We use AdamW (Loshchilov and Hutter, 2019) with a weight decay of 0.01 for optimization.

C Results on the Koh et al. (2021) dataset

To compare our results with previous work, we downloaded the data from Koh et al. (2021) from their github repository.[11] We found that, probably due to some preprocessing problem, the quasi-sentences in the dataset were not complete (see examples below). For a fair comparison, we proceeded as follows. First, we trained and tested our models on the original dataset of Koh et al. (2021), to assure that differences in results are not simply due to the missing tokens. We used the same train/test splits as specified in the data. Next, in order to evaluate the impact of the missing tokens on the results, we downloaded English manifestos from the Manifesto Project homepage[12] and recreated the dataset with manifestos from Australia, Canada, Ireand, New Zealand, South Africa, the UK and the US (Table 3). Our new dataset is substantially smaller than the original dataset and we did not balance the label distribution across the different splits. To ensure replicability, we will make our train/dev/test splits available upon publication.

A	Once people have what
B	Once people have offended, what next?
A	The manifesto is
B	The manifesto is comprehensive.
A	not has turned things
B	Choice, not chance, has turned things round.

Figure 2: Examples for missing tokens in the dataset (A: quasi-sentence taken from Koh et al.; B: recreated from the original manifestos data).

	lang	train	dev	test
Koh et al.	(EN)	69,500	14,888	14,894
recreated	(EN)	59,559	14,419	13,722
zero-shot	(DE)	–	–	88,694

Figure 3: Statistics for the recreated manifestos dataset (en) and for the German test set used for zero-shot prediction.

[11] https://github.com/allisonkoh/bertcnn-classifying-manifestos, (file: 02.FINAL_minor.csv).

[12] https://manifesto-project.wzb.eu

	CN-SIMILARITY	CN-ANTONYM	KELM-ADAP
Training Arguments			
batch size	32	32	16
number of epochs	10	30	1
learning rate	1e-4	1e-4	1e-4
warm-up ratio	0.1	0.1	0.1
weight decay	0.01	0.01	0.01
early stopping	True	True	False
patience	5	5	5
evaluation steps	15000	500	15000
gradient accumulation steps	1	1	4
Adapter Configurations			
adapter hidden size	96	96	96

Table 7: Training details for adapter training.

Model Setup		Major Topics Micro-F1	Major Topics Macro-F1	Minor Topics Micro-F1	Minor Topics Macro-F1
(Koh et al., 2021)	BERT-GRU (Base model)	59.3	47.9	43.2	23.9
	BERT-CNN (Base model)	59.1	47.3	44.8	26.0
Baselines	XLM-R	$61.7_{(0.4)}$	$50.6_{(1.0)}$	$48.6_{(0.2)}$	$34.1_{(1.7)}$
	PolSciBERT	$63.2_{(0.2)}$	$51.9_{(0.7)}$	$50.5_{(0.3)}$	$36.1_{(0.7)}$
CN-SYNONYM	Full	$61.7_{(0.3)}$	$52.0_{(0.3)}$	$49.4_{(0.3)}$	$37.4_{(1.0)}$
	AdapterStack	$63.5_{(0.1)}$	$52.2_{(0.5)}$	$51.0_{(0.2)}$	$37.7_{(1.1)}$
	AdapterFusion	$63.5_{(0.2)}$	$52.3_{(0.5)}$	$50.4_{(0.2)}$	$35.7_{(2.3)}$
KELM-ADAP	Full	$62.3_{(0.2)}$	$52.5_{(0.4)}$	$49.9_{(0.5)}$	$37.9_{(0.5)}$
	AdapterStack	$\mathbf{63.8}_{(0.2)}$	$\mathbf{53.5}_{(0.3)}$	$\mathbf{51.2}_{(0.2)}$	$\mathbf{38.5}_{(1.0)}$
	AdapterFusion	$63.5_{(0.2)}$	$52.2_{(0.1)}$	$50.8_{(0.2)}$	$37.0_{(1.6)}$
CN-SYNONYM & KELM-ADAP	AdapterStack	$62.8_{(0.5)}$	$51.5_{(0.9)}$	$50.6_{(0.3)}$	$37.0_{(0.7)}$
	AdapterFusion	$63.6_{(0.2)}$	$52.3_{(0.2)}$	$50.8_{(0.3)}$	$37.7_{(1.4)}$
Experiments with semantic dissimilarity knowledge					
CN-SYNONYM & CN-ANTONYM	AdapterStack	$62.1_{(0.8)}$	$50.7_{(1.0)}$	$50.3_{(1.1)}$	$36.3_{(2.2)}$
	AdapterFusion	$63.6_{(0.2)}$	$52.5_{(0.3)}$	$50.7_{(0.3)}$	$37.7_{(0.6)}$
CN-SYNONYM & CN-ANTONYM & KELM-ADAP	AdapterStack	$61.9_{(0.4)}$	$50.3_{(0.6)}$	$51.0_{(0.2)}$	$37.8_{(0.8)}$
	AdapterFusion	$63.5_{(0.3)}$	$52.3_{(0.2)}$	$50.9_{(0.1)}$	$38.4_{(0.9)}$

Table 8: Test set results for manifesto quasi-sentence policy domain classification (Koh et al., 2021). The results for Koh et al. (2021) were taken from Table 7 in their paper. The first column specifies the model setup, including the knowledge adapter(s) and the fine-tuning strategy applied. All evaluation metrics reported for our model setups were averaged over 5 random initializations. The numbers in parentheses indicate standard deviation over the 5 runs.

Author Index

Association for Computational Linguistics
209 N. Eighth Street
Stroudsburg, Pennsylvania 18360

ISBN 979-8-3313-1645-7

CURRAN ASSOCIATES INC.
proceedings.com